Psychology

oduction

Psychology
an introduction

EDITORS

Leslie Swartz
Cheryl de la Rey
Norman Duncan

OXFORD
UNIVERSITY PRESS

OXFORD
UNIVERSITY PRESS

Great Clarendon Street, Oxford OX2 6DP

Oxford University Press is a department of the University of Oxford.
It furthers the University's objective of excellence in research, scholarship,
and education by publishing worldwide in

Oxford New York

Auckland Cape Town Dar es Salaam Hong Kong Karachi
Kuala Lumpur Madrid Melbourne Mexico City Nairobi
New Delhi Shanghai Taipei Toronto

with offices in
Argentina Austria Brazil Chile Czech Republic France Greece
Guatemala Hungary Italy Japan Poland Portugal Singapore
South Korea Switzerland Thailand Turkey Ukraine Vietnam

Oxford is a registered trade mark of Oxford University Press
in the UK and in certain other countries

Published in South Africa
by Oxford University Press Southern Africa, Cape Town

Psychology an introduction
ISBN 0 19 578136 8

Publishing Manager: Marian Griffin
Editor: Stuart Douglas
Designer: Oswald Kurten
Illustrators: James Berrange and Rassie Erasmus
Indexer: Jeanne Cope

Published by Oxford University Press Southern Africa
PO Box 12119, N1 City, 7463, Cape Town, South Africa

Set in Minion 10.5pt on 13.5pt by Global Graphics
Imagesetting by Castle Graphics
Cover reproduction by The Image Bureau
Printed and bound by ABC Press, Cape Town

The authors and publishers gratefully acknowledge permission to
reproduce material in this book. Every effort has been made to
trace copyright holders, but where this has proved impossible,
the publishers would be grateful for information which would
enable them to amend any omissions in future editions.

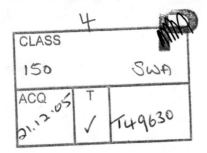

Table of Contents

List of contributors

Chapter 1   *Professor Leslie Swartz*
Director of the Child, Youth and Family
Development, Human Sciences Research
Council

Chapter 2   *Professor Tyrone Pretorius*
Vice-Rector (Academic Affairs), University of
the Western Cape
& Professor Cheryl de la Rey
Deputy Vice-Chancellor, University of
Cape Town

Chapter 3   *Ms Loraine Townsend*
Department of Psychiatry and Mental Health,
University of Cape Town

Chapter 4   *Professor Tokozile Mayekiso*
Head of the School of Human & Community
Development, University of the
Witwatersrand

Chapter 5   *Mr Sibusiso Ntshangase*
Department of Specialised Education,
University of the Witwatersrand

Chapter 6   *Associate Professor Tamara Shefer*
Department of Psychology and Director of
the Women and Gender Studies Programme,
University of the Western Cape

Chapter 7   *Professor Norman Duncan*
Psychology, School of Human and
Community Development, University of the
Witwatersrand
Mr Ashley van Niekerk
Crime, Violence and Injury Lead Programme,
Medical Research Council

Chapter 8   *Mr Mark Tomlinson*
Child Guidance Clinic, Department of
Psychology, University of Cape Town

Chapter 9   *Professor Mark Solms*
Department of Psychology, University of
Cape Town

Chapter 10   *Dr Oliver Turnbull*
Centre for Cognitive Neuroscience, School of
Psychology, University of Wales Bangor, UK

Chapter 11   *Professor Jaak Panksepp*
Department of Psychology, Bowling Green
State University, Ohio, USA

Chapter 12   *Ms Ronelle Carolissen*
Department of Psychology, University of
Stellenbosch

Chapter 13   *Dr Pam Naidoo*
Department of Psychology, University of the
Western Cape

Chapter 14   *Dr Ashraf Kagee*
Department of Psychology, University of
Stellenbosch
Professor Gideon de Bruin
Department of Psychology and Director,
Institute for Child and Adult Guidance, Rand
Afrikaans University (University of Johannesburg)

Chapter 15   *Mr Tshepo Tlali*
Department of Psychology, University of Fort
Hare

Chapter 16   *Professor Andrew Gilbert*
Department of Psychology, University of Fort
Hare

Chapter 17   *Mr David Neves*
Department of Psychology, University of
Kwazulu Natal

Chapter 18   *Mr Clifford van Ommen*
Department of Psychology, University of Fort
Hare

Chapter 19   *Ms Tanya Swart*
Institute for Social and Health Sciences/
Centre for Peace Action, UNISA

Chapter 20   *Dr Martin Terre Blanche*
Department of Psychology, UNISA

Chapter 21   *Garth Stevens*
UNISA Institute for Social and Health
Sciences

Chapter 22   *Dr Floretta Boonzaier*
Lecturer, Department of Psychology,
University of Cape Town

How to use this book

Psychology an introduction was written to meet the need for a psychology textbook that South African lecturers and students can identify with and that identifies and addresses key psychological issues as they occur not only in the world but also in South Africa.

There are a number of features in each chapter which will help the reader, whether a student, tutorial group leader, or lecturer.

Learning objectives

At the beginning of each chapter, you'll find a bullet-point list of learning objectives. These are skills-orientated. In other words, after studying the chapter, you should have enough information at your disposal to be able to express an informed opinion on the objective in question, and be able to demonstrate a related skill if this is relevant. An example is:

- After studying this chapter you should be able to introduce and discuss issues pertaining to culture and attachment theory.

Narrative

As mentioned in the introductory chapter of this book, the purpose of the short narrative section which is found before each chapter starts, is to place the following content into a South African perspective.

Parts

The Introduction indicates that there are 10 parts to the book. You'll see that each has its own introduction, too. The lead author for each part has indicated why the subject area addressed in each part – for instance, Social Psychology – is important, and how the chapters in the part fit together, relate to one another, and relate to the study of Psychology as a whole. An example is on page 151:

Part 4 – Personality. This part provides an overview of the way in which personality has been studied. It looks at the major personality theories and addresses the question, 'What is personality?'.

Boxes

The study of the content of this book is made more interesting by the inclusion of text boxes which contain interesting research facts, debates, or case studies.

Don't you agree that the box on page 422 –

Measuring stress – establishes the relevance of the theory in the text and its link to everyday living? The content of the boxes is meant to augment your understanding of the main text in any chapter. It can also be used by tutorial leaders and lecturers as the point of discussion in a classroom situation.

References

References at the end of each chapter are important because they show that the author of the chapter has read widely in compiling an up-to-date look at the subject area. The references include journal articles, books, and websites. As a student you can use the references to find other interesting information about a subject which you want to know more about.

Exercises

At the end of each chapter, there is a section which includes multiple choice questions and short answer questions. As a student, you can use these to test your own knowledge on the content of the chapter which went before. As a tutorial leader, you might want to use these as a classroom or assignment exercise.

Ancillary material

The answers to the questions in the book are included in a Solutions Manual for lecturers (0 19 576159 6). Each question is answered and lecturers and students are advised on how to approach and answer the short answer questions.

There is other ancillary material which will be made available by Oxford University Press SA to lecturers who confirm that they are prescribing this book for their classes.

Other materials are an Instructor's manual (0 19 576138 3), Question bank (0 19 576164 2) and Powerpoint slides (0 19 576166 9). These are available on CD and can be obtained from Oxford University Press SA through the Academic Sales Manager.

Further contact

Should you have any comments about the book, the publisher and authors would be pleased to receive these. Contact The Commissioning Editor, Academic Division, OUP SA, or contact OUP SA through the website at www.oup.com/za

Acknowledgments

A book of this size and scope would not be possible without the contribution of many people. We are very grateful to the many chapter authors, all of them busy people with multiple competing demands, for making this book happen. The range and depth of expertise of the authors speaks for itself. We are especially indebted to our lead authors, who each took charge of putting together a part of *Psychology an introduction*, approaching authors, collating material, and contributing actively to the editing process. The coherence and polish of the different parts is owing in no small measure to their work.

The only author whose name does not appear in the chapter headings is Kerry Gibson, who wrote the stories about Nosipho and her family and social circle. These stories are designed to give continuity to the text and immediacy to the issues, and we are very grateful to Kerry for her work.

Throughout the process of compiling this book, the editors have been ably supported by the sterling work of Loraine Townsend. Loraine's combination of dedication, tact, organizational skills, attention to editorial detail, and sheer perseverance would be hard to match. Loraine, assisted by Jonathan Ipser, also prepared the teacher support materials for this book. Further meticulous and incisive editorial support has been provided by René Brandt.

Arthur Attwell, formerly of Oxford University Press Southern Africa, commissioned *Psychology an introduction* and was very involved in the original conceptualisation of the book, its design and features. Marian Griffin ably took over the reins more recently, and has been both supportive and indefatigable in seeing this product to fruition. Stuart Douglas more than rose to the challenge of technically editing close to forty chapters, written by many authors, with differing styles. We would not have managed the task of completing the book without the considerable help of Stuart and Marian, and in the last stages of production, Lydia Wilson.

Finally, we should like to thank our colleagues, our students, participants in research we have conducted over the years, and our families and friends for all the contributions – obvious and less obvious – to making this book a reality.

Leslie Swartz
Cheryl de la Rey
Norman Duncan

Photo acknowledgments
p31 – SPSS-SA (Pty) Ltd.; p55, 57, 58, 60, 61 – T. Mayekiso; p56, 167, 171, 242, 277, 475 INPRA; p66, 70, 255, 322, 333, 337, 367, 412, PictureNET Africa – Henner Frankenfeld p66, 268 PictureNET Africa – Chris Marais; p84 iAfrika Photos – Justin Sholk p92 REUTERS/South – Mike Hutchings; p102 Science Photo Library p103, 173, 174, 176, 178, 190, 241, 277, 284, 476, 477 Corbis p156 iAfrika Photos – Desmond Steward; p157, 253, 259 Touchline Media p160 Trace Images/Cape Argus; p161 PictureNET Africa – Adil Bradlow; p162 AP Photo – NgHan Guan; p180 Kirtland Community College; p234, 267 Baileys African Archives; p244 PictureNET Africa – Steve Hilton-Barber; p264 South African Library; p256 PictureNET Africa – Greg Marinovich; p274 AP Photo – Ricardo Mazalan; p275 AP Photo – Hussein Malla; p275 iAfrika Photos – Lionel Soule; p283 AP Photo – John McConnico; p283 AP Photo – Lionel Cironneau; p283, 441 AP Photo; p305, 476 Trace Images – Benny Gool; p309 Gallo Images; p317 iAfrika Photos – Rob Whyte; p318 The Image Works – Mike Siluk; p323, 332 PictureNET Africa – Joao Silva; p334, 336, 351 iAfrika Photos – Per-Anders Pettersson; p346 iAfrika Photos – Eric Miller; p352 PictureNET Africa – Giacomo Pirozzi: p356 South Photos – Gisele Wulfshon; p365 PictureNET Africa – Nadine Hutton p393 Allsport/Touchline – Gary Matimore; p395 Allsport/Touchline – Anton Want; p399 Allsport/Touchline – Craig Jones; p402 iAfrika Photos – Adam Welz; p414 PictureNET Africa; p441 AP Photo; p444 PictureNET Africa – Paul Velasco; p454 PictureNET Africa – Neil van Niekerk; p472 REUTERS/South; p473 PictureNET Africa – Watson Mcoteli

Part 1

Introduction

Introduction: Finding Out about People

Leslie Swartz

Introduction

'Young people today do not have the same values their parents had.'

'Stress is making life unbearable for most people.'

'The trouble with politicians is that they are all dishonest.'

'Like it or not, men are more logical than women.'

'South Africa is a traumatised society.'

'If you want your child to speak properly, don't talk baby talk to her.'

'Only rich people can afford to become mentally ill.'

We hear these sorts of statements all the time – they are statements about people, opinions that are given as though they are facts. All of us hold views about people, and you may agree with some of the above statements and disagree with others. But how do we decide whether any of the statements are true? Can we decide? Are there ways we can come to have more confidence in our ideas about people? Can we become more specific in our claims than the above generalisations suggest?

There are many systems of belief about people, our behaviour, and what makes us who we are. Psychology is one of these belief systems, but it is not the only one. Many people, for example, look to religion to explain human behaviour. Others base their views on what older people in society say is true, from their years of experience. Increasingly, perhaps, many of us look to celebrities or famous people to give us lessons in life and knowledge about people. Psychology differs from many other systems of belief about people in one crucial respect: psychologists are concerned not only with *what* we know about people, but about *how we come to know these things*.

Let's think a little about what this implies. In many approaches to understanding people, approaches that differ from psychology, it is important to know *who* is making claims about people, their behaviour, and what makes them human. For example, in many systems of belief, the views of a recognised elder or expert are thought to be in themselves the best approximation we can have to true insight or wisdom about people. In such systems of belief, people will defend their views by saying that these views are similar to those of a recognised expert. In psychology, though, there are indeed experts, but the way in which we weigh up whether a belief about people is true, is rather different. Consider, for instance, the following statement, which is so broad that all psychologists would probably agree with it:

'How people develop in later life is related in some way to their early experiences.'

A psychologist who is influenced by the work of Sigmund Freud, the founder of psychoanalysis (see Chapter 37), may agree with this statement on the basis of having read Freud's work, and having been convinced that Freud's method of analysing adults and linking current behaviour to early experience provides useful information for our understanding of how people develop. This psychologist would not agree with the statement simply because Freud agrees with it, but would agree with it on the basis of being convinced by Freud's methods and approach to creating new knowledge about people.

By contrast, there are many psychologists who do not agree with Freud's approach. These psychologists cannot convince other psychologists that Freud was incorrect simply by saying that they do not like what Freud said. On the contrary, what they will need to do is to show how, in their view, the ways in which Freud came to his conclusions are lacking or incorrect. These psychologists would then make their own argument about how to find out about human behaviour. They could say, for example, that the only way we can know for sure whether early experiences affect later development is by observing babies, and seeing how they develop into adults. The method they use is different from Freud's – they believe that we need careful observation of people over a long period of time (what is known as a 'longitudinal design') in order to draw conclusions about human behaviour.

In focusing on methods of finding out things about people, psychology is similar to other approaches to understanding the world which fall under the broad heading of the 'human and social sciences'. Human sciences, which may include psychology, sociology and anthropology, for example, are similar to other sciences, such as physics and zoology, in that they are all concerned with collecting information in a particular way, using particular methods. But science is only partly about being confident about whether things are true. It is also about understanding *why* things are true.

Let's look again at the statement about human development:

'How people develop in later life is related in some way to their early experiences.'

Let's assume for the moment that we agree that the statement is true. *Why* is it true? *How* do we explain that it is true? We may have a lot of evidence that it is true, but this does not explain why. Let's think about two possible reasons why it is true. One reason could be that we learn patterns of behaviour in childhood which we continue to apply throughout life. Another could be that there is something about the way that we are made (the way our brains and bodies work) that determines both our early experiences and our later behaviour. Each of these two views represents the beginnings of a *theory* about how people develop.

In fact, as the section on developmental psychology (Part 2) in this book shows, most psychologists these days do not believe that we have to choose between a view that emphasises the influence of the environment on human behaviour (known as 'nurture') and one that emphasises the importance of our physiological make-up (known as 'nature'). But the way in which we decide between different theories of human behaviour depends upon methods that we use to test and develop theories. For example, psychologists have conducted a great deal of research on identical twins who have been raised in different homes. Why all this interest in identical twins? This is because these twins are identical to each other in terms of their genetic make-up. There is now a great deal of evidence that identical twins raised apart will tend to develop in ways which can

---

1.1   FINDING OUT ABOUT PSYCHOLOGY

This book may well be your first formal introduction to psychology. You will find many topics covered in the book, but because psychology is such a big field, there are also many aspects which are not covered. No single book can do anything more than introduce you to some of the key issues in psychology. To find out more, you must read more widely.

An enormous amount is written about every aspect of psychology. For a new learner, the amount of information can be overwhelming. Because psychology is a rapidly developing field in which new studies are conducted every day, it is important for you to try to read recent material in the field of psychology. It is probably true to say that every book in psychology, as soon as it is printed, is out of date. This is because new research is being conducted all the time – including the time between when the author has finished writing and the printed version of the book appears in the bookshops. In this book, we have tried to be up to date, but the fact is that new ideas are springing up in psychology all the time. It is always a good idea to look out for good books in psychology, and especially good new books, so you can keep up to date with the field.

Possibly even more important than books in the field of psychology are academic journals. Examples of these in *South Africa are the South African Journal of Psychology*, the *Journal of Industrial Psychology*, *Psychology in Society*, and *Psycho-Analytic Psychotherapy in South Africa*, to name just some. There are many excellent international journals as well, and many university libraries now offer on-line access to these through search engines like PsychInfo and PsychArticles. Psychologists in academic departments and research psychologists, as well as practitioners, will generally publish their work in academic journals. You will see references to articles in many psychology journals in the reference lists of the chapters that follow. A big advantage of reading articles printed in good psychology journals is that there is a standard process, before an article is accepted for publication, to assess whether the article is of good quality. The norm is that any article sent to a journal is reviewed by a number of experts in the field (this is called peer review). Articles which, in the view of the reviewers and the editor, are not up to standard academically will not be accepted for publication. This does not mean (unfortunately) that bad articles are never published, but there is a quality control filtering process.

The internet is a wonderful resource for gathering information easily, but there can also be problems with it. On the plus side, there are thousands upon thousands of websites which deal with every conceivable aspect of psychology. On the minus side, anybody can put any information or view on the internet – there is no quality control. A person who knows nothing at all about a subject can just as easily post an essay about that subject on an internet site as can somebody who is the world authority on that subject. It is for this reason that some university lecturers do not allow learners to access material from the internet, as learners sometimes have difficulty in making their own assessment of the quality of what they read. On the other hand, there are many excellent websites and on-line journals and discussion forums which are reviewed (similar to the way that journals use a review process). Many materials which would in the past have had to be sought on paper on library shelves can be easily accessed and read as electronic files. The key thing in using the internet (or any other knowledge source), is to assess critically the quality of what you are reading. This skill of critical assessment is not something which you will automatically have. In fact some old-fashioned educational techniques, where learners are forced to learn lists of things without evaluating how good arguments are, actually discourage critical thinking. A key purpose of training in psychology (and in other university subjects) is to develop your critical thinking skills.

When we read about psychology, how do we assess the quality of what we read? The first thing to note is that we cannot judge the quality of an argument on the basis of what it concludes to be true or false about people, or on the basis of whether we happen to agree with the author's beliefs about people or not. In fact, two excellent psychologists may differ very strongly about an aspect of human behaviour, but they may both provide excellent arguments and good evidence for reaching different conclusions. As you read more widely in psychology, you will find that there are many differences in opinion amongst researchers. It can even be the case that where two researchers conduct what looks like the same experiment in two different settings, they get very different results. This does not mean, necessarily, that either of the researchers did bad work. On the contrary, different findings in different contexts may give us important information.

A discipline like psychology thrives on debate. People are very complex, and different ways of studying people provide different sorts of information. It is through engaging with the debates that we all learn and the discipline of psychology moves forward. Learners studying psychology for the first time sometimes expect that psychology will tell them the 'facts' about people, and that psychologists 'know' everything there is to know about people. This is not the case. It is certainly true that there are principles about understanding human behaviour which are supported by good research evidence and strong theories, and you will learn about some of these principles in this book. But the discipline is developing all the time, and new evidence and arguments make for new views about people.

In order to assess whether an argument is well made in psychology (or in any other discipline), you have to be able to assess the methods used to support that argument. Studying methods of research – the processes whereby psychologists make systematic observations of people and use these observations to develop theories and conclusions about people, their thoughts, feelings and behaviour – is an important part of the training of a psychologist. This is why the second chapter of this book focuses on research methods. But even before you are skilled in understanding the many sophisticated methods psychologists use in their research, there are two basic questions you can ask about anything you read in psychology.

The first question is: 'Does the author provide evidence for what he or she claims to be true?' In psychology, we can't just make claims because we believe things to be so. Think, for example, of the claims made at the beginning of this chapter. A good psychologist will never make such claims without referring to research that provides evidence in support of them. Partly as a consequence of this, good psychologists rarely generalise too much – they make clear the extent to which there is good evidence to support their views.

The second basic question you can ask about any argument in psychology is: 'Does the author provide a clear and logical argument, linking what the author reports on having read and/or observed, to what the author concludes?' When you read in psychology, make an assessment as to how well the author builds an argument. When you read closely, you will find that authors often leave out steps in their argument, or jump to conclusions on the basis of insufficient, or incorrect, evidence.

Learning to read critically in psychology is not something which happens overnight, and it is not easy for some learners to make the leap from reading for lists of 'facts' (as they may have done in some schools) to reading in order to understand and evaluate what they read. But becoming a critical reader is crucial to becoming a successful learner in psychology – and it is also fun! As you develop your critical skills, you start to enter the world of scientific debate. You are no longer someone who just reads and accepts what you are told; you become a partner in creating your own knowledge.

be strikingly similar. This evidence has been used by those who favour genetic explanations for human behaviour (those who believe 'nature' is very important) to bolster their theoretical approach. But things are not necessarily so simple. Others, who are more convinced of environmental influences ('nurture'), have shown that even when twins are raised in separate households and never meet each other, those households are often quite similar to each other. And so the debates go on and on.

The approach of this book

The above arguments are a very quick introduction to ways of thinking about people. Many people study psychology in order to find out as much as they can about people, and in this book you will find no shortage of fascinating, and sometimes surprising, information about people (see Box 1.1 for more information about how to find out about psychology, and Box 1.2 to learn more about what psychology tells us about).

But more important than any of the information in this book, is that this book is an introduction to ways psychologists have come to know about people. As already mentioned, our knowledge about people changes all the time. This would be a very serious problem if our only concern were with telling you, the reader, what the latest knowledge in the field is. In fact, we are far more concerned with giving you, the reader, the basic tools whereby you can decide whether new information that comes to you is useful information or not, and, ultimately, the tools for you to join the ever-growing group of psychologists who are themselves creating new information, using good methods to extend our knowledge and to test our theories.

The authors of the chapters of this book are all experts in their fields who have studied psychology for a long time. All of them have made their own contributions to psychological knowledge through their own research and publications. But the impressive credentials of the authors are far less important than the quality of what they say. It is up to you, as a reader, to look at everything that is said in this book with a critical eye, and to come to your own opinions, based on clear arguments. If you agree with the authors (and we hope you often will!), it is not enough to agree with them just because you like their conclusions – you must be able to argue for yourself why their argument is convincing. How have they used evidence? What methods have they used? How good and useful are their theories? If you disagree with the authors (and again, we hope you often will!), it is not enough to disagree with them just because you don't like their conclusions. You have to be able to show why their arguments do not hold up.

Years	Number of citations in PsychInfo
1900–1909	8 220
1910–1919	12 909
1920–1929	31 786
1930–1939	65 062
1940–1949	53 078
1950–1959	85 893
1960–1969	133 381
1970–1979	272 195
1980–1989	440 030
1990–1999	602 476
2000–2009	707 060

Note: The drop in number for 1940–1949 is attributable to World War Two. For the decade 1990–1999 there were about as many entries (over 600 000) as for all of the preceding decades of the twentieth century. The decade 2000–2009 is a projection and extrapolation.

Table 1 Growth in output in psychology

This book, then, asks you to engage with the authors in finding out about people. There is so much to say

Many learners study psychology for one (or both) of two reasons. First, learners say, they want to become psychologists because they want to do psychotherapy with people (especially children) who have been hurt emotionally. Second, many learners say that they hope that as they study psychology they will learn more about themselves, and about how to improve themselves.

These wishes that psychology will enable us to help others and ourselves are not unusual. Many people in the street, when asked what psychologists do, believe that all psychologists are psychotherapists. The media provides constant images of psychotherapy in books, films and increasingly, on television (think of the popular programmes Frazier, Oprah and Dr Phil). Many people, in addition, expect psychologists to have better insights into themselves than other people, to be better at bringing up children and to be better at controlling negative emotions and behaviour. There is also, of course, the contrasting image of the psychologist as more 'crazy' than everyone else – many people mock psychologists and make jokes about them, scorning psychologists for not being more mentally healthy than those to whom, supposedly, psychologists give advice.

These images of psychologists and psychology are, of course, limited. Psychology is a very broad discipline and there are many aspects to it. The vast majority of people who begin studying psychology at undergraduate level will never become psychotherapists. This is partly because places in professional training courses in clinical and counselling psychology are very limited, but also because most people who study psychology do not choose to go in that direction.

Introductory psychology courses, such as the ones for which this book has been written, are generally designed not to help learners understand themselves more, nor as an introduction to psychotherapy. This book offers a very broad introduction to basic skills which first-year learners in psychology need to master before they go on to more advanced training, or to use in other disciplines if they do not go on with psychology. One of the key issues we are concerned with in psychology is the question of generalisability – the development of theories that apply to large numbers of people. No two people are the same, and studying psychology at first-year level cannot tell you specifically about yourself and your family, although it may set you thinking about the kinds of assumptions you have made about yourself and the world. A first-year training in psychology is designed to help you open your

mind to new ideas and, probably more importantly, to new ways of collecting and analysing information about people. Learn about these ways of thinking and you will, in time, be able to apply them to a range of situations. Often, the most exciting learning in psychology comes when learners study something that they are not especially interested in, and they come to see that the way the subject matter is approached is interesting or challenging. Keep an open mind, and you may well be surprised at the range of things you learn!

Learners from a wide range of disciplines take courses in psychology, not to become psychologists, but to learn ways of thinking about people which are helpful in their chosen fields, including health, education, business, management, and social development. Psychologists themselves work in a very wide range of contexts – in universities, schools, in the community, in hospitals, in business, in training sports personnel, in prisons, in police and military services, to name just a few. Undergraduate courses in psychology are usually quite general in nature so that they can provide a basis for work in a very wide range of contexts.

In South Africa, to become a psychologist registered with the Health Professions Council of South Africa (HPCSA), at present you have to have a masters degree in psychology and to have completed a recognised internship (which is like an apprenticeship in your particular branch of psychology). Even psychologists who have no special interest in the health field, and may practise as industrial and organisational psychologists focusing on management and staff training issues, must be registered with the HPCSA. To be accepted into a masters or doctoral programme in psychology, you need to have a first degree majoring in psychology and an honours degree. Places in masters and doctoral programmes are generally very sought-after – many more people wish to train as psychologists than there are places in courses. Learners who have done appropriate community or volunteer work, and who are able to speak a number of South African languages will generally have an improved chance of being accepted into postgraduate programmes. The fact is, though, that many people will not be accepted into such programmes, and every sensible undergraduate learner in psychology should consider professional training in psychology as only one of a possible range of options. Some universities in South Africa now offer a Bachelor of Psychology (B.Psych) degree, a four year undergraduate programme leading to registration with the

HPCSA as a counsellor in a specific area of practice, but once again, places on these courses are limited. As you study psychology, think about what interests you about the discipline and why, and think about what alternatives there may be to being a psychologist which will allow you to pursue these interests.

Training in psychology provides an excellent background for a wide range of careers – not just for psychotherapists! Even from your first year, start thinking about all the options open to you, and make use of career and curriculum advice to plan how best to use what you will learn in psychology to develop a fulfilling career, in whichever direction you choose.

1.3 WORDS, WORDS, WORDS

When you learn a new discipline (like psychology) you learn many new words. These words are sometimes referred to as the jargon of the discipline. Some words which are part of the jargon of psychology you will probably not have heard before – words like 'triarchic theory' (see Chapter 15 on intelligence). Other words you will probably have heard before, but they may have a slightly different meaning in the context of psychology – for example, in everyday talk, we may use the term 'depression' to refer to a wide range of emotions and experiences; when psychologists refer to 'depression' as a syndrome, however, they generally refer to a quite specific set of symptoms and behaviours (see Chapter 36). In some cases, professional people, like psychologists, use too much jargon – or use fancy words when simple ones will do. In this book, we have tried to keep the number of jargon words to a minimum, but it is important that you, as a reader, make sure that you understand how the authors of the chapters of this book are using words. There is a glossary at the back of the book to help you, and you can also consult dictionaries of psychology and the social sciences in your university library.

Words in psychology, as in other disciplines, change over time, and are used differently in different places. For example, Sinason (1992) has shown how different words have been used in different historical times for what today would be called intellectual disability in South Africa, learning disability in the United Kingdom and mental retardation in the United States. Though many of us would now disapprove of words like 'imbecile', 'moron', 'feeble-minded' and even the comparatively recent 'mental defective', there have been times when each of those words was quite acceptable to professionals working in the field. It is part of our job when using words in psychology to think of where these words come from, and what they can be taken to mean in the context in which they are used today.

There are two categories of words which cause considerable debate in psychology and other disciplines, and we now briefly look at these:

Subjects, respondents, participants or informants?

When we do psychological research, in most cases we are interested in aspects of human behaviour, thoughts, or emotions. But what do we call the people we are observing in order to study behaviour, thoughts and emotions? Thirty years ago there was little debate about this – psychological research was conducted on what were termed 'subjects'. More recently, however, there has been debate about the use of this term. There are two related major objections to the term 'subjects'. First, the term gives the impression that the people are being 'subjected' to research by psychologists, which implies coercion and the use of power by psychologists. Second, the term 'subject' tends to make us think of the person as a passive recipient of research, and not as a person acting in the world, actively making sense of the world. Many researchers prefer now to use the term 'respondents' as this more accurately gives a sense that we are interested in people who are responding to questions psychologists pose to them or situations in which psychologists place them. Other researchers prefer the term 'participants', which emphasises the active role people play in participating in psychological research, but some psychologists do not like this term as they see the psychologists who are conducting the research also as participants in the research process. Another term which is used for people psychologists study is 'informants' for people who give information to psychologists.

Many researchers nowadays avoid the subjects/respondents/participants/informants debates by referring specifically to the group being studied. For example, if we are studying cyclists' reaction times we can refer to the people we are studying as 'cyclists', and not use any other term – and similarly with studying adolescents, composers, lion-tamers, and so on. There is no hard and fast rule as to which term to use, but there are different conventions which tend to be adopted by users of different types of research method (see Chapter 2). Though it is possible to read too much into the ways in which researchers refer to the people they are studying, it is an interesting exercise to think about what may be implied by the use of different terms.

Patients or clients or consumers?

Clinical psychology, historically, has had strong ties to the practice of medicine, and clinical psychology texts have historically referred to the people clinical psychologists try to help as 'patients'. This remains an acceptable usage, but many psychologists have objected to it on the grounds that it implies that the people clinical psychologists work with are 'ill' when many would argue that the difficulties they face are not 'diseases' (see Chapter 36). There are very many alternative terms to 'patient', and the word 'client' is probably the one most commonly used in psychology. The term 'client' may be used to emphasise that the relationship between the clinical psychologist and the person the psychologist wishes to help may be different from that between doctor and patient, and more similar to that between a person offering services (such as legal services) and that person's clientele. Even within the health field, though, there is some debate about the word 'patient', and we sometimes see people who make use of health services referred to as 'consumers' or 'service users' or even simply 'users'. In counselling psychology for some time, the person doing the counselling was referred to by some writers as the 'helper', and the person receiving the counselling as the 'helpee' – an ungainly term, but one that shows the extent to which psychologists have struggled to find appropriate terms to refer respectfully and accurately to those with whom they work.

There is no single correct way to use language in a discipline as complex and diverse as psychology. In this book, we have not been prescriptive about many terms, and we have deliberately not imposed a uniform standard on the way all words are used. For this reason, for example, the term 'patients' is used extensively in the chapter on HIV/AIDS, TB and parasites (Chapter 35), but the term 'client' is used in the chapter on psychotherapy (Chapter 37), even though there are some who would object to both of those terms for different reasons. As an active reader of this book (and other writings in psychology) you will have to make up your own mind about what words are best used where. But remember: always have a reason or argument that supports your choice of words.

There is one area in which we have been consistent about the use of terminology, though, and this is in the use of non-sexist language. Until fairly recently, psychologists and others have happily used terms like 'man' to refer to all people, and pronouns like 'he' to refer to all people, male and female. Feminist theorists in particular have pointed out that this kind of usage subtly implies that we can assume that what is true for men is also true for women, which may not always be so, and that the male gender is taken as the standard for human behaviour. The use of sexist language has been prohibited in most journals in which psychologists publish (including the *South African Journal of Psychology* and all journals published by the American Psychological Association), and this book follows the tradition of non-sexist language use. Psychology learners, similarly, are expected to use non-sexist language in their writing.

---

about people that we cannot pretend to have said it all, but what we do hope to do is to help you become an informed and intelligent reader of the professional literature. Once you have worked through this book, you should be able to use the skills you have learned to apply to new material that you read, and, ultimately, to developing your own knowledge of people and how they work.

The organisation of this book

This book is a very general introduction to key issues in psychology, especially as they apply to our South African and developing country context. This first section of the book (which includes this chapter and the one that follows) focuses less on content in psychology than on the ways in which psychologists collect

and interpret information. This first chapter, as you have seen, talks generally about how psychologists look at the world and make sense of it. There is also an introduction to how psychologists use language (see Box 1.3) and to the question of how psychologists think about ethics and ethical behaviour (see Box 1.4).

Chapter 2 looks rather more formally at research methods in psychology and how we use these methods to develop new knowledge about people. At first reading, you may find this chapter rather difficult. Do not worry about this – research methods are often hard to grasp. You will probably find yourself returning to this chapter again and again through your studies in psychology, as you try to evaluate new things you learn. As you return again and again to Chapter 2, you will become more comfortable with methodological concepts.

In Part 2 of this book, we focus on human develop-

In Chapter 19 (on Group Concepts, Processes and Dynamics) of this book you will learn about the classic studies in psychology conducted by Milgram. Milgram wanted to understand how ordinary people come to be perpetrators of oppression and violence – an important question, and one which is as relevant today as it was in the early 1960s, when Milgram was doing his work. One method used by Milgram was to deceive people into believing that they were giving electric shocks to people who were failing at certain tasks. In fact, the people who apparently were receiving shocks were not being shocked at all – they were working with Milgram to deceive the research subjects. Milgram's findings as a result of this work were very important – Milgram was able to show that his subjects would continue, as far as they knew, to administer electric shocks to people as part of psychological experiments. On the basis of these findings, Milgram was able to conclude that we all have the potential to commit acts of atrocity when we are in situations in which we are obedient to others in authority. The difference between those who torture others, the implication goes, and those who do not, may lie less in the moral qualities of the torturers versus other people than in the situations in which people find themselves.

The importance of this line of argument to how we think about many contemporary problems – including those of violence, oppression, terrorism and genocide – cannot be overestimated. But let us think for a moment what it must have been like to have been a subject in Milgram's experiments. Imagine having to live with the knowledge that you are in fact quite capable of inflicting severe pain on others simply because somebody else says this is the right thing to do. Even if after you have believed you have given severe electric shocks to people it is explained to you that you did not really hurt anyone, you have found out something about yourself which, perhaps, you wish you did not really know.

There have been many debates in psychology about whether Milgram was ethically correct in deceiving people into believing they were hurting others. Was Milgram unethical in what he did? Or does what he found out, by conducting his work in this way, outweigh any concerns about harm to those who participated in his studies? Debates like this in psychology (and there is still debate about the ethics of Milgram's work) alert us to more subtle questions about the ethics of what we do.

In most, if not all, countries where psychology is organised as a discipline, there are codes of ethics which govern psychologists' behaviour and protect the public from abuses by psychologists. Psychologists must ensure in all their work that what they do in no way violates other people's human rights. Underlying most professional codes of conduct are principles which emphasise:

- beneficence, or acting in the best interests of the client;
- competence, or conducting work only for which one is trained and able to undertake;
- non-maleficence, or not causing harm;
- fidelity, or behaving in a trustworthy manner;
- integrity, or a commitment to the truth; and
- respect for human rights and dignity.

(Adapted from the Ethical Principles of Psychologists and Code of Conduct 2002 of the American Psychological Association: www.apa.org)

These principles apply to how psychologists are required to interact with the people they study, with the people they aim to help, with their learners and with colleagues. As you read the chapters in this book, think carefully about every study you read about and about what your view is on how ethical the study is. Under what circumstances, and to what degree, for example, is it acceptable to lie to people about the purposes of a research study? How ethical is it, for research purposes, to assess a child for learning problems if, once having found that there are such problems, you are not in a position to offer a way of remedying the problems? If you are concerned about the spread of HIV/AIDS through the sexual abuse of young children, what may be the ethical ramifications of finding out about this abuse? What, if anything, should you, as a researcher, do with the information that a child has been abused, and that abuse may be continuing? There is scarcely a question in psychology which does not raise ethical debates, and it is important to think about ethics at all times.

The question of ethics must be considered not only at the individual level. Given that we know, for example, that poverty can have devastating effects on human development (see Chapter 20), what is the responsibility of psychologists to contribute to the eradication of poverty? Should psychologists, as 'scientists', be politically neutral, or should we take stands on political issues in line with our professional ethics, and in line with what we know about human behaviour? But if we do align ourselves politically with certain positions, does this compromise our ability to make as broad as possible a contribution to society as experts in our field? An ethical dilemma which has confronted clinical psychologists in the aftermath of apartheid in South Africa has been that of whether these psychologists should offer support and help to those who committed gross human rights abuses. Do such people 'deserve' psychological help? Who has the right to decide who is 'deserving' of such help and who has no such right? Even if we feel we would rather not be helping perpetrators of abuse, what are the social consequences of our not giving this help? Could it be that psychological help to perpetrators of a range of crimes, including crimes such as rape and child abuse, may in fact help stop perpetrators from abusing again? How do we weigh up such questions?

When psychologists choose to work in the public domain, ethical questions raise their head again. Psychologists are often called in by courts of law as expert witnesses to help the courts decide on a range of questions. For example, the court may need to decide whether a person who has perpetrated a criminal act can be held legally responsible for his or her actions. Or a court may need to decide what the best custody arrangements are for children whose parents have decided to divorce and who disagree on what is best for the children. In the nature of the legal system, the courts often wish the psychologist, as expert witness, to give an opinion that is based on certainty. But psychologists are often not 100 per cent sure – it is in the nature of our discipline to be critical and to see shades of grey in human behaviour. In order to help the court achieve an outcome which they believe best for society, psychologists may be tempted to claim to be more certain than they are of something. But is this ethical? Is it honest?

Should psychologists offer their services to lessen the harmful effects of certain social practices? Imagine, for example, that you, as a psychologist, are called in to offer assistance to people who are participating in a reality television series in which these people are regularly humiliated, and feel the psychological consequences of this humiliation. What should you do? Do you offer help to these participants? If you do so, are you not subtly lending support and legitimacy to an unethical television show? Will the fact that a psychologist has been involved be used by the show's producers to say to the public that they are behaving ethically as they are providing psychological help to participants? Should you, instead, be arguing against the show as a whole? What do you do if you, as a psychologist, believe the show should not be aired, but a valued colleague of yours – your boss, say – feels differently, and is quite happy to provide psychological assistance to the show. Should you try to discuss your differences in private, or should you have a public debate with your colleague? What would such a public debate do to the image of psychology as a profession?

As you have no doubt gathered from the examples used in this box, ethical issues in psychology are not easy to address and resolve. What may appear to be a clear answer to an ethical dilemma may raise other ethical dilemmas which are far more complex. Psychologists can never claim to have resolved all of the ethical issues associated with their work, but what they can do is ensure that in everything they do they think carefully about ethical issues, and about how what they do affects the welfare of individuals, groups, communities and nations.

ment from before birth into late adulthood. It is important not only to gain an understanding of how people develop from being a collection of cells into social, emotional and intellectual beings, but also to know something about the kinds of influences there are on human development from before birth until the moment of death. An understanding of the basics of human development is essential for anyone wishing to conduct research within any field of psychology.

Historically, psychology has always had a connection with the study of the brain and the nervous system. At some times in the history of psychology, psychologists have tried to argue that we do not need to know much about the brain in order to understand people. In the past few years, however, it has become increasingly clear that an understanding of the brain and how it works is essential to a full understanding of our thinking, our emotions and what we do. The cutting edge approach taken by the authors contributing to Part 3 of this book shows that the traditional divisions between psychological and biological understandings of human behaviour have begun to break down, much to the benefit of psychology and cognitive science more generally.

Parts 4 and 5 of this book offer, to an extent, complementary views of how human beings work. Both views are essential for our understanding of psychology at present. Part 4 focuses on different theories of personality and on how psychologists see individuals operating in the world. In addition, it examines how psychologists go about assessing personality, and the methods we use to make our assessments as valid as they can be. Part 5, dealing with cognitive psychology, examines what happens 'in the mind' – in intelligence, thinking, language and memory. What is clear from this section, however, is that what happens in the mind also happens in a social context – to understand cognitive psychology we also have to understanding how thinking and similar functions operate in the context of the world around us.

This theme of the relationship between the internal world and the world around us is developed further in Part 6 of this book. Human beings are social animals, and social psychology focuses on how we change and are changed by our context. In this section, as in the others in this book, we focus on issues of particular relevance to South Africa and developing countries. We explore, therefore, the social psychology of groups, ethnicity and racism, gender and sex, poverty, violence and trauma and peacemaking – all crucial issues for social and community development in South Africa and similar countries.

In Africa, psychology is commonly taught as part of the training of educators. In many universities there is no department of psychology, but the discipline is taught in schools of education. For this reason, Part 7 of this book focuses on educational issues. Part 8 continues the educational theme by looking firstly at how psychology can contribute to career development across the life span. Psychology is making increasing contributions, furthermore, to understanding leisure activities and to developing people in the areas of physical activity and sport, and this is also dealt with in Part 8.

Linking with the previous section, Part 9 introduces the rapidly growing area of health psychology as applied to our context. The chapters in the section focus on behavioural and other influences on human health and development, including stress, risky behaviours and nutritional issues. It also focuses on key health issues facing the poorer countries of the world – HIV/AIDS, tuberculosis, and parasites (such as malaria and bilharzia (schistosomiasis)), and shows how psychology has an important role to play in the prevention and containment of these conditions, and in helping people adapt best to the consequences of them.

Part 10 opens with an introduction to the vast field of psychopathology, providing an outline of how psychology classifies mental disorder and the theoretical approaches which psychologists have taken to understanding mental health challenges. The rest of the section explores ways in which psychology and allied disciplines attempt to make a difference to people's mental health, and relates this to the worlds they live in. The different chapters in this section show how these interventions can be thought about at a range of levels, from the biological (psychopharmacology), through the individual and group (psychotherapy), to the community and social levels (community mental health).

What is different about this book?

There are many introductory textbooks in psychology, and many of them are of excellent quality. Why, then, have we put together this one? This book covers the same material as many introductory psychology textbooks, but it has some key features which set it apart. First, we have a very wide range of contributors, most of them from a diversity of southern African backgrounds. Traditionally, psychology textbooks have been written by authors based in the USA, and to a

---

1.5 PSYCHOLOGY FOR AFRICA?

This book has been written by African authors, with many African examples, and is designed to be used by learners mainly from Africa and developing countries. But does it reflect an 'African psychology'? What does the idea of an 'African psychology' mean? Does it make any sense to speak about an 'African psychology'? This is a much more complex question than may at first appear. In order to begin thinking about the question, let's go back to thinking about psychology itself.

The history of psychology is rooted firmly in Europe and North America. As you go further in your studies in psychology, you will learn more about this history, and it will become increasingly clear how the emergence of psychology as a robust international discipline in the twentieth century can be linked to intellectual traditions which go much further back in European history. As was the case during the twentieth century, the discipline is currently dominated by developments in North America, and in the USA in particular. This does not mean that there is not good work going on in psychology in Africa, Asia, Australasia and Europe, for example, but the sheer volume of work and resources put into psychology in the USA ensures that nobody working in psychology can ignore this influence.

Let's consider an example of how the dominance of European and North American ideas influences what we come to know of the world. A rapidly-growing field within psychology is that of infant development and attachment (see the Chapters 3 and 8). Well over 90 per cent of infants in the world are born in Africa and other developing parts of the world, but over 90 per cent of articles on infant mental health and development appearing in well-known international journals deal with infants in the USA, Canada, Europe, Australia and New Zealand (Tomlinson & Swartz, 2003). This means that there is an enormous imbalance between the context within which most babies live, and the knowledge that enters psychology about what we know about babies and their development.

Does this matter? There are two extreme responses to this question, neither of which is particularly helpful. The first extreme response is that all human behaviour is universal and subject to universal laws, and so it does not matter where we collect our information – it will be applicable everywhere. The opposing extreme response is that all human behaviour is context-specific, so what we learn in one context will not apply at all in other contexts. In fact, both these views have an element of truth, but neither provides a complete picture. International research in psychology has shown that certain basic principles of human behaviour apply everywhere, but there are also differences in how people grow up, and how they develop in different parts of the world. While it would be quite wrong, for example, to throw out all knowledge we have about people that comes from Europe and North America, it would also be wrong to think this knowledge can be applied without more thought to other contexts.

One of the difficulties with the debates about the appropriateness of psychological knowledge in different contexts is that when researchers work where there are many other researchers around, they may forget or even become blind to the importance of context. Many researchers based at North American universities, for example, conduct experiments using first-year psychology learners. The reasons for this are obvious: the learners are around, easy to involve in research, and may themselves learn a lot about psychology by participating in these experiments. There is no problem at all with this. The problem may arise, though, when all people working in the particular field of study are studying first-year psychology learners at North American universities. The researchers may forget that all the findings from very many studies come from research conducted on a group of people who are by no means typical of the world's population. They may be tempted to describe what they have found as universal, when they do not know this. Now, it may be the case that they have indeed found something universal – but they need to find proof for this by looking at the issue in a variety of contexts, and not just amongst North American psychology learners. Once they have done this work in a variety of places, and it is shown that context does not affect the outcome of the work, they can begin to speak about universals. When you read psychology books and articles, no matter where they are published or where the research has been conducted, every time you see a generalisation, try to make an assessment of the basis on which the generalisation has been made. Where does the evidence come from, and is the evidence enough to support the generalisation?

There is another sense in which we need to think about the debates about 'African psychology'. It is not enough simply to note that most information in psychology is being produced in North America and Europe. This situation did not come about by chance. The spread of psychology from these northern countries through the rest of the world has been associated with the spread of the influence – political and other – of these countries on the rest of the world. It is not simply a coincidence, for example, that just as North American ideas about psychology are known all around the world, the icon of Coca-cola is also known throughout the world. Psychology has been spread throughout the world in the context of other social processes, such as colonisation and globalisation. This raises interesting questions not only for psychology but also for other disciplines in the social sciences. To what extent is our professionally-constructed knowledge about people a product of the views of people who, for a range of reasons, have power? To what extent is our knowledge about people who do not have much power a product of how these people are seen by more powerful people? These are complex questions which cannot be answered fully here, but they are worth bearing in mind.

In the context of a country like South Africa, we need to ask other questions. Who, even within African countries, is producing psychological knowledge about Africa? Currently, for obvious historical reasons, most of the people who have written about psychology in South Africa have been White. The dominance of White voices in the production of knowledge about psychology is changing (and, indeed, the diversity of the authors of this book is testimony to this), but the dominance is still with us. We need to think, when we read what psychologists say about people, about the possible influences the psychologists' backgrounds may have on the conclusions they may draw about the people they study. There have been shameful examples in the history of psychology in South Africa and elsewhere where psychologists have deliberately produced 'scientific' knowledge in order to support repressive and racist policies. Examples of the use of psychology in the service of totalitarian regimes, and in the service of apartheid, are reasonably easy to find. But we need to ask a more subtle kind of question: To what extent are people who are outsiders to a group able really to understand that group? How should we interpret the many conclusions White South Africans have drawn about Black South Africans, for example? How do we factor into our analyses that in South Africa and many other countries psychologists try to understand people without even being able to understand the languages these people speak? Once again, there are no easy answers to these questions, and blanket generalisations – claiming that 'outsider' psychologists have nothing useful to say or, on the other hand, that 'out-sider' psychologists can say anything they wish without their 'outsider' status being a problem – are especially unhelpful. We need to keep thinking about these questions, bearing in mind how complex they are.

In this regard, it is probably not very helpful, as is sometimes done, to label all of psychology as 'Eurocentric', and to call for a more 'Afrocentric' psychology. Far more important than debates about labels like 'Eurocentric' and 'Afrocentric' are the more subtle questions about who is creating what kinds of knowledge about whom, and with what kinds of result. This book has a clear commitment to allowing psychologists from African backgrounds to help shape how learners of psychology on our continent are introduced to the discipline. But we cannot claim by any means to have answered all the questions that exist about what an 'African psychology' is, or could be. As you read this book, and as you study psychology further, you will return to these questions and debates, and your participation in these debates can help the field move forward.

lesser extent, in Europe. We believe that if psychology is to be of most use in South Africa and similar countries, it is important that people with experiences of different aspects of those societies are the ones writing about psychology – we need to be the ones writing about our discipline for our own colleagues and learners. This leads to the second way in which this book differs from others. We emphasise throughout this book the applications of psychological thinking to South Africa and similar contexts. Just about every section of this book has African examples, and we also emphasise fields of psychology which are often omitted or touched on only briefly in traditional introductory texts. For example, the section on social psychology focuses on social issues which are especially pertinent to South Africa and similar countries. The section on health issues extensively discusses issues of relevance to our part of the world – including HIV/AIDS, tuberculosis and parasites. We have an entire section on educational psychology, as many learners of psychology in Africa are involved in education. In addition to these features, we have included throughout the book stories of South Africans to help readers link the theory of psychology to lives typically lived in our part of the world (see Box 1.5).

In summary, we have tried to create a book which will equip you as a learner of psychology but will also relate to the lives of South Africans. Studying psychology is a great adventure – and we hope you enjoy it as much as we enjoyed writing this book!

And finally, we have included a narrative about Nosipho, a young South African woman, at the beginning of most of the chapters in this book in an effort to place the discussions which follow, in context. You'll meet Nosipho for the first time at the beginning of Chapter 2.

REFERENCES

Sinason, V. (1992). *Mental Handicap and the Human Condition: New approaches from the Tavistock*. London: Free Associations Press.

Tomlinson, M. & Swartz, L. (2003). Imbalances in the knowledge about infancy: The divide between rich and poor countries. *Infant Mental Health Journal*, 24:547–56.

A Brief Introduction to Research Approaches in Psychology

Tyrone Pretorius & Cheryl de la Rey

CHAPTER OBJECTIVES

After studying this chapter you should be able to:
- demonstrate a broad understanding of the research process
- understand the difference between qualitative and quantitative approaches to research
- use tables, graphs and basic statistics to summarise and describe a data set.

Nosipho liked the idea of research, finding out something new, perhaps an answer to an important question or information that would help to improve people's lives in some way. It seemed to her a little like being a detective. It was particularly interesting to think about discovering new things in a field like psychology when there was still so much mystery about why people felt, thought and behaved the way that they did. In some way, she supposed, she had always been a kind of researcher. She had always observed the people around her very closely and when she could, had asked them questions about their lives and how they saw the world. As she learned more about research at university, though, she realised that there were all sorts of useful ways of getting more accurate information and a deeper understanding of how things worked.

Introduction

During the early 1980s, the first clinical trials of the efficacy of azidothymidine (AZT) in slowing the development of the disease known as Acquired Immune Deficiency Syndrome (AIDS) were conducted. These trials showed that patients suffering from AIDS who were given AZT displayed increased appetite, weight gains and elevations in white blood cells related to the body's immune system. In addition, only one of 145 AIDS patients on AZT had died, compared to 19 of 137 patients in a control group who were given a placebo (Fischl *et al.*, 1987). On the basis of these clinical trials, the Food and Drug Administration in the United States gave approval for the use of AZT.

The above example provides an overview of the research process that could be illustrated in a very simplistic way, as shown in Figure 1.

The data collected in stage two can be either qualitative (words, themes) or quantitative (numbers, statistics) in nature. On the basis of this a rather crude distinction can be drawn between qualitative and quantitative approaches to research.

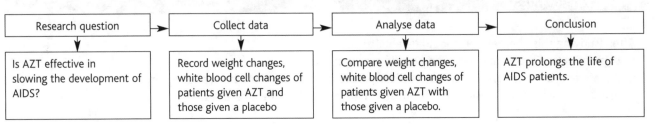

Figure 1 Research and AZT

2.1 WHY DO WE DO RESEARCH? KNOWLEDGE-DRIVEN VERSUS PROBLEM-DRIVEN RESEARCH

Apart from the distinction between quantitative and qualitative research, we also distinguish between knowledge-driven and problem-driven research based on the goals or purposes served by the research process.

Firstly, research enables us to increase our knowledge of human behaviour. By formulating questions and answering them through research, we increase our current levels of knowledge in two important ways. On the one hand, we are better able to describe the phenomenon that we study, and on the other, we are better able to explain it. Thus, research helps us to increase our knowledge of behaviour beyond mere descriptions of it. It helps us to explain, predict, and ultimately understand the phenomena that we study. In this regard it is referred to as knowledge-driven research, that is research that is directed towards the accumulation and testing of knowledge about human behaviour.

The long-term goal of research, however, is not simply to produce knowledge, but rather to produce knowledge that can be applied in some way in the real world. So, while the initial goal of research may be to increase our knowledge and understanding of some behaviour, a further goal is to use this knowledge and understanding to make appropriate changes in our personal and social environment. Research, then, is not confined to the production of knowledge alone, but extends beyond to the transformation of our world. Research that is directed towards such a goal is called problem-driven research.

There has been ongoing debate in the social sciences about which of these types of research are more important. The number of different labels attached to the two types of research has also increased over the years. Knowledge-driven research is also known as theory-driven or basic research, while problem-driven research is also known as decision-driven or applied research. Given the pressing social and economic problems in South Africa the debates about which type of research is more 'relevant' have become extremely intense with proponents of problem-driven research often scathingly referring to knowledge-driven research as 'ivory tower' research.

However, it is important to realise that while these two types of research can be clearly separated in theory, in reality it is not so easy. Research is often a combination of the two, and very rarely does one encounter a research project that does not consider either some dimension of theory or some dimension of behaviour as it exists in the real world. It is true that some research may be overwhelmingly biased towards the production of knowledge, while others may be overwhelmingly biased towards resolving some real problem, but the two types of research complement rather than contradict each other.

Thus, research studies may differ in terms of how much they emphasise the production of knowledge or the solving of problems, but the end goal is the same: we attempt to learn more about ourselves and the environments that we occupy, so that we may be better able to produce changes that enhance our well-being.

Quantitative research

Broadly speaking, quantitative methods are those methods that produce numeric data. These methods could include surveys, questionnaires, mechanical devices and experimental methodology (e.g., the experiment described above). Although these methods of data collection are quite diverse, the common denominator is the analytical procedures that are used to summarise and describe the data and draw conclusions. As such, a major part of this chapter deals with the analysis of quantitative data using statistical procedures. These statistical procedures are usually divided into two categories: descriptive and inferential statistics. *Descriptive statistics* are those analytical tools that are used to organise, summarise and describe data, for example, if we present the difference in weight gains for two groups in graphic form. *Inferential statistics* is that branch of statistics that is used to draw inferences about populations using data obtained from a sample. Thus, although the clinical trials mentioned earlier were conducted on only 282 AIDS patients (the sample), the researchers eventually want to draw conclusions about the efficacy of AZT for all AIDS sufferers (the population). This introductory chapter focuses only on descriptive statistics.

Lastly, the use of computerised statistical software has greatly reduced the laborious computation involved in data analysis. Some of the more popular software includes SPSS (Statistical Package for the Social Sciences) and SAS (Statistical Analysis System). Most universities and technikons have one or both of these systems available. In addition, in many spreadsheet applications (e.g., Microsoft Excel and Lotus) it is possible to obtain a wide range of statistics. The simplicity of use of this software could easily tempt us into adopting a 'cookbook approach' to statistics. However, we believe that a proper grounding in the conceptual and computational underpinning of a statistical procedure is important in assisting a learner or researcher to select, implement and interpret a statistical procedure.

Some concepts

Population and sample

In our example we have seen that instead of studying all AIDS patients, the researchers selected 282 AIDS sufferers to represent those living with AIDS. This sub-set of people is called the *sample*, while the larger group that includes every person with AIDS is called the *population*. To ensure that the sample adequately represents the population we use random sampling to select the members of the sample. *Random sampling* is a selection procedure in which all members of the population have an equal chance of being selected. However, in practice it is often logistically impossible or simply not feasible to draw a random sample, and very often researchers resort to using *convenience samples*. In such instances

---

2.2   YOU DON'T HAVE TO EAT THE WHOLE OX TO KNOW THAT THE MEAT IS TOUGH

The above saying is at the heart of sampling. It is often logistically impossible and extremely expensive to count every member of a population, and therefore we often gather information on the population by studying a selected sample. However, if it is possible to study the whole population would that increase the reliability of our findings?

By law, South Africa is required to have a census every five years. A census is an attempt to collect basic information from each household in the country, and the last census was undertaken in 2001. The results of the 2001 Census were officially released in July 2003. In addition to the census, a Labour Force Survey (LFS), which is based on a sample of 30 000 dwellings, is undertaken twice-yearly to collect information on employment and unemployment. Thus, for 2001 we have two sources of data on unemployment – the Census and the LFS. The 'Census in Brief', released in July 2003, contained both sets of data.

The Census 2001 puts unemployment at 41.6 per cent, whereas according to the LFS, the unemployment rate is 29.5 per cent. We would presume that since the Census represents an active attempt to cover all households, while the LFS is based on a sample of 30 000 dwellings, the Census rate would be seen as the official rate. However, in a footnote it is quite clearly stated that the LFS statistics are the official labour market figures. In the introduction to 'Census in Brief' the following warning is given:

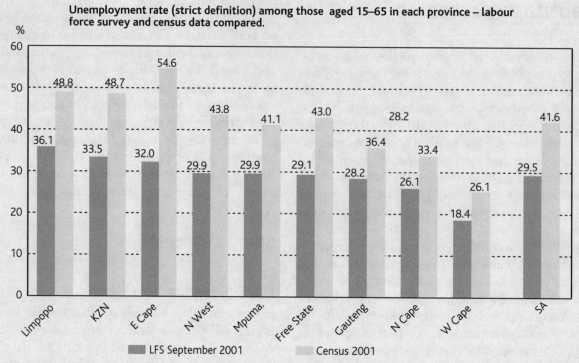

Unemployment rate (strict definition) among those aged 15–65 in each province – labour force survey and census data compared.

	Limpopo	KZN	E Cape	N West	Mpuma.	Free State	Gauteng	N Cape	W Cape	SA
LFS September 2001	36.1	33.5	32.0	29.9	29.9	29.1	28.2	26.1	18.4	29.5
Census 2001	48.8	48.7	54.6	43.8	41.1	43.0	36.4	33.4	26.1	41.6

■ LFS September 2001   ☐ Census 2001

Sources: Labour Force Survey, September 2001 and Census 2001: The LSF figures are the official labour market figures.
According to the LFS, the unemployment rate was 29.5 per cent for the country as a whole in September 2001. These calculations do not include the economically active.

Labour market data are included from both the Labour Force Survey of September 2001 and Census 2001. The Census produces lower estimates of labour force participation than the September 2001 Labour Force Survey. There is possible under-reporting of employment in the informal and subsistence agriculture sectors, particularly among those working only a few hours per week. The Labour Force Survey questionnaire includes more prompts to identify such people, which is not possible during Census enumeration. The United Nations and the International Labour Organisation note that Labour Force Surveys are expected to produce more reliable estimates of labour market variables than Censuses. Note that the Labour Force Survey figures are the official labour market statistics.

it is important to acknowledge the limitations in generalising our findings to the population.

Variables

The characteristics of people or objects that are the focus of our study (weight, white blood cells, etc.) are called variables. A *variable* is any property of an object or person that can vary from person to person or object to object. For example, the colour of a car is a variable since it is a property of an object (car) that can take on different values or labels (red, white, blue, etc.).

The choice of an appropriate statistical procedure rests on a fundamental distinction between discrete and continuous variables. *Discrete variables* are variables:

• that can take on a limited number of values;

• that are assessed only in whole numbers;
• where numbers often have no mathematical properties; and
• there is no sense of a continuum (i.e. high to low).

For example, numbers on a football jersey (1 to 11) are discrete since these numbers are used only for identification, they have no mathematical properties and there is no continuum (i.e. 1 is not lower than 11). *Continuous variables*, on the other hand, can take on any value, even a fraction of a value (for example, examination results). These values range from low to high (30 per cent is less than 50 per cent), and can be used in mathematical computations (i.e. we can calculate the 'average' examination results).

A further distinction can be drawn between dependent and independent variables. The *independent variable* is the variable selected, measured or manipulated by the researcher to determine its effect on another variable. In our example, AZT (absence or presence of it) is the independent variable. The *dependent variable* is the variable influenced by the independent variable (i.e. white blood cells, weight, life expectancy, etc.).

Descriptive data analysis

Let us assume that for the above study we have hypothetical data for 40 subjects on the increase in their protein intake (grams) over a period of four weeks. In an SPSS data file this data would be represented as follows:

The data of the 40 subjects are presented next to each other in three sets of columns. The first column is simply the row number and can be used to identify the subject. The second column is used to indicate whether it is an experimental or control subject (1 = control, 2 = experimental), while the third column indicates the increase in protein intake in grams. Thus, subject 1 was a member of the control group (received placebo) and had an increase of 11 grams in protein intake.

Condensing and summarising data

The table below contains only rows and columns of data, and thus does not communicate anything useful. The first step in data analysis is to organise and present the data so that the essential features of the

data are easily communicated. For this purpose we use tables and graphs. For example, if we were to present the information about the two groups in a table it would look as follows:

Category	f	%
Control	20	50
Experimental	20	50
N = 40		

The above table is called a *frequency distribution* since it indicates the frequency with which each value (or category) occurs. The symbol *f* is used to indicate frequencies, while the symbol N indicates the total number of participants.

Counting the number of times each category occurs is relatively straightforward in the above example since we only had two categories, namely experimental and control. This is called an *ungrouped frequency distribution* since it deals with the actual categories of the variable concerned. However, if we consider the values of protein intake we see that there is a range of values. The lowest value is 8 and the highest value is 37. Theoretically we would therefore have all the values between 8 and 37 listed and count the frequency with which each value occurs. Such a table would not be very informative and could be quite large. In such instances we could use a *grouped frequency distribution* in which the values of the variables are grouped

	Group	Protein		Group	protein		Group	Protein
1	1	11	15	2	24	29	2	31
2	1	23	16	2	26	30	1	13
3	1	25	17	2	30	31	2	27
4	2	26	18	2	24	32	1	33
5	2	37	19	2	25	33	1	30
6	1	10	20	1	26	34	1	12
7	1	10	21	1	12	35	1	14
8	1	11	22	2	25	36	2	14
9	2	11	23	2	26	37	2	29
10	1	12	24	1	24	38	1	16
11	1	13	25	2	27	39	1	31
12	1	13	26	2	32	40	2	31
13	2	14	27	2	15			
14	2	23	28	1	8			

into classes. For example, 8 to 12 would have the values 8, 9, 10, 11 and 12 in it. In deciding how to group scores into classes we could follow some pre-assigned categorisation. For example, if the variable was age we could use the various life stages as a guide to grouping the age scores into classes (for example, 0 to 5 early childhood, 6 to 12 middle childhood and 13 to 18 adolescence). In other instances, where no such theoretical basis exists, we would use the following procedure:

- Decide on the *number of classes*. It is recommended that we consider between 5 and 15 classes. Let us use 10 classes.
- Determine the range of scores. The *range* is the highest score minus the lowest score, that is 37–8 = 29.
- Determine the number of scores that will fall into each class. This is called the *interval size*, and is obtained by dividing the range by the number of classes: 29/10 = 2.9. If we round this off it would be 3. Thus each class would contain three scores.
- The first class should start with a score that is a multiple of the interval size. Since the lowest score for protein intake is 8, the first score below 8 which is a multiple of 3 would be 6. Thus, our first class would be 6 to 8, that is it would contain the scores 6, 7 and 8. The second class would be 9 to 11, that is scores 9, 10 and 11 would fall into this class. We will in fact end up with 11 classes because the lowest score is at the upper end of 6 to 8.
- Count the frequency of each class. We could simply run through the above list and count the number of 6s, 7s and 8s that would fall into the first class. An alternative and more systematic way, however, is to work our way down the list, and mark each score off as we enter it so that we make sure that no scores are missed. For example, taking the first 6 scores:

	Group	Protein		Class	Tally	f
1	1	11		6 to 8		
2	1	23		9 to 11	//	2
3	1	25		...		
4	2	26		...		
5	2	37		21 to 23	/	1
6	1	10		24 to 26	//	2
				...		
				36 to 38	/	1

The procedure that was followed above was:
- List the classes from lowest to highest.
- The first score is 11. Indicate this with a tally mark under the column called tally and delete the score in the table. Do the same with all other scores by indicating them with a tally mark in the appropriate class and deleting it in the table.
- Convert the tally marks to frequencies.

The final table with all the classes and without tally marks would look like the table below. We have added two extra columns.

Classes	f	%	Cum.f	Cum. %
6 to 8	1	2.5	1	2.5
9 to 11	5	12.5	6	15
12 to 14	9	22.5	15	37.5
15 to 17	2	5	17	42.5
18 to 20	0	0	17	42.5
21 to 23	2	5	19	47.5
24 to 26	10	25	29	72.5
27 to 29	3	7.5	32	80
30 to 32	6	15	38	95
33 to 35	1	2.5	39	97.5
36 to 38	1	2.5	40	100
	N = 40			

In analysing the above table:
- From the frequency column (*f*) we can see that one protein score fell into the class 6 to 8, five scores into the class 9 to 11, and so forth.
- The percentage column (%) indicates the percentage of scores falling into a particular class. Thus 2.5 per cent of all scores fell into the class 6 to 8. Percentage is obtained by dividing the frequency of the class by the total number of participants and multiplying by 100: (*f*/N) X 100. For example, for the class 24 to 26 it would be: (10/40) X 100 = 25 per cent.
- Cum.*f* is used to indicate cumulative frequency. *Cumulative frequency* is defined as the number of scores that fall *into and below* a particular class. Thus, for the class 6 to 8, one score fell into and below this class. For the class 9 to 11, six scores fell into and below this class. This is obtained by sim-

ply adding the frequencies of the classes cumulatively. For example, for class 12 to 14 add frequencies of this class and all the classes preceding it: $1 + 5 + 9 = 15$.

- Cum.% refers to *cumulative percentage*, which is the percentage of participants falling into and below a particular class. To find the cumulative percentage, we divide the cumulative frequency by the total number of participants, multiplied by 100: (cum.f/N) X 100. For the class 12 to 14 it would be $(15/40)$ X $100 = 37.5$. This means that 37.5 per cent of participants fell into or below the class 12 to 14.

Although the grouped frequency distribution provides a very useful summary, it suffers from the disadvantage that once scores are grouped they lose their individual identities. Thus one would not know whether the one score that falls into the category 36 to 38 is a 36, 37 or a 38. Therefore any calculations based on this frequency distribution could at best only be estimates. More about this later.

A very useful alternative to group frequency distributions is what is called *stem-and-leaf displays*. In such displays values are broken down into a leading digit (called the stem) and a trailing digit (called a leaf). For example, the value 37 would have a leading digit of 3 and a trailing digit of 7. The values of protein intake ranged between 8 and 37. Thus we could have stems of 0, 1, 2 and 3. In certain instances where there are many leafs to a particular stem, it is advisable to repeat stem values twice and thus divide leafs into low (0 to 4) and high (5 to 9) values. This is the approach followed below.

STEM	LEAF	f
0	8	1
1	0 0 1 1 1 2 2 2 3 3 3 4 4 4	14
*1	5 6	2
2	3 3 4 4 4	5
*2	5 5 5 6 6 6 6 7 7 9	10
3	0 0 1 1 1 2 3	7
*3	7	1
		N = 40

Traditionally, a stem-and-leaf display consists only of the first two columns. We have, however, added a

third column (f) to indicate another way in which these displays could be interpreted. In the above display, the stem of 0 and leaf of 8 indicates the value 8. The stem of 1 and leaf of 0 indicates the value 10. We thus have two 10s, three 11s, and so forth. The stems with an asterisk indicates higher value leafs. Thus a stem of *1 and a leaf of 5 indicates 15. Looking at the frequencies (f) we can see that 14 scores fell into the category 10 to 14 and two scores fell into the category 15 to 19.

Stem-and-leaf displays also provide an opportunity for an exploratory look at possible group differences. Thus, we could compare the scores of the control and experimental groups in the following bivariate stem-and-leaf display. Bivariate in this instance refers to two distributions of scores.

Control			Experimental
	LEAF	STEM	LEAF
	8	0	
	4 3 3 3 2 2 2 1 1 0 0	1	1 4 4
	6	*1	5
	4 3	2	3 4 4
	6 5	*2	5 5 6 6 6 7 7 9
	3 1 0	3	0 1 1 2
		*3	7

The display shows a clustering of the control group at the lower score values and the experimental group at the higher score values, suggesting higher intake of protein for the experimental group. Whether these observed differences are significant is the domain of inferential statistics.

Apart from tables, graphs can also be used to summarise data. The most commonly used graphs are the *bar chart*, the *histogram* and the *frequency polygon*. In the bar chart and the histogram, the frequencies of each score (or categories of scores) are displayed as a vertical bar with the frequencies listed on the y-axis (the vertical axis – also called the ordinate) and the scores (or categories of scores) listed on the x-axis (the horizontal axis – also called the abscissa).

The bar chart is normally used for discrete variables (such a gender), and the vertical bars do not touch each other. Thus, for the variable group we would have the bar chart presented in Figure 2.

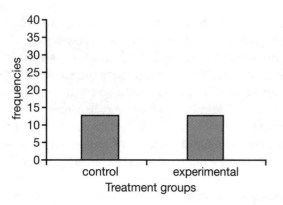

Figure 2 AZT treatment groups and frequencies

Since there were two equal sized groups the two bars are exactly the same height. The gaps between the bars indicate discrete categories. In the case of a histogram these bars touch each other since the histogram is used for continuous scores. However, instead of listing the categories of scores (e.g., 6 to 8) on the x-axis, we use the midpoint of each class (e.g., the midpoint of 6 to 8 is 7), as indicated below. The frequency polygon, on the other hand, is a graph in which the bars are replaced by dots, and these dots are then joined by a line. For this reason, the frequency polygon is often referred to as a line graph. A histogram and frequency polygon of protein intake are shown in Figure 3.

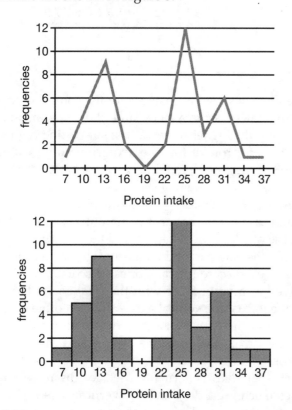

Figure 3 Protein intake and frequency histogram and frequency polygon

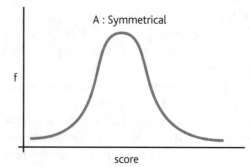

Figure A: Symmetrical

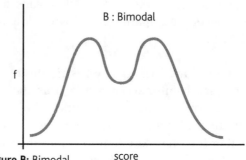

Figure B: Bimodal

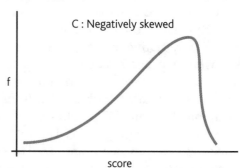

Figure C: Negatively skewed

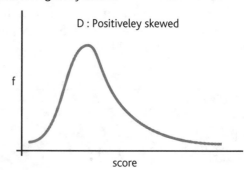

Figure D: Positively skewed

Apart from summarising and presenting data visually, graphs play an important role in describing the shape of the distribution of scores. The shape of a distribution plays a crucial role in the selection of appropriate statistical techniques. The following figures illustrate the most common shapes of a distribution of scores.

Figure A represents a very important distribution in statistics called the *normal distribution*. In a normal

Although the bar graph, histogram and frequency polygon are the most basic ways in which to present data visually, the use of word processing software with powerful graphic capabilities has enabled researchers to use innovative ways of communicating data.

The National Research and Technology Foresight Project of the Department of Arts, Culture, Science and Technology (1999) is part of a larger initiative aimed at reviewing and reforming the Science and Technology system in South Africa. One part of this broader project was the Health Sector report that attempts to address the science and technology challenges that would be faced in providing health care in South Africa from a medium- to long-term perspective. It was found that respondents in this research saw South Africa as unlikely to acquire the necessary technology or capacity for the period 2005-2009. The main set of reasons for why South Africa was perceived to be unable to acquire the necessary technology is shown in the following innovative graph:

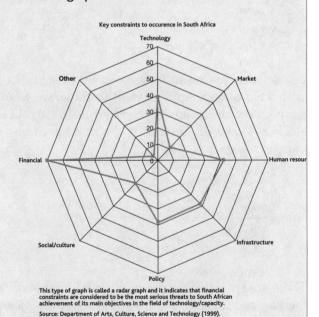

Key constraints to occurence in South Africa

This type of graph is called a radar graph and it indicates that financial constraints are considered to be the most serious threats to South African achievement of its main objectives in the field of technology/capacity.

Source: Department of Arts, Culture, Science and Technology (1999).

This type of graph is called a radar graph, and it indicates that financial constraints are considered to be the most serious threats to South Africa's achievement of its main objectives in the field of technology or capacity.

distribution the majority of scores are clustered in the centre of the distribution and trail off towards the upper and lower extremes. Thus, if this were examination results it would mean the majority of the class obtained marks in the middle range with a few extremely high achievers and a few extremely low achievers. The normal distribution is bell shaped, and called a symmetrical distribution since the left and right halves of the distribution are mirror images of each other.

Figures C and D, on the other hand, are *asymmetrical distributions*. In these distributions there is either a cluster of extremely high scores (*negatively skewed distribution*) or a cluster of extremely low scores (*positively skewed distribution*).

The peak of a distribution indicates where the highest frequency of scores is located. If a distribution has only one peak it is referred to as *unimodal* (Figure A). Distributions with two peaks (i.e. two clusters of scores with the highest frequencies) are referred to as *bimodal* (Figure B). Considering the graphs of our example of protein intake it is clear that there are in fact two distinct peaks, that is a bimodal distribution. This is not totally unexpected since the scores of two distinct groups have been combined into one distribution.

Numerical summary measures

In addition to tables and graphs we could also use some numerical indices to describe the essential characteristics of our data. These numerical indices are divided into:

- *measures of central tendency*: a single value that in some way represents all the values in a distribution; and
- *measures of variability*: a single value that describes the spread (variability) of scores in a distribution.

Measures of central tendency

There are three measures of central tendency, namely the mode, median and mean. The *mode* refers to that score which occurs most frequently in a set of scores. The *median* refers to that score in the middle of a distribution when scores are arranged from low to high, that is the score that halves a distribution in two. The *mean* is the measure of central tendency that most people talk about when they think of the average score. The mean is simply all the scores added together divided by the number of observa-

age' of these two scores are $(10 + 12)/2 = 11$. Thus the median is 11.

If this logic is applied to the set of protein scores we would firstly list the scores from lowest to highest:

8,10,10,11,11,11,12,12,12,13,13,13,14,14,14,15,16,23,23,
19 scores
24,24,
two scores
24,25,25,25,26,26,26,26,27,27,29,30,30,31,31,31,32,33,37
19 scores

We have an even number of scores (i.e. 40), and thus there is no exact middle score. The two scores in the middle with an equal number of scores above and below them are 24 and 24. Thus the median is $(24+24)/2 = 24$.

The mean is all the scores added together and divided by the number of scores. This is reflected in the formula:

$$\overline{X} = \frac{\sum X}{N}$$

where
$\overline{X}$ = *mean*
$\sum X$ = *sum of scores*
N = *number of obsevations*

In statistics, the mean is denoted by the symbol X with a bar on top. Applying this formula, we would simply add all the scores together (8+10+10+11+11, etc. = 844) and divide this by the number of observations which is 40. Thus:

$$\overline{X} = \frac{\sum X}{N}$$
$$= \frac{844}{40}$$
$$= 21.1$$

There are special formulas for calculating the mode, median and mean in the case of grouped frequency distributions where scores have been grouped into classes. However, as noted previously, whenever scores are grouped into classes these scores lose their individual identities. That is if we take the class 15 to 17 with a frequency of 2 we do not know exactly whether these two scores are 15, 16 or 17. In the case of grouped frequency distributions, the mode, median and mean calculated by means of these special formulae are always *approximate statistics* since they are not based on actual scores. In general, therefore,

Figure 4 Definition of a statistician: Someone who stands with their head in a refrigerator and their feet in hot water, and says, 'On average I feel fine'.

tions (N). If we were to use the SPSS program to determine the mode, median and mean of the set of scores relating to protein intake, we would have the following printout:

N	Valid	40
	Missing	0
Mean		21.10
Median		24.00
Mode		26

In the above table the mode is indicated as 26. If we run through our data table above we will see that the score of 26 occurs four times followed by several scores (e.g., 10, 11, 12 and 13) that occur three times. Since it is the score with the highest frequency, 26 is the mode.

The median for the set of protein scores is indicated as 24. If we have an odd number of scores, the middle score is easy to determine: 6, 9, 10, 12 and 16.

In this set of scores, 10 is the median since we have two scores above and below it. If we have an even number of scores we would take the 'average' of the two scores in the middle: 6, 9, 10, 12, 16 and 18.

The scores 10 and 12 are in the middle. The 'aver-

we should as far as possible avoid the computation of measures of central tendency for grouped frequency distributions. Fortunately it is now possible to calculate the mean of smaller distributions using handheld calculators, and for larger distributions, using spreadsheets (like Excel) and statistical software (like SPSS).

Although the mean is the statistic that most people associate with an average, in reality there are many kinds of 'averages,' and the family of averages is referred to as measures of central tendency. Thus, Mr Smooth in the picture below is not lying to his bank manager, his wife or COSATU – he is simply using different types of averages. To his bank manager he mentions the exact middle salary (median), to his wife he mentions the salary earned by most people in the company (mode) and to COSATU he

mentions the total salary costs divided by the number of people (mean).

Measures of variability

While measures of central tendency provide us with a single score that represents the whole distribution (i.e. the 'typical' score), measures of variability provide us with an index of the spread or variability of scores. It is also called measures of dispersion which means to 'scatter' or 'spread out'. When scores are spread out (e.g., 10, 20, 30) the variability is high, and when scores are clustered together (e.g., 9, 10, 11, 12) the variability is low.

The most common measures of variability are the *range*, the *variance* and the *standard deviation*. While the range indicates the difference between the high-

Wage bill: R25 000, R7 600, R5 500, R5 500, R2 500, R2 500, R1 500, R1 400, R1 400, R1 400, R1 400, R1 400

"As you can see Mr. Bank Manager, I do not overspend on wages. The average wage in my company is R1 500".

"Honey, don't worry. We will not go bankrupt. The average salary in my company is only R1 400".

"My workers are the best paid. The average salary in my company is R4 576".

Figure 5 The art of statisticulation (statistical manipulation): 'Figures never lie; liars figure'.

est and the lowest scores, the variance and standard deviation provides an indication of how far scores vary from the mean. The following is the SPSS printout for these measures of variability for our data on protein intake.

N	Valid	40
	Missing	0
Std. Deviation		8.252
Variance		68.092
Range		29

The range is defined as the highest score minus the lowest score. In the example, the highest score is 37 and the lowest score is 8. The range is thus: Range = 37–8 = 29.

Since the range depends only on two scores in the distribution it is considered a very crude measure of variability and is not used often. The variance, on the other hand, uses all the scores in the distribution and is a measure of the average deviation of all the scores in the distribution. For example, if we have the scores 2, 4 and 6, the mean would be 4. Thus, the deviation of these scores from the mean would be as follows:

Score	Mean	Deviation $(X - \bar{X})$
2	4	– 2
4	4	0
6	4	2

The symbol $X\text{-}\bar{X}$ is used to denote deviation from the mean, and it literally means score (X) minus mean ($\bar{X}$). The variance represents an average of these deviations, that is the sum of the deviations divided by the number of observations (N). However, if we were to sum these deviations we would find that they equal 0. To deal with this we simply square all the deviation scores and use these squared deviations in determining the variance. Thus we can computationally define the variance as:

$$\text{variance} = \frac{\text{sum of squared deviations}}{\text{number of observations} - 1}$$

Note that instead of N, N–1 is actually used since it has been demonstrated that for small samples using N–1 leads to greater accuracy. Statistically, we can write the above computational definition as:

$$s^2 = \frac{\sum (X - \bar{X})^2}{N - 1}$$

Using the scores on protein intake, we would go about it as follows. This can be demonstrated using only a few scores:

Score (X)	Mean ($\bar{X}$)	$X - \bar{X}$	$(X - \bar{X})^2$
8	21.1	–13.1	171.61
10	21.1	–11.1	123.21
...	21.1		
...	21.1		
11	21.1	–10.1	102.01
...	21.1		
14	21.1	–7.1	50.41
...	21.1		
29	21.1	7.9	62.41
37	21.1	15.9	252.81
			$\sum (X - \bar{X})^2 = 2655.6$

As an example: the score of 8 (first column) minus the mean of 21.1 (column 2) equals the deviation score (column 3) of 13.1. The deviation score squared (column 4) is equal to 171.61. The sum of the squared deviation scores is equal to 2655.6 (last row of table). Substituting these values in the formula:

$$S^2 = \frac{\sum (X - \bar{X})^2}{N - 1}$$
$$= \frac{2655.6}{40 - 1}$$
$$= 68.09$$

One of the difficulties with variance is that it is not based on the original deviations, but rather on the squared deviations. Thus, it is no longer in the original unit of measurement (in our example the original unit of measurement was grams), and as such has no direct interpretive meaning. Although it can be used to compare two distributions – for example, a distribution with a variance of 40 has greater variability than a distribution with a variability of 20 – it has no significance when it is considered on its own. One solution would be to convert the variance back into the original units of measurement, and this is achieved by taking the square root of the variance. This square root of the variance is called the standard deviation.

$$S = \sqrt{\frac{\Sigma(X - \overline{X})^2}{N-1}}$$

$$= \sqrt{\frac{2655.6}{40-1}}$$

$$= \sqrt{68.09}$$

$$= 8.25$$

Note that the symbol S is used for standard deviation. In the above formula, we have simply placed a square root sign above the previous formula for variance. Thus, we now have a measure of variability that is in the same units as the original scores. We can thus say that on average the various scores deviate 8.25 grams from the mean.

In summary, then, with the tables, graphs and numerical summary measures we have a rather good descriptive picture of our data. From the table and graphs we see that we are working with a bimodal distribution where there are two clusters of scores with the highest frequency. From the numerical summary measures we can say that the mean protein intake was 21.1 grams and that on average the scores deviate 8.25 grams from the mean.

Qualitative research

In the past psychology concentrated its research activities mostly on observable behaviour and on those phenomena that can be measured. The use of quantification and measurement alongside experimental-type methods of investigation were for a long time considered as the only scientifically legitimate methodologies. Initially, the emergence of qualitative research in psychology led to several years of polarised debate about the relative merits of qualitative and quantitative research. Unlike then, it is now broadly accepted that qualitative approaches to research are important and useful within psychology, as is the case in many other disciplines of the social sciences and humanities. It is currently generally accepted that both approaches are equally legitimate approaches, and that in many instances qualitative and quantitative approaches provide complementary insights.

Qualitative research methods are diverse and multidimensional. Although we can crudely define qualitative methods as those that lead to data that are more textual in nature (using words and language as opposed to numbers and figures) this is an oversimplification. The diverse methodologies of qualitative research, however, share certain broadly defined characteristics that distinguish it from quantitative research.

Defining characteristics

The most important defining characteristic is that qualitative methods focus on the study and the interpretation of meaning. Across the variety of qualitative approaches there is recognition that the meaning of human experience is worthy of examination. In short, qualitative research is the interpretive study of a particular issue.

Qualitative researchers point out that any research based exclusively on the examination of observable qualities is fundamentally limited. Instead, it is noted that human experience is always interpreted and can never be fully understood. Therefore, qualitative researchers work from the assumption that our understandings of the world are always mediated, and as a result there is always an interpretative component in research (Banister et al., 1994).

A common feature of qualitative research is the rejection of the possibility of objectivity as the ideal stance from which to generate knowledge. Qualitative researchers point out that language does not merely reflect reality, but it always also conveys something about our interpretation of reality. This means that human beings can never be totally objective. Similarly, qualitative researchers point out that as human beings themselves, researchers can never be totally objective and neutral. Researchers, like the rest of us, are always interpreting what they see, hear and experience. So, instead of trying to totally eliminate the influence of the researcher's understanding, qualitative methods have attempted to develop techniques which take into account the researcher's perspective and then address this as a component of the knowledge generation process.

Rather than objectivity, qualitative researchers use the concept of *reflexivity*. The meaning of reflexivity relates to the understanding of the person as self-reflecting (Smith, 1994). In the research process, reflexivity incorporates the capacity of both the researcher and the participants for self-reflection (Smith, 1994). As pointed out in Banister et al. (1994:150), 'the research topic, design and process, together with the experience of doing the research are reflected on and critically evaluated throughout' by both the researcher and those being researched. This means that research and its outcomes can never be totally objective, as they are necessarily filled with meaning.

This has implications for sampling in qualitative research. In the same way that quantitative methods always rely on a sub-set of the population (the sample), so too does qualitative research. However, it is accepted that because the focus is on meaning the sample can never be completely representative of everyone in the population. This means that the selection procedure is usually determined by the purpose of the study. But, as with quantitative research, and for practical reasons, convenience samples are also often used.

Another common characteristic of qualitative research is the focus on creating a collaborative and reciprocal relationship between the researcher and those being researched. Many creative strategies have been used to mitigate and challenge the power relations set up by the research itself. In psychology there has been a shift from designating people as subjects to participants or interviewees, and this reflects an attempt to do research 'with' as opposed to 'on' people (Banister *et al.*, 1994). The effort to create non-hierarchical relationships between the researcher and the researched has often resulted in attempts to incorporate participants as co-researchers by engaging in dialogic analytical exchange.

Data gathering

The main aim of most qualitative studies is to explain the ways people come to understand and account for issues, events and behaviours in their lives. In these studies, the researcher attempts to gain a holistic view of the issue being studied, and the view of the participant is therefore of central importance. The data gathered covers the perceptions, meanings and interpretations of the participants. An example of qualitative research is shown in the box overleaf.

In qualitative research there are a number of procedures or techniques of research that are relatively well established. Interviewing is one of the most frequently used techniques of gathering qualitative data.

Interviewing

In simple terms, *interviewing* involves the researcher asking questions, listening and analysing the responses. It is a process of gathering information for research using verbal interaction. The process typically begins with an approach being made to a potential participant. The researcher usually begins by giving some short information about him- or herself, such as name and institutional affiliation, and by describing the purpose of the study.

Interviews may differ in terms of the structure and format. In the most *structured* format the interviewer follows a set list and sequence of questions. In *semi-structured interviews*, the researcher ensures that certain areas of questioning are covered but there is no fixed sequence or format of questions. In *open-ended interviews* the researcher merely tries to remain focused on an issue of study without any pre-set list of questions. Typically, the interviewee will begin by asking a general, wide-ranging question on the issue of interest, but will allow the format and flow to be shaped by the interviewee. This type of interview is appropriate when the aim is to gain insight on the insider's (or participant's) meaning or interpretation.

Interviews may be conducted in a one-to-one situation or using a group setting. *Focus group interviews*, originally used in market research, are now widely used in psychological research. Focus group interviews basically entail a group discussion that explores a particular topic selected by the researcher. The discussion is facilitated by a moderator who enables and aids the discussion among the participants. A major advantage of focus groups is that it is a format that offers the researcher the opportunity to gather information in situations where participants are engaged in interaction with one another. In interactive settings, statements made by a participant may initiate a reaction and additional comments, thus offering a wider perspective of a topic or issue.

Interviews and focus groups are the most widely used techniques of gathering qualitative data. Other methods include the collection and study of documents, letters, entries in personal diaries and several other written sources of information. Audio and visual material is also used for research purposes, although these are usually converted to written format through transcriptions and note-taking.

Analysing qualitative data

There are several methods of qualitative data analysis such as thematic analysis, discourse analysis and narrative analysis. In all these techniques words constitute the basic unit to be analysed. All types of qualitative data analysis revolve around the analysis of meaning. Information gathered via interviews and other sources is usually transcribed. The analysis involves sifting through the transcripts in a systematic way so that conclusions may be reached about the issue under investigation.

Thematic analysis is the most commonly used method of qualitative data analysis. Audio-taped transcriptions are first broken down into units of meaning. The researcher then uses a technique to place the units of meaning into categories. In this way themes are systematically identified. When collated by the researcher, these themes will give insight into the particular issue being studied. In the past there was no computerised assistance for the researcher engaged in such qualitative analysis. However, in recognising the increasingly important role of qualitative research, some of the bigger statistical software companies have started developing tools to aid in this analysis. An example of SPSS's TextSmart is shown below.

Narrative analysis is a technique that approaches the transcript as if it were a story following some type of sequence. Reissman (1993), a well-known scholar of narrative, explained that a narrative always responds to the question 'and then what happened?'. Narrative analysis is especially useful for the study of changes over time. It may be used to explain how participants in a study understand past events and actions and also how they make sense of themselves and their own actions. Box 2.4 provides an example of a study which used narrative analysis to investigate how women make sense of abusive relationships.

Discourse analysis places a great deal of emphasis on the role of language. It is a technique through which the researcher analyses the use and structure of language to reveal representations of the world or sets of meanings. The researcher typically tries to

2.4   QUALITATIVE RESEARCH IN ACTION: SOUTH AFRICAN WOMEN'S NARRATIVES OF VIOLENCE

In South Africa, abuse of women is a pervasive problem affecting millions of families. Why do many women remain in relationships with men who abuse them? Boonzaier and de la Rey (2003) reported on a study in which 15 women living in Mitchell's Plain in the Western Cape in South Africa were interviewed. All the women who were interviewed had been married for periods from 5 to 26 years, and they had each experienced long-term abuse from their partners.

To gain a comprehensive picture of women's understandings of the violence, open-ended interviews were conducted. The issues covered in the interviews included specific woman's experiences of the abuse, how she responded, her feelings towards her partner and her reflections on staying or leaving. Prior to the interviews all the women were informed about the nature and procedure of the research, and the voluntary nature of their participation was explained.

During the interviews, the women described traumatic and painful memories of abuse. The interviewer took special care to establish rapport, show empathy and to convey sensitivity. At the end of each interview, the interviewer, who was from Mitchell's Plain herself, initiated a debriefing session in which the women could discuss the interview and the research process.

All interviews were tape-recorded and then transcribed. The interview transcripts were read many times, paying particular attention to the contents. These transcripts were then analysed to uncover the similarities and differences across and within cases. In analysing the transcripts, the gender identity of the roleplayers as women or men was particularly evident. Narrative analysis was used to show how the women's understandings of romantic love play an important role in binding them to their partners.

Many of the women viewed their partners as having two sides: a good side, which they loved, and then an abusive side. The women connected the appearance of the bad side to alcohol and drug abuse. Many of them described how their partners verbally abused them by calling them derogatory names. The authors show how these terms are examples of dominant cultural representations of women as either virgin or whore.

All of the women interviewed had sought assistance from various sources such as family, religious institutions and social agencies. The analysis revealed how these sources play contradictory roles, sometimes condemning the violent partner, but also encouraging the woman to be a good wife and remain in the relationship. Overall, the study shows how women's understanding of their experience of abuse is linked to the particular context in which their experiences occurred. Economic hardships, alcohol and drug abuse and dominant perspectives of masculinity and femininity all interact to shape women's responses and reactions.

A rental car company is considering selling its pre-driven vehicles. To sell the right car to the right buyer, the company undertakes an in-depth market survey. The rental car company asks a sample of people in its target market to describe — in their own words — what factors appeal to them when evaluating vehicles. The following procedure shows how well TextSmart works on the open-ended question: 'Why do you like the car/truck that you own?'

The analyst begins by importing the complete text of each response. TextSmart automatically filters the text by stemming, aliasing and excluding words. Plus, TextSmart offers powerful tools that give the analyst the flexibility to spell-check words, include or exclude terms and group terms into aliases. In a matter of minutes, the analyst acquires a thorough list of terms conveying her or his respondents' opinions and is now ready to begin analysis.

The Responses window (below left) shows responses that have been imported into TextSmart. The Included window (below right) displays the frequency of important terms in the responses. It also shows an example of a stemmed alias. TextSmart's stemming process automatically combines 'reliable' and 'reliability' into the alias 'rely'.

Next, the analyst cleans and refines this list of terms by excluding trivial terms and grouping synonyms into aliases. This process creates a list of terms that are suitable for categorisation.

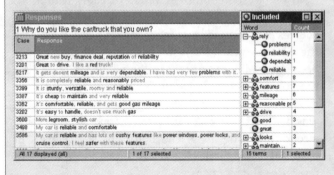

Sorting terms by frequency, the analyst discovers that a car's comfort is a priority to many respondents. The TextSmart window shows a custom alias created by the analyst by easily dragging and dropping terms into the alias window.

Using TextSmart's automatic categorisation feature, the analyst clusters terms that tend to occur together in responses. With TextSmart's powerful tools, she or he revises the categories to meet her or his specifications. She or he even has the flexibility to create custom categories.

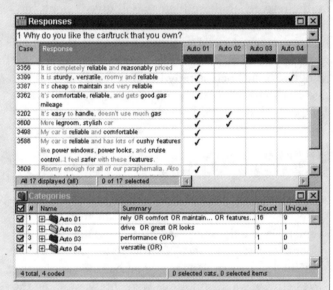

TextSmart created several categories automatically. The analyst now easily revises and labels the categories. The checkmarks indicate the responses that apply to each category.

Using TextSmart, the analyst codes the open-ended responses. She or he then exports these categories to a statistical package and merges them with other respondent data. By comparing and contrasting these coded responses, the analyst gets a clear, systematic representation of her or his respondents' attitudes and perceptions. With these results, the rental car company is able to create a focused marketing strategy that targets the best prospects for their pre-driven vehicles.

draw attention to dominant meanings of a particular phenomena as well as how these meanings may be contradictory and ambivalent. Överlien (2003), for example, examined how the staff members at a detention home for young women talk about them (the young women) as if they were still children, denying them any sense of sexuality.

In reality, many studies using qualitative methods use a mix of data analysis techniques. Most importantly, however, is that the researcher must be systematic in the analysis. There are several debates about the rigour of qualitative research which centre on questions such as: 'How can we trust the authenticity of qualitative research?' And, 'how can we be sure that such research is reliable and valid?'

Verification of qualitative data

There are many different perspectives on how to render qualitative data trustworthy and rigorous. A frequently used technique is correspondence checks. This may involve the use of colleagues and other researchers to analyse the data independently. This analysis is then compared with that done by the primary researcher to check for correspondence. Some researchers take the analysed data back to the participants to find out what they think of the analysis. Another technique that may be used is to openly consider alternative interpretations of the data and then report on these too. Whatever technique is used, all researchers in the end must show that the interpretation is not simply ad hoc but relates to the overall goals, theory and method of the study. In the final analysis, the researcher should provide sufficient information to show that a systematic procedure was followed so as to allow others to assess the merits and trustworthiness of the work (Reissman, 1993).

Conclusion

At the conclusion of this chapter we can now revisit the rather simplistic presentation of the research process that was provided at the beginning of this chapter. We can basically view the research process as consisting of the following six stages.

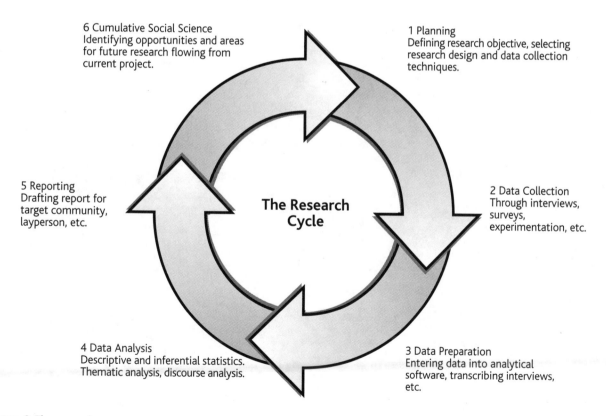

Figure 6 The research process

These stages apply equally to quantitative and qualitative research.

Banister, P. Burman, E., Parker, I., Taylor, M. & Tindall, C. (1994). *Qualitative Methods in Psychology: A research guide*. Buckingham: Open University Press.

Boonzaier, F. & de la Rey, C. (2003).'He's a man, and I'm a woman': Cultural constructions of masculinity and femininity in South African women's narratives of violence. *Violence Against Women*, 9(8):1003-29.

Department of Arts, Culture, Science and Technology. (1999). *National Research and Technology Foresight Project: Health*. Pretoria: Government Printer.

Fischl, M.A. (1987). The efficacy of azidothymidine (AZT) in the treatment of patients with AIDS and AIDS-related complex. *New England Journal of Medicine*, 317:185-91.

Överlien, C. (2003). Innocent girls or active young women? Negotiating sexual agency at a detention home. *Feminism & Psychology*, 13(3):345-67.

Reissman, C.K. (1993). *Narrative Analysis*. Newbury Park, CA: Sage.

Smith, J.A. (1994). Towards reflexive practice: Engaging participants as co-researchers or co-analysts in psychological inquiry. *Journal of Community & Applied Social Psychology*, 4:253-60.

SPSS. (2003). www.spss.com. TextSmart Online.

Statistics South Africa. (2003). *Census 2001: Census in brief*. Pretoria: Statistics South Africa.

Multiple choice questions

1. There is a relationship between duration of study or time spent studying and exam performance. In this sentence, 'exam performance' is the
   a) dependent variable
   b) sample
   c) population
   d) independent variable

2. Read the following sentences and indicate which is not true and incorrect
   a) the amount of soft drinks consumed at a party is variable
   b) the amount of nicotine in John Rolfe cigarettes is variable
   c) the sex of students in an all boys school is not variable
   d) a group of Grade 8 pupils is not variable

3. Read the following sentences and indicate which is true
   a) height and length are discrete variables
   b) occupation and marital status are continuous variables
   c) blood pressure is a discrete variable
   d) addresses and postal codes are discrete variables

4. Indicate which of the following statements relating to qualitative research is false
   a) the researcher aims to interact with and involve those being researched in a reciprocal relationship
   b) a qualitative researcher should ensure objectivity in research
   c) reflexivity, rather than objectivity, is central to the qualitative research process
   d) since our understandings of the world are always mediated, there is always an interpretive component in research

5. Which of the following pairs of statements describes the relationship between sample and population?
   a) learners in Psychology 1; all learners at the university
   b) players of Kaizer Chiefs soccer team; all players in the PSL
   c) lecturers at UWC; lecturers at Wits
   d) rural learners; urban learners

6. In a quantitative study, the research process may be described as a sequence of steps. These steps are
   a) conclusion; research question; data collection, data analysis
   b) data collection, research question, data analysis, conclusion
   c) data collection, data analysis, research question, conclusion
   d) research question, data collection, data analysis, conclusion

7. Which one of the following statements best describes a discrete variable?
   a) years of service of the psychology lecturers
   b) assessment in whole numbers only
   c) values ranging from low to high
   d) values ranging from high to low

8. The main difference between a measure of central tendency and a measure of variability is that
   a) the one is used for discrete variables and the other for continuous variables
   b) the first one reflects the population whereas as the other describes the sample
   c) the one represents all the values in the distribution whereas the other describes the spread of scores in a distribution
   d) the one is used in quantitative approaches and the other is used in qualitative approaches

9. The variance is calculated by
   a) subtracting the lowest score from the highest score in a distribution
   b) adding all the scores and then dividing by the total number of scores (N)
   c) computing the sum of the deviations divided by the number of scores (N)
   d) counting the frequency with each value occurs

10. In a normal distribution
    a) each member of the population has an equal chance of being selected
    b) there is a cluster of extremely high scores and a cluster of extremely low scores
    c) there are two clusters of fairly high scores or fairly low scores
    d) the majority of scores are clustered in the centre with few scores at the extreme ends

11. The defining features of qualitative research include
    a) a focus on meaning, reflexivity, minimising the power gap between the researcher and participants
    b) a focus on averages, reflexivity, minimising the power gap between researcher and participants
    c) a focus on meaning, objectivity, minimising the power gap between researcher and participants

d) a focus on variance, reflexivity, minimising the power gap between researcher and participants

12. Which of the following is a technique not used in qualitative research?
    a) discourse analysis
    b) interviewing
    c) central tendency analysis
    d) thematic analysis

13. Verification checks in qualitative data analysis may involve
    a) asking colleagues to analyse the data independently
    b) counting and tallying the frequency of variables
    c) providing sufficient detail of the procedure that was followed
    d) considering alternative interpretations

14. Discourse analysis involves
    a) grouping units of meaning into categories
    b) drawing attention to language usage to reveal dominant meanings
    c) tallying marks to frequencies
    d) examining changes over time

15) Which of the following statements is not typical of qualitative research?
    a) selection of the sample is determined by the purpose of the study
    b) the researcher reflects on the process of the study throughout
    c) the data gathered covers perceptions, meanings and feelings
    d) properties of persons are assigned different values

Short answer questions

1. Construct a frequency distribution for the following set of scores that reflect the number of times a ball was kicked by various rugby players. Use 12 class intervals:

   5, 5, 6, 7, 8, 8, 9, 9, 9, 9, 10, 10, 10, 10, 10, 13, 13, 14, 15, 15, 16, 18, 19, 19, 19, 21, 22, 23, 24, 26, 28, 29, 30, 31, 32, 33, 34, 35, 38, 38.

Use 12 class intervals and add columns for percentage, cumulative frequency and cumulative percentage. Then, using the above frequency distribution answer the following questions:

- What percentage of players kicked the ball between 21 and 23 times?
- How many players kicked the ball 18 times and less?
- What percentage of players kicked the ball 27 times or more?

Use the data in the previous exercise to construct an appropriate graph. Describe the shape of this distribution.

2. A control and experimental group were assessed in terms of reaction time. The control group received non-alcoholic beverages while the experimental group received a controlled amount of alcohol. The reaction time of the two groups are shown below:

   Control: 20, 21, 21, 21, 26, 29, 30, 31, 33, 35, 36, 37, 40, 40, 40, 41, 41, 41, 43, 43, 43, 43, 43, 43, 44, 44, 44, 47, 47, 49

   Experimental: 19, 19, 19, 19, 20, 20, 20, 20, 20, 20, 21, 21, 21, 21, 21, 21, 21, 21, 21, 24, 24, 25, 25, 25, 26, 28, 33, 38, 39, 44

   Construct a back-to-back stem-and-leaf display for the two groups. Repeat stem values twice. What preliminary conclusions are you able to draw on the basis of the comparison of the distribution of scores of the two groups?

   Now, use the stem-and-leaf display. Rotate the display so that the leafs are pointed vertically. Draw a line around the leaves and then describe the shape of the distribution for both groups. Once you have done this, combine the scores into one distribution and then describe the shape of the distribution.

3. For the following sets of scores determine the mode, median, mean, range, variance and standard deviation:

   18, 17, 22, 20, 25, 20, 16, 19, 18, 22, 26, 23, 23, 23, 24, 24, 22, 21, 19, 20, 20, 14, 18, 16, 28, 14, 14, 17, 18, 18, 6

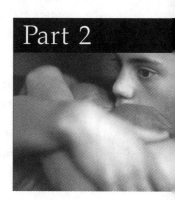

Part 2

Developmental Psychology

Norman Duncan

Developmental psychology can be described as a sub-discipline within psychology that broadly aims to describe and explain the on-going changes that people undergo throughout the human life span.

Largely to facilitate the description and explication of the complexities of human development, many developmental psychology volumes subdivide the human life span into developmental periods or stages. The criteria for this subdivision are normally chronological age and biological indicators of development change, such as the growth spurt at the beginning of the adolescent years, menarche and menopause[1]. While subdividing human development into stages may facilitate the description and explication of human development, this approach has various shortcomings, three of which are briefly outlined below.

Firstly, in this approach, the stages of development are most frequently based on North American models and criteria of human development. A too narrow application of the approach to contexts such as southern Africa may therefore be inappropriate and misleading. For example, it is accepted that the stages of adult development are based partly on predicted life expectancy rates. While the average life span in the United States was between 72 and 79 years during the 1990s[2], the average life span for the majority of South Africans was estimated to be 54 years during more or less the same time period[3]. Obviously, with such disparate age markers, what is conceived of as 'normal' adult development within the United States and similar high-income contexts cannot simply be transposed to lower-income contexts such as South Africa, as is frequently the case with the application of the 'stages of development' approach.

Secondly, the 'stages of development' approach tends to homogenise or gloss over the differences in development within stages, and in the process negates the uniqueness of individual development[4]. Actual development is much more complex than the 'stages of development' approach would lead us to believe because individuals sometimes grow in spurts or stops-and-starts, sometimes bit-by-bit, and at other times constantly[5].

Thirdly, the focus on the age- or biology-determined unfolding of development typical of the 'stages of development' approach, frequently leads to the role of the environment in human development being underplayed. Yet, as will become abundantly clear as you read through the chapters in this part of the book, environmental factors play a pivotal role in human development.

This part basically considers the human life span in five broad stages. However, it should be stressed that within the context of this volume, these stages should be seen as reflecting broad approximate developmental trends, rather than as a template for all human development in all contexts[6]. The broad stages of human development considered in this part are:

- The prenatal and neonatal period (Townsend's chapter).
- The preschool period (Mayekiso's chapter).
- The middle childhood period (Ntshangase's chapter).
- The period of adolescence (Shefer's chapter).
- Adulthood and aging (the chapter by Duncan and van Niekerk).

Thus, in essence, this part covers the entire human life span. As indicated, each of the above-mentioned periods is covered in a separate chapter. Largely to ensure a discussion of the key areas of development, as well as for the sake of overall coherence, development in each of the five life stages identified is presented in terms of the following three key developmental categories:

- Physical development, which includes physiological changes and motor development.
- Cognitive development, which includes the development of language and thought processes.
- Psychosocial development, which includes emotional development, personality development and the development of interpersonal relations[7].

Here it should be noted that while dividing development into these three domains might facilitate a comprehensive and coherent description of development during the various life stages covered in this part, in reality, people's behaviour and development cannot be divided into such neat categories[8]. People are 'whole' beings, and their development at any point in time involves a complex interaction of the three domains mentioned[9]. It should also be noted that throughout this part, Jean Piaget's theory is employed to describe various aspects of cognitive development, and Erik Erikson's psychosocial theory is used to discuss various facets of the individual's psychosocial development in the stages of development covered. The reader should, however, remember that Piaget's theory is merely one of several theories of cognitive development; and Erikson's theory is one of many theories of psychosocial development. The only reason why we focused on these theories throughout this part was to ensure a measure of continuity.

In addition to the five chapters covering the life stages referred to above, this part also includes Tomlinson's chapter focusing on the important developmental process of attachment.

While covering most of the key areas of development normally covered in standard developmental psychology texts currently available, in terms of its sharp focus on the contextual obstacles or challenges to optimal human development confronting many South Africans, this part differs from similar sections in these other texts. The HIV/AIDS pandemic (which at present is sweeping a path of human destruction through southern Africa) is one such contextual obstacle, and each chapter considers its impact on human development in South Africa. Apart from attempting to illustrate how this pandemic currently impacts on the lived reality of South Africans at various points in the human life span, the chapters in this part also illustrate how the pandemic, through the sheer extent of its destructive trajectory, will challenge and profoundly alter our basic assumptions and understanding of human development in years to come.

The notion of human resilience is another key issue taken up in all the chapters comprising this part. All the authors contributing to this part agree that because of human resilience, people do not necessarily succumb to the contextual obstacles confronting them. However, they generally also concur that because these obstacles may render people vulnerable to a range of risks and thereby undermine their optimal development, they should be eliminated. In this sense, the chapters in this part adopt what has been referred to as a critical social scientific stance[10]. In adopting this stance, these chapters obviously reject the outmoded notions of scientific or academic neutrality and detachment. Instead, through their attempts to lay bare some of the key contextual obstacles to optimal human development in South Africa – largely in an effort to encourage the reader to consider the ways in which these obstacles can be eliminated – they clearly support an agenda of social change[11].

Consequently, it is hoped that the content of this part will not only provide the reader with a broad understanding of development throughout the human life span, but that it will also motivate the reader to consider the ways in which the obstacles confronting many South Africans can be eliminated.

REFERENCES

1   Butterworth, G. & Harris, M. (1994). *Principles of Developmental Psychology*. Hove, Sussex: LEA; Duncan, N., Van Niekerk, A. & Mufamadi, J. (2003). Developmental psychology: A lifespan perspective. In L. Nicholas (Ed.). *An Introduction to Psychology*. Wetton: UCT Press, pp. 13-52; Hurlock, E.B. (1980). *Developmental Psychology: A life span approach*. New York: McGraw-Hill.

2   Berger, K.S. (1994). *The Developing Person Through the Life Span*. New York: Worth Publishers.

3   Dorrington, R. Bourne, D., Bradshaw, D., Laubscher, R. & Timaeus, I.M. (2001). T*he Impact of HIV/AIDS on Adult Mortality in South Africa*. Technical Report: Burden of Disease Research Unit. Tygerberg: Medical Research Council.

4   Berger, K.S. (1994). *The Developing Person Through the Life Span*. New York: Worth Publishers; Duncan, N., Van Niekerk, A. & Mufamadi, J. (2003). Developmental psychology: A lifespan perspective. In L. Nicholas (Ed.). *An Introduction to Psychology*. Wetton: UCT Press, pp. 13-52.

5   Berger, K.S. (1994). *The Developing Person Through the Life Span*. New York: Worth Publishers.

6   Duncan, N., Van Niekerk, A. & Mufamadi, J. (2003). Developmental psychology: A lifespan perspective. In L. Nicholas (Ed.). *An Introduction to Psychology*. Wetton: UCT Press, pp. 13-52.

7. Clarke-Stewart, A., Perlmutter, M. & Friedman, S. (1988). *Lifelong Human Development*. New York: Wiley; Hook, D. & Cockcroft, K. (2002). Basic concepts and principles in developmental psychology. In D. Hook, J. Watts & K. Cockcroft (Eds.). *Developmental Psychology*. Wetton: UCT Press, pp. 25-37.

8   Duncan, N., Van Niekerk, A. & Mufamadi, J. (2003). Developmental psychology: A lifespan perspective. In L. Nicholas (Ed.). *An Introduction to Psychology*. Wetton: UCT Press, pp. 13-52.

9   Clarke-Stewart, A., Perlmutter, M. & Friedman, S. (1988). *Lifelong Human Development*. New York: Wiley.

10 Neuman, W.L. (1997). *Social Research methods. Qualitative and quantitative research approaches*. Boston: Allyn & Bacon.

11. Duncan, N., Van Niekerk, A. & Mufamadi, J. (2003). Developmental psychology: A lifespan perspective. In L. Nicholas (Ed.). *An Introduction to Psychology*. Wetton: UCT Press, pp. 13-52.

Pre- and Neonatal Development

Loraine Townsend

CHAPTER OBJECTIVES

After studying this chapter you should be able to:
- describe the stages of prenatal development
- explain environmental factors that may place a foetus at risk for abnormal development
- present an account of development in the first two to four weeks of life.

Like so many others Nosipho had no recollections about her birth and being a newborn baby. She did however remember listening to the stories her mom and aunt told about this time. Her mom remembered really enjoying being pregnant with Nosipho. The family made sure she ate well and took care to have a rest when she could. They told her mom that this was important because proper nutrition and rest was important for the development of the baby. Nosipho's aunt told her of the young girl who lived down the road who fell pregnant and drank lots of alcohol during her pregnancy. The baby was very weak and ill when it was born and still had problems learning. Nosipho is always told that when she was born everyone exclaimed how fat and contented she looked. Although she slept a lot, when she was awake her mom remembers her being very alert and easily startled by loud noises. She would gaze into her mom's face and her mom believes that Nosipho recognised her voice from before she was actually born.

Introduction: Prenatal development

The foundations of adult health are laid down in prenatal development and childhood. This chapter will explore these foundations as they relate to prenatal and early neonatal development.

Each of us begins our life as a zygote, a single cell not much larger than the full stop at the end of this sentence, weighing approximately fifteen-millionths of a gram. If all goes well, just about 280 days later, at birth, we consist of some 2 billion cells and weigh more or less 3 kilograms. Clearly, then, during our entire lifespan, these 280 days (40 weeks or 9 months) of prenatal development inside our mothers' wombs are the most significant for our growth and development.

Conception

Approximately 14 days before a woman's menstrual period begins, she ovulates and a mature egg cell (ovum) is released from one of her ovaries into the fringed ends (called fimbria) of one of the two fallopian tubes. These fallopian tubes are no wider than a strand of human hair and are roughly 10 centimetres long. Within the tubes are thousands of cilia (hair-like projections) that constantly make waving movements, which move the ovum along the tube in the direction of the uterus.

During sexual intercourse, a man ejaculates millions of sperm cells, called spermatozoa, which are mixed with seminal fluid into a woman's vagina. Each

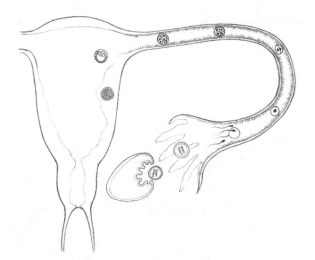

Figure 1 Early human development: From conception to implantation

cubic centimetre of ejaculation may contain as many as 18 million sperm cells. Each sperm cell is shaped much like a tiny tadpole, with a 'head' containing the cell nucleus and a thin 'tail' that thrashes about causing it to move along in a swimming motion. Of these millions of swimming sperm, only a few hundred will survive the relatively long journey to the fallopian tube containing the receptive ovum. Of these hundreds, only one will merge with, and fertilise the ovum. The merged cell is a single cell called a zygote.

However, in the case of twins or other multiple births, more than one egg cell is released from the ovaries and will be fertilised.

With dizygotic twins, two egg cells will be released and fertilised, while with identical or monozygotic twins, the single cell zygote splits into two identical, but separate zygotes. In rare cases, the single cell zygote does not split completely, and the two zygotes may continue to develop but remain joined in some way. In this instance, co-joined or Siamese twins develop. With triplets, quadruplets, etc. three, four or more egg cells are released and fertilised respectively.

Stages of prenatal development

The germinal stage

The first two weeks after conception are referred to as the germinal stage of prenatal development. It is a time when the zygote divides into a number of identical cells by means of a process called mitosis. It first divides into two cells, doubles to four, then eight and so on. About four days after conception, the cell mass, now comprising some 100 cells, emerges from the fallopian tube and gently descends into the uterus. Over the next few days, cell division becomes more organised and specialised and the cell mass is known as the blastocyst. It comprises two kinds of cells – the trophoblast and the inner cell mass, which play different roles in the development of the embryo and later the foetus.

After floating in the uterus for a day or so, the blastocyst settles in one spot. The lining of the uterus is rich with blood and is spongy, and is ready to receive the blastocyst which begins to burrow ever more deeply and implant itself into the mother's blood vessels and uterine wall. The cells in the uterine wall close over the hole through which the blastocyst burrowed and implantation is complete.

The embryonic stage

Once the blastocyst successfully implants in the uterus, the developing organism enters the stage of the embryo, which lasts for the next six weeks, until the eighth week or second month of pregnancy. During this time, the trophoblast and the inner cell mass develop further.

The trophoblast produces two membranes that will provide the developing embryo with its life support systems: protection and nutrition. The one membrane, called the amnion, begins to fill with amniotic fluid and surrounds the embryo. The amniotic fluid will protect the developing embryo and later the foetus by acting as a cushion against shock or injury as the mother moves about. The other membrane, called the chorion, becomes the foetal part of the placenta.

The placenta, which is a complex organ made of tissue from the embryo and the mother, is connected to the embryo by the umbilical cord. Along the length of the cord are veins and arteries that carry oxygen and nutrients such as sugars, fats, basic proteins and minerals to the embryo, and carry waste products, carbon dioxide and urea from the embryo to be disposed of by the mother's body.

At the same time, the inner cell mass begins to differentiate into the kinds of cells that will eventually become the organism's various body parts and organs. The cells multiply rapidly during this time and organise themselves into functional units, and new physical structures appear at astonishing speed (see Box 3.1).

By the end of the embryonic stage of development, the embryo is about 2 centimetres long. Despite its miniature size, the embryo is clearly recognisable as a human being: its face has eyes, nose, mouth, lips, ears and a jaw, all in the correct places. Its hands have fingers and thumbs; its legs have knees, ankles, feet and tiny toes; and the essential organ systems and the nerve cells of the spine have formed.

The foetal stage

During the foetal stage, which lasts from around eight weeks after conception until birth, the structure and systems that developed during the embryonic stage grow in size and efficiency. To give you an indication of the extensive and rapid growth that takes place during this period, some developments through each of the months are described.

3.1 DEVELOPMENT OF THE EMBRYO

End of second week
Amnion and chorion membranes emerge from the trophoblast and surround the developing embryo. The inner cell mass separates into three layers, the ectoderm, endoderm, and mesoderm, which become the body parts and organs.

Third week
The foundations of the brain, spinal cord, and nervous system develop. Rudimentary blood cells and blood vessels evolve. The heart develops, first as a tube then as a chambered pump. It begins to beat at the end of the third week.

Fourth week
A system for digesting food and kidney-like structures form. Arm and leg buds appear. Eyes and ears begin to take form. The formation of major veins and arteries is completed. The vertebrae of the spine become visible. Nerves begin to form in simple structures.

Fifth week
The umbilical cord, linking the embryo to the placenta, forms. Bronchial buds, which eventually become lungs, develop. Masses that become muscles appear in the head, trunk and limbs.

Sixth week
The head predominates in size. The outer ear takes shape. The lower jaw is complete; the upper jaw begins to form. The three main parts of the brain – the hindbrain, the midbrain and the forebrain – become quite distinct.

Seventh week
The face and neck begin to take definite form. Eyelids take shape. The stomach takes its final shape and position. Muscles are forming throughout the body and are beginning to assume their final shapes and relationships. The brain is developing thousands of nerve cells per second. A valve develops in the heart to separate the upper and lower parts.

Eighth week
The neck becomes distinct and the head elevates. The body assumes a more rounded appearance. The embryo is about 2cm in length. It is capable of some movement, and responds to stimulation around its mouth.

Procedure

During the final month and a half of pregnancy, 16 pregnant mothers were asked to read aloud a passage from a children's rhyming story. By the time their babies were born, they had 'heard' the passage many times. Two or three days after birth, the babies listened through headphones to either their mother or a stranger reading the same passage.

Results

As these neonates listened to the recorded voices, they quickly learned to use different sucking patterns on a specially designed dummy or pacifier to hear their mother's voice rather than the stranger's.

Conclusion

Foetuses can hear sounds, which they appear to remember and recognise soon after birth (DeCasper & Spence, 1986).

During the third and fourth months, male and female sex organs develop. From the fourth month of pregnancy, as skeletal structures harden and nerves begin to connect to muscles, the foetus becomes capable of movement, which the mother starts to feel. At roughly the beginning of the fifth month, the foetus is able to respond to sound and can orient itself to its mother's movements. Towards the end of this month, the part of the brain that will be responsible for complex, conscious thought – the cerebral cortex – is completed. During the sixth month, the foetus's eyelids open and its eyes begin to move. It is able to breathe and even cry. By the seventh month, the foetus's brain is able to control breathing, swallowing, and body temperature; it also has the nerve cell capacity to see, hear, smell and taste, as well as to vocalise (see Box 3.2). Many reflexes such as grasping and sucking, which are important for the newborn's survival, are now established. The foetus has now reached the 'zone of viability' (i.e. having a chance of survival should he or she be born prematurely). If the foetus is born at this time, with intensive medical care, it could have a 50 per cent chance of surviving. By the beginning of the ninth month, the foetus, which once floated with relatively weightless ease in the amniotic fluid, is so large that movements inside the uterus become restricted. He or she now curls up into the classic 'foetal' position and usually settles into a head-down position readying itself for birth.

Factors influencing prenatal development

What has been described thus far, is the progress of a normal pregnancy where the mother and foetus are both healthy, and the pregnancy progresses with no complications. However, this is not always the case, and there are many factors that may influence the prenatal development of the embryo and later the foetus, placing it at risk while in the mother's uterus and after birth. The mother and foetus are inextricably linked via the placenta, and the mother and her environment therefore become the prenatal environment of the foetus. The physical, social and psychological conditions, the behaviour of the mother, and her immediate environment affect the foetus in a variety of ways.

Maternal conditions

Maternal nutrition

It is essential that foetuses receive a variety of essential nutrients in order to develop normally. These nutrients are supplied directly from their mothers via the placenta and umbilical cord. Maternal malnutrition and/or under-nutrition before, during and after pregnancy increase the risk of birth complications and neurological deficits in newborn babies. Jones (1997) found that maternal under-nutrition could lead to low birth weight and sometimes miscarriage. Other researchers have provided evidence to suggest that undernourished foetuses are also at risk for heart disease, strokes and other illnesses (Godfrey, 1998).

Malnourished and undernourished mothers usually live in impoverished conditions. Whiteside and Sunter (2000) provide some statistics that demonstrate the extent of poverty in the South African context. They assert that about 50 per cent of South Africa's population live in the poorest 40 per cent of households and earn less that R355 per adult per month. A further 27 per cent of the population live in 20 per cent of the 'ultra poorest' households and earn less than R194 per adult per month. Clearly, the majority of South Africans, many of them pregnant women, live in impoverished conditions, and poor maternal nutrition is one of the foremost consequences of living in these conditions. This is one of the reasons identified by Steinberg and Meyer (1995) as contributing to the 15 times higher infant mortality rate in Africa as compared to the United States of America.

Some other maternal conditions and the effects they may have on the developing foetus are described in Box 3.3.

Teratogens

Through the placenta, foetuses are affected by what their mothers eat, drink or inhale. Many infections, bacteria and viruses are also transferred to the foetus across the placenta. These harmful external environ-mental agents, called teratogens, can cause changes in normal prenatal development, birth defects and even death:

- *HIV/AIDS*: Should a mother be infected with HIV – the virus that causes AIDS – her unborn baby may also become infected. The virus may be transmitted to the foetus either by passing through the placental barrier or through exposure to the mother's infected blood during birth. Approximately 30 per cent of babies born to HIV-positive mothers will be infected with the virus in this way (Cunningham

---

3.3 SOME MATERNAL CONDITIONS, ILLNESSES, INFECTIONS AND DISEASES, AND HOW THEY MAY AFFECT PRENATAL DEVELOPMENT

Maternal conditions

- Maternal stress: Premature birth and low birth weight are the most frequently found effects of maternal stress (Hedegaard *et al.*, 1993). As early as the 1940's, Sontag (1940, 1944) found that as babies born to severely stressed mothers grew into infancy, they were more likely to be irritable, rest-less, and experience digestive problems than babies born to non-stressed mothers.

- Attitudes towards pregnancy: David (1981) found that his sample of 220 unwanted babies were underweight and required more medical attention at birth than did a control group of wanted, planned babies (see Box 3.4).

- Mother's age: Teenagers are often physically imma-ture and psychologically unprepared for mother-hood. Babies of teenage mothers are often born pre-maturely and are underweight.

Maternal illnesses, diseases and infections

- Malaria: Babies born to these mothers may suffer from low birth weight (due to premature birth or stunted foetal growth), parasite exposure and infant mortality (Steketee & Nahlen, 2001).

- Worms: Approximately 44 million pregnant women in developing countries have hookworm infections (UNEP, UNICEF & World Health Organisation, 2002). The presence of these parasitic worms can adversely affect or even kill a foetus.

- Diabetes: Babies of diabetic mothers may be abnor-mally large at birth. There is also an increased risk of stillbirth, or of the newborn dying shortly after birth.

- Rubella (German measles): Researchers have found that rubella may cause heart defects, deafness, blindness, and/or mental retardation in 54 per cent of all babies born to mothers who contracted the infection during the first 12 weeks of their pregnan-cies (Boué, 1995).

- Rh incompatibility: When a maternal blood protein, Rh, is incompatible with the foetus's Rh, antibodies in the mother's bloodstream may destroy the foe-tus's red blood cells. The possible consequences for the foetus may include jaundice, premature birth, stillbirth and/or brain damage.

- Drugs: Thalidomide caused babies to be born with-out arms and/or legs. Tranquilisers and birth control pills can cause deafness, cleft palate and physical deformities. Large doses of aspirin can cause abnor-malities in foetuses.

- 'Recreational' drugs: Marijuana has been associated with low birth weight and premature birth. Babies born to cocaine-addicted mothers are more likely to be stillborn or premature, have low birth weight, to have strokes and/or other complications (Niebyl, 1994). They are irritable, uncoordinated and slow learners (Bendersky & Lewis, 1998).

- Caffeine: Large quantities of caffeine (found in cof-fee, tea and 'fizzy' drinks) are associated with increased rates of miscarriage and low birth weight (Dlugosz & Bracken, 1992).

- Radiation (X-rays, some medical treatment, atomic or nuclear fall-out): Foetuses exposed to radiation may develop physical deformities, heart disease, leukemia, retarded growth, mental retardation, chromosomal disorders, epileptic seizures and poor intellectual performance (Yamazaki & Schull, 1990).

- Chemicals (lead exposure): Foetal exposure to lead can raise the risk of low birth weight, abnormal organ development, foetal growth retardation, prenatal death and socio-behavioural problems in later infancy and childhood (Mathee & von Schirnding, 1999).

Procedure

In Czechoslovakia during the 1960s and 1970s, researchers investigated the lives of 220 unwanted children whose mothers had expressed strong negative attitudes to having them. These children were considered unwanted because their mothers had twice requested (and been refused) abortions. Once they were born, these children were matched with a control group of wanted children and their mothers. The children in the control group were considered wanted because their mothers had planned or accepted their pregnancies.

Results

At birth, the unwanted children weighed less and needed more medical care than the control group of wanted children.

Conclusion

Pregnant mothers' negative attitudes towards their pregnancies and their unborn children can affect their baby's development (David, 1981).

et al., 1997). Some of these babies may seroconvert to an HIV-negative status sometime during the first 18 months of their lives. Others will develop full-blown AIDS and, as there is no known cure for AIDS, will die most often within the first three years of their lives (Newman & Newman, 1995). When we consider that at least 4.7 million people are currently infected with the virus in South Africa (Department of Health, 2000), more than half of them being women, the risk to unborn children is considerable.

- *Sexually transmitted diseases (STDs)*: Gonorrhea may cause a baby to become blind unless treated immediately after birth. Blindness and severe brain damage can occur should a mother have genital herpes. An estimated 25 per cent of syphilis-infected foetuses are born dead. Those that survive may be deaf, mentally retarded or physically deformed. With over 4 million incidents of STDs occurring each year in South Africa (Department of Health, 1999), STDs are very likely to present a substantial risk to unborn children.
- *Tobacco (nicotine)*: Nicotine in tobacco smoke compromises the supply of nutrients and oxygen to the foetus. Babies born to tobacco smokers therefore tend to be smaller and weigh less than those born to non-smokers. In fact, the more a pregnant mother smokes, the less her baby will weigh at birth (Roquer *et al.*, 1995). Research has also shown that tobacco smoking is related to increased premature birth, miscarriage, and stillbirth (Roquer *et al.*, 1995).

Just how many unborn South African children are placed at risk due to their mothers' smoking is illustrated by the results of a survey. The survey found that '... approximately 47% of coloured women in South Africa smoke during pregnancy and previous research ... has found that a significant proportion of Black South African women are at risk for initiating smoking during their reproductive years' (Medical Research Council, 2002).

- *Alcohol*: Alcohol affects the foetus directly as it crosses the placenta and, because the foetus's liver is immature, remains in its system for a long time. One study found that 71 per cent of babies born to heavy drinkers were affected in some way (Jones *et al.*, 1973). Many of these babies suffered from foetal alcohol syndrome (FAS). FAS is a collection of symptoms presented by babies who are born to women who drank excessive amounts of alcohol during their pregnancies. Infants with FAS are born short relative to their weight. They have abnormally small heads and under-developed brains. Many have distinctly malformed faces: their eyes are spaced far apart, they have flat noses and under-developed upper jaws. They are mentally retarded and are slow in motor development. They have eye abnormalities, congenital heart disease and irregularities of the joints. Other symptoms include hyperactivity, learning disabilities and irritability. As it is unclear exactly how much alcohol will produce some, if not all these symptoms, pregnant mothers should abstain from drinking alcohol.

The seriousness of maternal alcohol consumption and FAS in South Africa, is suggested by evidence that the Western Cape has the highest incidence of FAS in the world, with approximately 1 in 14 children affected (Department of Health, 2001).

Other teratogens and their possible effects on prenatal development are described in Box 3.3.

Foetal vulnerability

Having reviewed the many risks that a developing organism may face, you may wonder how it is that so many babies are born without some lasting impairment. In fact, even when exposed to possible harm, the great majority of foetuses develop normally. This may be due to what is known as a self-righting tendency – a human tendency to develop normally under all but the most adverse conditions. A self-cleansing tendency also operates whereby severely malformed foetuses are spontaneously aborted within the first three months of pregnancy.

However, when damage from a harmful substance does occur, it may be severe – even fatal – or slight. The severity of the effect depends on a number of factors:

- When exposure occurs: Exposure to a harmful substance during the germinal stage of development may destroy the organism completely. During the embryonic stage, damage may be done to various organs and systems depending on the particular time they are being developed. In the foetal stage, exposure is likely to affect intelligence or behaviour.
- The constitution of the foetus: Foetuses react differently to the same harmful substance, depending to some degree on their genetic vulnerability to the substance: some may be severely affected, others only slightly, and still others may die.
- The mother's health: The risk of malformations is highest when a mother is younger than 20 and older than 40. Nutritional deficiency in a mother compounds the harmful effects of some substances.

- The type of exposure: Different harmful substances have different effects on the developing organism.
- The amount of exposure: As a general rule, the greater the exposure to the harmful substance, the more severe the effects on the developing organism.

The neonatal period of development

The neonatal period of development spans approximately the first two to four weeks after birth. With birth, the infant moves from the relatively safe environment of its mother's uterus to an environment where it must now breathe and feed on its own. It must begin to interact with its environment and make sense of this often bright, noisy and airy world. For many years it was thought that the newborn baby (known as a neonate) was a helpless, reflexive organism with limited motor skills, able to hear or see very little. One of the major achievements of developmental psychology has been to demonstrate that the neonate is much more competent than was previously thought. This section on neonatal development will begin by exploring some of the neonate's reported abilities. It will then go on to explore some risks to newly born infants – most often initiated during the prenatal period.

Assessing the newborn

Where babies are born in hospitals, their condition is assessed by means of simple standardised measures

Reflex	Stimulus	Response
Rooting reflex	Gentle stroke on cheek	Head turns towards stimulus; mouth opens; sucking starts
Sucking reflex	Place object in mouth	Rhythmic sucking of object & mouth movements
Babinski reflex	Gentle stroke of side of foot from heel to toes	Big toe flexes; other toes spread out; foot twists inwards
Palmar reflex	Press rod or finger into palm of hand	Grasps rod or finger firmly
Withdrawal reflex	Prick sole of foot with pin	Leg pulls up
Moro reflex	Make sudden loud noise	Arms & legs fling outwards. Fingers spread. Then fists clench & arms & legs pull back in

Table 1 Reflexes of the neonate

of physical well-being. One example of such a test is the Apgar scale where the newborn infant is given a score out of 10 based on conditions such as skin colour, heart rate, muscle tone, respiratory effort and responsivity. They are assessed twice, once immediately after birth and again 5 minutes later. A baby, whose score is less than 4, is considered to be in poor condition and requiring medical attention.

Reflexes

A newborn infant displays more than 20 reflexes over which he or she initially has no control: they are involuntary responses to specific stimuli from the external environment. Many of these reflexes are important for the newborn's survival. For example, the rooting, sucking and swallowing reflexes allow the newborn to take nourishment. The absence of reflexes may be an early indication of neurological problems. Some of these reflexes are described in Table 1.

Early sensory capacities

Normal, full-term babies enter the world with all their sensory capacities functioning to a certain extent. But anyone observing a baby during its first month will agree that it is difficult to assess exactly how well he or she is seeing, hearing, tasting, or smelling. However, recent ingenious research and experiments have allowed developmental psychologists to explore the sensory capacities of these few-week-old neonates. They have discovered that

3.5 INFANTS AND PREFERENCE FOR THEIR MOTHER'S MILK

Procedure
A pad soaked in the infants' mothers' breast milk and a pad soaked in stranger's breast milk were placed on either side of infants' heads.

Results
At 8 to 10 days old, the infants consistently turned their heads towards the pads soaked in their own mother's milk.

Conclusion
Infants prefer the familiar smell of their own mother's milk, which they must begin to detect and recognise from the first days of life (MacFarlane, 1975).

neonates are quite able to take in information from their environment via their senses.

Vision

Although anatomically the visual system is present at birth, certain parts of the eye and visual cortex are not fully developed; nor is the ability to co-ordinate the movement of their eyes. This means that newborn babies cannot focus properly and much of what they see is blurred. However, despite these shortcomings, they actively scan their surroundings (Bronson, 1997), and their visual system does function well enough for them to see objects about 21 centimetres away. They also show a distinct preference for looking at faces, patterned rather than plain stimuli and patterns with sharp contrasts (Bronson, 1997; Bushnell, 1998).

Hearing

Even in the first hours after birth, newborns can distinguish human speech from other sounds and even between human speech sounds – particularly demonstrating a preference for their mothers' voice (see Box 3.1). They appear to be particularly fascinated by 'baby talk' that is directed towards them (Werker & Tees, 1999).

Taste and smell

Neonates have a well-developed sense of smell. Experiments by Engen *et al.* (1963) demonstrated that newly born infants were not only sensitive to different smells, but could also distinguish between them (see Box 3.5). Their sense of taste is also well developed with a strong preference for sweet as opposed to sour tastes.

Risks to the neonate

The early capacities described above are those that are present in normal, healthy neonates who have had optimal prenatal developmental experiences and have encountered no serious problems during birth. However, not all newly born infants are healthy: some may have such poor physical condition that they die shortly after birth. Others are at risk for later developmental problems. These are most often those babies who are born prematurely, are underweight, or both.

Low birth weight

In the previous discussion on prenatal development, repeated reference was made to low birth weight (LBW). Low birth weight may occur in babies that are born before 35 to 40 weeks after conception, that is premature babies, or it may occur in full-term babies for any of the reasons already discussed in the section on prenatal development. At the one extreme, the risks to these LBW neonates can be extreme: stillbirth or death shortly after birth. Serious, but not fatal risks can include cerebral palsy, epilepsy, and other forms of brain damage. Less obvious effects may include later intellectual and learning problems. However, it is important to note that it is more often the combination of LBW and other biological and/or environmental risks that produce variations in the normal developmental sequences of the infant.

3.6 THE BONDING MYTH

Bonding between mother and infant describes a process popularly understood as the natural, customary and universal process of falling in love with one's child after birth. Because human infants are entirely dependent on their caregivers, particularly their mothers, for their survival, the development of a close and loving bond between mother and infant is thought to be vital for the well-being of the child. Bonding is therefore an essential part of the foundation on which all future development builds (Cole & Cole, 2001). Yet we have all read or been touched in some way by reports of the large numbers of babies, the world over, who are abused, neglected, abandoned and even murdered. This must surely lead us to question the popular notion that bonding is a universal, natural and expected occurrence. In an attempt to understand this contradictory evidence, the following discussion will introduce the more common explanations of how bonding is thought to develop and, in some instances, why it may be that such strong emotional ties fail to form.

Early explanations for bonding come from ethology – the study of animal behaviour and its evolutionary basis. In 1943, Konrad Lorenz, a German ethologist, noted the clearly distinctive facial features that almost all newborns, whether animal or human, have: heads seemingly too large for their bodies, prominent, rounded foreheads, large eyes and round, full cheeks (Cole & Cole, 2001). He proposed that this 'babyness' instinctively evoked strong caregiving responses in adults. From this perspective, bonding is an unconscious, instinctive behaviour, designed to ensure caregiving and therefore the survival of the species.

It is this perspective that may explain why mothers of some species of animals kill their malformed offspring. Presumably, these appearance-impaired offspring do not evoke positive caregiving behaviours, but quite the opposite. Indeed, Meira Weiss also found that (human) mothers of appearance-impaired infants found it difficult to care for, and in some instances abused and/or abandoned, their babies (Weiss, 1998:100). She suggests that deformed infants evoke strong negative emotions and even suspicion and '[t]his can result in the stigmatization of the appearance-impaired child as a "non-person", and lead to his/her rejection'. From this perspective, bonding does not occur because infants do not exhibit the 'babyness' essential for a positive response from parents (as identified by Lorenz).

However, Weiss offers an intriguing possibility that would account for her findings. She suggests that the relationship between parent(s) and infant(s) is informed by two decisions, namely whether to 'adopt' (to have, to care for, to bond to) and whether to love their biological child. In other words, bonding and loving are different and distinct processes that make up the relationship between parent(s) and child(-ren). In the case of 'normal' children, decisions to adopt and to love are interwoven, unconscious and unnoticed. In the case of appearance-impaired children, she suggests that often, only the first decision is made: the children are 'adopted', but not loved (leading to varying forms of neglect).

We also know that it is not only appearance-impaired infants who are rejected by their parents. In conditions of high infant mortality and female fertility, as is the case in parts of Brazil where Nancy Scheper-Hughes did research, failure to bond with newborn infants is not uncommon (Scheper-Hughes, 1992). Where a mother has a number of other children to care for, often in conditions of extreme poverty, she will only invest her limited emotional and physical resources in a child who will definitely survive. Often survival is only assured once the child is long past infancy. In these instances, what appears to be abandonment and neglect of newly-born and young infants should not be seen as evidence of a failure to bond, but as a survival strategy adopted by mothers in adverse social and economic conditions (Scheper-Hughes, 1992). For Scheper-Hughes, the common perception of bonding may well be relevant to middle- and upper-classes, but is an unaffordable luxury for many of the world's poor mothers.

Almost two decades after Lorenz's observations, Peter Klopfer and his colleagues observed the reactions of mother goats after being separated from, and reunited with their newborns (Klopfer *et al.*, 1964). It appeared that contact with the newly-born goats immediately after birth was essential for ensuring positive caregiving responses from the mother goats. This led Klopfer and colleagues to propose that the period immediately after birth was a sensitive period when mother and infant would become imprinted on each other. Following these observations, findings from research with human mothers and their babies confirmed a sensitive period for imprinting (or bonding) among humans. For example, research conducted by Marshall Klaus and John Kennell found that mothers who had not had the opportunity to bond with their newborns were more likely to neglect or abuse their infants (Klaus & Kennell, 1970). This led to the belief that hormones generated by mothers during birth may make them ready to form this important emo-tional bond with their infants. It also led to the belief that mothers and infants should have immediate physical contact after birth, before these hormones dissipated. From this perspective, bonding is a biologically-driven behaviour in response to physiological changes in mothers.

However, the thought that early contact is essential for successful bonding does not take into account the strong bonds that we know develop between mothers and infants who are separated for a time after birth, or between mothers and their non-biological, adopted infants, or between fathers and infants. Indeed, research conducted after Klaus and Kennell's original research, did not find any lasting differences among those mothers who were in immediate contact with their babies and those who were not (Eyer, 1992). Most developmentalists today therefore agree that early bonding is not essential to the creation of long-term positive relationships between mother and child, and that for many mother-infant pairs, bonding develops over time.

In conclusion, developmentalists agree that the great majority of parents do bond with their infants, whether immediately or over time, and in varying circumstances. But for those who do not, Weiss has suggested an explanation that would require researchers to re-examine the popular notion that describes bonding as a love affair between parent(s) and infant(s).

Malnutrition

Severely malnourished foetuses may be born suffering from an extreme form of starvation called marasmus. These infants hardly grow and their muscles wither. If they live, they do not catch up in growth, and are apathetic and unresponsive. They are at particular risk for later intellectual deficits. In parts of the world where famine and starvation are endemic, these risks to newborn infants are substantive.

These are just two of the risks that may threaten the normal development of neonates. However, these at-risk babies stand a better chance of overcoming these initial setbacks if they are born where there is ready access to medical interventions and treatment and/or if they are raised in comfortable socio-economic circumstances, and have supportive and attentive families. As we have already noted, many babies throughout the world are born without access to medical care and/or do not have favourable or supportive postnatal environments. The risks to their normal development are therefore considerable.

Conclusion

This chapter has explored prenatal development from the moment of conception, through each of the stages of prenatal development: the germinal, embryonic and foetal stages. Research has alerted us to the fact that the developing organism is not only affected by the immediate environment in its mother's womb, but also by the world outside the womb. Clearly, the period of prenatal development may be fraught with dangers, many of which will interfere with the optimal growth and development of the foetus. Despite this, the majority of babies develop within normal standards and go on to be healthy children and adults. The brief description of neonatal development has demonstrated that infants, from the moment of birth, actively begin to explore their new environments with a competency that was previously thought to be non-existent.

Bendersky, M. & Lewis, M. (1998). Arousal modulation in cocaine-exposed infants. *Developmental Psychology*, 34:3.

Boué, A. (1995). *Maternal Infection in Fetal Medicine: Prenatal diagnosis and management*. Oxford: Oxford University Press.

Bronson, G.W. (1997). The growth of visual capacity: Evidence from infant scanning patterns. *Advances in Infancy Research*, 11:109–41.

Bushnell, I.W.R. (1998). The origins of face perception. In F. Simon & G. Butterworth (Eds.). *The Development of Sensory, Motor and Cognitive Capacities in Early Infancy: From perception to cognition*. Hove: Erlbaum.

Cunningham, F.G., MacDonald, P.C., Gant, N.F., Leveno, K.J., Gistrap, L.C. Hankins, G.D.V. & Clark, S.L. (1997). *Williams Obstetrics* (20th edition). Stamford: Appleton & Lange.

Cole, M. & Cole, S.R. (2001). *The Development of Children* (4th edition). New York: Worth Publishers.

David, H.P. (1981). Unwantedness: Longitudinal studies of Prague children born to women twice denied abortions for the same pregnancy and matched controls. In P. Ahmed (Ed.). *Pregnancy, Childbirth, and Parenthood*. New York: Elsever, pp. 81–102.

DeCasper A.J. & Spence, M.J. (1986). Prenatal maternal speech influences newborn's perceptions of speech sounds. *Infant Behavior and Development*, 3:133–50.

Department of Health. (1999). 1998 seroprevalence survey in South African antenatal clinics. *AIDS Scan*, 11:5–9.

Department of Health. (2000). *National HIV and Syphilis Sero-prevalence Survey of Women Attending Public Antenatal Clinics in South Africa*. Pretoria: Department of Health.

Department of Health. (2001). *Developing World's First Genetic Birth Defects Conference*. Pretoria: Department of Health.

Dlugosz, L. & Bracken, M.B. (1992). Reproductive effects of caffeine: A review and theoretical analysis. *Epidemiologic Reviews*, 14:83–100.

Engen, T., Lipsitt, L.P. & Kaye, H. (1963). Olfactory responses and adaptation in the human neonate. *Journal of Comparative Physiological Psychology*, 56:73–7.

Eyer, D. E. (1992). *Mother-infant Bonding: A scientific fiction*. New Haven: Yale University Press.

Godfrey, K.M. (1998). Maternal regulation of fetal development and health in adult life. *European Journal of Obstetrics & Gynecology*, 78:141–50.

Hedegaard, M., Henriksen, T.B. & Sabroe, S. (1993). Psychological distress in pregnancy and preterm delivery. *British Medical Journal*, 307:234–38.

Jones, R.E. (1997). *Human Reproductive Biology*. San Diego: Academic Press.

Jones, K.L., Smith, D. W., Ulleland C.N. & Streissguth, A.P. (1973). Pattern of malformation in offspring of chronic alcoholic mothers. *Lancet*, 1:1267–71.

Klaus, M.H. & Kennell, J.H. (1970). *Maternal-infant Bonding: The impact of early separation or loss on family development*. St. Louis: Mosby.

Klopfer, P.H., Adams, D. K. & Klopfer, M.S. (1964). Maternal imprinting in goats. *Proceedings of the National Academy of Sciences*, 52:911–4.

MacFarlane, A. (1975). Olfaction in the development of social preferences in the human neonate. In *Parent Infant Interaction* (Ciba Foundation Symposium 33). Amsterdam: Elsevier.

Mathee, A. & von Schirnding, Y. (1999). *Environmental Lead Exposure and Child Health in South Africa*. Cape Town: Medical Research Council.

Medical Research Council. (2002). *Smoking Cessation Intervention for Disadvantaged South African Women of Reproductive Age*. Cape Town: Medical Research Council.

Newman, B.M. & Newman, P.R. (1995). *Development Through Life: A psychosocial approach* (6th edition). New York: Brooks/Cole.

Niebyl, J.R. (1994). Teratology and drug use during pregnancy and lactation. In J.R. Scott, P.J. DiSaia, C.B. Hammond & W.N. Spellacy (Eds.). *Dansforth's Obstetrics and Gynecology* (7th edition). Philadelphia: J.B. Lippincott, pp. 225–44.

Roquer, J.M., Figueras, J. Botet, F. & Jimenez, R. (1995). Influences on fetal growth of exposure to tobacco smoke during pregnancy. *Acta Paediatrica*, 84(92):118–21.

Scheper-Hughes, N. (1992). *Death Without Weeping: The violence of everyday life in Brazil*. Berkeley: University of California Press.

Sontag, L.W. (1940). Effect of fetal activity on nutritional state of the infant at birth. *American Journal of Diseases of Children*, 6:621–30.

Sontag, L.W. (1944). War and the fetal maternal relationship. *Marriage and Family Living*, 6:1–5.

Steinberg, L. & Meyer, R. (1995). *Childhood*. New York: McGraw-Hill.

Steketee, R.W. & Nahlen, B.L. (2001). The burden of malaria in pregnancy in malaria-endemic areas. *American Journal of Tropical Medicine and Hygiene*, 64(1–2 Suppl):28–35.

UNEP, UNICEF & World Health Organisation. (2002). *Children in the New Millenium: Environmental impact on health*. New York: United Nations Environment Programme.

Weiss, M. (1998). Conditions of mothering: The bio-politics of falling in love with your child. *The Social Science Journal*, 35(1):87–105.

Werker, J.F. & Tees, R.C. (1999). Influences on infant speech processing: Toward a new synthesis. *Annual Review of Psychology*, 50:509–35.

Whiteside, A. & Sunter, C. (2000). *AIDS. The challenge for South Africa*. Cape Town: Human & Rousseau Tafelberg.

Yamazaki, J.N. & Schull, W.J. (1990). Perinatal loss and neurological abnormalities among children of the atomic bomb. *Journal of the American Medical Association*, 266:605–9.

Multiple choice questions

1. Each of us begins our life as a single cell called a
   a) cell mass
   b) blastocyst
   c) zygote
   d) embryo

2. The first two weeks after conception are referred to as the _____ of prenatal development
   a) the embryonic stage
   b) the germinal stage
   c) the prenatal stage
   d) the foetal stage

3. What does the zone of viability refer to?
   a) the chances of survival should a foetus be born prematurely
   b) the tendency of the foetus to develop normally under all but the most adverse conditions
   c) the spontaneous abortion of a malformed foetus
   d) the amount of exposure to harmful substances to which a foetus may be exposed

4. Teratogens are
   a) elements of the internal environment that affect foetal growth and development
   b) the name given to the cell mass that provide the embryo with its life support systems
   c) the collection of symptoms displayed by babies and associated with excessive exposure to alcohol
   d) harmful external environmental agents that can affect foetal growth and development

5. According to Cunningham *et al.* (1997), approximately what percentage of babies born to HIV-positive mothers will be infected with HIV?
   a) 30%
   b) 50%
   c) 70%
   d) 100%

6. With regard to smoking cigarettes while pregnant, Roquer *et al.* (1995) found that
   a) smoking just a few cigarettes per day does not harm a developing foetus
   b) babies will be born deaf, mentally retarded or physically deformed
   c) the more a pregnant mother smokes, the less her baby will weigh
   d) none of the above

7. The severity of the effect of prenatal exposure to harmful substance(s) will depend on which five factors?
   a) the constitution of the foetus; when exposure occurs; the amount of exposure; the father's health; the type of exposure
   b) when expose occurs; the constitution of the foetus; the type of exposure; the mother's health; the amount of exposure
   c) the amount of exposure; when exposure occurs; access to medical care; the constitution of the foetus; the type of exposure
   d) the mother's health; when exposure occurs; the path of exposure; the constitution of the foetus; the type of exposure

8. The Apgar scale assesses a newborn's well-being by measuring its
   a) heart rate
   b) responsivity
   c) respiratory effort
   d) all of the above

9. Which of the following statements regarding the neonate's early sensory capacities is false?
   a) neonates have a well-developed sense of smell
   b) neonates can distinguish between their mother's and father's voices
   c) neonates can see quite clearly within hours of birth
   d) neonates show a strong preference for sweet-tasting substances

10. The _____ reflex in a neonate is produced by _____
    a) rooting; placing an object in the mouth
    b) sucking; a gentle stroke on the cheek
    c) withdrawal; placing a rod in the palm of the hand
    d) moro; making a sudden loud noise

Short answer questions

1. How does maternal nutrition affect the development of the foetus?

2. Why is it important that pregnant mothers should not consume alcohol?

3. The severity of the effect of exposure to harmful substance(s) during prenatal development depends on a number of factors. Describe each of these.

4. Briefly describe the neonate's early sensory capacities.

Preschool development

Tokozile Mayekiso

CHAPTER OBJECTIVES

After studying this chapter you should be able to:
- discuss the physical development of the preschool child in terms of body size and proportion, as well as overall growth changes
- describe the psychosocial development of the preschool child
- explain the development of gender identity of the preschooler
- explain the impact of child-rearing in general and parenting styles in particular on psychosocial development during the preschool period
- describe cognitive development in the preschool child
- list the sequence of language development in preschool children
- explain the contribution of early childhood development programmes to preschool development
- understand risk and resilience during the preschool period.

Nosipho had been looked after by her mother and her aunt at home before she had started preschool. Her aunt had stayed in the house with them, and Nosipho remembered crying when her mother had to go out somewhere. Although she was fond of her aunt, she had definitely preferred being with her mother. Nosipho realised now, though, that she had been very lucky to have two adults around like this to look after her. Her father had worked during the day, and although she knew he must have been around in the evenings, she couldn't really remember him much from this time.

Nosipho's recollections of this time were very incomplete but some moments stood out in her memory. Her happiest times were of being in the kitchen with her mother. Her mother would be making food and Nosipho would help her. Her mother would give her some of the bread dough to knead and Nosipho would feel very important. These days she watched her young nieces spreading flour and water across the table while her mother tried to cook and she realised that she, like them, had probably not been as helpful as she had imagined at the time. Nosipho watched her mother discretely tidy up and praise her nieces, thanking them for all their help and she saw how their faces lit up. 'She must have made me feel useful like that too,' Nosipho thought, realising why those memories of helping her mother felt so good. She wasn't just learning about cooking in those times with her mother – she was also learning how to feel good about what she could contribute, how to feel confident and capable. While there were some things that Nosipho felt quite unsure of, she realised she had a central core of belief in herself that had helped her get to university, and that helped her feel like she could manage her own life. It was interesting to think how all these small experiences in her childhood had helped to make her into the person she was now.

Figure 1 The preschool period is a time of incredible growth and learning

Figure 2 Preschool education is integral to successful physical, social and emotional-cognitive development

Introduction

This chapter provides an overview of development during the preschool period. For the purposes of this book, the preschool period covers the period from birth until six years of age. We will start by focusing on physical and motor development, followed by a discussion of some of the facets of emotional and social development during the preschool period. Lastly, preschool development in the sphere of cognitive and language development will be discussed. An overview of early childhood education is also provided. It is worth mentioning that while development during the preschool period will be discussed under three domains, namely physical, social and emotional and cognitive development, all development is interrelated and interactive.

Physical development

The preschool period is characterised by rapid growth during the first two years of life, and by a slower pattern of growth from two to six years. The growth of the infant continues to follow the cephalocaudal (from the head downward) and proximodistal (from the centre outward) patterns begun during the prenatal period. The trunk grows fastest during the first year. Babies gain control over muscles of the head and neck, then the arms and abdomen and finally the legs. They learn to control the movements of their shoulders before they can direct their arms or fingers (Hoffman *et al.*, 1994).

Birth weight is often doubled by four to six months and tripled by the end of the first year. The child's weight increases to about 14kg by the age of two years and to about 20kg at the age of six years. Height increases from about 51 to 52 centimetres at birth to about 96 centimetres at the age of two years. Height at the age of six years increases to about 113 or 114 centimetres.

The brain increases from 25 per cent of its eventual adult weight at birth to about 50 per cent of its adult weight at the age of twelve months. By two years of age it has attained 75 per cent of its adult weight, and by the age of five years, the brain has reached approximately 90 per cent of its eventual adult weight (Brierly, 1976). As a result of the rapid growth rate of the brain, children's ability to acquire new information increases. The development of the brain depends on experience, and thus early environmental influences can both enable and constrain brain development (Nelson, 2000).

Children improve their gross motor and fine motor skills (Clark *et al.*, 1989). Gross motor skills refer to capabilities involving large body movements such as walking, running, hopping and throwing. Fine motor skills refer to capabilities involving small body movements such as writing, handling a spoon and tying shoe laces. Gross motor skills develop faster than fine motor skills during the preschool period. Children develop and refine their motor skills mostly through activities such as play, drawing and cutting with a pair of scissors, etc.

Preschoolers start to show a preference for using one hand more than the other at about two years of age. However, handedness, which refers to which hand the child prefers to use, develops slowly and is only established at about five to six years (Shaffer, 1996).

Body proportions change during the preschool period. At the age of two years, the head is about one-fourth the total body size; by the age of five-and-a-half, it is one-sixth the body size (Cratty, 1970). The preschooler loses the chubby baby-like appearance as a result of the decrease in the amount of fat and the development of muscle tissue. Preschoolers engage in a number of physical activities such as running, walking, hopping, skipping, climbing and riding tricycles. Environments that facilitate the involvement of preschool children in these kinds of activities are crucial for preschool development.

Sustained periods of malnutrition are a signifi-

cant risk to normal physical development as they are associated with stunted physical growth, reduced activity levels and delays in maturation and learning (Waterlow, 1973).

Social and emotional development

Temperament

Each child is born with a temperament. Temperament refers to an individual's characteristic manner of responding to the environment (Thomas *et al.*, 1970). Research conducted by Thomas *et al.* (1970) identified three types of temperaments, namely 'easy' temperaments, 'difficult' temperaments and 'slow-to-warm up' temperaments. These categories were based on the children's difference in activity level, rhythmicity, approach-withdrawal, adaptability, intensity of reaction, threshold of responsiveness, quality of mood, distractibility and attention span. Children with easy temperaments are generally happy, adaptable, regular and easy to soothe. Children with difficult temperaments adapt slowly. They are also easily distractible, inflexible, exhibit intense reactions and cry a great deal. Children with a slow-to-warm up temperament take

Figure 3 Play is essential for the physical development of the preschool child

Figure 4 Caregiver involved in fostering the development of motor skills

some time to adjust to changes in their environment, but their reactions are not intense. By the age of two years, children have elaborated or restricted these response styles within their cultural context to develop what is called a personality (Craig, 1996).

Attachment

One of the major social and emotional milestones of preschool development is the development of attachment or affectional ties between children and their closest companions. The development of strong, positive, mutually enjoyable relationships with close caregivers is critical for social and emotional development during the preschool period.

At about seven to nine months, infants begin to actively seek proximity to the primary caregiver, and protest when separated from them. This wary or fretful reaction that infants and toddlers often display when separated from persons to whom they are attached is called separation anxiety. Separation anxiety peaks at 14 to 20 months and gradually becomes less frequent and less intense throughout the preschool period. Infants also exhibit a wary reaction to strangers i.e. stranger anxiety. Wary reactions to strangers peak at 8 to 10 months of age and gradually decline in intensity over the second year (Sroufe, 1977) (see also Chapter 8, this volume).

Figure 5 Positive mother-child interaction

Erikson's psychosocial stages of development

Erikson's first three psychosocial stages fall within the preschool period:

- *Basic trust versus mistrust*: During the first year of life, infants have to resolve the crisis of trust versus mistrust. The primary caregiver plays an important role in the resolution of this crisis. Infants need to be provided with consistent, reliable and predictable care-giving in order to learn to trust others to care for their basic needs. If caregivers are rejecting or inconsistent in their care, the infant may view the world as untrustworthy and may become mistrustful.

- *Autonomy versus shame and doubt*: The crisis that faces toddlers during the second and third year of life is that of autonomy versus shame and doubt. Toddlers start to show signs of independence by increasingly demanding to determine their own behaviour. This crisis is resolved favourably when caregivers provide their children with appropriate guidance that is based on the children's level of maturation and development. The quest for independence requires that young children try new skills. Children whose attempts at independence are met with approval, tolerance and understanding by caregivers develop a sense of autonomy. Toddlers who are constantly criticised and made to feel incompetent may experience a sense of shame and doubt.

- *Initiative versus guilt*: The crisis that faces young children from the age of three to six years is initiative versus guilt, which relates to issues of mastery and competence. Young children are considered to possess an eagerness to tackle new tasks, interact with peers, caregivers and other members of the family. Children who are punished or criticised for expressing their desires and plans may develop a sense of guilt, which leads to fear and a lack of assertiveness (Papalia & Olds, 1998).

Development of the gender concept

By age two-and-a-half to three years, preschoolers acquire a basic gender identity. They can label themselves as either boys or girls. They begin to acquire sex-role stereotypes at this age. The sex-role stereotypes are usually reinforced by the caregivers' differential treatment of boys and girls. Caregivers in many cultures encourage nurturing behaviour from girls while expecting boys to play a more instrumental role. In many African contexts, girls, for instance, are expected to assist with the upbringing of younger siblings and to perform domestic chores. African boys, on the other hand, are expected to assist with looking after livestock (Mwamwenda, 1995). Although many three-year-olds have acquired a basic gender identity, they do not understand that gender is constant. A three- to four-year-old boy may make statements that suggest that he could be a mother when he gets old. Children normally begin to understand that gender is constant at the age of five to seven years, and that boys will grow to become men and girls will become women.

Child rearing

A secure and loving environment is necessary for children's optimal growth and development. Children need guidance, love and care in order to develop as stable well-adjusted and sociable human beings. The key to good care-giving is sensitivity and emotional responsiveness to the initiative of the child (World Health Organisation/International Child Development Programme, 1997).

Caregivers, the state and society at large have an important role to play in ensuring that the rights of the young child to survival, growth and development are promoted and protected. The rights of the young child span the areas of health, nutrition, a safe environment, and psychosocial and cognitive development (See Boxes 4.1 and 4.2).

- Opportunities to begin to learn to care for themselves.
- Daily opportunities to play with a variety of objects.

The rights of preschool aged children
All of the above, plus:
- Opportunities to develop fine motor skills.
- Encouragement of language through talking, being read to, singing.
- Activities that will develop a sense of mastery.
- Experimentation with pre-writing and pre-reading skills.
- Hands-on exploration for learning through action.
- Opportunities for taking responsibility and making choices.
- Encouragement to develop self-control, co-operation and persistence in completing projects.
- Support for their sense of self-worth.
- Opportunities for self-expression.
- Encouragement of creativity (UNICEF, 2001).

Another important aspect of child rearing is the transmission of cultural beliefs. Caregivers impart to children aspects of their culture and traditions that are important to give children a sense of identity and a better understanding of the world around them. For example, children often first acquire an understanding and appreciation of the value of 'ubuntu' (compassion) within the context of parent-child interactions.

4.1 THE RIGHTS OF YOUNG CHILDREN

The rights of young children (0–3 years)
- Protection from physical danger.
- Adequate nutrition and health care.
- Appropriate immunisations.
- An adult with whom to form an attachment relationship.
- An adult who can understand and respond to their signals.
- Things to look at, touch, hear, smell, taste.
- Opportunities to explore their world.
- Appropriate language stimulation.
- Support in acquiring new motor, language and thinking skills.
- A chance to develop some independence.
- Help in learning how to control their own behaviour.

Figure 6 Fathers involved in child rearing can contribute greatly to the development of the child

Many children are exposed to a lot of violence at home, in their communities and on television. One of the important tasks of caregivers is to bring up children who are going to contribute towards decreasing the levels of violence in their communities.

A positive caregiver-child relationship facilitates the development of an emotional tie that is the building block of human cognitive capacity, the acquisition of language and empathic identification with other human beings (Richter, 2000). Relationships in which love is shown and in which children are provided with opportunities to learn are crucial for child development. Positive relationships between caregivers and young children facilitate the development of a positive sense of self, in that they affirm the child's sense of self.

Not all caregivers are able to establish positive relationships with their infants. Caregiver-child relationships can become disturbed for a number of reasons, some of which are related to the child (e.g., prematurity, difficult temperament, mental or physical disability), and others related to the caregiver (e.g., depression, stress, teen motherhood and a his-tory of child abuse). The environment in which children are brought up does impact on the caregiver-child relationship. Poverty is the most important risk factor for very young children and correlates of poverty affect children's development throughout their critical years.

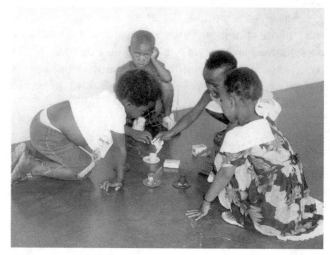

Figure 7 Preschoolers learning to listen, interact and co-operate with each other

4.2   ARE THE NEEDS OF CHILDREN AFFECTED AND INFECTED BY HIV/AIDS BEING ADEQUATELY ADDRESSED?

The plight of children affected and infected by HIV/AIDS is a crisis that continues to escalate on a daily basis. It is estimated that the number of children orphaned by HIV/AIDS increased by 400 per cent between 1994 and 1997. It is further estimated that by 2010 orphans, both due to HIV/AIDS and other causes, will comprise about 17 per cent of South African children. The question that still remains unanswered is how are the rights of the large numbers of orphans and vulnerable children going to be adequately addressed? A study conducted under the auspices of the Gauteng Department of Education (1999) identified the following categories of children at risk:
- Children designated as coming from 'ultra-poor' families whose income falls in the lowest 20 per cent of the income bands in South Africa.
- Children living in informal settlements.
- Children with special educational needs or disabilities.
- Children exposed to domestic violence or abuse.
- Children exposed to violence in the community.
- Children of teen mothers without family support.
- Undernourished children.
- Children living in families with HIV/AIDS.
- Children living in families severely affected by TB and other debilitating diseases.

- Children in families suffering from severe 'hardships'.

The constitution of South Africa states that a child's best interests are of paramount importance in every matter concerning the child. It is a guarantee that has far-reaching implications. The 'matters' that concern children are extensive. They include education, housing, food, health, sanitation, water and peace. Even though the rights of children are entrenched in the constitution, the call to 'put children first', 'batho pele', remains just as urgent today as in the past.

Although there have been a number of responses to the growing and impending crises facing children, the rights of many children are not adequately addressed, despite the fact that they are guaranteed in the constitution. A number of preschool children, especially in rural areas, still have no access to early childhood development programmes. Approximately 40 per cent of young children in South Africa grow up in conditions of abject poverty and neglect.

All sectors of society, including government departments at national and provincial level, local government, non-governmental organisations (NGOs), community based organisations (CBOs), FBOs (faith-based organisations) and international organisations need to co-ordinate their efforts so that the rights of children that span the areas of health, nutrition, a safe environment, psychosocial development and cognitive development

can be protected. There is a need for coordination between different sectors of government, at local, district, provincial and national levels, to ensure the implementation of policies on the identification of children in need, and access to social grants and alternative care.

The premature death of parents from HIV/AIDS-related conditions deprives children of love, support and care. The Joint United Nations Programme on HIV/AIDS (UNAIDS) estimated that 660 000 children in South Africa have been orphaned due to AIDS (UNAIDS, 2002).

Parenting style

Baumrind (1967, 1971) identified three styles of parenting used by parents of preschool children:

- *Authoritarian parents*: Authoritarian parents set absolute standards and rules for their children. There is very little communication between the parent and the child regarding rules and regulations. These parents rely on force and punishment to enforce their standards. They show very little warmth towards their children. Children do not

get involved in family decision-making, even in matters that involve them. Baumrind found that preschoolers of authoritarian parents were generally anxious, withdrawn and unhappy.
- *Authoritative parents*: Authoritative parents are warm and responsive to the needs of their children. They set limits for their children and explain the reasoning behind these limits. These parents have open communication with their children and involve them in family decision-making in an age-appropriate manner. These parents listen to the concerns of their children and are flexible when it is deemed appropriate. Authoritative parents encourage autonomy based on the child's level of maturity. Baumrind found children of authoritative parents to be self-reliant, self-controlled and soundly competent.
- *Permissive parents*: Parents who use the permissive

4.3 DEVELOPMENT AND IMPLEMENTATION OF A PRIMARY CARE MODEL TO PROMOTE POSITIVE INTERACTIONS BETWEEN CAREGIVERS AND YOUNG CHILDREN

Research shows that the course of a child's cognitive and social-emotional development is strongly predicated by the quality of early mother-child interaction. The need to pilot a programme on the development and implementation of a primary care model to promote positive interactions between caregivers and young children in the Eastern and Western Cape Provinces was identified by the National Department of Health through its National Plan of Action for Violence Prevention and also by the intersectoral Victim Empowerment Programme (VEP), a project of the National Crime Prevention Strategy (NCPS). It was anticipated that the development and implementation of the model would lead to the reduction of the levels of violence as a result of empowering parents with effective parenting skills to enrich their interaction with their children. The project was implemented through the use of both professional staff and community workers. The intervention was conducted at low intensity (weekly or two-weekly contacts with care-

givers) using professional staff and non-professional staff in communities with multiple problems, most notably poverty, for a period of four to five months. The community workers conducted home visits as well as providing support to caregivers in the primary health care centres. The programme highlighted the need to integrate the caregiver-child support programme into other services, especially the integrated management of childhood illness, maternal health and nutrition.

The programme was based on the following World Health Organisation/International Child Development Programme (1997) guidelines for good interaction:
- Show your child you love her.
- Talk to your child. Get a conversation going by means of emotional expressions, gestures and sounds.
- Follow your child's lead.
- Praise and appreciate what your child manages to do.
- Help your child to focus her attention and share her experiences (Richter, 2001).

style of child-rearing are warm and nurturing. Very few demands are made on the children and rules are not enforced. Children are permitted to express their impulses and parents do not monitor their children's activities. Permissive parents allow children to make many of their own decisions at an age when they are not yet capable of doing so responsibly. Children of permissive parents are often found to be generally immature and impulsive.

Cognitive development

The preschool period is characterised by dramatic cognitive development. Infants develop a basic understanding of the world around them during the first two years of life. They learn to recognise objects and people, to search for objects that are not in their field of vision, to understand cause and effect, and to appreciate the concept of space (Kaplan, 1998). As the horizons of the preschool child widen, they are increasingly exposed to new social situations and activities that impact on their cognitive development. Although cognitive and language development occurs in a predictable sequence in almost all children, environmental factors can affect development if there is significant early deprivation. When deprivation is severe and prolonged, intervention may be necessary (Craig, 1996).

Piaget's stages of cognitive development

The sensorimotor stage (0–2 years)
During Piaget's first stage of cognitive development, infants learn about their environment through their senses and motor activity. The infant develops the ability to co-ordinate sensory input with motor actions. Symbolic representational ability develops between the ages of 18 months and 24 months. One of the most important achievements during the sensorimotor stage is the development of object permanence. Infants are considered to have attained an understanding of permanence when they realise that objects continue to exist when they are no longer visible. The development of this ability is gradual; it appears between 4 and 8 months and is completely achieved between 18 to 24 months. Infants who have attained object permanence search for hidden toys. Deferred imitation – the ability to reproduce the behaviour of an absent model – appears between 18 and 24 months.

The preoperational stage (2–7 years)
Piaget called this stage the preoperational stage because children have not yet acquired the cognitive operations that are required for logical thinking. The preoperational stage is characterised by the increasing use of symbolic thought expressed through language and scribbles. Children engage in pretend play and may even invent imaginary playmates. For example, boys in the rural areas of South Africa often build wire cars and then pretend to be driving cars.

Piaget identified a number of limitations of preoperational thought:
- Children's thinking often displays animism. They attribute human-like qualities to inanimate objects.
- Their thinking is characterised by transductive reasoning, i.e. reasoning from one particular event to another particular event. If a child usually visits her grandparents on a Sunday, for example, she will think that it is not Sunday if one particular Sunday she is unable to pay the grandparents a visit.
- Children at this stage lack the capacity for thought conservation. Conservation involves the ability to understand that quantities may remain the same regardless of changes in their appearance (Piaget & Inhelder, 1969). For example, when children are presented with two balls of dough of the same size, they will understand that the quantities of the dough are the same. However, if one of the balls is changed into a sausage in front of the child, the child no longer understands that the amounts of dough are the same in the ball and the sausage. The lack of conservation in preschool

Figure 8 Preschoolers engaged in pretend play

children is attributed to centration (i.e. the inability to focus on more than one aspect of an object or process at a time), as well as irreversibility (i.e. the inability to mentally reverse perceived actions – e.g., the child does not understand that one can change the sausage back into a ball).

- Preoperational thought is also characterised by egocentrism, that is the tendency to view the world from one's own perspective and to have difficulty recognising another person's point of view.

Early childhood ... (ECD)

... urs in the ... and infor... mostly ... od devel... commu... thin the ... vidence ... pol peri... ring the ... es that ... devel-opm... where the majo... ... up under conditions of poverty and stress. ECD programmes play a critical role in complementing and supplementing learning experiences at home and in the community, and are intended to promote the development of children to reach their full cognitive, emotional, social and physical potential (Mwamwenda, 1995).

The exposure of young children to early childhood development programmes facilitates the early identification of barriers to learning, assessment, and intervention for growth, health and psychological development. Preschoolers that experience severe barriers to learning during the preschool years can be identified and provided with the necessary support. A number of preschools in South Africa have introduced life skills programmes on HIV/AIDS and child abuse and neglect.

The preschool years are an ideal phase for the transmission of values, such as the appreciation of diversity and tolerance of and respect for others – core values that are essential for a peaceful and democratic society. Values such as the need to help people who are less fortunate than oneself, are important for young children to learn in order for

Figure 9 Preschool children acquire literacy, numeracy and social skills through early childhood programmes

them to develop a sense of caring and responsibility towards other people (Richter, 2001).

Language development

At birth, babies use undifferentiated crying as a means of communicating their needs to their caregivers. After the first month, caregivers can distinguish cries of pain, hunger, discomfort, tiredness and boredom by listening to the pitch of the cry. At the age of six to eight weeks, babies start making cooing sounds.

Around four months, babies utter consonant-vowel combinations in long strings, such as 'babababa' or 'mamamama'. These babbling sounds are universal and even deaf babies produce them. However, human interaction is necessary for babbling to develop further. Around six to seven months, babbling starts to resemble the child's home language.

Most children utter their first word at the age of 12 months. They start by using one-word sentences (holophrases) to convey the meaning of a whole sentence. The child may say, 'baby', meaning 'mommy look at the baby'. The child's vocabulary increases to about 50 words at the age of 18 months.

At about 24 months of age, babies use telegraphic speech, which contains only those words that are necessary to communicate meaning and which omit less significant words.

The language of toddlers progresses from two-word utterances to three-word utterances. From the age of three years to six years the child's vocabulary and sentence length increase such that by the age of six the child uses all parts of speech and can use language much more effectively and efficiently (Craig, 1996). At this age, children are capable of producing sentences that are complex and adult-like.

4.4 DIFFICULT SOUNDS FOR PRESCHOOL CHILDREN IN ISIXHOSA

Children aged between 1 and 4 years have difficulty with articulating palatal sounds. They opt for a related sound that is articulated by another part of the mouth. The parts that the children are comfortable with in articulating are the velar (soft palate) (/g/), the alveolar (/s/, the lips (/m/) and the lower lip together with upper teeth (/f/). It is also difficult for a child to articulate the borrowed sounds like /r/, as in /irula/ (a ruler). The word is articulated as a /ilula/.

If a child is faced with pronouncing a sound /gq/ or /ngq/ in a word like/umngqusho/ (stamped mealies), she usually articulate the word as something like either /umgusho/ or /incusho/

There are palatal sounds that are articulated through the side of the mouth, that is the air stream goes through the side of the mouth, with the teeth tightly closed. One of those sounds is /hl/ as in /hleka/ (laugh). This sound is articulated by pushing the tongue downwards, so that it shapes like a bowl, thereby opening a space for more air to be contained in the mouth; and then pushes the air towards the side-teeth, which are tightly closed, so that the air is forced to leave through the side of the mouth. Instead of going through this entire process, the child uses an alternative alveolar sound, /s/. This /s/ sound is a very soft, hissing one, between /s/ and /sh/. So, if the child wants to say, /uyahleka/ (she is laughing), she will say /yaseka/.

Conclusion

Many children in South Africa are growing up under conditions that predispose them to future problems (see Box 4.5). Studies on risk and resilience have shown that three broad factors seem to offer protection from the damaging effects of stressful life events (Berk, 2001):

4.5 A STUDY INTO THE SITUATION AND SPECIAL NEEDS OF CHILDREN IN CHILD-HEADED HOUSEHOLDS

Procedure

This study was conducted in Gauteng, Northern Province, Mpumalanga and KwaZulu-Natal Province in South Africa. Data was collected through focus group discussions, interviews and structured questionnaires with service providers and community leaders. A total of 117 AIDS orphans from 34 child-headed households were also interviewed.

Results

The study identified physical, material and educational needs as the top priority of children in child-headed households, followed by emotional support or sense of belonging. One of the major challenges facing preschool children in child-headed households is growing up without parental love, care and s upport. Additional challenges included children's vulnerability to physical, sexual and emotional abuse, a poor health status, as well as diminished opportunities to receive education.

Conclusion

The study highlights the need to develop adequate mechanisms to support, empower and strengthen communities and families as they address the needs of the increasing number of AIDS orphans (Nelson Mandela Children's Fund, 2001).

- *Personal characteristics*: Personal characteristics like temperament can mediate the impact of stressful events. Children with calm, easy-going, adaptable, sociable dispositions who are willing to take initiative have a special capacity to adapt to change and elicit positive responses from others.
- *A warm caregiver relationship*: A close relationship with at least one caregiver who provides affection and assistance and introduces order, stability and organisation into the child's life fosters resilience.
- *Social support outside the immediate family*: A person outside the immediate family like a grandparent or a member of the extended family, or a neighbour, who has a special relationship with the child can promote resilience. Children at risk can also benefit from interventions, such as early childhood development programmes, nutrition programmes and psychosocial interventions to improve health, physical growth and psychological development.

Baumrind, D. (1967). Child care practices anteceding three patterns of preschool behaviour. *Genetic Psychology Monographs*, 75:43–88.

Baumrind, D. (1971). Current patterns of parental authority. *Developmental Psychology Monographs*, 4(1):1–103.

Berk, L.E. (2001). *Development Through the Lifespan* (2nd edition). Boston: Allyn & Bacon.

Brierly, J. (1976). The growing brain. In P. Kaplan (Ed.). *The Human Odyssey: Life-span development*. Pacific Grove: Brooks/Cole.

Clark, J., Phillips, S. & Petersen, R. (1989). Developmental stability in jumping. *Developmental Psychology*, 25:929–35.

Craig, G. (1996). *Human Development*. New Jersey: Prentice Hall.

Cratty, B. (1970). *Perceptual and Motor Development in Infants and Children*. New York: Macmillan.

Gauteng Department of Education. (1999). *Report on Impilo: A holistic approach to early childhood development*. Johannesburg: Gauteng Department of Education.

Hoffman, L., Paris, S. & Hall, E. (1994). *Developmental Psychology Today* (6th edition). New York: McGraw-Hill.

Kaplan, P. (1998). *The Human Odyssey: Life-span development* (3rd edition). Pacific Grove: Brooks/Cole.

Mwamwenda, T. (1995). *Educational Psychology*: An African perspective. Durban: Butterworths.

Nelson, C. (2000). The neurobiological bases of early intervention. In J. Shonkoff & S. Meisels (Eds.). *Handbook of Early Childhood Intervention* (2nd edition). Cambridge: Cambridge University Press, pp. 204–31.

Nelson Mandela Children's Fund (NMCF). (2001). *Report on a Study into the Situation and Special Needs in Child-headed Households*. Johannesburg: NMCF.

Papalia, D. & Olds, W. (1998). *Human Development*. New York: McGraw-Hill.

Piaget, J. & Inhelder, B. (1969). *The Psychology of the Child*. New York: Basic Books.

Richter, L. (2000). Interventions for child development: Caring for health. Paper presented at the *WHO Seminar Series*, 26 May 2000, Geneva, Switzerland.

Richter, L. (2001). *Development and Implementation of a Primary Care Model to Promote Interactions Between Caregivers and Young Children in the Eastern and Western Cape Provinces*. Pretoria: Department of Health: Directorate for Mental Health and Substance Abuse.

Shaffer, D. (1996). *Developmental Psychology: Childhood and adolescence* (4th edition). Pacific Grove: Brooks/Cole.

Sroufe, L.A. (1977). Wariness of strangers and the study of infant development. *Child Development*, 48:1184–99.

Thomas, A., Chess, S. & Birch, H. (1970). The origins of personality. *Scientific American*, 223:102–9.

UNAIDS. (2002). *Report on Global HIV/AIDS Epidemic*. Geneva: UNAIDS.

UNICEF (2001). *The State of the World's Children, 2001*. Geneva: UNICEF.

Waterlow, J. (1973). Note on the assessment and classification of protein energy malnutrition in children. *Lancet*, 2:87–9.

World Health Organisation/International Child Development Programme. (1997). *Improving Mother/Child Interactions to Promote Better Psychosocial Development in Children*. Geneva: World Health Organisation.

Multiple choice questions

1. Which of the following describes the cephalocaudal pattern of development?
   a) from the head downward
   b) from the left to the right
   c) from the center outward
   d) from the periphery inward

2. Walking, throwing, writing and tying shoe laces are capacities collectively known as
   a) gross motor skills
   b) fine motor skills
   c) integrated motor skills
   d) none of the above

3. At about what age does handedness develop in a pre-school child?
   a) it is present at birth
   b) at about two years of age
   c) between three and four years old
   d) at about five to six years old

4. Thomas *et al.* (1970) identified three types of temperaments, namely
   a) easy, complex, slow-to-warm-up
   b) easy, difficult, slow-to-warm-up
   c) easy, difficult-to-warm-up, stubborn
   d) easy, difficult, slow

5. According to Erikson, which three psycho-social stages of development fall within the preschool period of development?
   a) basic trust versus mistrust
      initiative versus shame and doubt
      industry versus inferiority
   b) autonomy versus shame and doubt
      initiative versus guilt
      integrity versus despair
   c) basic trust versus mistrust
      autonomy versus shame and doubt
      initiative versus guilt
   d) basic trust versus guilt
      autonomy versus role confusion
      initiative versus inferiority

6. Which of the following was not described by Baumrind (1967, 1971) as a parenting style used by parents of pre-school children?
   a) authoritarian
   b) autocratic
   c) authoritative
   d) permissive

7. According to Piaget, the stage during which infants learn about their environments through their senses and motor activity, is called the
   a) sensorimotor stage
   b) transductive stage
   c) preoperational stage
   d) egocentric stage

8. During preschool development, the inability to focus on more than one aspect of an object or process at a time is known as
   a) concentration
   b) conservation
   c) centration
   d) conservatism

9. At what age do most children have a vocabulary of about 50 words?
   a) 9 months
   b) 12 months
   c) 18 months
   d) 24 months

10. Which of the following statements regarding risk and resilience in pre-school children, is/are true?
    a) personal characteristics like temperament can mediate the impact of stressful events
    b) a close relationship with at least one caregiver fosters resilience
    c) a close relationship with a person outside the child's immediate family can promote resilience
    d) all of the above

Short answer questions

1. Describe, with the aid of examples, the infant's pattern of physical development during the first two years of life.

2. Write brief notes on the limitations of preoperational thought according to Piaget.

3. Briefly describe the course of language development during the preschool period.

4. Discuss the different types of parenting styles according to Baumrind the child's school competence or incompetence.

5. Briefly discuss the factors associated with resilience in children.

Middle Childhood

Sibusiso Ntshangase

CHAPTER OBJECTIVES

After studying this chapter you should be able to:
- demonstrate a basic understanding of what middle childhood entails
- understand the factors that influence the physical development of children during middle childhood
- describe the factors that influence the social and emotional development of children during middle childhood
- describe the factors that influence the cognitive development of children during middle childhood
- explain the risk and resilience factors that are likely to have an impact on development during middle childhood.

One of Nosipho's clearest and earliest memories of being a young child was her first day at primary school. She didn't think she was as frightened as she had been when she started at the educare centre, but she had vivid recollections of sitting at a desk for the first time, feeling stiff and uncomfortable. Even thinking about it now, she could still feel the tightness of her new school shoes on her feet and how the material of her dress felt strange and hard against her skin. The rest of the day was a blur, but thinking back on it, she could imagine how hard it must have been for her, a child who loved running and doing handstands, to have to sit quietly in a classroom all day.

Of course, reading and writing were second nature to her by then, but it was really mind-blowing to think about how much she must have had to learn through those first years of school. Naturally, only some of that learning was of the kind the teachers were trying to teach. In Nosipho's mind, what stood out were not the lessons themselves, but rather some of the teachers she had liked – and those she disliked! In particular, she remembered her Grade 5 teacher who had encouraged her to voice her opinions in class, and recalled how this had made her feel much more confident that she had felt before. She also remembered an unpleasant man who

had taught her maths and put her off it altogether. He seemed to think that only the boys needed to learn maths and teased the girls, saying they should rather concentrate on learning to cook for their husbands. Thank goodness her high school maths teacher had got her interested again and helped her to realise it was actually something she was quite good at. If she hadn't kept on with it she would not have been able to get into psychology!

Most of the things she remembered from primary school, though, had happened outside of the classroom altogether. She had had a best friend, Thandi, for the first three years of school, and they had walked around the school grounds arm in arm. It was at the beginning of Grade Four that another girl had joined the pair, and she had watched jealously as Thandi got more and more friendly with her. She remembered crying one day after Thandi had finally chosen to sit next to her new friend at the break and Nosipho had found herself wondering around the playground on her own. She remembered the difficulty of trying to find her way into another group of girls, and her relief when they had finally accepted her. It was funny the way that everyone talked about childhood being such a happy time. If you thought about it, it was actually pretty difficult and hard work at times.

Introduction

Middle childhood generally refers to the developmental period between 6 and 12 years. Unlike the first five years, which are largely characterised by a spurt in physical development, during this developmental stage the child experiences a relatively slower, but steady rate of growth. However, this becomes an important period in children's cognitive, social and emotional development (Louw *et al.*, 1998). In South Africa, just like in the rest of the world, children start their schooling during this stage; hence this period is often referred to as the 'school years'. As a result, during this stage, children's environment expands beyond their homes and care centres, providing them with frequent opportunities to interact with a wider range of people in more places than when they were younger (United Nations Environment Programme, 2002).

Figure 1 A daily trip to school

Physical development

As mentioned above, an important characteristic of this stage is the slower average growth rate of children, compared to the earlier preschool period and the later period of adolescence. During this stage, the average annual growth rate in terms of height and weight is about 6cm and 2kg, respectively. On average, the child's height increases from approximately 1.20m at the age of six to approximately 1.50m at the age of twelve years, while mass increases over the same period from approximately 20kg to approximately 40kg (Louw *et al.*, 1998).

The brain also continues to mature, although again at a pace far slower than that seen during the

prenatal period or during the pre-primary school years. The milk teeth are replaced by permanent teeth, a process that is largely completed by the end of middle childhood.

Physical growth is accompanied by improved gross and fine motor skills as a result of an increase in strength, co-ordination and muscular control. Examples of improved gross motor skills include the ability to walk in a straight line, to run fast and to stop and execute turns, to skip, to balance on one foot, to jump, and to throw at targets. Despite the rapid progress they make, children, particularly boys, often overestimate the physical feats they can perform, and the bolder or less inhibited ones are likely to be somewhat accident prone, resulting in bruises, burns, cuts, scrapes, and an assortment of other injuries (Shaffer, 2002).

The child's improved fine motor skills are aided by an improvement in hand-eye co-ordination or motor-perceptual functioning that accompanies middle childhood. Fine motor skills include skills like buttoning a shirt, tying shoelaces, holding a pen correctly, being able to write, and copying simple designs.

Figure 2 Learning to ride a bicycle is one of the significant accomplishments of middle childhood

Physical development during middle childhood plays an important role in the development of children because it allows them to engage in play, which is a source of their balanced existence in their environment. Various perspectives hold that a lack of physical play during middle childhood could be indicative of certain developmental difficulties. For example, according to Erikson's (1963) perspective, it could be an indication of unresolved early crises involving feelings of mistrust, doubt and guilt (see Chapter 4, this volume). Secondly, according to a more medical orientation, it could be an indication of a motor skills disorder, such as Developmental Co-ordination Disorder (American Psychiatric Association, 1994). It could also be due to learning disabilities.

According to Shaffer (2002), three kinds of environmental influences can have a major effect on physical growth and development during middle childhood: nutrition, illnesses and the quality of care that children receive.

Research on the nutritional status of children, both local and abroad, indicates that under-nutrition and over-nutrition can play a significant role in physical development during middle childhood (e.g., Richter *et al.*, 1999; Valenzuela, 1997). The National Research Foundation Unit for Research in Child Development in South Africa in its Annual Report (2003) noted that malnutrition remains the most prevalent problem affecting young children in South Africa, with more than a third of children showing stunted growth.

Accordingly, a number of community-based nutrition research projects have been conducted by the Medical Research Council of South Africa, in an attempt to monitor the growth and nutritional status of children in the country. For instance, the Medical Research Council (2003) is currently involved in exploring dietary calcium deficiency as a cause of rickets in the country. The ultimate objective of this study is to establish effective methods for prevent-

5.1 HOW BENEFICIAL IS PLAY?

In contrast to earlier views that childhood play activities are a frivolous waste of time, studies done in the early 1950s (e.g., Piaget, 1959) indicated that play in fact allows children to practice and strengthen a range of competencies.

Intellectually, play provides a context for using language to communicate and the mind to fantasise, plan strategies and solve problems. Indeed, children often show more advanced intellectual skills during pretend play than they do when performing other activities, suggesting that play fosters cognitive development (Lillard, 1993). Consequently, children who regularly engage in pretend play (or who are trained to do so) often perform better on tests of Piagetian cognitive development, language skills and creativity than children who 'pretend' less often (Fisher, 1992; Johnson, 1991).

Pretend activities may also promote social development. To be successful at social pretend play, children must adopt different roles, co-ordinate their activities, and resolve any disputes that may arise. Children may also learn about, and prepare for adult roles by 'playing house' or 'playing school' and stepping into the shoes of their mothers, fathers, or school teachers (Gleason *et al.*, 2000). Perhaps because of the social skills they acquire (e.g., an ability to co-operate) and the role taking experience they obtain, school children who participate in a lot of social pretend play tend to be more

socially mature and popular with peers than age mates who generally play without partners.

Finally, play may foster healthy emotional development by allowing children to express feelings that bother them or to resolve emotional conflicts. Children who are from socio-economically disadvantaged and deprived environments, such as informal settlements, could often be found happily playing and making noise at the top of their little voices, to the amazement of an observer who might be surprised by the awful conditions under which they are living. One of the main reasons for their happiness could be that they often spend a lot of time playing together and thus having a chance to act out their emotions. Another example could be that of a little girl who has been scolded at lunch for failing to eat her fruit, and who may gain control of the situation at play as she scolds her doll for picky eating or persuades the doll to 'eat healthy' and consume the fruit. Indeed, playful resolutions of such emotional conflicts may even be an important contributor to children's understanding of authority and the rationales that underlie all the rules they must follow.

Let it never be said, then, that play is useless. Although children play because it is fun, not because it sharpens their skills, play indirectly contributes to their physical, social, emotional and intellectual development (adapted from Shaffer, 2002:231).

ing the development of rickets in affected communities, and to treat children with the disease.

Furthermore, research has indicated that play or physical activity substantially reduces the risk of developing some illnesses. The Birth to Twenty (2003) study, for instance, indicated that regular physical activity could help to reduce symptoms of anxiety and depression, and is associated with fewer hospitalisations, visits to the doctor and medications (see Box 5.2).

5.2 BIRTH TO TWENTY

Procedure
The Birth to Twenty study is a longitudinal research project studying child health and development in Africa, following them from birth to twenty years. The Birth to Twenty study examined whether South African children are physically active enough.

Results
More than 40 per cent of children (in Grades 4 and 5) do not regularly engage in vigorous physical activity. Also, physical activity is less common among girls than boys and among those with lower income and less education.

Conclusions
South African children are not sufficiently physically active and would benefit from more physical activity and sport participation (Birth to Twenty, 2003).

Social and emotional development

As indicated in Box 5.1, physical growth and social development are interrelated. A long-absent aunt who cries, 'My, how you've grown!' may summon a grin from the wary seven-year-old or a blush from the self-conscious eleven-year-old, but she is confirming for them the social importance of this sign of increasing physical maturity (Bukatko & Daehler, 1995). Based on their level of physical growth, the environment assigns children particular roles and has certain expectations of them. For instance, a six-year-old boy may be expected to cry less easily and frequently than when he was younger. Furthermore, children of school-going age are expected to do certain chores, which might not have been seen to be suitable for them when they were younger. For instance, they may now be sent to buy goods at a shop. They may also be expected to perform certain basic cooking and house cleaning tasks. Often too, they may now be asked to look after their younger siblings while their parents are away. Whether the tasks frequently expected of children are appropriate for their development is of course debatable.

Figure 3 Young girls, particularly if they are the oldest in their families, are often expected to take care of their younger siblings

Erikson (1963), in his psychosocial theory of development, describes the middle childhood stage as that of industry versus inferiority (see chapter 4 of this volume). He describes this stage as the period during which children must master important social and educational skills. It is a period when the child compares him- or herself with peers. As children encounter the challenges of school, positive outcomes lead to a valuing of personal accomplishments and a sense of competency, or industry. In this way, they acquire the social and academic skills to feel self-assured. On the other hand, negative outcomes lead to a sense of failure and feelings of inferiority. During this stage, teachers and peers are significant environmental or social agents (Goldstein, 1994; Shaffer, 2002).

The social messages that children receive as they interact with the environment play an important role in developing their self-concept. According to Louw et al. (1998), the middle childhood period could be regarded as a sensitive period for the development of the self-concept because specific kinds of experiences have significant consequences for its development. Children of school-going age begin to define themselves in psychological terms; they develop a concept of who they are (i.e. the real self) and also of how they would like to be (i.e. the ideal self). Freud suggests that the ideal self develops with the super-ego. For instance, as much as they can define themselves according to their family circumstances, they can also define themselves according to the norms they have learned, and it helps them to control their impulses so that they can be seen to be the 'good' person they would like to be (Louw *et al.*, 1998).

Children, during this stage, develop a sense of their own competencies, the things they are good at and the things they feel unable to do. This is derived partly from what others tell them and partly from comparing themselves to others, whether it be in running, completing puzzles, reading or sewing. These competencies as well as the degree of liking or respect that others show toward them, are likely to contribute to their self-esteem (Tyson, 1987).

Currently, school-going children are confronted by a variety of social factors, which are more demanding and more likely to put them at risk (see Box 5.3). It is during this stage of development that the socially defined gender dimensions are likely to have an impact in defining a child's future. According to UNICEF (2003), in many countries, the state of girls' education still presents a broad social crisis. Girls are reported to be the ones most likely to become the victims of gender-related barriers. UNICEF (2003) notes that girls currently constitute the majority of children in and out of school. However, the number of those out of school generally increases significantly in times of conflict, social crisis and natural disaster. Traditionally in southern African countries, if a choice has to be made between sending a boy or a girl to school, often due to poverty, the boy will usually be given precedence.

Again, in the face of the HIV/AIDS pandemic currently devastating South Africa, girls of school-going age are more often likely to find themselves having to care for sick family members and eventually becoming heads of households in the event of their parents dying of AIDS.

Middle childhood is also a period of greater emotional maturity. Children have now outgrown the period of helplessness and are expected to be independent and self-sufficient. This, according to Louw *et al.* (1998), implies greater emotional flexibility and greater emotional differentiation.

Compared to the limited emotional expression of babies, emotional expression during middle childhood is more specific, more diverse and more

5.3 INVESTING IN CHILDREN: ADVANCING SUSTAINABLE DEVELOPMENT

As the world meets on the critical issues of sustainable development, some countries in southern Africa are reeling from cumulative shocks and disasters that have put nearly 13 million people at risk of dying. More than half of those at risk are children.

The disasters include searing droughts and crop failures, entrenched poverty and the ravages of the HIV/AIDS pandemic. The results are, amongst others, a food crisis, a water crisis, a health crisis and an education crisis all at once, with each element feeding on the others.

Organisations such as UNICEF are responding by trying to save children's lives and safeguard their rights. Support is needed for various measures, including therapeutic feeding centres, immunisation efforts, vitamin A distribution, new wells and water purification equipment, school lunches to keep children in school, and help for families and children affected by HIV/AIDS, especially those at risk of exploitation.

Investing in children is a crucial way to intervene in these crises and to advance sustainable development. For example, it has been argued that children below 14 years of age offer a 'window of hope' to stop the spread of HIV/AIDS. Many of them are still not infected, and with proper awareness about preventing disease and behavioural change linked to this awareness, they have a better chance of protecting their own lives and other people.

According to Carol Bellamy, Executive Director of UNICEF (2003:1): 'Ensuring the rights and well-being of children is the key to sustained development in a country and to peace and security in the world. Meeting this responsibility, fully, consistently and at any cost, is the essence of leadership. Heads of State and Government hold the lion's share of this responsibility but commitment and action are also called for across the board.'

sophisticated (Louw *et al.*, 1998:345). However, although children at this stage are better able to express their emotions, social gender-role stereotyping often prevents such expression. For instance, boys are often taught not to cry and not to show fear, while girls are often criticised if they become aggressive. Such gender-role stereotyping has the potential of preventing children from exploring and experimenting with their full repertoire of emotions

(Louw *et al.*, 1998). The resultant 'bottling up' of emotions, particularly among boys, has been established as a potential contributing factor in mood disorders (such as depression and suicidal ideation) among children (Kaplan & Sadock, 1998).

As should be clear from the earlier discussion, the school becomes a powerful agency of socialisation during middle childhood. Schools are the site where cultural values and norms that will be adhered to and treasured for years are formally transmitted. One of the purposes of schools is to extend the socialisation process begun by the family. At school the child is expected to relate to a new form of authority, namely teachers, follow a new of set of rules, make new friends and learn to get along with those who are not his or her friend. He or she is also expected to develop an interest in the acquisition of knowledge in a formal and structured manner. Ultimately, the school provides the child with the knowledge and skills necessary for social and economic adjustment (Behr *et al.* in Mwamwenda, 1995).

Figure 4 School is where many friendships are formed

As much as there is an agreement that social factors such as the home and school environment contribute substantially to the child's development, one has to consider that there has been a long-standing debate among developmental psychologists regarding the role of the biological makeup versus the role of the environment in determining children's capabilities (see Box 5.4).

5.4 HOW DO HEREDITY AND ENVIRONMENT INTERACT?

Question: Is child development primarily the result of nature (genetic forces) or nurture (environmental forces)?

There are opposing viewpoints:
- 'Heredity and not environment is the chief maker of people ... Nearly all of the misery and nearly all of the happiness in the world are not due to environment ... The differences among people are due to differences in germ cells with which they were born' (Wiggam, 1923:45).
- 'Give me a dozen healthy children, well formed, and my own specified world to bring them up in, and I will guarantee to take any of them at random and train them to become any type of specialist I might select – doctors, lawyers, artist, merchant, chief, and yes, even beggar and thief, regardless of talents, penchants, tendencies, abilities, vocations, and race of their ancestors. There is no such thing as an inheritance of capacity, talent, temperament, mental constitution, and behavioral characteristics' (Watson, 1925:82).

What is your position? How often do your hear parents saying they prefer certain schools because they believe their children will be better socialised in them? Do you think children exposed to violence are more likely to be violent and bully at school? Do you think children who grow up in the absence of their parents are worse off than their peers who can rely on their parents? (Adapted from Shaffer, 2002.)

Cognitive development

By far the most influential theory in the description of cognitive development is Piaget's theory (Shaffer, 2002). In Piaget's theory, the stage of cognitive development that coincides with the middle childhood period is the concrete operational period. During this stage a number of basic cognitive abilities emerge. Some of these abilities are described in Box 5.5.

However, it is important to note that although Piaget's theory has had a strong impact, particularly on the education sector where it informs the discovery-based curriculum in primary schools, other theorists with different views have challenged it.

Reversibility

Reversibility is achieved when the child realises that certain operations can be reversed. For example, given the numbers 12 and 6, they can supply the answer '2' as the number that when multiplied by 6 equals 12 and that when divided into 12 equals 6.

Decentration

Instead of focusing on just one aspect of an object or event, the child can simultaneously focus attention on several attributes of an event or object and realise that those attributes can be separated. The child realises, for example, that although a balloon may be large, it can also be light.

Conservation

Conservation is the ability to recognise that properties of objects or substances do not change because their form changes. For instance, children will understand that the amount of water does not change when the shape of the container holding it changes. The realisa-tion that pouring water from one container to another does not change the amount of water requires both *reversible* thinking (with the child reasoning that if the water were poured back to its original container it would look the same as before), and *decentration* (with the child taking into account both the height and width of the containers).

Seriation

Seriation is the ability to arrange objects in order along quantitative dimensions, such as weight, length, or size. During the stage of concrete operational thought, the child can arrange a series of dolls in order of height, whereas a four-year-old child, for instance, might alter-nate tall and short dolls, or arrange them more randomly.

Transitivity

Transitivity is the ability to recognise relations among a number of ordered objects, for example, recognising that if Nokuphila is taller than Thobeka and Thobeka is taller than Anele, then Nokuphila must also be taller than Anele (adapted from Goldstein, 1994:387).

One of the first important challenges to Piaget's theory came from the Russian developmentalist, Lev Vygotsky. Vygotsky's socio-cultural theory focused on how culture – the beliefs, values, traditions, and skills of a social group – is transmitted from genera-tion to generation. Rather than depicting children as independent explorers or scientists who make criti-cal discoveries on their own (as articulated within Piaget's theory), Vygotsky viewed cognitive growth as a socially mediated activity, one in which children gradually acquire new ways of thinking and behav-ing through co-operative dialogues with more knowledgeable members of society.

Vygotsky's theory is relevant in understanding cognitive development during the middle child-hood period because it highlights the potential role of the schooling system as a social structure that transmits cultural values and beliefs to children (Shaffer, 2002). It is this theory that has mostly informed the new Outcomes Based Education (OBE) curriculum that is currently being introduced in South African schools. In essence, OBE is based on the principles of co-operation, critical thinking and social responsibility, and defines children as active participants in the acquisition of knowledge.

Recognising the role of culture in cognitive devel-opment, Mwamwenda (1995) states that cognitive abilities cannot be defined out of context. For instance, the value that the West attaches to Piagetian concepts may not be the same as the value the vast majority of African people would attach to them. As a result, the way in which 'Africans' and 'non-Africans' are likely to relate to these concepts may differ significantly and may affect their corre-sponding child-rearing practices.

Conclusion

Middle childhood is an extremely important period in the social, emotional and cognitive growth of chil-dren. It is a foundational period, when the basis is laid for social values and norms. Middle childhood is a formative period in establishing and cementing moralilty, integrity and respect. Cultural context and social situation are integral factors in shaping the course of middle childhood.

American Psychiatric Association. (1994). *Diagnostic and Statistical Manual of Mental Disorders* (4th edition). Washington: American Psychiatric Association.

Birth to Twenty. (2003). *Are South African Children Active Enough?* www.wits.ac.za/birthto20 (accessed 26 February 2003).

Bukatko, D. & Daehler, M.W. (1995). *Child Development: A thematic approach.* Boston: Houghton Miffin Company.

Erikson, E.H. (1963). *Childhood and Society* (2nd edition). New York: Norton.

Fisher, E.P. (1992). The impact of play on development: A meta-analysis. *Play and Culture*, 5:159–81.

Gleason, T.R., Sebanc, A.M. & Hartup, W.W. (2000). Imaginary companions of preschool children. *Developmental Psychology*, 36:419–28.

Goldstein, E.B. (1994). *Psychology.* California: Brooks/Cole Publishing Company.

Johnson, E.P. (1991). Searching for the social and cognitive outcomes of children's play: A selective second look. *Play and Culture*, 4:201–13.

Kaplan, H.I. & Sadock, B.J. (1998). *Synopsis of Psychiatry: Behavioural sciences/Clinical psychiatry* (8th edition). Baltimore: Lippincott Williams & Wilkins.

Lillard, A.S. (1993). Pretend play skills and the child's theory of mind. *Child Development*, 64:348–71.

Louw, D. , van Ede, D. & Louw, A. (1998). *Human Development* (2nd edition). Pretoria: Kagiso Publishers.

Medical Research Council of South Africa. (2003). *Dietary Calcium Deficiency as a Cause of Rickets in Developing Countries*, www.mrc.co.za (accessed 2 June 2003).

Mwamwenda, T.S. (1995). *Educational Psychology: An African perspective* (2nd edition). Durban: Butterworths.

National Research Foundation Unit for Research in Child Development in South Africa. (2003). *2000 Annual Report*, www.psychology.unp.ac.za/NRFUNIT.HTM (accessed 2 June 2003).

Piaget, J. (1959). *Play, Dreams, and Imitation in Childhood.* New York: Norton.

Richter, L., Griesel, R. & Rose, C. (1999). The psychological impact of a school feeding project. In D. Donald, A. Dawes & J. Louw (Eds.). *Addressing Childhood Adversity*. Cape Town: David Philip, pp.74–93.

Shaffer, D.R. (2002). *Developmental Psychology: Childhood and adolescence* (6th edition). Belmont: Wadsworth Group.

Tyson, G.A. (1987). *Introduction to Psychology.* Johannesburg: Westro Educational Books.

UNICEF. (2003). *Barriers to Girls' Education: Strategies and interventions*, www.unicef.org/programme/girlseducation (accessed 20 February 2003).

United Nations Environment Programme. (2002). *Children in the New Millennium: Environmental impact on health*, www.unep.org (accessed 20 February 2003).

Valenzuela, M. (1997). Maternal sensitivity in a developing society: The context of urban poverty and infant chronic undernutrition. *Developmental Psychology*, 33:845–55.

Watson, J.B. (1925). *Behaviorism*. New York: Norton.

Wiggam, A.E. (1923). *The New Decalogue of Science*. Indianapolis: Bos-Merrill.

Multiple choice questions

1. According to Shaffer (2002), which three kinds of environmental influences can have a major effect on physical growth and development during middle childhood?
   a) pollution, quality of care, and crime
   b) nutrition, illnesses, and quality of care
   c) nutrition, schooling, and peers
   d) illness, pollution, and schooling
2. According to Erikson, which of the following statements regarding the middle childhood stage of development is/are true?
   a) it is a period during which children must master important social and educational skills
   b) it is a period when the child compares him- or herself with peers
   c) it is a time when teachers and peers are significant environmental or social agents
   d) all of the above
3. What did Erikson term the psychosocial conflict that children during middle childhood need to resolve?
   a) industry versus inferiority
   b) industry versus inability
   c) superiority versus inferiority
   d) authority versus inferiority
4. When a young boy is told, 'boys mustn't cry, they must be strong and brave', this is an example of
   a) social sanctioning
   b) positive reinforcement
   c) gender-role stereotyping
   d) punitive parenting
5. When a child realises that although a balloon may be large, it can also be light, he or she is demonstrating the ability called
   a) decentration
   b) conservation
   c) seriation
   d) reversibility
6. Transitivity is the ability to
   a) arrange objects in order along quantitative dimensions, such as weight, length, or size
   b) the ability to recognise that properties of objects or substances do not change because their form changes
   c) recognise relations among a number of ordered objects
   d) none of the above

7. Key finding(s) from the Birth to Twenty study found that regular physical activity
   a) could help to reduce symptoms of anxiety and depression
   b) is associated with fewer hospitalisations, visits to the doctor, and medications
   c) both a and b
   d) neither a nor b
8. Which cognitive development theory has mostly informed the new Outcomes Based Education (OBE) curriculum that is currently being introduced in South African schools?
   a) psychosocial theory
   b) psychodynamic theory
   c) biological-maturation theory
   d) socio-cultural theory
10. The theory focusing on how culture – the beliefs, values, traditions and skills of a social group – is transmitted from generation to generation can be attributed to which influential theorist?
    a) Lev Vygotsky
    b) Jean Piaget
    c) Sigmund Freud
    d) Erik Erikson
11. According to which early developmental psychologist is development primarily the result of nature (genetic forces)?
    a) S. Freud
    b) J.B. Watson
    c) D.R. Shaffer
    d) G.A. Tyson

Short answer questions

1. Briefly outline the physical development of children during the middle childhood years.
2. What did Erikson (1963) mean when he described the middle childhood stage in terms of industry versus inferiority?
3. According to UNICEF (2003), in many countries, the state of girls' education still presents a broad social crisis. Discuss this statement.
4. Critically discuss the role of culture in cognitive development.
5. Childhood play activities are a frivolous waste of time. Provide a convincing argument against this assertion.

Adolescence

Tamara Shefer

CHAPTER OBJECTIVES

After studying this chapter you should be able to:
- demonstrate an understanding of traditional theories and literature on adolescence as a life stage
- unpack the central themes of adolescent development on a physical, psychological and social level
- outline some of the key areas of contemporary research on adolescents in the southern African context
- highlight current areas of risk and challenges for change within the lives of this group of youth in South Africa.

Nosipho's adolescent years were not full of the conflicts and rebellions that other teenagers seemed to have. Her parents were very strict, and she had few opportunities to get into trouble. The typical adolescent dangers of drugs and sex seemed a long way from her, and she spent most of her afternoons doing homework and helping around the house. At the time she resented this and imagined her friends having so much more fun than her. But looking back, she was grateful that she had been protected in this way. So many of the kids she was at school with had fallen pregnant or had got involved with a bad group and ended up dropping out of school. These days it must be even more difficult for teenagers, with HIV/AIDS being such a big part of life. Nosipho wondered how kids were managing to deal with it.

But, while everything appeared on the surface to be quite orderly during Nosipho's adolescence, there was a great deal going on that her parents certainly would never have guessed. She remembered the excitement with which she had begun to think about 'boys'. She was very shy about speaking to any directly, but would often find herself daydreaming about a particular boy over quite a long period – sort of like an imaginary boyfriend. Not all these imaginings were pleasant, though, and she often had doubts about whether anyone would actually fall in love with her. She recalled also spending ages in front of the mirror trying to imagine if someone could find her attractive and wondering how she compared to the beautiful women she saw in magazines and on television. Thank goodness she no longer believed that you had to conform to some particular idea of beauty in order to be loved – it would have been so awful to have to try and live up to some impossible ideal. When she looked at where she was now, Nosipho could certainly see how things were much more settled inside herself than they had been when she was a teenager. She felt somehow much more comfortable with her beliefs, her values and her sense of herself – and of course she had a real boyfriend now!

Introduction

'She's so moody lately, a real teenager!'

'He won't listen to a thing I say, just sits in his room and sulks all day, listening to loud music!'

Figure 1 Popular culture constructs a stereotypic picture of this stage of development as troublesome for the individual, his or her family and society at large. There is a growing argument in developmental psychology that adolescence is not necessarily a traumatic process

These are some of the everyday comments you may have heard about adolescents. Popular culture constructs a stereotypic picture of this stage of development as a troublesome one for the individual, his or her family and society at large. Similarly, traditional developmental psychology has reinforced the idea that, universally, this is an emotionally turbulent and 'difficult' stage of development. G. Stanley Hall (1844 to 1924), known as the 'father' of adolescent psychology, coined the term 'storm and stress' to describe what he saw as the natural moodiness of adolescents (Dacey & Travers, 2002). But is it really so for every culture? There is a growing argument in developmental psychology that adolescence is not necessarily a traumatic process (e.g., Steinberg, 1990). It is now more widely accepted that there may not be one universal experience of adolescence, but rather that this stage may take on different forms across different cultures and even within different families and for different individuals.

In traditional developmental psychology, adolescence refers to that stage of human development that follows middle childhood, and that serves as the transition from childhood to adulthood. It is generally viewed as beginning with the onset of the biological changes of puberty and ending with the cultural identity of adulthood. While adolescence may not necessarily be universally traumatic, as described by much of the literature, and in some communities does not even constitute a clear-cut developmental stage, a wide range of physical, emotional and social changes are associated with this stage of development. In most cultures, the beginning of biological puberty, and the social and cultural expectations and pressures which come with this, tend to signify an important transition for the child.

This chapter presents some of the central theories and documentation of adolescence in traditional developmental psychology. It looks at this development through the lenses of biology, psychology and society, while recognising that these levels of experience are never separate in the lived experiences of the human subject. The chapter draws on the South African context, as well as local literature and research on adolescence to create a more contextualised picture of the South African adolescent. The chapter attempts to raise some the key areas of challenge, that is, areas of potential risk and difficulty, for South African adolescents in contemporary South Africa.

Physical development

Physical development in adolescence centres on the physical and hormonal changes that take place in puberty. Puberty has been defined as 'a period of rapid physical maturation involving hormonal and bodily changes that occur primarily during early adolescence' (Santrock, 2002:349). Puberty begins with hormonal increases, which manifest in a range of internal and external bodily changes. These are known as the *primary and secondary sex characteristics* that signify sexual maturation and gender differentiation. These changes coincide with a growth spurt in height and weight which lasts about four-and-a-half years (Newcombe, 1996), and which peaks at eleven-and-a-half years for girls and thirteen-and-a-half years for boys (Santrock, 2002). As evident from Box 6.1, there are many factors that impact on the onset of puberty, such as nutrition, health, heredity and body mass (Santrock, 2002), which means that the onset of puberty may vary greatly from person to person, and across different cultures.

Puberty is usually presented as a biological and universal fact of change that heralds adolescence. Biology is not something outside of culture. Rather, it is becoming more evident that the social world has a complex impact on humans' biological and physiological lives. Reports of the effect of hormones used on animals in the production of meat represents one of the most frightening indicators of the way in which biology and culture are interwoven in the experience of puberty. In Puerto Rica in the 1980s, there were reports of girls as young as the age of 4 developing breasts and beginning to menstruate (Henriques et al., 1984). The acceleration of sexual maturation was believed to be the result of the use of oestrogen in the feed of chickens, which forms part of the staple diet of this group of Puerto Ricans. Henriques et al. (1984:21) comment how the 'effect of these biological changes is utter confusion of the children, their peers and adults regarding appropriate behaviour and expectations, so that they are caught in the limbo of child-woman'.

A further example of the way in which puberty is affected by environmental context is evident through cross-cultural and historical differences in the onset age of puberty. Santrock (2002:349) highlights the following examples of such differences across time and culture:

- In Norway, the average age of menarche is just over 13 years of age, compared to 17 years of age in the 1940s.
- In the United States of America, the average age of menarche is 12 years of age and has been declining at about 4 months per decade for the past century.

See Ruth Ozeki's *My Year of Meat* for a fictionalised account of the use of hormones in meat.

The most noted changes in puberty include the following:

- Ovaries enlarge, and all parts of the reproductive system, including the fallopian tubes, uterus and vagina become more developed. The beginning of the menstrual cycle or *menarche* for young women emerges out of these changes.
- The testicles, penis, scrotum, prostate gland and seminal vessels are further developed. The beginning of sperm production or *spermarche* and experiences of ejaculation, often in erotic dreams ('wet' dreams), are associated with these changes in young men.
- The growth of bodily hair, primarily pubic and under-arm, but also facial and upper torso hair, especially in boys.
- The development of breasts in girls.
- The deepening of voices.
- Changes in skin texture, which may result in skin infections, such as acne.

While all of these changes appear quite dramatic, puberty actually takes place gradually, and it is difficult to identify its exact starting point. Hormonal changes, for example, may begin some years before they are evident in bodily changes.

The body changes in adolescence clearly have multiple psychological consequences as well. By all accounts, this stage brings on a new awareness and concern with the body for the developing child. Adolescents are *preoccupied with their bodies*, particularly during the changes of puberty (Santrock, 2002). The focus on the body is also clearly gender differentiated, with pressure on males to develop their bodies, while young women are expected to conform to the slim media image. It is not surprising, then, that the eating disorders of anorexia nervosa and bulimia nervosa most frequently begin in adolescence. Much of the psychological literature on these disorders highlights the significance of the social pressures on girls to achieve the slim ideal image, as well as the socio-psychological meanings of developing into adult women (see, for example, the seminal works of Bruch, 1974; Orbach, 1978; Palazzoli, 1974).

Although it has been argued that eating disorders are only present in affluent societies or middle-class families, there is growing evidence that South African youth, particularly adolescent girls, in all communities are at risk (Goosen & Klugman, 1996). For example, a recent study found that the prevalence of abnormal eating attitudes is equally common in South African schoolgirls from different ethnic backgrounds (Caradas et al., 2001).

Cognitive development

Within Piaget's developmental framework, adolescence is characterised by the development of *formal operational thinking*. This form of cognition suggests an ability to think more abstractly, more idealistical-

Figure 2 'I wish I was thinner ...' Sometimes imposed, sometimes self-inflicted, the demands of adolescence can be taxing

ly and more logically (Santrock, 2002). Formal operational thinking involves more abstract, less concrete conceptualisation, with the ability to hypothesise and use logical reasoning. The abstract component of this thinking is reflected in problem-solving abilities, such as the ability to solve abstract mathematical equations. The idealisation component, which is linked to the dominance of abstract thinking, is evident in the tendency of adolescents to construct ideal images of themselves, others and the social world. Idealism emerges out of the adolescent's increased ability to apply reason, and manifests in an attraction to political and humanitarian causes (Hughes, 2002). The logical component, which Piaget called 'hypothetical-deductive' thinking, is manifested in an ability and desire to actively plan and problem-solve. Furthermore, according to information-processing theorists, the adolescent is also capable of quicker, more complex processing, linked to their increased concentration ability as well as their development of a range of information-processing strategies (such as problem-solving rules) (Newcombe, 1996).

Developmental psychologists have described a number of implications of these cognitive changes in adolescents. *Adolescent 'egocentricism'*, which refers to the adolescent's preoccupation with the self and related self-consciousness, constitutes one of the primary sequelae of these changes (Elkind, 1967, 1976).

Theorists describe how the adolescent's focus on reflection extends to a preoccupation with thoughts about the self, which may exacerbate their growing self-consciousness due to physical changes in their bodies (Newcombe, 1996).

The effects of egocentricism in formal operational thinking have been described using the concepts of the 'personal myth', the 'invincibility fable', and 'the imaginary audience' (Dacey & Travers, 2002; Hughes, 2002). The personal myth refers to adolescents' fantasies about themselves as unique and special, while the related invincibility fable involves unrealistic ideas about themselves as invincible and untouchable. The latter is obviously particularly dangerous in the current context of HIV/AIDS, as an adolescent may believe, as many studies have shown, that 'it can't happen to me' – which may facilitate increased risk-taking behaviour (Dacey & Travers, 2002). The imaginary audience refers to the self-consciousness and self-centredness, already described, which stems from the belief that the adolescent is always the centre of focus in any situation.

As emphasised earlier, it should be remembered that culture and social norms and expectations also impact on cognitive development. Some theorists have focused on the impact of culture, gender and other social forces on cognitive development, and have argued that culture may not only influence the rate of cognitive development, but also the mode of thinking that develops (Rogoff in Shaffer, 1999). Others have shown that our ideas of mature cognition may be sexist because they idealise what is considered positive for mature men rather than what is expected of women. For example, Carol Gilligan (1982) criticises Kohlberg's theory of moral development as being based on a male definition of morality, arguing that gender socialisation creates different standards of morality for men and women. Mature cognitive development is generally viewed as characterised by rationality, independence and self-sufficiency, which are traditionally male characteristics, as opposed to 'emotional sensitivity', sensitivity to relationships, and dependence on others, which are traditionally seen as feminine qualities.

Critical thinking is another spin-off of formal operational thought that has been widely documented in the literature. Theorists differentiate between *convergent* and *divergent* thinking, the former referring to a strategy of focusing on one correct answer to a problem, while the latter refers to solving a problem with many possible answers (Dacey & Travers, 2002). Critical thinking allows the young person to begin questioning aspects of his or her life that were previously assumed, and is more likely to facilitate creative thinking as well.

Psychological and emotional development

Theories of adolescent personality development

Identity is the key issue highlighted in theories of adolescent personality development. Erik Erikson has provided one of the most comprehensive accounts of identity development through the life span (Santrock, 2002). In his theory, adolescence falls into the fifth of eight stages, namely identity versus identity confusion. According to Erikson, each stage that we pass through involves a crisis for the developing self. For the adolescent this crisis refers to struggling and experimenting with conflicting identities as the individual moves from the security of childhood to develop an autonomous adult identity. Those who do not adequately resolve the conflict of this stage will suffer from 'identity confusion', which may take a range of problematic forms such as social isolation and loss of identity in groups, amongst others. The successful resolution of the identity crisis will mean the achievement of a settled, stable and mature identity.

Erikson has been criticised for the rigid way in which he has theorised identity, as well as the idea that identity formation is largely established in ado-

---

6.2 IDENTITY VERSUS SUBJECTIVITY

Most traditional psychological theories assume a process whereby all human psyches develop into stable, unitary and rational personalities. Although some theorists, like Freud, see this as a complex, partly unconscious process, for most personality theorists the personality is viewed as fixed by the age of 5 years. The idea of an inherent and unchanging personality is evident in the wide range of psychological assessment tools that measure types of personality (e.g., introvert versus extrovert), cognitive ability (e.g., IQ tests), gender identity (e.g., androgynous versus stereotypic male and female), amongst others. Many of these assessment tools will be carried out at an early age and, based on the outcomes, the child will be categorised and channelled in different ways. These instruments are believed to identify inherent (genetic, biological) traits and life-long, enduring and unchanging characteristics of the personality. There is little space in this construction of identity for change and multiplicity.

Following a broader philosophical shift in social theory, some psychologists are beginning to question the rigid way in which we view identity. Social constructionist psychologists, for example, highlight the way in which the self is constructed in culture and may shift and change in different social contexts. This explains why a child may appear to be introverted and shy in the school classroom, yet noisy and confident in the home environment. Currently, psychological theories themselves are being evaluated and shown to reflect broader ideologies that regulate and control human behaviour. For example, it has been well illustrated how the entire field of IQ testing has served to legitimise racism and reproduce social inequalities between different groups of people across the lines of colour, class and gender.

In a challenge to traditional psychological theories, contemporary critical psychologists argue that the self is not a stable, unchanging, rational, coherent and fixed identity. Instead, it is a 'subject' that is constructed within different contexts and in relation to others and the social world, that shifts and changes, that is multiple (or has many forms) and is also partly unconscious and irrational. Based on this understanding, some contemporary psychologists prefer to use the term subjectivity (as opposed to identity) to highlight how we are all subjected to the social world and its power in constructing how we view ourselves and others. On the other hand, the term subjectivity also acknowledges that we are active agents that may resist dominant meanings of who or what we are and, to some extent, reconstruct ourselves and ways of being in the world.

On the other hand, we all experience ourselves as a single 'I' and speak of ourselves as having a central core of self. Think of how often we talk about our 'true', 'real' or 'inner' self. The idea of being fluid, multiple, shifting and irrational, without a central inner core, is frightening to those of us who have grown up believing in these ideas. Social constructionists will argue that these ideas are so common and 'normal' that we cannot think of a reality outside of them. What do you think?

lescence. Newer theories of identity, including post-modern notions of subjectivity, increasingly view identity as far more flexible, fluid and changing across different contexts and the life span, than previously thought.

Gender and sexual identity

The physical changes in the body have multiple psychological correlates for young people and will differ from one individual to another, depending on the responses from those around them. Much of the literature points to the way in which boys and girls experience the onset of puberty differently (Hughes, 2002). While some international work highlights difficulties for young men around their first ejaculation if they have not been warned of this, generally menstrual bleeding for young women has been shown to be a more dramatic experience (Hughes, 2002). International work highlights the importance of puberty in the transition to womanhood, and the role of menstruation in learning the regulations and requirements of adult femininity (Holland *et al.*, 1996; Tolman, 1997; Ussher, 1989). Furthermore, it is argued that menstruation 'is the crucial moment in the development of psychological disempowerment for many women' (Tolman, 1997:173), and that puberty signifies 'the beginning of the process which links female reproduction to weakness and debilitation' (Ussher, 1989:13). Similarly, in a local historical study, Mager (1996) maintains that the gendering of girls was established at the beginning of puberty in Eastern Cape African society. Following this, girls' sexuality was legitimated through sexual play with older boys, in preparation for marriage.

Clearly, adequate and positive information is a key aspect of how an adolescent will experience these physical changes. Young women in particular have been shown to lack basic knowledge about their bodies, reproductivity and sexuality (Bassett & Sherman, 1994; Bhende, 1995; Uwakwe *et al.*, 1994; Vasconcelos *et al.*, 1995). This lack of knowledge appears to be reinforced by global ideas about morality and gendered ideas about female sexuality, both of which require girls to be virgins and sexually naïve (Weiss *et al.*, 1996). Thus, even if women have sexual knowledge, they face social pressure to maintain an image of innocence, particularly with men, who may interpret knowledge as an indication of past sexual activity. Consequently, it is very difficult for women to protect themselves against sexually transmitted infections (STIs) and AIDS since taking these measures will be interpreted as them having an active sexual life.

In the South African context, both historical and contemporary studies point to young women having difficult experiences of puberty. Practices of forced and immediate placement of girls on contraception, and warnings against boys and men at the onset of menstruation are apparently common in many South African communities (Lesch, 2000; Mager, 1996; Shefer, 1998). These studies show the way in which girls are seen as needing to be protected during their development because they are 'sexually vulnerable' to 'dangerous' male sexuality at the onset of menstruation. In this way, young girls are taught that they are passive and vulnerable to men or boys, and that menstruation is a negative, dangerous transition (Shefer, 1998, 1999). As a result, young women are often unprepared for sexual relationships and lack useful knowledge as well as a positive sexual identity (Thomson & Scott, 1991).

Boys, on the other hand, appear to be socialised positively into their 'manhood', with puberty signifying a transition to active (hetero)sexuality. Nonetheless, manhood appears to be rigidly associated with heterosexuality and the ability to be sexual with many women. Therefore, those who do not conform or who are not successful in this area may be punished or stigmatised. Alternative sexualities, either homosexual or those resistant to traditional macho masculinity, are still not well tolerated in South African communities. For men and boys, the feminist argument about the close ties between heterosexual and masculine identity are supported by empirical studies. For example, when asked what it means to be a man, a 12-year-old boy replied 'to have sex with a woman' (National Progressive Primary Health Care Network, 1995:35).

It is clear that adolescence is a central stage during which the young adult acquires gender and sexual identities. In particular, fitting in with stereotyped gender roles becomes essential for the developing child. Sexual identity is also interwoven with gender identity, so that different sexual behaviours and roles are expected of young men and women. A great deal of local literature highlights the way that traditional gender roles are reproduced in heterosexual relationships (e.g., National Progressive Primary Health Care Network, 1995; Shefer, 1999; Strebel, 1993; Varga & Makubalo, 1996). It is also evident that being a successful man and woman implies being heterosexual. South Africa, like the rest of the world, in spite of protecting the rights of all sexual orientations, remains a homophobic and heterosexist society. Many young

Puberty may be constructed as opening up a world of danger for young women:

When my mother came to know about my menstruating, she sat me down and gave me a talk about the facts of life. One thing that I clearly remember and that I know I will never forget is her telling me that *a woman is like a delicate, fragile piece of glass and that once that glass is broken, it can never be put back together*. That was her way of telling me that I was now a woman ... (young woman, my emphasis).

There is much pressure in adolescence to conform to stereotyped gender roles. However, this is not always a positive experience for all young people:

Frill dresses did not suit me, I could not put on socks and get my hair done. I was different. I was always dirty. My mother tried to punish me for that behaviour ... As I grew up, I found myself in a complex situation. People no longer associated with me. They could not play with or around me. I was in darkness, loneliness ... At school it was the same situation. There was playing in groups of boys and girls. They would tease you for playing with the wrong gender group. I would be a victim all the time. I felt inferior and neglected (young woman).

Menstruation is frequently constructed as a dangerous transition for girls, as they are viewed as vulnerable to male sexuality and pregnancy. For many young women this has meant having to take contraception at the onset of menstruation:

My granny saw stains of blood on my dress ... She told me that I was reaching adulthood. She told me that I was menstruating. She told me that if I could use contraception I would not have a baby. She asked me to go with her to the family planning clinic whereby I was comforted by the sister. The sister discussed with me the importance of family planning and teenage pregnancies and also about sexually transmitted diseases. Then the sister discussed with me [the] injection and advantages of it. But the feeling I was having didn't change, the feeling of embarrassment and anger (young woman).

There is a strong pressure on young men to take on macho masculinity, which means learning to repress any display of emotion:

At primary school I was a very quiet boy ... People said that I was a sissy. When I fail[ed] a subject I would cry like a baby because in our family you must be 'perfect' like my brother. So I knew that my mother would beat me when I arrived at home. At that time I knew a little of gender. Always that men are superior to females. Only females can cry. Men must be brave, and men must wear the pants in the house. From that day I tried to change ... Sometimes I get a bad mark or get beaten by the teacher, I will try not to cry and keep it in ... (young man).

Source: A study by T. Shefer (1999), conducted with University of the Western Cape (Cape Town) Psychology students based on autobiographical essays on their gender and sexual development.

---

people 'come out' as gay or lesbian in adolescence, and the handful of available studies show that this is an experience full of challenges and difficulties (Kowen, 2001; Potgieter, 1997).

Reproductive health risks

It is now widely recognised that HIV/AIDS is one of the biggest challenges facing South Africa. The sexual behaviour of young people, especially adolescents, has increasingly come under the spotlight. According to loveLife (2002), a project that specifically addresses HIV/AIDS and lifeskills education for adolescents and young adults, HIV mostly affects young South Africans, with around 60 per cent of all adults who acquire HIV becoming HIV positive before the age of 25. Based on annual surveys of national representative samples of South African adolescents, they maintain that the proportion of teenagers who had penetrative sex increased expo-

nentially between the ages of 12 and 17. Among sexually active 12 to 17-year-olds, 51 per cent reported their first penetrative sex at 14 years or earlier, with such young people also reporting a high number of sexual partners. It is not surprising that teenage pregnancy has long been highlighted as extremely high in many South African communities. Both STIs and unwanted pregnancies are related to the widespread practice of unsafe sex among young people.

Socio-economic factors aside, traditional gender roles clearly play a significant role in the barriers to safe sex practices. The central role that cultural practices of gender power and inequality play in creating barriers to the negotiation of safe and equitable heterosex has received increasing attention in international research and academic contexts. Similarly, in South Africa a number of key studies have highlighted the way in which gender power relations manifest in the negotiation of heterosex (e.g., Miles, 1992; Shefer, 1999; Strebel, 1993). Studies show how women's lack of negotiation is strongly associated with socialised sexual practices which require women to be passive, submissive partners, while men must initiate, be active and lead women in the realm of sexuality (Shefer, 1999; Varga & Makubalo, 1996).

Community, family and peers

Theorists highlight adolescence as a time when the developing child strives for autonomy from the family and parents, 'pulling away' from parents and investing more in the peer group. Parent-adolescent conflict has received a lot of attention in the literature on adolescent development. Santrock (2002) asserts that this conflict frequently involves adolescents becoming disillusioned with their parents and parents attempting to hold onto their control and authority. It has been argued that the conflict between parents and adolescents has been overemphasised, and is not necessarily a universal phenomenon. For example, a study in India found minimal parent-adolescent conflict, and adolescents do not appear to go through the phase, described in Western studies, of constantly challenging their parents (Larson in Santrock, 2002). Moreover, it has been suggested that these everyday conflicts serve an important function in the development of the adolescent into an autonomous adult (Santrock, 2002).

While there has been little work in the South African context on the relationship between adolescents and their parents, anecdotal evidence suggests that there is frequently a lack of communication between the two generations (Ramphele, 2002). On the other hand, it should be remembered that many South African children have not grown up in a stereotypic nuclear family, and have frequently been separated from both mother and father (Bozalek, 1997; Ramphele, 2002). It is expected that very different dynamics may exist in South African families from those described in the Western literature that predominates in research on adolescents. Furthermore, community has historically played a significant role for South Africans, both because of the oppression of apartheid and the importance of community in indigenous cultures. Many young South Africans grew up with a sense of struggle and community that may have impacted very differently on their identities and intra-familial relations.

Peer group pressure is seen as very powerful in adolescence, and the adolescent has been shown to spend far more time with peers than anyone else. Santrock (2002) argues that conforming to peers is not necessarily negative, as peer groups may also inspire pro-social behaviours. On the other hand, some of the areas of risk for adolescents, such as teenage pregnancy, substance abuse and violence, are clearly areas where peer pressure plays a large role.

Notwithstanding peer pressure, the role of peers in the adolescent's life is central. Sullivan's (1953) work is still cited today as highlighting the psychological significance of friendships beginning in early adolescence. Sullivan's argument that friends play a large role in the well-being of the child, and that this role increases in adolescence is supported by contemporary research (e.g., Furman & Buhrmester, 1992). In addition, given the emphasis on sexuality in the peer group, dating and romantic relationships become a primary focus for many adolescents. It is not surprising, then, that sexuality develops rapidly and becomes a primary emphasis for young adolescents. This emphasis on sexuality is clearly seen in the way in which romance and sexuality are interwoven in current cultures, and sexuality and erotica are widely used to sell consumer products.

Risk-taking behaviours

Historically, adolescence has been viewed as a problematic phase and much of the literature and research seems to focus on the 'problems' as opposed to the positive developments of this stage. As mentioned earlier, this stage is not necessarily a 'stormy' one for the individual. Sexuality is obviously a key area of risk-taking behaviour, especially in the context of the current HIV/AIDS pandemic, but also with respect to STIs and unplanned pregnancies. Another two areas of risk-taking behaviour which are particularly widespread in the South African context, are substance abuse and participation in criminal or gang-related violence.

Substance abuse

The abuse of alcohol and drugs has been recognised as a major problem among South African teenagers (Flisher et al., 1993; Morojele, 1997). Substance abuse appears to be on the increase in South Africa, as it is in other countries such as the USA (Hughes, 2002), particularly among adolescents who make up about a quarter of all those currently abusing substances in the country. Based on data obtained from three sites of the South African Community Epidemiology Network on Drug Use project (Cape Town, Durban and Gauteng) in 2000, it was found that in a three month period the proportion of adolescents relative

6.4 RITES OF PASSAGE

Most cultures have rituals linked to the transition from child to adulthood. Puberty and adolescence have frequently been viewed as a taking on of the mantle of culture itself. In many indigenous South African cultures, a circumcision ritual carried out in groups and in a remote area ('in the bush') has been traditional for late adolescent males. Ramphele (2002:57) details an account of a Xhosa initiation ritual as experienced by one of the young men she interviewed, highlighting the centrality of 'discipline and fortitude in the face of physical and emotional strain'.

There are many other examples of puberty rites across the globe. Robinson (2002) details some examples:

- Navajo young men make a solo journey into the mountains to attain their manhood.
- Australian aboriginal adolescents are given tattoos in late puberty as preparation for adulthood, and the transition is viewed through the metaphor of the 'death of childhood' and the 'rebirth into adulthood'.
- Girls of the Arapesh tribe in New Guinea stay in menstrual huts in early puberty for six days without food or water.
- The majority of North Americans mostly do not celebrate overt rituals at the time of puberty, except for those in religious families who may have a religious ceremony, like Confirmation (in Christian families) or a Barmitzvah (in Jewish families).

For further reading, consult Nelson Mandela's *Long Walk to Freedom* and/or Mamphela Ramphele's *Steering by the Stars.*

to the total number of patients in treatment for alcohol and other drug (AOD) abuse, was 24 per cent in Cape Town, 21 per cent in Durban, and 18 per cent in Gauteng (Myers & Parry, 2002).

Adolescent substance abuse obviously holds multiple risks for young people and their future. It has been well illustrated that such abuse is strongly associated with academic problems, both in achievement and attendance. Furthermore, substance abuse is related to increased mental health problems, including psychiatric disorders, and other disorders, and for some culminates in suicidal desires and/or actions. Substance abuse is also closely associated with sexual risk-taking, further increasing adolescents' vulnerability to HIV/AIDS and other STIs, as well as unwanted pregnancies (Morojele, 1997; Myers & Parry, 2002).

Violence and criminal activities

South Africans have long been exposed to a violent society, and young people in particular have paid the price for such violence (e.g., Duncan & Rock, 1997). We are still recovering from the violence of apartheid which the majority of South Africans, who are today adults, grew up with as part of their day-to-day lives. In contemporary South Africa, violence is still enmeshed in the fabric of our society, especially as the divisions of wealth and poverty continue to exist and indeed deepen. One of the areas where young people are drawn into violence, both internationally (Dacey & Travers, 2002) and in South Africa, is through gang cultures. For several decades there has been a growing focus on gangsterism in South Africa (e.g., Pinnock, 1982, 1984), and more recently, on the way in which gender power inequalities manifest in gang cultures (Salo, 2001). One South African study among men found that men who had been involved with gangs were twice as likely to have abused women as well (Abrahams *et al.*, 1999). The socio-psychological literature on gangs argues that the gang provides adolescents with a structured life that they might not have had at home, and fulfils a wide range of functions, such as protection, belonging and status (Dacey & Travers, 2002).

Given the high rate of violence against women in all societies, and the way in which men and women are socialised to accept traditional gender roles in their relationships, adolescents are also at risk of being victims or perpetrators of gender violence, including coercive sexuality, rape and physical and emotional abuse. In a recent survey of men in Cape Town, it was found that more than 40 per cent of the men in the sample of 1 394 male municipal workers reported having physically and/or sexually abused their female partners within the last ten years (Abrahams *et al.*, 1999). Some authors have highlighted the way in which violence is used to maintain control over women, and how this control and power are central to what it means to be a 'real man' in many communities (Wood & Jewkes, 2001). The significance of being a successful 'man' in the transition to adulthood may mean that male adolescents are vulnerable to the use of violence if this is interwoven with hegemonic male identity.

Figure 3 In many places young people live with the continual threat of violence and destruction

Conclusion

Adolescence has been viewed historically as a volatile, 'stormy' and ultimately problematic stage of life in which the developing person is vulnerable to a wide range of risks. In many ways, the adolescent is viewed in traditional literature as controlled by his or her developing body and the physiological changes that take place during this time. This is a very rigid picture of adolescence, which presents adolescence as biologically determined, ignores history and may also ignore cultural diversity.

While there are clearly risks related to growing up as a teenager in contemporary South Africa, we also need to look critically at the assumptions we make about adolescence and adolescents. This stage of life, like all stages, is one accompanied by multiple changes. There are multiple experiences of being an adolescent that differ across communities, families and individuals. In addition, we should be able to acknowledge the young people's resilience and strength in the face of adversities, as well as their vulnerabilities and the risks that they are exposed to as they grow up.

Abrahams, N., Jewkes, R. & Laubsher, R. (1999). *'I do not believe in democracy in the home': Men's relationships with and abuse of women*. Tygerberg: Medical Research Council.

Bassett, M. & Sherman, J. (1994). Female sexual behaviour and the risk of HIV infection: An ethnographic study in Harare, Zimbabwe. *Women and AIDS Program Research Report Series*. Washington, DC: International Center for Research on Women.

Bhende, A. (1995). Evolving a model for AIDS prevention education among underprivileged adolescent girls in urban India. *Women and AIDS Program Research Report Series*. Washington, DC: International Center for Research on Women.

Bozalek, V. (1997). Representation of the family and South African realities. In C. de la Rey, N. Duncan, T. Shefer & A. Van Niekerk (Eds.). *Contemporary Issues in Human Development: A South African focus*. Johannesburg: International Thompson Press, pp. 7–24.

Bruch, H. (1974). *Eating Disorders*. London: Routledge & Kegan Paul.

Caradas, A.A., Lambert, E.V. & Charlton, K.E. (2001). An ethnic comparison of eating attitudes and associated body image concerns in adolescent South African schoolgirls. *Journal of Human Nutrition and Dietetics*, 14:111–20.

Dacey, L. & Travers, B. (2002). *Human Development: Across the lifespan* (5th edition). New York: McGraw-Hill Higher Education.

Duncan, N. & Rock, B. (1997). The impact of political violence on the lives of South African children. In C. de la Rey, N. Duncan, T. Shefer & A. van Niekerk (Eds.). *Contemporary Issues in Human Development: A South African focus*. Johannesburg: International Thompson Press, pp. 133–55.

Elkind, D. (1967). Egocentricism in adolescence. *Child Development*, 38:1025–33.

Elkind, D. (1976). *Child Development and Education: A Piagetian perspective*. New York: Oxford University Press.

Flisher, A.J., Ziervogel, C.F., Chalton, D.O. & Robertson, B.A. (1993). Risk taking behaviour in Cape Town Peninsula high school students. *South African Medical Journal*, 83:430–82.

Furman, W. & Buhrmester, D. (1992). Age and sex differences in perceptions of networks of personal relationships. *Child Development*, 63:103–15.

Gilligan, C. (1982). *In a Different Voice: Psychological theory and women's development*. Cambridge, MA: Harvard University Press.

Goosen, M. & Klugman, B. (Eds.). (1996). *The South African Women's Health Book*. Cape Town: Oxford University Press.

Henriques, J., Hollway, W., Urwin, C., Venn, C. & Walkerdine, V. (Eds.). (1984). *Changing the Subject: Psychology, social regulation and subjectivity*. London: Metheun.

Holland, J., Ramazanoglu, C. & Thomson, R. (1996). In the same boat? The gendered (in)experience of first heterosex. In D. Richardson (Ed.). *Theorising Heterosexuality*. Milton Keynes: Open University Press, pp. 143–60.

Hughes, L. (2002). *Paving Pathways: Child and adolescent development*. Belmont, CA: Wadsworth/Thomson Learning.

Kowen, D. (2001). *An Exploratory Study of the Experiences of Female Youth Who Identify as Lesbian*. Unpublished Masters Dissertation, University of the Western Cape, Cape Town.

Lesch, E. (2000). *Female Adolescent Sexuality in a Coloured Community*. Unpublished Doctoral Dissertation, University of Stellenbosch, Cape Town.

loveLife (2002). loveLife sees behavioural changes in teenage sex, www.doh.gov.za/docs/news/2002/nz0813.html (accessed 15 November 2002).

Mager, A. (1996). Sexuality, fertility and male power. *Agenda*, 28:12–24.

Mandela, N. (1994). *Long Walk to Freedom: The autobiography of Nelson Mandela*. London: Little, Brown and Company.

Miles, L. (1992) Women, AIDS, power and heterosexual negotiation: A discourse analysis. *Agenda*, 15:14–27.

Morojele, N. (1997). Adolescent alcohol misuse. In C. de la Rey, N. Duncan, T. Shefer & A. Van Niekerk (Eds.). *Contemporary Issues in Human Development: A South African focus*. Johannesburg: International Thompson Press, pp. 207–32.

Myers, B. & Parry, C. (2002). Fact sheet – substance use by South African adolescents. *South African Health Info*, www.sahealthinfo.org/admodule/substance/htm (accessed 15 November 2002).

National Progressive Primary Health Care Network. (1995). *Youth Speak Out for a Healthy Future: A study on youth sexuality*. Braamfontein: NPPHCN/UNICEF.

Newcombe, N. (1996). *Child Development: Change over time* (8th edition). New York: HarperCollins College Publishers.

Orbach, S. (1978). *Fat is a Feminist Issue*. New York and London: Paddington Press.

Ozeki, R.L. (1998). *My Year of Meat*. London: Picador.

Palozzoli, M. S. (1974). *Self Starvation: From the intra-psychic to the transpersonal approach to Anorexia Nervosa*. London: Human Context Books.

Pinnock, D. (1982). *Towards an Understanding of the Structure, Function and History of Gang Formation in Greater Cape Town*. Unpublished MA thesis, University of Cape Town, Cape Town.

Pinnock, D. (1984). *The Brotherhoods*. Cape Town: David Philip.

Potgieter, C. (1997). *Black, South African, Lesbian: Discourses of invisible lives*. Unpublished Doctoral Thesis, University of the Western Cape, Cape Town.

Ramphele, M. (2002). *Steering By the Stars: Being young in South Africa*. Cape Town: Tafelberg.

Robinson, M.A. (2002). Cross cultural differences. In *Adolescent Directory Online* (ADOL). Website of Center for Adolescent Studies, School of Education, Indiana University, Bloomington, http://education.indiana.edu/cas/adol.welcome.html (accessed 15 November 2002).

Salo, E. (2001). Amandla awethu, die casspirs ga' nou kerk toe. Continuing the culture of militarism in Cape Flats townships. *African Gender Institute Newsletter*, December 2001.

Santrock, J.W. (2002). *Lifespan Development* (8th edition). New York: McGraw Hill.

Shaffer, D.R. (1999). *Developmental Psychology: Childhood and adolescence* (5th edition). Brooks/Cole Publishing Company: Pacific Grove, CA.

Shefer, T. (1998). 'Girl's stuff': Stories of gender development in a local context. *Psychology Bulletin*, 8(2):1–11.

Shefer, T. (1999). *Discourses of Heterosexual Identity and Relation*. Unpublished Doctoral Dissertation, University of the Western Cape, Cape Town.

Steinberg, L. (1990). Autonomy, conflict, and harmony in the family relationship. In S.S. Feldman & G.R. Elliot (Eds.). *At the Threshold: The developing adolescent*. Cambridge, MA: Harvard University Press, pp. 255–76.

Strebel, A. (1993). *Women and Aids: A study of issues in the prevention of HIV infection*. Unpublished doctoral thesis, University of Cape Town, Cape Town.

Sullivan, H.S. (1953). *The Interpersonal Theory of Psychiatry*. New York: W.W. Norton.

Thomson, R. & Scott, S. (1991). Learning About Sex: Young women and the social construction of sexual identity. *WRAP Paper 4*. London: Tufnell Press.

Tolman, D. L. (1997). Doing desire: adolescent girl's struggles for/with sexuality. In M.B. Zinn, P. Hondagneu-Sotelo & M.A. Messner (Eds.). *Through the Prism of Difference: Readings on sex and gender*. Boston: Allyn & Bacon, pp. 173–85.

Ussher, J.M. (1989). *The Psychology of the Female Body.* London and New York: Routledge.

Uwakwe, C.B.U., Mansaray, A.A. & Onwu, G.O.M. (1994). A Psycho-educational Program to Motivate and Foster AIDS Preventative Behaviors Among Female Nigerian University Students. Unpublished final technical report, *Women and AIDS Research Program*. Washington, DC: International Center for Research on Women.

Varga, C. & Makubalo, L. (1996). Sexual non-negotiation. *Agenda*, 28:31–8.

Vasconcelos, A., Neto, A., Valenca, A., Braga, C., Pacheco, M., Dantas, S., Simonetti, V. & Garcia, V. (1995). Sexuality and AIDS prevention among adolescents from low-income communities in Recife, Brazil. *Women and AIDS Program Research Report Series*. Washington, DC: International Center for Research on Women.

Weiss, E., Whelan, D. & Gupta, G.R. (1996). *Vulnerability and Opportunity: Adolescents and HIV/AIDS in the developing world.* Washington, DC: International Center for Research on Women.

Wood, K. & Jewkes, R. (2001) 'Dangerous love': Reflections on violence among Xhosa township youth. In R. Morrell (Ed.). *Changing Men in Southern Africa*. Pietermaritzburg: University of Natal Press, pp. 317–36.

Multiple choice questions

1. _____, known as the 'father of adolescent psychology', used the term '_____' to describe adolescence.
   a) Sigmund Freud; 'the phallic stage'
   b) G. Stanley Hall; 'storm and stress'
   c) Erik Erikson; 'identity versus identity confusion'
   d) H.S. Sullivan; 'the importance of friends'

2. Adolescence is a period of hormonal imbalance and emotional turbulence for all adolescents
   a) this statement is universalistic and deterministic
   b) there is a growing body of research that shows that not all adolescents across all cultures experience adolescence as a 'stormy' period
   c) different cultures have different meanings for adolescence and this may impact on how an adolescent experiences this phase
   d) all of the above

3. Puberty begins with
   a) hormonal increases which manifest in a range of internal and external bodily changes or what are know as *primary and secondary sex characteristics* that signify sexual maturation and gender differentiation
   b) the knowledge that one is now a man or a woman
   c) social rewards for being an adult
   d) all of the above

4. Changes in puberty coincide with a growth spurt in height and weight which lasts about ____ with the peak rate occurring at ___ for girls and ___ for boys
   a) 2 years; 10; 12
   b) 5 years, 12; 14
   c) 4.5 years; 11.5 years; 13.5 years
   d) 3.5 years; 9.5; 11.5

5. In Puerto Rica in the 1980s it was discovered that girls were beginning to develop breasts and menstruate at the premature age of 7 years. This was found to be related to
   a) the pressure in this culture to become sexually active at an early age
   b) genetic abnormalities related to in-group marrying
   c) hormones in the food that the community was eating
   d) all of the above

6. According to Piaget, the adolescent is capable of _____ which refers to an ability to _____
   a) concrete operational thinking; carry out practical and material based thinking
   b) formal operational thinking; think more abstractly, more idealistically and more logically
   c) systemic thinking; see things in context
   d) imaginery thinking; visualise the future

7. One of the implications of cognitive developmental changes in adolescence is referred to as '_____', referring to _____
   a) adolescent egocentricism; a preoccupation with the self
   b) adolescent fundamentalism; the development of conservative ideologies
   c) adolescent rebelliousness; the tendency to challenge social norms and parents
   d) none of the above

8. The *personal myth* refers to adolescents'
   a) unrealistic notions of invincibility and untouchability
   b) belief that they always the centre of focus in any situation
   c) obsession with their body image
   d) fantasies about themselves as unique and special

9. According to Erikson _____ is the key issue for the adolescent who is in the ___ stage of development, in which the crisis is one of _____
   a) peer pressure; 7th; individuality versus sociability
   b) differentiation; 6th; dependence versus independence
   c) identity; 5th; identity versus identity confusion
   d) parental disengagement; 8th; self versus family

10. Some of the key issues that appear to emerge in adolescence and have been documented in the literature include
    a) parent-adolescent conflict
    b) risk-taking behaviours
    c) peer pressure and the importance of friends
    d) all of the above

Short answer questions

1. Reflect on your own adolescence and identify the areas of challenge and change for you.

2. How is adolescence understood and experienced in your community – how is it similar or different to the way in which adolescence has been understood in the traditional predominantly Western psychological literature?

3. How do you think HIV/AIDS impacts on the contemporary experience of adolescence? Or, reflect on how apartheid may have impacted on the experience of adolescent development.

4. Gender and sexual identity development are a key part of adolescent development. Discuss this and draw on your own experiences of becoming a man or woman in your community.

5. If you are not yet a parent, imagine yourself as one with an adolescent son or daughter, and write a letter to them advising them on what you think are the important messages they might need. Draw on the literature on adolescence as well as the particular conditions in your broader social community to explain why you highlighted the issues you did.

7

Adulthood and Aging

Norman Duncan & Ashley van Niekerk

CHAPTER OBJECTIVES

After studying this chapter you should be able to:
- describe the key physical, cognitive and psychosocial developmental issues associated with early, middle and late adulthood
- describe and discuss the main South African social, environmental and economic challenges that impact upon and constrain adult development
- identify the different health risks that apply over the early, middle and late adulthood periods
- discuss the scope and impact of the epidemic of violence on South African men and women
- discuss the impact of the HIV/AIDS pandemic on the familial and economic roles of older South African adults.

When Nosipho first heard that they would be discussing ageing in class she felt a little disappointed. Perhaps this section would be less interesting and less relevant to her own life than the material they had covered in the course so far. But after reading a little on the subject, Nosipho found her thoughts turning to her grandmother who lived out in the rural areas with her mother's sister. She only saw her about once a year but 'Gogo' was still a very important figure in her family's life. Having respect for older people was something her mother had impressed on her right from when she was a young child.

The course material prompted some discussion about growing old with her friends. Some spoke about how their grandparents stayed in homes that were fashionably called 'retirement complexes'. She had seen these blocks of flats herself. Often there was a small garden out the front where some of the elderly people could be seen sitting out in the sun. It looked like quite a comfortable life, but Nosipho also wondered whether it might be lonely to be living without family. She tried to imagine herself old and wondered what it might be like to know that one was approaching the end of one's life. She hoped that for herself she would have lived a good and interesting life by the time she got to that point. She also hoped she would have some people around who loved her. Thinking of all this made her feel like writing to her grandmother. Gogo's eyesight was not very good these days but perhaps her daughter would read it to her and she would know that Nosipho was thinking of her.

...the crime of our society. Its 'old-age policy' is scandalous. But more scandalous still is the treatment that it inflicts upon the majority of [people] during their youth and maturity. It prefabricates the maimed and wretched state that is theirs when they are old. It is the fault of society that old age begins early, that it is rapid, physically painful and because [people] enter it with empty hands... (Simone de Beauvoir, 1975:177).

Introduction

As we read through this chapter on adulthood and the aging process, it might be useful to bear in mind that what happens in the later stages of life is not merely the result of the unfolding of a biological 'blueprint' of development. Rather, as Simone de Beauvoir (1975) reminds us in the quotation presented above, these life stages are largely built on foundations laid earlier in life, and are significantly conditioned by people's current life circumstances. Obviously, the quality of these foundations and circumstances will determine the quality of life during the period of development to which we now turn our attention.

Adulthood

Lasting from the age of 20 years, approximately, to the end of life, the period of adulthood is generally considered the longest stage in the human life span. It is also viewed as the stage when individuals reach full biological and psychosocial maturity. Although the nature and onset of adulthood may vary considerably from one individual to the next and across societies, most developmental psychology textbooks describe adulthood as consisting of three distinct and consecutive phases, namely early adulthood, middle adulthood and late adulthood. Generally, these three stages are seen as lasting from approximately 20 to 39 years, 40 to 59 years, and 60 years and older, respectively (Craig, 1989; Kaplan & Sadock, 1998).

Largely in order to facilitate the description and clarification of development during adulthood, this chapter will address the key aspects of adult development in relation to these three stages. However, these stages will merely serve as a broad framework for the discussion to follow, and not as a pre-set template for all adult development; for as observed in the introduction to this section, a too narrow and rigid adherence to the stages identified above has

several limitations (see Berger, 1994; Craig, 1989; Duncan et al., 2003; Laubscher & Klinger, 1997).

Early adulthood

Physical development

With regard to physical development, the early years of adulthood are generally considered to constitute the prime of life (Berger, 1994). For example, at approximately 25 to 30 years, physical growth – especially shoulder width, height and chest size – as well as muscular strength and manual dexterity reach a peak (Papalia & Olds, 1995). With regard to overall health status, early adulthood is generally also considered to be one of the more problem-free periods in the human life cycle. In fact, as Berger (1994:444) observes, 'even the common cold is less frequent in this stage than in any other [period] of the life span'.

However, while the individual generally reaches the peak of physical development during early adulthood, paradoxically, this period also announces the first visible signs of aging. For example, because of hormonal changes and a reduced flow of blood to the skin, hair may already grow less abundantly as from the late 20s. Additionally, as the skin begins to lose its elasticity, facial wrinkles may also start making their appearance at this stage (Berger, 1994; Papalia & Olds, 1995; Rogers, 1979).

Health Risks

Even though under normal circumstances, early adulthood is generally considered the period when the individual is least likely to experience health problems or to die as a result of disease, it is also the period when the individual is most at risk of death or injury through almost all forms of violence, including violent assault and suicide, and motor vehicle collisions (Berger, 1994; Burrows et al., 2001; Dorrington et al., 2001). While both young males and females have a very high exposure to violent crime in South Africa, recent studies conducted by Burrows et al. (2001) and Dorrington et al. (2001) indicate that homicide currently constitutes the single major cause of fatalities amongst young adult South African males. A similar gendered pattern of heightened susceptibility to death as a result of violence has also been observed in other countries, such as the United States, where it has also been found that homicide amongst young males is more likely in lower-income than upper-income communities (Berger, 1994; National Center for Injury Prevention and Control, 2003; World Health

COUNTRY	YEAR	0–4 years		5–14 years		15–29 years		30–44 years		45–59 years		> 60 years	
		M	F	M	F	M	F	M	F	M	F	M	F
Canada	1997	14	10	65	32	784	189	1091	303	758	233	510	156
Colombia	1995	56	34	310	151	12169	982	7272	575	2141	218	737	83
Mauritius	1999	2	2	3	3	40	29	66	26	22	7	11	3
USA	1998	396	326	894	613	12511	2297	11688	3524	6885	2170	6600	1682

Table 1 World Health Organisation database on mortality caused by intentional injury: Data for selected countries

Source: World Health Organisation (2002)

Organisation, 2002) (See Tables 1 and 2). Some of the more insidious consequences of these high levels of violence include the constraints imposed on the personal development of individuals, the often-irreparable damage to relationships, the disruption of family and communal life, and the inappropriate allocation of scarce community resources (Butchart et al., 2000).

According to Miedzian (in Berger, 1994), the gendered patterns of injury and death due to violence are the result of a complex interaction between a range of biosocial factors. These factors include the higher levels of testosterone and drug abuse found amongst males, as well as early socialisation and the dominant (fairly destructive) representations of masculinity which sometimes sanction various forms of violence perpetrated by men against other men and against women and children (Angless & Shefer, 1997; Berger, 1994; World Health Organisation, 2002). Ongoing socio-economic inequities and social fragmentation have also been identified as two of the key factors contributing to the continuing high levels of violence in South African society (Butchart et al., 2000).

Age Group	Male	Female
0–4 years	477	437
5–14 years	1849	1209
15–29 years	10189	2512
30–44 years	16555	3892
45–59 years	7864	2196
> 60 years	4009	2472
	40943	12718

Table 2 Medical Research Council statistics on registered fatal injuries (intentional or unintentional) in South Africa for 1996

Source: Dorrington et al. (2001)

HIV/AIDS is another major health problem currently facing young adults in South Africa. Recent research found that young adults, particularly young adult women, are most at risk of contracting the disease (Dorrington et al., 2001; Schonteich, 1999; United Nations, 2001). For example, it was found that approximately 25 per cent of young women aged between 20 and 30 were infected with HIV (United Nations, 2001). Pauw and Brener (1997) also found that, partly because of physiological factors, the heterosexual transmission of the virus from men to women is two to four times more likely than from women to men. As will become clearer later in this chapter, the alarming spread of this pandemic will have a significant impact on the manner in which many young South Africans will embark on two of the more crucial life tasks of early adulthood, namely establishing an intimate relationship with a life-partner and parenting.

Cognitive development

According to Piaget (in Butterworth & Harris, 1994; see also Cockcroft, 2002), the peak of cognitive development is reached when the individual becomes capable of formal operational (logical) thinking, that is during the period of adolescence. However, this position is contested by Berger (1994) and Craig (1989). During early adulthood, according to these writers, cognitive development progresses beyond formal operational thinking. Furthermore, they argue, thinking during early adulthood is more complex, more global and more adaptive than what the formal operational thinking of adolescence generally allows for. They argue that during early adulthood, thinking is less absolute and abstract than during adolescence, and therefore allows the individual to deal with the unpredictable and the practical problems of life much more effectively (Papalia & Olds, 1995).

Psychosocial development

Early adulthood is generally characterised by the assumption of many critical social roles and responsibilities, including marriage and partnerships, parenting, and earning an income to sustain ourselves and our dependents. These roles and responsibilities both influence and are influenced by various aspects of psychosocial development during early adult development.

Marriage and partnerships

Erik Erikson (in Ryckman, 1993) described the central psychosocial challenge of the earlier adulthood period as the resolution of a tension between the drive towards intimacy, on the one hand, and isolation, on the other. As part of their quest for intimacy, many young adults may marry in their mid-20s, although this varies considerably across settings. For example, in many Western societies, there is a growing tendency for young adults to opt for cohabitation rather than marriage, and for marriages to take place later in life (Papalia & Olds, 1995). In other societies (in parts of India, for instance) marriages involving teenagers are not uncommon.

For many young people, marriage leads to the enhancement of their relationships with their partners and an improved sense of identity and fulfilment. Indeed, studies have shown that married people appear to be more contented and satisfied with life than single people (Orford, 1992), with the most contented being married women in their early twenties who do not have children (Papalia & Olds, 1995). Nonetheless, for many young adults marriage could also result in relationship conflicts, disillusionment with partners, constraining attachments (Kaplan & Sadock, 1998) and even violence. Indeed, in South Africa, women face extraordinarily high levels of violence and sexual assault from their partners. It has been reported that as many as one in every three women is abused by her partner (Angless & Shefer, 1997; see also Jewkes *et al.*, 2001). Additionally, these women frequently face an indifferent judicial and police system that routinely denies them assistance and redress (Nowrojee & Manby, 1995; Suffla *et al.*, 2001). Obviously, violence within the family will influence the development and expression of intimacy as well as psychosocial development more generally during early adulthood.

Currently, violence is not the only potential threat to the expression and development of intimacy dur-

Figure 1 Demonstrating against abuse of women

ing this stage. Given the interconnectedness of intimacy and adult sexuality (Erikson in Ryckman, 1993), the high levels of HIV/AIDS infection in this country, particularly amongst young people (Schonteich, 1999), may also have a profound impact on the expression and development of intimate partnerships during early adulthood (see Van Dyk & Van Dyk, 2003). However, in order for any definitive statements to be made regarding the relationship between the current high levels of HIV/AIDS infections and patterns of intimacy during early adulthood, there is a need for more focused research specifically examining this relationship.

Parenthood

The formalisation of partnerships in institutionalised arrangements, such as marriage or co-habitation, is often followed by parenthood. Although this perception appears to be changing, child rearing is still perceived to be women's work in many societies. Given that for both women and men, earning an income is widely recognised as a priority activity, the opposing demands of working and child-rearing may generate considerable frustration and anxiety for many women. While some women may successfully negotiate and integrate these tasks (which may result in a sense of independence and achievement for many) (Bernstein *et al.*, 1994), the ideal is a situation in which both women and men assume equal responsibility for the care of their children.

The task of parenting young children is normally associated with young adulthood. However, the decimation of this age group as a result of the HIV/AIDS pandemic will severely distort this association. Already South African society is confronted by large numbers of young children who are currently parented by older siblings and grandparents because of the death of their parents due to AIDS-related diseases (Schonteich, 1999). Indeed, it is predicted that by 2010, South Africa will have approximately two million AIDS orphans who, in the absence of adequate social security services, will either have to be cared for by relatives or will be left to fend for themselves and their siblings (Hook, 2002; Schonteich, 1999).

Work

Work plays a crucial role in the development of the young adult. Not only does it provide a source of income, and thereby allow for a measure of self-sufficiency, but it can also provide an outlet for creative accomplishment, and serve as the source of stimulating relationships with colleagues and increased self-esteem (see Fromm, 1949/1975). A range of factors, including socio-economic status and gender, affect the choice and timing of an individual's work or occupation (Rogers, 1979; Wilkinson & Marmot, 1998). Currently, in South Africa, the availability of employment plays a critical role in an individual's choice or lack of choice in relation to work or occupation. It is worth noting that during the last decade of the twentieth century South Africa had an average unemployment rate of 30.3 per cent, with the majority of the unemployed being from the poorest sector of South African society (55.4 per cent), from rural communities (55.5 per cent), and female (56.9 per cent) (Kinsella & Ferreira, 1997; May et al., 2000).

Research has shown that the inability to find employment, or the loss of employment and income, is extremely stressful and places individuals at a high risk for alcohol dependence, violence, suicide and psychological illness (Kaplan & Sadock, 1998; Wilkinson & Marmot, 1998). In addition, the intense competition and instability in the job market, largely as a result of globalisation, also leaves many young adult South Africans vulnerable to exploitation, which obviously has an impact on their well-being.

Middle adulthood

In terms of chronological age, middle adulthood is traditionally reported to extend from roughly the age of 40 to 60 years, with a range of physical, biological and social 'cues' or indicators generally marking its onset. Some of these indicators are considered below.

Physical development

Middle adulthood is generally characterised by an increasingly perceptible decline in physical attributes and functioning, such as a decrease in muscle size, the gradual shrinkage and stiffening of the skeleton, an increase in body fat retention, and a decline in dexterity and flexibility, and sensory and perceptual abilities (Bernstein et al., 1994; Craig, 1989; Kaplan & Sadock, 1998). For example, a decline in visual capacities is prominent from about the age of 40, while taste, smell and sensitivity to pain and temperature generally decline from about 45 years (Papalia & Olds, 1995). Additionally, during this period, there is also a decline in the functioning of the digestive system; a decrease in the flow of blood to the brain; women reach menopause (which refers to the end of menstruation, and consequently, the capacity to bear children); and males experience a decline in sexual responsiveness (Craig, 1989).

Here it should be noted that the physical experience of middle and late adulthood generally occurs earlier among lower-income unskilled workers than among higher-income professionals. This is largely a result of the fact that lower-income groups, compared to their upper-income counterparts, are generally more frequently exposed to health risks (such as exposure to industrial chemicals, long hours of strenuous work, inadequate health facilities, and stress) that hasten the 'aging' process (Craig, 1989; see also Mathers et al., 2001).

While middle adulthood is the stage when the first signs of significant physical decline appear, many developmental experts believe that regular exercise and a good diet can slow the aging process substantially and allow the individual to continue to function with vitality and a sense of well-being (Craig, 1989). However, in a country and a world where the gap between the rich and the poor is getting bigger, with the poor becoming gradually poorer (May et al., 2000), the question is, how many people would be privileged enough to enhance their quality of life in this way?

Health Risks

During middle adulthood the individual becomes increasingly susceptible to the risk of various diseases, such as cardiovascular diseases (which include cardiac disorders, arteriosclerosis and hypertension), various forms of cancer, arthritis and respiratory diseases (Berger, 1994; Craig, 1989). This increased susceptibility to illness and disease during this stage of development is largely a result of the increasing degeneration of the body. Nonetheless, research evidence shows that people's living conditions and lifestyles have a significant influence on their health. For example, heavy smoking and drinking have been implicated in various cardiovascular diseases (Craig, 1989). Furthermore, it appears that stress associated with certain lifestyles (such as hyper-competitiveness and social isolation) and living conditions (such as unemployment and living in poverty-stricken and violent communities) contribute significantly to the health problems of middle adulthood, particularly cardiovascular diseases and depression (Wilkinson & Marmot, 1998). However, the way in which individuals perceive and respond to the stressful events with which they are confronted also influences the impact on their health. For example, the individual who perceives a potentially stressful event as a challenge that he or she can deal with is much less likely than others to be adversely affected by it (Faure & Loxton, 2003).

Cognitive development

Contrary to a belief held by many, cognitive functioning does not show any dramatic decline during middle adulthood. On the whole, during middle adulthood, the individual's cognitive abilities may be as good as during early adulthood. Some research even shows that reasoning and verbal skills may actually improve during this stage (Schiamberg, 1985). Furthermore, studies reveal that for scholars and scientists, the period from 40 to 60 years is characterised by fairly steady intellectual productivity or output, which is generally well above the levels attained by their counterparts who are in their twenties (Dennis in Schiamberg, 1985). To a certain extent, this trend can perhaps be explained by the idea of 'crystallised intelligence' (Craig, 1989) (See Box 7.1).

7.1 FLUID VERSUS CRYSTALLISED INTELLIGENCE

One theory suggests that there are two kinds of intelligence, namely fluid intelligence and crystallised intelligence. Fluid intelligence is said to influence speed of thinking, inductive reasoning and short-term memory, and is thought to be based primarily on the speed and efficiency of neurological factors. Thus, this kind of intelligence is thought to depend on the functioning of the nervous system. It is believed to increase until late adolescence and then decline throughout adulthood, as the nervous system deteriorates (Berger, 1994; Craig, 1989).

Crystallised intelligence, on the other hand, refers to the individual's acquired abilities to process information, including analysis and problem solving. Vocabulary and general information are seen as examples of crystallised intelligence. Unlike fluid intelligence, crystallised intelligence is believed to increase throughout the life span or for as long as people are capable of absorbing information (Berger, 1994; Craig, 1989).

Psychosocial development

According to Erikson (in Kimmel, 1974; see also Ryckman, 1993), the primary psychosocial challenge during middle adulthood is to strike a balance between generativity and self-absorption or stagnation. Simply stated, generativity refers to the urge and commitment to take care of the next generation, and may be expressed in various ways, including nurturing, teaching, guiding and mentoring children and young adults (Clarke-Stewart *et al.*, 1988). Generativity is also expressed in attempts to contribute to and improve society. According to Erikson's theory, people in middle adulthood who do not express a sense of generativity generally are self-centred to the point of indulging themselves 'as if they were their own children' (Clarke-Stewart *et al.*, 1988:485). Obviously, the individual's capacity to express her or his generative urges could be compromised by factors such as poverty. For example, the individual who is constantly battling to keep body and soul together will not have sufficient personal resources and energy to invest in caring for and mentoring others.

Life cycle squeeze

Many people in middle adulthood find themselves in a situation where they do not only have to take responsibility for maturing children, but also for their aging parents. Oppenheimer (in Clarke-Stewart *et al.*, 1988) refers to this situation as the 'life cycle squeeze'. It is generally assumed that the poorer the person who is caught in this situation is, the greater the stress he or she is likely to experience in financial terms, that is in situations where his or her parents' income cannot sustain them. Paradoxically many poor communities in South Africa are currently faced by a situation where entire families are dependent on aged family members' social grants (May *et al.*, 2000).

Late adulthood

Developmental psychologists have traditionally used the age of 60 years as a marker for the onset of late adulthood. The commencement of late adulthood coincides with senescence – the increasing decline of all the body's systems, including the cardiovascular, respiratory, endocrine and immune systems (Kaplan & Sadock, 1998). However, the actual rate of ageing may vary greatly among individuals. Furthermore, the belief that old age is always associated with profound intellectual and physical infirmity is a myth. The majority of older people retain most of their physical and cognitive abilities (Kaplan & Sadock, 1998). The general increase of living standards and medical technology has led to an increase in longevity in many societies and, therefore, a significant number of older persons. However, for many low-income countries, this is not the case. For example, while the average life span in the United States was between 72 and 79 years during the 1990s (Berger, 1994), the average life span for the majority of South Africans was estimated to be 54 years at more or less the same time (Dorrington *et al.*, 2001). Furthermore, recent research shows that while the disability-adjusted life expectancy, or DALE (which measures the average number of years specific populations are expected to live in full health), in 1999, was 70 years for Americans, it was 39.82 years for South Africans (Mathers *et al.*, 2001). This difference in the average life spans and the disability-adjusted life expectancies between populations of low-income countries, such as South Africa, and high-income countries, such as the United States, is largely a result of the differences in their standards of living. Needless to say, this difference will increase even more markedly over the next few decades as a result of the HIV/AIDS pandemic (Dorrington *et al.*, 2001; Mathers *et al.*, 2001; Schonteich, 1999).

Physical development

With senescence, there is a decline in sensory and psychomotor abilities, although with a great deal of individual variation (Bernstein *et al.*, 1994; Kaplan & Sadock, 1998). The loss of vision and hearing are common, and may have particularly serious psychological impacts since they hinder a range of daily living and social activities, and therefore the individual's independence (Berger, 1994; Branch *et al.* in Papalia & Olds, 1995). There may also be a sharp drop in sensitivity to a range of tastes and smells, with older people often complaining that food is less tasty and, consequently, eating less. Furthermore, older people experience a decline in strength, muscular co-ordination and reaction times, resulting in higher proportions of home and traffic accidents (Sterns *et al.* in Papalia & Olds, 1995). With senescence, there is a shortening of the spinal column, a consequent decrease in height, and an increased vulnerability to osteoporosis, especially among women. Generally, the organs, especially the heart, become less efficient. There is also an increasing decline in the immune system, with greater susceptibility to infectious illnesses. For both men and women, there is an increased decline in sexual function and responsiveness (Kaplan & Sadock, 1998).

Health Risks
Research indicates that despite the onset of some physical decline, most individuals in the late adulthood period rate their health as good or excellent (United States Bureau of the Census in Papalia & Olds, 1995). However, in South Africa, the experience of health may vary widely, depending on socioeconomic status, gender and urban or rural location (Kinsella & Ferreira, 1997). Adults in this age group may experience a decline in health conditions due to injuries and infections, and an increase of non-communicable diseases. Generally, the increased susceptibility to illness during this stage of development is largely a result of the progressive degeneration of the body. In South Africa, however, many older people who have experienced a lifetime of poor diet, arduous physical labour, multiple pregnancies and inadequate reproductive health care, have an even greater susceptibility to ill-health (Bradshaw & Steyn, 2001). In this age group, major causes of illness, disability and death are stroke, tuberculosis, heart disease, diabetes and cancer (Bradshaw *et al.*, 2002a). About 90 per cent of older adults have considerable annual medical expenses, with few having

any medical insurance. Many older adults rely upon the assistance of their family and the state to meet rising medical expenses (Kinsella & Ferreira, 1997).

Cognitive development

The older adult may experience a decrease of some cognitive abilities, in particular his or her ability to rapidly and flexibly manipulate ideas and symbols. Reasoning, mathematical ability, comprehension, novel problem solving and memory all decline over late adulthood (See Box 7.1). However, repetition and some memory-based activities remain intact, although there may be a decrease in the complexity of thought (Bernstein *et al.*, 1994; Kaplan & Sadock, 1998). Despite this decline, many psychologists have asserted that a general intelligence decline in old age is a myth, and argue that new abilities, such as wisdom, emerge to compensate for the decline in others. Others have described this position as optimistic (Papalia & Olds, 1995). Many people over the age of 65 years report a decline in cognitive functioning (between 6 and 10 per cent), and even more over the age of 85 years (20 to 50 per cent), because of Alzheimer's disease alone. Alzheimer's disease is a degenerative brain disorder that results in a decline in intelligence, awareness and the ability to control bodily functions. There are various theories as to the cause of this disease which is the most prevalent and feared of the dementias (i.e. the various forms of intellectual and personality deterioration sometimes associated with old age) that may affect older people (Berger, 1994; Papalia & Olds, 1995).

Psychosocial development

The older adult has to face and deal with declining independence, retirement and often a reduction in financial resources, transitions in relationships with siblings, and the task of constructing a meaningful understanding of her or his life achievements. In addition to these normative developmental challenges, many older adults in South Africa often also have to deal with a number of very difficult social problems, such as high levels of crime, poverty and HIV/AIDS infection levels. Of all these problems, at the moment the HIV/AIDS pandemic, and its staggering and pervasive impact on the health and stability of households and familial relationships appears to be the most salient and daunting. Already it is clear that the consequences of the HIV/AIDS pandemic are profoundly impacting on

the social and familial demands of the surviving older adults, particularly in relation to care-giving responsibilities ('Our loss has brought us together', *Mail & Guardian*, 24 to 30 January 2003; see Box 7.2).

Year starting 1 July	Estimated % of deaths due to AIDS
1995	9%
1996	14%
1997	19%
1998	26%
1999	33%
2000	40%

Table 3 Estimated percentages of adult deaths due to AIDS, based on Actuarial Society of South Africa statistics

Source: Dorrington *et al.* (2001)

Retirement and economic adjustments

During this period, the older adult is likely to have retired from a full-time occupation. There may be a range of economic adjustments. The physical decline brought on by ageing reduces individual ability to contribute to inter-generational households, and to remain economically self-sufficient. Older people, particularly those living in rural areas, are often the poorest and most vulnerable group in developing countries (Bradshaw *et al.*, 2002a).

In South Africa, 4.5 per cent of the population receives a government pension. Many households with at least one elderly member are poor by most standards, and rely on state-funded social and medical support. As previously noted, these households often rely on the pensions of their elderly members. Indeed, at a rate of 1:7, the dependence on state-sponsored old age financial grants in South Africa is very high (Kinsella & Ferreira, 1997). Moreover, current estimates suggest that 40 per cent of households are headed by an older person, with this proportion rapidly increasing because of the HIV/AIDS pandemic.

The old-age financial grant is arguably a lifeline to a substantial number of households in South Africa. Unfortunately, this often opens the way to the abuse of the elderly for access to this money. This abuse may take the form of neglect, or physical or psychological abuse, especially of more dependent older adults. Neglect may involve the withholding of food, shelter, clothing or medical care. Abuse may involve psychological torment such as a scolding, insults or threats of physical violence, as well as physical violence such as beatings, punching or burning (Papalia & Olds, 1995). While anecdotal information points to widespread elder abuse in South Africa, very limited research-based and empirical data are available regarding the extent of this abuse.

Family and social roles

As indicated earlier, for many, old age remains a period of continued emotional and social growth (Kaplan & Sadock, 1998). For others, late adulthood often becomes a more inward-looking, cautious and conforming time. Family roles appear more androgynous, with males appearing more nurturing and females becoming more assertive. This may be especially apparent in grandparenting roles (Kaplan & Sadock, 1998; Papalia & Olds, 1995).

As already observed, in South Africa, the psychological challenges for many older people will change profoundly with the HIV/AIDS pandemic, with a marked and more sustained 're-reversal' of care roles (see the discussion on the 'life cycle squeeze'). The HIV/AIDS pandemic is likely to put considerable pressure on the older and especially poorer South Africans, who will be more likely to have to care for their adult children who suffer from AIDS as well as their orphaned grandchildren ('Our loss has brought us together', *Mail & Guardian*, 24 to 30 January 2003; see also Box 7.2). As the pandemic matures and AIDS mortalities increase, it is anticipated that the number of AIDS orphans (particularly maternal orphans younger than 15 years of age) will increase significantly (Bradshaw *et al.*, 2002b).

There will also be increasing pressure on aged grandparents to deal with the psychological, social and income losses within their children's families, especially if there is a limited state response. These individuals are likely to be emotionally exhausted with the loss of, and care for their children, and the demands of the altered family structure. Instead of being cared for themselves by their adult children or the social security system, they will be back in the role of caregiver (Adjetaye-Sorsey in Bradshaw & Steyn, 2001). Therefore there is a need for alternative models of community care to be further developed together with forms of state assistance in caring for adult AIDS sufferers and eventually their orphaned children and indigent parents (Bradshaw *et al.*, 2002b).

7.2 GRANNIES AND ORPHANS

Magdalene Segomela lives in a tiny, one-roomed house in Alexandra, with her two grandchildren, Mpho and Paul. Though old and sickly, Magdalene Segomela conveys an image of determined strength and a sense that she has come to accept her life. She laughs a lot, even though her laughter tends to be tinged with sadness.

Granny Segomela and her grandchildren moved into her little house in Alexandra after they were forced out of their previous home by the malicious taunting of their neighbours. The taunting was a result of the fact that her daughter was HIV-positive, and had died of AIDS-related illnesses in 1999. Her granddaughter, Mpho, 10 years old, was born with the virus, and Granny Segomela does not possess the wherewithal to obtain all the necessary medication for Mpho. The reality is that Segomela has to support herself and her grandchildren on her monthly pension of R650.

Granny Segomela is also one of many grandmothers who are part of a support group, started and organised by nursing sister, Rose Letwaba of the Alex-Tara Children's Clinic. Letwaba had seen that there was a need to provide some form of support for grandmothers who had to look after their children orphaned by AIDS. 'Every time when the grannies were bringing the children, I could see the sadness. So I thought maybe by bringing the grannies together and sharing their experience of loss, they could really comfort each other,' Letwaba explained ('Our loss has brought us together', *Mail & Guardian*, 24 to 30 January 2003).

Death and dying

Death and dying are realities that humans face throughout their lives. However, at no time in their lives are people as conscious of their own mortality as during late adulthood, when they start losing a growing number of their peers to death, and when they increasingly become aware of the frailty of their own bodies, largely as a result of a growing susceptibility to illness.

According to Erikson *et al.* (in Fadiman & Frager, 1994; Ryckman, 1993), late adulthood is typically characterised by a re-examination and integration of past events and experiences. They argue that older people need to confront a tension around integrating their life experiences and stories versus a despair over the inability to relive their lives differ-

How do people typically relate to life and social functioning during late adulthood? Do they become more withdrawn from life now that they are in retirement and no longer capable of the same levels of activity as earlier in life, or do they become more spontaneous because they now no longer have the responsibilities of caring for dependent children and working? Developmental psychology has produced various theories that attempt to answer these questions. We will consider two of these theories:

Disengagement theory: According to this theory proposed by Cumming and Henry (in Berger, 1994), during late adulthood, the aging individual progressively disengages from society, and society, in turn, increasingly disengages from the individual. According to Cumming and Henry, this disengagement is reflected in the fact that people normally retire from work at this age and they become more passive, and their social circles become more restricted. Generally, many developmental psychologists have opposed this theory quite strongly because, as they argue, while disengagement may occur in some areas of life during late adulthood, re-engagement may simultaneously occur in other areas of life. For example, after retirement, people may start developing new hobbies and finding new friends and other social activities.

Activity theory: In direct opposition to disengagement theory, activity theory posits that the elderly want, and in fact need to remain active and that they consequently substitute new roles and activities to replace those they are forced to relinquish due to retirement and withdrawal from certain social functions. One of the primary criticisms of this theory is that heightened levels of social activity are not necessarily synonymous with psychosocial well-being, as implied by the theory.

Obviously, proponents of these opposing positions would view the new roles that many people in late adulthood would have to assume as a result of the AIDS pandemic in many southern African countries in fundamentally different ways.

ently. People who succeed in resolving this tension are able to meaningfully integrate their past experiences, often into a wisdom that Erikson (cited in Ryckman, 1993:196) described as an 'informed and detached concern with life itself in the face of death itself'. When death is imminent, people generally wish to die with dignity, love, affection, physical contact, and with no pain, and may wish to be comforted by their religious faith, their achievements, and the love of their family and friends (Bernstein *et al.*, 1994).

Conclusion

In this chapter you were introduced to some of the basic concepts and ideas central to our understanding of adulthood and aging. This introduction to adult development has outlined some of the key attributes of physical, cognitive and psychosocial development that are reported to mark adult development. Additionally, the chapter has examined some of the key social threats that constrain optimal adult development in contemporary South Africa, including the high levels of violence, unemployment, poverty and HIV/AIDS infection characterising the South African social landscape. Through its examination of these threats to development, the chapter has attempted to show how optimal human development is systematically compromised for particularly lower-income groups, women and the aged in South Africa – notwithstanding the resilience frequently shown by the groups. We hope that the content of this chapter will not only provide you with a greater understanding of the development of the maturing adult in general, but that it will also serve as a foundation for your study of adult development in a context such as South Africa.

Angless, T. & Shefer, T. (1997). Children living with violence in the family. In C. de la Rey, N. Duncan, T. Shefer & A. van Niekerk (Eds.). *Contemporary Issues in Human Development: A South African focus.* Johannesburg: ITP, pp. 170–86.

Bernstein, D. A., Clarke-Stewart, A., Roy, E.J., Srull, T.K. & Wickens, C.D. (1994). *Psychology.* Boston: Houghton Mifflin.

Berger, K.S. (1994). *The Developing Person Through the Life Span.* New York: Worth Publishers.

Bradshaw, D. & Steyn, K. (Eds.). (2001). *Poverty and Chronic Diseases in South Africa.* MRC Technical Report. Tygerberg: MRC.

Bradshaw, D. , Johnson, L., Schneider, H., Bourne, D. & Dorrington, R. (2002a). *Orphans of the HIV/AIDS Epidemic; The time to act is now.* MRC Policy Brief (No. 2). Tygerberg: MRC.

Bradshaw, D. , Schneider, M., Laubscher, R. & Nojilana, B. (2002b). *Cause of Death Profile, South Africa 1996.* Burden of Disease Research Unit Report May 2002. South African Medical Research Council. www.mrc.ac.za/bod/profile.pdf (accessed 10 January 2003).

Burrows, S, Bowman, B, Matzopoulos, R. & Van Niekerk, A. (2001). *A profile of fatal injuries in South Africa 2000; Second Annual Report of the National Injury Mortality Surveillance System.* Tygerberg: Medical Research Council.

Butchart, A., Terreblanche, M., Hamber, B. & Seedat, M. (2000). Violence and violence prevention in South Africa: A sociological and historical perspective. In T. Emmett & A. Butchart (Eds.). *Behind the Mask.* Pretoria: HSRC, pp. 29–54.

Butterworth, G. & Harris, M. (1994). *Principles of Developmental Psychology.* Hove, East Sussex: LEA.

Clarke-Stewart, A., Perlmutter, M. & Friedman, S. (1988). *Lifelong Human Development.* New York: Wiley.

Cockcroft, K. (2002). Theories of cognitive development: Piaget, Vygotsky and information-processing theory. In D. Hook, J. Watts & K. Cockcroft (Eds.). *Developmental Psychology.* Lansdowne: UCT Press, pp. 175–99.

Craig, G.J. (1989). *Human Development.* Englewood Cliffs: Prentice-Hall.

De Beauvoir, S. (1975). Old age: End product of a faulty system. In J. Dyal, W. Corning & D. Willows (Eds.). *Readings in Psychology. The search for alternatives.* pp. 175–78. New York: McGraw-Hill.

Dorrington, R., Bourne, D. , Bradshaw, D. , Laubscher, R. & Timaeus, I.M. (2001). *The Impact of HIV/AIDS on Adult Mortality in South Africa. Technical Report: Burden of Disease Research Unit.* Tygerberg: Medical Research Council.

Duncan, N., van Niekerk, A. & Mufamadi, J. (2003). Developmental psychology: A lifespan perspective. In L. Nicholas (Ed.). *An Introduction to Psychology.* Landsdowne: UCT Press, pp. 13–52.

Faure, S. & Loxton, H. (2003). Anxiety, depression and self-efficacy levels of women undergoing first trimester abortion. *South African Journal of Psychology,* 33(1):28–38.

Fadminan, J. & Frager, R. (1994). *Personality and Personal Growth.* New York: Harper Collins College Publishers.

Fromm, E. (1949/1975). *Man for Himself.* Norfolk: Routledge & Kegan Paul.

Hook, D. (2002). Critical issues in developmental psychology. In D. Hook, J. Watts & K. Cockcroft (Eds.). *Developmental Psychology.* Lansdowne: UCT Press, pp. 343–66.

Jewkes, R., Penn-Kekana, L., Levin, J., Ratsaka, M. & Schrieber, M. (2001). Prevalence of emotional, physical and sexual abuse of women in three South African provinces. *South African Medical Journal,* 91(5):421–8.

Kaplan, H.I. & Sadock, B.J. (1998). *Synopsis of Psychiatry: Behavioral sciences/clinical psychiatry* (8th edition). Baltimore: Williams and Wilkins.

Kimmel, D. (1974). *Adulthood and Aging.* New York: John Wiley & Sons.

Kinsella, K. & Ferreira, M. (1997). *Aging trends: South Africa.* International Brief: United States Department of Commerce, . http://www.census.gov/ipc/prod/ib-9702.pdf (accessed 1 June 2002).

Laubscher, L. & Klinger, J. (1997). Story and the making of the self. In C. de la Rey, N. Duncan, T. Shefer & A. Niekerk. (Eds.). *Contemporary Issues in Human Development: A South African focus.* Johannesburg: ITP, pp. 58–79.

Mathers, C., Sadana, R., Salomon, J., Murray, C. & Lopez, A. (2001). Healthy life expectancy in 191 countries, 1999. *Lancet,* 357:1685–91.

May, J., Woolard, I. & Klasen, S. (2000). The nature and measure of poverty. In S. May (Ed.). *Poverty and Inequality in South Africa: Meeting the challenge.* Cape Town: David Phillip, pp. 19–50.

National Center for Injury Prevention and Control (NCIPC) (2003). *Youth Violence Facts,* www.cdc.gov/ncipc/factsheets/yvfacts.htm. (accessed 17 February 2003).

Nowrojee, B. & Manby, B. (1995). South Africa: *The state response to domestic violence and rape.* Human Rights Watch, www.hr.org.reports/1995/Safricawm–02.htm (accessed 1 May 2002).

Orford, J. (1992). *Community Psychology: Theory and practice.* Chichester: Wiley.

Papalia, D. E. & Olds, S.W. (1995). *Human Development.* New York: McGraw-Hill.

Pauw, I. & Brener, L. (1997). Women & AIDS in South Africa. In C. de la Rey, N. Duncan, T. Shefer & A. van Niekerk (Eds.). *Contemporary Issues in Human Development: A South African focus.* Johannesburg: ITP, pp. 250–75.

Rogers, D. (1979). *The Adult Years. An introduction to aging.* Englewood Cliffs, NJ: Prentice-Hall.

Ryckman, R.M. (1993). *Theories of Personality.* Pacific Grove, California: Brooks/Cole.

Schiamberg, L.B. (1985). *Human Development.* New York: Macmillan.

Schonteich, M. (1999). Age and AIDS: South Africa's crime time bomb? *African Security Review,* 8(4), www.iss.co.za/Pubs/ASR/8No4 Schonteich.html. (accessed 8 January 2003).

Suffla, S., Seedat, M. & Nascimento, A. (2001). Evaluation of Medico-legal Services in Gauteng: Implications for the development of best practices in the after-care of rape survivors. *MRC Policy Brief, No. 5.* Tygerberg: MRC.

United Nations (2001). *United Nations Special Session of HIV/AIDS: Global crisis-global action fact-sheet.* New York: United Nations.

Van Dyk, A.C. & Van Dyk, P.J. (2003). 'What is the point of knowing?': Psychosocial barriers to HIV/AIDS voluntary counselling and testing programmes in South Africa. *South African Journal of Psychology,* 33(2):118–25.

Wilkinson, R. & Marmot, M. (Eds.). (1998). *Social Determinants of Health. The solid facts.* Copenhagen: World Health Organisation.

World Health Organisation. (2002). *World Report on Violence and Health.* Geneva: World Health Organisation.

Multiple choice questions

1. Recent South African research by Dorrington *et al.* (2001) indicates that
    a) homicide constitutes the single major cause of fatalities amongst young adult South African males
    b) homicide constitutes the single major cause of fatalities amongst young adult South African females
    c) suicide constitutes the single major cause of fatalities amongst young adult South African females and males
    d) motor vehicle crashes constitute the single major cause of fatalities amongst young adult South African females

2. Recent South African research indicates that currently ___ are most at risk of contracting HIV/AIDS
    a) women in the stage of young adulthood
    b) men in the stage of young adulthood
    c) women in the stage of middle adulthood
    d) men in the stage of middle adulthood

3. Studies cited by Orford (1992) indicate that married people are more contented with life than single people, with the most contented being
    a) men in their late thirties who do not have children
    b) women in their early forties who have children
    c) women in their early twenties who do not have children
    d) men in their late twenties who have children

4. Recent research by Kinsella and Ferreira (1997) and May *et al.* (2000) indicates that in South Africa
    a) urban communities are hardest hit by unemployment
    b) young adult males are hardest hit by unemployment
    c) women are hardest hit by unemployment
    d) women are least affected by unemployment

5. The physical experience of middle and late adulthood
    a) generally occurs earlier among lower-income unskilled workers than among higher-income professionals
    b) generally occurs earlier among higher-income professionals than among lower-income unskilled workers
    c) is determined exclusively by genetic factors
    d) cannot be slowed by diet and exercise

6. According to Erik Erikson's theory, the primary psychosocial challenge during middle adulthood is
    a) to strike a balance between generativity and self-absorption or stagnation
    b) to strike a balance between intimacy and isolation
    c) to confront the tension between identity achievement and identity diffusion
    d) to confront the tension between integrating their life experiences and the despair resulting from possible missed opportunities in life

7. Senescence refers to
    a) the synthesis between feminine and masculine traits
    b) the decline in the body's systems during late adulthood
    c) the individual's improved intellectual functioning during middle adulthood
    d) the improved efficiency of neurological processes during middle adulthood

8. According to the research conducted by Bradshaw *et al.* (2002b) _____ constitute(s) the major cause(s) of illness, disability and death during late adulthood
    a) tuberculosis
    b) strokes and heart disease
    c) diabetes and cancer
    d) all of the above

9. Fluid intelligence is said to
    a) decline throughout adulthood
    b) increase throughout adulthood
    c) remain stable throughout adulthood
    d) refer to the individual's learned ability to analyse and solve problems

10. According to the disengagement theory
    a) the individual gradually withdraws from society as she or he ages
    b) society gradually withdraws from the individual as the latter ages
    c) both (a) and (b)
    d) with disengagement in some areas of life, re-engagement occurs in others

Short answer questions

1. Describe the key features of physical development and decline over early, middle and late adulthood.
2. Discuss the major health risks associated with ill-health and mortality in each of the three periods.
3. Outline the development of cognitive and intellectual attributes and skills across the three periods.
4. The current HIV/AIDS pandemic will profoundly affect the social roles and responsibilities of adults. Critically discuss this assertion.
5. Critically discuss the psychological, social and economic impacts of violence on South Africans.

8

Parent-infant Attachment: Theory and Implications

Mark Tomlinson

CHAPTER OBJECTIVES

After studying this chapter you should be able to:
- provide a broad overview of the basic concepts of attachment theory
- introduce and discuss issues pertaining to culture and attachment theory
- explain and discuss the long-term implications of early attachment relationships
- briefly discuss the implications of attachment theory for understanding the concept of resilience.

While Nosipho had often thought about experiences in her childhood, she had hardly ever thought about herself as a baby. Of course, not being able to remember anything about this time, it was hardly surprising that she had dismissed its significance. But after learning about the importance of infancy for development, she felt she wanted to know more about her own early years. She found a couple of photographs of herself – along with some of her sister and brother. Looking at the photos it was hard to imagine what, if any, psychological processes might have been going on behind the smiling plump, baby faces. In photographs all babies looked happy, and often, she thought, looking across to her sister's photo, they actually looked pretty much the same. But speaking to her mom later that night she got quite a different idea about babies – and about herself!

She realised that she hadn't really ever sat down and asked her parents what she had been like as a baby. There were, of course, the usual passing remarks about how 'sweet' she had been and how early she had walked and talked, but nothing more. Now, with a bit of prompting, her mom started to talk about how Nosipho had been a premature baby and rather ill at first. She had actually spent the first two weeks of her life in hospital – something she had not known. 'I hated to leave you there, you looked so little and lonely', her mom said, explaining that she had had to go home to take care of her sister and brother. When she came home, Nosipho was mainly content – that is, if her mom was with her. 'If I tried to go and make a cup of tea in the kitchen you would cry and when you got a bit older you would crawl right behind me everywhere I went', her mom told her. I don't think you ever really liked to be on your own, her mom added, reminding Nosipho of how she had cried and refused to let her mom leave the classroom on the first day of pre-school. This was a bit of a surprise for Nosipho who had got used to thinking of herself as quite independent and grown up these days – but as she thought about it she realised that perhaps she still had a little of that kind of insecurity in herself – she preferred being with people to being alone and often felt a little shaky when her boyfriend had to be out of town for a few days. 'So much for my "independence"', she thought ruefully.

Introduction

As has been discussed previously, the infancy period is characterised by extensive physical, sensory and cognitive development. Central to emotional development during infancy is the process of developing an attachment relationship between the infant and his or her caregivers.

Brief history

The central figure in the emergence of attachment theory was John Bowlby, a British theorist writing in the second half of the twentieth century. In 1948, Bowlby hired James Robertson to assist him in the observation of children who had been separated from their caregivers as a result of a stay in hospital. Hospital policy in the United Kingdom at that time stipulated that parents were only to visit their sick children for a very short period each day. The distress of the infants during separation from their parents was interpreted as atypical until they became settled and uncomplaining (Bretherton, 1995). The result of Robertson's observations was a film entitled, *A Two-year-old Goes to Hospital*, which not only contributed to the development of attachment theory, but also helped improve the fate of children in hospitals around the world (Bretherton, 1995).

As a result of the large numbers of homeless children in post-war Europe, Bowlby was commissioned by the World Health Organisation to write a report on the mental health of these children (Bretherton, 1995). The report was published as *Maternal Care and Mental Health* (Bowlby, 1951), with the major conclusion being that for the child to develop optimally, a warm, intimate and continuous relationship with a mother (or permanent mother substitute) was needed (Bowlby, 1969). Another influence on Bowlby's theory was the field of ethology, particularly Lorenz's account of imprinting in geese (Bretherton, 1995). Harlow's research with Rhesus monkeys, which showed that warmth and contact between the mother and infant (and not simply nourishment) was critical in the formation of social relationships (Lamb *et al.*, 1985), also played its part in the genesis of attachment theory.

The emergence of attachment theory

Biological foundations

As is evident from the discussion above, Bowlby drew on an impressive number of domains of knowledge and fields of inquiry in developing attachment theory. Central, however, was Bowlby's focus on what he considered to be the universal biological endowment of humans derived from the natural history of humankind (Grossman, 1995). Belsky and Cassidy (1994) consider the most fundamental aspect of attachment theory to be its focus on the biological bases of attachment behaviour, while Simpson (1999) states that attachment theory is in fact an evolutionary theory.

The evolutionary biological model emphasised natural selection in shaping the behavioural repertoire of a species (Lamb *et al.*, 1985). Bowlby argued that in the savannah grasslands where humans evolved, proximity to a caregiver was vital for protection from predation, and thus, for survival. In his observations, Bowlby noted (of both infants and various primate species) that upon separation from a caregiver, infants displayed fairly specific sequences of behaviour, such as crying and throwing temper tantrums (Simpson, 1999). If these behaviours were unsuccessful in ensuring the return of the caregiver, the infant would move into the second stage and become despondent. This despair (which resulted in the infant becoming silent, and with slowed motor movements) served the dual purpose of conserving energy and minimising injury, but perhaps most importantly, ensured that movement and sound did not attract predators (Simpson, 1999). If separation from the caregiver persisted, the infant would then move into a final stage of detachment, and display behaviour suggesting heightened coping and inde-

Figure 1 Konrad Lorenz is best known for his work on signalling in ducks and imprinting in goslings

pendence. However, in reality, the infant was clearing the way for the development of other affectional bonds with another caregiver, a partial relinquishing of the old bond to enable the new (Simpson, 1999).

Attachment behaviours

In order to understand the environment of evolutionary adaptedness (Bowlby, 1969), an important question is how the infant achieves proximity to the caregiver so as to ensure survival. Human beings are not born with the physical ability (as many animals are) to seek proximity to their mother by means of their own locomotion (movement). The infant has a number of attachment behaviours that have the predictable outcome of increasing the proximity of the infant to the mother (Cassidy, 1999). One example of attachment behaviour is signalling. Behaviours such as smiling and vocalising are crucial elements of the behavioural repertoire of infants to signal distress. Other attachment behaviours include aversive behaviours, such as crying, that are designed to bring the mother to the infant in order to end the crying. As the infant develops, the nature of the attachment behaviours that are utilised will change, since once locomotion has been achieved, the infant will be able to follow the mother in order to achieve proximity (Belsky & Cassidy, 1994). Equally, for attachment behaviours to be effective, adults must also be equipped with responses that ensure care taking of the infant (Lamb *et al.*, 1985). Mutual responsiveness, caregiver sensitivity and parent-infant interaction are thus crucial aspects of the behaviour of human beings, as they provide the foundation that ensures prompt response to signals of distress from the infant (Lamb *et al.*, 1985:13).

Stages of growth of the attachment system

Bowlby outlined four main phases in the development of the attachment system (Ainsworth, 1969). The first occurs from birth to about 8 to 12 weeks of age and is characterised by orientation and signalling by the infant, but without the ability to discriminate one person from another. The second phase is a period of discriminating sociability (Thompson, 1998) and occurs between six and eight months. The infant still behaves in the friendly fashion characteristic of the first phase, but now the infant is far more discriminating towards his or her mother. The next phase is attachment proper (Thompson, 1998) where the infant actively seeks

Figure 2 Kangaroos provide an excellent example of intimate mother-child attachment

proximity to the mother, uses the mother as a secure base from which to explore the world, and where behaviour begins to become organised on a goal-corrected basis (Ainsworth, 1969). The final stage entails the formation of a reciprocal relationship between the infant and caregiver, and occurs between the third and fourth year of life. During this phase the child begins to understand other people's motives and feelings (Ainsworth, 1969; Thompson, 1998).

Attachment organisation

Attachment is not a static trait residing in the infant in a fixed amount (Sroufe & Waters, 1977). Instead, it is an affective tie between infant and caregiver that is influenced and mediated by feelings and the context. Weinfield *et al.* (1999) stress the distinction between the *presence* and the *quality* of an attachment relationship. It is only in rare circumstances such as harsh institutional rearing (e.g., in an overcrowded and understaffed orphanage) that a child will fail to develop an attachment relationship. If there is somebody to attach to, the infant will attach. However, the form that the attachment takes will depend on the nature of the care that the infant has received (Weinfield *et al.*, 1999).

The Strange Situation is an experimental procedure comprising seven three-minute episodes of the entrance of an unfamiliar female, separation from the mother, and then reunion with the mother. The reunion behaviour of the infant in this unfamiliar environment is then coded, providing a description of the important elements of the interaction. Ainsworth *et al.* (1978) classified the behaviour of the infants upon reunion into three attachment patterns: Secure, insecure-avoidant and insecure-resistant. Main and Solomon (1986) subsequently developed a fourth category, namely disorganised, which is an attempt to account for those children whose behaviour did not easily fit into the three classic Ainsworth categories. Disorganised children showed marked and pervasive fear in the presence of the parent (Steele, 2002).

As children get older, the form that their attachment behaviour takes will change. For instance, the distances that the child will travel from the attachment figure will increase with age. Much of this is facilitated by other developmental changes that the growing child undergoes at the pre-school level. These changes would include the improvement in the child's cognitive ability in representing, and thus anticipating, the various moment-to-moment changes in proximity with the attachment figure. The increasing need for individual mastery and the ability to make use of communication to regulate contact with the caregiver, also facilitate the child's decreasing need for a 'physical' secure base.

Security of attachment

Mary Ainsworth developed the Strange Situation procedure in an attempt to operationalise and provide a measure for Bowlby's attachment ideas (See Box 8.1). Ainsworth *et al.* (1978) distinguished between two general types of attachment relationships – secure and insecure. The three initial categories (Box 8.1) are all seen as organised strategies to deal with the environment and care-giving that the infant has received. They reflect the experiential shaping of a genetically pre-programmed, inborn attachment system (Siegel, 1999). Secure infants are upset by the departure of their mother, but upon reunion are soothed, and fairly quickly resume exploratory play. Insecure-avoidant infants appear unperturbed by the departure of the mother, and

present as independent and self-sufficient. Insecure-resistant infants are upset by the departure of the mother, but upon reunion display ambivalent behaviour alternating between seeking comfort and then becoming rejecting of that comfort (e.g., pushing toys away and angry kicking).

Attachment theory and culture

Both the concept of attachment and (more specifically) the Strange Situation paradigm have had to establish their cross-cultural applicability. An in-depth discussion of the question of cross-cultural patterns of attachment is not within the scope of this chapter (for a comprehensive review see Van IJzendoorn & Sagi, 1999), but some brief points should be noted.

Van IJzendoorn and Sagi (1999) argue that there are two crucial issues in this debate that need to be considered. The first is the universality of the infant-mother attachment relationship, while the second is the applicability of the Strange Situation paradigm cross-culturally. Ainsworth *et al.* (1978) developed the Strange Situation with a middle-class White sample from the United States, immediately raising the possibility that the procedure is not applicable to non-Western samples. Considerable research over the last 25 years has tested the cross-cultural validity of the Strange Situation. Important differences have emerged that might suggest limitations of the cross-cultural use of the Strange Situation. For example, in Japan, researchers have claimed that resistant attachments are over-represented and avoidant attachments under-represented (Miyake *et al.*, 1985; Takahashi, 1986). Part of the reason presented to explain this has been the argument that the Strange Situation is an invalid instrument to assess Japanese infants, as they are used to continuous close proximity to their mothers (Van IJzendoorn & Sagi, 1999). Upon separation these infants became highly distressed (for many of the infants this was the first time that they had been separated from their caregiver). The separation episodes in this research were not curtailed (as has now become the norm), resulting in a 'more than mild' stress level induced in the Japanese Strange Situation procedure (Van IJzendoorn & Sagi, 1999). However, these differences fell away through variations in the actual procedure (shortening separation episodes), adapting assessments to the particular culture, as well as through the use of naturalistic home observations to explain differences.

According to Van IJzendoorn and Sagi (1999), cross-cultural studies have not refuted the bold claims of attachment theory about universality and normativity, and in fact the studies are remarkably consistent with the theory. The three basic attachment patterns of secure, avoidant and resistant have been found in all cultures studied thus far (albeit with differing proportions). In addition, there does appear to be a general cultural pressure towards the selection of the secure attachment pattern in most children (Van IJzendoorn & Sagi, 1999). With regard to the use of the Strange Situation in South Africa, research has been limited. (For a discussion of a South African attachment study see Box 8.2.)

Internal working models

In view of what has been discussed above, an important question begs an answer: How do early attachment experiences come to have a bearing on emotional development through the life span? Bowlby argued that infants, based on their early experiences of the availability and responsiveness of their caregivers, build mental representations of the attachment figure. Bowlby called these 'internal working models', which are acquired through interpersonal interaction (Bretherton, 1995). Essentially, internal working models are 'maps' or 'operable models' (Bretherton & Munholland, 1999) of the self and the attachment partner, which are based on the interactions of infants with their primary caregivers – their relationship history (Bretherton & Munholland, 1999). These maps then become the

'filters' through which new relationships and interactions are perceived (Thompson, 1998), and provide the 'rules' by which infants predict the likelihood of a particular behaviour of either the caregiver or somebody else, and thus plan their response (Bretherton, 1995).

An important element of these internal working models is that they can be revised based on new environmental information or experiences (hence the word, 'working', i.e. open to revision). In this respect, they are not static and rigid constructs of how caregivers and others always interact. Rather, they are a template that predicts and regulates the attachment-related behaviour of both the infant and the attachment figure, and the basis for reflection on joint interaction and relationship conflict (Bretherton & Munholland, 1999). If the mother is consistently unresponsive to the infant, the infant will not only develop a working model of the mother as rejecting, and thus plan future behaviour accordingly, but also develop a sense of him- or herself as unlovable and not worthy of the love of the mother. (See Box 8.3 for a brief account of an adult measure that attempts to access adult states of mind with regard to attachment.)

Attachment security as a predictor of developmental outcome

Attachment theory postulates that a secure attachment will ensure that the infant and child will develop confidence in the availability (psychological and physical) of the caregiver, and that healthy independent exploration of the environment will arise as a result of this knowledge. In terms of a developmental trajectory, this knowledge then provides the foundation for social and emotional development, and is argued to exert an influence on the formation of later relationships by way of the internal working models (Coleman & Watson, 2000). Avoidant individuals may minimise attachment behaviours and feelings, and present a picture of being immune to hurt or even the need for emotional intimacy (Carlson & Sroufe, 1995). Major losses or separations are experienced as confirming the worst expectations about the psychological availability of attachment figures (Carlson & Sroufe, 1995). Resistant individuals may struggle with managing anxiety, exaggerate emotion, maintain negative beliefs about the self, and respond to loss with unusually intense anger and depression that may persist (Carlson & Sroufe, 1995).

Conclusion

In the light of these findings, what are the implications for the development (or non-development) of resilience? Does a secure attachment protect against the development of later emotional difficulties or psychopathology? Substantial research has shown that a secure attachment may protect against later difficulties, with the child (and adult) developing a belief that they are worthy of love and effective in gaining it from others (Carlson & Sroufe, 1995). However, is the protective function of a secure attachment the same as resilience? Weinfield *et al.* (1999) state that resilience should not be seen as a static trait residing in an individual, but rather as a process. Seen in this light, a secure attachment may be seen as one element in the process of a child developing resilience. Being securely attached alone does not make a child resilient, but is without doubt a component of resilience. Lewis *et al.* (1984:123) describe this succinctly when they state: 'Infants are neither made invulnerable by secure attachments nor are they doomed by insecure attachments to later psychopathology.'

The longer an individual has experiences of insensitive and unresponsive care-giving, poverty, abuse, neglect and an altogether hostile environment, the more likely the long-term consequences. The greater the accumulation of risk, and the fewer the protective factors (such as a secure attachment), the more likely the development of later difficulties or psychopathology.

Ainsworth, M.D.S. (1969). Object relations, dependency, and attachment: A theoretical view of the infant-mother relationship. *Child Development*, 40:969–1025.

Ainsworth, M.D.S., Blehar, M., Waters, E. & Wall, S. (1978). *Patterns of Attachment: A psychological study of the Strange Situation*. New Jersey: Lawrence Erlbaum.

Belsky, J. & Cassidy, J. (1994). Attachment: Theory and Evidence. In M. Rutter & D.F. Hay (Eds.). *Development Through Life: A handbook for clinicians*. Oxford: Blackwell Scientific Publications, pp. 373–402.

Bowlby, J. (1951). *Maternal Care and Mental Health*. Geneva: World Health Organisation.

Bowlby, J. (1969). *Attachment and Loss: Volume 1, Attachment*. New York: Basic Books.

Bretherton, I. (1995). The origins of attachment theory: John Bowlby and Attachment Theory. In S. Goldberg, R. Muir & J. Kerr (Eds.). *Attachment Theory: Social, developmental, and clinical perspectives*. London: The Analytic Press, pp. 45–84.

Bretherton, I. & Munholland, K.A. (1999). Internal working models in attachment relationships: A construct revisited. In J. Cassidy & P.R. Shaver (Eds.). *Handbook of Attachment: Theory, research and clinical applications*. New York: Guilford Press, pp. 89–111.

Carlson, E.A. & Sroufe, L.A. (1995). Contribution of attachment theory to developmental psychopathology. In D. Cicchetti & D. J. Cohen (Eds.). *Developmental Psychopathology. Volume 1: Theory and methods*. New York: John Wiley, pp. 581–617.

Cassidy, J. (1999). The nature of the child's ties. In J. Cassidy & P.R. Shaver (Eds.). *Handbook of Attachment: Theory, research and clinical applications*. New York: Guilford Press, pp. 3–20.

Coleman, P. & Watson, A. (2000). Infant attachment as a dynamic system. *Human Development*, 43:295–313.

George, C., Kaplan, N. & Main, M. (1985). *Adult Attachment Interview*. Unpublished manuscript, University of California, Berkeley.

Grossman, K.E. (1995). The evolution and history of attachment research and theory. In S. Goldberg, R. Muir & J. Kerr (Eds.). *Attachment Theory: Social developmental and clinical perspectives*. Hillsdale, NJ: The Analytic Press, pp. 85–121.

Hesse, E. (1999). The adult attachment interview: Historical and current perspectives. *Handbook of Attachment: Theory, research and clinical applications*. New York: Guilford Press.

Lamb, M.E., Thompson, R.A., Gardner, W. & Charnoy, E.L. (1985). *Infant-Mother Attachment: The origins and developmental significance of individual differences in strange situation behaviour*. London: Lawrence Erlbaum Associates.

Lewis, M., Feiring, C., McGuffog, C. & Jaskir, J. (1984). Predicting psychopathology in six-year-olds from early social relations. *Child Development*, 55:123–36.

Main, M. & Solomon, J. (1986). Discovery of a new, insecure-disorganized/disoriented attachment pattern. In T.B. Brazelton & M. Yogman (Eds.). *Affective Development in Infancy*. Norwood, NJ: Ablex, pp. 95–124.

Miyake, K., Chen, S.J. & Campos, J.J. (1985). Infant temperament, mother's mode of interaction, and attachment in Japan: An interim report. In I. Bretherton & E. Waters (Eds.). Growing points of attachment theory and research. *Monographs of the Society for Research in Child Development*, 50(1–2, Serial No.209):276–97.

Siegel, D. (1999). *The Developing Mind: Toward a neurobiology of interpersonal experience*. New York: Guilford Press.

Simpson, J.A. (1999). Attachment theory in modern evolutionary perspective. In J. Cassidy & P.R. Shaver (Eds.). *Handbook of Attachment: Theory, research and clinical applications*. New York: Guilford Press, pp. 115–40.

Sroufe, L.A. & Waters, E. (1977). Attachment as an organizational construct. *Child Development*, 48:1184–99.

Steele, H. (2002). State of the art: Attachment. *The Psychologist*, 15:518–22.

Takahashi, K. (1986). Examining the strange situation procedure with Japanese mothers and 12–month-old infants. *Developmental Psychology*, 22:265–70.

Thompson, R.A. (1998). Early socio-personality development. In W. Damon & N. Eisenberg (Eds.). *Handbook of Child Psychology. Social, emotional, and personality development* (5th Edition), Volume 3. New York: John Wiley & Sons, pp. 25–104.

Tomlinson, P., Cooper, P., Swartz, L. & Molteno, C. (2002). *Challenges in assessing attachment and associated factors in a South African peri-urban settlement*. Symposium presented at 'The baby birth to three': Prevention, parents, poverty, and policy conference. World Association for Infant Mental health, Amsterdam, Netherlands.

Van IJzendoorn, M.H. & Sagi, A. (1999). Cross-cultural patterns of attachment: Universal and contextual dimensions. In J. Cassidy & P.R. Shaver (Eds.). *Handbook of Attachment: Theory, research and clinical applications*. New York: Guilford Press, pp. 713–34.

Weinfield, N.S., Sroufe, L.A., Egeland, B. & Carlson, E.A. (1999). The nature of individual differences in infant-caregiver attachment. In J. Cassidy & P.R. Shaver (Eds.). *Handbook of Attachment: Theory, research and clinical applications*. New York: Guilford Press, pp.68–88.

Multiple choice questions

1. Which one of the following is not an attachment behaviour?
   a) crying
   b) crawling
   c) signalling
   d) playing
2. Who developed the strange situation procedure?
   a) Bowlby
   b) Freud
   c) Ainsworth
   d) Piaget
3. Which of the following two theorists outlined the disorganised attachment category?
   a) Main and Solomon
   b) Ainsworth and Bowlby
   c) Robertson and Harlow
   d) Van Ijzendoorn and Sagi
4. Which of the following is not a feature of the repertoire of human beings that contribute to ensuring caregiver response to infant distress?
   a) caregiver sensitivity
   b) high IQ
   c) mutual responsiveness
   d) parent-infant interaction
5. Who made the film entitled *A Two-year-old Goes to Hospital*?
   a) Robertson
   b) Ainsworth
   c) Bowlby
   d) Harlow
6. Which of the following attachment categories was not developed by Mary Ainsworth?
   a) secure
   b) disorganised
   c) resistant
   d) avoidant
7. Which of the following fields of inquiry was central to Bowlby's development of the attachment theory?
   a) adolescent theory
   b) ethology
   c) psychoanalysis
   d) game theory
8. At what approximate age do children become able to understand the feelings and motives of other people?
   a) 18 months
   b) at five years of age
   c) between two and three years
   d) between three and four
9. For what organisation did Bowlby write an influential report following World War Two?
   a) United Nations
   b) British government
   c) World Health Organisation
   d) UNICEF
10. Which theorist observed imprinting behaviour in geese?
    a) Robertson
    b) Lorenz
    c) Harlow
    d) Ainsworth

Short answer questions

1. What is the difference between attachment and an attachment behaviour?
2. Briefly describe what an internal working model is.
3. Outline the four main phases in the development of the attachment system.
4. Outline the similarities and differences between the adult attachment interview and the strange situation.
5. Outline the major theoretical influences on Bowlby in his development of the attachment theory.

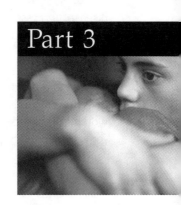

Part 3

Brain and Behaviour

Mark Solms and Oliver Turnbull

How do we know that the brain is the organ of mental life – apart from the fact that this is the received knowledge transmitted to us by high school biology teachers? Perhaps some other region, for example, the liver, the leg, or the lung is actually the body part that we use for thinking? To test this claim, you would need evidence, perhaps evidence from damage to the brain (and indeed the liver or leg) – together with evidence of the effects that such damage would have on mental life. This, then, is the task of neuropsychology – using science to understand the part of the body that 'produces' that thing we use for thinking, the thing which we experience as the mind. Of course, it is not merely a matter of knowing that the organ of the mind is the *brain*. Actually, the brain and the mind are not exactly the same thing – if for no other reason than because there are parts of the brain that have little to do with what we experience when we think a thought.

To know that the mind is 'produced' by the brain is knowledge no more sophisticated than to say that the power for driving a car comes from its engine. This is a basically accurate answer, but entirely lacking in detail. It tells us nothing of the specifics of *how* your car manages this remarkable process. How do the different parts of the engine work – what does the distributor do, what role is played by the spark-plugs, what is a compression cycle? Why does a car need petrol, oil and water, why does it produce exhaust fumes?, and so on. Most people who drive cars have little idea of the specifics of how an engine functions – just as most people can use their minds without knowing the first thing about how the organ of mind really operates.

If you are member of the general public, not knowing much about the brain is a luxury that you can probably afford. However, if you are sufficiently interested in the mind to sign up for a university-level course in psychology, then you must surely be interested in knowing how mental experience is produced. This is the topic of the series of chapters in this section. Of course, trying to explain how mental life is 'produced' by the brain is a challenging task for an introductory chapter. The brain is a remarkably complex organ, and there is still a great deal more that we have yet to understand about how it operates. Our situation in neuroscience is quite unlike our understanding of the way motorcars work – probably because, in the case of the brain, we are not the people who 'designed' the instrument! Indeed, part of the task of neuropsychology is trying to understand what the basic 'design principles' of the brain might be. However, though our understanding of brain function is incomplete, there is much that we *do* know. To achieve a high level of understanding of brain function, one needs to grasp a substantial amount of biochemistry and anatomy, as well as have an understanding of the many disease processes that can affect the brain. However, there is no need for those who have a limited background in those areas to be concerned in a series of introductory chapters such as these ones. We hope to provide enough detail to show you that neuropsychology is not only inherently interesting, but also that a basic working knowledge of the topic is absolutely essential for anyone who hopes to be a psychologist.

The first chapter of this section, by Mark Solms, briefly reviews some the history and development of the neuropsychology – which has an enviable record of some 150 years of scientific investigation. There have been several landmark discoveries during this time period, which have progressed together with a range of theoretical and technical developments, and Solms' chapter briefly covers these. The chapter also provides some idea of the practical work that is carried out by neuropsychologists, in their day-to-day encounters with those who have suffered some form of brain disease or brain damage.

The earlier phases of research in neuropsychology focused largely on *cognition*, as well as on domains such as language and memory. However, neuropsychologists have long been aware that *emotion* has an important place in the mental apparatus (although neuropsychology seemed to avoid work on emotion for most of the last century) for a range of both theoretical and technical reasons. The motivation for the field to focus on emotion has now become increasingly clear, and the last decade or two has seen an enormous growth in our understanding of the neural basis of emotion. In the second of the neuropsychology chapters, Jaak Panksepp has produced a brief review of this vast field. The most exciting aspect of this work has been that neuropsychology now has a growing understanding of the biological basis of many 'psychiatric' disorders (such as schizophrenia, depression and autism) whose neurobiology has much to do with disorders of emotion systems.

In the third chapter of this section, Oliver Turnbull briefly reviews some of the many discoveries that have been made about the neural basis of vision. This topic is chosen as a thematic example in neuropsychology – probably because vision is the best investigated (and, arguably, the most important) of the senses. The chapter reviews what we have come to understand about the way in which we recognise objects in the world and interact with them. It shows the ways in which neuropsychologists use the evidence provided by patients with focal brain lesions – which produce a range of selective disorders of visuo-perceptual and visuo-motor ability.

Hopefully, this series of chapters will explain part of the huge growth in understanding that is currently taking place in the neurosciences. For millennia, intelligent human beings have been able to understand a great deal about the way the human mind operates – often developing profound insights into psychology. For this reason, we are able to experience a range of universal 'truths' of human nature in literatures from around the world. (An example of this is found in Nelson Mandela's Robben Island copy of Shakespeare's collected works. Mandela marked a section of Act II, Scene II of *Julius Caesar*, a statement on the topic of courage and mortality that he found relevant and inspirational – even though the words were written almost 400 years earlier, across the breath of two continents, and were read by someone raised in an entirely different culture.) When Hamlet considers suicide, for example, in the famous 'To be, or not to be ...' speech, he encounters the same range of choices, and has the same range of experiences, as a suicidal teenager in our present age. Without question, Shakespeare understood a great deal of the operation of the human mind. However, like the motorist who understands nothing of how the car's engine works, all Shakespeare's insights into human experience lay unconnected to a knowledge of how the mind was produced. After centuries of neglect, we are at last becoming aware of the neural basis of mental life, and we should feel rightly privileged to live in an era when such knowledge is becoming available. Hopefully, this section will make it clear that neuropsychology is a fascinating field, and one that is central to any well-rounded understanding of human psychology.

Neuropsychology

Mark Solms

After studying this chapter you should be able to:
- identify or describe the origins and basic assumptions of neuropsychology
- identify or describe the various methods used in modern neuropsychology, and describe the circumstances under which they are used.

Being a neuropsychologist was not something that Nosipho had ever contemplated as a career choice. Like most people she hadn't really known such a profession existed or what it was that they might do. She knew that there were medical specialists that operated on the brain – called neurosurgeons, but she hadn't really thought about how a psychologist might be involved in working with people who had experienced some kind of neurological problem. But as Nosipho discovered how important the brain was for all our human experiences, she found herself growing increasingly fascinated with this relatively new but rapidly growing area in psychology.

People often spoke about the centre of themselves being their 'heart', but Nosipho began to realise that it was more likely your brain that made who you were. A brain injury could change everything about you, who you felt you were and how you experienced the world. Psychologists could be involved in diagnosing different kinds of damage to the brain and helping people with the effects of these. Understanding more about this amazing organ might make it possible not only to help people who had suffered brain disease or injury, but it could also help explain the complex processes that went on in the minds of normal people as well. Understanding these better might help with all sorts of psychological problems.

Introduction

As its name suggests, neuropsychology straddles two disciplines: *neurology* and *psychology*. Neurologists would describe the subject matter of neuropsychology as *the mental functions of the brain*, while psychologists would describe it as *the neurological basis of the mind*. Either way, neuropsychologists seek to correlate the structure and functions of the mind with the anatomy and physiology of the brain.

Broadly speaking, neuropsychology can be divided into two major divisions: *clinical* and *research*. Although in reality there is considerable overlap between the two, research neuropsychologists are primarily concerned with pure knowledge about how mental functions are organised in the brain, and what the study of the brain (in health and disease) can reveal about the organisation of the mind, whereas clinical neuropsychologists are more concerned with the practical application of this knowledge – to the diagnosis and management of the mental aspects of neurological disease.

The disciplinary link between psychology and neurology reflects the special relationship that exists between the mind and the brain. Unlike any other organ of the body, the functions and dysfunctions of the brain have immediate and direct effects on the mind – so much so that the view is commonly expressed that 'the brain is the organ of the mind' (in much the same way as the stomach might be described as the organ of digestion, or the lungs as organs of respiration). On the basis of this intimate connection, everything that we deal with in psychology is ultimately also an aspect of neurology. (The specific nature of this connection has troubled philosophers since ancient times, in the form of the 'mind-body problem'. Ultimately, the connection between brain and mind is not far removed from the connection between body and soul, and it is therefore also linked to far-reaching theological problems.) Needless to say, however, many aspects of what we deal with in psychology do not readily lend themselves to neuropsychological methods.

The question might well be asked: How does *psychiatry* fit into this interdisciplinary picture? Neurology and psychiatry have a problematical relationship with each other. As the neurological basis of psychiatric disorders has increasingly yielded to advances in medical science, so the distinction between the two specialities has appeared increasingly arbitrary. The distinction is now essentially a matter of convention, justifiable only on historical grounds. In the nineteenth century (when this distinction first arose), physicians classified as 'neurological' those mental disorders which were associated with *structural* changes in the brain – that is changes that could be observed at autopsy – and as 'psychiatric' those disorders for which no such changes could be observed. The latter were described as disorders of brain *function*. Hence the distinction between 'structural' (neurological) and 'functional' (psychiatric) disorders, which remains an accepted part of medical nosology to this day. The problem with dividing 'nervous' patients up this way arises from the fact that modern psychiatrists attribute many of the 'functional' disorders they deal with to micro-structural changes (e.g., over-activity or under-activity in a particular neurotransmitter system), and accordingly they treat them with medications which target particular neurochemical pathways. Many 'neurological' disorders have a similar basis and treatment (e.g., epilepsy and Parkinson's disease). The difference between structure and function is therefore by no means clear-cut anymore. In future, the distinction between psychiatry and neurology might well, therefore, disappear. In line with this trend, the discipline of neuropsychology is becoming increasingly relevant to psychiatry. To make matters worse, some psychiatrists now specialise in what they call 'neuropsychiatry' (i.e. they specialise in the psychiatric or 'functional' aspects of 'structural' neurological disease!). For the most part, however, in practice, clinical neuropsychology is still concerned primarily with 'neurological' (as opposed to 'psychiatric') disorders, insofar as it attempts to delineate the mental effects of structural changes in the brain. In this respect, the difference between neuropsychology and neuropsychiatry coincides roughly with the distinction between *cognition* and *affect*. Clinical neuropsychology focuses primarily (but by no means exclusively) on cognitive rather than emotional disorders. The same does not apply to research neuropsychology, however. Today our 'pure' knowledge of how mental functions are organised in the brain rests heavily on knowledge we have gained (at the micro-structural level) about brain functions. The distinction between cognitive and affective neuroscience is well illustrated by the chapters in this textbook on visual perception (a cognitive function) and motivation (an affective function). The distinction between neuropsychology and neuropsychiatry, too, will probably eventually disappear.

Since the two chapters just mentioned (Chapters 10 and 11 of this volume) may also readily serve as examples of the current state of knowledge in neuropsychological research, this chapter will focus primarily on *clinical* neuropsychology. This emphasis reflects the fact that neuropsychology in South Africa is very much a clinical discipline (for an introduction to neuropsychology, see Bradshaw & Mattingley, 1995; Feinberg & Farah, 1997; Solms & Turnbull, 2002).

Early history of neuropsychology

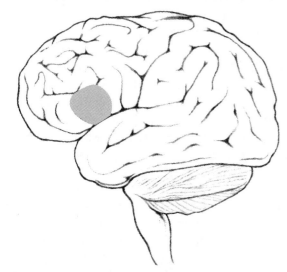

Figure 1 Broca's area

The birth of neuropsychology is traditionally linked with the discovery in the 1860s, by Pierre Paul Broca, of the fact that damage to a particular part of the left hemisphere of the human brain – today known as 'Broca's area' (see Figure 1) – results in loss of the faculty of speech. Since speech (i.e. symbolic vocalisation) is an unequivocally mental function, and moreover a specifically human one, this discovery caused considerable excitement in European scientific circles at the time. On the basis of his famous observation, Broca concluded that the faculty of language could be 'localised' in a particular part of the brain. This isolation of the physical basis of an aspect of the 'soul' led to a flurry of similar observations over the next several decades, with respect to a host of other mental functions. For example, Heinrich Lissauer localised visual knowledge to the occipital lobe (at the back of the brain; see Figure 2), and Hugo Liepmann localised motor knowledge to the left parietal lobe (Figure 3). (It is important to distinguish between simple vision and visual knowledge or 'gnosis'; the former is a physical function, the latter a mental one. Patients with occipital lobe damage causing 'visual agnosia' accordingly are not blind. They can see but they cannot derive meaning from what they see. Such a patient might describe a frying pan, for instance, as a 'circular piece of metal with upturned edges attached to a cylindrical plastic shaft', but the patient would have no idea what such an object is used for. The same applies to motor knowledge versus simple movement, etc.) These classical localisations, like Broca's, were made on the basis of correlations between specific mental changes observed during life and focal areas of brain damage detected at autopsy. This was called the method of clinico-anatomical correlation. The lost mental functions were – logically – considered to be the normal functions of the parts of the brain that had been damaged. Proceeding in this way, by the middle of the twentieth century, the surface of the brain was divided up into a mosaic of component 'centres', with each centre being described as the 'locus' of one or another mental faculty.

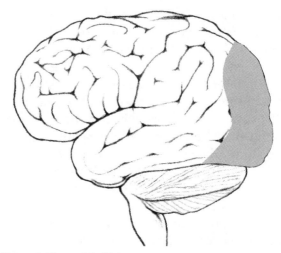

Figure 2 The occipital lobe

Opponents of this simple interpretation of clinico-anatomical correlation (known as 'localisationism') soon appeared. The young Sigmund Freud, for example, wrote a scathing critique in 1891 of the authoritative works of Broca, Carl Wernicke and Ludwig Lichtheim, on the basis of which the various components of language – spontaneous speech, comprehension, repetition, reading and writing – had been localised in a patchwork of centres on (and just below) the surface of the left hemisphere. Other prominent critics of the localisationist school, which nevertheless absolutely dominated the early history of neuropsychology, were John Hughlings Jackson, Pierre Marie, Henry Head and Kurt Goldstein. These authorities all criticised the 'diagram makers' for their propensity to reduce the dynamic complexities of the mind to simple box-and-arrow models of nervous centres and their connections.

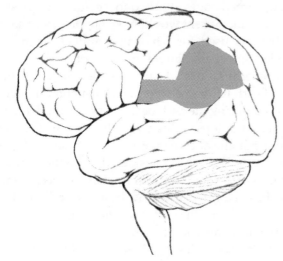

Figure 3 The left inferior parietal region

The 'box-and-arrow' approach still dominates much of modern neuropsychology (due primarily to the influence of Norman Geschwind in America and of cognitive psychology in Europe; see below), but today our information processing models are far more sophisticated. A major turning point came after the second world war – which, sadly, produced a wealth of focal brain injuries for neuropsychologists to study. The leading figure in this revolution was the Soviet neurologist and psychologist, Aleksandr Romanovich Luria. Luria recognised that there was truth in both of the extreme positions taken by the early neuropsychologists.

Whereas the *localisationists* sought to identify the 'seat' of each mental function in a particular part of the brain, the rival *equipotentialists* argued that mental functions were dynamic things which depended on the concerted functioning of the brain as a whole. Luria pointed out that although it was true that a whole mental faculty cannot be reduced to the activities of a circumscribed cortical zone, it was also true that different cortical zones performed different functions – the different parts of the brain were not 'equipotential'. His compromise position, called 'dynamic localisation', sought to specify the constellations of multiple cortical zones that functioned together to produce each complex mental faculty. He argued that mental faculties were composites of multiple elementary functions, and that only the component elements could be narrowly localised. The faculties themselves were produced by dynamic interactions between the components; hence the faculties themselves could not be localised. They existed, as it were, between the component 'centres' of the brain rather than within them. The task of neuropsychology, Luria argued, was to identify the localisable components of each complex faculty. This provides insight into the composition of mental faculties and into the mechanism of the mental disorders that are produced by damage to different cortical zones (for a good indication of Luria's approach, see Luria, 1973a, 1973b, 1979.)

Luria's approach is perhaps best illustrated by way of an analogy. Digestion, for instance, is not a function of the stomach alone; it depends on concerted interaction between multiple organs, such as the musculoskeletal organs of mastication that render solid foodstuffs digestible, the neuromuscular mechanisms involved in swallowing these products, the gastric juices that break them down for absorption purposes (thereby involving the liver, gall-bladder and pancreas in the process, alongside the stomach), the peristaltic mechanisms that transport the decomposed end-products to the intestines, etc. It is apparent that digestion is not the function of any one of the elements in this process; rather it is the resultant of a dynamic interaction between all of them. Nevertheless it is also apparent that the different elements that participate in the overall process do so unequally – with each contributing a specific sub-function. The same, according to Luria, applies to mental functions vis-à-vis the component zones of the brain. Mental functions are produced by multiple brain regions working in a concerted fashion, with each region contributing a specific sub-function, and with other brain regions not contributing at all.

This notion – that is that our complex mental functions are produced by dynamic 'neural networks' as opposed to static 'centres' – rapidly gained ground, and it represents the standard conceptualisation in neuropsychology today.

On the basis of this conceptualisation of mind-brain relations, Luria developed a sophisticated approach to clinical neuropsychological diagnosis and assessment. The task of the neuropsychologist, according to Luria, is not simply to identify which mental functions are 'lost' or 'preserved' as the result of a brain lesion in any given case – nor even to measure the degree to which particular functions are 'impaired' or 'intact' – but rather to characterise, psychologically, the specific way in which the affected functions have broken down, in order to identify the underlying mechanism of the disorder in question. This locates the component part of the complex functional system that is impaired, which aids diagnosis, and in turn provides a rational basis for designing a rehabilitation strategy.

Thus, for Luria, neuropsychology is of necessity theory-driven. Every neuropsychological assessment is directed by a theoretical understanding of mind-brain relationships on the part of the clinical investigator. Moreover, every new assessment potentially contributes to our theoretical understanding of the internal structure of mental faculties. For this reason, among others, it is not unusual to find single case reports in leading neuropsychological journals (e.g., Brain, Cortex, Neuropsychologia, Nature Neuroscience and Neurocase).

Combining our ever-evolving theoretical knowledge of mind-brain relationships with the classification of neuropsychological disorders (neuropsychological nosology), as well with the myriad specific ways in which the brain is damaged by particular neurological diseases and varieties of trauma (neuropathology), it is readily apparent that a clinical neuropsychologist must of necessity be a highly trained specialist. There is very little overlap between the specialist skills required to practice as a clinical neuropsychlogist and the broader skills of the general clinical psychologist. For this reason, it is perhaps not surprising to learn that not all practioners of neuropsychology are equally (or even adequately) well trained (for more on the history of neuropsychology, see Finger, 1994).

Two approaches to clinical neuropsychology

The qualitative approach to neuropsychology, outlined above, is derived more from the clinical traditions of internal medicine than those of clinical psychology or psychometry. The specialist neuropsychologist starts from a particular clinical question and proceeds flexibly, selecting the assessment tools he or she needs as the answer to the question at hand declares itself and the clinical picture unfolds. The aim is to identify a particular pattern of cognitive symptoms and signs that makes clinico-anatomical sense, thereby integrating (1) the observable clinical picture, via (2) its causal mechanism, with (3) the underlying neuropathology. The general clinical psychologist or psychometrician, by contrast, typically applies a standardised battery of tests,

which (1) measures the patient's performance across a range of mental functions, and (2) compares this measure to an established population norm. This approach precisely quantifies the degree of abnormality in the functions assessed, but it typically does not answer the clinical questions that prompt neurologists (or neurosurgeons, or paediatricians, etc.) to refer patients for neuropsychological assessment in the first place.

For purposes of illustration, consider the hypothetical referral in Box 9.1.

9.1 QUALITATIVE AND QUANTITATIVE NEUROPSYCHOLOGICAL ASSESSMENT

An eight-year-old girl slipped while playing next to her parents' swimming pool, banged her head, and fell into the water. It is unclear how long she was submerged in the water before she was found by her mother. However, by the time she was found she was unconscious and blue in the face. The mother administered mouth-to-mouth resuscitation, whereafter the child vomited violently and resumed breathing. She was taken to casualty, semi-conscious, and was admitted for a period of observation. The laceration over her right forehead required six stitches. Although she passed through a period of confusion and drowsiness, she appeared to have recovered completely by the following day. An MRI scan of her brain showed no abnormality. She was therefore discharged home on the following day and, a few days later, she returned to school. However, her teachers noticed a change in her. She was no longer her bright and cheerful self, she seemed far less confident both academically and socially, and at the end of term she performed poorly in her examinations. Both parents and teachers attributed the change to the near-drowning incident. However, the question remained: Was the change attributable to neurological or emotional factors?

If this child was referred to a clinical psychologist trained only in standard psychometric assessment techniques, the psychologist would submit her to a battery of standardised intelligence tests such as the SSAIS (South African Individual Scale – see Chapter 15, this volume), perhaps supplemented by projective tests or behavioural inventories. If the results were – as they would be in this case – low average scores on the IQ tests (with the performance scales being worse than the verbal ones) and evidence of anxiety and insecurity on the projective tests, how would that help a psychologist answer the question that prompted this referral? For one thing, we would need to know how this child might have scored on these same tests had they been administered to her before her accident. A clinical psychologist would therefore compare her scores on sub-tests of the SSAIS which are known to be resistant to brain damage and therefore to correlate highly with premorbid intelligence (e.g., the information sub-test) with those that rely more heavily on current problem-solving ability and are therefore more vulnerable to brain damage (such as block design); or he or she might decide to administer a standardised test of pre-morbid IQ, such as the NART (National Adult Reading Test). But still we would be left only with a gross measure of the degree to which her current intellectual functioning compares with her pre-accident potential. Assuming that the tests reveal a drop-off in this respect, have we really learned anything that we did not already know before the assessment? A documented decline in her academic performance was, after all, the reason she was referred for psychological assessment in the first place! The question is not so much whether or how much the accident affected her academic ability but rather why it was affected: Was the change neurological or emotional or both? (Neuropsychology is often best appreciated by understanding individual cases. A good and accessible case description can be found in Sacks (1985).)

In order to answer this question, the specialist neuropsychologist would begin with the differential-diagnostic possibilities: either the change in the child was due to (1) brain damage or (2) emotional trauma, or (3) both. In the first case, two subsidiary possibilities exist: the brain damage may be due to either closed head injury or cerebral anoxia (or both). Next, he or she would test these possibilities by assessing the cognitive functions that are typically affected by head injury and anoxia, looking for a recognisable constellation of symptoms and signs (known as a 'syndrome') that makes clinico-anatomical sense in this context. For example, in anoxic brain damage, three brain regions are particularly vulnerable: the occipital association cortex (due to the high metabolic rate of these cells, they require more oxygen), the hippocampal formation and the superior dorso-lateral convexity of the hemispheres (due to the latter two regions being supplied by the terminal branches of major cerebral blood vessels, they are the most vulnerable to compromised oxygen supply). Damage to

each of these regions produces specific localising syndromes: visual agnosia (usually of the apperceptive type), general amnesia (of the mesial temporal variety) and dysphasia (of the mixed transcortical type). If the child is found to be normal in all of these respects – with normality being defined as the absence of the requisite symptoms and signs, rather than a particular cut-off score (for the reason that human brain functions are species-specific functions) – then it is reasonable to conclude that she is unlikely to have suffered cerebral anoxia, since even the most vulnerable brain areas appear intact. Next, the neuropsychologist would assess for typical features of closed head injury, and so on. If this syndrome too cannot be demonstrated, then it would be reasonable to infer – by method of exclusion – that the child's academic difficulties were most likely attributable to functional (i.e. emotional) rather than structural (i.e. organic) causes. However, here too the neuropsychologist would be more secure about this diagnosis if positive features of an appropriate psychiatric disorder (e.g., post-traumatic stress disorder) can be demonstrated.

This extreme comparison of the two main approaches to neuropsychological assessment is illustrative only. It is not meant to imply, for example, that specialist neuropsychologists never use standardised psychometric tests. That is far from true. For example, in the assessment of age-related memory decline, where the diagnosis of a dementia of the Alzheimer type might be entertained, it would be critical to quantify a patient's memory performance on standard tests for purposes of comparison over time. The essential difference between the two approaches is this: in specialist neuropsychological assessment, measurement and standardisation are servants of the assessment process, not its masters. In general psychometric assessment, by contrast, the structure of the assessment is determined by the fixed requirements of the tests rather than the flexible, unfolding clinical picture in relation to the referral question.

The role of theory

It should be apparent from what has been said already that theory plays an important role in clinical neuropsychological practice. When Broca first described his classical cases of loss of speech due to focal brain damage, he conceptualised his observations in the nomenclature of the dominant psychological theory of his day, namely, 'faculty psychology', a close relative of the French phrenological tradition. This theory literally shaped what he saw;

because he believed that the mind is subdivided into a number of component 'organs' or faculties, of which speech was one, it was only reasonable that he should conceptualise his cases as instances of loss of speech as a whole, and that he should on this basis have localised the entire faculty of speech in a circumscribed 'centre'. The next generation of neuropsychologists (e.g., Wernicke and Lichtheim) subscribed to a different psychological theory, namely the 'association psychology' of the British empiricist philosophers. They accordingly conceptualised the speech and language disorders they observed as disorders of association ('disconnection') between the cortical projection zones of the major senses, and of damage to the centres of 'memory images' that cluster around these sensory zones – and thereby structure our subjective representation (or 'apperception') of the world. For these observors, it was not simply a matter of which faculty was affected, but rather of which aspect of the faculty: Which memory image centres were affected and which spared, and which centres were disconnected from which?

Neuropsychological nosology was accordingly reconfigured. Broca's unitary 'aphemia' (loss of speech) was subdivided into a host of sub-types of 'aphasia' (loss of language), such as Wernicke's aphasia (damage to the 'centre for sensory word images' which was located adjacent to the projection zone of the auditory nerve), conduction aphasia (disconnection between Wernicke's centre and Broca's 'centre for motor word images'), and transcortical sensory aphasia (disconnection between Wernicke's centre and the 'centre for concepts' which was superimposed over all the unimodal centres).

The rival interpretation of the aphasias proposed across the English channel by John Hughlings Jackson was shaped by another British intellectual tradition, namely the evolutionary biological tradition of Charles Darwin and Herbert Spencer. In accordance with this tradition, Jackson conceptualised disorders of language as consequences of damage to the highest (most recently evolved) cortical centres, and he drew attention to the fact that more primitive aspects of speech (so-called 'emotional speech', such as swearing and singing) were preserved with aphasia, due to the fact that these functions were performed by lower (less recently evolved) centres. Aphasia, Jackson famously pointed out, was a disorder of language ('propositionising') not merely of speech.

The next major development in neuropsychological theory was the influence of Gestalt psychology, associated mainly with the work of Kurt Goldstein, followed by Pavlovian reflex theory and American behaviourism. In this way, layer upon layer, as our theoretical understanding of the psychology of speech and language gradually evolved, so too did our capacity to recognise and conceptualise the vast complexity of empirical phenomena that comprises the disorders of speech and language that actually exist in nature. The same also applies the other way around; the rich complexity of actual neuropsychological disorders was an abundant source of new theoretical insight into the laws that govern the structure and functions of the human mind. To the extent that our mental faculties were observed to break down in ways that did not coincide with our theoretical expectations, our theories were recognised to be in need of revision. As the father of neurology, Jean Martin Charcot, once put it: 'Theory is good, but it does not stop things from existing'!

In modern times, neuropsychology has been dominated by the theories of cognitive psychology more than any other. Accordingly, cognitive psychology has also benefited more than any other school of psychology from the advance in understanding that accrues from testing any theory in the crucible of neuropsychology. Cognitive psychology has served neuropsychology so well because it offers an almost unlimited means of fractionating the information processing algorithms that comprise our various cognitive capacities into ever smaller processing units (or 'modules'), which accordingly approximate ever more closely to the specific physiological functions of the individual processing units of cortical tissues. Not surprisingly, therefore, the place of cognitive theory in neuropsychology has recently almost imperceptibly given way to other computer-based approaches, such as the 'parallel distributed processing' (PDP) models of neural network theorists, which seem to approximate more closely to actual patterns of cerebral activity at the microscopic, cellular level.

However, in very recent years, as neuropsychology has begun to tackle some of the most complex (and most interesting) problems of human psychology connected with the 'visceral underbelly' of the mind, such as emotion, motivation and the structure of personality – as well as the subtleties of subjective and intersubjective experience, like 'empathy', 'free will' and 'the self' – so cognitive and other information-processing models have inevitably begun to fail us. Computer-based models are ill-equipped to describe the sorts of physiological process that govern the instinctual and subjective poles of the mind. For these aspects of neuropsychology, molecular biological, ethological, and perhaps even psychoanalytical theories might offer more appropriate conceptual and observational tools for the neuropsychology of the future (see Chapter 10, this volume).

Research methods in neuropsychology

For more than a century, clinico-anatomical correlation (already described) provided the methodological backbone for all neuropsychological research. In the early years of neuropsychology, clinicians meticulously documented the mental abnormalities observed in individual cases of neurological disease or damage, and then correlated the changes with the anatomical site of the lesion that could be observed at autopsy. The great advances in neuropsychology that occurred during the two world wars were attributable partly to the fact that it was possible to infer the site of a patient's brain damage during life by tracking the entry and exit points of bullet or shrapnel wounds. The possibility of visualising the location of bullets, shrapnel and skull fragments embedded in the brain by means of X-rays provided further localising information.

Against this crude background, the advent of *in vivo* brain imaging, by means of which the soft tissues inside the skull could be visualised during life, was bound to represent a major methodological advance. This technology enabled neuropsychologists to correlate their clinical observations immediately and directly with the underlying pathological changes in brain anatomy. The huge clinical and research benefits that this development brought to neuropsychology are obvious. The first generation of such imaging technology – computerised tomographic (CT) scanning – became widely available in the 1970s. It is no accident that this ushered in a sustained period of progress in neuropsychology which still continues to this day. By the late 1980s, CT scanning had been widely replaced by a second generation of *in vivo* technology known as magnetic resonance imaging (MRI). This technology yielded much better resolution and therefore far greater precision and accuracy in clinico-anatomical correlation.

The latest advance was *functional* brain imaging. This comes in two major forms: positron emission tomography (PET) and functional MRI (fMRI). In different ways, both of these technologies measure differences in the rate of metabolic activity in the brain.

This makes it possible to infer which parts of the brain participate most actively in producing a particular mental function or state *while the patient (or research subject) is actually performing the relevant activity.* Again, the methodological advantages are huge and obvious. Now it is possible, using PET or fMRI technology, to image the differential levels of metabolic activity in all regions of the brain simultaneously, while the subject is doing just about anything the researcher cares to study, and thereby to literally obtain a 'photograph' of the parts of the brain that generate the mental activity in question. Typically, researchers use this technology within a 'subtraction' paradigm; that is, subjects are imaged performing control task A, imaged again performing experimental task B, and then the difference between the two tasks is 'subtracted'. This supposedly isolates the part(s) of the brain that specifically produce the target mental operation, which distinguishes the control from the experimental task. For example, the control task might involve the subjects gazing at black and white pictures whereas the experimental task involves them gazing at colour pictures; the difference between the two brain images then represents the specific brain regions that are involved in colour vision (as opposed to vision in general).

Although it is easy to follow the logic behind this research paradigm, it is also easy to see the potential for misinterpretation of its results. All too often one reads reports of functional imaging research which identifies the 'subtracted' brain region as if it alone performed the mental function of interest. Thus a technology which, more than any other, is suited to demonstrating the hard-won truth of previous generations of neuropsychologists, to the effect that mental functions are produced not by circumscribed cortical 'centres' but rather by dynamic constellations of cortical and sub-cortical zones working in concert, risks plunging neuropsychology back into the misconceived narrow localisationism of the pre-World War Two era!

Functional imaging technology (which is terribly expensive) is only now, at the time of writing, beginning to become available to South African neuropsychologists.

Neuropsychology in South Africa and around the world

Neuropsychology is still a very young science, and for this reason its official professional status is still evolving in relation to the other, more established psychological specialiaties. Thus the educational requirements for registration as a specialist neuropsychologist vary quite widely from one country to another. Moreover, local conditions have dictated somewhat different training requirements and assessment practices in different countries.

In South Africa, for example, where clinicians have to contend with a very heterogenous population as regards language, socio-economic status, culture and educational level, standardised psychometric techniques are of more limited value than they are in the highly developed economies and homogenous populations of Western countries. For this reason, the approach to neuropsychological assessment that was pioneered by Aleksandr Luria in the former Soviet Union, where social conditions were similar to those of modern South Africa, seem particularly appropriate. In the United States of America, by comparison, the psychometric approach to assessment has far greater currency.

Because it is such a young field, the influence of individual practitioners who pioneered the field in particular centres and contexts is also more strongly felt than it is today in other branches of psychology. Thus, for example, in the United States, the influence of Norman Geschwind – who was deeply impressed by the box-and-arrow models of the classical German behavioural neurologists mentioned above – is still strongly felt, and propagated today by the generation of behavioural neurologists (known as the 'Boston school') who trained under him. The character of Australian neuropsychology today was similarly shaped by the direct, personal influence of Kevin Walsh, a psychiatrist based at the Austin Hospital in Melbourne who had deep respect for the dynamic theories and clinical practices of the Soviet school of neuropsychology. (Walsh has in fact written a very good general introduction to neuropsychology. See Walsh, 1985.) British clinical neuropsychology has likewise been molded by the particular approach to neuropsychology of Elizabeth Warrington, a cognitive psychologist at Queen's Square in London, with a strong psychometric bent. In South Africa, Michael Saling – a research psychologist from the University of the Witwatersrand in Johannesburg – played a similar pioneering role, and his qualitative, Lurianic approach to neuropsychological assessment continues to be practiced and propagated by his erstwhile pupils today.

The reader will notice that the pioneers of modern neuropsychology around the world were drawn from a diversity of professional backgrounds. This too reflects the relative youth of the profession. In some countries, such as Italy, most of the present generation of clinical neuropsychologists are drawn from the ranks of neurology. In America, the pioneers of the field were predominantly behavioural neurologists, but the vast majority of practioners today are psychologists. In Britain, where psychology is divided into 'clinical' and 'research' categories (among others), the development of neuropsychological theory has been powerfully driven by research psychologists – almost exclusively in the cognitive mold – whereas clinical practice is the preserve of 'psychometric' clinical psychologists. Nevertheless, these two groups are united under a single 'Clinical Neuropsychology' division of the British Psychological Society. (A parallel British Neuropsychological Society exists, which is predominantly research based.) In South Africa, at the time of writing, a specialist category for neuropsychology has not yet been established by the Professional Board for Psychology of the Health Professions Council. However the reality on the ground is (paradoxically) that the most highly trained clinical neuropsychologists in South Africa are drawn mainly from the ranks of research psychology, despite the ambiguous legal framework within which they practice.

It should not be surprising under these circumstances to learn that neuropsychological training programmes, too, vary widely from one country to another. In South Africa today the most highly elaborated programme is offered by the University of Cape Town at Groote Schuur Hospital. This programme (convened by the author, a research psychologist, and Ozyman Ameen, a neurologist) trains specialist clinical neuropsychologists primarily in the 'qualitative' tradition outlined above – although, ironically, because the appropriate professional category still does not exist, this programme is officially described as a training in Psychological Research. South African psychology graduates seeking training abroad are advised to apply in the first instance to the University of Melbourne in Australia, which offers a specialist-registration course in clinical neuropsychology that can readily be transplanted to South African conditions.

Professional roles of the clinical neuropsychologist

Neuropsychologists work in a variety of settings, but most typically in hospitals and private practice settings. (Neuropsychologists also sometimes consult in educational, industrial and primary-health settings.) In hospitals, neuropsychologists are usually based in neurology, neurosurgery and psychiatry departments, although they frequently receive referrals from paediatrics and geriatrics, as well as from casualty and other medical departments (for example, occasional referrals are received from cardiology and pulmonology).

In neurology departments, neuropsychologists frequently play a direct role in the diagnosis of neurological disease. This reflects the fact that characteristic cognitive and behavioural changes appear in the early stages of many neurological diseases, and are sometimes the first symptoms or signs to appear. In these cases, the role of the neuropsychologist is to recognise these changes for what they are, and in this way to contribute to the accurate identification of the disease process in question. This role frequently involves the differentiation of 'organic' (i.e. structural) from 'non-organic' disorders. The differentiation of organic and non-organic disorders frequently represents the specific referral question in cases sent for neuropsychological assessment from geriatric and psychiatric departments. As regards geriatric referrals, the question typically revolves around the differentiation of normal aging (which is of course associated with memory loss and word finding difficulties, and – which is not frequently recognised – depression). As regards psychiatric referrals, functional psychotic and mood disorders can easily be confused with neurological disorders, and vice-versa. Korsakoff's disease, which is caused by a nutritional deficiency usually associated with chronic alcoholism, for example, might easily be confused with a functional psychosis; and yet it is in fact a reversible condition if it is diagnosed and treated early enough. The same is true of Wernicke's aphasia; these patients frequently do not realise that something is wrong with their audioverbal comprehension and that their own spontaneous speech is highly bizarre (replete with neologisms and 'word salad'). Conversely, hysterical conversion disorders (which are quite commonplace in developing countries like South Africa) closely mimic neurological disorders such as paralysis, dystonia, amnesia and epilepsy. The same applies, albeit to a lesser extent, to some forms of schizophrenia and some mood disorders. It is also important to recognise that neurological disorders (and normal aging) are frequently complicated (or 'elaborated') by psychiatric disorders. For example, genuine epilepsy is very frequently accompanied by hysterical epilepsy (so-called 'pseudoseizures'). It also needs to be remembered that many neurological disorders are accompanied by 'pseudopsychiatric' features which are in fact a direct manifestation of the primary brain disease (e.g., the early personality changes in Huntington's chorea, the depression in Parkinson's disease, the hypomania in multiple sclerosis, and the anti-social or obsessive-compulsive behaviours in Pick's disease).

Complex combinations of psychiatric and neurological problems are particularly common in paediatric cases, mainly for the reason that a child's personality necessarily develops around (or in reaction to) his or her neurocognitive strengths and weaknesses and neurobehavioural propensities. Epilepsy, tic disorders and specific learning disabilities (such as developmental dyslexia and dyspraxia) are particularly common examples. It is easy to see why it is essential for neuropsychologists to have extensive training, not only in clinical neurology but also in educational, paediatric and psychiatric issues.

Conclusion

In all of these settings, the role of the neuropsychologist also extends beyond diagnosis to include assessment or evaluation in a broader sense; that is, neuropsychologists are frequently called upon to characterise the cognitive status of a patient with known brain disease, in order to determine the specific implications of the disease for that particular patient in relation to his or her specific circumstances.

In private practice, this role of the neuropsychologist is frequently put to medico-legal use, to assist with the determination of damages, loss of earnings and quantification of future rehabilitation and palliative needs. Assessment of mental competency is another common medico-legal task of the neuropsychologist, not only in cases of generalised dementia, mental retardation and the like, but also in acute-care settings in the determination of a patient's capacity to provide informed consent for (or against) surgery, for example.

The careful characterisation of a patient's cognitive status is also essential for the rational planning of a rehabilitation programme. However, for some reason, such programmes are not typically executed directly by neuropsychologists (in South Africa at least); rather, the neuropsychologists designs and supervises a programme which is actually carried out by occupational therapists (in conjunction with nurses, speech therapists and others).

Neuropsychologists have additional, sometimes highly specialised roles in neurosurgical settings. Here neuropsychologists not only play a general evaluative role in the pre- and post-surgical workup, they also sometimes play a role during the operation itself. In epilepsy surgery, for example, it is important to ensure that the part of the brain that is to be surgically resected is not performing an essential cognitive function. This can frequently only be determined with certainty intra-operatively, when the designated tissue can be temporarily ablated (either pharmacologically or electrically) by the surgeon or anaesthetist, giving the neuropsychologist a brief opportunity to assess the cognitive consequences of the contemplated resection.

Last but not least, it is important to draw attention to the role of the neuropsychologist in counselling neurological patients and their families. The value of expert explanation and advice (and calm, sympathetic understanding) cannot be overestimated in situations where cognitive and behavioural changes that are perfectly familiar and explicable to us are experienced by patients and their families as humiliating, frustrating, confusing and frightening, or even as unacceptable indulgences, failings or 'misbehaviour' by patients and their families. Especially in paediatric cases, the neuropsychologist's role seldom terminates at the end of the assessment session, but can continue for many years, as the patient confronts new complications and challenges at every stage in their developmental trajectory.

There are of course many other roles for neuropsychologists, but these are the main ones. There is a huge demand for neuropsychological expertise in South Africa, as there is in so many other walks of life. It is to be hoped that this chapter will have encouraged some readers to devote their psychological skills and energies to this absolutely fascinating profession.

REFERENCES

Bradshaw, J.L. & Mattingley, J.B. (1995). *Clinical Neuropsychology: Behavioural and brain science*. SanDeigo: Academic Press.

Feinberg, T.E. & Farah, M.J. (1997). *Behavioral Neurology and Neuropsychology*. New York: McGraw Hill.

Finger, S. (1994). *Origins of Neuroscience: A history of explorations into brain function*. New York: Oxford University Press.

Luria, A.R. (1973a). *The Working Brain*. Basic Books.

Luria, A.R. (1973b). *The Man with a Shattered World*. Basic Books.

Luria, A.R. (1979). *The Making of Mind: A personal account of Soviet Psychology*. Cambridge, MA: Harvard University Press.

Sacks, O. (1985). *The Man Who Mistook His Wife for a Hat*. London: Picador.

Solms, M. & Turnbull, O.H. (2002). *The Brain and the Inner World: An introduction to the neuroscience of subjective experience*. London: Karnac.

Walsh, K.W. (1985). *Neuropsychology: A clinical approach*. London: Churchill Livingstone.

Multiple choice questions

1. Which of the following psychological abilities is usually disrupted after damage to Broca's area?
   a) spatial ability
   b) numerical skills
   c) vision
   d) speech

2. The technique of relating specific mental changes observed during life to focal areas of brain damage detected at autopsy is known as the
   a) hypothetico-inductive method
   b) clinico-anatomical method
   c) dissociative method
   d) uniformitarian method

3. The attempt to identify the 'seat' of each mental function in a particular part of the brain is known as
   a) localisationism
   b) equipotentialism
   c) mind-body dualism
   d) second-order phrenology

4. Whom of the following were not involved in the early history of aphasia research?
   a) John Hughlings Jackson
   b) Kevin Walsh
   c) Pierre Paul Broca
   d) Carl Wernicke

5. Which of the following practitioners is most likely to apply a standardised battery of psychological tests?
   a) psychotherapist
   b) psychometician
   c) psychoanalyst
   d) neurologist

6. Which brain regions are not commonly damaged in anoxic brain damage?
   a) occipital association cortex
   b) hippocampal formation
   c) superior dorso-lateral convexity of the hemispheres
   d) Broca's area

7. Which of the following topics has been the first to be addressed in detail by neuropsychology?
   a) cognitive abilities
   b) personality
   c) emotion
   d) motivation

8. Which of the following methods has been in longest use in neuropsychology?
   a) magnetic resonance imaging (MRI)
   b) 'parallel distributed processing' (PDP) models
   c) X-rays
   d) clinico-anatomical correlation

Short answer questions

1. Describe the sorts of methods that are used in modern neuropsychology.

2. Discuss the localisationists versus equipotentialists debate.

10

Motivation: From Intrinsic Psychobiological to Extrinsic Cognitive-Cultural Approaches

Jaak Panksepp

After studying this chapter you should be able to:
- provide an historical overview of the concept of motivation, and a taxonomy of affects
- introduce a hierarchical view of motivation from basic emotional to higher cognitive process
- discuss whether there are evolved systems for emotional processes that can be localised within the brain
- introduce seven basic emotional systems of the mammalian brain that mediate affective processes that energise behaviour and cognitions
- share details of three social-emotional systems that mediate sexual urges, maternal care, and separation-distress and bonding that constitute an integrated core system for social motivation.

When Nosipho thought about the driving forces in her life, she immediately identified things like her desire to do well, to please her parents and, in her more unselfish moments, her wish to do something 'useful for her community'. She generally thought about herself as someone who made carefully thought out and rational choices about what to do. Nosipho also prided herself on the way she tried to stick to her principles about what was right and to let these principles guide her actions.

As Nosipho started to learn more about motivation she, at first, felt quite reluctant to accept that she could be motivated by such basic needs as hunger or pleasure. It made human beings sound no different to animals! It was also difficult to admit to herself that emotions like fear, anger or love could overrule her more rational self. But as Nosipho learned more about neurology she could see how these basic wants were almost hardwired into the brain to help people survive. How could people stay alive if they didn't eat, drink, have sex, look after their babies and protect themselves? When you looked at it like that, it was quite natural and understandable to have

these primitive, 'animal-like' impulses in addition to more noble motivations.

While it disturbed her slightly to think that people were not as different from other animals as she had thought, it also helped her to understand how she sometimes had a powerful impulse to act in a way that seemed to by-pass her thinking processes. At these times the main motivation for Nosipho was not what she thought, but how she felt. These overwhelming feelings often happened in response to some threat that seemed to trigger an almost instinctive internal reaction from her. The next time she found herself feeling a rush of anger as someone pushed in front of her after a long wait in a supermarket queue she would try to be more forgiving of herself. Perhaps her rush of anger was just part of an 'instinct' to make sure she got what she needed. Of course being human rather than animal also meant that Nosipho had the capacity to control this kind of feeling rather than simply act on it with the kind of aggression a dog might show if someone got in between it and its bone.

Introduction

Motivation is one of those intrinsically ambiguous but critically important constructs in psychology that has been neglected during the recent 'cognitive era' of psychology. In prior times it was studied with enthusiasm, followed by periods of stagnation and despair about our ability to really understand what seems so easy and natural to talk about. The study of motivation currently aims to clarify not only the basic urges of our bodies, but also the highest aspirations of our minds. In short, the issue of motivation boils down to the study of why and how humans, as well as other animals, initiate and persist in certain behavioural (and in humans cognitive) patterns rather than in others. Why are we sometimes eager to eat, to drink, to take off clothes or to put on more, or to have any of a variety of social contacts or thoughts? Why are some interested in some activities, and others in different activities?

As it turns out, much of this requires a physiological analysis. While cognitive science has told us a great deal about how human beings receive, integrate, store, access, and compare information from the environment, it has had a more difficult time explaining what it is in the brain-mind that biases our attention to receive information selectively and how stored information is selected for further cognitive processing. Motivational urgency, driven often by shifting brain emotional states, helps do that. We now have neuroscientific ways to address these questions, and thereby to conceptualise how related cognitions become structured.

Motivation is intrinsically a multi-dimensional concept, similar to *emotions* and *consciousness*. It is a broad category name for a diverse set of brain-mind processes rather than any unitary construct or single entity. Traditionally, *motivations* referred to processes that help take care of our bodily needs, while *emotions* referred more to our mental needs and challenges, but this distinction is no longer commonly used. Here we will simply use the term generically to cover all varieties of mental activity that 'energise' organisms to do what they do. Motivation has many conscious and unconscious components, with the former being easier to talk about and to study than the latter. Although we know less about such matters, many unconscious brain processes underlie everything we do and think about. It is increasingly recognised that our actions often precede our thoughts about what we have done (Wegner, 2002).

The most forward looking current approaches take a hierarchical systems approach including discussion of both higher and lower brain-mind processes, embedded in a discussion of the types of evolutionary mechanisms that generate our various emotional feelings about the world – the many affective processes that help guide our actions. Although motivation is typically conceptualised as an intrinsic aspect of our mental apparatus, it also has a long history of being linked indirectly to various types of learning and cognitive processes, including memory formation, from which motivation is sometimes hard to distinguish (see Box 10.1). The viewpoint developed in this chapter is that many of our higher as well as everyday motivations remain tethered to ancestral mechanisms that we still share with many other animals of the world, especially mammals to whom we are most closely related. In this chapter we will specifically focus on the neural underpinnings of our basic social motivations, an area that is now bridging many areas of mind-brain research.

10.1 MOTIVATION AND MEMORIES

The topic of human motivation is never very far from the issue of the degree to which our actions and thoughts are purposefully directed toward certain types of goals above others. Obviously, it is hard to discuss higher human motivations without considering cognitive and memory processes, and hence learning theory. Indeed, motivation has been the ghostly process that often wreaks havoc with research in learning and memory. Practically every apparent deficit in memory, especially in animal models, could be interpreted as a deficit in motivation. How can we know whether an animal has forgotten something as opposed to having lost the motivation to behave?

Organisms surely will not perform what they have learned if they are not motivated to exhibit what they know. For instance, when learned responses are extinguished, it does not mean that either animals or humans have forgotten previously acquired associations. Often they are no longer motivated to exhibit unrewarding, unrewarded or under-appreciated behaviours, often because of frustration or other negative emotional feelings. And when we include the many unconscious motivations that are not readily visible to our cognitive apparatus, it is understandable that the psychological concept of motivation has had such a mixed and difficult history (see Bolles, 1967).

The psychobiological view of motivations

While motivation is not a unitary process of the mind, the simple motivations that have solid physiological causes, such as thirst and hunger, are much easier to understand scientifically than the subtle ones that arise from our cognitive aspirations. Indeed, we can learn much about those basic human motivations by studying our fellow animals. The shared foundational processes were laid down early in brain evolution – including fundamental processes ranging from fear and anger, to brain sources of separation distress (sadness) and playfulness (social joy).

In this chapter we will focus on the basic emotional systems that have been revealed by cross-species brain research rather than the various systems that mediate our bodily needs, such as hunger and thirst. These deeply *intrinsic* systems have been largely clarified by neuro-behavioural research in other animals, while the more externally directed (*extrinsic*) cognitive-psychological systems with which they interact, remain much easier to study in humans. Both intrinsic and extrinsic control factors are highlighted in Figure 1, which summarises how powerfully rough-and-tumble play in rats (an intrinsic motivation which requires a willing partner) is inhibited by the smell of a cat (an extrinsic factor that operates through an intrinsic fear system), leading to a reappraisal of the environment. Even though only a small sample of cat hair was introduced into the test chamber on a single day, the effects dramatically outlasted that event. Emotional learning (in this case contextual fear conditioning) can be very rapid and robust.

The *intrinsic-extrinsic* dimension of motivational structures has been one that psychologists have discussed for well over a century, with one or the other gaining favour at different times. During the early years when psychology was emerging as a scientific discipline, instinct theories of motivation prevailed. Human instincts, from aggression to shyness, were postulated rather too liberally (McDougall, 1908). This mode of intrinsic theorising was abandoned when investigators realised how circular such ideas were and how little such words, without really defining what they meant in neuropsychological terms, explained in complex creatures such as humans (Beach, 1955). This led to the search for extrinsic and learned causes of behaviour, including motivation, leading to a behaviouristic era where

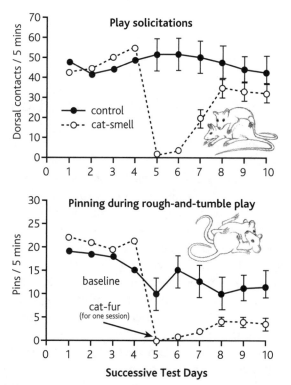

Figure 1 Play: Solicitations and fully-fledged
Following four baseline days of play, cat smell was introduced into the play chamber for a single test day (i.e. during a standard five-minute play session). Although the chamber had no cat smell on all subsequent days, play solicitations (i.e. dorsal contacts, top graph with target behaviour indicated) were markedly reduced for three days, while pinning (i.e. bottom graph, with target behaviour indicated) was reduced for all five subsequent days. The control group (solid lines) was not exposed to any cat smell. Data are means and plus and minus standard errors of the mean. The figure is from *Affective Neuroscience* (Panksepp, 1998, reproduced with permission).

many internal processes were denied recognition as sources of behavioural control. However, after a few generations of focus on stimulus-response associationism (the 'behaviourist revolution') followed subsequently by a focus on the cognitive controls of human behaviour (the 'cognitive revolution'), a dissatisfaction emerged with a psychology that did not wish to consider the deeper inner causes, leading to another intellectual backlash (the 'affect revolution') which is currently bringing basic motivational and emotional concepts back to the foreground of psychological thinking.

One of the most productive ways to envision emotional urgency (for instance the desire to play and to easily become scared, as depicted in Figure 1), is to conceptualise the kinds of 'instinctual' *brain systems* evolution provided organisms as basic tools for learning, and to figure out how they operate. In sum, all of the above schools of thought have considerable utility, and they must eventually be blended if we aspire to understand the whole person or the whole organism.

The hierarchical view of motivations

Now, after 30 years of the cognitive revolution during which the study of the many intrinsic motivational and emotional aspects of organisms was neglected, we are entering an era of a full bio-psychosocial synthesis, where psychologists aspire to blend all relevant levels of analysis. We all recognise that the body has a host of behavioural processes that are essential for the harvesting of environmental resources. We recognise that many animals, especially humans, have complex symbolic capacities, which enable the construction of vast cognitive structures that permit us to intend to behave in a large variety of ways. And we no longer neglect the evolutionarily based systems of the brain upon which all bodily survival is premised, ranging from the brain's ability to monitor how much water and metabolically useable energy is contained in our bodies (e.g., core thirst and hunger systems) to how much the social environment is supporting our emotional feelings (e.g., basic sadness and social joy systems of the brain). Of course, these genetically ingrained emotional and motivational systems can only carry out their evolutionarily appointed functions in the context of relevant environments. It is very hard to socially play with oneself. The evolutionary mandate is that we do it with a willing other. This is why we cannot tickle ourselves.

Indeed, the acceptance of a multi-layered hierarchy of motivations was built into the most influential view of motivation ever offered by a psychologist, namely Abraham Maslow's (1970) *hierarchy of needs* (see Chapter 13, this volume). This view systematised the idea that as we fulfill basic needs (such as keeping body temperature within certain limits) we open up possibilities for fulfilling more complex desires. Maslow's 5-tiered conceptualisation, included: 1) physiological/bodily needs at the bottom, followed by 2) our need for safety, 3) belongingness and love, 4) self-esteem and achievement near the top, all of which permits 5) self-actualisation – aspirations to achieve our highest potential. The higher motivational structures could only prevail if the lower ones had first been satisfied.

Unfortunately, this conceptual scheme did not promote much research, partly because it failed to fully recognise that all of the first three items were of such fundamental importance that they could not really be understood without brain research on the nature of our core affect systems, most of which emerged early in brain evolution. Regrettably, for most of the twentieth century, psychologists were not especially interested in studying the brain – the primary organ of the mind. This has changed dramatically because of the emergence of modern brain imaging technologies (Murphy *et al.*, 2003; Phan *et al.*, 2002).

For present purposes, we will discuss motivation in terms of this two-tiered approach, which breaks down into: 1) the motivations that emerge from our basic affective structures which we share in remarkably similar brain ways with other mammals, and 2) those which reflect our cognitive nature, where we recognise ourselves as agents who wish to fit in positively within certain social structures and who typically wish to excel within those structures. The psychological representatives for the first category are the basic feeling states that we can experience, from irritable anger to panicky loneliness, along with their simple learning tendencies (i.e. classical and instrumental conditioning). The psychological representatives for the second category are the more complex cognitive structures that must include concepts such as *imagination*, whose conceptual products are subsumed by the term *creativity*, and whose actualised products are brought into the world through *ambition* and *dedication* to sustained practice and personal work.

Of course, more biological information is available about the first set of factors because they can be studied in detail in other animals. However, people are commonly more intensely interested in the latter, because these concerns seem closer to their mental aspirations. A tension between these approaches is also evident in the emergence of the new discipline known as evolutionary psychology, which seeks intrinsic cognitive-type motivational systems in the higher regions of the human brain (i.e. our massive cortical 'thinking cap' that mushroomed dramatically several million to several hundred thousand years ago, giving us the facility of language), while typically neglecting what we already know about the sub-neocortical motivational systems we share with other animals (see Box 10.2). Since a lasting science of cognitive motivations must be built on a solid science of affective motivations, the present coverage will focus on the core emotional processes that serve as motives for many of our cognitive deliberations (i.e. thoughts).

One of the most robust intellectual movements in psychology during the past two decades that is relevant to our understanding of motivated behaviour is the evolutionary psychology tradition that emerged in social psychology (Barkow *et al.*, 1992). To some extent this movement has been dissociated from the neuroscientific and biological understanding of basic emotions and motivations, and it has made many of the mistakes that are common when one tries to 're-invent the wheel'. It has been postulating evolved specialisations for motivated cognitive activities in the absence of any credible evidence for such specialised 'modules' existing in the brain (Panksepp & Panksepp, 2000), highlighting once more the conceptual problems that may emerge when psychologists do not connect their thinking to evidence already available from other scientific approaches. Each of the three 'classic' discoveries of evolutionary psychology, can be readily understood from the perspective of a multi-tiered, biologically based emotional/motivational analysis:

- A *cheater detection module* was postulated by Cosmides and Tooby (1992) on the basis of clever experiments indicating that certain logical inferences which most people find very difficult to make correctly as a bare-bones logical problem, are easy to solve when re-cast in real-life terms involving people attempting to fool other people. This clever line of evidence, suggesting that people easily solve problems when they have something to lose as opposed to when they do not, suggests our cognitive apparatus has specialised abilities to identify those who attempt to fool us. Of course, the alternative is that when we experience negative affect in a social interaction, as would occur if we are cheated, then our general purpose cognitive apparatus is influenced by motivational 'energies' that help us focus clearly on the details of a specific cognitive problem.

- Another key concept is that we have *mate selection modules*. Males tend to focus on the desirability of youth and beauty (as markers of reproductive fitness), while females tend to focus on the desirability of having a rich mate who is willing to share their riches (as markers of capacity and willingness to invest in rearing a family) (Buss, 1999). Of course, both of these may again simply reflect learned strategies based on the different emotional strengths and weaknesses of males and females. Male sexual feelings are rapidly aroused, which would tend to focus the males' attention to signs of sexual attractiveness. Female arousal is slower and less predictable, which would allow more deliberation over other issues that are relevant in establishing long-term relationships that could be costly (i.e. lead to pregnancy) and lead to other difficulties unless the male was sincerely committed to participating in rearing a family. Although one could postulate that males and females have evolutionarily determined cognitive modules for these choices, in the absence of evidence, it is just as easy to postulate that learned cognitive strategies could easily emerge from the different erotic tendencies of males and females.

- A third classic finding is that humans have *kin selection modules*. Parents are much more likely to exhibit aggressive behaviours (child abuse) toward step-children than their own biological offspring (Daly & Wilson, 1988), leading to the possibility that people have evolutionarily pre-disposed cognitive mechanisms to reduce harm to their close genetic kin than toward those with whom they do not share as much genetic material. Although the basic data on which this argument is premised is quite robust, there are obvious alternative explanations. Stronger social attachments, as would occur when parents have nurtured a child from birth, produce strong anti-aggressive neurochemical responses than would be possible for a new parental unit that joins an established parent-child unit. It is well established that brain chemicals such as opioids and oxytocin are strong inhibitors of aggression, and it is possible that such primitive emotional influences strongly limit the amount of aggression exhibited while caring for our own biological children. A new adult entering an established family structure would not have the same neurochemically-based social bonding safeguards.

These examples highlight some important motivational findings from evolutionary psychology (i.e. the results are not in dispute), but also indicate that in science every finding has multiple interpretations. Generally scientists believe that a more simple explanation (one that is *parsimonious*) is better than a more complex one. Thus, when a variety of relevant emotional findings have been established in lower animals, it is not necessary to seek more complex interpretations for human behaviour, such as the evolution of specialised cognitive modules. This does not mean that the more complex interpretation, such as the emergence of a specialised *cognitive module*, is necessarily wrong, but that it is the responsibility of investigators who advance such ideas to provide an extra measure of evidence that such complex genetically-controlled brain mechanisms do exist and that the findings cannot be explained in simpler ways.

A taxonomy of core bodily and emotional needs

Affective states are the various ways we can feel. There are a large number of basic feelings, but they tend to fall into three natural categories: 1) There are those that reflect the basic bodily needs that are essential for survival. The main ones include the need to breathe (suffocation), the need for maintaining body water balance (thirst), body temperature balance (feelings of cold and overheating) and energy needs (hunger). Generally, when these bodily needs are being restored, we feel pleasure and when they are taken farther away from the stable (*homeostatic*) bodily level, we experience displeasure. Some of the pleasures are very distinct, such as the large number of smells and tastes that indicate whether the substance may be good or bad for our bodies. 2) As bodily needs are satisfied, background feelings emerge that generally do not have clear psychological labels, but are typically background feelings such as satisfactions and feelings of relaxation and being at peace. And, 3) there are a large number of basic emotional feelings that are not directly linked to bodily needs but more to emotional issues about which both humans and animals feel strongly because they are needed for safety and survival, and to assure social support and social continuity. Since this is such an important set of brain processes for understanding mental life as well as psychiatric disorders (Panksepp, 2004), let us first consider the main systems and then select a few for more detailed coverage.

The core emotional systems allow organisms generate adaptive instinctual behaviours during various life-challenging situations. Thus, all mammals, including humans, have brain systems for:

- becoming angry if access to resources are thwarted (a *rage* system);
- becoming scared when bodily well-being is threatened (a *fear* system);
- sexual desires that are somewhat different in males and females (*lust* systems);
- urges to exhibit loving attention toward our offspring (a *care* system);
- feelings of separation distress when we have lost contact with loved ones (a *panic* system);
- the boisterous joyousness of rough and tumble playfulness (a *play* system); and
- exploratory activity directed at searching and foraging for resources (a *seeking* system).

In the above scheme (Panksepp, 1982, 1998), italicised labels are used to highlight that we presently only have preliminary knowledge about the psychobiological details of these systems, especially in humans, and thereby hopefully to minimise part-whole confusions (i.e. one slice does not make a pie). Currently, psychobiological studies using various animal models provide the most robust causal strategies to identify brain mechanisms that generate the basic affects that all mammals share as an evolutionary heritage, and hence which also must exist in humans, even though good evidence is scarce for our own species. Good human research on such brain systems is almost impossible to do, at least ethically.

Each emotional response is manifested through characteristic action patterns, with various brain characteristics and psychological dimensions that reflect the dynamics of the associated feelings (see Box 10.3). There has been considerable historical resistance in psychology to considering that there exist any emotion-specific localisation of functions within the human brain. However, all of the above emotions can be provoked by electrically stimulating specific circuits in sub-cortical regions of the animal brain, which highlights their intrinsic nature. There is also sufficient human data that emotional feelings are aroused by such localised stimulation (Heath, 1996; Panksepp, 1985). Of course, these 'trigger spots' activate many higher areas of the brain that also become aroused when human brains get emotional (Murphy *et al.*, 2003; Phan *et al.*, 2002). The animal data highlights the fact that there are evolutionarily created underlying operating systems for certain emotions in primitive sub-cortical limbic areas of all mammalian brains. If there are 'neurochemical codes' for these systems, as the animal data now indicates, then there are a large number of new targets for psychiatric medicine development (Panksepp & Harro, 2004).

10.3 DEFINITIONS AND DIMENSIONAL THEORIES OF EMOTIONS

One of the most famous psychological definitions of emotions was provided by Kleinginna and Kleinginna (1981:355), where they argued that: 'a formal definition of emotion should be broad enough to include all traditionally significant aspects of emotion, while attempting to differentiate it from other psychological processes.' After an extensive discussion of over 200 past definitions, and related controversies in the literature, they suggest the following working definition: 'Emotion is a complex set of interactions among subjective and objective factors, mediated by neural/hormonal systems, which can (a) give rise to affective experiences such as feelings of arousal, pleasure/displeasure; (b) generate cognitive processes such as emotionally relevant perceptual effects, appraisals, labeling processes; (c) activate widespread physiological adjustments to the arousing conditions; and (d) lead to behavior that is often, but not always, expressive, goal-directed, and adaptive.' The emotional systems discussed here have been conceptualised to have neuronal properties that fit all of these criteria (Panksepp, 1982).

It should also be noted that each of the emotional processes have certain energetic *dimensions*, and often psychologists seem to think these dimensions are the primary aspects from which the more basic concepts are constructed (Russell, 2003). However, it is just as reasonable to simply envision that every basic affect has each of these three dimensions. They traditionally include the *valence* of a feeling – how it is positive (feels good) or negative (feels bad). The next most salient dimension is *activation* level, since one can feel either more or less aroused/invigorated or relaxed/sleepy during each affective state. Finally there is a more subtle dimension that has been called *potency* (also at times called *power* or *surgency*) which essentially reflects how large or small a feeling seems to be in filling one's mental space. Although the use of dimensional approaches to study animal emotions (e.g., Rolls, 1999) is less common than the more categorical basic systems approach (Panksepp, 1998), recent work on self-report measures that utilise various natural emotional vocalisations that animals readily make, has found simple dimensional schemes useful (Knutson *et al.*, 2002).

The localisation of motivational functions in the brain

Although emotions are broadcast widely in the brain, there are some highly specific neurochemical controls for specific emotional and other motivational tendencies in the brain. This goes against a great deal of received 'wisdom' from behavioural and cognitive science, where practically everything in the mind was constructed by experience. It is consistent with more recent evolutionary views (see Box 10.3), but it is worth pausing to reflect why there has been such a resistance in psychology to envisioning *intrinsic*, albeit experientially refined, mental specialisations within the brain.

Ever since the nineteenth century, there has been a heated debate among investigators of mind-brain relations: Are psychological processes organised diffusely in the brain (the equipotentiality view that any given brain area can support any of a large variety of functions), or are psychological processes organised in specific areas of the brain (the localisationist view, that specific psychological abilities are elaborated by distinct parts of the brain)?

The equipotentiality view long had a certain socio-political appeal, especially among the new breed of free-thinkers who brought their vibrant views of human nature to center stage during the fast-paced social change of the eighteenth century, culminating in the American and French revolutions. The central ideas of those revolutions were 'all men are created equal' and 'liberty, fraternity and equality'. With such rallying cries, they helped destroy the longstanding tyrannies that had arisen from the concept of 'royal blood' – the self-gratifying idea that some had God-given rights to lord it over others while others had the obligation to serve. One way the democracy-entranced revolutionaries several hundred years ago sought to destroy the dubious claims of royalty was to assume that all people started with the same potentials, and that all subsequent differences were learned. Hence, if we could change the environment we could change the people of the world. Give everyone an equal chance at a quality education, and all can rise to the top. Through this early version of 'political correctness', humanists sought to change social institutions so that all individuals could be brought to similar high standards of daily existence. Indeed, considerable evidence supports the view that humans do have exquisitely malleable and plastic brain structures, especially in our mushrooming 'thinking cap' of neocortex (Panksepp & Panksepp, 2000), but now we also know that these functions are built upon highly specialised lower brain structures (Panksepp, 1998), and that there are powerful biological constraints over the human spirit (Konner, 1982).

The neuroanatomical version of this debate revolved around the claims that specific psychological functions are elaborated by specific parts of the brain versus the view that the brain was an equipotential tissue in which various functions were evenly spread through a homogeneous substance resembling a blank slate (or *tabula rasa* as John Locke, the renowned British philosopher (1632-1704) called it). This view prevailed through most of twentieth century behavioural and cognitive psychologies.

During the past few decades, most have come to realise that the localisationist perspective to brain function is certainly as close to the truth as any other view. However, this conclusion can only be asserted with the recognition that what is localised in neuronal circuits is the potential for certain types of cognitive and emotional activities. All the specific details of life are learned. What is inherited are specialised tools (I like to call them 'gifts of nature') for allowing us to feel, behave and think in various ways, while all of our individual memories and refined skills are learned. This new, data-supported view, forces us to confront one of the greatest unresolved problems of psychology, namely, what are the natural inherited functions of the brain? Only when we understand what is inherited can we fully understand why and how things are learned (see Boxes 10.1 and 10.2).

We can be sure that there are various types of attentional dispositions, special abilities for generating specific types of memories (e.g., spatial navigation), and many specific emotions and motivations. With regard to the issue of 'royal blood' raised above, we can be quite certain that dominance (power) urges are a natural function of the brain, especially the male brain 'fueled' by high levels of testosterone. People have a natural tendency to assert their influence so as to gain an advantage in the competition for available resources, and this often requires being more pushy, aggressive, intimidating and powerfully 'royal' than the next fellow. Conversely, we also know that humans can be nurturing and helpful and, as we will see, such tendencies are facilitated very much by female-specific patterns of neurochemical change that promote feelings of maternal care at the end of pregnancy.

We now know a great deal about how specific emotions are elaborated by anatomical and chemical processes in animal brains, and many investigators now agree that those findings are relevant for understanding the human condition as well. For instance, as we shall see, the neuropeptides vasopressin and oxytocin have been implicated in the control of human sexuality (mainly male and female, respectively), and even though we cannot monitor release of these substances within human brain circuits, they can be monitored in the blood-

stream (since they are also circulating hormones released from the pituitary). Just as would be expected from the animal data, vasopressin is released during the initial appetitive phase of male sexual arousal, while oxytocin, the more female principle, is released, even in males, during the consummatory pleasure, or orgasmic, phase of the sex cycle (Figure 2).

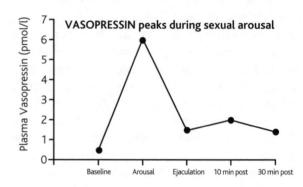

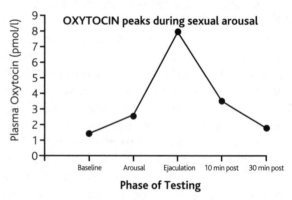

Figure 2 The varieties of love and lust
Effects of masturbatory sexual arousal, ejaculation and various post-ejaculatory intervals on average plasma oxytocin and vasopressin levels in human males. Data adapted from Murphy *et al.* (1990). Figure from *Affective Neuroscience* (Panksepp, 1998, reprinted with permission).

Of course, the study of the sources of the basic animal emotions and motivations only provide general principles for understanding fundamental human issues. Such research has little chance of clarifying the details of individual human beings. We can make more choices than any other creature on the face of the earth. No matter how well general principles of core emotions and motivations translate across species, the detailed expressions of those principles will vary widely from one individual to another. Each of the evolutionarily provided psychological tools that evolution has created in brains is subject to genetic selection, and hence a considerable degree of intrinsic biological variability. Modern research, based on evolutionary principles, is recognising that the core affective/emotional states are very similar in animals and humans, even though humans can re-symbolise these states into higher cognitive structures that construct more subtle higher motivational structures (e.g., self-actualisation). We can regulate the motivational dictates of these systems with our higher mental processes. Most other animals cannot. They apparently have less of that subtle and mysterious process called free will, which is generated by our capacity to enjoy conscious self-awareness and reflection.

Seven core emotional systems and related motivational structures

Let us now consider the core emotional systems shared by all mammals that are important for some of the basic human motivations. The details of these systems will not be discussed, but have been extensively explored in animal models (Panksepp, 1998):

- The world has abundant dangers, many of which we need to learn about, and others which we intrinsically *fear*. Although the stimuli that provoke fearfulness in different species are often different (e.g., darkness in humans and light in rats; we like cats, but rats have an intrinsic fear of cat smells), the core structures of the *fear* system are remarkably similar across all mammalian species. Neuroscientists have unraveled the details of the brain circuitry that mediate some fears, and many have focused on information that enters the *fear* system via so called 'high-roads' (more cognitive-perceptual inputs to sub-cortical brain areas such as the amygdala), and via the so-called 'low-road', the more primitive sensory inputs to the same brain regions, from which descends what might be called the 'Royal Road' – the evolved *fear* system itself, which governs the instinctual action apparatus that intrinsically helps animals avoid danger (Panksepp, 1998). There may be several distinct anxiety systems in the brain, but the *fear* one appears to be the one that is inhibited by modern anti-anxiety drugs that are used clinically in humans. These same drugs reduce the affective-motivational impact of fearful stimuli and situations in animals, and there are many new anxiety-generating neuropeptide chemistries that have been identified in animal brains (Panksepp, 2004).

- Fear is commonly evoked by the anger and threats of other, bigger and stronger people and wild animals. Where does anger come from? It is commonly aroused by frustration and the inability to behave freely. An easy way to make babies angry, to arouse their *rage* system, is by restraining their free movements. Likewise, if adults do not get what they want, they are likely to become enraged. Of course adults can modulate their anger in ways that children and animals cannot. Just like every sub-cortical emotional system, higher cortico-cognitive ones are able to provide inhibition, guidance and other forms of emotional regulation. Psychiatry presently has no psychotropic medications that can specifically control pathological anger, but the neuroscientific analysis of *rage* circuitry in animal brains may eventually yield such tools.

- Where would we mammals be if we did not have brain systems to feel *lust* for each other? Male and female sexual systems are laid down early in development, while babies are still gestating, but they are not brought fully into action until puberty, when the maturing gonadal hormone systems begin to spawn male and female sexual desires. However, because of the way the brain and body get organised, female-type desires can exist in male brains, and male-type desires can exist in female brains (see Pfaff, 1999). Of course, learning and culture persistently add layers of control and complexity that cannot be disentangled by neuroscience.

- Where would we mammals be if we did not have brain systems to take *care* of each other? Extinct. The maternal instinct, so rich in every species of mammal (and bird too), allows us to propagate effectively down generations. To have left this to chance, or the vagaries of individual learning, would have assured the end of our line of ascent. These hormonally governed urges, still present in humans, have produced a sea-change in the way we respond to newborn babies. The changing tides of peripheral estrogen, progesterone, prolactin and brain oxytocin figure heavily in the transformation of a virgin female brain into a fully maternal state (see Numan & Insel, 2003). Because males and females have such large differences in these brain and body systems, males require more emotional education to become fully motivated, and hence engaged, care takers.

- When young children get lost, they are thrown into a *panic*. They cry out for care, and their feelings of sudden aloneness and distress may reflect the ancestral codes upon which adult sadness and grief are built. A critical brain system is that which yields separation distress calls (crying) in all mammalian species. Brain chemistries that exacerbate feelings of distress (e.g., Corticotrophin Releasing Factor) and those that powerfully alleviate distress (e.g., brain opioids, oxytocin and prolactin) are the ones that figure heavily in the genesis of social attachments and probably amelioration of depression (Nelson & Panksepp, 1998). These are the chemistries that can assist or defeat us in our desire to create inter-subjective spaces with others, where we can learn the emotional ways of our kind.

- Young animals *play* with each other when they feel safe (see Figure 1), in order to navigate social possibilities in joyous ways. The urge to play was also not left to chance by evolution, but is built into the instinctual action apparatus of the mammalian brain. We know less about this emotional system than any other, partly because so few are willing to recognise that such gifts could be derived as much from mother nature as our kindest nurturer. It is even harder to conceive that such systems can even promote a joyous 'laughter' in other species (Panksepp & Burgdorf, 2003). But these are 'experience expectant' systems that bring young animals to the perimeter of their social knowledge, to psychic places where they must pause to contemplate what can or cannot be done to others. Human children that are not allowed safe places to exercise their ludic energies – these urges for rough-and-tumble engagement – may express such ancient urges in situations where they should not. To be too impulsive within the classroom is to increase the likelihood of being labeled as a troublemaker (e.g., with Attention Deficit Hyperactivity Disorder (ADHD)) who can be quieted with anti-play drugs (i.e. all the psychostimulants currently used to treat ADHD). Perhaps it would be wiser to entertain the idea that many of these children, especially when they are very young, would find better benefits from extra rations of rough-and-tumble activities each and every day.
- A remarkable system that has emerged from brain research is one that mediates the appetitive desire to find and harvest the fruits of the world. The chosen label for this general-purpose desire network was the *seeking* system. Animals 'love' to self-activate – to self-stimulate – this system in addictive ways. Indeed, because of the remarkable evolutionary neural similarities of such systems, all other mammals are attracted to the

drugs that humans commonly overuse and abuse, and they also generally dislike similar drug-induced experiences (Panksepp *et al.*, 2002). For decades, the *seeking* system was considered to be a reward-pleasure system, but it is now generally agreed that it is better conceptualised as a basic, positively motivated action system that helps mediate our desires, our foraging and our positive expectancies about the world, rather than the behaviouristic concept of 'reinforcement' (for a summary see Panksepp & Moskal, 2004). This system is presently being intensively studied in animals as a general purpose learning system, since it is essential for animals to pursue all the fruits of their environment, including the satisfactions to be had through the emotional systems already discussed – such as the seeking of safety when one is scared or seeking retribution when one is angry. This system can even energise dreams (Solms, 2000). The fact that this system can be used for so many seemingly distinct motivations, operating in both positive and negative emotional situations, has been a difficult finding for psychology to assimilate, and it is a reasonable way for evolution to have constructed a general purpose motivational urge that is needed in many situations, helping maintain a fluidity in behaviour as well as the operations of the cognitive apparatus (Ikemoto & Panksepp, 1999).

In addition, there are well-studied brain systems for various homeostatic bodily needs (hunger, thirst, etc.) that interface with the world through the *seeking* system that will not be discussed here. All these systems interact with higher cognitive processes, but much more research will be needed before we understand those emotion-cognition interactions at a neural level. However, just from a psychological analysis we can expect that much of what we do cognitively is based on how we feel emotionally. Even our will-power may be substantially a part of our affect-guided decision-making apparatus. When we actively try to reign in our passions, our restraint may itself be motivated by affect. For instance, our tendency to hold off smacking someone when we are angry may be largely premised on our cognitive ability to avoid the negative affect that may arise from being attacked in return, or socially excluded from future activities or even legally charged with assault. The reason we may avoid eating the whole carton of just-opened ice-cream is because we know it may make us feel ill or perhaps make us feel guilt, shame, and embarrassment at putting ourselves at risk of becoming overweight and another coronary statistic.

Because of the limited space available, we will not discuss such emotion-cognition interactions, but just focus on the basics of three of the above social emotional-motivational systems, including:

- the *lust* systems that regulate sexual urgency;
- the maternal *care* system; and
- the one that generates the *panic* of separation distress, which motivates social bonding.

A focus on these three social systems should provide a flavour of how basic emotional/motivational systems have been discovered and studied. Details for each are available in Panksepp (1998). This selective focus does not mean that most human motivations are not highly cognitivised and concerned with complex social and economic issues. They are. For instance, for the first topic, sexuality, our real-life concerns often focus on: How does one begin to feel about sex if children are unwanted? If one desires abortions? If one has AIDS? Neuroscience has little to say directly about such social concerns, but at the same time they would usually not be pressing issues if we did not have powerful motivational forces in our minds and bodies. Here, we will restrict our focus to those deep psychobiological forces rather than socio-cultural concerns.

Brain control of sexuality

Animal brain research has indicated that the male and female poles of sexuality reflect two extremes of a gradient that readily allows for various intermediary variants. In other words, although the basic circuits for male and female sexuality are distinct to a substantial extent, male-typical *lust* circuits can exist in female brains, and female-typical *lust* circuits can exist in male brains. This, along with our capacity to choose, allows sexual urges to become quite complicated in the real world.

In simplest terms, the biological side of the story goes like this (Pfaff, 1999): Although one is typically born either genetically female (with the XX pattern of sex chromosomes) or genetically male (with the XY pattern), the actual manner in which brain and body development proceeds is determined by hormonal organisational signals which control development while the baby is still in the womb. The same principles operate in humans and other animals. The major variants are fourfold. In addition to male

brains within male bodies and female brains within female bodies, nature can promote male-typical erotic urges within the body of a woman and female-typical erotic urges within the body of a man. The essential accuracy of this view has been affirmed by years of scientific research on the nature of sex-circuits within animal brains.

The fact that individuals who look like men on the outside can come to feel like women on the inside, and people in women's bodies can come to feel like men, can emerge from a well established biological fact: certain areas in male and female brains are differently organised before birth. Thus, not only are the bodies of boys and girls different, but so are their brains, and distinct biochemical signals trigger babies' brains and babies' bodies to take their respective gender-characteristic paths.

The signal that typically tells the developing *bodies* of young mammals to masculinise is a metabolic derivative of testosterone called dihydrotestosterone, while the signal which tells their *brain* to become masculinised is estrogen (which is also derived from testosterone, but through a different metabolic step called aromatisation). Thus, if a female brain is exposed to too much testosterone (or its metabolic end-product, estrogen) during the sensitive periods of development (the precise time varies from species to species), initially female brains will assume male-like characteristics while leaving the body feminine. Conversely, in the absence of either testosterone or estrogen, but in the presence of sufficient dihydrotestosterone, an evidently male body can come to contain a female-type brain, which would *promote* a homosexual type of gender identity at maturity. Although nature is strongly disposed toward creating relatively clear-cut male within male and female within female brain-body forms, it is biologically possible to have many gradations between the traditional poles of maleness and femaleness.

Thus, gender choice is not just a matter of cultural and early learning influences, as many psychologists used to believe, but also a matter rooted heavily in biology. Although it would be foolish to conclude that gender identity is controlled completely by biology, we now know how things can get quite mixed up within the brain. Indeed, if mothers are heavily stressed during pregnancy, it can set in motion internal biochemical changes that tend to leave the brains of their sons in a feminised form. Such effects of stress have been intensively studied in animal models. If rat mothers are exposed to excessive stress during their third trimester (i.e. the last week of their three-week gestation period), their male offspring are typically homosexual or bisexual, since the timing and strength of organisational processes was disrupted. Basically, the timed release of testosterone and related biochemical processes such as the production of aromatisation enzymes (both of which help masculinise the brain) are thrown off, and male brains tend to retain female-like characteristics. That this also happens to humans during stress has even been documented historically: There was a higher than expected incidence of homosexual males born during the period 1943 to 1945 in East Germany (when that country was losing World War Two) than either before or after the war.

However, the adult consequences of such brain *organisational* effects need to be brought out by the *activational* effects of adult gonadal hormones. The distinctions between the organisational and activational components of sexual development have clarified our understanding of what it means to be biologically eroticised in male and female ways. A photographic analogy helps us image the two processes. The hormones secreted during fetal development help 'expose' the brain and body as male or female, while the hormones secreted at the onset of puberty eventually 'develop' the exposed negative, thereby activating the latent male or female sexual tendencies that had been laid down within their brain circuits when they were new-born babies. In short, if brain and body organisational signals do not match up, the individual will have to discover, through experience, which gender was predominantly imprinted within their brains.

The details of the *activational* brain changes are also well documented in animals, and the brain chemistries that promote adult male sexual urges (for instance, vasopressin in the anterior hypothalamus) are activated by testosterone, and those that are more influential in mature female sexual urges (for instance, oxytocin in the medial hypothalamus) are activated by estrogen. However, oxytocin also promotes male orgasms (see Figure 2). There is a certain beauty in the fact that oxytocin is an especially important player in the terminal orgasmic components of male sexual behaviour, for it may allow the sexes to better understand each other. Indeed, sexual activity can invigorate this chemical system in the male brain which may then help promote nurturing and non-aggressive behaviours later in life.

While oxytocin has a comparatively limited role in the control of male sexuality, in females oxytocin is important throughout both the courting and copulatory phases of sexual behaviour. Do these same systems also participate in human sexuality? There is abundant evidence that they do (see Figure 2), but of course, we have much more behavioural flexibility than rats because the power of our cognitive habits can sustain sexual motivation when hormonal supports have weakened. These same chemistries are re-utilised in nearby brain areas to construct circuits via which parents become intrinsically motivated to take care of their offspring. As we will see, oxytocin and vasopressin help establish attachment bonds between mother and child, and to cement adult friendships.

Care circuits for parental behaviours

Hormonal changes which herald birth prepare the mother to exhibit maternal behaviour several days before the actual birth. Human mothers commonly exhibit a compulsive flurry of house-preparation several days before the baby is due, and rat mothers begin to build nests and become substantially more eager to interact with baby rats. This heightened maternal desire corresponds to the time when three characteristic hormone changes are beginning to occur. Estrogen, which has remained at modest levels throughout pregnancy, is rapidly increasing. Progesterone, which has been high through pregnancy, is beginning to plummet. And, of course, there has been a rise in prolactin to encourage breast tissues to manufacture milk. If we produce this pattern of hormone change via injection, we can artificially instigate maternal urges in virgin rats. This is partly because oxytocin systems of the brain are strengthened. If brain oxytocin systems are blocked at the onset of the first birth, maternal behaviour, at least in rats, is weak and inconsistent. If all the conditions are right, oxytocin administered right into the brain is quite effective in evoking maternal behaviour in virgin females, but it is certainly not the only necessary ingredient. For instance, administration of prolactin into the brain (a hormone which instigates the manufacture of milk within breast tissue) also facilitates maternal tendencies. This is because certain brain circuits exist in these brain regions that use prolactin to instigate specific kinds of emotional tendencies. There is a great deal of chemical coding (usually via neuropeptides, short chains of amino acids, such as the ones just discussed).

It must be emphasised that well established maternal behaviour no longer requires oxytocin, even in rats. Once the mother rat has had several days of maternal experience, blocking this neuro-chemical system no longer impairs the desire to act maternally. This demonstrates that the learning which transpires from the activity of an intrinsic brain operating system rapidly becomes functional-ly autonomous, that is, it becomes partly independ-ent of the system that initially got the ball rolling in the first place, just as we saw for human sexual behaviour. Of course humans are smart enough to initiate care-giving behaviours completely cogni-tively and instrumentally, but it is unlikely those behaviours will be accompanied by emotional grati-fications of the kind that the ancient care-giving sys-tem of the brain help create in the mind. (Please con-sider this information as well as that in the next sec-tion in the context of coverage of attachment in Chapter 8.)

Brain systems for separation-distress and social bonds

Until recently, we knew nothing about the neuro-chemical nature of social bonds. Even though all of us feel the intensity of our friendships, family attachments, and romantic relationships, there was practically no way of studying how they might be constructed from specific brain activities. Then there were two breakthroughs: 1) the discovery that neu-ral circuits which mediate separation distress – the feeling of being isolated from sources of social sup-port – are under the control of brain opioids (intrin-sic brain neuropeptides that act just like morphine or heroin), and 2) as already discussed, the develop-ing understanding of the oxytocinergic basis of maternal and sexual behaviours. These two lines of inquiry proceeded separately, but are now coming together in interesting ways.

The first neurochemical systems discovered to exert a powerful inhibitory effect on separation dis-tress were brain opioids, neuropeptides that provid-ed a powerful new way for conceptualising social attachments. There are powerful similarities between the dynamics of opiate addiction and social dependence (including addictive, drug tolerance, and withdrawal symptoms), and it is now clear that positive social interactions derive part of their pleas-ure from the release of opioids in the brain. Not only can opioids inhibit feelings of separation distress in young animals, but the opioid systems of young animals are quite active in the midst of rough-and-tumble play. Also, when older animals share friend-

Figure 3 Care and comfort
When held gently in human hands, newborn chicks exhibit a com-fort response consisting of the cessation of vocalisations and eye closure. These effects are attenuated by opiate receptor blockade with naltrexone and amplified by low doses of morphine. Figure from *Affective Neuroscience* (Panksepp, 1998, reprinted with per-mission).

Considering the importance of oxytocin for maternal behaviour, it was of immediate interest to determine if this molecule could also inhibit the negative emotions that arise from separation. Indeed, oxytocin turned out to be an extremely powerful inhibitor of the separation calls, further affirming that social comfort was produced by the same brain chemistries that help mediate mater-nal and sexual behaviours. Also, it is noteworthy that the oxytocin molecule has special properties that help increase the sensitivity of the brain opioid-induced feelings of pleasure. Perhaps the secretion of oxytocin in nursing animals blocks opioid tolerance, and thus provides a way for the maternal experience to sustain social reward on the basis of increased activity of internal opioids within the brain. It would be disastrous if mothers lost their ability to experience intense social reward when children were still quite young.

ly time grooming each other, their brain opioid sys-tems become especially active. The pleasure of touch is partly due to the release of opioids in the brain (see Figure 3). Similarly, sexual gratification is, at least in part, due to opioid release within the brain. From all this, it is tempting to hypothesise that one reason certain people become addicted to opiates is because they are able to replace with drugs the pos-itive feelings that are normally derived from social interactions. Indeed, opiate addiction in humans is most common in environments where social isola-tion and alienation, and other kinds of psychological pain, are endemic. We can also increase opiate con-sumption in animals simply by separating them from companionship. Recently it has been demon-strated that human sadness is accompanied by reduced brain opioid activity (Zubieta *et al.*, 2003). In sum, it is now clear that positive social emotions and social bonds are to some extent mediated by opiate-based addictive processes in the brain, and addicts often take these molecules just to feel emotionally normal. But opiates also mediate the pleasure of other rewards such as food and drink.

At the present time, oxytocin and opioid systems appear to be prime movers in the construction and maintenance of social bonds. Indeed, animals prefer to spend more time with other animals in whose presence they have received infusions of oxytocin or opiates into the brain. Similarly, males exhibit preferences for females in whose presence they received vasopressin infusions. It seems almost as if friendships are cemented by the same chemical systems which mediate maternal urges. Perhaps this is one of the primitive emotional reasons we are more likely to help family and friends than strangers (see Box 10.2). Not only do we feel better about them than strangers, but we also have their faces and voices and ways of being engraved in our memories, partly because neurohormones such as oxytocin solidify social memories.

There is a final piece to the social puzzle that is worth sharing. The chemistries that promote pleasure and family values, are also ones which reduce irritability and aggressiveness. It has long been known that human societies which encourage touching and the free flow of intimacy are among the least aggressive in the world. This, of course, makes a great deal of evolutionary sense. If you are well satisfied, there is little reason to fight. However trite this may sound, the principle is supported by brain research: Both opioids and oxytocin (but not the male sexual urge facilitator vasopressin) are powerful anti-aggressive molecules.

Do such findings have implications for understanding social dynamics in human societies? Surely they do, but that will be very hard to demonstrate. What has been found, however, is that horrible tendencies (such a child abuse) are related to the degree of relatedness among individuals (see Box 10.2). Parents are generally much less likely to abuse their children than more distant relatives, and 'strangers' such as baby-sitters and new mates in reconstructed families, are more likely than biological kin to be individuals who indulge in child abuse. In other words, as the degree of social bonding diminishes, the probability of violence toward others increases, and generally more so in males than females. Perhaps this principle even extends to the types of interactions that can exist among societies. Would social policies that promote bonding between diverse social groups decrease the amount of aggression in our world?

The implications of these neurochemical findings are profound. They demonstrate not only the subtle tinkering ways of evolution, but also indicate how complex behaviours are controlled by ancient neural systems we still share with all of our fellow mammals. These findings also provide a dramatic example of the pervasive interactions of nature and nurture. Maternal behaviour and sexuality can become habits, which, through experience, become partially independent of the primitive motivational substrates from which they were initially constructed. The data suggest how basic 'family values', and perhaps even 'love', are constructed within the brain. Tender loving care of their pups by rat mothers has life-long consequences for the emotional vigour of their offspring (Meaney, 2001), which highlights a general principle that is emerging. Life experiences have lasting effects on the basic circuits that control our emotions and motivations, making better emotional education in societies a matter of foremost concern (Panksepp, 2001).

On the importance of affective processes in motivation

The central importance of affect in our mental lives is finally being recognised in psychology (Russell, 2003), and more and more investigators are beginning to accept (and sometimes explicitly acknowledge) that this topic simply cannot be adequately understood scientifically without neuroscientific approaches. Conversely, neuroscientists have often also been slow to recognise the importance of mental processes, such as affective feelings, in understanding what the brain does. An understanding of motivation and the brain simply cannot be achieved without a forthright confrontation with basic psychological processes such as affective states. Here is a telling example: Through the careful neurochemical controls of feeding behaviour in animals, researchers have identified dozens of putative 'satiety' agents that effectively reduce eating in animals. Of course, the key question for future medicinal development (i.e. discovery of useful appetite control drugs) is clarification of which of these agents actually reduces the desire to eat because they mimic the nice feeling of being well fed – the natural feeling of satiety.

Researchers who study feeding in animals know that there are many abnormal ways to reduce feeding, the most obvious being making the animal feel sick. This is commonly studied with *conditioned taste aversion* tests, whereby animals learn to avoid foods that have been followed by feelings of malaise or illness (typically experimentally produced by injections of drugs such as lithium chloride that make the animals feel bad). However, animals also show *conditioned satiety* – with plenty of food available, they eat less and less of items that are very concentrated in energy, since normal brains take pains to regulate overall bodily energy balance. One reason some people become obese is because these brain mechanisms for long-term energy regulation are not working properly.

Thus, there need to be better ways to sift those agents that produce natural feelings of satiety from those that may disrupt feeding because they induced various aversive feelings. An ideal solution to this would be to identify some type of positively motivated behaviour that would actually *increase* when animals feel pleasantly satiated. One such behaviour is rough-and-tumble play in young animals. As has long been known, children who are hungry, especially those in the midst of a famine, rarely have the desire to play, and young rats are no different. However, a single satisfying meal brings back the urge to play, which could serve as a motivational marker for a normal satiety, and hence a test to evaluate the true satiating capacity of potential new appetite control agents (Siviy & Panksepp, 1985). Although this test has not been widely used, that only indicates that neuroscientists are lagging behind psychologists in recognising the important role of affective states in governing motivated behaviour.

The one place where they are beginning to recognise affective feelings is in the brain mechanisms that generate drug addictions: One of the most striking discoveries in addiction research has been that other animals enjoy the same drugs as humans (Bevins, 2004). This means that we biologically share very similar basic motives. Even crayfish like to return to places where they were injected with cocaine or amphetamine (Panksepp & Huber, 2004). Does this mean that they also have affective experiences, and that these psychological processes emerged very deep in evolutionary time? We do not yet know, but we do now have a more solid scientific understanding of human motivation through the analysis of brain systems that evolution provided each and every organism so that they could spontaneously look after their ancient survival needs. Although there are many differences in the details of these systems, because of many evolutionary divergences, basic principles do remain remarkably similar in all living mammals that have been studied closely (Panksepp, 1998).

As usual, more research will be needed before we really understand how higher human motivations are actually constructed from personal experiences with those powerful and ancient brain mechanisms that allow organisms to feel very strongly about what is happening in their bodies and the world. But we can be sure there is some connection, for when the lower substrates of our emotions and motivations are damaged, then our highest aspirations also tend to dissolve (Watt & Pincus, 2004).

Conclusion

Motivation is a multifaceted process that needs to be broken down into component processes for adequate scientific understanding. There are a large number of basic biological processes, ranging from the brain's ability to detect bodily needs and stressors, to basic emotional processes that include a variety of core social emotions, that need to be studied if we want to understand why people and other organisms do what they do. The complex evolutionary baggage that we all carry with us from an ancestral past cannot be deciphered without a careful study of the motivational structures that we share with the other animals. These foundational processes do not diminish the need to recognise the evolution of more sophisticated cortical-cognitive structures that help parse the many differences and distinctions that exist in the world.

New layers of motivational control have emerged in the human mind. These higher cognitive type motivations are much harder to understand at a biological level, as they create many subtle motivational and personality differences that exist in different humans. Within the hierarchical structures of our brains, there is abundant re-representation of functions permitting increasing flexibility of behaviour. Primitive mind functions may become more subconscious as higher mechanisms take over the outward navigation of behaviour (Freud, 1933; Wegner, 2002). However, this does not mean that those systems do not continue to influence our behaviour.

We can utilise those peri-conscious emotional energies to take us mental spaces of the highest human aspirations. It is certain that human imagination and creativity reflect new qualities of mind, often passionately engaging, that allow us to aspire to levels of self-actualisation that are beyond the ken of other animals. Future work must attempt to reveal how the cognitive apparatus is channeled by such ancient energetic emotional systems that help drive so many of our behaviours. In this chapter we have only passingly focused on how human behaviour patterns can become independent of the primitive neural mechanisms that were necessary for the initial creation of certain basic behavioural tendencies that we share with the other animals.

In short, every felt need of our bodies and every emotional passion of our nervous system, can serve as a basic motivational framework for the emergence of complex cognitive structures that are unique to each person. At the lower levels, a motivational analysis seeks to understand the basic nature of why we do what we do; at higher levels it attempts to clarify our more subtle aspirations. The former level of analysis seeks clarity about that which is biologically *intrinsic* to the organism; the latter seeks to describe how those evolutionarily inbuilt processes interact with the *extrinsic* aspect of the world. The science of psychobiology currently aims to describe those patterns that are sufficiently similar across different individuals and species, so that lasting general principles of organisation may eventually be revealed. Psychology and neuroscience desperately need each other to make such progress.

REFERENCES

Barkow, J.H., Cosmides, L. & Tooby, J. (Eds.) (1992). *The Adapted Mind: Evolutionary psychology and the generation of culture*. New York: Oxford University Press.

Beach, F.A. (1955). The descent of instinct. *Psychological Review*, 62:401-10.

Bevins, R.A. (Ed.) (2004). *50th Nebraska Symposium on Motivation: Motivational factors in the etiology of drug abuse*, Lincoln: Nebraska.

Bolles, R.C. (1967). *Theory of Motivation*. New York: Harper & Row.

Buss, D. (1999). *Evolutionary Psychology*. Boston: Allyn & Bacon.

Cosmides, L. & Tooby, J. (1992). *Cognitive adaptations for social exchange*. In J.H. Barkow, L. Cosmides & J. Tooby (Eds.). The Adapted Mind: Evolutionary psychology and the generation of culture. New York: Oxford University Press.

Daly, M. & Wilson, M. (1988). *Homicide*. New York: A. de Gruyter.

Freud, S. (1933). *New Introductory Lectures on Psycho-analysis*. New York: Carlton House.

Heath, R.G. (1996). *Exploring the Mind-body Relationship*. Baton Rouge, LA: Moran Printing, Inc.

Ikemoto, S. & Panksepp, J. (1999). The role of nucleus accumbens DA in motivated behavior: A unifying interpretation with special reference to reward-seeking. *Brain Research Reviews*, 31:6-41.

Kleinginna, P.R. & Kleinginna, A. (1981). A categorized list of emotion definitions, with suggestions for a consensual definition. *Motivation and Emotion* 5:345-59.

Knutson, B., Burgdorf, J. & Panksepp, J. (2002). Ultrasonic vocalizations as indices of affective states in rats. *Psychological Bulletin*, 128:961-77.

Konner, M. (1982). *The Tangled Wing: Biological constraints on the human spirit*. New York: Hold, Rinehart and Winston.

Maslow, A.H. (1970). *Motivation and Personality* (2nd edition). New York: Harper & Row.

McDougall, W. (1908). *Introduction to Social Psychology*. London: Methuen.

Meaney, M.J. (2001). Maternal care, gene expression, and the transmission of individual differences in stress reactivity across generations. *Annual Review of Neuroscience*, 24:1161-92.

Murphy, F.C., Nimmo-Smith, I. & Lawrence, A.D. (2003). Functional neuroanatomy of emotions: A meta-analysis. *Cognitive, Affective, & Behavioral Neuroscience*, 3:207-33.

Murphy, M.R., Seckl, J.R., Burton, S., Checkley, S.A. & Lightman, S.L. (1990). Changes in oxytocin and vasopressin secretion during sexu-al activity in men. *Journal of Clinical Endocrinology and Metabolism*, 65:738-41.

Nelson, E.E. & Panksepp, J. (1998). Brain substrates of infant-mother attachment: Contributions of opioids, oxytocin, and norepinephrine. *Neuroscience & Biobehavioral Reviews*, 22:437-52.

Numan, M. & Insel, T.R. (2003). *The Neurobioogy of Parental Behavior*. New York: Springer.

Panksepp, J. (1982). Toward a general psychobiological theory of emotions. *The Behavioral and Brain Sciences*, 5:407-67.

Panksepp, J. (1985). Mood changes: In *Handbook of Clinical Neurology*. Volume 1, Issue 45: *Clinical Neuropsychology*. Amsterdam: Elsevier Science Publishers, pp. 271-85.

Panksepp, J. (1998). *Affective Neuroscience: The foundations of human and animal emotions*. London: Oxford University Press.

Panksepp, J. (2001). The long-term psychobiological consequences of infant emotions: Prescriptions for the 21st century. Infant *Mental Health Journal*, 22:132-73.

Panksepp, J. (Ed.). (2004). *Textbook of Biological Psychiatry*. New York: Wiley.

Panksepp, J. & Burgdorf, J. (2003). 'Laughing' rats and the evolutionary antecedents of human joy? *Physiology & Behavior*, 79:533-47.

Panksepp, J. & Harro, J. (2004). The future of neuropeptides in biological psychiatry and emotional psychopharmacology: Goals and strategies. In J Panksepp (Ed.). *Textbook of Biological Psychiatry*. Hoboken, NJ: Wiley, pp. 627-59.

Panksepp, J., Knutson, B. & Brugdorf, J. (2002). The role of emotional brain systems in addictions: A neuro-evolutionary perspective. *Addiction*, 97:459-69.

Panksepp, J. & Moskal, J. (2004). Dopamine, pleasure and appetitive eagerness: An emotional systems overview of the trans-hypothalamic 'reward' system in the genesis of addictive urges. In D. Barsch (Ed.). *The Cognitive, Behavioral and Affective Neurosciences in Psychiatric Disorders*. New York, Oxford University Press, in press.

Panksepp, J. & Panksepp, J.B. (2000). The seven sins of evolutionary psychology, *Evolution and Cognition*, 6:108-31.

Panksepp, J.B. & Huber, R. (2004). Ethological analyses of crayfish behavior: A new invertebrate system for measuring the rewarding properties of psychostimulants. *Behavioural Brain Research*, in press.

Pfaff, D.W. (1999). *Drive: Neurobiological and molecular mechanisms of sexual motivation*. Cambridge, MA: MIT Press.

Phan, K.L., Wager, T., Taylor, S.F. & Liberzon, I. (2002). Functional neuroanatomy of emotion: A meta-analysis of emotion activation studies in PET and fMRI. *Neuroimage*, 16:331-48.

Rolls, E.T. (1999). *The Brain and Emotion*. Oxford: Oxford University Press.

Russell, J.A. (2003). Core affect and the psychological construction of emotion. *Psychological Review*, 110:145-72.

Siviy, S. & Panksepp, J. (1985). Energy balance and play in juvenile rats. *Physiology & Behavior*, 35:435-41.

Solms, M. (2000). Dreaming and REM sleep are controlled by different brain mechanisms. *Behavioral and Brain Sciences*, 23:843-50.

Watt, D.F. & Pincus, D.I. (2004). The neural substrates of consciousness: Implications for clinical psychiatry. In J. Panksepp (Ed.). *Textbook of Biological Psychiatry*. New York: Wiley, pp. 75-110.

Wegner, D.M. (2002). *The Illusion of Conscious Will*. Cambridge, MA: MIT Press.

Zubieta, J.K., Ketter, T.A., Bueller, J.A., Xu, Y., Kilbourn, M.R., Young, E.A. & Koeppe, R.A. (2003). Regulation of human affective responses by anterior cingulate and limbic mu-opioid neurotransmission. *Archives of General Psychiatry*, 60:1145-53.

Multiple choice

1. A key transmitter in the so-called seeking emotional system is
   a) norepinephrine
   b) serotonin
   c) dopamine
   d) acetylcholine

2. Which of the following is not one of the levels in Maslow's hierarchy of motivations?
   a) need for stimulus-seeking
   b) belongingness and love
   c) self-esteem
   d) self-actualisation

3. Which of the following brain neurochemical system in mammals is least important for specifically mediating social attachments and social feelings?
   a) opioids
   b) dopamine
   c) oxytocin
   d) prolactin

4. Which of the following enzymes would be deficient in a male whose body is physically feminised at birth?
   a) aromatase
   b) oxytocin
   c) 5-alpha-reductase
   d) prolactin

5. If the body of a human male is unable to manufacture aromatase during fetal development, he is more likely to
   a) exhibit feminine sex desires with normal masculine body characteristics
   b) masculine sex desires and masculine body characteristics
   c) masculine sex desires and feminine body characteristics
   d) feminine sex desires and feminine body characteristics

6. Which of the following does not have much evidence for being a basic emotional systems?
   a) care
   b) panic
   c) play
   d) shame

7. Which of the following neurochemical agents is not especially effective in reducing separation calls in young animals?
   a) opioids
   b) vasopressin
   c) oxytocin
   d) prolactin

8. Which of the following emotional systems seems to be least important in the elaboration of social attachments?
   a) lust
   b) panic
   c) play
   d) fear

9. An emotional system that is especially important for helping mediate a motivated approach to many different rewards and goals is
   a) intrinsic
   b) seeking
   c) play
   d) extrinsic

10. Which of the following is not one of the main three attributes of dimensional theories of emotion?
    a) valence
    b) surgency
    c) activation
    d) homeostasis

Short answer questions

1. Describe:
   • some of the main tenets of evolutionary psychology;
   • some of the major empirical achievements of evolutionary psychology; and
   • some potential criticisms of evolutionary psychology.

2. Discuss two major ways that emotions are defined, and highlight the seven basic emotional systems of the brain that have been revealed so far.

3. Discuss the basis for positing various intrinsic social-emotional systems in the brain, and discuss some of the relevant data for how at least three of the systems operate.

11

The Biological Basis of Perception and Disorders of Vision

Oliver Turnbull

CHAPTER OBJECTIVES

After studying this chapter you should be able to:
- identify and describe the anatomical basis of various aspects of human vision, and discuss the theoretical assumptions about the organization of vision that underlies the division of labour between systems
- identify and describe the principal categories of neuropsychological disorders of vision that are observed after brain lesion
- evaluate the role of this evidence in our understanding of the psychology of these processes.

Nosipho found it fascinating to think of all the complicated brain processes that allowed her to be able to perform the simple task of seeing. She was lucky enough to have no problems with vision, and using her sight felt completely natural to her. She looked around at everyone sitting in the lecture hall and then at the bit of clear blue sky she could see out the window. It was hard to imagine what it must feel like to not be able to see these things, to see them in confusing ways or, perhaps worst of all, to see them but not be able to make sense of them. As she learned about how many neurological problems could affect vision, her ability to see felt even more amazing. 'Imagine being able to "see" faces but not recognise them!' Nosipho imagined that this must be a very disturbing experience. It was quite frightening to think about how much could go wrong with the complex workings of the brain, but learning about these helped her to understand and appreciate the remarkable things her brain was able to do.

Introduction

In the general subject area of perception, we could choose to look at all the senses, such as hearing and touch, and the biological basis for each of these. After all, the study of perception is about how we organize information received by our body through our eyes, ears, nose, tongue, and skin surfaces to make meaning. Instead, in this chapter we have chosen to focus primarily on one sense – vision – because this is the part of the field of perception where the greatest gains have been made in recent years, and because it forms a good case study.

One of the most important ways by which we learn about the organisation of complex systems is through the way that they break down. This is as true of our understanding of perception as it is for our understanding of the human digestive system, the complexities of the eco-system or the organisation of societies. This section will investigate the way our perceptual abilities operate, by investigating what happens when the organ of the mind, the brain, is damaged. By understanding how our ability to see and act on the world might be disrupted, we gain valuable insights into the way that this system operates under normal circumstances.

This section reviews the many disorders of perceptual ability that are seen after damage to the brain. The general principles that hold true for the organisation of visual abilities hold true for other sense organs, such as hearing and somato-sensation (touch).

What are these general principles? Firstly, it seems that visual abilities are organised hierarchically – that is there are some brain regions, which we often refer to as 'primary' visual areas (see Figure 1), that carry out relatively 'low-level' or elementary tasks – such as the perception of light intensity and edge detection. While these are important abilities, this section will focus more on the higher level, or more psychologically sophisticated brain regions, sometimes referred to as 'secondary' and 'tertiary' areas. A highly simplified diagram of the arrangement of this system is shown in Figure 1.

The lower-level, or less psychologically-complex, areas – often known as primary visual cortex, lie at the back of the occipital lobes (labeled '1' in Figure 1). These areas are more-or-less directly connected to the retina, with the reversal of left and right seen in other aspects of brain organisation – such that the left visual cortex gathers information from the right side of the visual world. Primary visual cortex is the 'input' end of the visual system – the place were the more elementary aspects of processing occur. In front of this zone lies a more psychologically sophisticated system, sometimes referred to as 'secondary' areas, which are dedicated to a range of specialised visual processing tasks (labeled '2' in Figure 1). Colour and motion processing, object recognition, and so on appear to take place here. Finally, the highest level of the visual system, the tertiary area, operates the most abstract and psychologically sophisticated aspects of visual processing (labeled '3' in Figure 1). These areas are also dependent upon several other sensory modalities, such as hearing and touch (i.e. they are poly-modal or hetero-modal). These brain regions appear to be involved in important aspects of arithmetic, writing, constructional operations and spatial attention, and in some respects represents the 'output' end of the normal perceptual system.

Damage to the primary visual area causes so-called 'cortical blindness'. Visual experience stops because key aspects of the 'input' end of the visual system are disrupted. Damage to the middle, or secondary zones causes more complex disorders of visual processing. As might be imagined from the material discussed in the last paragraph, patients with damage to secondary areas lose the ability to perceive colour, or movement, for example, or they lose the ability to recognise specific objects. Damage to the tertiary does not affect visual perception *per se*, but rather causes more abstract disorders which transcend concrete perception: an inability to calculate, to write, or to construct complex forms.

A second key principle of the organisation of visual abilities has already been implied by the arguments of the last few paragraphs. It appears that various aspects of visual ability (and our abilities in other senses) are operated by dedicated sub-components – such that the overall task of vision seems to

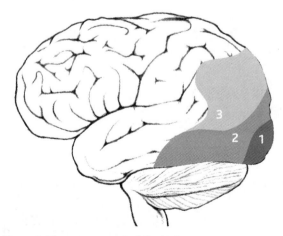

Figure 1 The arrangement of the brain

be carried out by relatively independent sub-systems. We know this because these individual sub-components can be selectively damaged. It is through a better understanding of the way that these sub-components operate, and the brain areas that run the various aspects of vision, that we have come to the modern understanding of the organisation of vision and its neurobiological basis.

We will briefly review these many different disorders to better understand the ways in which the complex tasks of vision are divided up.

Various types of visual disorder

The traditional understanding of the breakdown of disorders of vision has been one of a bewildering variety of disorders. There are, for example, disorders with exotic names, such as agnosia (a disorder of object recognition), alexia (a disorder of reading) and topographical disorientation (a disorder of route finding). There are many disorders of this type in the neuropsychology of vision – probably more than a few dozen in total. In order not to become bogged down in complexity, we will discuss only a few examples of these disorders in more detail below. Firstly, however, a few words about the classification of these systems.

Neuropsychologists have long discussed the many types of visual disorders independently – without trying to group them together. The complexity and diversity of the clinical disorders seemed to make it difficult to understand their relationship to the *overall* manner in which the visual system operates. Certainly, there are many disorders of vision, but are there any underlying trends or patterns that might help us to understand the *general* landscape of the visual system?

One such useful distinction would be to differentiate between the tasks of object recognition (*what* an object is) and spatial abilities (*where* an object is). There

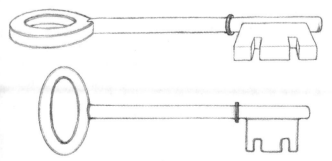

Figure 2 Some objects are always identifiable, regardless of perspective and spatial location

is some intuitive appeal in contrasting these two 'visual' tasks, partly because changing one dimension has so little effect upon the other. Thus, a key remains a key independent of its spatial location (see Figure 2). Even when it moves around in the world, and no matter which angle we see it from, it remains a key.

However, consider this situation with respect to space. In Figure 3, only *one* of the two keys is 'inside' the mug. This remains true even if I, as a viewer, observe the arrangement of mug and keys from a different position. However, if the key is removed from the mug it remains stable in terms of its identity (it is still a key) but changes in terms of its spatial properties (it is no longer in the mug). Thus, object identity and spatial location seem to operate in quite independent ways – and these two aspects of perception might be tackled in different ways by different parts of the visual system.

Figure 3 While objects may be recognisable, their spatial location may be difficult to determine

Another intuitive reason for promoting the distinction between location and identity is the fact that the tasks of object recognition and spatial knowledge seem to demand the use of rather different properties from vision. Object recognition relies on knowing about an object's shape, texture and colour, and this information remains relatively stable across time (chameleons being one rare exception to this). In contrast, spatial abilities have no need to rely on colour or shape information. Instead they rely on knowledge of the precise location of objects in the world, including the way that objects in the world change their position when either you move, or when an object moves in relation to you. Thus, the spatial domain is one where moment-by-moment changes in the position of either object or observer are critical.

An example of a disorder of recognition: Prosopagnosia

To discuss this issue in more detail, we will now focus on one aspect of the problem – that of object recognition. Neuropsychology has identified many classes of object recognition problem – from a general failure to recognise all types of visual objects (visual object agnosia) to more specific problems relating to sub-categories, such as faces (prosopagnosia), colours (achromatopsia), or words (alexia). Recent work suggests that recognition problems might also be restricted to categories such as animate or inanimate objects, scenes, body parts and even particular types of emotional expression, such as fear.

Trying to survey all of these disorders runs the risk of providing too much detail for a person new to the field (see Farah, 1990 for a useful review). It is a better introduction to human neuropsychology to focus on one class of visual recognition deficit, and show in more detail the many things that it can teach us about the way the visual system is organised. We will focus on perhaps the best investigated of the visual disorders – the selective loss of facial recognition ability, known as prosopagnosia. Given the immense importance of face recognition for humans, it seems an especially useful topic to focus on.

Prosopagnosia is a disorder of the recognition of *familiar* faces. It represents a failure to map a new perceptual experience onto a pre-existing memory of things learned before. Like other agnosias, the elementary perceptual abilities of these patients are normal, or near-normal. Therefore, they can usually judge the location, size and orientation of visual objects accurately. In fact, patients with prosopagnosia generally have such good visual abilities that they can tell that they are looking at a face, and can usually point to the various parts of the face (the eyes, mouth, etc.). This makes them quite remarkable people to interact with – if they can 'see' so well, how on earth can they not see well enough to know who they are looking at? Nevertheless, in spite of these good elementary visual abilities, they fail to recognise familiar faces – the faces of famous persons, friends, members of their own family, and sometimes even their own face viewed in a mirror! However, it is not simply a problem of naming – the problem that we all have sometimes when we recognise a face but can't recall the name. We know this because of the many *preserved* abilites that prosopagnosics have.

Like other agnosias, prosopagnosia is a disorder which is specific to a single sense modality – in this case vision. This is clearly demonstrated by the fact that they can usually recognise a person as soon as they hear the voice. They can also recall the biographical details of the person who they cannot visually identify. A typical patient's description might be 'of course I know who my brother is, I'd normally recognise him in an instant. But I didn't recognise him when he walked into the room to visit me the other day. Still, as soon as he spoke, then I knew it was him immediately'. So, they can recall the name and biographical details of the person without difficulty – the problem seems to be using *visual* information to recognise people. They can easily recognise people from auditory information. In fact, they could probably easily recognise people by touch alone, if humans were in the habit of recognising people in this way. These data suggest that prosopagnosics have a disorder of recognition that is specific to the visual modality.

This is an appropriate time for us to consider the site of lesion which produces prosopagnosia. The lesion site seems to involve a particular part of the occipito-temporal regions – that of the inferior surface – which is best visualised when the brain is viewed from below. These brain regions, the inferior surfaces of the occipito-temporal region, appear to be crucially involved in visual object recognition (see Figure 4). When there are bilateral lesions of these areas, patients suffer profound deficits of object recognition – for all categories of object, including faces. Until some ten or twenty years ago, it was believed that this was also the lesion site in cases of prosopagnosia – that is, that prosopagnosics had bilateral lesions of the inferior surface of the temporal lobes (Kertesz, 1983). Because it appeared that the lesion site in prosopagnosia was the same as that which disrupted the recognition of *all* categories of visual object, it was widely held that face recognition used the same cognitive apparatus as that employed for all other kinds of object. However, in recent years it has become clear that the lesion site in prosopagnosia need not be bilateral, but that a lesion of the inferior surfaces of the temporal lobes, on the *right* side only, is sufficient (see Farah, 1990). This has opened the way for the suggestion that face recognition is a relatively specific deficit of visual ability.

Thus, it seems that prosopagnosia is a rather specific sort of neurological disorder, consistent with the claim that certain classes of neuron seem to be selectively activated by faces (Perrett *et al.*, 1992).

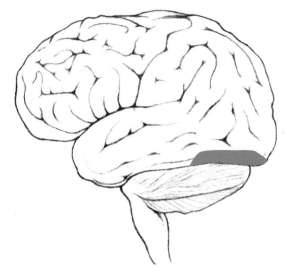

Figure 4 The inferior surfaces of the occipito-temporal region of the brain are where object recognition is located

Prosopagnosia is certainly a disorder only of *visually* presented faces, because patients can recognise people by voice. However, there is evidence that the recognition of other classes of object, even within the visual modality, is often preserved in such patients. One clear example of this is the fact that prosopagnosics can often use other types of purely visual information to recognise people. They are often able to recognise friends or family when they are wearing familiar and distinctive clothing, and they can sometimes recognise people when they use a particular gesture or have an unusual way of walking, such as a limp. Also, these patients can generally perform the task of object recognition quite well for other classes of visual object.

One example is the fact that prosopagnosics can often still read. Also prosopagnosics can also often accurately recognise so-called 'common' objects (natural objects and artefacts which are not part of a specialist category – for example, horses, telephones or houses). In summary, it seems remarkable that *some* kinds of visual object recognition should be spared – for written words and common objects, and recognising people by means of their gestures or clothing – while the recognition of faces is so severely disrupted.

Evidence of this kind has, perhaps understandably, led to the suggestion that perhaps faces are 'special'. In other words, that we have particular cognitive systems, and presumably different brain regions, for dealing with the problem of face recognition. This question, of whether there is a 'specialised' part of the mental apparatus, is the sort of question that cognitive neuropsychology seems especially well designed to answer. Of course, we should always be cautious in relation to dramatic conclusions about specialisation. Nevertheless, it is reassuring to see that there also appear to be good non-neurological reasons to suppose that faces are 'special'. For example, there are many reports of infants showing preferential looking at faces (for a review see Gauthier & Nelson, 2001). In addition, we have long known that the inversion of faces disrupts the recognition of faces far more than that of (most) other visual objects (e.g., Yin, 1969). So, it might seem that any neurological arguments which supported a claim for a specialised face recognition system would have good converging evidence from nearby disciplines.

11.1 FACES, MODULES AND DISSOCIATIONS

How might we demonstrate that there are special systems (or 'modules') for face recognition? Cognitive neuropsychology looks for differing levels of performance between tasks, called dissociations. If a prosopagnosic can recognise common objects (e.g., scores 90/100 on an object recognition task), but fails to recognise faces (e.g., scores 30/100 on a face recognition task), then faces and common objects are said to be 'dissociated' (as you'll see below, this is a single dissociation, where a patient is impaired on Task 1, but not Task 2). This might suggest that faces are 'special'.

However, there is a possible problem of task difficulty – perhaps faces are harder stimuli to recognise than common objects? There is also good reason to suspect this. Damasio *et al.* (1989), for example, point

out that recognising a common object (e.g., a shoe) is very different from the requirements of a face recognition task (recognising your friend Susan). For example, faces are 'visually confusable' because they all have the same component parts (eyes, mouth, nose, etc.). In contrast, a shoe is composed of different parts compared with the objects you're asked to discriminate it against (trousers, dogs, etc.). Identifying common objects might also be regarded as simpler because it is recogniton at a supra-ordinate level (the category 'shoe' has many exemplars in the world), but face recognition requires the identification of a single instance of an object (only one person is your friend Susan). How might we equate the difficulty of the tasks? One type of 'equivalent' task would be to see if prosopagnosics can recognise faces from trousers and dogs (like the supra-ordinate task of shoe recognition). As we saw above, prosopagnosics can do this (they know that they're looking at a 'face', but they just can't recognise it). Another type of 'equivalent' task would be recognising Susan's shoe from an array of other people's shoes. It turns out that prosopagnicics have difficulty with other 'visually confusable' categories too, such as makes of car, buildings, or flower-types – and prosopagnosic bird-watchers can no longer tell different bird species apart. Perhaps faces aren't so 'special' after all, and don't have a special 'module'.

So, note that the 'task difficulty' argument can cope with a patient who shows:

- impaired recognition on both tasks (faces and common objects); and
- impaired recognition on the 'more difficult' task (faces) with preservation of the 'simpler' task (objects).

However, the 'task difficulty' argument can't tolerate the final alternative:

- impaired recognition on the 'simpler' task (objects) with preservation of the 'more difficult' task (faces).

Taken together, the first two points represent polar opposites – doing well with faces and badly with objects, and vice versa. Of course, this can't be found in one patient, but we might find two patients with such contrasting performances. These represent a double dissociation. Here, patient A is impaired on Task 1, but not Task 2. In contrast, patient B is impaired Task 2, but not Task 1.

Perhaps double dissociations within the 'confusable stimuli' class would be better evidence for faces being 'special'? Some cases have been reported, for example a farmer who couldn't recognise his cows (zooagnosia), but had intact face recognition abilities. In contrast, another farmer could not recognise faces, but could tell his cows apart. Because of this double dissociation, it can't be that task difficulty is a problem (cows can't be merely more easy to recognise than faces, or vice versa). Does this imply that faces are 'special', and that there are face recognition 'modules'? More worryingly, does it imply cow recognition 'modules'? Perhaps we have accepted these 'dissociation' arguments too readily?

Believing the arguments about double dissociations and modularity requires that we accept a number of assumptions about brain injury – assumptions that are necessary if we are to believe that pathological performance provides a basis for conclusions about normal function. Many neuropsychology texts introduce discussions on these issues, but these assumptions are typically taken for granted by cognitive neuropsychologists, and are pretty much untestable.

Disorders of spatial ability

Just as there are many classes of disorder of object recognition, so there are many ways in which spatial ability might be disrupted. Of course, the word 'spatial' can be applied to 'the position of objects' in a wide variety of contexts. In one sense, it means the *relative* position of things (so that one box can be 'inside' another, or is 'smaller' than it). Other spatial relationships depend very directly on the position of the observer, such that something to my left might be to your right: This sort of spatial knowledge is especially important for the process of acting on the world, so that we can reach for an object like a ball. Amazingly, we can do this even when both the ball and ourselves are moving, as happens in sports such as cricket and rugby, which suggests that the systems producing this ability are of great complexity. Finally, there are complex ways in which we use special types of spatial knowledge to represent sophisticated concepts used in language or arithmetic. Examples would be the way in which 'b' and 'd' refer to quite different sounds, even though they are so similar in structure as to be mirror-images. Or the way in which adding '2' to a number such as '9' (both single digits) somehow produces '11' (a double digit, which strangely contains two number '1's).

Interestingly, it seems that each of these separate types of spatial ability has some relatively independent part of visual cortex, or more accurately a connected network of parts, dedicated to its function – in much the same way as was true for different sorts of object recognition. As in that example above, there is no space to review each of the different disorders (for reviews see, e.g., De Renzi, 1982; Milner & Goodale, 1995; Turnbull *et al.*, 1997), and we will learn more considering a smaller number of cases. In describing each, we will draw some examples from a remarkable book which is based on the personal descriptions of a patient, called Zazetsky (Luria, 1972), who was injured in the left parietal region by a bullet during the Second World War. Zazetsky suffered from many deficits in his spatial ability, and his personal descriptions will help to clarify the nature of each of them.

One area of Zazetsky's difficulties was with the assignment of the verbal labels 'left' and 'right' within a spatial co-ordinate frame. In some ways this seems relatively simple: 'left' is the side that people generally wear their watch on. Zazetsky was examined by a physician to test his vision, and was asked to tell in which direction a semicircle was facing – a question that he should have easily been able to answer as he had been training to be a scientist and technician before the war. As he described this experience, he simply couldn't begin to think of an answer, and merely looked at her, so that she became annoyed with him: 'Why don't you answer? Which direction is the semicircle pointing – to the right or the left?' It was only then that he understood what she was asking: 'I looked at the semicircle but couldn't judge since I didn't know what 'left' or 'right' meant ... I could see [the semicircle] ... it was so clear you couldn't miss it. But I didn't understand the doctor's question ... I just sat and stared at the figure but wasn't able to answer her since I didn't know what the words meant' (Luria, 1972:54).

Zazetsky also seemed to have 'forgotten' the shapes that we normally use to represent particular sounds. He was quite familiar with the sound 'bee', to the extent that he might be able to produce it, repeat it, even tell you that it is the sound that starts the word 'boat'. However, he had great difficulty remembering the shape which we normally make on a page which we use to represent the sound 'bee' – the ability to recall that it consists of one vertical and a curved line: b. He described himself as having 'forgotten how to use a pencil ... all I could do was draw some crooked lines across the paper ... It looked like the scribbling of a child who still hasn't learned the alphabet' (Luria, 1972:71–2). Some time later, when he had recovered a little, he recalled 'Even after I thought I knew the letters, I couldn't remember how they were formed. Each time I wanted to think of a particular letter I'd have to run through the alphabet until I found it' (Luria, 1972:72). It seems that Zazetsky had suffered a disturbance of the ability to generate and recognise even individual letter shapes. Similar to that seen in at least one type of dyslexia.

It is clear, therefore, that profound disorders of spatial ability can be observed after lesion to the brain regions concerned with vision. Are these independent of perceptual disorders – such as those described above?

11.2 WHAT IS MODULARITY?

Many reasons have been put forward to support the idea that the cognitive system is 'modular'. Some arguments come from the perspective of artificial intelligence, for example, authorities such as David Marr, who noted that other complex systems (such as radios, telephones, or motor cars) have separate component parts. This makes such a system efficient because (Marr argues) it is easier to detect and correct errors in a modular system. Thus, in evolution, changing the properties of one component would have limited repercussions on the entire system, making it easier to 'debug'. However, it may be that the logic of engineering does not readily apply to biology.

What exactly do we mean by 'modularity'? The best description has been provided by Fodor, in his celebrated (though very dense) book *The Modularity of Mind* (published in 1983). He suggests five properties of a cognitive module:

- Informational encapsulation: that the module should operate in isolation and ignorance of the rest of the cognitive system.
- Domain-specificity: that modules accept only one form of input. Obvious examples are the modality-

specific primary sensory areas. Less obviously, language systems would deal only with 'language' input, unless the module happens to be one of the systems specialised for 'translating' to-or-from the perceptual and motor systems. The operation of such systems must also be:

- Mandatory: that the operation of the system is unstoppable once it has begun. An example might be that we can not stop ourselves from recognising someone once we have seen them. Of course this can not be true for the whole mental apparatus: we can stop ourselves from naming someone we see. But (if Fodor's modularity is correct), the 'face recognising' system itself should be unstoppable – perhaps things can be stopped later on.
- Innate: modules are a result of genetics, as modified by evolution. This is one of Fodor's more controversial suggestions. What about reading and writing? Well, it turns out that Fodor doesn't think that all systems are modular. In fact, he claims that:
- Input and output processes alone are modular. Thus, perceptual and motor abilities (the parts closely

connected to the outside world) are thought to be modular in Fodor's scheme. They are also 'innate', using the argument in the previous point. However, so-called 'central' systems, such as reasoning, arithmetic, and so on, are not modular.

What do these rules say about cognitive neuropsychology? Authorities such as Tim Shallice argue that cognitive neuropsychology is viable if, and only if, the assumptions in the first two points, above, are true. However, he feels that the last three points, above, need not be true for cognitive neuropsychology to be a workable enterprise. Indeed, most of cognitive neuropsychology involves the investigation of so-called 'central' systems – so Shallice has a vested interest in testing, and disproving, the final point. Shallice also adds a further assumption, required for making neuropsychology viable – that there is neurological specificity, so that different parts of the cognitive system are run by different brain regions, and hence can be disrupted in isolation.

What evidence do we have for modularity? Well, there is abundant neuropsychological evidence for regional specialisation – the argument that different parts of the brain do different things. The fact that disorders like prosopagnosia occur in relative isolation from other neuropsychological disorders, and occur reliably after injury to the same brain regions, make regional specialisation virtual certanties. But regional specialisation is not the same as modularity. Modularity implies 'walls' or 'boundaries' or 'borders' between cognitive systems. Only with a system with boundaries can we have informational encapsulation. So, how might brain injury affect the function of two modular systems? This depends on whether damage to a 'module' implies total loss of function or a loss proportional to the extent of lesion (called 'graceful degradation'). Evidence from clinical neuropsychology emphatically suggests graceful degredation. Patients usually don't lose all of their face recognition capacity – rather, their performance is reduced to a greater or lesser extent. This suggests some kind of 'distributed network' architecture, of the sort found in connectionist networks (or parallel distributed processing computers). Does graceful degredation 'disprove' modularity? No. We might argue that a module has boundaries, but has a 'distributed network' internal organisation. Such a mixture of distributed and modular architecture, which would be 'hard-on-the-outside, soft-on-the-inside', seems unlikely, but is theoretically possible. Several neuropsychology texts have introductory chapters that touch on these important issues, and are worth following up.

Two visual systems for spatial and object knowledge

Are object recognition and spatial skills somehow 'independent' abilities? There is some reason to believe that we might loosely lump together the many visual agnosias (disorders of object recognition), including perhaps some of the specialised losses of face recognition (prosopagnosia) and word recognition (alexia), and consider their independence from spatial abilities. For example, spatial abilities (as defined by tasks of orientation, size, location and distance judgements) have been tested in many patients with visual agnosia, and these abilities appear to be relatively intact, in spite of the deficits of object recognition (Damasio *et al.*, 1989; De Haan & Newcombe, 1992; Farah & Ratcliff, 1994). Similarly, the 'spatial' category would also include a variety of neuropsychological disorders: loss of topographical orientation, and impairments in domains such as attention, reaching, and voluntary gaze. In many patients with such disorders, object recognition seems relatively intact (De Renzi, 1982;

Newcombe & Ratcliff, 1989). Thus, there is precedent for considering object recognition and spatial abilities as operating independently.

An influential attempt to unify perceptual and spatial disorders in a model which might account for the neuropsychological findings (as well as findings with normal participants), has grown out of the idea that there are two 'cortical visual systems': one specialised for spatial, and the other for object, perception. The original formulation was presented by Ungerleider and Mishkin (1982), based on work on monkeys, and was more-or-less unrelated to the work on cognitive models of the recognition process in normal humans that the growing disciplines of cognitive psychology and neuropsychology were developing (see Turnbull, 1999). More recently, the two visual systems account has been highly influential in relating work on the neural substrate of recognition to issues of object representation (Farah, 1992; Kosslyn *et al.*, 1990; 1994; Logothetis & Sheinberg, 1996).

The key hypothesis of the Ungerleider and Mishkin (1982) account can be summarised by the simple idea that the many areas of visual cortex are organised into two relatively independent pathways. One system, the so-called 'dorsal stream', runs from occipital to the parietal cortex, and is primarily concerned with the perception of spatial information, in particular the spatial location of the object (i.e. "where"). The second system, the 'ventral stream', runs from occipital to the infero-temporal cortex, and is concerned with the recognition of objects as members of a familiar class (i.e. "what") (see Figure 5).

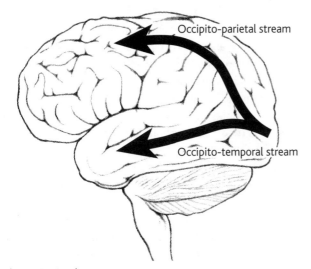

Figure 5 Visual cortex streams

One problem with Ungerleider and Mishkin's (1982) scheme is the fact that the two visual systems hypothesis is a generalisation about the monkey visual system, which cannot be applied indiscriminately to human vision (for review see Eidelberg & Galaburda, 1984; Ungerleider & Haxby, 1994). However, the two visual systems approach appears to be consistent with the large body of knowledge acquired in human neuropsychology. Lesions of the temporal cortex, particularly on the ventral surface of the temporal lobe, produce disorders of object recognition (Damasio *et al.*, 1989; Kertesz, 1983) which are similar to the deficits seen after experimental lesions of the infero-temporal cortex in the monkey (e.g., Walsh & Butler, 1996), and there has long been evidence for an occipito-temporal lesion site in prosopagnosia, and in some cases of visual agnosia (Damasio *et al.*, 1989; Kertesz, 1983).

Similarly, parietal lesions result in disorders that may be broadly characterised as 'spatial'. These include visuo-spatial neglect, the spatial aspects of drawing and constructional tasks, peri-personal spatial disorders such as left-right orientation and ideo-motor apraxia, disorders of reaching (optic

ataxia) and voluntary gaze (ocular apraxia) (De Renzi, 1982; Kertesz, 1983; Newcombe & Ratcliff, 1989; Perenin & Vighetto, 1988). Thus, to a first approximation, the Ungerleider and Mishkin (1982) model seems an accurate account of the gross differences between occipito-parietal and occipito-temporal neuropsychological syndromes.

Vision for action: Milner and Goodale's account

The original suggestion that there may be two visual systems has been modified in the last decade, following the work of Milner and Goodale (1993, 1995). They have suggested a substantial reinterpretation of the original two visual systems account, agreeing that there is strong evidence for separate 'dorsal' and 'ventral' systems of processing in the monkey and human visual systems. However, they suggest that the dorsal stream appears to be more directly tied to the visuo-motor processes than to identifying the spatial location of an object. Milner and Goodale (1993, 1995) also acknowledge the possibility that inferior parietal regions in humans may play a role in many visuo-spatial cognitive tasks, which could require the use of information from both streams.

An interesting series of investigations was published by Milner and Goodale in the 1990s (Goodale *et al.*, 1994; Goodale & Milner, 1992; Milner & Goodale, 1993) which suggests that some classes of spatial ability are remarkably independent from perceptual abilities that seem almost identical in their fundamentals. In their most famous case, a visual agnosic, referred to as DF, was asked to perform two types of task. The first tested her 'perceptual' ability – which, as a visual agnosic, we might expect to be impaired. Consistent with this, she was unable to describe the size, shape and orientation of visual targets, yet was able to use the same types of visual information to guide her motor responses. The opposite pattern has been demonstrated in a patient with optic ataxia (RV) who could describe the shape of objects but could not accurately reach for them (Goodale *et al.*, 1994). These data, and others related to them, have been taken as evidence that the dorsal visual system is dedicated to visuo-motor guidance, rather than simply all classes of spatial information.

Neuropsychology has an interesting, and rather surprising, approach to the rather uninspiring methodological issue of sample size. We might expect that neuropsychology would adopt the same solution to the problem of individual variability as the rest of experimental psychology. The problem of variation in a population is usually solved, in experimental psychology, by collecting large numbers of subjects and averaging the group data. For example, find as many patients as possible who have visual problems, and give them all tests of face and common object recognition. Average the data because, as in the rest of psychology, you want to get rid of variability so as to lessen the influence of data points that are outliers. The result is rather uninteresting: on average, patients with visual problems after brain damage do poorly on both measures, relative to controls. If this approach were adopted, one might never be able to claim that there are specialised systems for face or common object recognition!

In contrast, cognitive neuropsychology would regard one case of a dissociation between face and common object recognition (i.e. a single subject) as sufficient to demonstrate a dissociation. You would need one more (a mere two subjects) for the full double dissociation. Not only are such single cases sufficient for cognitive neuropsychology, but they are actually preferred over the traditional group study. Why? Because instances of dissociation are often hidden by the data from other subjects when we average across a group. When we average the scores from a group of patients with visual impairment on tests of face and common object recognition, the group does poorly, on average, on both. But there may be single cases of good performance on one task but not the other. In the last paragraph these data (in conventional experimental psychology) were called 'outliers', and we said that they were a cause of variability that we wanted to get rid of. Now, viewed from the perspective of cognitive neuropsychology, these 'outliers' are the interesting cases, rather than the group average – they are the raw material of dissociations. Traditional group studies are seen as a poor approach to neuropsychology, and the literature is full of important single cases, usually identified by their initials (for example: HM or HJA).

Does this mean that cognitive neuropsychology has a problem with collecting decent-sized samples? Surely it's a bad thing to base a science on just a few instances of a phenomenon, rather than on a range of the normal population? Neuropsychology does run the risk of focusing on unusual and rare dissociations. Note, however, that neuropsychologists are prepared to accept group studies – of a particular sort. They prefer multiple single-case studies, where each subject is analysed at the individual subject level: patient 1 does badly on both Tasks A and B; patient 2 does badly on Task A, but well on Task B. In this way a dissociation of interest, such as that seen in patient 2, is not missed.

Conclusion

The work reviewed in this section clearly demonstrates a number of principles of modern cognitive neuroscience, and of vision in particular. In a few decades of highly productive work, it has been possible to identify the general neuroanatomical correlates of different aspects of vision, and demonstrate that there is a great deal of specificity in the way the visual system seems to be designed. This is most notable in the specialisation of individual brain regions, as in the example of selective face recognition deficits (prosopagnosia) described above. The field also appears to be generating some theoretical advances on the back of the empirical work – with the 'two visual systems' account being the best example. We should note that such accounts are probably always destined to be oversimplifications of complex issues. Nevertheless, generating simple models which explain a wide range of phenomena has been the cornerstone of work in the natural sciences, and advances in neuroscience are a welcome, and a necessary stepping-stone to a complete understanding of the way the visual system operates. Our understanding of the biological basis of perception remains therefore at a relatively early stage, but there is no question that great progress has been made, and it appears that the discipline has a bright future.

Damasio, A.R., Tranel, D. & Damasio, H. (1989). Disorders of visual recognition. In F. Boller & J. Grafman (Eds.). *Handbook of Neuropsychology* (volume 2). Amsterdam: Elsevier, pp. 317–32.

De Haan, E.H.F. & Newcombe, F. (1992). Neuropsychology of vision. *Current Opinion in Neurology & Neurosurgery*, 5:65–70.

De Renzi, E. (1982). *Disorders of Space Exploration and Cognition*. Chichester: Wiley.

Eidelberg, D. & Galaburda, A.M. (1984). Inferior parietal lobule: Divergent architectonic asymmetries in the human brain. *Archives of Neurology*, 41:843–52.

Farah, M.J. (1992). Agnosia. *Current Opinion in Neurobiology*, 2:162–4.

Farah, M.J. (1990). *Visual Agnosia*. Cambridge: MIT Press.

Farah, M.J. & Ratcliff, G. (1994). *Neuropsychology of High-level Vision*. Hillsdale, New Jersey: Lawrence Earlbaum Associates.

Gauthier, I. & Nelson, C.A. (2001). The development of face expertise. *Current Opinion in Neurobiology*, 11:219–23.

Goodale, M.A., Meenan, J.P., Bulthoff, H.H., Nicolle, D. A., Murphy, K.J. & Racicot, C.I. (1994). Separate neural pathways for the visual analysis of object shape in perception and prehension. *Current Biology*, 4(7):604–10.

Goodale, M.A. & Milner, A.D. (1992). Separate visual pathways for perception and action. *Trends in Neuroscience*, 15(1):20–5.

Kertesz, A. (1983). *Localization in Neuropsychology*. New York: Academic Press.

Kosslyn, S.M., Flynn, R.A., Amsterdam, J.B. & Wang, G. (1990). Components of high-level vision: A cognitive neuroscience analysis and accounts of neurological syndromes. *Cognition*, 34:203–77.

Kosslyn, S.M., Alpert, N.M., Thompson, W.L., Chabris, C.F., Rauch, S.L. & Anderson, A.K. (1994). Identifying objects seen from different viewpoints: A PET investigation. *Brain*, 117:1055–71.

Logothetis, N.K. & Sheinberg, D. L. (1996). Visual object recognition. *Annual Review of Neuroscience*, 19:577–621.

Luria, A.R. (1972). *The Man With a Shattered World*. Cambridge, USA: Harvard University Press.

Milner, A.D. & Goodale, M.A. (1993). Visual pathways to perception and action. *Progress in Brain Research*, 95:317–37.

Milner, A.D. & Goodale, M.A. (1995). *The Visual Brain in Action*. Oxford: Oxford University Press.

Newcombe, F. & Ratcliff, G. (1989) Disorders of visuospatial analysis. In F. Boller & J. Grafman (Eds.). *Handbook of Neuropsychology* (Volume 2). Amsterdam: Elsevier, pp. 333–56.

Perenin, M.T. & Vighetto, A. (1988). Optic ataxia: A specific disruption in visuomotor mechanisms: Different aspects of the deficit in reaching for objects. *Brain,* 111: 643–74.

Perrett, D.I., Hietanen, J.K., Oram, M.W. & Benson, P.J. (1992). Organisation and functions of cells responsive to faces in the temporal cortex. *Philosophical Transactions of the Royal Society of London*, Series B, 335:23–30.

Turnbull, O.H. (1999). Of two minds about two visual systems. *Psyche*, 5(8):1–5.

Turnbull, O.H., Carey, D. P. & McCarthy, R.A. (1997). The neuropsychology of object constancy. *Journal of the International Neuropsychology Society*, 3:288–98.

Ungerleider, L.G. & Mishkin, M. (1982). Two cortical visual systems. In D. J. Ingle, M.A. Goodale & R.J.W. Mansfield (Eds.). *Analysis of Visual Behavior*. Cambridge, Massachusetts: MIT Press, pp. 549–86.

Ungerleider, L.G. & Haxby, J.V. (1994). 'What' and 'where' in the human brain. *Current Opinion in Neurobiology*, 4:157–65.

Walsh, V. & Butler, S.R. (1996). The effects of visual cortex lesions on the perception of rotated shapes. *Behavioural Brain Research*, 76:127–42.

Weiskrantz, L. (1986). *Blindsight*. Oxford University Press.

Yin, R.K. (1969). Looking at upside-down faces. *Journal of Experimental Psychology*, 81:141–5.

Multiple choice questions

1. Neurological patients who cannot recognise familiar faces, but have normal elementary visual abilities (and can recognise people by non-visual means) are said to have
   a) prosopanomia
   b) prosopamnesia
   c) prosopagnosia
   d) achromatopsia

2. According to Ungerleider and Mishkin, the ventral and dorsal streams can be thought of as processing what aspects of visual information?
   a) what and where
   b) where and who
   c) when and where
   d) what and who

3. Patients with prosopagnosia cannot
   a) recognise colours
   b) attend to one side of the visual world
   c) move one side of the body
   d) recognise familiar faces

4. Which of the following is false?
   a) the critical lesion site in prosopagnosia is a lesion in the inferior occipito-temporal region
   b) prosopagnosia is a disorder of the recognition of familiar faces
   c) most prosopagnosics have difficulties recognising people's voices
   d) some prosopagnosics show preserved recognition of common objects (e.g., dog, bicycle, etc.)

5. Which of the following is not a spatial ability impaired after occitpito-parietal lesions?
   a) left-right discrimination
   b) writing
   c) sentence production
   d) double-digit addition

6) Which of the following best describes the function of the dorsal visual system?
   a) the recognition of common objects
   b) visuo-motor guidance
   c) sentence comprehansion
   d) colour perception

7. Which of the following was not suggested by Fodor (1983) in relation to modularity?
   a) that 'modularity' is a useful concept in helping us understand the organisation of the mental apparatus
   b) that modules are 'innate'
   c) that all cognitive systems are modular
   d) that the operation of modules should be mandatory

8. Which is the minimum required to produce a double dissociation?
   a) one patient, performing a test of function X
   b) one patient, performing two tests of function X
   c) two patients, each performing a test of function X
   d) two patients, each performing two tests: one of function X and one of function Y

Short answer questions

1. Describe one example of the sorts of evidence that has been reported to show that faces are 'special'.
2. Which sorts of evidence would be required in order to argue that a part of the cognitive apparatus was 'modular'?
3. What is agnosia?
4. What are the primary neuropsychological disorders that follow from lesion to the 'ventral' visual system, and what do these tell us about the role of this system in vision?

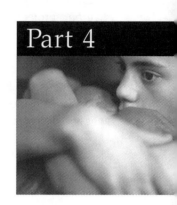

Part 4

Personality

Ashraf Kagee

The study of personality forms an integral part of the work of psychologists. The variety of approaches to this subject conveys a sense of the richness and diversity of ideas that may be found in psychological science. Accompanying these varied approaches to understanding personality is the wide variation in the method of inquiry. Thus, methodological diversity in many ways parallels the diverse manner in which pioneers in the discipline have approached personality studies.

This part provides an overview of the way in which personality has been studied. The first chapter provides an overview of major personality theories. Any serious study of personality needs to pay homage to the major theorists such as Freud, Jung, Adler, Erikson, Skinner and Bandura. Admittedly, these theorists developed their ideas in Europe and North America, which are cultural and geographical contexts that are at variance with those that developing countries are presently experiencing. Yet, their contribution to the understanding of the human being has a role to play in conceptualizing personality dynamics in all social contexts.

The modern world is no longer culturally monolithic, and divisions between Western and non-Western cultures are porous and continually shifting. The study of personality, which is complexly related to culture, class and historical era, necessarily has to take into consideration the way in which individuals are located within their social contexts. Thus, the chapter by Naidoo examines the major theoretical orientations to the study of personality and critically engages with the notion of their relevance to the developing world context.

The chapter that addresses the question 'What is personality?' seeks to gain an understanding of the many factors that affect the development of personality. Thus, cultural, political, economic and social factors are considered major influences in shaping personality development. The distinction between individualistic and communal cultures provides a challenging backdrop within which the personality is considered. Within this debate, critical psychology makes important contributions to contextualising personality studies in a country like South Africa, with its history of political oppression, economic exploitation and racial segregation. Carolissen sketches the problems and pitfalls inherent in the study of personality in South Africa and other developing countries, while highlighting the continued need for personality to be considered in the study of psychology.

As a discipline and profession, psychology has always been concerned with the measurement of mental and behavioural phenomena. The measurement of personality is therefore an important concern to personality theorists. The third chapter in this section addresses the question of personality assessment by examining objective and projective methods. Most research conducted on personality assessment has emerged from industrially developed countries. Thus, again, contextual and cultural factors necessarily impact the study of personality assessment in countries where questions of literacy, individuality and interdependence have alternative meanings and different levels of importance to those in Europe and the United States of America. Kagee and De Bruin provide an overview of the technical details of personality assessment, including an introduction to psychometric theory.

The following part of the book therefore has been developed to provide the reader with the rudimentary conceptual elements to understanding human personality, while calling attention to the complexity of the subject in the social context in which we live. Some of the perspectives, models and theories described in this part are potentially contradictory with one another, while others may be seen as conceptually compatible. We present the mix of approaches and methods in the study of personality to indicate the heterogeneity and richness of the debates regarding the subject.

12

What is Personality?

Ronelle Carolissen

CHAPTER OBJECTIVES

After studying this chapter you should be able to:
- distinguish between different approaches to personality
- understand the varied influences on personality
- have a perspective on personality in the South African context.

Learning about personality and personality assessment made Nosipho feel both interested and nervous at the same time. It was exciting to think that it was possible to accurately identify, interpret and measure her own personality traits. On the other hand, it was a bit scary to think that someone could test her and discover what she was 'really' like – maybe that they could even see things about herself that she didn't know.

Nosipho felt that she could identify at least some of her own personality characteristics. She was quite a perfectionist and hard working, but she was also loyal and kind. But most of what she knew about herself had, as she thought about it, come from other people's reactions to her. Over the years various people had told her how she came across and how they experienced her. Some of these insights were, at the time, quite surprising to her. Nosipho particularly recalled one friend telling her angrily that she was often 'distant' and didn't let others know how she felt. At first Nosipho had just felt her friend was being unfair, but later realised that she must have seen her shyness and misinterpreted it. Perhaps it wasn't so easy to understand what people's personalities were like from the outside. But then again it was equally difficult to really get know yourself!

Nosipho spoke to some friends after class about this whole idea of being able to establish a person's personality characteristics. They agreed that personality tests were not magical tools that you could use to read people's minds, but that they might be helpful in the complicated task of trying to find out who somebody is and what they are capable of. Nosipho and her friends had ended up laughing about how personality tests might have come in useful in checking out some of their less successful romantic partners. Afterwards, though, Nosipho thought more seriously about how she might be able to make better choices about jobs, careers and courses – maybe even relationships – if she understood a bit more about herself.

Nosipho was also aware that there was much more to understanding personality than applying or undertaking tests. Like most people, Nosipho had of course heard about Freud before she had begun to study psychology. What she had heard, though, was not very promising! People often made jokes about Freud and sex and, of course, his strange ideas about 'penis envy' made it hard to take him seriously. But as she began to learn more about psychoanalytic theories of development, Nosipho realised that to dismiss Freud's thought and theories completely would mean missing out on some really interesting ideas about how people come to be who and what they are. Perhaps the clues to understanding more about herself really were hidden away in her childhood, and if she understood more about her past she might be to make some sense of how she experienced things in her present life.

One of the things that most people pointed out to Nosipho about herself was about how self-critical she was. Friends often told her not to be so hard on herself, but she just couldn't seem to help it. When she got a low mark on an essay, she would find herself thinking about it for ages, what she must have done wrong, how she should have done it differently, and so on. She felt quite envious of the way some of her friends could just let these sorts of things go. Her parents had expected quite a lot of her academically, and she had tried hard to please them as a child. It was strange, though, that now they even thought she was too demanding of herself and encouraged her to take time off from working. She was quite surprised the other day when she had told her father how disappointed she was about a test mark and he had said that he thought it sounded like she had actually done quite well enough. 'Perhaps your standards are too high', he had added. Maybe it was possible that she had recognised her parents' expectations of her as she was growing up, but had exaggerated them in her own mind. Perhaps it was really her own superego that demanded so much of her? It was interesting, but a bit unnerving to think that her superego might be harsh not just because of her parents' expectations of her but also because she unconsciously felt guilty about some long forgotten childhood wishes.

Introduction

Commonsense definitions of personality often refer to sets of characteristics particular to individuals. Notions such as 'his personality will prevent him from becoming a good psychologist' or 'her personality makes up for what she lacks in looks' can be overheard in everyday conversations. People generally refer to a characteristic or set of characteristics that is inherent to individuals and that makes them different from others. It is precisely this notion of what makes one person different from another that concerns personality psychologists. While superficially, the notion of identifiable individual characteristics suggests that definitions of personality are easy to derive, quite the opposite is true.

This chapter will provide a comprehensive overview on understandings of personality, which will include mainstream approaches such as psychoanalytic and behaviourist approaches to personality, as well as cultural and critical approaches (which can be classified as non-mainstream approaches). Non-mainstream approaches are seldom included in Euro-American texts on personality, whereas mainstream approaches are predominantly represented in these texts. Euro-American psychology usually emphasises the centrality of the individual, intrapsychic processes and occasionally interpersonal relationships and family structures when considering influences on personality. The impact of community and societal norms and values are seldom regarded as equally significant in influencing personality.

The negligence in failing to consider community and societal factors as also being formative in personality definition, is important, as the relevance of applying only American and European psychological theory in the South African context has been questioned extensively (Anonymous, 1986; Berger & Lazarus, 1987; Dawes, 1986; Moll, 2002; Vogelman *et al.*, 1992). The current chapter will therefore provide an overview of both mainstream and non-mainstream approaches, and provide illustrative examples which can begin to situate understandings of personality within a South African context.

Personality psychology and its relevance in South Africa

The essence of the debates around personality has revolved around the fact that mainstream psychological theory has developed in particular socio-historical contexts with specific class groupings in mind. Historically, studies of personality have reflected the worldviews characteristic of European or Euro-American middle to upper middle-class societies. Thus they may not be totally applicable to groups that fall outside these categories. Questions concerning the relevance of the concept of personality for non-Western populations may include: 'Can behaviour in Japan be understood in the same way that we understand behaviour in America?' or 'Can behaviour in a working-class community in Khayelitsha, South Africa, be sufficiently explained by theoretical constructs developed in the American context?' An extension of the debate suggests that psychological theories and practice reinforce the social and political status quo and contribute significantly to maintaining oppressive power relations in society. This occurs through an almost exclusive focus on intrapsychic and interpersonal relations, often ignoring the psychosocial context in which individuals live.

This means that processes happening inside of people, such as thoughts and emotions and how they function within their families, receive predominant focus while understanding broader contexts for behaviour receive little attention. By extension, this approach suggests that traditional psychological

Figure 1 Euro-American psychology emphasises the individual, intrapsychic processes, interpersonal and family structures when considering influences on personality

practice fixes people to adapt to their (unequal) roles in society, rather than also to challenge the social inequality (Holmes & Lindley in Hook, 2002). A good example of this phenomenon is the institution of patriarchy where women generally are cast into roles that are inferior and less powerful than those accorded to men in society. Multiple roles often involving women primarily caring for and nurturing others, limited access to leisure time and self-care and a general societal devaluation of women's roles, all contribute to women's psychological distress (Holmshaw & Hillier, 2000; Jewkes, 2002; Worrell, 2001). While the World Health Report on Mental Health (World Health Organisation, 2001) acknowledges the interdependence of biological, psychological and social factors in the aetiology of mental health problems such as depression, mental health difficulties among women are often addressed through individual drug therapy and psychotherapy alone rather than also engaging these women in empowering activities which may allow them to change their social conditions in their respective communities (Holmshaw & Hillier, 2000). Drug and non-transformative psychotherapies are criticised for relieving only symptoms, while the factors which maintain the mental health problems remain intact. These debates raise questions central to any psychological research and therefore understandings of personality in the South African context.

Psychoanalytic approaches suggest that peoples' unconscious contains an aggregate of past experiences, conflicts and drives, and determines individual differences in personality. In this theoretical framework there is little opportunity for freedom of choice. Major theorists within this tradition are Freud, Jung, Adler and Lacan. Biological theorists explain differences in individual behaviour by referring to neurophysiological processes seated in the brain, genetic predisposition and genetic inheritance. Eysenck is the main proponent of this approach. More recently theorists, such as Buss (1991), have also argued for evolutionary processes impacting on behaviour. Cognitive theorists, like Kelly, argue that differences in the way in which people process information explain individual differences.

Theorists such as Skinner and Bandura use behavioural explanations to explain individual differences. They argue that behaviour patterns are established as a result of consistent conditioning. Allport belongs to a school of trait theorists who identify how a person may rate on a continuum of personality traits such as aggression or friendliness. Humanistic approaches, as reflected in the work of Rogers and Maslow, place great value on personal responsibility and experiences of acceptance in determining individual difference (Brody & Hayes, 1995; Burger, 1997; Hjelle & Ziegler, 1981).

Mainstream or traditional approaches and personality

Personality is a very complex concept, and there are many competing definitions. These definitions are informed by the psychological theory subscribed to by their respective proponents. Theories attempt to understand and explain questions about human nature. It is beyond the scope of this chapter to delve fully into detail about the various personality theories, but a brief overview of the central approaches is provided.

It is common in many areas of psychology to have various theories about the relationships between constructs. However, these theories do not combine to form a holistic understanding of personality. The six main approaches to personality, namely psychoanalytic, biological, humanistic, behavioural or learning, cognitive and trait approaches form the crux of personality theorising within mainstream psychology.

Figure 2 Trait theorists emphasise personality traits, such as aggression and friendliness

An example drawn from social psychology can perhaps illustrate how theorists from various traditions will describe a consistent pattern of empathy, a phenomenon common in psychology. Empathy often results in altruistic behaviours that especially involve helping others in need. Psychoanalytic approaches explain this by arguing that individuals may experience shame and guilt if they do not help, hence they are implicitly co-opted into helping. Biological approaches suggest that helping behaviour is biologically inherent in people as early human survival depended on co-operation. During these times humans needed to form co-operative groups and altruism increased their chances of survival. A careful assessment of the rewards and costs of the decision to help before choosing how to act, will be central to cognitive theorists' views of helping behaviour. The greater the costs of helping, the less likely people will be to help. For example, if great danger or potential loss of life is involved, people may be apprehensive and reluctant to help. Behavioural approaches argue that reinforcers and punishers dictate whether people help or not. People often look good when they display helping behaviour, or money given to charity may result in a tax rebate. Social learning approaches view modelling of prosocial behaviours as the essential determinant of empathetic behaviours such as helping. Children learn prosocial behaviours when they are exposed to other children and adults who engage in these behaviours. Learning theorists suggest that some people do not like to witness pain and suffering as this may cause personal distress. To avoid this experience, they engage in helping behaviour. Trait theorists see empathy as existing as a consistent trait on a continuum of established personality traits. Humanistic approaches argue that people are essentially good and will help others if they have grown up in a supportive environment that has fostered self-actualisation (Horowitz & Bordens, 1995).

While the various approaches do seem to differ considerably, they are however bound together by certain areas of commonality. These are:

- The idea that behaviour is an outcome of an internal personality structure. An internal personality structure suggests that that there is an enduring core in each individual that will affect behaviour.
- The need to understand and explain individual differences. It is argued that only through the study of personality can this endeavour be pursued.

- The importance of understanding personality within the context of an individual's development, be it biological, social or environmental (Hjelle & Ziegler, 1981).

These theories seldom elaborate on cultural factors impacting on personality (Burger, 1997). A further exploration of personality and culture will therefore examine the profound interconnectedness between the two areas.

Personality and culture

Culture itself has multiple definitions. For our purposes, it can be defined as:

> A set of guidelines (both explicit and implicit) which individuals inherit as members of a particular society, and which tells them how to view the world, how to experience it emotionally, and how to behave in relation to other people, to supernatural forces or gods, and to the natural environment. It also provides them with a way of transmitting these guidelines to the next generation – by using symbols, language, art and ritual (Helman, 1994:2-3).

Culture involves rules shared by members of a group. It is an abstract concept but is enacted and made practical through behaviours that can change over time. It is also not static, as rules change over periods of time (Swartz, 1998). In this definition, culture is a central aspect of an individual's identity, personality and social experience. Cultural values, mores and norms are internalised to become part of individuals' psychological make-up, and therefore strongly influence behaviour.

How does culture influence personality?

Various theorists such as Hofstede (2001), Matsumoto (1996) and Triandis (2001) have conceptualised an individualist-collectivist continuum of culture. Societies encourage values that place individuals along different points on the continuum. The concept of individualistic cultures refers to 'the degree to which a culture encourages, fosters, and facilitates the needs, wishes, desires, and values of a unique self over those of a group' (Matsumoto, 1996:24). Individualistic cultures, therefore encourage individuals to think of themselves as independent selves. In collectivist cultures, individuals see themselves as intricately linked to and dependent upon others.

Regions	Traits	Culture
North America, Europe	independent, self-driven individuals	Individualistic
Asia, Africa	interdependent, concrete definitions of self	Collectivist

Table 1 Regions and values: Recent research has suggested a continuum of individualism and collectivism, suggesting a less static view and more fluidity of these concepts

Dominant mainstream American culture is highly individualistic, and individuals are deemed to be successful when they meet personal goals, are separate from others and are self-contained (see Table 1). In this context, personal characteristics such as personality, individual ability and intelligence are highly prized. In collectivist cultures, individualism is given less salience. Interdependence among individuals, empathy and a strong sense of belonging to a supportive group, are encouraged. This impacts on the way 'individual' characteristics such as personality are construed (Markus & Kitayama, 1991; Ritts, 2001). Asian, Japanese and parts of South African culture have generally been thought of as having a collectivist ethos. In South Africa, African people value the concept of 'umuntu umuntu Ngabantu' which, when roughly translated, means: 'A person is only a person amongst other people' (Higson-Smith & Killian, 2002). This essentially means that a person is a social being only because she or he is able to exist and function in a complex and interconnected way with other people. Individual characteristics are deemed less prominent, and the social context of interaction is more highly valued.

Ritts (2001) furthermore argues that collective cultures do not attend to the needs of all others but

rather to those whom they deem to be part of the in-group, such as immediate and extended family members and long-term work and interest groups. An example from the South African context may illustrate this well. During the apartheid era in South Africa, the National Party divided the oppressed population into White, Coloured, Indian and African groupings. Apartheid involved a hierarchical system of privileges based on racial grouping. Most social and individual privileges were accorded to Whites. Coloureds and Indians were generally granted more privileges than Africans in terms of access to education, job preferences, area of residence, and freedom of movement. Black appearance, ability and experience were devalued in relation to that of White.

This devaluation had a profound negative impact on Black self-definition, and therefore personality traits such as assertiveness were discouraged and suppressed by dominant social norms (Fanon, 1967). In this context, the political reaction of Black consciousness, which originated in the 1970s, served to raise awareness about Black pride as espoused by the Black Consciousness Movement. This movement made an attempt to counteract deep levels of shame instilled in Black people about their experience. For example, the use of skin lighteners and hair straighteners amongst Black people to resemble the ideal White person was actively discouraged, and

Figure 3 Institutional racism was devaluing to Black people in South Africa

an historical emphasis was placed on the achievements of Black people (Fanon, 1967; Ncgobo, n.d.). Political thrusts such as the Black Consciousness Movement therefore created opportunities to reconstitute a fragmented collectivity and provide opportunities both for the construction of a positive collective identity and positive self-evaluation. The construction of behaviour through social experience does not, however, imply that individual characteristics such as personality do not exist. They will only be viewed differently in cultures that view collectivism as important.

12.3 INDIVIDUALISM-COLLECTIVISM AT SOUTH AFRICAN UNIVERSITIES AND IN KENYA

Eaton and Louw (2002) aimed to examine the impact of individualism-collectivism on constructions of self among English speakers and African language speakers at universities in South Africa. They administered the Twenty Statements Test to 78 African language speakers and 77 English speakers at South African universities. They found that African language speakers used more interdependent and concrete descriptions characteristic of collectivism than English language speakers.

Ma and Schoeneman (1997) examined the self-concepts of Kenyans in Nairobi. Participants were divided into the following categories: Urban and formally educated Kenyans, traditional and informally educated Kenyans and American university students. Urban, formally educated Kenyans showed self-concepts with some individualistic tendencies, whereas traditional Kenyans had the most collective self-concepts. Americans had the most individualistic tendencies. The researchers argued that urbanisation, development and education influenced self-concepts of Kenyans in Nairobi and resulted in decreased levels of collectivism.

Culture and the structure of personality

One definition of personality offered by Burger (1997:4) is that it is 'consistent behaviour patterns and intrapersonal processes originating within the individual'. This definition rests on several assumptions. It assumes a relatively stable core component to personality that is individual in nature and that is consistent from one context to another. The definition also refers to intrapersonal processes, in other words, processes internal to individuals as opposed to processes between individuals. It is assumed that factors external to the individual are important but are always mediated by individual differences. The notion of factors external to the individual is linked to a central concept within personality theory: locus of control. Loci of control are thought to be internal or external (Rotter in Matsumoto, 1996). If personality is determined by an internal locus of control people view the outcome of their behaviour as being controlled by factors deemed to be intrinsic to the individual, such as motivation. For example, if we excel in a sports competition, the assumption is that we are talented and have practiced extensively. An external locus of control assumes that the outcomes of behaviour are dependent on forces outside of the individual and beyond individual control. If a person excels in a competition, a person may believe it is because others assisted and supported him or her in preparation, thus ensuring success.

Eurocentric cultures tend to have an internal locus of control, whereas collectivist cultures tend to have an external locus of control (Matsumoto, 1996; Triandis, 2001). Ritts (2001) cites studies conducted by a variety of researches to support an internal locus of control amongst Americans (individualistic culture) as opposed to an external locus of control amongst Chinese, Japanese, Zambians and Zimbabweans, respectively (collectivist cultures).

Figure 4 Are the achievements of winning sprinters determined by an internal or external locus of control?

Some work has also been done on conceptualisations of the structure of personality within collectivist cultures. Berry *et al.* in Matsumoto (1996), for example, describe a three-tiered model of African personality. The first tier represents spirituality at the person's core; the second tier, psychological aspects; and the third tier represents physiological aspects. The body provides a casing within which these three core layers reside. Family, community and social factors affect core aspects of personality on different levels. Ncgobo (n.d.) supports the concept of an African personality. While Berry *et al.* and Ncgobo argue that the structure of personality is different in African people, this kind of argument needs to be evaluated critically in order to prevent a racially or culturally biased, and therefore limited, understanding of personality.

A more useful way of integrating culture, race, class and gender with personality is to view personality as an integration of an individual's construction of meaning using cultural values, products and behaviour integrated with biological and psychological factors such as evolution and temperament. This view of personality allows for both individual differences and cultural influences to coexist.

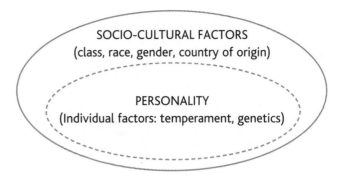

Figure 5 Visual representation of an integration of mainstream and cultural approaches to personality

Critical psychology: A critique of the concept of personality

Critical psychology is an approach that challenges established assumptions about psychology from the perspectives of social justice and liberation. Critical psychologists argue that traditional theories about personality that are drawn from Eurocentric and American contexts are presented and accepted as the only legitimate theories. Concepts of personality are also represented as value-free. Sloan (1997) suggests that mainstream approaches maintain the status quo of social inequality largely by placing overdue emphasis on individualism in understandings of personality. Firstly, concepts of personality that focus on individual core values such as aggression, greed and lack of empathy, situate these characteristics within individuals. In doing this it does not encourage us to examine and possibly change the society that inculcates these values. Instead, it encourages us to intervene at an individual level.

Sloan (1997) furthermore argues that personality theories are individualistic, as they encourage people to define problems of living as private matters, despite the fact that these problems often have social origins. This once again prevents attempts to find solutions at a communal or social level. Instead, interventions are typically aimed at the level of the individual or family.

Sloan (1997:98) defines personality as 'socially produced aspects of identity and affective experience that impede self-reflection, agency, autonomy, mutuality and other capacities that characterize meaningful living.' This definition is very different from mainstream understandings of personality that place emphasis on an individualistic core. It suggests that the concept of personality is an impediment to be overcome, as it limits positive experiences in daily living.

Figure 6 Theorists critical of the concept of personality suggest that it focuses on individualism and blames the victim, therefore deviating blame from societies that encourage values and practices that create homeless people

Critical approaches to personality can be seen as a holistic critique of personality rather than an explanatory approach to personality, as they suggest that the concept of personality is in itself flawed to the core and merely serves as a mask to obscure self-reflection on oppressive social relations.

Conclusion

This chapter has provided an overview of personality by classifying perspectives on personality into mainstream, cultural and critical perspectives. It demonstrated how traditional Euro-American views on personality are but one perspective, and that there is variation in the way in which personality is defined across different cultures. It was suggested that an integration of individuals' abilities to make meaning, in conjunction with psychobiological influences can allow for a successful marriage between individual and cultural conceptions of personality. Critical perspectives suggest that personality is a negative construct to be transcended, and can therefore be seen as a critique of personality rather than an attempt to explain individual differences. It is therefore important to view traditional approaches within a broader framework, so that the cultural, racial and class-based lenses with which we often approach the study of personality can be acknowledged and overcome.

REFERENCES

Anonymous. (1986). Some thoughts on a more relevant or indigenous counseling psychology in South Africa: Discovering the socio-political context of the oppressed. *Psychology in Society*, 5:81-9.

Berger, S. & Lazarus, S. (1987). The views of community organizers on the relevance of psychological practice in South Africa. *Psychology in Society*, 7:6-23.

Brody, R. & Hayes, N. (1995). *Teaching Introductory Psychology*. Sussex: Lawrence Erlbaum Associates.

Burger, J.M. (1997). *Personality*. California: Brooks/Cole Publishing.

Buss, D.M. (1991). Evolutionary personality psychology. *Annual Review of Psychology*, 42:459-91.

Dawes, A.R.L. (1986). The notion of relevant psychology with particular reference to Africanist pragmatic initiatives. *Psychology in Society*, 5:28-48.

Eaton, L. & Louw, J. (2002). Culture and self in SA: Individualism and collectivism predictions. *Journal of Social Psychology*, 140:210-17.

Fanon, F. (1967). *Black Skin, White Masks*. Harmondworth: Penguin.

Helman, C. (1994). *Culture, Health and Illness: An introduction for health professionals* (3rd edition). Oxford: Butterworth.

Higson-Smith, C. & Killian, B. (2002). Caring for children in fragmented communities. In D. Donald, A. Dawes & J. Louw (Eds.). *Addressing Childhood Adversity*. Cape Town: David Philip.

Hjelle, L.A. & Ziegler, D.J. (1981). *Personality Theories: Basic assumptions, research, and applications* (2nd edition). Auckland: McGraw-Hill.

Hofstede, W. (2001). *Culture's Consequences: Comparing values, behaviors, institutions and organizations across nations*. California: Sage.

Holmshaw, J. & Hillier, S. (2000). Gender and culture: A sociological perspective to mental health problems in women. In D. Kohen (Ed.). *Women and Mental Health*. London: Routledge.

Hook, D. (2002). Psychotherapy, discourse and the production of psychopathology. In D. Hook & G. Eagle (Eds.). *Psychopathology and Social Prejudice*. Lansdowne: UCT Press, pp. 20-54.

Horowitz, I.A. & Bordens, K.S. (1995). *Social Psychology*. California: Mayfield Publishing.

Jewkes, R. (2002). Intimate partner violence: Causes and prevention. *Lancet*, 359:1423-9.

Ma, V. & Schoeneman, T.J. (1997). Individualism versus collectivism: A comparison of Kenyan and American self-concepts. *Basic & Applied Social Psychology*, 19:261-73.

Markus, H.R. & Kitayama, S. (1991). Culture and the self: Implications for cognition, emotion, and motivation. *Psychological Review*, 98:224-53.

Matsumoto, D. (1996). *Culture and Psychology*. California: Brooks/Cole Publishing Company.

McCrae, R. (2001) Trait psychology and culture: Exploring intercultural comparisons. *Journal of Personality*, 69(6):819-46.

Moll, I. (2002). African Psychology: Myth and reality. *South African Journal of Psychology*, 32(1):9-16.

Ncgobo, D. (no date). Nihilism in Black South Africa: The new South Africa and destruction of the black domestic periphery. http://singh.reshma.tripod.com/alteration/alteration6_1/10NCGOBO.htm (accessed 10 March 2003).

Realo, A. & Allik, J. (2002). The nature and scope of intra-cultural variation on psychological dimension. In W.J. Lomer, D.L. Daniel, S.A. Hayes & D.N. Sattler (Eds.). *Online readings in psychology and culture*. www.edu/culture (accessed 24 May 2003).

Ritts, V. (2001). *Personality, the self and culture*. www.stlcc.cc.mo.us/mc/users/vritts/self.html (accessed 12 February 2003).

Sloan, T. (1997). Theories of personality: Ideology and beyond. In D. Fox & I. Prilleltensky (Eds.). *Critical Psychology: An introduction*. London: Sage.

Swartz, L. (1998). *Culture and Mental Health*. Cape Town: Oxford.

Triandis, (2001). Individualism-collectivism and personality. *Journal of Personality*, (69)6:907-24.

Vandello, J. & Cohen, D. (1999). Patterns of individualism and collectivism across the United States. *Journal of Personality & Social Psychology*, 77:279-92.

Vogelman, L., Perkel, A. & Strebel, A. (1992). Psychology and the community: Issues to consider in a changing South Africa. *Psychology Quarterly*, 2(2):1-9.

World Health Organisation. (2001). *The World Health Report 2001. Mental health: New understanding, new hope*. www.who.int/whr/2001 (accessed 2 February 2002).

Worrell, J. (2001). Feminist interventions: accountability beyond symptom reduction. *Psychology of Women Quarterly*, 25(4):335-43.

Multiple choice questions

1. Personality is
   a) a reflection of the core characteristics within an individual
   b) a reflection of world-views characteristic of Euro-American middle-class societies
   c) a reflection of a person's culture
   d) all of the above
2. Mainstream approaches to personality
   a) provide a comprehensive understanding of personality
   b) provide a limited understanding of personality
   c) provide a South African understanding of personality
   d) all of the above
3. The study of personality in South Africa has involved
   a) traditional approaches
   b) cultural approaches
   c) critical approaches
   d) none of the above
4. Biological approaches to personality focus on
   a) explaining individual differences in behaviour
   b) neurophysiological process seated in the brain
   c) genetic predisposition
   d) all of the above
5. Personality within a cultural context
   a) involves rules shared by members of a group
   b) is mediated by internalised rules and values
   c) is determined by social norms
   d) none of the above
6. Individualistic cultures
   a) are American
   b) value the self above the group
   c) value the group above the self
   d) none of the above
7. Collectivist cultures
   a) are Japanese
   b) value the broader societal group above the self
   c) value the self above the group
   d) view individuals as linked to each other and interdependent

Short answer questions

1. Discuss the main approaches that characterize mainstream personality theorising, using illustrative examples.
2. What unites the various approaches within mainstream personality theory?
3. How has culture impacted on your personality?
4. Is it possible to integrate individual and cultural conceptions of personality? Discuss.
5. What separates critical perspectives on personality from other approaches?

Personality Theories

Pam Naidoo

After studying this chapter you should be able to:
- understand how each personality theorist attempts to answer the question of individual similarities and differences
- know what set of assumptions underpin the various approaches to personality
- know the theoretical concepts that are unique to each theorist, namely Freud, Jung, Horney, Erikson, Maslow, Skinner and Bandura
- understand the influence of the concept of the unconscious, first introduced by Freud, in mainstream personality theories, particularly in the neoanalytical explanations of human behaviour
- critically evaluate the personality theories within the framework of scientifically acceptable criteria
- apply your mind to the applicability and non-applicability of the mainstream theories to the African, Asian and other contexts.

Introduction

It is not uncommon that when reference is made to someone, this description often includes aspects of the person's personality. Consider the following quotation: 'I met Solomon Ngcobo yesterday. He has not changed a bit. He is still the calm, patient, and sociable person that he has always been.' One can also deduce from this quotation that it is implied that people tend to present themselves consistently over time. This means that there are certain stable personality characteristics that endure. You may describe your colleague, Jeff, as always being the quiet, responsible dependable person ever since you met him 20 years ago. However, while you may also be able to describe another colleague, Marlene, in the same way you describe Jeff, Jeff and Marlene may be different in other ways besides the fact that Jeff is male and Marlene is female. Marlene, for example, may be able to express her dissatisfaction about certain work conditions to her seniors at work, that is, she is able to assert her rights. Jeff, on the other hand may not be able to be assertive about matters that he truly has strong opinions about.

We can see clearly, therefore, that while people may have similar characteristics, they are also different in other ways. The study of personality and the development of personality theories attempt to address the question of individual similarities and differences.

What is it, then, that makes individuals unique? Many factors influence the development of personality. These factors include social ones (such as economic resources and educational experiences) and cultural ones (such as family norms and values and religious influences).

Many theorists have attempted to explain personality development. In the discipline of psychology, individuals who have attempted to build a personality theory using various constructs are called personologists. In the following section various theoretical approaches to personality will be discussed. The first attempts in psychology to explain behaviour were based on what was observable. This method of trying to understand people's behaviour was based on the methods used in the natural sciences.

Freud first introduced the relationship of consciousness to unconscious processes into psychology. After keen observation of his patients, in the late nineteenth century, Freud concluded that unconscious mental processes account for the behaviour of individuals. Despite not being able to subject his

theory to any level of scientific rigour, Freud had many followers whose theories included both conscious and unconscious aspects to their theory of personality. Other personologists, however, namely the behaviourists developed theoretical constructs based only on those behaviours that were observable. Their theories, therefore, did not include unconscious processes.

It is also interesting to note that although most theories of personality were developed through some scientific method, albeit 'loosely', the way in which personologists have developed and refined their theories must also be understood from their personal circumstances and events in their formative years that have shaped their lives. By tracing the development of the various theories by first providing a very brief personal history of each theorist you will be able to understand the relationship between the personal life of the theorist, the spirit of the time (or the Zeitgeist) during which the theorist lived, and how this relationship influenced and contributed to the development of the respective theories.

The first formal study of personality was psychoanalysis, initiated by Freud in the late nineteenth century. The basic premise of psychoanalytic theory is that behaviour is determined by unconscious drives and motives. While Freud was influenced by many, for example, Breuer and Charcot (Pervin, 1980), he is still considered to have revolutionised understanding of human behaviour and human mental processes. Freud began to formulate his theory of personality after studying the cases, mostly middle to upper income women, that he treated in his practice. Factors that appeared to be common in the lives of these women, according to Freud, included the life long experiences of early childhood influences, the existence of early infantile sexuality, the significance of the content of dreams, and finally the factors that influenced their lives of which they were not consciously aware.

Theorists such as Jung, Adler and Horney are considered to be neopsychoanalysts because they have used Freud's theory as a frame of reference to build their own. The neopsychoanalysts have challenged some of Freud's concepts, particularly his overemphasis on sexuality as a driving force for behaviour. They have, however, alluded to the existence of the concept of the unconscious.

Other approaches to the study of personality include the life span approach, the trait approach, the humanistic approach, the cognitive approach, the behavioural approach and the social learning approach. Erikson, one of the proponents of the life span approach emphasises the psychological polarities (e.g., trust versus mistrust in early infancy) that exist in each psychosocial stage. Cattell and other trait theorists have a relatively more scientific approach to the study of personality. They have employed the statistical technique of factor analysis to develop personality traits. Humanists, such as Maslow and Rogers, stress the importance of the self and recognise the potential of humans to self-actualise. Cognitive theorists such as Kelly focus on the role of individuals' cognitions. These theorists are concerned with conscious mental processes and the way an individual thinks about and perceives the world, solves problems and makes decisions. The behaviourists, such as Skinner, reject any notion of unconscious factors in motivating human behaviour. Behaviourists are only interested in behaviour that is observable. Finally, the social learning theorists, such as Bandura, explain the relationship between cognitive factors and learning. They show how cognitions mediate between stimulus and response in the development of personality.

Approaches to personality development: An overview

The psychoanalytic approach

The main proponent of the psychoanalytic theory of personality was *Sigmund Freud* (1856-1939). Freud was born in Monrovia into a Jewish family. His father was a wool merchant and his mother, a homemaker. Together they had seven children, including Freud, who was their first-born. Freud was a genius, excelling academically. He was said to have mas-

Figure 2 Sigmund Freud

tered many languages. He was married to Martha. Anna Freud, one of their daughters, succeeded in becoming a respected psychoanalyst.

Freud completed a medical degree at the University of Vienna and established a practice in clinical neurology in 1881. At this time he began to explore the personalities of those suffering from emotional disturbances. His work in Paris with Charcot, a psychiatrist who was also a pioneer in hypnosis, alerted him to the fact that there might be a sexual basis for neurosis.

By 1896, after several years in practice, Freud was convinced that sexual conflicts were the primary cause of all the neuroses. He observed that many women patients reported sexually traumatic events in which older male figures, or father figures, were reported to be the seducers. He later admitted, though, that some of these events may have been a fantasy of the individual, but seemed very real to the patient.

Freud continued to develop his theory of personality using case material and engaging in dream

Theoretical approaches and corresponding theorists at a glance

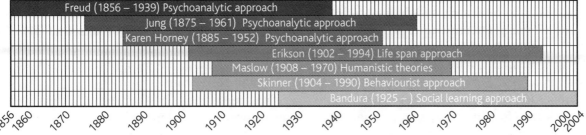

Figure 1 Theoretical approaches to personality development and corresponding theorists

analysis. By documenting data over time he was able to construct a fairly comprehensive theory along rational and empirical lines. At this stage in his career he attracted such people as Carl Jung and Alfred Adler. Psychoanalytic schools were initiated in the United States. Although Freud visited and lectured in the US, he preferred to remain in Vienna.

During the German occupation of Austria in World War Two, Anna Freud, Freud's daughter, was arrested. At this point Freud left Austria to live in London, and later died in 1939.

Freud's view on personality development

Instincts, according to Freud, are the basic motivational drives that determine the basis for personality, and are conceptualised as mental representations of internal stimuli, such as hunger, that drive a person to take certain actions (Freud, 1901). This means that a basic internal need (such as hunger) initiates a physiological reaction. This bodily need then gets translated into a mental representation (a wish) of how we should behave in order to fulfill that need (e.g., looking for food to satisfy our hunger).

Freud postulated that individuals always experience a certain amount of tension based on instinctual needs, and that we always act in a way that will reduce the tension. Individuals, therefore, are always looking to satisfy their needs. To illustrate this point further consider the sex drive. We may satisfy the sex drive by engaging in heterosexual, homosexual, or autosexual behaviour, or we might channel or re-direct the sexual energy in another direction by engaging in a different type of activity. Psychic energy, then, according to Freud, may be displaced onto another substitute object. This principle of displacement is the key to understanding the development of personality and explains why individuals are different and often have such diverse interests.

Instincts have been grouped into two broad categories by Freud, namely the *life instinct* and the *death instinct*. The life instinct serves survival needs and individuals' need to constantly satisfy the needs for food, water, air and sex to ensure growth and development. The psychic energy manifested by the life instinct is called *libido*. The libido can be attached to or invested in objects. Freud termed this cathexis.

Freud regarded sex as our primary motivation. Erotic wishes arise from the body's erogenous zones that include the mouth, anus, and sex organs. Freud suggested that most of our behaviour is pleasure-seeking and we are constantly striving to suppress our sexual desires.

The *death instinct* represents the destructive force of human nature. Biologically we are all programmed to die, but Freud went on to say that people have an unconscious wish to die. This wish to die, Freud suggests, is transformed into an aggressive drive in which individuals act out their aggression on others. This implies that we all have the potential to be destructive.

The conscious, preconscious and the unconscious: The three levels of personality

The term 'conscious' corresponds to the sensations and experiences that we are aware of at any given moment in time. Freud thought that our conscious was a limiting aspect of our personality because it only included a small portion of our thoughts, sensations and memories. He therefore stated that it was the tip of the iceberg.

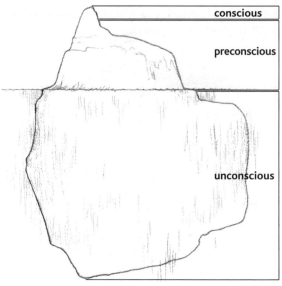

Figure 3 The conscious, preconscious and unconscious: The conscious is the tip of the iceberg

Of particular importance in Freudian theory is the concept of the unconscious. The unconscious is that part that is below the conscious and contains the instincts, those wishes and desires that direct our behaviour. The unconscious is the focus of psychoanalysis because it the most powerful driving force behind all behaviours.

The preconscious lies between the conscious and the unconscious, and is the level of personality most readily available to our consciousness. It houses our thoughts, memories and perceptions that we may be able to recall if we shift from the present state of consciousness to the preconscious level.

Id, ego and superego: The structure of personality

The id

The id corresponds to the unconscious and houses the instincts and libido. It is a forceful structure of the personality and provides the impetus for the other structures. Because of the location of the instincts within the id, the id is directly related to the satisfaction of bodily needs. Tension arises in the quest to fulfil bodily needs, and the id is said to operate in a way to reduce tension in order to maintain a homeostatic balance. The id is said by Freud to operate according to the *pleasure principle* to increase pleasure and avoid pain. It seeks immediate gratification and is as such selfish and inconsiderate of the needs of others.

The id has no awareness of reality. The only way the id can attempt to satisfy its needs is through reflex action and wish-fulfilling hallucinatory or fantasy experience, which Freud labelled as *primary-process thought*.

The ego

Children soon learn that they cannot always act on their immediate needs. They learn how to interact with the outside world to develop mental functions such as perception, recognition, judgement and memory in the way that adults do. Freud termed these abilities *secondary-process thought*.

These rational elements are contained in Freud's second structure of personality, the ego. The ego therefore guides by reason. It helps to reduce tensions created by id functioning by finding means based on the *principle of reality*. Through the ego's consistent contact with reality, id impulses are satisfied in socially appropriate ways at the right time and place using acceptable objects.

The id therefore is controlled by the ego. No attempt is made by the ego to prevent satisfaction of the id, but the ego does manipulate and redirect environmental factors in order to control the ultimate expression of id needs. The id and the ego are seen to have a conflictual relationship because the ego has to constantly heed to demands of the id, which is the structure that provides the energy for itself and the ego structure.

The superego

Components of the superego are largely unconscious, and it contains the ideas of right and wrong that we have learned during our childhood. This internal moral code or conscience Freud called the *superego*. By the age of 5 or 6 most children learn from significant others, such as their family members, what behaviours are punishable. This leads to the development of the conscience, one component of the superego. The behaviours that have been praised and rewarded lead to the development of the *ego-ideal*, a second component of the superego.

Figure 4 The work of the superego

The process of internalisation of what is good and what constitutes bad is a powerful unconscious recognition of parental influence, albeit parental control. Once the process of internalisation occurs, the rules of right and wrong are self-administered. Self-control then replaces parental control. Consequently, when we engage in behaviours that are contrary to the individual moral order, we suffer guilt and shame.

The superego is seen by Freud to be harsh in its insistence for moral order. Unlike the ego, the superego serves to obliterate certain id drives such as sex and aggression. The ego therefore serves as a go-between, and is pressured by the id, reality and the superego. When the ego cannot cope with the demands of the id, reality and the superego, anxiety develops.

Anxiety

Freud described anxiety as an objectless fear, and often we cannot point to the source of our anxiety. Anxiety, stated Freud, is fundamental to the development of neurotic and psychotic behaviour. He suggested that the prototype of all anxiety is birth trauma. The child leaves the warmth and security of the mother's womb to face a harsh and hostile world.

Freud describes three types of anxiety: reality anxiety, neurotic anxiety, and moral anxiety (Hall & Lindzey, 1978). The basic type of anxiety is reality anxiety, which is a fear of real dangers in the external world. Neurotic and moral anxiety are derived from reality anxiety. Neurotic anxiety is the fear that the instincts will get out of control and cause us to behave in a way that could be amenable to being punished. We therefore are more afraid of the punishment than of the loss of control of the instincts. Moral anxiety is fear of the conscience. People with well-developed superegos are afraid to behave in ways that are contrary to the moral code in which they were raised.

Anxiety serves to alert us that the ego is in danger. Freud believed that we are always defending against anxiety, to a lesser or greater degree. Various defense mechanisms are employed to protect the ego.

We defend against anxiety by using more than one defense mechanism. Although they are different in many ways, *defence mechanisms* share two fundamental qualities: (1) they are denials or distortions of reality, and (2) they operate unconsciously. Freud mentions a number of defense mechanisms, which include repression, denial, reaction formation, projection, regression, rationalisation, displacement and sublimation (for an in-depth reading on each of the defense mechanisms see Freud (1901) and Schultz and Schultz (2001)).

Psychosexual stages of personality development

Freud stated that a child makes every attempt to satisfy the id, while the parents make every effort to impose moral demands and those demands that govern the law of reality. Freud was convinced that an individual's personality forms by the age of five.

Freud observed that children's conflicts seemed to revolve around certain regions of the body. Each stage of development is associated with conflicts around specific body parts. Freud based his theory of psychosexual development around this. Each stage of development is associated with an erogenous zone, and it is only if the conflicts at each stage are resolved that the individual will go on to the next stage.

If an individual is unable to resolve conflicts at a certain stage they remain fixated at that stage. This means that libidinal energy gets invested in that particular stage, leaving less energy for the stages that follow.

The oral stage

This first stage is from birth to 2 years of age. The mouth is the source of pleasure. The activities of sucking and biting are indicative of erotic pleasure for the child.

A child during this period is dependent on the caretaker, who becomes the object of his or her libidinal energy. Since the caretaker is usually the mother, through this process of receiving gratification from the mother the child learns to love her.

There are two ways of behaving during this stage: oral incorporative behaviour and oral aggressive or sadistic behaviour. Individuals fixated at the oral stage are excessively concerned about activities such as eating and drinking. If infants are excessively gratified they may become overly optimistic and dependent. They tend to be gullible, relying on others for gratification. Such people are labelled oral-passive personality types.

The oral-aggressive or oral-sadistic personality type develops during the frustrating period when a child is cutting his or her teeth. These infants experience both love and hate towards their mothers. People fixated at this stage tend to be excessively pessimistic, hostile and aggressive. They tend to make biting remarks, and are not usually good towards others. Instead, they are manipulative and exploitative in order to dominate.

The anal stage

Demands made by adults on a child are few until the need for toilet training arises. This usually happens around 18 months. It is this phase, termed the anal stage, which Freud believed made a significant impact on personality development. The process of defecation gives the child erotic pleasure but this is interfered with for the first time due to toilet training when the parents begin to set the rules about when and where the child may conduct the habits of the bowel.

The child soon learns that he or she has for the first time some control over the parents, and consequently also learns to use this power of control to manipulate the parents. If toilet training is not successfully carried out, the child is faced with excessively demanding parents, which leads to the child reacting in one of two ways. Firstly, the child may react by defecating at inappropriate times and in inappropriate places, much to the disapproval of the parents. If the child needs to employ this reactionary method to toilet training and regulation frequently, this may lead to the development of an anal-aggressive personality. In adult life this may translate into an individual becoming sadistic and hostile.

The second reaction to toilet training may be the retention of faeces. This gives the child erotic pleasure and a further sense of control over the parents, particularly if the child has not defecated for a few days. Parents express their concern in this instance and satisfy the child's intention of securing parental attention. This may lead to the development of an anal-retentive personality. These individuals are typically stubborn and stingy, and tend to hoard things as their security depends on the possessions they have and the order in which both their possessions and life are maintained. These people tend to be rigid, compulsively neat and overly conscientious.

The phallic stage

This stage is between three to six years, when we begin to feel pleasure in the genital region. The *Oedipus complex* is an important phenomenon during this stage. Freud used the Oedipus complex as a means to explain a boy's sexual attraction to his mother and accompanying feelings of rivalry towards his father. When a boy realises that girls do not have a penis, the resulting anxiety is the *castration complex*. A boy's identification with his father occurs when he represses his sexual strivings toward his mother and tries to please his father.

The *Electra complex* was used by Freud to explain female sexual development. Girls feel a sexual attraction to their father and therefore experience rivalry towards their mother. Girls, Freud stated, also experience penis envy and want a penis of their own.

The latency and genital stages

The latency stage is between six years and puberty, and is a period of relative sexual quiet. From puberty on there are many hormonal changes that mark the stage called the genital stage. During this psychosocial stage the individual enters into heterosexual relationships outside the family.

Evaluation of Freud's theory

The concept of the unconscious is considered to be Freud's most important and valuable contribution. The fact that, according to Freud, our conscious thoughts and behaviour are directed by repressed thoughts revolutionised theoretical formulations about human behaviour. Freud also brought to attention the importance of early childhood influences on later development.

The controversial aspects of Freud's theory centres around his emphasis on the sexual drive as a primary motivating force for human behaviour. His perception of women has also received criticism. Freud stated that women were anatomically inferior because they do not have a penis, psychologically inferior because they do not experience the Oedipal conflict or castration anxiety (as a result of not having a penis), morally inferior because they do not develop as strong a superego as boys do (due to not having had the aforementioned conflict), and culturally inferior because they are not able to sublimate (as they do not have a strong superego) and use their creative energy to become productive (Papalia & Olds, 1988).

Other criticisms come from humanistic theorists who believe that Freud did not acknowledge human courage. Finally, Freud's theory has been criticised because it cannot be scientifically validated.

Neoanalytic approaches

Carl Gustav Jung

Figure 5 Carl Gustav Jung

Jung (1875-1961) was born in Switzerland into a family of clergymen. His childhood was marked by strife and unhappiness. Although Jung shared a close relationship to his father, he experienced him as a weak man. His mother was seen to be the stronger of the two parents, but was emotionally unstable and often unable to contain her emotions.

Jung's parents apparently did not enjoy a good marital relationship, which resulted in him spending many hours alone. He continued to be a lonely child even after the birth of his sister when he was nine years old. It is thought that Jung's interest in dreams and fantasies is directly related to his isolated and solitary existence as a child.

Like Freud, Jung also became a medical doctor. He completed his medical degree at the University of Basil and specialised in psychiatry, working under the psychiatrist Bleuler, famous for naming the mental disorder schizophrenia.

In 1907, Jung began his association with Freud (Jung, 1909). They shared many professional interests, including the concept of the unconscious.

Jung's view on personality development

Jung differed from Freud in one important way. He rejected the idea of sexuality as a major determinant of behaviour. Instead he believed that behaviour in large part is driven purposefully and in a way that allows people to grow and develop throughout life. In the process of growth and development individuals are also searching for meaning in their lives. He placed emphasis on the individual's ancestral past, and contended that the foundations of personality are archaic, primitive, innate, unconscious and universal (Jung, 1927, 1928).

In order to gain an in-depth understanding of the way personality evolves, Jung focused on a person's racial past. He studied such fields as religion, mythology and philosophy.

The structure of personality

Jung disagreed with Freud on the latter's emphasis on sexuality, and viewed libido as a generalised life force, which he saw from two different perspectives (Schultz & Schultz, 2001). The first perspective was that libido was a general life energy, and the second perspective was that libido was focused psychic energy that facilitates personality dynamics, which Jung called the psyche.

Jung added to Freud's concept of the unconscious, the concept of the *collective unconscious*. The collective unconscious refers to the cumulative experiences of past generations, which are shared by all human beings by virtue of our common ancestry. According to Jung, psychic life is the mind of our ancient ancestors, the way in which they thought and felt, the way in which they conceived of life and the world, of gods and human beings.

Those recurring experiences and images that are contained in the collective unconscious are called the *archetypes* (Jung in Schultz & Schultz, 2001). Archetypes are expressed in our dreams and fantasies. Significant archetypes mentioned by Jung include the mother, the hero, the child, God, power, death and the wise old man. Jung adds that these archetypes are universally represented among different cultures from past and present time periods.

Jung emphasised the principle of opposites, and stated that people often struggle with opposing forces within their selves. We struggle, for example, with the mask we present to others (*the persona*) and the private or personal self. If we persistently present the persona at the expense of the personal self, we may begin to doubt our sense of self. We also struggle with the masculine and feminine parts of ourselves. According to Jung, every woman has a masculine part (*animus*) and every man has a feminine part (*anima*) to his personality as a result of centuries of living together and internalising aspects of the opposite sex. Jung contended that it is essential that a man express his female side, and a woman her masculine side, in order to reach optimal growth as a human being.

Jung also distinguished between *introversion* and *extroversion*. An individual relates to the world primarily as an introvert or as an extrovert, but also possesses the qualities of the opposite orientation. The introvert has an inner orientation, toward the self, and is cautious and reflective. The extrovert has an outward orientation, toward the outside world, and is sociable, active and seeks adventure.

In developing our personalities, therefore, we are constantly trying to find the balance between opposing forces to achieve a fully realised self.

Evaluation of Jung's theory

Jung's approach to personality has influenced a number of disciplines, such as psychiatry, history, sociology, economics, political science, philosophy and religion (Schultz & Schultz, 2001).

Jung has made some important contributions to psychology. The words 'association test' are a recognised projective technique with which the development of the Rorschach Inkblot test has been associated. The concepts of introverted versus extroverted personalities are used with some conviction in psychology today. Jung's concepts such as individuation and self-actualisation have influenced personologists, namely Maslow, Adler, Cattell and Erikson.

Critics of Jung state that the concept of the archetype is said to be metaphysical and with no proof that it exists (Glover, 1950). Further, critics argue, the concept of the archetype cannot be scientifically validated.

Karen Horney

Figure 6 Karen Horney

Horney (1885-1952) was the first personologist to challenge Freud on issues of gender. She argued that Freud formulated a theory of personality from a man's point of view. In addition, she disputed the deterministic theory as put forward by Freud. Horney argued that the social and cultural influences on personality development were more important than the biological drive theory as proposed by Freud.

Horney is regarded to have initiated feminist psychological thinking. Her views on gender are better understood in the context of her personal history. She was born in Germany and had an older brother whom she envied because he was her parents' favoured child. She recognised that she was intellectually more capable than he was, though. In addition, she also realised at a young age that boys received more recognition than girls did.

Horney, it is said, had always craved her father's love and attention. She found him to be intimidating and inaccessible. The way she related to men reflected her constant need to find love and security.

In order to guarantee her entry into university, Horney worked hard and pursued her academic life with certainty. She became a medical student in 1906, at the University of Freiburg, and completed her medical degree in 1913, at the University of Berlin. In the early twentieth century it was both difficult and unusual for a woman to balance both marriage and career. She had three daughters during her marriage, which lasted 17 years. The marriage ended because she felt an overwhelming degree of oppression. It was at this point that she went into psychoanalysis. This experience spurred her on to theorising about personality development.

Horney's view on personality development

Horney placed great emphasis on cultural factors in personality development. She was interested in how individuals coped with basic anxiety – the feeling of isolation a child has in a hostile world. According to Horney's theory of neurosis, in the neurotic person there is a conflict among the three ways of responding to basic anxiety. These three patterns (*neurotic trends*) are: moving toward other people (the compliant personality), moving against other people (the aggressive personality) and moving away from other people (the detached personality). All three are characterised by rigidity and inhibition of the person's full potential.

The compliant personality has a persistent need to be loved and protected, and constantly seeks approval. People with compliant personalities need at least one dominating person in their life who will take charge and offer protection and guidance. Horney postulated that the behaviour of compliant personalities is a result of repressed hostility. They have, she said, a desire to control and manipulate others, but repress this and instead portray themselves as subservient and pleasing. The aggressive personality views their world as hostile. They are also motivated to alleviate anxiety, but behave in a way that reveals that they are not afraid of rejection. Aggressive personalities are domineering, have a need to excel and have their achievements affirmed by others. Finally, the detached personality moves away from others to maintain an emotional distance. They become self-sufficient and rely on their own resources. Detached personalities place emphasis on reason, logic and intelligence.

Horney states that in the neurotic individual, only one of the personality types are dominant and the other two are repressed. However, conflict arises when one of the repressed personalities tries to express itself because the neurotic individual makes every attempt to retain their dominant personality.

Neurotic persons, Horney said, construct an idealised self-image to unify their personality, but often struggle because they are unable to attain the ideal. The idealised self-image further alienates the neurotic from the true self. In an individual who is not neurotic, however, all three personalities are expressed at different times and are usually people who are flexible in nature.

Feminine psychology

Horney revolutionised psychological thinking by becoming the first woman to present a paper on feminine psychology in 1922 (Schultz & Schultz, 2001). She challenged Freud's notions of penis envy and counter-argued that men envied women because of a woman's ability to fulfill the role of motherhood so adeptly. Further, she rejected Freud's explanation of the Oedipus complex as having a sexual origin. Instead she said the Oedipus complex is a conflict the child experiences because of the simultaneous feeling of both dependency and hostility they feel toward their parents. She postulated that social and cultural influences played a more influential role in the development of personality than biological influences, as suggested by Freud. Women, according to Horney, are particularly subjected to cultural forces.

Evaluation of Horney's theory

Horney used the case study method to develop a theory of personality, and has therefore received similar criticisms to those directed at Freud, Jung and Adler. However, research has been conducted on Horney's three proposed neurotic trends: moving against people, moving away from people, and moving toward people (see Caspi *et al.*, 1987, 1988).

Although Horney has influenced feminist psychology, very little research has been conducted to support her notions.

The life span approach

The first major theory of personality to cover the entire life span is Erik Erikson's (1902-1994) theory of psychosocial development. Erikson (1950) retained and developed Freud's concept of the ego to further understand society's influence on the developing personality. He theorised about eight stages of psychosocial development and the individual's ability to successfully resolve the conflict with which he or she is confronted in each stage.

Erikson was born in Frankfurt, Germany, of Danish parents. His parents were not married, and his father left before Erikson was born. His mother married Erikson's paediatrician, Dr Homburger. Erikson was unaware for many years that Dr Homburger was not his biological father. When he did become aware he was distressed by this news.

During his school years in Germany, he underwent another crisis that pertained to his heritage. Although he was of Danish descent, he grew up in Germany, and as such regarded himself as a German. His peers did not accept him as a German because his step-father was a Jew. This was another instance in which his identity came into question.

Throughout his schooling Erikson did not excel. He was thought of as more of an artist than an academic. At age 25, after extensive travel, he moved to Vienna to teach in a small school that was attended by Freud's patients and friends. At this point a relationship between himself and Freud developed. Erikson's professional career began here and he has openly acknowledged the influence of Freud's psychoanalytic theorising on his work.

Anna Freud, Freud's daughter, psychoanalysed Erikson and he later became a member of the Vienna Psychoanalytic Institute. He enjoyed a life long marriage.

Erikson's view on personality development

Erikson's theory takes into account both the psyche and society in describing the eight psychosocial stages of development throughout the life span (see Box 13.1). He emphasised the conflict between what is instinctual in nature and societal demands. Erikson explained the consequences of resolving or not resolving the conflict, which presents as a crisis, in each stage of development.

Figure 7 Erik Erikson

Stage one: Basic trust versus mistrust (birth to 12 months)

If an individual has consistently good and reliable care during the first twelve months of his or her life, Erikson postulated that there will be successful resolution of the first crisis: basic trust versus basic mistrust. If the primary caregiver adequately attends to the dependency needs of the child, such as feeding and comforting, then a basic sense of trust develops. The child then uses this pattern of interacting with significant people in its life to measure their relationships and the development of trust with others (Erikson, 1950).

Stage two: Autonomy versus shame and doubt (12 months to 3 years)

During this stage of development, a child begins to explore his or her environment and develop language. The child also learns a degree of independence while simultaneously coming to terms with his or her limitations.

If over-controlling parents thwart a child's independence, feelings of self-doubt set in and a feeling of shame develops when interacting with others. When a child is allowed to express his or her free will but also exercises self-restraint in the face of society's demands then a healthy resolution of this stage has occurred.

Stage three: Initiative versus guilt (3 to 6 years)

As the child becomes more adept in dealing with him- or herself and the outside world, then he or she initiates their own activities. If a child is punished harshly for taking the initiative then the child develops a sense of guilt in self-directed activities, which lasts throughout life.

Stage four: Industry versus inferiority (6 years to puberty)

When the child attends a place where formal instruction takes place, issues of competency arise. The child also compares him- or herself against his or her peers. Children who feel inferior to their peers develop a sense of inferiority, and those who achieve and develop confidence about who they are and what they can achieve, become industrious.

Stage five: Identity versus role confusion (puberty to young adulthood)

The most important life task during this stage of development, according to Erikson, is to establish an identity. Teenagers are faced with having to answer to the question: Who am I?

This period is seen to be a particularly difficult time for teenagers because even if they have successfully resolved the previous four stages, they are faced with bodily changes in keeping with the growth spurt they experience, as opposed to subtle and unobtrusive changes.

This stage is often marked by confusion. People have difficulty in deciding what their life goals should be, for example, career decisions. Erikson states, however, that falling in love helps to establish identity.

Stage six: Intimacy versus isolation (young adulthood)

During this stage individuals have the capacity to form a close and intimate bond with someone special in their lives. This requires intermittent ego loss in our intimate interactions because we have to share space and feelings (such as during love-making or marriage).

Stage seven: Generativity versus stagnation (middle adulthood)

By the time an individual reaches the age of 40, he or she would have accumulated many life experiences to be able to guide and mentor young people. People who guide and nurture their children and other young people toward their future are said to be engaging in the process of generativity. Generativity also involves being productive and creative in our work, whether paid work or voluntary work for social upliftment. Stagnation, on the other hand, leads to a further decrease in our creativity, which ultimately leads to self-indulgence.

Stage eight: Ego integrity versus despair (late adulthood)

Ego integrity is achieved with the successful resolution of the previous seven crises. It means that individuals have little regret about the way they have lived their lives. If they are consumed with what they should have done or what they would have done differently, they experience despair because they realise that they cannot 'turn back the clock'.

Evaluation of Erikson's theory

Erikson's most important contribution was his consideration of development issues throughout the life span. His recognition of the need to successfully resolve a major developmental conflict within each important stage of growth in order to achieve the level of maturation for maximum functioning, is widely acknowledged.

Some of the criticisms against Erikson include the fact that his developmental theory does not apply to women (Tavris, 1992). Further, questions arise about whether his theory applies to people in depressed financial conditions who are not able to go through the stages in the way that Erikson theorised (Slugoski & Ginsburg, 1989). In addition, it is argued that Erikson does not consider or explain homosexual relationships.

Despite the criticisms, Erikson's theory widely influences social and educational policies and therapeutic approaches.

13.2 ERIKSON'S FINDINGS ON GENDER DIFFERENCES IN PLAY CONSTRUCTIONS

In the 1960s Erikson used play therapy, which he called play constructions, to conduct research on his theory. In one study, 300 boys and girls, ages 10 to 12, were asked to create a scene from an imaginary movie using dolls, toy animals, automobiles and wooden blocks.

Girls tended to build scenes that did not reflect movement, were peaceful and that contained low, enclosed structures. Intruders (males or animal figures) tried to force their way into the interior of the construction. Boys, on the other hand, focused on exteriors, action and height. Their constructions were action-oriented, with tall towering structures and cars and people in motion.

Erikson came under fire for his interpretation of his findings of this study. He stated, using the psychoanalytic tradition, that the play constructions depicted the biological, genital differences between boys and girls. Boys had an external organ: erectable and intrusive in character, and girls' genitalia is internal. Erikson was criticised for the view that suggests that women are victims of their anatomy, and their personalities are determined by the absence of a penis.

Humanistic theories

Humanistic psychology focuses on internal motivators of behaviour and has an optimistic view of human nature, believing that all humans have a positive nature. Humanists emphasise self-determination and free will (Papalia & Olds, 1988). The humanistic approach may be conceptualised as a phenomenological one because it stresses the importance of the 'subjective, unique experiences of each person and the potential all of us have for self-fulfillment through spontaneity, creativity, and personal growth' (Papalia & Olds, 1988:464).

Abraham Maslow

Figure 8 Abraham Maslow

Maslow (1908-1970), the oldest of seven children, was born in Brooklyn, New York. He had a difficult childhood and did not respect his parents much. His mother was apparently an aggressive woman, who constantly rejected him. To escape the poverty in which he grew up, he developed a love for reading and scholarship. Maslow married young.

During his studies of psychology at university he was influenced by the behaviourist, James B. Watson. He received a PhD in 1934 at the University of Wisconsin, and thereafter enjoyed a successful professional life.

Maslow's view on personality development
Maslow showed most interest in healthy individuals. He focused on the positive aspects of human nature such as joy, enthusiasm, love and well-being, and did not go into any depth on the negative aspects such as conflict, shame, hostility and unhap-

piness (Maslow, 1968). Maslow studied creative, high functioning individuals, and then drew conclusions about healthy personality development.

Human motivation, according to Maslow, rests on a hierarchy of needs. There are two types of needs: D needs and B needs. D needs are to correct deficiencies, and B needs are to achieve a higher level of being. Basic survival needs must be met first before higher order needs can be considered. Higher order needs provide the most intense kinds of spiritual and psychic gratification. Figure 9 illustrates the hierarchy of needs as described by Maslow.

Maslow's Hierarchy of Needs

Self-actualisation needs

Esteem needs

Social needs

Safety needs

Physiological needs

Figure 9 Maslow's hierarchy of needs

Maslow described the hierarchy of five innate needs as instinctoid, meaning that they have a hereditary component. These needs are physiological, safety, belongingness and love, self-esteem and self-actualisation, and are arranged from strongest to weakest. Lower needs must be satisfied to some degree before higher needs become influential. Only one need will, however, dominate our personality depending on which of the other needs have been satisfied.

The physiological need (a lower need) serves to motivate behaviour if, for example, an individual is starving and not able to satisfy his or her hunger. In a middle-class community it is unlikely that there would be a concern to satisfy individuals' physiological needs. The needs for safety and security are important drives for infants and neurotic adults. Their needs for safety still dominate their personality. Infants and neurotic adults need to have structure in their lives to ensure a high degree of predictability. Normal individuals are also concerned about safety needs, such as ensuring a good financial future, but they are not overwhelmed by these needs.

The need for belongingness and love is the next need in the hierarchy of needs. In order to satisfy this need, we form close one-to-one relationships (with a friend, for instance) or develop a close relationship with a group of individuals. Esteem need is a relatively higher need in the hierarchy of needs. With respect to esteem needs, individuals not only need to develop feelings of self-worth but also respect and recognition from others.

The need for self-actualisation is the highest order need, according to Maslow. Self-actualisation refers to the complete development of the self. Conditions necessary to satisfy the need to self-actualise include being free of self-imposed and societal constraints, not being distracted by lower order needs, being able to love and be loved, and acknowledging our strengths and weaknesses (Maslow, 1970, 1987). Maslow considered Albert Einstein, among others, to be a self-actualiser.

Evaluation of Maslow's theory

Maslow has been acknowledged for highlighting the characteristics of the healthy personality. He deserves credit for having initiated the humanistic approach to human development, and provided an alternative to those who were disillusioned with behaviourism and psychoanalysis.

His theory has been criticised, however, for not meeting the rigours of science and specifically for being vague about how he derived the concept of self-actualisation.

Critics have questioned whether the order of the hierarchy of needs as described by Maslow occurs in that sequence. People tend to differ in terms of their higher-order needs (e.g., some may consider focusing on career (esteem need) as a higher order need as compared to developing a relationship (love need)).

The behaviourist approach

The basic premise in behaviourism is that newly born children are born void of any semblance of personality. Environmental experiences from the moment of birth are seen to be the strongest influence in impacting on the development of personality. Environmental factors are seen as so powerful by behaviorists because they believe that it can shape personality throughout life, from childhood to adulthood.

B. F. Skinner

Figure 10 B. F. Skinner

B. F. Skinner (1904-1990) was born in Pennsylvania, USA. He was raised in a family with strict moral codes, and one in which you were punished for bad behaviour and rewarded for good behaviour! Skinner tried his hand at writing, but failed. In 1928 he entered Harvard, and earned his PhD three years later.

Skinner's view on personality development
Skinner believed that the way in which people behave depends on whether they have been rewarded or punished for a particular behaviour in the past and the consequences they expect in the future. Rewards are seen to have a stronger influence in shaping behaviour than punishment. Human behaviour follows the principles of learning, and is the result of a series of stimulus-response sequences. Even if a behaviour does not enhance a person's life, as long as the behaviour is rewarded it will continue to be part of a person's behavioural repertoire.

The concept of reinforcement
Skinner, based on many hours of well controlled research, came to the conclusion that behaviour can be controlled by its consequences, that is, by what follows the behaviour. He believed that any human being or animal could be trained to perform any act based on the type of reinforcement provided following the desired behaviour.

Respondent behaviour and operant behaviour
Respondent behaviour is the response to a specific stimulus. It is an automatic response, which is not learned, such as a knee jerk if one is tapped on the knee. Respondent behaviour may also be learned, and this learning is called conditioning, according to Pavlov, a Russian physiologist, introduced the term conditioning in the early 1900s. Watson built on Pavlov's ideas of conditioning and subsequently used this concept as the basic research method for behaviourism (Schultz & Schultz, 2001).

Pavlov discovered through his experiments with dogs, that these animals would salivate to a neutral stimulus and not only to the sight of food as previously thought. Through systematic research, Pavlov discovered how to condition (or train) the dogs. When he sounded a bell before feeding the dog, the dog did not salivate. However, when he paired the sound of the bell with the food (the bell first followed by the food) consistently over a period of time, the dog began to salivate at the sound of the bell. He soon realised that he had conditioned the dog to respond to the bell, the neutral stimulus, and not the food.

The experiment by Pavlov, as described above, established the importance of reinforcement. The dogs only responded to the sound of the bell because they were rewarded for doing so (food was the reward in this instance). In the same vein, an established conditioned response will not be maintained in the absence of reinforcement. If, for example, the dogs in Pavlov's experiment stopped receiving food after the sound of the bell, the frequency with which the dog would salivate would decrease over time and would soon stop altogether. This process is called *extinction* and is the process of eliminating a behaviour by withholding reinforcement.

Skinner observed that not all behaviour can be accounted for on the basis of respondent behaviour. Behaviour also appears to be spontaneous and not really traceable to a specific stimulus or set of stimuli. For Skinner, such behaviour is emitted rather than elicited by a stimulus. *Operant behaviour* acts on the environment and changes it, in contrast to respondent behaviour.

The famous Skinner box experiment helps to illustrate the concept of operant behaviour. When a food-deprived rat is placed in a box its behaviour is random in that it explores its environment, without responding to a particular stimulus. During this exploration the rat will depress a lever on the wall of the Skinner box, causing a food pellet to drop into the trough. The rat has therefore changed its environment. The food becomes the reinforcer for the behaviour of pressing the bar. This leads the rat to behave in a more controlled manner. If, however, the food pellets are withheld (removing the reinforcer) the rat will cease to press the lever.

Skinner postulated that most human and animal behaviour is learned through the process of operant conditioning. The more *positive reinforcements* a child receives, the more the child will display the behaviour. Continued disapproval of the particular behaviours of the child would soon lead to the extinction of those behaviours.

13.3 BEHAVIOUR MODIFICATION: A CLASSIC REPORT

A woman with a 4-year-old son sought treatment for him because she thought him to be unruly. Two psychologists observed the mother and child in their home to establish the nature and frequency of the child's undesirable behaviours, when and where they occurred, and the reinforcers the child received for the behaviours.

The psychologists' observation revealed that there were nine undesirable behaviours, including kicking and biting. It was also observed that the mother reinforced the child by giving him toys or food when he behaved badly, which instead of stopping him from displaying bad behaviour (which was her intention), was reinforcing his behaviour.

A behaviour modification programme was designed for this mother that emphasised attention and approval as reinforcers when the child behaved in positive ways and no rewards when the child displayed any one of the nine undesirable behaviours. (Hawkins *et al.*, 1966)

Schedules of reinforcement

Skinner further observed that in every day life, behaviour is rarely reinforced every time it occurs. A baby, for example, is not pacified every time it cries. Using rats, Skinner investigated different *reinforcement schedules* in controlling behaviour. He tested the following rates of reinforcement:
- fixed interval;
- fixed ratio;
- variable interval; and
- variable ratio.

The *fixed interval schedule of reinforcement* means that the reinforcer is given following the first response after a fixed time interval has elapsed. The timing of the reinforcement has nothing to do with the number of responses. Receiving a weekly or a monthly salary is an example of a fixed interval schedule. The response rate declines, however, if the time between the response and the reinforcer is too great.

In the *fixed ratio schedule of reinforcement*, reinforcers are given only after the person or animal has made a specified number of responses, such as a salesperson receiving a commission based on his or her selling a certain number of items.

The *variable interval schedule of reinforcement* refers to the time that a reinforcer is presented after varying time intervals, such as fishing. The *variable ratio schedule of reinforcement* is based on an average number of responses between reinforcers, such as playing the slot machine in a casino. Variable reinforcement schedules result in consistent and enduring behaviours that tend to resist extinction.

Successive approximation

To explain more complex behaviours, such as learning to speak, Skinner used the term *successive approximation*. This applies to reinforcing behaviour only as it comes to approximate the final desired behaviour.

Evaluation of Skinner's theory

Skinner was concerned with assessing behaviour. His assessment approach is called functional analysis, which involves three aspects of behaviour. These three aspects include the frequency of the behaviour, the situation in which the behaviour occurs, and the reinforcement associated with the behaviour. These factors have to be evaluated in order to plan and implement a behaviour modification programme. The ability to change undesirable behaviour and reinforce desired behaviours, based on Skinner's behavioural approach, is seen as the main contribution of this approach to understanding human behaviour.

Humanists criticise Skinner's approach because they say that humans are far more complex than Skinner suggests. Skinner's emphasis on observable behaviour ignores human qualities based on internal self-control and conscious free will. It is suggested that he discounts thoughts, feelings and other such phenomena.

Interestingly, Verwoerd, the architect of apartheid was a behaviourist, and was said to have used behaviourist principles to divide and rule people in South Africa.

The social learning approaches

Albert Bandura

Figure 11
Albert Bandura

Albert Bandura (1925- present) was born in Alberta, Canada. He earned a PhD from the University of Iowa in 1952 and later joined the faculty at Stanford, where he became a full professor in 1964. In 1980 Bandura received the American Psychological Association's award for Distinguished Scientific Contributions. Bandura was said to be extremely popular with his students because of his warm disposition (Allen, 2000).

Bandura's view on personality development

Bandura is considered to be a social learning theorist. His basic premise is that personal factors (such as cognition and biological variables), behaviour, and external environmental variables influence each other and are influenced by the Other (Bandura, 1977; see also Chapter 21, this volume).

Behaviour, he says, goes beyond basic learning principles, and the social context is important in the ultimate expression of that behaviour. Individuals tend to copy other people's behaviour and when they repeat the same behaviour, and are rewarded for it, that particular behaviour will persist. If the behaviour is not rewarded we stop the behaviour. Bandura goes on to suggest that when an individual observes a model they learn the value of a behavioural performance in terms of what it will achieve.

In observational learning, both social and cognitive components are important. When an individual copies the behaviour of another, the individual thinks (cognitive process) about the outcome of his or her behaviour in relation to the outcome of the model's behaviour.

The process of imitating or copying other people's behaviour is called modelling. This is particularly the case with children. If they observe aggressive behaviour there is a strong possibility that they will act aggressively. Similarly, if they watch altruistic behaviour, they are more likely to act in a helpful and gentle manner. If the individual whose behaviour the child is imitating is rewarded for the behaviour, this appears to have a stronger influence on the child than if the person is not rewarded at all or there is no consequence of the person's behaviour.

Bandura also makes a point, however, that people do not passively adopt a model's behaviour (Bandura, 1989). People may turn information into a symbolic form so that it can translate into action at a later time. Models do not have to be 'real' people in the act of doing something; in symbolic modelling verbal and pictorial means are used to convey information that lead to certain behaviours associated with rewards (such as a TV advertisement).

Characteristics of the models are also important in determining what is learned. People are drawn to models whose attractiveness is a combination of certain characteristics (such as appearance, style and confidence), and their success in general and on specific tasks. However, whatever is learned from a model will also depend on a person's capabilities prior to observing the model.

Bandura (1991) also points out that in considering whether to adopt the behaviour of another, the learner (observer) takes into account the incentive it provides in receiving a reward for the copying of the behaviour. Personal goals will also determine which behaviours an individual will adopt. Goal attainment can only be achieved if it is guided and governed by the self-regulatory process (internal cognitive/affective functions), which include, among other factors, self-persuasion, self-praise and acceptance of challenges.

According to Bandura, *self-efficacy* is one of the most powerful self-regulatory processes. Self-efficacy is a belief that concerns our ability to perform behaviours producing an expected, desirable outcome. When we are high on self-efficacy it means that we are confident that we can control our behaviour in a difficult situation. Bandura recommends participant modeling to individuals low on self-efficacy.

It is not only behaviour that we learn from models, according to Bandura. In *vicarious expectancy* learning people adopt other people's expectancies concerning future events, especially those with whom they share a common experience. In response facilitation, our previous abilities (that were inhibited) may re-emerge by watching our model use those behaviours that we have inhibited. Sometimes a model tries out something new and displays its benefit to others. Bandura terms this *diffusion of innovation*. Others may therefore adopt the new innovative behaviour displayed by the model and pursue the cause depending on its future benefits.

Behaviour is acquired through modeling, but it is maintained by rewards. *Extrinsic rewards* are those that originate outside the individual, such as money. *Intrinsic rewards* are from within the individual, such as self-satisfaction.

Finally, Bandura states that individuals adopt defensive behaviours in order to cope with unpleasant events that are anticipated on future occasions, such as avoiding a situation because we believe it will be unpleasant.

Evaluation of Bandura's theory

Social learning theory has many advantages. Its concepts are amenable to laboratory investigation. Bandura's approach, in particular, has vast appeal, and many of his concepts enjoy empirical support. In particular, self-efficacy is the most researched of the self-regulatory mechanisms. There is much supporting evidence for the concept of self-efficacy. In treating a spider phobia, Bandura *et al.* (1982) showed that there is a direct relationship between self-efficacy and behavioural performance after the treatment. Bandura *et al.* (1996) also demonstrated the relationship between high self-efficacy and high academic achievement.

Due to overwhelming research support for Bandura's social learning theory, and its applicability in many spheres of life such as crime and health, explicit criticisms of his theory are not noteworthy.

13.4 THE RELATIONSHIP BETWEEN SELF-EFFICACY AND PAIN TOLERANCE

The basic premise in this study is that coping techniques that improve self-efficacy produce substantial increases in endorphins, which are the body's natural painkillers. A pain-rating scale and self-efficacy rating scale were administered to 45 chronic low back pain patients. These patients were enrolled in a 3-week rehabilitation programme.

Six months later those patients higher in self-efficacy reported better physical functioning and less back pain than did patients lower in self-efficacy. (Altmaier *et al.*, 1993)

Conclusion

Figure 12 Non-Westerners: Are the various personality theories discussed in this chapter applicable to them?

The theories mentioned thus far are considered to be mainstream Western theories of personality. The applicability or non-applicability of these theories within African, Asian and other cultures, therefore comes into question. We might argue, for instance, that the psychoanalytic approach to understanding personality development is not applicable within the South African context because the theory was built on case histories of middle-class Viennese women, and further, the theory locates women in an inferior position (both socially and psychologically).

Despite the apparent non-applicability of mainstream Western theories, these theories nevertheless continue to inform and influence the way in which personality is constructed in other cultures. A common thread running through each theory is the consideration of the interaction between intrinsic (that which is inherent in an individual) and extrinsic (that which lies outside the individual) factors. In personality formation, therefore, external factors (such as social, cultural and political influences) interact with internal factors (such as intelligence and biological predispositions). We can therefore extrapolate from existing personality theories of the various theoretical persuasions to develop a framework for understanding the psychological development of individuals outside the Western context.

In exploring contemporary issues in human development, particularly in the South African context, Laubscher and Klinger (1997) conceptualise the terms 'personality' and 'the self' within the same framework. They favour using the terms interchangeably to convey a 'sense of me' that is developed experientially.

Laubscher and Klinger suggest the use of the narrative approach, within the South African context, to study 'the self'. Story telling, according to Laubscher and Klinger (1997), provides an experiential account of the individual that lends itself to better understanding the development of personality (see De La Rey *et al.* (1997) for contextual developmental issues within the South African situation).

Laubscher and Klinger (1997) also raise the importance of gender in personality development. They are critical of life span approaches in particular, because they argue that women follow a different development path as compared to men.

This chapter has presented a summary of the mainstream Western personality theories and theorists. The applicability or non-applicability of these theoretical postulations must be critically considered for use outside of Western cultures. While at a broader level there is little doubt that there are striking similarities between individuals from various cultures, there are also important differences. It is important, therefore, to contextualise and situate knowledge. We must take into account social, cultural, and political nuances in the development of personality.

13.5 ONE PROBLEM, MANY PERSPECTIVES

In this chapter, it is clearly demonstrated that the personologists discussed are or were committed to their particular theoretical approach in attempting to understand human behaviour. This means, therefore, that there can be many possible explanations for the same behavioural scenario. Consider the following example. John is said to have his father's 'personality'. He is dominating, intelligent, arrogant and inconsiderate. He happens to also physically resemble his father. What explanations can be offered to understand why John is the way he is, given the fact that he was raised in a nuclear family with both his biological parents and two younger siblings?

Analysts will interpret John's behaviour within the context of his developmental history, from birth onward. John's early childhood influences will be seen to have impacted on his personality development. In the process of resolving the Oedipus complex, John would have internalised his father's behaviour to obtain the emotional and physical bond he so desired with his mother. Of course, the behaviourists will totally reject such an explanation for John's behaviour, because the process of internalisation cannot be empirically validated. The behaviourists would say that John is the way he is because he has modelled his father's behaviour, and certain environmental conditions (including human interactions) helped to reinforce these behaviours. A life span personality developmental theorist would argue that during the crucial years of identity formation, John's familial influences, especially that of his father, were more powerful than his peer group and other ideological and philosophical influences. African and Asian social scientists may argue that none of the postulations put forward by the various Western-based theories make any sense. John's behaviour they may suggest, is a reflection of his sense of 'self', socially constructed from the various influences on his development, including familial and other outside social agents.

Allen, B. (2000). *Personality Theories: Development, growth, and diversity*. Boston: Allyn & Bacon.

Altmaier, E.M., Russell, D.W., Kao, C.F., Lehmann, T.R. & Weinstein, J.N. (1993). Role of self-efficacy in rehabilitation outcomes among chronic low back pain patients. *Journal of Counselling Psychology*, 40:335-39.

Bandura, A. (1977). *Social Learning Theory*. New Jersey: Prentice-Hall.

Bandura, A. (1989). Social cognitive theory. *Annals of Child Development*. New York: Jai Press.

Bandura, A. (1991) Social cognitive theory of self-regulation. *Organizational Behaviour & Human Decision Making Processes*, 50:248-87.

Bandura, A., Reese, L. & Adams, N. (1982). Microanalysis of action and fear arousal as a function of differential levels of perceived self-efficacy. *Journal of Personality & Social Psychology*, 43:5-21.

Bandura, A., Barbaranelli, C., Caprara, G.V. & Pastorelli, C. (1996). Multifacted impact on self-efficacy beliefs on academic functioning. *Child development*, 67:1206-22.

Caspi, A., Elder, G.H. & Bem, D.J. (1987). Moving against the world: Life course patterns of explosive children. *Developmental Psychology*, 23:308-13.

Caspi, A., Elder, G.H. & Bem, D.J.(1988). Moving away from the world: Life course patterns of shy children. *Developmental Psychology*, 24:824-31.

De la Rey, C., Duncan, N, Shefer, T. & Van Niekerk, A. (Eds.). (1997). *Contemporary Issues in Human Development. A South African focus*. Johannesburg: International Thompson Publishing, pp. 58-79.

Erikson, E.H. (1950). *Childhood and Society*. New York: Norton.

Freud, S. (1901). *The psychopathology of everyday life*. In, The Standard Edition of the Complete Works of Freud (volume 6). London: Hogarth Press.

Glover, E. (1950). *Freud or Jung?* New York: Norton.

Hall, C.S. & Lindzey, G. (1978). *Theories of Personality*. New York: John Wiley & Sons.

Hawkins, R.P., Peterson, R.F., Schweid, E. & Bijou, S.W. (1966). Behaviour therapy in the home: Amelioration of problem parent-child relations with the parent in a therapeutic role. *Journal of Experimental Child Psychology*, 4:99-107.

Jung, C.G. (1909). *The association method*. In The Collected Works of C.G. Jung (volume 8). New Jersey: Princeton University Press.

Jung, C.G. (1927). *The structure of the psyche*. In The Collected Works of C.G. Jung (volume 8). New Jersey: Princeton University Press.

Jung, C.G. (1928) *On psychic energy*. In The Collected Works of C.G. Jung (volume 8). New Jersey: Princeton University Press.

Laubscher, L. & Klinger, J. (1997) Story and the making if the self. In De La Rey, C., Duncan, N., Shefer,T. & Van Niekerk, A. (Eds.). *Contemporary Issues in Human Development. A South African focus*. Johannesburg: International Thompson Publishing, pp. 58-79.

Maslow, A.H. (1968). *Toward a Psychology of Being*. New York: Van Nostrand Reinhold.

Maslow, A.H. (1970). *Motivation and Personality* (2nd edition). New York: Harper & Row.

Maslow, A.H. (1987). *Motivation and Personality* (3rd edition). New York: Harper & Row.

Papalia, D.E. & Olds, S.W. (1988). *Psychology*. USA: McGraw-Hill Book Company.

Pervin, A. (1980). *Personality: Theory, assessment and research*. New York: John Wiley & Sons.

Schultz, D.P. & Schultz, S.E. (2001). *Theories of Personality*. California: Wadsworth/Thompson Leaning.

Slugoski, B.F. & Ginsgurg, G.P.(1989). Ego identity and explanatory speech. In J. Shotter & K.F. Gergen (Eds.). *Texts of Identity*. London: Sage, pp. 36-55.

Tavris, C. (1992). *The Mismeasure of Women*. New York: Simon & Schuster.

Multiple choice questions

1. _____ introduced the concept of the unconscious and highlighted the relationship of consciousness to the unconscious
   a) Jung
   b) Skinner
   c) Bandura
   d) Freud

2. One of the following theorists is a neoanalyst
   a) Bandura
   b) Jung
   c) Skinner
   d) Watson

3. Which one of the following statements is correct?
   a) Skinner was known to have formulated the psychosocial stages of development
   b) Erikson was known to have formulated the psychosocial stages of development
   c) Jung was known to have formulated the psychosocial stages of development
   d) Bandura was known to have formulated the psychosocial stages of development

4. Only one of the following statements is correct. Freud stated that
   a) material in the preconscious is readily available to consciousness
   b) material in the unconscious can never be brought to consciousness
   c) feminists readily accept Freud's notion of the Oedipal Complex
   d) the id, ego, and superego function independently of each other

5. The neorotic trend of moving toward other people as described in Horney's theory depicts
   a) the aggressive personality
   b) the detached personality
   c) the introverted personality
   d) the compliant personality

6. Which of the following statements correctly depicts Maslow's hierarchy of needs arranged from basic needs to higher order needs?
   a) safety, belongingness and love, self-esteem, self-actualisation and physiological
   b) physiological, safety, belongingness and love, self-esteem and self-actualisation
   c) self-esteem, self-actualisation, belongingness and love, physiological and safety
   d) self-actualisation, belongingness and love, physiological, safety and self-esteem

7. Using rats, Skinner investigated different reinforcement schedules in controlling behaviour. He tested the following rates of reinforcement
   a) fixed interval
   b) fixed ratio
   c) variable interval and variable ratio
   d) all of the above

8. Which of the following statements does not reflect the concept of self-efficacy as described by Bandura?
   a) it is a characteristic possessed by one or a few persons
   b) it is one of the most powerful self-regulatory processes
   c) it is a belief that concerns one's ability to perform behaviours producing an expected outcome that is desirable
   d) it differs as a function of gender and age

9. One of the following concepts does not belong within the framework of behaviourism
   a) reinforcement
   b) token economy
   c) behaviour modification
   d) self-actualisation

Short answer questions

1. Freud described the structures of personality to include the id, ego, and superego. Describe the id, ego, and superego and explain how they are interrelated.

2. Describe the principles of opposites, equivalence and entropy, as stated by Jung.

3. Why is identity formation important during adolescence, according to Erikson?

4. How does Skinner explain the difference between respondent behaviour and operant behaviour?

5. Why do Laubscher and Klinger (1997) use the terms 'personality' and 'the self' interchangeably within the South African context?

14

Personality Assessment

Ashraf Kagee & Gideon De Bruin

CHAPTER OBJECTIVES

After studying this chapter you should be able to:
- understand the process of psychological assessment
- differentiate between a clinical interview, objective assessment and projective assessment
- be familiar with the commonly used personality inventories
- understand basic psychometric theory
- be familiar with some of the controversies in the area of personality assessment.

Introduction

The best way to introduce personality assessment is by example. Examine the following scenarios: First, Dr Radebe, a clinical psychologist, wants to get to know her patient in a short space of time in order to optimise the time that she spends with him in therapy. Knowledge of her patient will enable her to understand his perception of his problems and identify the most appropriate form of treatment for him. Dr Radebe conducts an interview in which she asks specific questions and requests that her patient responds to a battery of tests aimed at assessing his personality. This information will assist Dr Radebe to gain a better understanding of her patient, his problems and the most effective manner to address them.

Second, Ms Mhlaba is a human resource director in a large South African mining company. She wants to ensure that she makes the correct decision in hiring a field manager. This is a position that is highly stressful, and requires good leadership skills and rapid decision-making. The successful candidate should be able to handle pressure and communicate articulately. The human resource director short-lists five candidates for the position and invites them for an interview with a panel of six managers. The interview involves a series of questions and answers directed at assessing each candidate's personality characteristics to determine whether they are suitable for the position. Each interviewer rates his or her impressions of the candidate's performance on a scale of 1 to 5. This information helps Ms Mhlaba to make a decision about who should get the job.

These scenarios are examples in which *psychological assessment* plays an important role. Assessment is the process of obtaining information from people in order to help make decisions to solve problems. Usually this information is gathered from individuals or groups, but sometimes also from organisations or even communities.

Assessment often, but not always, involves *measurement*. Measurement of psychological *constructs* or phenomena is based on the assumption that if a construct exists, it exists in some amount and we should therefore be able to quantify or measure it. Many assessment exercises involve the use of interviews and questionnaires.

This chapter is primarily concerned with the assessment of personality. Therefore, the constructs of interest relate to the personality characteristics of people. Psychologists who work in a variety of settings such as industrial, mental health, forensic, educational, and community settings, often conduct personality assessments. In such settings, important questions might be related to individuals' strengths and weaknesses, typical ways of interacting with others, and the manner in which they are unique and therefore different from others.

What is personality?

There are various ways of defining personality. Most often someone's personality is described by noting how unique that person is, that is how he or she is different from other people, and what patterns of behaviour are characteristic of that person. For the purpose of this chapter, personality is defined as 'the complex set of unique psychological qualities that are said to influence an individual's characteristic patterns of behaviour across different situations and over time' (Zimbardo *et al.*, 1995:443). While it is true that there are many similarities between people, there are also differences that are of interest to researchers and practitioners in psychology.

An important concept in understanding personality is the *trait* (see Chapter 13, this volume). Traits are tendencies that people have in varying degrees that are more or less stable across different situations and across time. Theories that draw on the concept of traits are called trait theories. Trait theories suggest that human beings have certain characteristics that vary in their quality or intensity. For example, On Monday you lend money to a friend; on Tuesday you share a chocolate with a classmate during break time; and on Friday you offer a ride home to an acquaintance going your way. It might therefore be said that you are a generous person and the trait that you possess is generosity.

Psychological assessment

Psychological assessment is a fundamental activity in many settings in which psychologists work. For example, a mental health professional can only know how to offer psychological treatment to someone if he or she knows what the chief concern is. Information from assessments in this context is used to help form initial diagnostic impressions about the patient, to assess whether he or she is ready for clinical interventions, to monitor his or her progress during the course of therapy, and to assess the outcome of treatment when the course of therapy is complete.

We can define psychological assessment, then, as an activity in which a psychologist gathers a wide variety of information about a person by using assessment tools (tests) as well as other methods. These methods might include interviews, school, university or hospital records, and the impressions of people who know the person well, such as family members. The psychologist then brings all this information together to reach a conclusion or make a decision about the person. Some psychologists hold the view that personality assessments should be conducted in a highly individualised manner, with little concern for information beyond the patient being assessed. Other psychologists prefer quantitative assessment, which may be compared to group norms. The use of norms allows the psychologist to understand the patient in relation to others who are similar to him or her in terms of demographic characteristics. Thus the test scores of a 10-year-old boy will be compared to the average score of a representative sample of 10-year-old boys in order to determine whether or not his score is significantly different to that of the sample. Such data allows the clinician to make a determination about how similar or different the boy is compared to his peers. This view is concerned with individual differences, because data yielded by quantitative assessment tell us in what ways an individual is different or similar to other people on a particular trait or characteristic.

The process of assessment

The assessment process involves many sources of information. For this reason it is considered to be multi-dimensional, and the data obtained from the different sources have to be synthesised or put together in an orderly way in order to be used effectively. A thorough assessment involves the use of:

- more than one measure, including tests, interviews, and rating scales;
- more than one source of information, such as the client, teachers, parents and other persons who know the client; and
- more than one occasion, so that patterns of functioning may be identified over a period of time rather than only on a single occasion.

The three most popular ways of conducting an assessment of personality are the *clinical interview*, *objective tests*, and *projective tests*.

The clinical interview

The most common method of assessing the nature of a patient's personality is the interview. The purpose of an interview is to evaluate the patient's verbal and non-verbal behaviour in order to understand what might be done to help the patient. An interview usually involves at least two people: the interviewer and the patient or patients. An assessment interview is a conversation with the purpose of gaining an understanding of the personality dynamics of the interviewee.

The challenge then is for the psychologist to have a clear goal in mind and to proceed with the interview in a way that will achieve that goal.

Often people seek psychological help for serious personal problems, often brought about because of certain personality traits. The interviewer begins by asking the patient to describe his or her problem and pays special attention to the way he or she understands and interprets the problem. The interviewer may ask about the history of the problem, and in this way gain insight into the circumstances surrounding the origin of the problem, when the problem becomes worse, and situations in which the patient is less bothered by the problem. This kind of information is useful in deciding about treatment options to help alleviate the problem or disorder that the patient is found to have. Information of this nature is also likely to be informative about the personality of the person and how he or she engages with the world.

Assessment interviews may be unstructured, semi-structured, or highly structured. An *unstructured interview* often takes the form of a conversation in which any issue that comes up is pursued in conversation. The interviewer is minimally directive and considers most of what the client says as important information that will help the interviewer gain a better understanding of the patient. A *semi-structured interview* involves the use of some questions to provide structure to the interview and may help guide the patient's responses. The interviewer is interested in the patient's general responses to the questions and considers them to be a way to get the patient to talk about him- or herself. Open-ended questions are typical in semi-structured interviews, that is questions to which the patient might respond in any way, for example: 'How do you feel about school?' This kind of conversation is helpful for the interviewer to get to know the patient better.

Unstructured or semi-structured interviews have been criticised for being overly subjective and therefore lacking in reliability. For the purposes of this chapter, reliability means replicability – if interviewer A interviews a patient, he or she should arrive at the same conclusion as interviewer B or interviewer C. If there are wide discrepancies between the results of the various interviewers, then the interview method is said to be unreliable.

A *structured interview* is exactly that – a highly structured encounter in which the interviewer asks only a specific set of questions to which exact answers are of interest. In many ways a structured interview is a questionnaire that is verbally administered. Questions are asked that will elicit responses that can fit into pre-determined categories, and therefore the questions are closed, for example: 'Do you feel sad or depressed a lot of the time?' The answer to a question such as this may either be yes or no, or possibly sometimes. Because specific answers are elicited by structured interviews, they often have much better reliability than unstructured or semi-structured interviews.

Structured interviews usually provide the interviewer with the exact words to use when asking questions as well as highly specific guidelines about how to score or code the respondent's answers. A popular structured interview that is used in both clinical and research settings is the *Structured Clinical Interview for the DSM-IV (SCID)* developed by Spitzer and his colleagues. Structured interviews of this nature are often used in research or clinical settings to establish whether or not a patient has a particular psychological diagnosis or not. The interview questions are designed to elicit responses from the patient that would allow the interviewer to determine whether the patient has the symptoms that constitute a particular disorder. For this reason, interviewers have to undergo specific training in psychology with a particular emphasis on *psychopathology* (the psychological functioning of disordered persons), as well as training in the administration of the specific structured interview that is used.

Objective personality assessment

Objective assessment instruments refer to psychological tests which consist of highly structured and standardised questions, possible response options, scor-

ing procedures, and methods of interpretation. For this reason they can be administered, scored and even interpreted in a reliable and accurate manner by both professionals and trained lay persons. Objective tests are used to assess either persons functioning within the normal range, such as job applicants, or those considered to be psychologically disordered, such as residents in a psychiatric hospital. Psychological testing refers to the measurement of behaviour, and is one of the important aspects of the assessment process.

Considerable research data are available for many objective tests. These data have been used to develop standardised rules to interpret test scores in relation to previously establish criteria, such as *group norms*. An important benefit of objective tests is that they permit the comparison of people on various personality dimensions. Thus, an objective test that has been standardised and normed may help an evaluator make statements about whether an individual has more or less of the characteristic in question. The use of *cut-scores* is important here. Cut-scores are points on a scale that indicate below which most people would score. If a person's score falls above the established cut-score, their performance would be interpreted as lying outside the normal range.

14.1 ASSESSMENT: THE CHECKLIST OR QUESTIONNAIRE

As part of an assessment procedure a clinician asks a patient to complete the Hopkins Symptom Checklist (HSCL-25). The HSCL is a paper and pencil test intended to provide health care providers with a means of detecting symptoms of anxiety and depression in their patients. Possible scores on this measure range from 25 to 100. Previous research suggests that most people in the normal range of functioning score below 44 on the HSCL and therefore persons whose scores fall above 44 may require more intensive attention from a mental health professional. The patient's score is 55, clearly higher than the cut-score of 44. This would suggest that the person may have an elevated level of distress and therefore be eligible for a psychological diagnosis of anxiety or depression. In such a case, assessment using a structured interview is necessary to determine whether or not the person has a clinical diagnosis.

A major benefit of objective tests is their efficiency. Whereas an interview must usually be administered by a trained professional, an objective test does not, and in many cases is self-administered by the respondent. Tests that do not require an examiner for administration, and are therefore self-administered by the test-taker, are called *self-report inventories*. This makes objective tests much more cost effective than interviews, especially when large numbers of people need to be assessed in a short amount of time. A large variety of tests are available for use in clinical, research, educational and vocational settings. The Mental Measurements Yearbook (Buros Institute of Mental Measurements, 2003), now in its fifteenth edition, is a catalogue of available tests and brief evaluations of their quality and usefulness. Each entry includes descriptive information about the test, reviews by professional reviewers, and a list of references to literature that is pertinent to the test.

Objective tests are useful if their *psychometric properties* are good. Psychometrics is the word used for the measurement of psychological functioning. It involves the use of specific statistical procedures to determine whether a test is appropriate for use in a particular context. Social desirability is sometimes a problem with objective tests, as a client might endorse an item which assesses a positive characteristic, even if he or she does not have that characteristic. Similarly, he or she may fail to endorse an item assessing a negative characteristic despite having that characteristic. These are examples of *faking good*. The opposite problem, *faking bad*, occurs when clients endorse negative characteristics, despite not having them. This may occur during a mental health assessment when the presence of psychopathology may entitle a patient to financial benefits such as disability payments or insurance claims. For these reasons, some psychologists prefer to use projective assessment procedures, which disguise what the test actually assesses.

The following are two examples of an objective personality test. First, the *Minnesota Multiphasic Personality Inventory* or MMPI, as it is more commonly known. The MMPI is a widely used paper and pencil personality test that has 566 items of statements which respondents have to endorse as either true, false, or undecided. The MMPI is based on an empirical approach to test construction. The content of respondents' answers to individual test items is usually of little interest to the psychologist. Instead the developers matched the patterns of people's answers to the patterns of responses of 'criteri-

on' groups. These criterion groups were people who had characteristics of special interest, for example, a psychological diagnosis such as depression or schizophrenia. Thus if individual respondents showed a pattern of responses similar to a criterion group of depressed individuals, this would constitute important data that the respondent might be at risk for depression him- or herself. The MMPI is therefore an example of what is called a *criterion-based* approach to personality assessment. Items on the MMPI were not selected on the basis of what their content seemed to mean, but on the basis of empirical findings. One of the innovative aspects of the MMPI is the inclusion of a validity scale designed to detect suspicious response patterns such as misrepresentation, dishonesty, defensiveness, and evasiveness. An interpreter of an MMPI profile would first check the validity scale and determine whether the results are valid before proceeding to interpret the rest of the profile.

Second, the Neurotic-Extraversion-Openness Personality Inventory or NEO-PI (or NEO for short). The NEO-PI was originally designed to assess personality characteristics in adult normal populations. The NEO is based on the assumption that there are five basic dimensions underlying the traits that people use to describe themselves and others (De Raad, 2000; McCrae & Costa, 1989). Some available research suggests that these five basic dimensions may be found in cultures other than those considered to be Western. The five dimensions of personality, or the Big Five (Costa & McCrae, 1992), are: extraversion, agreeableness, conscientiousness, neuroticism and openness to experience. The *extraversion* dimension discerns between people who are gregarious, warm, and positive versus those who are quiet, reserved and shy. The *agreeableness* dimension describes people who are straightforward, compliant, and sympathetic versus those who are quarrelsome, oppositional, and unfeeling. The *conscientiousness* dimension refers to achievement-oriented and self-disciplined people compared to those who are frivolous and irresponsible. The *neuroticism* dimension differentiates between people who are anxious and depressed, on one hand, and those who are calm, contented and self-assured, on the other. Finally the *openness* to experience dimension refers to those persons who are creative, open-minded and intellectual versus those who are unimaginative, disinterested and narrow-minded. These dimensions are not based on any specific psychological theory, and the strength of the Big Five model is that it is easy to understand because the dimensions were derived from natural language. The NEO-PI, which assesses the Big Five dimensions, has been tested with samples using different languages and has been shown have some validity in a variety of cultures (McCrae, 2000).

Projective personality assessment

Projective assessment techniques use stimuli that are ambiguous and the patient is asked to offer any response that comes to mind. The assumption with projective techniques is that responses are likely to reflect aspects of the patient's personality that are usually concealed. Psychologists who use projective assessment methods find them useful because it is difficult for patients to provide *socially desirable responses*. This is because the content of the test is ambiguous, and it is therefore less apparent what the psychologist wants to find out. Thus, the person might be given a series of stimuli that are deliberately ambiguous, and asked to provide interpretations or responses to them, for example, abstract patterns or incomplete pictures that may be interpreted in a variety of ways. Responses to these stimuli are said to be 'projections' of the person's inner feelings, personal motives, and conflicts derived from prior life experiences that are considered to be unconscious and therefore unable to be assessed directly. One famous projective instrument is the *Rorschach Test*, which

uses symmetrical inkblots as ambiguous stimuli to which the patient is asked to respond. These respons-

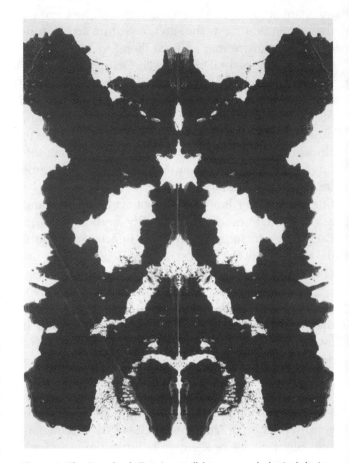

Figure 1 The Rorschach Test is a well-known psychological device

---

14.2 PERSONALITY AND/IN THE NEW SOUTH AFRICA

The political changes that occurred in South Africa since 1994 were accompanied by an increase in opportunities for gambling. Peltzer and Thole (2000) examined the relationship between attitudes to gambling and personality traits such as conservatism and risk taking among a sample of African university students. The results showed that men held more positive attitudes towards gambling than women. A positive attitude towards gambling was related to personality attributes such as willingness to take risks, liberalism, and the course of study that students chose.

Heuchert *et al.* (2000) examined the five factor personality model among a sample of White, Black, Indian, and Coloured South African university students using the NEO-PI. They found that the five factor model was well reproduced for persons of all racial backgrounds. They found significant differences between Black and

White students in terms of openness to experience, with Black students scoring low, White students scoring high, and Indian students scoring in the intermediate range on this domain. Heuchert and colleagues speculated that these differences were primarily due to social, economic and cultural differences between racial groups, rather than due to race itself.

Taylor and Boeyens (1991) compared Black and White samples on the South African Personality Questionnaire (SAPQ) in an attempt to determine whether the instrument was suitable for cross-cultural applications. They concluded that the SAPQ was an inappropriate measure to use in cross-cultural contexts in terms of the performance of the items on the scale between the various samples. This research resulted in the suggestion of a strategy for the creation of a personality inventory that is more suitable for cross-cultural use in South Africa.

Can psychological experiences be measured in the same manner as physical objects? Many psychologists believe that if a psychological phenomenon exists, it also exists in some amount and thus one should be able to measure it. Therefore all personality attributes, if they exist at all, should be observable in some way and measurable. Other psychologists dismiss this notion and are critical of the practice of reducing complex psychological experiences to a set of numbers. These psychologists feel that the quantification of personality results in a loss of meaning and may even dehumanise the person.

Consider this: Some companies administer a battery of psychological tests to job candidates and, on the basis of their performance on these, invite them to interview for the job. Those candidates whose scores fall in an undesirable range may not be invited for an interview. Defenders of this practice say that interviewing is a resource intensive and time consuming task and therefore employers want to be reasonably sure that interview candidates are within the acceptable range in terms of their personality attributes. Opponents of this practice feel that one can only really get to know someone in a face-to-face context, and that pre-testing with personality tests is reductionistic and dehumanising. They feel that the human

personality exists in relation to other people, and that the interaction between the interviewer and the candidate best represents how the candidate will perform in a work environment.

The question of how to measure compatibility between romantic partners, trust between soldiers on a battlefield, or the bond between a parent and a child seems to defy quantification. Some psychometricians view these situations as challenges for their field, while many psychologists acknowledge the futility of trying to measure these kinds of concepts. In psychotherapy process research, for example, empathy of the therapist towards the client has been the focus of measurement. Many psychologists have criticised this effort, saying that empathy is an intangible phenomenon that cannot be reduced to a single number. Yet, it may be said that therapist A is consistently more empathic than therapist B. This kind of statement automatically assumes some form of quantification, even if this is less precise than the measurement of length, weight, or volume. Thus, those psychologists who are determined to measure as many constructs as possible, advocate for the development of psychometric instruments that assess phenomena such as empathy, love, and trust. What do you think?

es are then interpreted and statements are generated regarding the person's underlying personality traits. Clearly, the reliability and validity of projective tests is much lower than objective tests, but they continue to be used in some clinical settings.

Criticisms of personality assessment

Not all psychologists are in favour of personality assessment. Some consider personality tests to be dehumanising in that they force respondents to choose answers from a range of options that are imposed by the person who constructed the test. Thus the criticism is that tests try to pidgeon-hole people into pre-existing categories using forced choice response options.

Personality assessment may also be culturally inappropriate in some contexts. For example, in many highly industrialised societies, values such as individual independence and autonomy are highly regarded. However, in some less technologically developed countries, many people value interde-

pendence and communalism as the bases for the functioning of their society. Thus a personality assessment procedure developed in an industrialised country may place a great emphasis on independence, and high scores on this measure may be regarded more positively than low scores. When administered in a culturally different context, respondents may score low on this measure and may be revealed to have personality problems such as difficulty individuating or separating from their families of origin. The usefulness of various assessment procedures should be considered from the perspective of local traditions, customs, values, and beliefs.

Tests that require the ability to read are biased against non-literate persons. In societies in which the literacy level is low, it may not be appropriate to use paper and pencil personality tests. Instead, the interview-based method of assessment may be more appropriate. However, interviews are more resource intensive to administer than self-report measures, as they require the interviewer to be trained and a specific meeting time to be arranged. It is also important to conduct an interview under conditions of confidentiality. Self-report measures are easier in that a secretary or assistant may administer these, a patient may complete them in a clinic waiting room if necessary, and usually no words are exchanged so that privacy becomes less of an issue.

The reliability of personality questionnaires

An important quality of a satisfactory psychometric instrument is that it reveals differences between people in terms of the characteristics or traits that it seeks to evaluate. In other words, if an individual has less of a certain trait or ability than another person, an instrument that measures that trait or ability in a satisfactory manner will reflect these differences. Unfortunately, no instrument is perfect, and scores on even the best-known psychometric instruments are influenced by error to a greater or lesser degree. These shortcomings of psychometric instruments are summarised neatly in one of the most fundamental equations of classical psychometric theory. The equation is as follows:

Observed score = True score + Error score

This equation makes an important distinction between *observed scores* and *true scores*. The scores obtained for respondents on psychometric instruments are observed scores. If one person is evaluated with the same scale on a number of different occasions, it can be expected that his or her scores will not be exactly the same every time. However, they should be similar. If it were possible to evaluate a person with the scale an infinite number of times, the mean (or average) of these scores would represent his or her *true score*. As it is impossible to test people an infinite number of times, the true score is thought of as a *hypothetical score*.

There are many reasons why respondents' observed scores might differ from their true scores. These reasons are largely due to measurement error, represented by the *error score* indicated in the equation above. Different sources of measurement error (that could lead to differences in scores of over-repeated test administrations) are listed below:

- The instructions are not clear or are not followed consistently over subsequent test administrations. The best solution for this type of measurement error is to make sure that each testee receives exactly the same instructions. This is the reason that any good psychometric test supplies *standardised instructions* in the manual.

- The mood of a person on a particular day may be of such a nature that he or she would not answer the questionnaire as he or she 'usually' is.
- The items of the test do not provide an accurate reflection of the characteristic being measured. In this regard, it is important to note that each item in a test or scale must have relevance to the attribute being measured. This implies that all the items in a given scale should have at least a moderate correlation with all the other items in the scale. Sometimes it happens that some items that do not provide accurate reflections of the attribute being measured are included in the scale. Responses to these items therefore do not have any relevance to the characteristic in which the investigator or therapist is interested, but this item still contributes to the grand total of the particular scale. A poor correlation with other test items usually indicates that this item's contribution is mostly error variance.

The relative influence of error in a set of observed scores can be determined by means of the reliability coefficient. Reliability coefficients reflect the proportion of observed variance that consists of true variance. There are four types of reliabilities that are often reported in the manuals of psychometric instruments.

Test-retest reliability

This type of reliability is related to the degree to which individuals' scores remain constant over repeated test administrations. The coefficient is calculated by correlating individuals' scores for the first test administration with those of the second test administration. As for any other correlation coefficient, the reliability coefficient can vary between −1.00 and +1.00, but in practice, this coefficient will always lie between 0 and 1.00. A value of 1.00 indicates that the instrument is perfectly reliable, and that measurement error has no influence on the scores whatsoever. In such a case, the observed score would be equal to the true score. However, it never happens that measurement error can be completely eliminated. A general rule has developed over time that coefficients of 0.80 and higher are regarded as satisfactory for scores on personality questionnaires, whereas coefficients of 0.90 and higher are regarded as satisfactory for ability measures. Coefficients above 0.70 are also acceptable, but scores on scales with such reliability coefficients should be approached with some caution. It should be noted that the greater the interval between test administrations, the lower the reliability coefficients will be, in most cases. The test-retest reliability coefficient should only be computed if it can be assumed that the trait of interest is relatively stable and does not change too much over time.

Equivalent-forms reliability

Another important method used to calculate reliability coefficients is the comparison of equivalent forms of a specific instrument. Two instruments can be shown to be equivalent if they consist of the same number of items and measure precisely the same construct. Consider that for each specific construct or characteristic that can be measured, a *universum* of possible items exists. It is the duty of the test constructor to cover this universum in a satisfactory manner through the items selected. Any two tests that cover this universum in a satisfactory way should be measuring the same construct and scores for the two tests should show a high correlation (Nunnaly & Bernstein, 1994). As with test-retest reliability, the equivalent forms reliability is calculated as the correlation between two test administrations, but here two equivalent tests are administered. Therefore, if a researcher thus constructs a test that supposedly provides an accurate reflection of individuals' scores for a particular characteristic, these scores should correlate highly with an equivalent test.

Split-half reliability

It is also possible to determine the reliability of a test or scale by means of a single administration of the test or scale. In this regard it is important to know whether different parts of the test measure the same characteristic or construct. What researchers typically do is divide the items of the scale randomly in two, and correlate the scores from the one half with scores from the other. Just as in equivalent tests, a high correlation indicates that the two halves measure the same construct.

The reliability of a scale increases as more items are added to it (provided that the items are relevant to the construct of interest). Taking into consideration that the split-half method divides a scale into two shorter parts, the possibility exists that the reliability coefficient could be low, because it is based

on scores from two shorter tests. It is possible to correct for this shortcoming using a simple formula known as the Spearman-Brown correction formula. The formula is as follows:

$$r_{tt} = 2r/1 + r$$

where r_{tt} is the corrected correlation, and r is the correlation between the two halves of the tests. This correction provides an estimation of what the reliability would be if the two halves of the test were as long as the original scale.

Internal consistency reliability

Considering that it is possible to divide a test in a variety of ways, it would be useful to have a single coefficient that reflects the average of all the split-half reliability coefficients of a particular scale. This statistic is known as Cronbach's alpha coefficient. It is also sometimes referred to as the Kuder-Richardson coefficient when the items are answered in a dichotomous format. This coefficient provides an indication of the degree to which the items in a scale are all related to the same construct, and it is therefore desirable that it be as high as possible. In the field of personality measurement, coefficients of 0.80 and higher are desirable. A general formula for the internal consistency of a set of scores is as follows:

$$\text{Reliability}_{coefficient\ \alpha} = \frac{k\,(\bar{r}_{ij})}{1 + (k - 1)\bar{r}_{ij}}$$

where k = the number of items in the test, and r_{ij} = the mean intercorrelation of the items. This formula clearly shows that the reliability of a set of scores increases as the number of test items increase and as the intercorrelations between these items increases. One can therefore improve the reliability of a test by including more items and by making sure that all the items are related to one another.

The validity of psychological test scores

Reliability is an important characteristic of any psychological measuring instrument, but there is no guarantee that valid scores can be obtained with it. Validity is the extent of correspondence between what the test measures and what it is supposed to measure. The validity of test scores therefore depends on the degree to which they achieve their goal. This implies that tests that have more than one purpose must be valid for each of these purposes. It is not uncommon for a test to be valid for one purpose, but invalid for another. There are several types of validity. We discuss some of the main types:

Criterion-related validity

The criterion-related validity of test scores refers to the degree to which the test can accurately predict some criterion of interest. A criterion can refer to any aspect that a psychologist wishes to measure, for example, aggressive behaviour, school performance, job satisfaction, etc. Criterion-related validity is usually evaluated by means of the correlation between test scores and criterion scores – the higher the correlation, the better the criterion-related validity of the test.

We can distinguish between two types of criterion-related validity, namely *predictive* validity and *concurrent* validity. *Predictive validity* requires that the criterion scores be obtained some time after the test scores are obtained. For example, if an employer wants to see whether introversion-extroversion is a predictor of job satisfaction, he may ask a *representative sample* of his employees to complete an introversion-extroversion test and then at a later time, say six months later, he will evaluate the workers' job satisfaction. The next step would then be to obtain the correlation between the introversion-extroversion scores and the job satisfaction scores. An important consideration in predictive validity is that appropriate criterion scores are not always available. Such criterion scores should also be reliable and valid, but in many work situations, for example, the criterion scores are judgements made by supervisors of which the reliability and validity is unknown.

With *concurrent validity*, the criterion scores are obtained at the same time as the test scores. In this regard, psychologists are often interested in whether the test can distinguish between groups that are known to differ in terms of the criterion. As an example, consider a psychologist who wishes to evaluate the concurrent validity of a Superego Strength Questionnaire. Based on Freud's theory, one would expect juvenile delinquents to have less well developed superego's than non-delinquents. The psychologist thus administers the test to a group of delinquents and to a group of non-delinquents, and then correlates the test scores with group membership. The higher the correlation, the better the concurrent validity of the test scores. Psychologists who wish to evaluate the concurrent validity of a test sometimes follow the strategy of administering two tests that measure the same trait (e.g., an old Superego Strength Questionnaire and a new Superego Strength Questionnaire) at the same time, and then obtain the correlation between the scores for the two tests.

Content validity

The content validity of test scores refers to the degree to which they represent the domain of interest. One thus asks whether or not the test has been properly constructed. Two aspects are important in this regard: no important aspects of the domain of interest should be left out, and no aspects should be included that are not part of the domain of interest. This implies that content validity depends on the definition of the domain or construct of interest. The content validity of a test is evaluated by systematically and logically inspecting the content of the items. The issue of content validity should be addressed at the beginning of the test construction process, when the items that are to be included are considered. This implies that the person constructing the test should have a thorough theoretical knowledge of the construct to be measured. The content validity of a test is satisfactory only if the chosen items adequately represent the domain of interest. It cannot be expressed numerically and can only be judged by experts in the particular domain of interest.

Construct validity

Construct validity refers to the degree to which a test succeeds in measuring what it purports to measure. A construct refers to a hypothetical variable that, together with other constructs, forms a theory of which the goal is to explain observable behaviour. Construct validity is especially important in basic scientific research where predictions are made about the relationship between constructs (as measured by tests) and other variables. If the predictions are confirmed, it provides support for the construct validity of the test.

As an example, consider a researcher who is interested in the construct validity of a neuroticism questionnaire. Based on theory, the researcher expects that people with high scores for the questionnaire will have more sensitive autonomic nervous systems than people with low scores. If scores for the test succeed in distinguishing between people with sensitive and less sensitive autonomic nervous systems, it will provide support for the construct validity of the test. Another approach would be to correlate the scores for the neuroticism test with scores for other neuroticism tests. If a satisfactory correlation is obtained it shows that the two tests measure the same construct and therefore provide support for the construct validity of the neuroticism tests. When a test correlates as expected with another test that measures the same construct, it shows *convergent validity*. We might also decide to correlate the neuroticism test with tests that measure different constructs, such as extroversion and intelligence. On the basis of personality theory, we would expect a low or zero correlation between the neuroticism test and the extroversion or intelligence test. If such a correlation is found the test is said to show *divergent validity*.

It is clear that construct validity employs some of the same methods that are used to evaluate predictive and concurrent validity. The difference is based on the reason for which it is evaluated – concurrent and predictive validity are mostly evaluated to assess the practical utility of the test, whereas construct validity is evaluated to assess the scientific utility of a test. Contemporary psychometricians, however, view all different types of validity as different manifestations of construct validity. Hence, if a test predicts a criterion in a theoretically meaningful way and the content validity of the test is judged to be satisfactory, then this evidence also supports the construct validity of the test.

Conclusion

This chapter is concerned with personality assessment. We have shown that the assessment of personality can take several forms, such as interviews, standardised psychometric tests and projective techniques. Most often projective methods of assessment have limited utility because of inadequate reliability and validity. The interview is probably the most thorough method of personality assessment in that it permits the interviewer to take time to get to know the person in a face-to-face encounter. An important limitation is that it is time consuming and interviewers need to be trained professionals. For this reason, self-report psychometric measures are often used for personality assessment. Two of the most popular instruments are the MMPI and the NEO-PI. When using a psychometric instrument to assess personality it is important that the measure has good reliability and validity, otherwise the assessment may yield inaccurate results. Generally, persons who conduct personality assessments should be trained in personality theory, psychopathology, psychometric theory and statistics.

REFERENCES

Buros Institute of Mental Measurements. (2003). *The Fifteenth Mental Measurements Yearbook*. USA: University of Nebraska Press.

Costa, P.T. & McCrae, R.R. (1992). The five-factor model of personality and its relevance to personality disorders. *Journal of Personality Disorders*, 6:343-59.

De Raad, B. (2000). *The Big Five Personality Factors: The psycholexical approach to personality*. Seattle: Hogrefe & Huber Publishers.

Heuchert, J.W.P., Parker, W.D., Stumpf, H. & Myburgh, C.P.H. (2000). The five-factor model of personality in South African college students. *American Behavioral Scientist*, 4:112-25.

McCrae, R.R. (2000). Trait psychology and the revival of personality and culture studies. *American Behavioural Scientist*, 44:10-31.

McCrae, R. & Costa, P.T. (1989). More reasons to adopt the five-factor model. *American Psychologist*, 44:451-52.

Nunnally, J.C. & Bernstein, I.H. (1994). *Psychometric Theory* (3rd edition). New York: McGraw Hill.

Peltzer, K. & Thole, J. (2000). Gambling attitudes among Black South African university students. *Psychological Reports*, 86:957-62.

Taylor, T.R. & Boeyens, J.C. (1991). The comparability of the scores of Blacks and Whites on the South African Personality Questionnaire: An exploratory study. *South African Journal of Psychology*, 21:1-11.

Zimbardo, P., McDermott, M., Jansz, J. & Metaal, N. (1995). *Psychology: A European Text*. USA: Harper Collins.

Multiple choice questions

1. An important concept in understanding personality is
   a) human nature
   b) attribute
   c) trait
   d) disorder
2. Please state the answer that is not correct. Popular ways of assessing personality are
   a) clinical interviews
   b) projective tests
   c) objective tests
   d) free association
3. One of the problems associated with objective measures is
   a) social conformity
   b) social desirability
   c) social pressure
   d) social attitudinal patterns
4. One famous projective test is the
   a) Minnesota Multiphasic Personality Inventory
   b) NEO Personality Inventory
   c) Hopkins Symptom Checklist
   d) Rorschach Inkblot Test

5. Which of the following is not an form of reliability?
   a) test retest reliability
   b) equivalent forms reliability
   c) split half reliability
   d) convergent reliability
6. The extent of correspondence between what a test measures and what it is supposed to meaure is called
   a) reliability
   b) validity
   c) test confidence
   d) the correlation coefficient

Short answer questions

1. Discuss the most popular methods of personality assessment.
2. What is objective personality assessment?
3. Name and describe two examples of objective personality assessment.
4. What are the advantages and disadvantages of using objective methods of assessment?
5. What are the advantages and disadvantages of using objective methods of assessment?

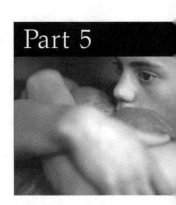

Part 5

Cognitive Psychology

Andrew Gilbert

Cognitive psychology is a term used to describe that field of psychology that studies what goes on 'in the mind'. Cognition concerns the mental process or capacities that exist when people are engaged in activities such as thinking, remembering, being creative, planning, analysing, reasoning and solving problems.

At different times in the history of psychology, different aspects of cognition have received particular attention. As a result, there are a number of specific areas of focus within the broad field of cognitive psychology. Among these are:

- Thinking, which has a more general focus on how people reason, solve problems and think in their everyday lives.
- Language, which focuses on the relationship between thought and language.
- Memory, which is concerned with how and why people remember or forget things.
- Intelligence, which attends to the measurement of individual differences in the capacity for intellectual activities.

In the following four chapters, each of these foci in cognitive psychology is given attention in a separate chapter. Tlali examines intelligence, Gilbert looks at thinking, Neves considers language and van Ommen explores memory.

Despite the different traditions in cognitive psychology there are a number of cross-cutting theories, themes and issues. You will find them constantly reappearing, sometimes in disguised ways, as you work your way through the four chapters. It is possible, therefore, to read these chapters in a different way by focusing on the debates and dilemmas that are present in cognitive psychology as a whole.

To help you see some of the common threads in the four chapters, three particular issues are highlighted here.

First, all four chapters work with the assumption that thinking is a mental process. Mental processes are generally understood as internal processes going on 'in the mind' (However, also consider the second theme below). The study of such processes creates a huge challenge because how is it possible to study something that cannot be directly observed? One of the ways psychologists address this problem is to develop theories which make assumptions of what these internal process might be like. These assumptions guide:

- What aspects of cognition are regarded as important.
- How cognition can be investigated.

You will find as you read these chapters the presence of a number of very different assumptions about these internal processes. Some psychologists use the computer as a metaphor for looking at mental process (e.g., the information processing approach). Others consider thinking to be a mental process linked to the individual's adaptation to the environment (e.g., the constructivist approach and Piaget). Still others see mental processes as being the internalisation of cultural ways of doing things (e.g., the socio-historical approach and Vygotsky). Comparing how these three different sets of assumptions influence what is studied, how it is studied and how psychologists apply their insights, should help you deepen your understanding of the complexity of psychology.

Second, while historically the focus in cognitive psychology has been on internal mental processes, a growing number of psychologists recognise that this focus is based on an artificial separation of the personal internal world from the outside social or cultural world. This inside-outside tension is one of the dualisms we grapple with in contemporary psychology. You will find, as you read these chapters, that some theories focus mainly on the 'internal' (e.g., the information processing approach) while others seek to break down the internal-external distinction (e.g., the socio-historical approach). The latter theories provide a critique of mainstream views of cognition and open up new possibilities for understanding cognition. Some examples of where you will find this debate follow. In the chapter on intelligence, the growing awareness of the importance of context in the measurement of internal intellectual capacity has led to an interest in the assessment of 'learning potential', rather than fixed mental capacity. In the chapter on memory, the idea of 'distributed cognition' is discussed, which suggests that remembering something is linked to resources in social settings that facilitate internal memory processes. In the chapter on language, the link between language and social identity is considered, and in the chapter on thinking, the nature of everyday thinking is discussed.

Third, linked to the above two themes is another tension to be found across the chapters. This is a tension between whether it is important to seek universal or local understandings of cognition. The former concerns the establishment of concepts, laws and principles of cognition that are true for everyone everywhere. You will find that Piaget's theory in the chapter on thinking, Chomsky's ideas in the chapter on language, and information processing in the chapter on memory follow this idea. In contrast to this are psychologists who are more interested in how cognition is influenced by the local or specific social settings. Thus, for example, in the chapter on thinking there is discussion on practical everyday thinking that seems to differ from formal logical thought. In the chapter on language, this issue appears in the form of the cultural relativity debate: 'Do different languages, vocabularies and linguistic resources determine the way people think?' In the chapter on intelligence it appears in the debate about whether there is a general intelligence 'g' or multiple intelligences that relate to specific skills.

Keep these themes and debates in mind, and seek other common themes, as you read these chapters. Doing so will bring out a deeper understanding of the promise and prospects of cognitive psychology.

15

Intelligence Testing

Tshepo Tlali

CHAPTER OBJECTIVES

After studying this chapter you should be able to:
- trace the historical development of intelligence testing
- demonstrate your understanding of the concept of intelligence and intelligence testing, and the tensions that exist in this field
- demonstrate your understanding of the use of intelligence tests
- identify various theoretical approaches to intelligence tests and testing
- demonstrate your understanding of the historical development of intelligence tests in South Africa
- identify various individual tests used in South Africa
- demonstrate your understanding of racial and cultural issues involved in psychological testing.

Nosipho, like most people, knew something about IQ tests. She had done one at school along with everyone else in her class. She didn't really understand at the time what the test was going to be used for, but had listened to some of the other kids making jokes about one or two pupils who they were sure would be discovered to be 'really, really dumb'. She felt a bit nervous doing the test herself and wondered if it would show her up to be reasonably intelligent or not. In the end the test had involved some tasks that seemed different to normal school work, but weren't all that difficult. She never got any results from the test itself, but she imagined her teachers may have seen them because they kept telling her that she was 'under-achieving'. She didn't seem to be able to live up to what they had expected of her. A friend of her father's had had the opposite problem. He had told her that he had been advised not to go to university because his IQ score was below normal. As it happened, he ignored the advice his school counsellor had given him and successfully completed an engineering degree. Perhaps, Nosipho thought, the tests were not quite as objective and accurate as people thought. She had once overheard some of the teachers at her school suggesting that IQ tests might even be racist – that they

had been invented for White people by White people and that they didn't recognise the different ways that different cultures approached intellectual tasks.

At the same time Nosipho thought, it might be valuable to try and make some sense of the slightly mysterious concept of 'intelligence'. People often made assumptions about who was 'clever' or 'stupid' and maybe if more was understood about these things there wouldn't be so much negative stereotyping. Also, Nosipho imagined, if you could measure intelligence properly it might really help teachers direct children to appropriate career paths or understand why a child was struggling with schoolwork. Nosipho's much younger cousin had been taken to see a psychologist after he had had trouble learning at school. The psychologists did some tests on him – including an IQ test – and helped to diagnose a problem he had in 'processing visual information'. The psychologist had referred the boy to an occupational therapist and he was now doing much better at school. 'Looking carefully at a person's intellectual abilities and knowing their strengths and weaknesses might be helpful, provided it was used carefully and sensitively,' Nosipho thought.

Introduction

Cultures everywhere and throughout history have had words for describing some people as smart, clever or bright. In doing this they are often referring to an assumed difference in mental ability or capacity across people. Psychologists who study intelligence have taken these everyday distinctions and developed formal theories about the characteristics of intelligence and constructed tests to measure mental ability.

In the same way that different cultures have different criteria of what it means to be clever or bright, so psychologists differ in their understanding of intelligence depending on their particular theoretical and conceptual frameworks. Box 15.1 gives a list of definitions taken from central theories of intelligence. Consider how much they differ.

15.1 SOME DEFINITIONS OF INTELLIGENCE

Binet (in Sattler, 1992:45)
'The tendency to take and maintain a definite direction; the capacity to make adaptations for the purpose of attaining a desired end; and the power of autocriticism.'

Spearman (1923:300, 63)
'... everything intellectual can be reduced to some special case ... of educing either relations or correlates.'

'The mentally presenting of any two or more characters [education of relations] ... tends to evoke immediately a knowing of relation between them.'

Das (1973:27)
'... the ability to plan and structure one's behavior with an end in view.'

Gardner (1993:x)
'the ability to solve problems, or to create products, that are valued within one or more cultural settings.'

Sternberg (1984:312)
'... mental activity involved in purposive adaptation to, shaping of, and selection of real-world environments relevant to one's life.'

While the problem of the definition of intelligence remains (Maloney & Ward, 1976), all approaches treat intelligence as a hypothetical construct referring to some mental capacity, power or process linked to actual performance.

The study of intelligence has taken two related but conceptually different roads. The one has followed a practical agenda of producing reliable tests that measure individual differences in intellect. One use of these tests is to obtain a score that can predict behaviour in some other sphere of life, for example, academic or work performance. This is known as the psychometric approach. The second approach has worked more theoretically to provide answers to the question: 'What is intelligence, its nature and composition?' In this chapter these two themes are examined separately. At the end of this chapter, however, which looks at the issues of race, culture and intelligence, we will pose the question: How can we use the theories to make sense of some of the more controversial findings produced by the application of tests?

First, however, let us look at some international and national milestones in the conceptualisation and the development of intelligence tests.

A brief history of psychological testing

Interest in intelligence and intelligence testing can be traced back to the latter part of the nineteenth century. A scientific movement to establish psychology as a distinct discipline of study characterised this period. To measure mental capacity requires appropriate ways of analysing and representing scores. British mathematician, Sir Francis Galton (1822-1911), a younger cousin of Charles Darwin, conducted pioneering work, at this time, to develop the statistics that are required for the measurement of intelligence. He is regarded as the father of the testing movement.

The American psychologist James M. Cattell (1860-1944), however, is given the credit for coining the term 'mental test'. He worked under the German experimental psychologist Wilhelm Wundt (1832-1920), and believed that general laws of behaviour could be established by examining differences in mental operations among individuals. He proposed that mental abilities could be measured objectively through formalised testing (Ittenbach et al., 1997).

At the turn of the twentieth century, when the French government opened public schools to every child, Binet (1857-1911), Victor Henri (1872-1940), and Theodore Simon (1873-1961) were commissioned to develop a scale to identify those children who had the ability to benefit from formal education. Prior to their work, intelligence was seen as the sensitivity of perception. Binet and his colleagues took a different view by arguing that the measurement of intelligence should focus on higher mental processes (Herrnstein & Murray, 1994). They regarded the ability to reason, draw analogies and identify patterns as central to intelligence. The Binet-Simon Scale they developed in 1905 reflected the age-based cognitive development of these abilities. It objectively identified degrees of mental ability and became the prototype of many subsequent scales.

Their work had a major impact on psychology. Jenkins and Paterson (in Sattler, 1992:81) note 'probably no psychological innovation has had more impact on the societies of the Western world than the development of the Binet-Simon Scale'. There was, however, some discontent with the age-scale format, that is creating scores for each age group. Robert M. Yerkes (1876-1956) and his colleagues developed an alternative format called the point-scale format, which allocates a person's score to a specific index or point that is assumed to represent the intellectual functioning of individuals. This forms the basis for contemporary testing.

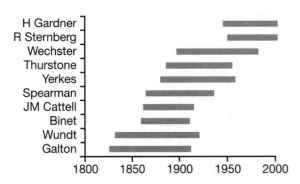

Figure 1 The historical sequence of major role players in the history of intelligence testing

David Wechsler is another important figure in the historical map of intelligence testing. In the USA he constructed three important tests: the *Wechsler Intelligence Scale for Children* (WISC) in 1949; the *Wechsler Adult Intelligence Scale* (WAIS) in 1955; and the *Wechsler Preschool and Primary Scale of Intelligence* (WPPSI) in 1967 (Ittenbach *et al.*, 1997). These have formed the basis for many other tests, including some of those used in South Africa. Wechsler believed that intelligence was a unitary trait and could best be explained through performance over a wide range of intellectual activities. Like the Binet-Simon scale, the Wechsler scales were not based on

any theoretical considerations, they merely provided the clinician with information needed for service delivery.

Testing in South Africa

The historical development of psychological testing in South Africa followed a similar pattern to that in the US and Europe. According to Foxcroft and Roodt (2001), the early psychological tests in South Africa were adaptations of overseas psychological measures.

For example, C. Louis Leopoldt and J.M. Moll took the Binet-Simon scale and standardised it on 1 400 pupils from the then Transvaal. This test became officially known as the Binet-Simon-Goddard-Healy-Knox Scale. Similarly, E. Eybers of the University of Free State, revised the Binet scale as well as the 1924 Egerton-Bridge Scale, which was an adaptation of the Yerkes-Bridges scale developed in the USA, to become the 1925 Eybers Scale (Louw & Edwards, 1997). Both these scales were standardised for use with English- and Afrikaans-speaking South Africans.

The following three individual scales for intellectual assessment for different age groups are presently used in South Africa: The Junior South African Individual Scale (JSAIS) assesses the intellectual functioning of children between the ages of three to seven years; the Senior South African Individual Scale-Revised (SSAIS-R) assesses the intellectual abilities of children from roughly eight to seventeen years; and the South African Weschler Adult Individual Scale (SAWAIS-III) covers all age groups between seventeen and sixty five years. The SAWAIS-III has recently being standardised for all population groups with a minimum educational level of Grade 9. A description of the SSAIS-R is given in Box 15.2.

The measurement of intelligence

The challenge when measuring intelligence is to produce an index that indicates intellectual functioning. It is not adequate to describe a person by their score on a test. It is necessary to compare this score with the scores of other people of a comparable background. For example, if Manoke scores 80 out of a 100 this might appear to be a good score, but

The aims of the SSAIS-R are: to obtain a measure of general intellectual ability in order to predict scholastic achievement; and to provide a profile of scatter analysis, for diagnostic and prognostic purposes (Owen, 1998).

This scale was initially constructed for Afrikaans and English-speaking Whites, Coloured and Indian learners between 7 and 16 years of age. A socio-economic disadvantagement scale, named the 'SED questionnaire', has to be used in all the cases where disadvantage is suspected. Interestingly, the designers of this scale argue that the term 'intelligence' only applies in those cases where no disadvantagement has been detected. Recently, the 'Individual Scale for Zulu/Xhosa/North-Sotho/Sesotho/Tswana-speaking learners' has been standardised for Black children in their home languages (Owen & Taljaard, 1995). This scale uses the same nine sub-scales of the SSAIS-R, but in addition has a mazes sub-test.

The SSAIS-R consists of verbal and non-verbal sub-tests. A description of these follows. The five verbal sub-tests along with an optional sixth are:
- Vocabulary: verbal intelligence, verbal concepts ability, and receptive language development.
- Comprehension: comprehension of social situations and judgment based on knowledge and use of conventional rules.
- Similarities: verbal concept formation on a concrete-perceptual level, and abstract reasoning.
- Number problems: numerical reasoning, logical-analytic and deductive reasoning underlying this ability.
- Story memory: attention and short term auditory memory for meaningful verbal learning material.
- Memory for digits (optional): attention, concentration, working memory and auditory short-term memory for numerical symbols.

The four non-verbal sub-tests along with an optional fifth are:
- Pattern completion: visual concentration, non-verbal concept-formation, as well as deductive and inductive reasoning ability.
- Block design: the ability to visualise and reason in terms of spatial relationships.
- Missing parts: visualisation of reality situations and concrete reality-testing.
- Form board: visual organisation and integration, concept-formation, and visual-perceptual speed in discerning relationships between parts.
- Coding (optional): cognitive functions involved in learning unfamiliar task and applying what has been learned.

if everyone else in his class scores 90 out of 100, we would not want to say Manoke was brighter than everyone else! How have psychologists established an index of intelligence?

Binet used the idea of mental age (MA) as an index for the intellectual capacity of children. The Binet-Simon test was divided into sets of five items, one set for each age group. The difficulty of the items was adjusted so that an average child of a particular age could just complete all five items. If a child could complete all the items in the set for a particular age – say, for example, those for seven-year-olds – but not those items of the next level (the set for eight-year-olds) then child was said to have a mental age (MA) of seven. (Flanagan *et al.*, 1997). This index is useful because if a child has a mental age that is higher than their chronological age then they can be said to be functioning at a higher mental level than their peers. This index, however, had a problem because a lowering of MA relative to CA (chronological age – the actual age of the person) is far more significant the younger the subject. For

example, a one year deficit in development in a three-year-old implies a far greater level of developmental retardation than does a one year deficit in a 12-year-old.

In 1912, Stern developed the concept of Intelligence Quotient (IQ) (Maloney & Ward, 1976). He argued that the ratio of MA to CA would provide a better index of mental functioning. The formula for computation of this ratio became established as:

$$IQ = \frac{MA}{CA} \times 100$$

According to this formula, an eight-year-old child with a MA of eight years obtains an IQ of 100. The same child would receive an IQ of 50 if his or her MA was four, or 150 if his or her MA was 12. On the basis of this ratio an IQ of 100 can regarded as the average IQ for a child of any age.

The IQ ratio, however, as an index for adult intelligence, is problematic. Research has shown that scores of intellectual ability do not increase after about the age of 16, that is MA will remain constant after 16. Given the IQ ratio, this means that IQ scores will go progressively down as CA increases, and adults will increasingly appear to have IQs that suggest severe mental retardation. Wechsler resolved this problem by proposing that the ratio method should be replaced by a deviation method (Maloney & Ward, 1976). This has become the basis for calculating IQ scores for most contemporary tests.

In the deviation method, a distribution of scores of a representative sample of people of the same chronological age is obtained. The test scores are recalculated using this distribution so that the average score for the group becomes 100 and every score changed to represent a deviation from this mean (hence the term deviation method). This approach enables a score on a test to be converted to an IQ score with a mean of 100 so that it is possible to compare all individuals on the same standard. The deviation IQ therefore gives the relative position of a person compared to his or her peers. How IQ scores have come to be traditionally classified in terms of the description of intellect is given in Table 1.

IQ score	Descriptive categories
140+	Extremely gifted
130 – 140	Highly gifted
120 – 130	Gifted
110 – 120	High average
90 – 110	Average
80 – 90	Low average
70 – 80	Borderline mental retardation
50 – 70	Mild mental retardation
35 – 55	Moderate mental retardation
20 – 40	Severe mental retardation
Less than 20	Profound mental retardation

Table 1 The classification of IQ scores

Using the deviation method requires that every intelligence test has age-based norms. These are tables of values which reflect the distribution of scores for particular age groups from which a standard IQ score can be calculated. Developing an intelligence test requires applying it to a large sample which is representative of a particular popula-

tion, so that these norms can be established for this population. This process is called standardisation. When a test is used to assess intellectual functioning it is crucial that the person's score is compared against appropriate norms. Failure to do this invalidates the findings. We will return to this issue when we look at cultural problems with testing.

Uses of intelligence tests

Obtaining an index of intellectual capacity is of little use if this index is not able to predict performance or achievement in some other aspect of life. Maloney and Ward (1976) argue that a test possesses predictive validity if it can be shown to correlate with a prescribed set of socially defined 'success' criteria. Thus if it can be shown that people with above average IQ scores are more likely to get their degrees without failing a course then IQ is predictive of university success.

This is one way in which intelligence tests are used. In line with Binet's approach, intelligence tests are still widely used to provide information to guide the decision-making of parents, educators and other professionals (Owen, 1998). Information gained from individual intellectual tests is used to assess such issues as:
- school readiness;
- the need for appropriate remedial programmes for learners with learning problems and/or disabilities; and
- deciding upon special and/or specialised educational programmes for a child.

A second way in which intelligence tests are used is to assist in diagnostic processes. Some tests, such as the SAWAIS and SSAIS-R, can provide useful clinical hypotheses concerning the person's organic, emotional and psychological status (Flanagan *et al.* 1997; Nell, 2000). These tests consist of a number of sub-scales (see Box 15.2). Discrepancies in performance across these sub-scales as well as patterns in the scatter of scores can indicate problems. Thus, for example, large differences between scores on the verbal and non-verbal sub-scales may help identify, along with other forms of assessment, organic problems in the brain.

It should be noted that there is a distinction between the practical utility and the scientific validity of IQ tests (Lezak, 1983). Many tests were developed for specific practical purposes rather than to verify a theory of intelligence. The following sections outline more theoretical approaches.

Theories of intelligence

Theories of intelligence can be divided into four groups, namely psychometric, information processing, eclectic and learning potential theories. Each of these is considered in the following sections.

Psychometric theories

Psychometric theories have been constructed from the Psychometric approach to intelligence testing that has been outlined in the preceding sections. This approach has focused on describing the structure of intelligence by examining the relationships between test items or sub-tests of psychological tests. This involves conducting a statistical analysis, called a factor analysis, in which the patterns of correlations between the various elements of the test are studied. If certain elements appear to relate to each other and form a cluster (these clusters are called factors) then it is assumed that the factors are measuring different aspects of intelligence.

Psychometric theories have sparked a debate about whether intelligence is a general capacity or many different abilities. Charles Spearman, a British psychologist working at the beginning of the last century, argued that intelligence consisted of two factors: a general intelligence and specific intelligence (Sattler, 1992). General intelligence, named 'g', is a general capacity for inferring and applying common sense to experiences drawn from various situations (Herrnstein & Murray, 1994). Spearman argued that people who possess a high general intelligence are usually successful across differing activities. For example, they may be good at both languages and science. With further research he found that some people possess specific kinds of ability which enable them to excel in particular activities but not others. He called this specialised ability-specific intelligence 's'. Performance on any particular task would include a mixture of 'g' and 's'.

In contrast, an American psychologist, Thurstone, in the 1930s, identified seven primary mental abilities in his factor analysis of test scores (Thurstone, 1931). His research, therefore, did not support the idea of 'g' but rather a series of special abilities, such as verbal comprehension as opposed to reasoning.

It is important to keep in mind that the data upon which the psychometric theories are constructed are based on the performance of people on particular tests. This is limiting because what goes into the tests will determine what is discovered. Psychometric theories are, therefore, as much a reflection of the way tests have been constructed as they are of the actual underlying nature of intelligence. A second challenge to the psychometric approach concerns the static nature of the measurement process. Many psychometric tests measure a person's performance on one test completed at one moment in time. They are, therefore, not sensitive to intelligence as a dynamic process. The learning potential approach, which is outlined in more detail later in the chapter, attempts to address this issue.

Information processing theories

Unlike the psychometric approach which describes the pattern of responses on tests, the information processing (IP) approach attempts to investigate what might lie behind the apparent differences in intelligence. Details of the principles behind the IP approach are given in Chapters 16 and 18. A brief look at Sternberg's (1984) theory of intelligence highlights the IP approach to intelligence. Examples of other IP theories are: Das (1973), Das *et al.* (1994), and Naglieri (1989, 1997).

Sternberg's triarchic theory of intelligence

Sternberg's approach (1984) focuses on how people process and control information. It is called the triarchic theory of intelligence because it contains three sub-theories which describe different dimensions of information processing: the componential, experiential and contextual.

The componential sub-theory is concerned with the internal mental processes that underlie human intelligence. It is comparable to the traditional notions of intelligence, in the sense that a person with high componential intelligence is expected to do well in traditional intelligence tests. There are three kinds of information processing within this system:

- Metacomponents, which are the higher-order, executive processes (which control the other two components) used in planning, monitoring and evaluating performance (Sattler, 1992). Examples of metacomponents include abilities such as problem identification, and making strategic decisions.

- Performance components are the processes involved in the execution of a given task, which has been conceptualised or planned by the metacomponent (Sternberg, 1997).
- Knowledge-acquisition components are those involved in learning and storing new information.

The experiential dimension concerns those aspects of intelligence involved in handling different tasks and situations (Sattler, 1992). Performing new tasks that do not rely on past experience requires intellectual processes different from those used when conducting complex tasks that have become automatic. How well people do on these two contrasting tasks will be an indication of experiential intelligence. It is this kind of intelligence that led Sternberg (1984) to believe that it is difficult to compare levels of intelligence fairly across socio-cultural groups.

The contextual dimension conceptualises intelligence in relation to the external world. Sternberg (1984) argued that it is also necessary to view intelligence in terms of adaptive behaviour in the real world environment. Adaptive behaviour can be understood as skills that are needed to survive in particular environments. As these adaptive requirements will differ from one culture to another, this aspect of intelligence can only be evaluated in context (Sattler, 1992).

An interesting example of contextual intelligence is demonstrated in the work of Serpell (1994) in Box 15.3. Sternberg's approach makes an important contribution to intelligence because it argues that people can be intelligent in different ways, and that everyday intelligent behaviour is an important aspect of intelligence. Sternberg's idea of contextual intelligence encourages sensitivity to intelligence in multicultural societies, such as South Africa.

Eclectic approaches

Howard Gardner's (1993) theory of intelligence is presented here as an eclectic theory, because he draws ideas from across the spectrum of approaches to cognition.

Multiple intelligence theory

Gardner (in Flanagan *et al.*, 1997:106) defines intelligence as 'the ability to solve problems, or to create products, that are valued within one or more cultural setting.' Like Thurstone, he argued that there is more than one form of intelligence, but he goes beyond the description of scores to seek evidence for different intelligences. He has identified seven intelligences: linguistic, logical-mathematical, spatial, musical, bodily-kinaesthetic, interpersonal and intrapersonal (Gardner, 1983, 1993).

The first three are similar to what is assessed in psychometric tests (see Box 15.2). The other four are different. Musical intelligence involves operations such as pitch, rhythm, timbre and the ability to understand and manipulate musical symbols. Bodily-kinesthetic intelligence involves the abilities used in skilled movements such as dancing or athletics. Interpersonal and intrapersonal intelligences refer to the ability to understand others and relationships and the ability to understand and have insight into our own behaviour, respectively.

Gardner argued that these intelligences are largely autonomous. Each has particular information processing capacities, problem-solving features and

---

15.3 THE INFLUENCE OF ENVIRONMENT ON INTELLIGENCE

Serpell (1994) and his co-workers sampled two contrasting, low-income neighbourhoods (one in Lusaka, Zambia, the other in Manchester, England) to test the hypothesis that environment plays a pivotal role in moulding our intelligence. Eight-year-old boys and girls were asked to reproduce a standard pattern, such as a square with diagonals, a human figure, or a flower. In the drawing version of the task, the child was given a blank sheet of paper and a pencil and asked to copy a printed standard. In the wire-modelling task, the child was handed a strip of wire and asked to make a model just like a standard wire model. They also administered a clay-modelling version of the same task, which they predicted would be of equal difficulty for both samples, since many Zambian children make models from natural clay during the rainy season, and many English children play with industrially produced modelling clay. As they had predicted, the English children performed significantly better on drawing task, the Zambian children performed much better on the wire-modelling task, and there was no group difference on the clay-modelling task.

Figure 2 Gardner's seven types of intelligence

developmental trajectories. As a result, assessment should be designed to examine the cognitive potential or competence in each of these intelligences. It also implies that the development of intelligences may proceed at different rates and individuals can display an uneven profile of abilities across intelligences. According to Gardner, assessment should be sensitive to what individuals are capable of accomplishing.

Although Gardner's theory offers an interesting alternative and, in the context of South Africa, opens up the promise of greater sensitivity to differing intelligences arising out of different contexts, it has a number of limitations. First, it is not clear why particular intelligences are primary. Why, for example, is musical ability a primary intelligence? Why are other forms of intelligence, for example, religiosity and the ability to make sense of rituals and mystical life, not considered as intelligence? Second, it argues against the idea of 'g', which many psychologists have come to accept underlies all forms of cognition.

Learning potential theories

The psychometric approach views intelligence as a relatively fixed capacity. Intelligence tests measure this capacity in a static way, in that a person has an opportunity to demonstrate how they think by responding to a standardised test at one moment in time. Starting from a developmental perspective, however, with a focus on the changing nature of thought, a very different view of intelligence emerges. From this perspective it is not what has been achieved that is important but rather the potential for change that is given priority. The learning potential approaches understand intelligence as the potential for change rather than some fixed capacity.

This idea is captured in Vygotsky's concept of the zone of proximal development. (See Chapter 16, this volume, for more on the socio-historical theory that informs this approach). This 'zone' is the 'gap' that exists between what the learner can achieve unassisted and what she or he can potentially achieve with the assistance of another person (Vygotsky, 1978). The potential individuals have concerns how they gain from the way others mediate their experience for them.

From this view, the measurement of intelligence should focus on how people can respond to interventions or opportunities to improve their performance rather than on a normative test (Lidz, 1997). Unlike psychometric tests which are based on achievement and assume that subjects have had equal opportunities to learn, learning potential approaches employ psycho-educational assessment procedures that follow a pretest-intervention-posttest format (Haywood & Brown, 1990).

Feuerstein's Mediated Learning (Feuerstein *et al.*, 1980) is an example of this approach. After World War Two, thousands of war orphans and young immigrants from over 70 countries were sent to Israel. By traditional measures of intelligence, the majority of these children appeared to be extremely low functioning. Feuerstein and colleagues argued, however, that this was due to the traumatic experiences these people had experienced and the lack of adequate mediation due to the context of the war, rather than due to inherent cognitive abilities. Feuerstein conducted numerous studies to demonstrate that task-specific training designed to promote metacomponential thinking, amongst other things, could change performance so that these children could achieve 'normal' levels of cognitive development (Laughon, 1990). As Laughon (1990:462) argues, 'Feuerstein believes that a lack of mediated learning experience is the single most important cause of retarded performance.'

Bradbury and Zingel (1998) have demonstrated the effectiveness of mediated learning in South Africa in their implementation of a method of facilitating peer interaction with a sample of primary school children from diverse cultural backgrounds. Craig (1989) has used this approach for assisting students to bridge the gap between school and university in South Africa.

An example of a dynamic assessment using the ideas of the learning potential approach is given in Box 15.4.

Race, culture and intelligence

From the time intelligence tests were developed, through to the present there has been evidence that there are racial and cultural differences in measured

15.4 DYNAMIC ASSESSMENT IN ACTION

Juan is a 10-year-old boy who presented with a number of behavioural problems, including conduct difficulties, an oppositional, defiant attitude, stubbornness and poor interpersonal behaviour. According to his maternal grandmother, Juan had never attended any formal schooling except for three months he spent in Grade 1 a little more than 18 months ago. Juan had been living with his maternal grandparents since he was three-and-a-half months old. His biological mother left him in the care of her sickly parents and contributes nothing (materially and/or otherwise) for him. He lives in a rural area. His grandparents are uneducated and very poor, and struggle to make ends meet. His main chore in the family is to look after his grandfather's cattle, and he vehemently refuses to do any other thing. He dislikes everything that has to do with school and is teased by his peers for being the only child in the village who does not go to school. He seldom plays with other children because he often gets into physical fights with them.

In sessions with Juan, a thorough assessment was made using numerous psychological tests such as the SSAIS-R, Draw-a-Person Test (DAP), Kinetic Family Drawing (KFD) and the Beery Test. Both his SSAIS-R and DAP full scale IQ was around 61, which suggested that he was mildly mentally retarded. The Beery test indicated that his mental age was 3-and-a-half years below his chronological age. In his drawing of the KFD he only drew himself with the rest of other family members omitted, which possibly indicate his sense of not belonging in that family.

During the sessions, Juan was uncooperative and resistant to most activities. He showed little interest in what we were doing and he also appeared to be anxious and exhibited a negative attitude toward being tested. After a few sessions when the therapeutic rapport was fully established, Juan started engaging in a number of activities such as reading, drawings and completing different puzzles. Engaging in these activities was based on self-instructional training methods, which allowed the tester to model suitable behaviour and/or appropriate ways of approaching certain activities or tasks for him. Also, sessions consisted of modelling for him how to draw a picture of a human being, some arithmetic and reading and spelling exercises.

In the seventh session Juan did a post-test of all the tests mentioned above (except the KFD) and his scores had improved drastically. His SSAIS-R's full-scale score was around 78 and his IQ estimate on the DAP was now 87. Apart from changes in the tests scores, there was a tremendous improvement in his adaptive functioning skills. His attitude toward school had changed and he was looking forward to starting school the following year.

cognitive abilities *as determined by performance on tests*. The italicised part of the sentence is important, as the following section will reveal. The challenge for psychologists studying this construct is how should we understand these differences? One question we need to ponder is whether intelligence tests reflect real differences in intellect across cultures.

To be able to answer this question we have to be sure of a number of things: First, the test must be reliable. Reliability concerns whether or not a person tested on different occasions would receive the same score. In other words, how consistent is a person's score? Without some confidence that a test is reliable we cannot be sure that intelligence is being measured accurately.

Second, the test must be valid. Validity is whether a test measures what it is supposed to be measuring. This is a complex matter because determining a test's validity rests on a number of issues. One of these concerns whether the test relates to the hypothetical construct it is measuring. This is called construct validity. Early sections highlighted the debate about whether intelligence is one or a number of abilities. If the assumption was that a test measures 'g', but in fact it is measuring only one specific ability, then the test would not be valid. A second concern is whether or not the norm tables that are used while testing are appropriate for the person being tested. Using norms standardised on a group that does not represent the testee's background would make the results invalid.

A third issue concerns what is sometimes referred to as the 'face validity' of the test: are the assumptions that have been made about the nature of intelligence appropriate for the particular culture being studied? Gardner's idea of multiple intelligences and Sternberg's contextual intelligence suggest that intelligence will be influenced by what abilities are promoted and supported in different settings. If a test is measuring a specific ability, for instance, musical ability, but this is not one highly regarded in the particular setting, then the test would have limited validity for that culture.

This raises an important issue about testing and culture. Can any test be regarded as free of cultural influences? The idea of a culture-free test comes from the assumption that a test measures some basic fixed capacity. Thus, Anastasi (1990:357) refers to culture-free testing as the 'efforts by psychologists to develop psychological tests that would measure hereditary intellectual potential independently of the influence of cultural backgrounds'. It is general-

Figure 3 'Who was the Lion of Ethiopia?' 'Well, who captains the Springboks?' Culturally fair questions?

ly accepted now that attempts to develop a culture-free test are futile. Two strong arguments can be given for this. First, developments in genetics have revealed that heredity and environmental factors operate jointly at all stages of the organism's development and so their effects are inextricably intertwined and cannot be separated (Owen, 1998). Second, intelligence tests do not generally access this underlying hereditary ability.

If we are unable to develop culture-free tests then the alternative is to ensure the tests are culturally fair. Culture-fair tests are those which focus on experiences that are common to different cultures and eliminate cultural bias and prejudice. In developing culture-fair tests the items in the test should not favour or disadvantage individuals from different cultures. For example, an item that asks: 'Who is the vice-president of the United States of America?' would favour citizens of that country and disadvantage citizens of South Africa. However, fairness is more complex than this.

Consider again the research in Box 15.3. The actual materials used for the task had a profound and different impact on the performance of the children from Britain and Zambia. Some forms enhanced their performance, other forms lowered the performance. So the nature of the task must be culturally fair. More is needed than this, however. The whole context of the assessment must be considered. For example, a person not familiar with being tested in the company of an 'expert' who reads out instructions and expects the task to be done silently in a closed room and away from friends (the normal conditions for intelligence testing) is likely to be very stressed. Can this be regarded as a culturally fair assessment? The ideas of the learning potential theorists are relevant here. They would argue that in such circumstances it is what people learn from such situations rather than the assessment itself that might be more informative of their intellect.

To return to the earlier question: When differences on scores are found across cultures do these reflect real differences in intellect across those cultures? With the above points in mind, it would only be possible to says 'yes' to this question if there is certainty that the test is reliable and valid, and that both the test and the circumstances surrounding the testing are culturally fair to the persons being tested. These are very complex and difficult conditions to satisfy perfectly.

There has been a history in South Africa in which tests have been improperly used to draw invalid conclusions (Nzimande, 1995). For example, Fick (1929) administered individual measures of motor and reasoning abilities standardised for White children, to large sample of African (Black), Coloured, Indian and White school children. He found that the mean score of African children was inferior to that of Indian and Coloured children, with the White children having a mean score superior to all groups. He attributed the inferior performance of African children to innate differences. Although these findings were strongly disputed by Biesheuvel (1943), Fick's findings stood and served as an important impetus for the formulation of the notorious Bantu Education Act of 1953. This particular instance clearly indicates the inappropriate use of psychological testing because the instrument used was not standardised for African, Indian, Coloured and White children.

To date, most tests have been developed in particular settings for particular people. In South Africa, the focus has been mainly on literate, schooled people who have English or Afrikaans as their home language. Clearly, a lot more research needs to be done on intelligence and its measurement in South Africa, and great care must be taken in understanding the cultural dynamics around testing. The theories of intelligence, however, provide rich and useful ways of giving direction to this research.

Conclusion

While the idea of intelligence has been around since time immemorial, it is still a subject of debate and controversy. In the early history of modern psychology, intelligence was seen as the capacity for thinking and attempts were made to measured this capacity. This started the psychometric movement of psychological testing, which continues to this day. Parallel to this thrust has been alternate conceptions of intelligence which include the information processing, multiple intelligence and learning potential approaches. These perspectives on intelligence offer insights into how the nature and quality of individual thinking are related to the internal processing of information and engaging in different social and cultural activities. All these approaches to intelligence, and the debates between them, enable psychologists to determine the value of using intelligence tests for predictive and diagnostic purposes. At the same time, they reveal the limitations and misuse of testing, especially when this is considered in relation to cultural and social contexts. This chapter has also highlighted how intelligence and its measurement has been used and abused in the particular context of South Africa.

Anastasi, A. (1990). *Psychological Testing*. New York: Macmillan.

Biesheuvel, S. (1943). *African Intelligence*. Johannesburg: Macmillan.

Bradbury, J. & Zingel, J. (1998). Learning through peer interaction in a multi-cultural primary school classroom. *South African Journal of Education*, 18(4):231-40.

Craig, A. (1989). The conflict between the familiar and unfamiliar. *South African Journal of Higher Education*, 3(1):166-72.

Das, J.P. (1973). Structure of cognitive abilities: Evidence for simultaneous and successive processing. *Journal of Educational Psychology*, 65:103-8.

Das, J.P., Naglieri, J.A. & Kirby, J.R. (1994). *Assessment of Cognitive Processes: The PASS theory of intelligence*. Needham Heights, MA: Allyn Bacon.

Feuerstein, R., Rand, Y., Hoffman, M.B. & Miller, R. (1980). *Instrumental enrichment*. Maryland: University Park Press.

Fick, M.L. (1929). Intelligence tests results of poor white, native (Zulu), coloured and Indian school children and the educational and social implications. *South African Journal of Science*, 26:904-20.

Flanagan, D.P., Genshaft, J.L. & Harrison, P.L. (1997). *Contemporary Intellectual Assessment: Theories, tests and issues*. New York: The Guilford Press.

Foxcroft, C. & Roodt, G. (2001). *An Introduction to Psychological Assessment in the South African Context*. Oxford: Oxford University Press.

Gardner, H. (1993). *Multiple Intelligence: The theory in practice*. New York: Basic Books.

Haywood, H.C. & Brown, A.L. (1990). Dynamic approaches to psychoeducational assessment. *School Psychology Review*, 19(4):411-23.

Herrnstein, R.J. & Murray, C. (1994). *The Bell curve: Intelligence and class structure in American life*. New York: Free Press Paperbacks.

Ittenbach, R.F., Esters, I.G. & Wainer, H. (1997). The history of test development. In D.P Flanagan, J.L. Genshaft & P.L. Harrison (Eds.). *Contemporary Intellectual Assessment: Theories, tests and issues*. New York: The Guilford Press, pp. 17-31.

Laughon, P. (1990). The dynamic assessment of intelligence: A review of three approaches. *School of Psychology Review*, 19(4):459-73.

Lezak, M.D. (1983). *Neuropsychological Assessment* (2nd edition). New York: Oxford University Press.

Lidz, C.S. (1997). Dynamic assessment approaches. In D.P. Flanagan, J.L. Genshaft & J.L. Harrison (Eds.). *Contemporary Intellectual Assessment: Theories, tests and issues*. New York: The Guilford Press, pp. 281-97.

Louw, D.A. & Edwards, D.J.A. (1997). *Psychology: An introduction for students in southern Africa*. (2nd edition). Johannesburg: Heinemann.

Maloney, M. & Ward, M. (1976). *Psychological Assessment: A conceptual approach*. New York: Oxford University Press.

Naglieri, J.A. (1989). A cognitive processing theory for the measurement of intelligence. *Educational Psychologist*, 24:185-206.

Naglieri, J.A. (1997). Planning, attention, simultaneous, and successive theory and the cognitive assessment system: A new theory-based measure of intelligence. In D.P. Flanagan, P.L. Genshaft & P.L. Harrison (Eds.). *Contemporary Intellectual Assessment: Theory, tests and issues*. New York: The Guilford Press, pp. 247-67.

Nell, V. (2000). *Cross-cultural Neuropsychological Assessment: Theory and practice*. London: Lawrence Erlbaum.

Nzimande, B. (1995). To test or not to test? *Paper presented at the Congress on Psychometrics*, CSIR, Pretoria, 5 to 6 June 1995.

Owen, K. (1998). *The Role of Psychological Tests in Education in South Africa: Issues, controversies and benefits*. Pretoria: Human Science Research Council.

Owen, K. & Taljaard, R. (1995). *Manual for the Senior South African Individual Scale – Revised (SSAIS-R): Background and standardisation*. Pretoria: Human Science Research Council.

Sattler, J.M. (1992). *Assessment of Children: Revised and updated edition*. San Diego: Jerome M. Sattler.

Serpell, R. (1994). The cultural construction of intelligence. In W.J. Lonner & R. Malpass (Eds.). *Psychology and Culture*. Boston: Allyn and Bacon.

Spearman, C.E. (1923). *The Nature of Intelligence and the Principles of Cognition*. London: Macmillan

Sternberg, R.J. (1984). A contextualist view of the nature of intelligence. *International Journal of Psychology*, 19:307-34.

Sternberg, R.J. (1997). The triarchic theory of intelligence. In D.P. Flanagan, J.L. Genshaft & P.L. Harrison (Eds.). *Contemporary Intellectual Assessment: Theories, tests, and issues*. New York: The Guilford Press, pp. 92-104.

Thurstone, L.L. (1931). *Multiple Factor Analysis*. Chicago: University of Chicago Press.

Vygotsky, L.S. (1978). *Mind in Society: The development of higher psychological processes*. Cambridge, MA: Harvard University Press.

Multiple choice questions

1. Who is credited with coining the term 'mental test'?
   a) Binet
   b) Cattell
   c) Galton
   d) Weschler
2. In psychological testing, what IQ score is regarded as average?
   a) 50
   b) 75
   c) 150
   d) 100
3. Which one of the following approaches conceptualises intelligence as the possibility for change rather than as a fixed capacity?
   a) the eclectic
   b) learning potential
   c) information processing
   d) the psychometric
5. Which one of the following is true?
   a) the Senior South African Individual Scale-Revised (SSAIS-R) is a culturally fair test that can be used for all South Africans, regardless of the socio-economic or language background
   b) most IQ tests are culturally free tests that can be applied to people in many different countries
   c) an item in an South African IQ test which asks 'Who is the vice president of the United States?' would be an example of a culturally fair test item
   d) an IQ test can never be culturally free as IQ tests do not only measure inherited ability
5. The ability to survive in a particular environment is referred to as
   a) coping ability
   b) adaptive behaviour
   c) intelligent ability
   d) mental age
6. What are the two main uses of intelligence tests?
   a) for diagnostic and predictive purposes
   b) for school readiness and remedial programmes
   c) for determining disability and specialised educational programmes
   d) none of the above
7. One of the major criticisms levelled against Gardner's theory of multiple intelligence is that
   a) it is too long and over-elaborate
   b) it does not take the context into account
   c) it argues against the idea of 'g'
   d) it identifies too few types of intelligences
8. What are the two types of intelligence identified by Spearman in his two-factor theory?
   a) multiple and single
   b) linguistic and logical-mathematical
   c) general and specific
   d) general and musical
9. In his triarchic theory of intelligence, Sternberg identifies three different dimensions of information processing: the componential, experiential and contextual. Which of these dimensions emphasises higher-order executive processes in planning, monitoring and evaluating performance?
   a) contextual
   b) experiential
   c) contextual and experiential
   d) componential
10. The concept of Intelligent Quotient was developed by
    a) Stern
    b) Binet
    c) Cattell
    d) Wechsler

Short answer questions

1. Explain the term standardisation in relation to the construction of intelligence tests.
2. How do Learning Potential Theories differ from standard psychometric approaches in terms of how they conceptualise the nature of intelligence?
3. Explain the following terms in relation to intelligence testing:
   - reliability
   - validity
   - culture-free tests
   - culture-fair tests
4. In what ways can culture negatively impact on the validity of an intelligence test outcome (i.e. IQ score)?
5. There are many instances in South Africa's history of intelligence testing where tests have been misused. Give examples of such instances and identify the challenges related to culture and the testing of intelligence.

16

Thinking

Andrew Gilbert

CHAPTER OBJECTIVES

After studying this chapter you should be able to:
- demonstrate an understanding of representation and describe different building blocks of thinking
- identify and describe three different approaches to thinking and outline their different underlying assumptions
- discuss what cognitive psychology has contributed to an understanding of problem solving, reasoning and everyday cognition
- demonstrate an understanding of the tension that exists between thinking as an internal mental process, as opposed to a social process embedded in activities.

Introduction

As you begin to read this chapter, what are you thinking? Are you wondering what you might learn about thinking? Perhaps you are planning how to structure your reading and making decisions about which parts of this chapter you will read? Alternatively, you may be aware of not attending at all to what is on this page. Are you imagining what you could be doing; visualising your friends drinking coffee at the mall?

Stop here for a moment. Look back at the words that have been used: 'wondering', 'planning', 'making decisions', 'being aware of', 'attending to', 'imagining', 'visualising'. All these refer to some form or aspect of thinking. Thinking is not one but many kinds of activities.

Given its many forms, defining thinking is problematic. The above words, however, do have some things in common. They are all verbs and suggest an activity or process. They all allude to this process occurring at an internal, mental level. They suggest that the outcome of the process leads to insight, understanding or the manipulation of ideas or knowledge. In general terms, then, thinking is the mental processes or capacities which enable people to solve problems, to reason, to make sense of things or to use their knowledge to understand situations, events, other people or themselves.

As we go further we will see that the idea that thinking is only about mental processes is challenged by some psychologists, but this is an adequate working definition with which to start.

This chapter explores how psychologists have come to understand thinking. Three themes will be followed. First, the problem of representation will be examined. If thinking happens at an internal level, then it is important to understand how objects and ideas are represented mentally.

Second, the constructivist, the information processing and the socio-historical approaches to the study of thinking will be discussed. Each of these approaches opens very different windows onto thinking.

Third, three different types of thinking will be described: reasoning, problem solving, and everyday thinking. These descriptions will be woven into the different sections on the theories of thinking.

Representation and thinking

Look at Figure 1.

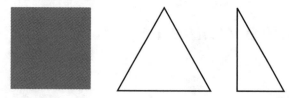

Figure 1 What are these?

What do you see? A square and two different triangles? Would it surprise you if you were told that in a study conducted by Gilbert (1987) in rural Kwazulu-Natal a number of respondents saw the 'square' as a wall of a house, the 'equilateral triangle' as a roof or poles for a house and the 'right-angled triangle' as a saw needed to cut the poles? Figure 1 is nothing more than lines and shading on white paper, but mentally these come to represent different things for different people. When something stands in for or refers to the thing we are thinking about, this is called representation. How do humans represent things?

Categories

One powerful way of representing the world is to place things that have similar characteristics or properties into categories. Shape, colour and form, for example, are three ways in which we classify objects.

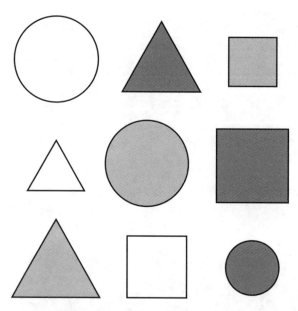

Figure 2 Consider how complex categorisation can become even with three simple categories

The symbols in this diagram have the properties of shape, size and shading. How many different combinations of these images can you create using just three categories?

The term 'concept' is used for the mental categories by which people classify not only objects and events but also abstract ideas and processes. Democracy, for example, is an abstract concept used to describe a particular quality of social and political life.

Concepts are important building blocks for thinking for a number of reasons. First, they lead us into sets of linked knowledge. Using the concept of democracy to describe South Africa, for example, evokes the ideas of free speech, the rule of law and the right to free association.

Conversely, concepts promote cognitive economy (Rosch, 1978). Concepts on their own can be used for thinking instead of having to use all the separate ideas to which they are linked. Having a sense of all that the concept 'democracy' means enables us to use the term 'democracy' as the basis for the further development of ideas.

Third, categories combine with other categories to form hierarchies, which then provide complex pictures of phenomena (see Figure 3). Botany is an excellent example of this. Linnaeus (1707-78) started classifying plants in terms of the structure of flowers and seeds. On this simple criterion all known plants have now been incorporated into a hierarchical taxonomy. For example, a species of rose – the 'dog rose' (*Rosa canina*) – is classified under the genus Rosa, within the family Rosaceae, within the order Rosales, and the class Angiospermopsida, the division Tracheophyta, and the kingdom Plantae, which refers to all plants in the living world (Stace, 1989). This taxonomy is now a powerful resource. A South African botanist, for instance, can visit the jungles of Panama and discover a new plant which, given its flower structure, may be categorised as being closely related to a rose. Once this is done, without any further information, a whole set of generalisations about the new species can be made including: 'Beware of the thorns!'.

Reflect on how important categorisation is in making assumptions about people, events and

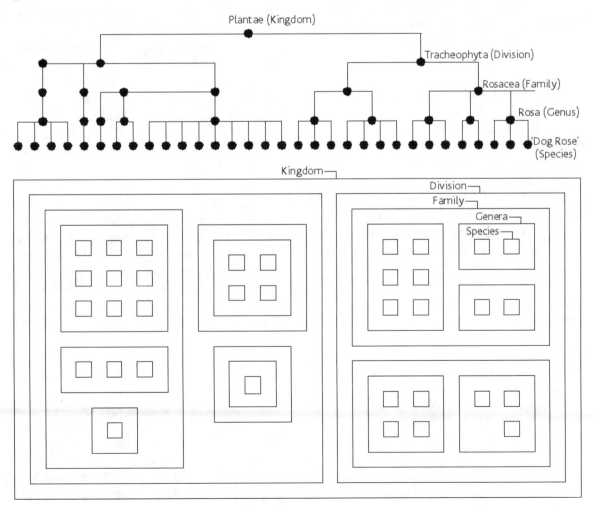

Figure 3 Classification and/as taxonomy – the case of the 'dog rose'

places. At the same time, note how rigid and unfounded categorisations can be the source of racism and sexism.

Imagery

Consider this: 'In what ways are an elephant and a *dassie* (rock rabbit or hydrax) similar and different?' In thinking about this question did you use visual images of these animals? (In terms of zoological taxonomy these two animals, despite the images you might have of them, are closely linked species!) Visual imagery, seeing the images of objects represented in your mind's eye, is an important form of representation.

One common and fairly durable form of imagery is a cognitive map. This is an internal representation of the spatial arrangements of the environment. If someone asks you for directions to a lecture venue on campus you are likely to hold some image of the route in your head while giving directions. You would be using your cognitive map of the campus. Box 16.1 identifies some systematic distortions that appear to lie behind cognitive maps.

Schemas, scripts and models

Read the following paragraph:

Nomabaso entered the computer room at the university and sat down in front of the screen. 'Oh damn it', she said, 'I left my student card in the library.'

What was happening here? There is nothing in the paragraph that tells you what the link is between the student card and sitting in front of the computer. However, if you were familiar with working on a university computer and having to input your student number when you log on, then the above description would make complete sense to you. What you will have done is used a script of 'working on a university computer' to make sense of the description.

A script is a set of information that provides guiding principles about what normally to expect in a specific situation (Sanford, 1987). A script is one kind of schema or network of knowledge about procedures, sequences of events or processes. Schemas refer to the more over-arching bodies of knowledge that are central in our thinking. Scripts or models refer to the more practical aspects of schemas used in particular contexts (Shore, 1996). For example,

16.1 COGNITIVE MAP DISTORTIONS

Using your own internal cognitive map of South Africa, answer these:
* In your head, draw a line directly south from Johannesburg until it crosses the coastline. Which coastal city is nearest to this line and about how far away?
* In your head, draw a line between Cape Town and Port Elizabeth. Draw another line between Port Elizabeth and Durban. Roughly, do these two lines form a continuous straight line running in a northeast direction? Is Port Elizabeth roughly northeast of Cape Town and Durban northeast of Port Elizabeth?

Get out a map and check your own cognitive map. Does it surprise you that neither Cape Town, Port Elizabeth nor Durban are close to being south of Johannesburg? East London is directly south. Does it also surprise you that Port Elizabeth is almost as far south as Cape Town, that is that a line between the two is a horizontal one, whilst Durban is north east of Port Elizabeth?

Matlin (1994) argues that while cognitive maps are reasonably accurate, they reflect systematic errors. We use heuristics, or rules of thumb, to estimate things and these are biased to make things more orderly than they really are. The *rotation heuristic bias* occurs when figures that are slightly tilted (such as the map of the coastline between Cape Town and Durban) are 'seen' as more vertical or more horizontal than they really are. If you thought Cape Town, Port Elizabeth and Durban were on a straight line running northeast this would be evidence of a rotation bias to the vertical. A second bias is the *alignment heuristic*. In this bias there is a tendency to line up two objects in a straight line close to the lines of latitude or longitude. Pulling Cape Town or Durban closer to a southern line from Johannesburg than they actually are, would be an example.

diagnostic models enable one to 'read' important phenomena. Meteorologists have models of cloud formations, which enable them to read whether or not it is likely to rain (see Figure 4).

Task models provide a schedule for getting practical things done (Shore, 1996). When cooking a meal, do you peel and start cooking the potatoes before grilling the meat? This is evidence of a task model.

Figure 4 Diagnostic models enable one to 'read' important phenomena. Meteorologists use models of cloud formations to predict the weather.

Scripts and models enable one to make assumptions about what will happen in particular situations. They can create problems, however, when they are used in the wrong contexts or are applied rigidly when a situation rapidly changes.

The constructivist approach to cognition

A Piagetian perspective

Jean Piaget (1896-1980), a Swiss scientist, is the central theorist in this approach. He started his scientific life as a zoologist, and was interested in how organisms are transformed in response to the demands of the environment. He used this idea of adaptation to explain how logical abstract thinking develops in humans.

His metaphor for thinking is that it is 'interiorised action'. He argued we are not born with the structure of our thought already in place; thinking is not

Figure 5 Jean Piaget, one of the great thinkers of the twentieth century

innate (or inherited). We construct our ability to think as we interact with the world. For this reason his approach is known as constructivism.

Adaptation involves two related processes that change our thinking in opposite directions: assimilation and accommodation. Assimilation is 'the integration of external elements into evolving or completed structures' (Piaget, 1970:7). Coming across a new object and incorporating it into an existing category would be assimilation, for example, discovering a new flower in Panama and classifying it in the genus *Rosa*. Sometimes, however, action requires the 'modification of a … structure by the elements it assimilates' (Piaget, 1970:8). This is accommodation. In this process, new information transforms cognitive structures. Discovering a new flower that does not fit into any existing genus and requires a revision of plant taxonomy would be an example of accommodation.

Through these dual processes, Piaget argued, thinking is constantly transformed. At first, thinking involves 'thinking by doing', that is putting together simple patterns of action while manipulating objects (the sensorimotor stage). Out of this come mental schemas – mental operations that are sequences of actions that have come to be represented mentally. Once such schemas are in place, the quality of thinking changes. Now a problem can be solved by 'thinking about' the action rather than having to physically take the action. This is the concrete operational stage. Adding 104 and 250, in your head, by imagining yourself doing it on paper, is an example of the concrete internalisation of action.

Do the task outlined in Box 16.2 before going further.

Piaget goes one step further in arguing how thought is internalised action. Interacting with more complex phenomena (e.g., volume rather than area

Cut a piece of string 60 cm long. Tie the two ends together. Place the loop on a table. Using your thumb and forefinger of both hands make a rectangle. Start by making a square. Now reduce the space between your thumb and forefingers while moving your hands apart so that the square becomes a rectangle. Do you think that the surface area of the table enclosed by the string, for the two shapes you created, is approximately the same? Will the area always be roughly the same no matter what rectangle you create? Explain your answer.

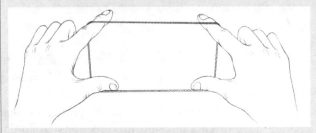

If you said, 'Yes, the area is approximately the same because the length of string is always the same', or

'because the area within the rectangles looks similar', then you are making an error!

Let's work this out logically. A square made by string 60 centimeters long would have sides 15 centimeters by 15 centimeters (assuming that tying the knot does not shorten the string). The area of this square is 15 x 15 = 225 square centimeters. If you close up your fingers a little to make a rectangle 18 centimeters by 12 centimeters (the string is still 60 centimeters long) then the area will be 18 x 12 = 216 square centimeters. This is still roughly the same area. If, however, you make a rectangle with sides 25 centimeters by 5 centimeters (this still has a perimeter of 60 cm.) then the area is 25 x 5= 125 square centimeters! If you were a farmer grazing cattle you would quickly know that there is much less land to graze in a rectangle with uneven sides than there is in a square, with the same perimeter!

This task captures the Piagetian idea that thinking has to become more and more distant from actual manipulations, and logical as tasks become more complex.

as depicted in Box 16.2) requires the construction of new forms of thinking. Instead of 'thinking about' action, thinking now involves manipulating the mental schemas that are in place. This requires thinking in terms of abstract, logical principles, making deductions and formulating hypotheses. Such thought is formal operational thinking – disembedded thinking based on abstract schemas now free from the immediate physical context.

Reasoning

Piaget's focus on abstract, logical thinking came out of his interest in the nature of scientific thinking. Reasoning, which is systematically drawing conclusions from statements or facts, is a characteristic of thinking in science. The study of this form of thinking has a history that goes back to the early Greek philosophers who developed the formal rules of logic. Modern philosophers and psychologists continue to see reasoning as thinking which works according to the principles of logic.

Two kinds of reasoning have received considerable attention: deduction and induction. Deductive reasoning involves working from general statements to draw particular conclusions that are true in relation to these statements. The following sequence of reasoning would be deductive:

All humans die before they are thirty.

I am a human.

I will die before I am thirty.

Logically, this conclusion is true, even though the general statement from which it was derived is obviously false. Induction is reasoning which draws conclusions from particular cases. It is based on relationships between real events. Every day you observe that the sun rises from the sea. Inductively you might, therefore, conclude that the sun will always rise from the sea. Inductive reasoning produces hypotheses, which are tentative conclusions, which can then be scientifically tested. Both forms of reasoning are central to science.

Tasks A & B in Box 16.3 are examples of a deductive reasoning task. In both these tasks you had to draw a number of specific conclusions from a general statement. In Task A this was 'If a label has a Y on the front then a 1 is printed on the back'. Which of the labels did you decide you needed to turn over?

Task A

Imagine you work at a label factory. Labels have either an X or a Y printed on the front and a 1 or 2 printed on the back. Unfortunately the printer malfunctioned and some of the labels were incorrectly printed. You have the job of checking to ensure that if a label has a Y on the front then a 1 is printed on the back. You have the following labels in front of you. Which labels would you turn over to be sure that every label with a Y on the front has a 1 on the back?

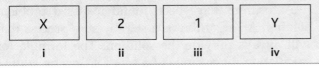

X	2	1	Y
i	ii	iii	iv

Task B

Imagine you are employed by your local supermarket. You have to check receipts made out by sales staff. If any sale involved an amount of R100 or more it has to be approved by the sales manager. The amount of the sale should be written on the front of the receipt and the manager's approval on the back. You have the following receipts in front of you. Which would you turn over to be sure that the sale clerk has followed the rule?

1 pot R20.00	Approved: Signed by manager	Approved: Not signed by manager	1 dress R140.00
i	ii	iii	iv

Logically, the answer is labels ii and iv. It is possible you did not get this answer. Do not worry! D'Andrade (1995), from whose study this task is taken, found that about 80 per cent of the graduates in his study also got it wrong. (Note: If you got it wrong, the general rule, 'If a label has a Y on the front then a 1 is printed on the back', is not the same as, 'If a label has a 1 on the back then a Y is printed on the front'. We cannot assume the latter from the former.)

What answer did you give to Task B? If you said iii and iv you would be correct. In contrast to Task A, D'Andrade (1995) found that more than 70 per cent of his students got the answer correct on this task. Tasks A and B are identical in terms of logic, so why is there this discrepancy in responses? D'Andrade argues that while people can reason deductively, whether or not they use this form of thinking accurately will depend on the cultural schemas that they have available to them. The difference between the two tasks is that the second is a more familiar one and makes more sense because cultural schemas for this kind of task are present.

Challenges to the constructivist perspective

The constructivist approach is concerned with establishing universal principles that lie behind thinking. All humans of normal intellect are faced, at a general level, with the same forms of adaptation and will, therefore, move in the direction of more and more abstract thought. The thinking with which Piaget is concerned is domain-general knowledge – abstract thinking that applies across all situations and contexts. As the following sections reveal, not all psychologists share this view.

From Piaget's perspective, logical reasoning is the pinnacle of human thinking. D'Andrade's (1995) experiment reveals that the picture may be more complex than this. When required to think abstractly we often fail to do so, but given a culturally appropriate context for such thinking, our ability to think abstractly is revealed. This interaction between thinking and context is explored under the socio-historical approach.

The information processing approach

In the 1960s, developments in the fields of computer and information science began to revolutionise the world. Computers became highly efficient and effective processors of information. Perhaps then, psychologists thought, the computer might be a useful metaphor for understanding how humans process information. This produced the information processing (IP) approach, which is the major perspective in cognitive psychology (see Chapter 18, this volume).

Before you go further with this section try and solve the problem given in Box 16.4.

Try and solve this problem (which is an adapted form of a problem proposed by Bransford & Stein, 1984):

Two cars A and B are travelling in a straight line towards each other at 50 kilometres per hour. When the cars are 100 kilometres apart a fly takes off from Car A in the direction of Car B at the speed of 80 kilometres per hour. When it meets Car B it turns around and flies back to Car A and then turns and flies back to Car B. It continues doing this between the two cars until they meet. How far does the fly travel? (Assume the cars and the fly travel at a constant speed and never have to slow down.)

In the IP approach, the challenge is to produce process models that describe the step-by-step ways that humans process information. Newell and Simon's (1972) view of problem solving provides an example of this approach to thinking. They see problem solving as searching through a problem space, that is processing information to achieve a goal. This space is defined by a starting state and an end state (the goal of the task). Steps have to be taken (sub-goals achieved) to reach the end state. How these steps are sequenced forms the strategy that is used to solve the problem. A state-action analysis, in other words, a description of the states, steps and strategies taken within a problem space, would, in the IP approach, be a description of the thinking that has taken place.

A state-action analysis of the problem, 'How far did the fly fly?' is demonstrated in Box 16.5.

Problem solving from an information processing perspective

A number of important insights into problem solving have come from the IP approach.

Algorithms have been found to assist problem solving. An algorithm is a step-by-step process that will always provide the solution. The formula for calculating the average of a set of scores by adding up all the scores and dividing by the number of scores in the set, is an algorithm. The seven steps for solving the 'fly problem' in Box 16.4 constitute an algorithm. Applying known algorithms to problems helps solve them.

When a problem space is large, then applying an algorithm may be too time consuming. In such instances, using a heuristic may be preferable. A

Let us use the problem of 'How far did the fly fly?' (Box 16.4) as an example of how the IP approach would construct a state-action analysis to understand your thinking.

You were required to calculate the distance the fly travels. This is the end state. The starting state is the information given in the problem: the speed of the cars and the fly, and the distance the cars are apart. The gap between these states creates the problem space. To solve the problem requires transforming the starting information into a form that provides an answer to: 'How far does the fly fly?' There are a number of possible steps that can be taken. Here is one strategy.

Step 1: The starting state tells us the fly travelled at 80 kilometres per hour. So if we know the amount of time the fly flew for we would know the distance it travelled.

Step 2: From the starting state we know the fly and the cars travelled for the same length of time. So if we know how long the cars travelled for we will know how long the fly travelled for.

Step 3: From the starting state we also know the speed of the cars. If we can calculate the distance the cars travelled then we can work out how long they travelled for.

Step 4: We know that the cars travelled in a straight line towards each other at 50 kilometres per hour and that they were 100 kilometres apart. We can, therefore, calculate the distance the cars travelled. The cars must have met after 50 kilometres.

Step 5: With this information return to Step 3. If the cars travel at 50 kilometres per hour for 50 kilometres they will travel for an hour.

Step 6: With this information return to Step 2. If the cars travel for an hour, the fly travelled for an hour.

Step 7: With this information return to Step 1. We know the fly travelled at a speed of 80 kilometres per hour. In one hour it must travel 80 kilometres.

Problem solved!

Does this description capture the way you thought?

heuristic is a short-cut method, a rule of thumb that reduces the problem space.

Breaking down a problem into a series of sub-goals is a useful heuristic. Working backwards from the end to the starting state is another. Did you do this when solving the 'Fly problem'? Unlike algorithms, heuristics do not guarantee success, even though they can be very useful. Allowing a particular heuristic to dominate our thinking is known as a mental set. Mental sets can block problem solving, particularly when the heuristic is an inappropriate one.

The comparison of the thinking of experts and novices has been a useful source of information for the IP approach. Experts are people who perform well on a particular task. Novices are new to the task. Research has shown novices and experts across a wide range of domains of knowledge represent problems differently. Experts use more abstract ideas and interpret what they see in terms of rules and principles. Physicists working on physics problems, for example, group them on the basis of underlying principles rather than on the similarity of the information that is presented to them (Chi *et al.*, 1988). Chess experts see moves in terms of configurations, such as 'defence strategies', while novices focus on the movement of individual chess pieces (Chase & Simon, 1973). Experts spend more time trying to understand the nature of the problem before starting to solve it and are more aware of when they are making an error (Chi *et al.*, 1988).

Challenges for the information processing approach

Many of the insights from the IP approach have come from studies of problem solving. The reason for this is that it is possible to systematically manipulate the elements of problems in experiments. There are, however, at least two kinds of problems: well- and ill-defined problems. In a well-defined problem the original and end state and the rules are clearly defined. (The 'Fly problem' is a good example.) In an ill-defined problem one or more of these elements are unclear. In everyday life many problems are ill defined because there are no clear solutions. Sometimes we do not even know what the starting point is or what kinds of questions we should be asking ourselves. This raises the question of how applicable are the findings of the IP approach for understanding the thinking behind the everyday problems of human life?

Figure 6 'I see a battle scene, Shaka Zulu on the rampage, ambushing the enemy from the side.' 'Well, I thought I saw a duck and a sheep, but now I am not so sure.' An expert-novice interaction?

The socio-historical approach

Lave (1991:67) argues that 'learning, thinking and knowing are relations among people engaging in activity in, with and arising from the socially and culturally structured world.' This suggests a very different view of thinking. While it does not deny the existence of internal mental processes, it suggests that thinking is a social process and linked to the interaction between the individual and the setting in which the thinking occurs (Resnick, 1991).

This view is known as the socio-historical or situated cognition approach. Lev Vygotsky (1896-1934), a Russian psychologist, is often regarded as the founder of this approach. He argued that thinking has its origins in the social world within which people live (Vygotsky, 1976). His idea can be captured in the phrase 'thinking is internalised culture'.

In describing the cognitive development of children, he stated:

Any function in the child's cultural development appears twice: first, on the social level, and later, on the individual level; first between people (inter-psychologically) and then inside the child (intra-psychologically) … All the higher functions [of thinking] originate as actual relations between human beings (Vygtosky, 1976:57).

Two important ideas are contained in this statement. First, that thinking has its origins in interaction with others. Second, that what is learned in interaction with others is taken over by the individual and used as the base for his or her own thought. In other words, the symbols, schemas and scripts for thinking that are internalised become the tools for our own thinking.

This view suggests that thinking cannot be separated from the social context in which it is used. The social setting often provides the structure and resources for thinking. Complete the task in Box 16.6.

16.6 A WEIGHT WATCHER'S DILEMMA

Imagine you want to lose weight. You use a Weight Watcher's recipe to make a meal, which includes cottage cheese as an ingredient. The recipe says you should use two-thirds of a cup of cottage cheese. You go to the fridge and fill a cup two-thirds with cottage cheese. Just before you are about to use it you remember that your diet table says that today you are allowed only three quarters of what the recipe says. How would you go about working out three quarters of a two thirds of a cup of cottage cheese? (Example taken from Lave, 1988).

How did you arrive at an answer? Seen as a mathematical problem, the solution is simple. Three quarters of two thirds of a cup can be represented arithmetically as $\frac{3}{4} \times \frac{2}{3} = \frac{1}{2}$ a cup! It is that easy. Perhaps, however, you were like the weight watcher reported by Lave (1988) who solved the problem as follows. He filled the measuring cup two-thirds full with cottage cheese then turned up the cup onto a chopping board. He then patted it into a circle, marked a cross on it and scooped away one of the quarters. The remaining portion was his allocation. What is interesting about this person's action was that Lave reports that man had sophisticated mathematical skills but did not think about using them. Such behaviour is not uncommon. In this case, the setting provided a structure for his thinking, in which his standard mathematical skills were not 'called upon'. It also provided resources for resolving the problem

in novel ways – the board and utensils. These formed part of his thinking.

Everyday thinking

The above is an example of everyday thinking – the kind of thinking that occurs as we deal with the mundane, practical things of life. Such thinking does not happen in experiments or laboratories but occurs in the everyday settings of daily life. It needs to be studied in these settings.

Studies of everyday thinking have revealed that it differs from the kind of thinking that is studied in more formal settings. Everyday thinking incorporates aspects of the task environment into problem solving. Scribner (1986) reports, for example, that dairy workers in the USA required to fulfill an order for 31 bottles of chocolate milk restructured the problem in relation to the ways the milk was packaged. Working with crates that contained 32 pints, they saw the problem as one crate minus one pint. In other words, the way they calculated arithmetic problems in the work situation was not based on standard mathematical algorithms but on the way the items were packaged. Similar findings of everyday thinking were found among child street vendors in Brazil, as demonstrated in Box 16.7.

What the study of everyday thinking suggests is that thinking is not just a mental activity; it is spread across the context in which the thinking takes place and cannot be separated from it. The term, 'distributed cognition', describes this idea. It is a growing area of interest in cognition (see Chapter 18, this volume).

Challenges to the socio-historical approach

It contrast to the constructivist approach, which argues for a domain-general approach to thinking, the socio-historical approach argues that thinking will change across contexts and will be affected by the resources for thinking that are available in that context. This kind of thinking is regarded as domain-specific thought – thinking that is tied to the particular sphere of life or context. The term 'local knowledge' is often used for this kind of thinking (Gilbert, 1997b).

The socio-historical approach raises the question: If thinking is tied to context does this mean people from different contexts will think differently? This issue is the cultural relativism debate, which is examined in

Carraher *et al.* (1985) have done interesting research on everyday thinking. They studied the way child vendors in Brazil solved the day-to-day problems of marketing their products – sweets and fruit. They found numerous examples of how the manner in which items were structured in their environment was used as a resource for solving problems. Thus, for example, coconuts, which were priced at 35 cruzerios, were normally sold in lots of three. When a customer (the researcher) asked for the price of 10 coconuts, the child vendor would use this knowledge as the base for their thinking. Their calculation, therefore, took the following line of reasoning: 'Three coconuts are 105 cruzeiros, three more will be 210, three more 315 and then one more to make ten will be 350'. Common with the weight watcher example, the vendors used the way the items were 'naturally' structured in their environment, rather than alternate algorithms, such as 'ten times 35', to solve the problem.

the chapter on language (Chapter 17). While the socio-historical approach argues that thinking is tied to context, it also suggests that thinking is flexible, for as we change contexts so does our thinking. From this position the socio-historical approach provides a positive view of human thought, since it suggests that given opportunities to understand what is required in new situations and access to new tools for thinking, people can overcome the limitations to thinking that they may have. Craig (1989) has used this approach to understand and help students to bridge the gap between school and university tasks. Gilbert (1997b) has used it to look at the local knowledge and its importance in community development.

Conclusion

Thinking is not one kind of activity and does not have one form. There are many kinds of thinking, and the structure and nature of thought changes depending on the context within which it occurs. It is inevitable, then, that psychologists will approach thinking from different perspectives and each approach will tend to investigate the type or form of thinking that relates to that approach.

As a result, there is no simple answer to the question: What is thinking? This chapter has tried to capture some of the fascinating and insightful ways psychologists answer this question. They all add up to a rich picture of the complex and changing nature of human cognition.

REFERENCES

Bransford, J.D. & Stein, B.S. (1984). *The IDEAL Problem Solver*. New York: W.H. Freeman.

Carraher, T.N., Carraher, D.W. & Schliemann, A.D. (1985). Mathematics in the streets and in the schools. *British Journal of Developmental Psychology*, 3:21-9.

Chase, W.G. & Simon, H.A. (1973). Perception in chess. *Cognitive Psychology*, 4:55-81.

Chi, M.T.H., Glaser, R. & Farr, M.J. (1988). *The Nature of Expertise*. Hillsdale, NJ: Lawrence Erlbaum.

Craig, A. (1989). The conflict between the familiar and unfamiliar. *South African Journal of Higher Education*, 3(1):166-72.

D'Andrade, R.G. (1995). *The Development of Cognitive Anthropology*. Cambridge: Cambridge University Press.

Gilbert, A.J. (1987) *Psychology and Social Change in the Third World: A cognitive perspective*. Unpublished doctoral thesis, University of South Africa, Pretoria.

Gilbert, A.J. (1997a). Thinking. In D.A. Louw & D.J.A. Edwards (Eds.). *Psychology*. Johannesburg: Heinemann, pp. 375-420.

Gilbert, A.J. (1997b). Small voices against the wind: Local knowledge and social transformation. *Peace & Conflict Journal of Peace Psychology*, 3(3):275-92.

Lave, J. (1988). *Cognition in Practice. Mind, mathematics and culture in everyday life*. Cambridge: Cambridge University Press.

Lave, J. (1991). Situated learning in communities of practice. In L.B. Resnick, J.M. Levine & S.D. Teasley (Eds.). *Perspectives on Socially Shared Cognition*. Washington: American Psychological Association, pp. 63-84.

Matlin, M.W. (1994). *Cognition*. Fort Worth, Texas: Harcourt Brace.

Newell, A. & Simon, H.A. (1972). *Human Problem Solving*. Engelwood Cliffs, NJ: Prentice Hall.

Piaget, J. (1970). Extracts from Piaget's theory. In K. Richardson & S. Sheldon (Eds.). *Cognitive Development to Adolescence: A reader*. Hove: Lawrence Erlbaum, pp. 1-17.

Resnick, L.B. (1991). Shared cognition: Thinking as social practice. In L.B. Resnick, J.M. Levine & S.D. Teasley (Eds.). *Perspectives on Socially Shared Cognition*. Washington: American Psychological Association, pp. 1-20.

Rosch, E. (1978). Principles of categorization. E. Rosch & B. Lloyd (Eds.). *Cognition and Categorization*. Hillsdale: Lawrence Erlbaum.

Sanford, A.J. (1987). *The Mind of Man*. New York: Harvester.

Scribner, S. (1986). Thinking in action: Some characteristics of practical thought. In R.J. Sternberg & R.K. Wagner (Eds.). *Practical Intelligence: Nature and origins of competence in the everyday world*. Cambridge: Cambridge University Press, pp. 13-30.

Shore, B. (1996). *Culture in Mind: Cognition, culture and the problem of meaning*. New York: Oxford University Press.

Stace, C.A. (1989). *Plant Taxonomy and Bio-systematics* (2nd edition). Cambridge: Cambridge University Press.

Vygotsky, L.S. (1976). *Mind in Society: The development of higher psychological processes*. Cambridge, MA: Harvard University Press.

Multiple choice questions

1. Representing objects by classifying them into categories
   a) assists in the creation of complex hierarchies
   b) connects the object or idea to a body of related knowledge
   c) places an object into a taxonomy
   d) all of the above

2. Sitting in a lecture and having a fairly accurate idea of the sequence of events that will happen during the lecture period would be evidence of
   a) a script
   b) a state action analysis
   c) an algorithm
   d) a heuristic

3. Which one of the following is a characteristic of the way novices think in comparison to experts?
   a) novices use more abstract ideas
   b) spend more time trying to think about the problem before starting to solve it
   c) are more aware of making an error
   d) group problems on the basis of similarity of the information available rather than underlying principles

4. Which one of the following is associated with the socio-historical approach to thinking?
   a) Piaget
   b) Vygotsky
   c) Linnaeus
   d) Newell

5. Seeing a new object and including it into an existing classification system is an example of
   a) assimilation
   b) visual imagery
   c) concrete operational thinking
   d) none of the above

6. The view that thinking and knowing are linked to relations between people and the activity they are engaging in, would be supported by which approach in cognitive psychology?
   a) the information processing approach
   b) the constructivist approach
   c) the behaviourist approach
   d) the socio-historical approach

7. Which one of the following is the term used for a step-by-step process that will ensure the achievement of a goal?
   a) heuristic
   b) schema
   c) mental set
   d) algorithm

8. Persistent use of an inappropriate heuristic is known as
   a) a rotation heuristic bias
   b) an alignment bias
   c) a mental set
   d) schema repetition

9. A model that identifies the states, steps and strategies used in solving a problem would be characteristic of which one of the following approaches to thinking?
   a) the constructivist approach
   b) the information processing approach
   c) the behaviourist approach
   d) the socio-historical approach

10. You observe that every morning the sun rises in the east, from the sea. If you hypothesise, therefore, that the sun will rise tomorrow from the sea, this would be an example of what kind of thinking?
    a) inductive thinking
    b) everyday thinking
    c) deductive thinking
    d) sensorimotor thinking

Short answer questions

1. Give three reasons why representing the world in terms of concepts can be regarded as the building block for thinking, and give an example for each reason.

2. What does the study of the way that experts and novices differ in the way they think tell us about how humans process information?

3. Briefly, give an example of 'everyday thinking' in your life. Why is it important to study such thinking in comparison to the study of formal reasoning?

4. What is the difference between an algorithm and a heuristic? Give an example of when you would use each one of these when solving a problem.

5. Using an example, explain how Piaget argues that thinking is constantly transformed by the processes of assimilation and accommodation.

17

Language

David Neves

CHAPTER OBJECTIVES

After studying this chapter you should to be able to:
- define what language is and describe its most important characteristics
- demonstrate an understanding of the relationship between language and thought
- identify the various components of language and be able to illustrate these with appropriate examples
- describe the process of language acquisition
- demonstrate an understanding of the debates surrounding the origins of language
- have an appreciation of southern Africa's rich linguistic diversity.

For Nosipho the subject of language was a particularly interesting one. She had grown up speaking Xhosa at home but had spoken English when she started pre-school. She didn't remember having to learn English but had just seemed to pick it up from hearing it spoken around her. It was amazing how much easier it had been to learn a language as a young child than it was now! Nosipho had taken an introductory course in French when she started university and had found it surprisingly difficult to learn. Her adult mind seemed to struggle much more to learn new words and grammar.

Nosipho still spoke both Xhosa and English fluently, but used them in different situations. She tended to speak Xhosa at home with her family and English at university. She and her friends often spoke a mixture of both languages, moving between them depending on what they were talking about. Because her textbooks and lectures were in English, Nosipho found herself thinking about psychology in English. But when she was telling her parents about something she had learned in a lecture, she would sometimes struggle to find the equivalent Xhosa word to describe it. Often there didn't seem to be a word that meant exactly the same as the concept she was trying to explain and she simply had to slot in the English word. There were also times she struggled to find the English equivalent of an experience she could describe so easily in Xhosa. This was particularly frustrating when she was trying to describe a strong feeling, for example. Speaking two languages seemed to have made Nosipho especially aware of the way that language could affect the way a person saw and described the world. With so many different languages spoken in South Africa it would be all the more important to understand how people developed and used language.

Introduction

Reflect for a minute on the phenomenal power of language. At the moment you are scanning patterns of squiggles by which someone in another time and place, and whom you may never have met, is able to communicate with you. The ability to represent and manipulate information by means of symbolic systems such as language is among the most remarkable cognitive achievements of our species. In evolutionary terms, language enabled human beings to organise society and transmit knowledge across generations (Pinker & Bloom, 1990). Having language means we no longer have to learn from trial and error which poisonous plants or predators to avoid, nor do we need to reinvent the wheel, antibiotic medicines or democracy with each new generation. Language is, therefore, a powerful resource for thought and action.

What is language?

Language is a system of representation that enables us to encode and convey meaning through the production and combination of signs. Language has the following qualities:

- *Language is highly symbolic.* The relationship between words and the entities to which they refer is arbitrary and a product of social convention. There is, for example, nothing inherent in the word 'giraffe' that looks, sounds or walks like a giraffe.
- *Language is infinitely generative.* It entails the production of infinite meanings from a finite set of discrete elements. For example, in English, from an alphabet of 26 characters, 44 sounds and approximately 100 000 words, sentences expressing an endless range of meanings can be created.
- *Language is rule-governed.* The infinite meaning-making power of language does not make all combinations of language elements acceptable. Language is governed by various rules that enable people to produce and interpret meaning in a consistent and largely shared way.
- *Language is specific.* Although we can communicate ideas and feelings by non-verbal means such as music, mime or visual images, how would you convey the specific idea 'psychopathology is my third favourite section of psychology' or 'I think you are not standing next to a penguin' without using language?
- *Language is widespread and complex.* The fact that language is found in all societies and effortlessly acquired by young children obscures its hidden complexity. Consider, for instance, that any average English speaking five-year-old child knows whether to use 'a' or 'the' when referring to an object, despite the fact that the grammatical rules for this are extremely abstract and complex.
- *Language can be written.* Not all languages are written, but those that are have their representational power vastly expanded. The technology of writing enables language to transcend time (many religious texts are thousands of years old) and distance (think of an e-mail message instantly sent to a friend across the world).

17.1 WHEN WILL WE BE ABLE TO SPEAK WITH ANIMALS?

Do animals use language, and when will be we able to speak with them? The answer to this question depends largely on how one defines language. Animals use complex systems of communicative signalling: bees do a dance to tell other bees where to find pollen, while insects, birds and many mammals emit warning, territorial and mating calls. In some respects we already communicate with animals: perhaps you call your cat to feed it or have witnessed a Border Collie dog obey its handler's commands and round up a flock of sheep. However, animal communication lacks several of the features of language, identified at the beginning of this chapter:

- The communicative units used by animals lack the arbitrary or symbolic quality of human language and are directly related to their semantic content. For example, a dog's growling and bearing of its teeth at you is directly related to its potential future action – it will bite if you come any closer!
- Animals' communicative units are not discrete (think of a dog barking or cat purring) and cannot be combined into longer utterances. Animals' communicative acts tend to be relatively continuous and repetitive.
- Animal communication lacks the productive, generative quality of human language and can only convey limited meanings.

Most efforts to teach animals language have focused on our closest living relatives, primates such as chimpanzees. Attempts to teach even intelligent animals such as chimpanzees language have been largely unsuccessful. Chimps do not share our vocal apparatus, so the efforts to teach them have used sign language or systems of manipulating plastic signs (Premack & Premack, 1972). Several decades of research have revealed crude language use that can be accounted for in terms of stimulus-response learning and lacks the syntactical quality that characterises human language (Terrance, 1980). Humankind's long-standing dream of talking to animals, therefore, seems unlikely to be fulfilled anytime soon. Considering the significant evolutionary advantages of language use, perhaps the most compelling argument against primates using language is: Why do they not already use it? Chomsky concludes, 'It's about as likely that an ape will prove to have a language ability as that there is an island somewhere with a species of flightless birds waiting for human beings to teach them to fly' (cited in Fromkin & Rodman, 1988:410).

Language and thought

Language is a powerful resource for representation and thought, but what is the precise relationship between language and thought? Does language shape our thought, or vice versa?

Is it possible to think without language? Many famous artists and scientists have described how they thought by means of visual images, numbers or even abstract logic. Pioneering genetics researchers Watson and Crick visualised and built physical models of the structure of DNA in a double spiral shape, which enabled them to confirm their theory (Watson, 1980). Similarly, Albert Einstein described how he developed his theory by imagining himself dropping coins in rapidly descending lifts or timing beams of light flashed within fast moving railway carriages (Gleick, 1999; Pinker, 1994). Thinking is thus not dependent on language. On the other hand, it is possible to have language without thought. If you have ever rote-learned a poem or listened to a parrot mimic human speech you might have a sense of this.

The debate over the complex relationship between language and thought remains unresolved and perhaps it will never be put to rest, as separating each from the other is extremely difficult. Researchers have typically tried to unravel the complex relationship between thought and language in one of two ways. They have either investigated how thought and language develop in children or, alternatively, they have looked across cultures that use different languages, to understand how these affect peoples' thinking. In what follows we explore the development of thought and language in children by considering a debate between Piaget and Vygotsky. We then examine how different languages affect their speakers' thinking, by discussing Whorf's cross-cultural work.

Child development studies

Have you ever had the frustrating experience where you have a thought, but cannot find the words to express it? Or perhaps you have written a sentence and felt it is not exactly what you want to convey? If so, you might be tempted to say that thought precedes language. Examining children's intellectual development, Jean Piaget said much the same thing. Piaget classified language amongst the developing child's other symbolic abilities such as play, deferred imitation and memorisation (Piaget, 1968). He noted that these abilities only emerge in the child's second year of life, at the conclusion of the sensorimotor stage. Piaget maintained that language is similar to the child's other cognitive abilities as it requires the construction of the underlying conceptual structure, but language and thought are not the same thing, and developmentally, thought precedes language.

In contrast, Soviet psychologist, Lev Vygotsky, argued that the development of thought follows that

Figure 1 'Mummy said: left over right, then twist and make a loop . . .' Young children, and occasionally even adults, talk themselves through unfamiliar or complex tasks

of language. Describing thought and language as distinct systems for representing information, Vygotsky said these systems develop alongside each other until the age of approximately two, when 'thought becomes verbal and speech rational' (Vygotsky in Byrnes & Gelman, 1991:20). In Vygotsky's view, thought is a form of inner, self-directed speech. So, to think is to silently talk to yourself. If you have ever overheard children (or even adults) talking themselves through a complicated or unfamiliar task, you may well have a sense of this. In Vygotksy's view language, and therefore thought, are heavily influenced by the social systems in which the child grows up.

The issue of children's private or egocentric speech illustrates the differences between Piaget and Vygotsky's respective theories. Pre-school children often talk aloud to themselves, paying minimal attention to those around them. In groups they tend to engage in collective monologues where they talk past each other. This egocentric or private speech declines and disappears around the age of six years. Why? Piaget and Vygotsky's respective explanations are revealing. Piaget argues that, with the child's mental maturation, socialised speech (used by people in everyday life) comes to replace egocentric speech. The latter form of speech simply dies out. Vygotsky, in turn, argues that all speech is by definition *already social* and private speech has become silent and internalised as thought. Consequently, 'the true direction of the development of thinking is not from the individual to the social, but from the social to the individual' (Vygotsky, 1986:36).

Cross-cultural studies

Benjamin Whorf (1956), influenced by his teacher Edward Sapir, advanced an even stronger view of the relationship between language and thought. Linguistic determinism (or the Sapir-Whorf hypothesis) states that different languages incorporate radically different worldviews, which ultimately determine how people think. Whorf is best known for his cross-cultural research that documented the large number of words (over a dozen) that the Inuit (or Eskimo) have for snow, while people living in warmer regions have fewer or no words for snow. Linguistic determinism states that developing particular words for an object or phenomenon enables one to perceive differences, make distinctions and categorise information in ways that would otherwise not be possible. So, the Inuit would be capable of communicating, seeing and thinking about differences related to snow that people living in sunny South Africa could not. But linguistic determinism does not only operate at word level – even the grammatical structure of language influences our thought.

Whorf (1956) described the manner in which the Native American Hopi's language does not make the same rigid distinctions between past, present and future tense as languages of European origin. As a result he argued the Hopi have a conception of time that is continuous and circular, much like the recurrent cycles of the seasons. In contrast, in industrial societies time is linear, ordered into discrete units, frequently referred to and tracked by timepieces strapped to our wrists! Having particular linguistic resources at our disposal therefore enables us to make certain conceptual distinctions (Halliday & Matthiessen, 1999). Although experiments have not always found evidence for linguistic relativism (see Au, 1983, 1988; Heider, 1972), a weaker view of this idea, that language influences rather than determines thought, is better supported (Hardin & Banaji, 1993).

Figure 2 Linguistic relativism: A group of isiXhosa-speaking counsellors identified the metaphoric term *mthungululi* (removing mud from someone's eyes) to describe the practice termed 'counselling' in English

Linguistic relativism – the idea that we perceive the world within a framework conferred by our language – is particularly apparent in a multilingual society like South Africa. Consider, for instance, that isiXhosa does not have a precise equivalent for the English word 'counselling'. Work with a group of isiXhosa-speaking counsellors identified the metaphoric term *mthungululi* (removing mud from someone's eyes) to describe the supportive, yet non-advice-giving, practice of counselling (Tutani, 2000). So, were these Xhosa speakers unable to understand the practice of counselling? No, but in this instance their language was unable to help them in the same way as English, and a suitable term had to be found.

On the other hand, isiXhosa has a wide range of terms describing kinship (family) relations that are largely unavailable to native English speakers. isiXhosa speakers often describe paternal uncles and aunts as mother and father, terming the paternal uncle *utatomncinci* (small father) and paternal aunt *udadobawo* (small mother). In isiXhosa first cousins are often termed brothers and sisters, and a distinction can even be made between brothers who are older *umkhuluwa*, and younger *umninawa* (Kaschula & Anthonissen, 1995). Complex kinship terms suggest members of isiXhosa-speaking communities have a keen understanding of communal relations and a marked 'social intelligence'.

The components of language

Language is made up of a number of components. Ranging from the small to large, these include sounds, words, sentences and the broader pragmatic context of language use. The production of meaning is a product of all of these elements.

Sounds

Phonetics is the study of the physical sounds of language. The sound units that make up spoken language are termed phonemes. Phonemes only roughly correspond with the written alphabet, for instance, the written English term, 'psycho' has six letters but is made up of four sounds ps-y-ch-o. Spoken phonemes are produced by our vocal apparatus, which includes the tongue, lips, larynx (voicebox), trachea (windpipe) and lungs. The phonological or sound quality of language even determines its written form because most written alphabets are phonetic – they encode sound units. Notable excep-

tions to phonetic alphabets are Chinese logograms and ancient Egyptian hieroglyphs, where the written characters convey ideas (see Figure 3).

Phonological differences are an important source of variety amongst the world's languages, and part of what makes learning a foreign language difficult (Miller, 1996). If you have ever tried to write down an unfamiliar spoken language you will know that it is difficult deciding where individual words even begin and end! Phonological differences can be heard amongst South Africa's diverse languages. English contains 44 phonemes, above average in global terms, but far below the 141 of the Khoisan people of the Northern Cape and Namibia (Pinker, 1994). Certain phonemes are altogether absent from some languages. For instance, a native Japanese speaker visiting South Africa would not readily be able to distinguish between the 'r' and 'l' sounds. English also has the 'th' sound (as in 'there'), which is largely unknown in other languages, while Afrikaans has strong, guttural and rasping 'g' and 'r' sounds that speakers of other languages struggle to pronounce. Can you say the South African national motto? Written in an almost extinct dialect of Khoisan (spoken by the first inhabitants of South Africa), it reads: !KE E:/XARRA//KE. (Pronounced: click-eh-air-click-gaara-click-eh) and means 'diverse people unite' (see Figure 4). The Xhosa, Zulu and Khoisan people's language have up to 48 click sounds, found

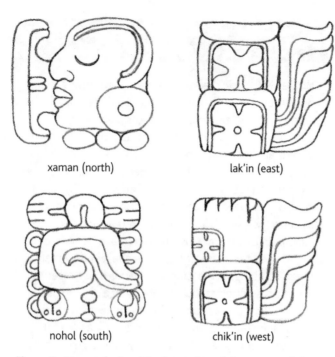

xaman (north)

lak'in (east)

nohol (south)

chik'in (west)

Figure 3 Mayan glyphs of the four points of the compass (where the glyph represents the entire idea rather than a collection of sounds)

nowhere else in the world (Pinker, 1994).

Words

Words represent the next level of language, and are made up of morphemes. Morphemes are the smallest meaningful units of language and include root words, suffixes and prefixes. Consider the following example: the 'establishment' is often used to describe the dominant social and political structures in society – so what would the word, 'antidisestablishmentarianism' mean? The longest word in the English language, its morphological elements can be broken down as: anti/dis/establish/ment/arian/ism. This word describes a viewpoint or philosophy ('ism'), which is opposed to ('anti'), the people who follow a philosophy ('arian'), which is against ('dis'), the 'establish/ment'. Phew! Essentially the people (or viewpoint) described by this word are against those who are against the establishment. As morphemes combine to create meaning, each morpheme changes the meaning of this word.

Sentences

Sentences are not random collections of words because the words within a sentence interact to generate specific meanings. The rules of syntax determine how words are ordered. For example, the sentence, 'The man bit the dog.' has a very different meaning from, 'The dog bit the man'. Or, as Pinker (1996) reminds us, a Venetian blind is very different from a blind Venetian! The rules of syntax are often emphasised in grammar classes in school.

Have you ever tried to translate an extract of language into another language? If so, you might know that it is practically impossible to do this on a word-for-word basis and still make sense. A better strategy is to sum up the general meaning of each sentence. This is because the individual words and syntax of a sentence alone cannot account for its meaning. We need another concept to understand language. Semantics examines the way in which words and underlying meanings are related. Consider linguist Noam Chomsky's famous nonsense sentence, 'Colorless green ideas sleep furiously'. This example illustrates how the syntax of a sentence can be perfect, while its semantic content (or meaning) is not. (How can something be green and colourless? What does it mean for ideas to sleep – especially furiously?). Successfully comprehending and producing sentences therefore demands that we be sensitive to both syntax and semantics.

Figure 4 The South African coat of arms: Can you pronounce the motto?

Pragmatic context

The final aspect that needs to be noted in order to understand language is the pragmatic context of language use. Although meaning is a product of language's formal properties (phonology, morphology, syntax and semantics), it is created in a context understood by both speaker and hearer. Imagine you are eating dinner and somebody asks you, 'Would you be so kind as to pass the potatoes?' You pause for a moment and reply, 'Yes, I probably would', without passing the potatoes. This would be inappropriate because the speaker is not actually asking you how kind or polite you are; they are requesting the potatoes! Misjudging the pragmatic context of language use is a frequent source of confusion between speakers of different languages.

The process of language acquisition

Psycholinguistics is the discipline that examines the relationship between language and mind, including the process of children's language acquisition.

Birth to one year

A newborn baby's angry screams, whimpering cries, contented grunts and cooing noises cannot be regarded as language as these are involuntary and spontaneous responses. Although these responses do convey the infant's emotional state, they lack the systematic and generative qualities that we earlier identified as being part of language. Communication and language, therefore, are not quite the same thing. There is evidence that even in the womb unborn babies can hear their mother's voice and newborn babies can distinguish their mother's speech (see Figure 5).

Babies' first language production is babbling. These are the repetitive *dee-dee-dee, ba-ba-ba* sounds produced from between the ages of three to six months, until the child's first birthday. Babbling is remarkably universal and unrelated to auditory stimulation. Deaf children babble, as do hearing children of deaf parents. In addition, infants born to Kikuyu- and Spanish-speaking parents produce the universal 'ba' and 'pa' babbling sounds, even though these languages do not have these phonemes (Pinker, 1994). In many cultures caregivers talk to their infants in 'motherese' or infant-directed speech, which is a grammatically simplified language characterised by repetition and a higher-

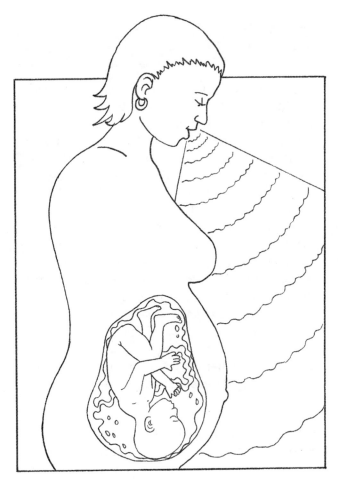

Figure 5 Unborn babies can hear their mother's voices

than-normal pitched voice. But the production of more meaningful sounds requires both physical maturation of the infant's vocal apparatus, and plenty of babbling practice.

Ages one to two years

Children typically start producing holophrases (*holo* means 'complete') at about 12 months of age, where single words come to function as sentences. In English, these are single words such as: *up, ma, juice* or *kitty*, which serve a naming function but also express emotion. For example, a child's utterance 'juice', might not just identifying the object but be a statement signifying thirst (Fromkin & Rodman, 1988). By their second birthday children produce telegraphic speech (so named because people kept telegrams brief by leaving out all the unimportant words). What is noteworthy is that telegraphic speech, for the most part, is syntactically and semantically correct. For example, children say 'juice gone' rather than 'gone juice'. At this stage children also tend to make the overextension error, applying the same words to multiple contexts. For example, they

English verbs come in two forms, regular and irregular. Regular verbs are turned into past tense by adding the suffix 'ed'. Today we *walk* and *talk*, yesterday we *walked* and *talked*. It even works with made-up or nonsense examples. Tell a child that today we '*maulk*' and ask them what we did yesterday. They will probably say '*maulked*'. The English language has about 180 irregular verbs: today we *come* and then *go*; yesterday we *came* and then *went*. Irregular verbs have to be memorised, but we fortunately get a lot of practice, as these are amongst the most frequently used verbs in the English language (e.g., be, have, do, say, make, go, take, come, see, get, know, give, find) (Pinker, 1999). However, having had less opportunity to memorise them, children tend to overgeneralise the 'ed' suffix, and say their sister '*hitted*' them, they '*holded*' the kitten, or they '*hearded*' a noise.

might call a four-legged, brown creature such as a cow by the more familiar term 'doggy'.

Age three years and beyond

After telegraphic speech there is no three-word stage, because from this point on children start producing the extended sentences adults use and their vocabulary grows at a phenomenal rate. Between their second and sixth birthday children add five to nine words to their vocabulary daily (Dromi, 1987). Furthermore, they become skilled users of grammar. In fact, many of the grammatical mistakes preschool children make come from over-applying rather than under-applying grammatical rules. This can be illustrated by examining English-speaking children's use of irregular verbs (see Box 17.3).

These kinds of patterns of language acquisition are an important issue in the theories of language acquisition, which we will look at next.

The origins of language acquisition

Having considered the elements of language as well as the process of its acquisition, we now consider the processes and structures that enable its acquisition.

Behaviourism dominated the early history of psychology and emphasised that all behaviour is determined by environmental influences. Behaviourist B.F. Skinner (1957) accordingly described language as a form of learned 'verbal behaviour' and explained its acquisition in terms of operant conditioning processes. As children imitate the language of those around them, correct language utterances receive reinforcement and become conditioned. For example, a child's parent might give the child a toy when he or she names it correctly, thereby setting up a relationship between the object and its name. Conversely, children's incorrect utterances are either not understood or deliberately ignored by caregivers. As incorrect responses receive no reinforcement they are extinguished.

The behaviourist or learning theory view of language acquisition can be criticised on a number of grounds:

- It cannot account for the innovative, generative quality of children's language. Children could not have previously overheard and remembered all the grammatically correct sentences they produce.
- It cannot explain children's tendency to overgeneralise grammatical rules, such as placing the 'ed' suffix on irregular verbs. If language were simply a product of their environment, where would children have learned to say '*hitted*', '*holded*' or '*hearded*'? Adults do not to make these mistakes.
- It does not explain how children learn language when the stimuli are often so poor. Listen carefully to adults' everyday language; it is full of fragments, false starts and incomplete sentences.
- It does not explain how children learn language when the reinforcement they receive is so indirect and improbable. Adults tend to correct the semantic rather than grammatical content of children's utterances. So when a young child exclaims 'Look at that doggy eat the field', the child's caregiver would probably explain that it is a horse rather than dog, instead of correcting the grammar.

Noam Chomsky (1959) noted these criticisms and revolutionised psycholinguistics with an alternative view of language acquisition. Arguing that the capacity for language use is not learned but rather innate (hence the fact that Chomsky's theory is referred to as a '*nativist*' theory), Chomsky hypothesised the existence of a *language acquisition device*, and described humans as genetically pre-programmed to learn language. Chomsky (1980:134) explained, 'in certain fundamental respects we do not really learn language; rather grammar grows in the mind.' Chomsky described what he termed a 'universal grammar', the deep structure common to all language. (This is different from the prescriptive grammars you learned in school.) It is from this universal grammar that the rules for our everyday, 'natural' languages (e.g., Japanese, isiZulu, Portuguese, etc.) are derived. Universal grammar therefore is the complex capacity for language that gets filled by the particular languages we acquire. Thus, while the particular languages children acquire depend on their linguistic context, children are predisposed to learn language and do so in a relatively effortless manner and invariant sequence.

Nativist theory also accounts for specific features of the language acquisition process, such as critical language acquisition periods. The critical language acquisition period can be illustrated as follows: when families move to new countries where different languages are spoken, children acquire (often multiple) languages faster and easier than their parents.

Even deaf children, who spontaneously use sign language, do so better when they learn it at a young age. Further evidence for the existence of a critical language acquisition period are the few documented cases of feral (wild) or severely deprived children. These are children who have grown up in total social isolation, either through severe parental neglect or abuse. Even after intensive efforts at rehabilitation these children fail to develop normal language abilities, because they have missed the critical 'window periods' for language development (Bernard, 2000; Curtiss, 1977).

Language in South African society

Language is not only a resource for thought, it is an important element of people's cultural heritage and identity. Language can therefore be an extremely contested political issue. Learners' resistance to the introduction of Afrikaans as the medium of instruction in Black schools led to the 1976 Soweto riots.

The political significance of language and its role in fostering multiculturalism is reflected in post-apartheid South Africa expanding its number of official languages from two (English and Afrikaans) to eleven (isiZulu, isiXhosa, SeTswana, SePedi, SeSotho, XiTsonga, SiSwati, IsiNdebele and TshiVenda, English and Afrikaans). But many other non-official languages and dialects (a spoken variation of a language) are spoken in South Africa. These range from religious languages such as Arabic and

Figure 6 The relative ease and speed with which children are able to acquire new languages, for instance in a foreign environment, supports the notion of critical language acquisition periods

17.4 LANGUAGE ACQUISITION AND MULTILINGUALISM IN SOUTH AFRICA

Although research supports the effectiveness of early education conducted in the child's home language (or mother-tongue), many South African parents are keen for their children to access the educational and economic opportunities associated with English. As schools themselves now decide language policy, this leads to the following dilemma. How much emphasis should be placed on English, and how much on the learner's home language? This is a key debate surrounding multilingualism: How do we affirm and support linguistic heritage, without denying learners the opportunities associated by the dominant (English) language? While there is no easy resolution to this question, many caution against the elevation of English and the growing neglect and marginalisation of South Africa's indigenous languages (Alexander, 1989, 2000; McLean, 1992).

Figure 7 Language is about power: School children's resistance to being taught in Afrikaans precipitated the 1976 Soweto riots and mounting opposition to apartheid

Hebrew, the European, Asian and African languages spoken in immigrant communities, to dialects such as Tsotsitaal, a secret language spoken by township tsotsis (criminals). Furthermore language, particularly in multicultural settings, is dynamic and marked by much borrowing and exchange. Even the influential English language has borrowed terms such as 'indaba' (meeting) and 'veld', from other South African languages. In fact, as a global *lingua franca* English has appropriated many words from other languages, for example 'thug', 'patio' and 'bouquet' come from Hindi, Spanish and French respectively (Kaschula & Anthonissen, 1995:74).

As a valuable part of people's cultural heritage and an important resource for thinking, there are no inferior or primitive 'natural' languages. In fact, people with simple material technologies often have highly complex languages (e.g., the Khoisan). A South African example of a primitive, non-natural, language would be Fanagalo. Fanagalo is a type of simplified language (called a pidgin, by linguists) that is spoken

on mines to enable migrant workers to communicate with each other. It has a vocabulary of about 2 000 words, of which 500 are reportedly swear-words!

Conclusion

Describing the characteristics, components and acquisition of language, this chapter sought to show how language is interwoven with cognition. Language embodies a range of striking paradoxes: its individual sign elements (words) are innately arbitrary, yet become combined in profoundly meaningful ways; it is firmly rule governed, yet facilitates infinite creativity and innovation; and it is biologically 'hard wired', yet infused with clear political and social dimensions. The product of all these paradoxes, language use, and the kinds of cognitive gains it confers, is arguably one of the distinctive characteristics of our species.

Alexander, N. (1989). *Language Policy and National Unity in South Africa/Azania.* Cape Town: Buchu Books.

Alexander, N. (2000). *English Unassailable but Unattainable. The dilemma of language policy in education in South Africa.* PRAESA Occasional Papers, No.3. Cape Town: Praesa/University of Cape Town.

Au, T. (1983). Chinese and English counterfactuals: The Sapir-Whorf hypothesis revisited. *Cognition,* 15:155-87.

Au, T. (1988). Language and cognition. In R.L. Schiefelbusch & L.L. Lloyd (Eds.). *Language Perspectives: Acquisition, retardation, and intervention.* Austin, Texas: Pro-Ed, pp. 125-46.

Bernard, C. (2000). From potential to realization: An episode in the origin of language. *Linguistics,* 38(5):989-1004.

Byrnes, J.P. & Gelman S.A. (1991). Perspectives on thought and language: Traditional views and contemporary views. In S.A. Gelman & J.P. Byrnes (Eds.). *Perspectives on Language and Thought.* Cambridge: Cambridge University Press, pp. 3-27.

Chomsky, N. (1959). Review of Verbal Behaviour by BF Skinner. *Language,* 35:26-58.

Chomsky, N. (1980). *Rules and Representations.* New York: Columbia University Press.

Curtiss, S. (1977). *Genie: A psycholinguistic study of a modern-day 'wild child'.* New York: Academic Press.

Dromi, E. (1987). *Early Lexical Development.* Cambridge: Cambridge University Press.

Fromkin, V. & Rodman, R. (1988). *An Introduction to Language.* Fort Worth, Texas: Holt, Rinehard & Winston.

Gleick, J. (1999). Albert Einstein. *Time,* 29 March:40-3.

Halliday, M.A.K. & Matthiessen, C. (1999). *Construing Experience Through Meaning: A language-based approach to cognition.* London: Continuum.

Hardin, C. & Banaji, M.R. (1993). The influence of language on thought. *Social Cognition,* 11(3):277-308.

Heider, E.R. (1972). Universals in color naming and memory. *Journal of Experimental Psychology,* 93:10-20.

Kaschula, R.H. & Anthonissen, C. (1995). *Communicating Across Cultures in South Africa: Towards a critical language awareness.* Johannesburg: Hodder & Stoughton.

McLean, D. (1992). Guarding against the bourgeois revolution: Some aspects of language planning in the context of national democratic struggle. In R.K. Herbert (Ed.). *Language in Society: The theory and practice of sociolinguistics.* Johannesburg: Witwatersrand University Press, pp. 151-61.

Miller, G.A. (1996). Some preliminaries to Psycholinguistics. In S.A. Gelman & J.P. Byrnes (Eds.). *Perspectives on Language and Thought.* Cambridge: Cambridge University Press, pp. 405-13.

Piaget, J. (1968). *Six Psychological Studies.* New York: Vintage Books.

Premack A.J. & Premack, D. (1972). Teaching language to an ape. *Scientific American,* 227:92-9.

Pinker, S. (1994). *The Language Instinct.* New York: William Morrow.

Pinker, S. (1996). Rules of language. In S.A. Gelman & J.P. Byrnes (Eds.). *Perspectives on Language and Thought.* Cambridge: Cambridge University Press, pp. 558-69.

Pinker, S. (1999). Horton hearded a who! *Time,* 1 November:65.

Pinker, S. & Bloom, P. (1990). Natural language and natural selection. *Behaviour and Brain Sciences,* 13:707-84.

Skinner, B.F. (1957). *Verbal Behavior.* New York: Appleton-Century-Crofts.

Terrance, H.S. (1980). *Nim.* London: Meuthen.

Tutani, L. (2000). *Nurses' Experience of Contesting Discourses in HIV/AIDS Activities in the Primary Health Care Setting.* Unpublished master's research report, Rhodes University, East London.

Vygotsky, L.S. (1986). *Thought and Language.* Cambridge, MA: M.I.T Press.

Watson, J.D. (1980). *The Double Helix: A personal account of the discovery of the structure of DNA.* New York: Norton.

Whorf, B.L. (1956). *Language, Thought and Reality.* Cambridge, MA: M.I.T Press.

Multiple choice questions

1. Which of the following is not true of language?
   a) the relationship between words and what they refer to is arbitrary
   b) primitive or traditional societies use primitive languages
   c) language is one of several ways by which ideas can be communicated
   d) language is a rule-governed system

2. The prefix 'anti' in the word 'anticlockwise' is a
   a) morpheme
   b) suffix
   c) word
   d) phoneme

3. Which of the following is characteristic of child-centred speech?
   a) lower tone
   b) grammatically simple sentences
   c) increased volume
   d) using the hands to gesticulate

4. The study of how language is used in a particular context is called
   a) semantics
   b) phonology
   c) syntax
   d) pragmatics

5. A three-year-old child says that 'he holded a rabbit at the farm today'. This shows that
   a) he cannot yet understand grammar
   b) he learned his language from his environment
   c) he is still in the imitation stage of language acquisition
   d) none of the above

6. B.F. Skinner explained that children acquire language through
   a) their innate biological capacity
   b) trial and error
   c) reinforcement
   d) going to school

7. Which of the following statements concerning the 'language acquisition device' is false?
   a) it is transmitted through reinforcement and learning
   b) this notion was advanced by Chomsky
   c) it is common to all people
   d) it is the foundation for the everyday 'natural languages' we eventually acquire

8. Which of the following statements concerning egocentric speech is false?
   a) egocentric speech declines and dies out around 6 years of age
   b) egocentric speech demonstrates that young children tend not to consider other people's perspectives
   c) Vygotsky argued that egocentric speech is replaced by mature, socialised speech
   d) none of the above

9. Feral children often struggle to learn language, even in later life.
   This is evidence of
   a) the longlasting psychological effects of their trauma
   b) the existence of a critical language acquisition period
   c) the importance of biological factors
   d) none of the above

10. Linguistic relativity thesis suggests that
    a) language enables us to think
    b) language determines how we think
    c) language influences how we think
    d) language is evidence of thinking

Short answer questions

1. People who talk to their animals (such as some pet owners, or farmers who talk to their prize livestock) are often adamant that their communication constitutes language. In view of what you have learned about the characteristics of language, how would you respond to such a claim?

2. What is the nature of the relationship between thought and language?

3. Describe the various components of language and suggest how they work together to produce meaning.

4. Describe the process and stages of language acquisition children go through to finally become competent users of language.

5. The early behaviourist psychologists argued that language use and acquisition could be accounted for simply in terms of learned behaviour. Critically evaluate this view.

18

Memory

Clifford van Ommen

CHAPTER OBJECTIVES

After studying this chapter you should be able to:
- demonstrate that there are a variety of approaches to studying memory
- understand the basis of the information processing (IP) approach
- explain the IP concepts of acquisition, storage and retrieval
- define cueing, recognition and free forms of recall
- describe the concepts used in, and the differences between, the two-store, multi-store and working memory models of memory
- explain the process of list learning and the effects associated with this
- define forgetting and some of the concepts developed in investigating this process
- describe the basis of the ecological approach to studying memory
- outline the importance of context and culture in the process of remembering
- describe some of the criticisms of laboratory-based research and memory research more generally.

This section of the course made Nosipho think about her own memory and how she used to struggle to memorise her work for tests and exams while she was at school. She hadn't seemed to be able to keep information in her head. Often she would think she had learned properly for a test, only to find the answers disappearing the moment she tried to put them down on paper. Early on at university she had decided to take the problem in hand and had gone to the learning centre to ask for some help. There she had been taught various tricks and strategies for being able to remember more effectively. She knew now that it wasn't enough just to read over her notes when she learned as she had done at school. Instead, if she was going to be able to remember something she needed to be more actively involved in repeating back the information to herself while she was learning and sometimes even writing things down and testing herself. This active kind of remembering seemed to work much better. She also learned ways of triggering her memory during tests and exams. She found that if she took the first letters of a list of ideas and made them into a word it was much easier to recall the whole list. Sometimes she drew a funny picture of the material she was trying to learn and in the exam she would find herself smiling as she visualised it. It not only cheered her up during exams it also found that remembering the picture jogged her memory for the information she needed!

Now that Nosipho was feeling more relaxed about her ability to remember information for exams she recognised in fact how amazing people's memories – including her own – actually were. She could remember things that had happened to her, places and people right back from when she was about five years old. She could remember several poems she had learned in primary school and all the children she had been friends with. She could remember the names of all sorts of products on the supermarket shelves, movie actors and actresses, different makes of car, countries and directions for how to get around in the city. 'It really is incredible when you think about how much complicated information each person remembers in a lifetime,' she thought to herself.

Introduction

Take a moment and jot down what you understand by the term 'memory'. It is a word in common use in contemporary society so you should already have some idea of what it may refer to.

Let us consider some definitions provided in two online dictionaries. The *Cambridge Dictionary of American English* (2003) defines memory as the 'ability to remember', while the *One Look Dictionary Search* (n.d.) describes it as 'the power of retaining and recalling past experience'. Both of these definitions refer to some capacity (power or ability) to bring (a mental) something from the past into the present. Is this similar to what you have jotted down?

If you work through the questions and tasks detailed in Box 18.1, you may realise that the something that is recalled, and from when that something dates, can vary greatly. It can, for example, be a number, a name, a melody, a story, an image, or even a movement. Furthermore, this may be from a second ago, a year ago, or even from your early childhood. What should also become clear, as you consider this diversity, is that it is a phenomenon that is deeply part of our lives. Without the capacity to retain and remember, our existence would be radically different, if not impossible.

Modern psychology has always been concerned with the study of memory and, consequently, a vast field of memory research has developed. This chapter will introduce you to a variety of core terms, consider some contemporary research and demonstrate how various psychologists have developed the concept of memory.

The information processing approach to understanding memory

A useful way to frame our current understanding of memory is to use the inside-outside binary discussed during this part's introduction. Using this, several successive approaches to the study of memory can be distinguished.

Very influential, and the primary focus of this chapter, is the information processing (IP) approach (see Chapter 16, this volume). Here there is a primary focus on memory as something that takes place in our heads. Memory is mostly studied as an internal brain (mental) process, which is regarded as consisting of distinct and interconnected stages (Hammond, 1987). There have, however, been numerous debates regarding some of the concepts that have been developed within this approach. This has lead to expansions both within and outside the IP school, some of which will be detailed in the second half of this chapter. The main trend has been toward an ever-increasing break from the 'inside' emphasis, a shift toward greater inclusion of the context (the environment, culture and society) in which memorising and remembering take place. With this has come a decreasing emphasis on the distortions and accuracy of memory (how poorly and well we remember things) and a greater acknowledgement of the practical (everyday) nature of what we remember, and when.

18.1 MEMORY QUESTIONS AND TASKS

Take a few minutes and tackle the following questions and tasks:

- What primary school did you attend?
- What is your current telephone number?
- What is the capital of Zimbabwe?
- Try and picture, in as much detail as possible, what your bedroom looks like.
- Read the following set of numbers once, cover them up, and, write them down on a piece of paper without looking at them again: 219391945

- In one minute, try and write as many words as you can that begin with the letter 'T'. Proper nouns, sentences and numbers are not allowed.
- Open up a phonebook, look down the list of names, and keep count of the number of names you associate with someone you know or have known.
- Get up and pretend that you are kicking a soccer ball or swinging a golf club.
- Writing no more than a few lines, summarise a story you were recently told or read.

Input, storage and output

I am sure many of you think about computers when you hear the word 'memory' mentioned. This typically refers to the computer's storage capacity, that is, the amount of information it can retain without loss when switched off. Generally, since extremes of size seem to impress people, the larger the memory, the better the computer. In the same way, the quicker and greater the amount of detail a person can remember, the more impressed we are.

Computers have been used as a powerful analogy with which to understand memory. In the IP approach, the memory process consists of three aspects:

- An *input or acquisition stage*, such as when you type words on a keyboard.
- A *storage stage*, such as when you save a file on a computer's hard drive to use again later.
- An *output or retrieval stage*, such as when you call up a file from the hard drive and view it on your screen (Groome, 1999).

So, in a similar fashion to the computer, the brain is regarded as a complex information processor of which memory is a very important part.

To give you an example: One morning a close friend invites you to a party at her house that night. The IP approach would describe the basic memory process that accompanies and follows the invitation in this way: Your friend invites you to the party, you hear (sense and perceive) and understand (comprehend) her words. Input has thus occurred, the information your friend has given you is said to have been *encoded*. You retain (store) this information during the day while you attend lectures. That night, while driving home, you remember her invitation; you are said to have retrieved or *recalled* the information from storage. This recollection is the output of the process. The fifth item in Box 18.1 gives you another illustration of this sequence.

Retrieval can be assisted. To continue with the above example: just after being invited you jot down 'party' in your diary. That night you notice the word you have written down and recall (retrieve) the memory about the invitation. Your diary note is said to have acted as a *cue*, a trigger for you to remember a specific piece of information. The seventh item in Box 18.1 is another example of cueing.

Short-term and long-term memory

Early IP theorists conceptualised memory as consisting of two types of memory store: *short-term memory (STM)* and *long-term memory (LTM)*. This became known as the two-store model of memory (Haberlandt, 1994). According to Groome (1999), STM refers to information that is currently in our awareness, while LTM refers to the information of which we are not currently conscious but which is being kept in storage. To use the bedroom example (Item 4) from Box 18.1, if you are picturing your bedroom in your imagination, that information is in your STM. You are currently aware of this information. You have retrieved this from your LTM, so prior to being cued with the bedroom task, the image you evoked in your STM was being kept in storage. Information has thus passed from LTM to STM.

According to Lezak (1995), STM only retains information for a few seconds, unless it is *rehearsed*, that is, unless you continuously repeat the information to yourself. You are probably most aware of this process when trying to remember a phone number without having a pen and paper at hand to jot it down. STM was, however, also regarded as a route through which information can be stored in LTM. If rehearsed enough, information would be stored in LTM, where it can be retained for a long time, from hours to even decades. The telephone number question in Box 18.1 is an example of LTM information.

Atkinson and Shiffrin (1968) extended the two-store model by adding a third component called the *sensory register*. This structure was understood as receiving the initial input (e.g., visual, tactile or acoustic stimuli) from the environment prior to it being recognised. Reed (1992) reports that the sensory store for vision is only 250 milliseconds, a quarter of a second. Once, however, a stimulus is recognised and open to rehearsal it was regarded as being in STM. Because Atkinson and Shiffrin's (1968) model included several memory stores, it became known as a *multi-store model of memory*.

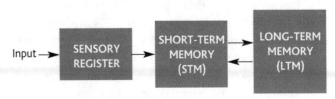

Figure 1 Atkinson and Shiffrin's (1968) multi-store model of memory (simplified)

Working memory

Despite its initial popularity, the store-type model has gradually been replaced by the *working memory model* (Haberlandt, 1994). Part of the reason for this was the growing experimental evidence that indicated the shortcomings of the store model. For example, it was found that simply rehearsing material (called *maintenance rehearsal*) did not necessarily increase a person's ability to recall material; rather it seemed that recall was related to the level at which the material was being processed. Craik and Tulving (in Haberlandt, 1994) demonstrated that the more detailed the analysis of material when rehearsing (called *elaborative rehearsal*), the more likely you were to recall it.

For example, if you take the list of words you generated for the sixth item in Box 18.1, and merely repeated them to yourself, you would probably recall less words than if you tried to remember the sequence in which you first generated the words or what you were thinking of when first producing the words. Perhaps you could check which of the words sound similar or have similar meanings. Thus, by analysing the words in a variety of ways, you are engaging in an elaborative form of rehearsal that should maximise later recall.

What this demonstrates is the need for a more dynamic understanding of memory, one that goes beyond the passive flow of information from one store to another. By the late 1970s, STM was replaced by the concept of *working memory* (Haberlandt, 1994). Like STM, working memory stores information temporarily and is limited in capacity, but it is also more than a store, it is also a place where information is manipulated and transformed (Psychological Corporation, 1997).

For example, read the digit list (the fifth item) in Box 18.1 once, try and keep this list in mind (no peeping at the page!) and reverse its sequence. Write down your reversed list. Keep at it until you manage to remember it accurately. What you will have managed is to both store and transform (in this case, reverse) information. Working memory refers to this active and dual process.

Elaborating on this, Baddeley and Hitch (in Groome, 1999) have argued that working memory consists of three components: A *central executive* where manipulations occur, a *phonological loop* and a *visuo-spatial sketchpad*, which enables the temporary storage of verbal (word) material and images respectively. Thus, the working memory model is essentially an elaboration of the STM component of the multi-store model, which retains the LTM concept from the store model.

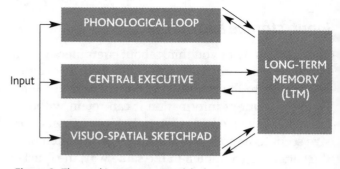

Figure 2 The working memory model of memory

The primacy and recency effects

A common test used to assess memory in people that have sustained brain damage is the Rey Auditory Verbal Learning Test (Lezak, 1995). A list of fifteen words is repeatedly read to the person who then, after each reading, has to try and recall as many of the words as possible, a process known as free recall. Some interesting things are usually noted when considering which words a person tends to recall. Usually the words that are read out first and last tend to be recalled more often than the words in the middle of the list. These phenomena have been referred to as the *primacy effect* (the tendency to recall words heard first), and the *recency effect* (the tendency to recall words heard last) (Groome, 1999). How do we explain this effect?

Research has shown that people are limited in terms of the amount of discrete bits of information they can hold in awareness at any one time. This is sometimes referred to as a person's immediate memory span or simple span (Groome, 1999). A test used to assess this is the Digit Span Forward (Psychological Corporation, 1997). An approximate example of an item from this test is provided in Box 18.1 (fifth item). A general finding is that people have a span for between five to nine bits or chunks of information, with seven being a common average (Miller in Groome, 1999).

Clearly, fifteen items is beyond the immediate memory span of most people, and yet many people manage to recall most of these items after only a few readings of the list. It is argued that the recency effect is a function of the immediate memory span (STM capacity), while the primacy effect is due to material being temporarily rehearsed (working memory) or stored in LTM, later being recalled as you recite the list. Thus, using both stores, a person is able to recall more than seven items on the list.

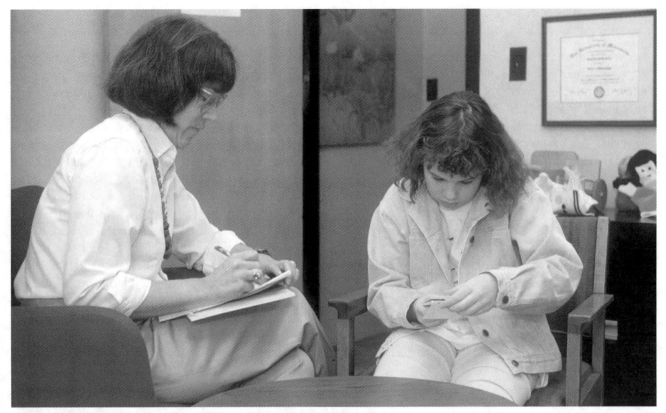

Figure 3 Neuropsychological assessments usually include asking the client to recall a series of discrete numbers so as to determine their simple span

Forgetting

Having spent some time on the concepts of STM and working memory, the final part of this section will focus on LTM. More specifically, we will briefly consider forgetting, or the loss of information once it is stored in LTM. Learning may be defined as the storage of material in LTM.

Hermann Ebbinghaus (1850-1909) was one of the first persons known to have scientifically studied memory (Groome, 1999; Haberlandt, 1994; Shuttleworth-Jordan, 1997). He was the first to observe and graphically plot the forgetting curve, a typical pattern of forgetting where material which has just been learned is rapidly forgotten at first and is then forgotten at a more gradual pace afterwards (Groome, 1999).

Two explanations for this pattern were considered: spontaneous decay, where material is lost due to not being used across time, and interference, where some other input disrupts these memories (Haberlandt, 1994). The interference explanation has proved more popular primarily due to the argument that time alone is an inadequate explanation of forgetting, and that it is the things that happen across time that are responsible for this process (McGeoth in Haberlandt, 1994).

Two forms of interference have been distinguished:

- *Retroactive interference* is where new material disrupts older information (Haberlandt, 1994). For example, you are introduced to two people at a party, the one early in the evening and the other an hour later. The next day you find that whenever you try to recall the name of the first person, the name of the second keeps coming to mind. A frustrating experience!
- *Proactive interference* is where previously learned material interferes with the learning of new material (Haberlandt, 1994). Let us take the party example again: you are introduced to the first person who happens to be from Hungary and has an unusual name. After some effort you manage to recall the name at will. A while later you are introduced to her partner with an equally difficult name. You find that you struggle immensely to memorise the second name since the first name seems to interfere. Prior learning has impeded your current rate of learning.

Generally, memory research has focused on auditory and visual memory, the ability to acquire and recall, either immediately or after some delay, that which is heard and seen. This is usually assessed using two forms of material: verbal (such as words, sentences and symbols) – which may be either auditory (listening) or visual (reading) or visuo-spatial (such as recalling two- or three-dimensional patterns and designs) – which is usually visual. But there are forms of memory for the other senses as well, including tactile and olfactory (smell) memories. These, however, tend to enjoy less attention in memory research.

What is interesting about the type of remembering just described is that it involves a conscious process, that is, you are aware that you are recalling some form of information. This type of memory has been referred to by a variety a names, including *explicit, propositional* or *declarative* memory. More recently, there has been increasing interest in conducting research on those memories that we are less aware of having (Groome, 1999), the so-called *implicit* or *procedural* memories.

Such memories also come in a variety of forms. The eighth item in Box 18.1 draws on implicit memory. You probably think of complex movements, such as kicking a ball, swinging a golf club, or even shuffling a deck of cards, as a skill that you have to practice to perfect. But if you consider that this involves a process of acquisition, rehearsal, storage and recall, you will realise that skills (and habits for that matter) are all forms of memory.

Research has shown that implicit memories are usually acquired by engaging in (doing) the activity and that they are less easy to forget (Shuttleworth-Jordan, 1997). For example, even though you may not have ridden a bicycle for years, you would probably be able to cycle without much trouble if you were asked to do so today.

Figure 4 Memory never rests. Even at parties we are encoding new information which may be open to proactive interference

The expansion of understandings of memory

In this section we will be discussing some of the responses to the basic IP model.

Meaning and memory

Without looking back, try and recall the nine digits that you learned from Box 18.1. Chances are that, if you used rote (parrot) learning, you will be unable to do so. Now look back at the numbers and use the following sentence, 'World War Two started in 1939 and ended in 1945' to memorise the sequence. Chances are that you will still remember the numbers (219391945) by the end of the chapter. This is impressive since, at nine numbers, this is at the upper limit of the immediate memory span. How is this possible?

What has happened is that the digits have been made meaningful; they have been linked to other information that enables the sequence to be retained in a more enduring form (Groome, 1999). It is difficult to retain these nine numbers when they are meaningless, but when linked to historical 'facts', recalling these numbers becomes less demanding. Thus, in understanding memory, we need to understand the role of meaning and past learning.

The work of Frederic Bartlett (1886-1979) becomes significant here, since he argued that our long-term memory is organised according to meaning frameworks, known as *schemas* (Shuttleworth-Jordan, 1997). Our past experiences (past learning) act as frameworks that structure the learning of new information (Groome, 1999).

Let us use the 2003 Cricket World Cup as an example. Imagine you watched all the South Africa matches with two friends, one who knew little about cricket and the other who had an in-depth knowledge of the game's rules, strategies and players. If you discussed the Cup with these two friends now, you would probably find that the second friend would be able to recall much more about each match than your less-informed friend. According to Bartlett's theory, the reason for this is that your friend who is an avid fan has a more detailed and developed schema that assists him in encoding and retaining cricket information.

The accuracy of memory

The schema concept has profound consequences for our understanding of memory. If what we remember depends on our previous learning, then the type of detail that each person recalls will vary, since no two people share the same learning history. The memories you recall during discussions or while quietly reminiscing are thus constructed; they are the product of a meeting of your schemas with the event you are remembering.

Therefore, to think of memory as a video recording of events in your life, which you then replay in your mind's eye when remembering, is inaccurate. Instead, remembering is a reconstructive exercise using information retained within the frameworks of relevant schemas (Neisser, 1984). This means that memories are not accurate depictions of the events of the day and are prone to distortions.

The context of remembering

The idea that memories are inherently inaccurate or 'constructed' has lead to a significant shift in memory research. Some researchers have retained a focus on the inaccuracy of our recollections and have tried to identify factors that maximise the accuracy of schema-based memories. Most of this research has been experimental and conducted in the laboratory. Others have argued that this is too limited and research needs to move into everyday life. This departs from the basic IP model with its emphasis on the internal processes of memory. The net is now thrown more widely to include the haphazardness of daily existence, the very thing that experimental psychologists tried to exclude by conducting research in laboratories.

This shift in focus in memory research has been called the *ecological approach* and is closely associated with work of Ulric Neisser (Edwards & Potter, 1995). Neisser argued that rather than being concerned with the inaccuracy of remembering we should be intrigued by its functionality, that is, how it is accurate enough to allow us to successfully manage our daily lives. For example, Neisser refers to 'gist' memory, the ability to recall the main points or central themes of an event or story (Edwards & Potter, 1992), a skill often called on in daily life. The ninth item in Box 18.1 calls on this ability.

Neisser thus argues for a shift away from the computer analogy to a focus on the person-in-context. Memory thus becomes a social rather than an exclusively mental process. This has also been described as a shift from a central-processor model to a distributed-processor model (Laboratory of Comparative Human Cognition, 1983).

The significance of the role of context in remembering is not something new and unique to the ecological approach. We all know that some contexts will evoke strong recollections for us (Groome, 1999). Let us work with the bedroom exercise (fourth item) from Box 18.1 to demonstrate this. Imagining your bedroom (context) may result in you recalling various events that took place there; a discussion with your mom the previous day, a song you listened to a week before, or even a fight with your brother several years before. The memories may come flooding back.

Research has shown that remembering is context-dependent. An example of this is a study by Greenspoon and Reynert (in Groome, 1999) who found that children who were asked to recall what they had learned in the same room in which they had originally learned it, tended to recall more information than children who had to recall the same information in a different room. One explanation for this is that there are various features in the learning context that serve as triggers for remembering. In this experiment, such triggers would have been absent in the room where learning had not taken place.

Society and culture as context

It is important to realise that context refers to more than our physical surroundings but extends to the socio-cultural background of the person doing the remembering. Mistry and Rogoff (1994) argue that the 'inaccuracy' and 'distortion' that is evident in people's remembering may be better understood as a product of their context than as an indication of the functioning of some internal process. They argue that persons learn particular remembering skills within their specific cultural context. For example, in Western formal schooling we are taught strategies for remembering unrelated bits of information (as in the fifth item in Box 18.1). These strategies may be absent in other contexts where such skills are not in demand.

This idea places the IP approach in an interesting position. Since it has been very concerned with the remembering of discrete, meaningless bits of information, the IP approach thus locates itself within the concerns of Western culture. It then becomes possible to ask to what extent are the findings of this approach relevant to those in positions outside of this dominant culture?

Let us consider the following: Frederic Bartlett found that Swazi herdsman were very good at remembering details of the cattle under their care but did less well at remembering a 25-word message (Mistry & Rogoff, 1994). Using the above idea, it can be argued that the herdsmen had well developed skills for remembering cattle, very significant animals in Swazi culture, but were less skilled in carrying messages which would probably be more valued in a Westernised culture.

Figure 5 Cultural context plays a role in determining what type of memory skills we develop

Another example from work by Mistry and Rogoff (1994) refers to work done with Mayan children who were asked to remember a culturally relevant story and then retell it to an adult. The researchers found that the Mayan children did far worse than a group of American children. Rather than assuming that some cultures have poorer memories, the cultural context should be taken into consideration. Outspokenness is a skill valued in middle-class US culture (Markus & Kitayama, 1991) but speaking freely to an adult is considered inappropriate for Mayan children, since one should not claim greater knowledge than an adult. It is thus not surprising to note a poorer performance amongst such children.

Living in a world of action: A critical approach to memory research

In closing this chapter, let us briefly consider Edwards and Potter's (1995) critique of Neisser's ecological approach. They agree with Neisser that laboratory studies provide limited insight into the process of remembering since such research is so removed from the context of the everyday world. Where they differ from Neisser is that his, and all previous memory research, is built on the assumption that an accurate and indisputable record of the original events exists which can be used to judge the accuracy of a person's recollections. For example, a videotape recording of a conversation would be judged to be a reliable record of what was actually said by someone in a particular place. Although he is interested in studying memory in its natural context, Neisser still shares the IP concern for determining the accuracy of people's recollections.

But, say Edwards and Potter (1995:32), 'there can be no neutral, interpretation-free record against which to check claims'. In order to help you understand this statement, let us take the example of a student (see Box 18.3) who was involved in a car accident with the Dean of Humanities. The box demonstrates how the memory of the event varies according to the context: to whom, where and when the story is told.

The story as told to friends is quite different to the story written down at the police station. Edwards and Potter (1995) argue that how it is told each time would aim at achieving different effects. This does not mean that the student is lying (the same facts may be reported each time), or that he or she is conscious of these variations, but what Edwards and Potter (1995) are saying is that the student is creating ver-

Figure 6 A story told to friends may be quite different to the story told to a policeman. No version of the same event is ever neutral and free of context and interpretation.

sions to meet the demands of the situation. This is a process we are all continuously concerned with. Since we are always recollecting in a context, we can never tell the one final true version of what happened. There is no situation outside of society and others.

What are the consequences of this idea for memory research? Edwards and Potter (1995) do not condemn Neisser's work. They see his research as making a valuable contribution, but they argue for the importance of studying how people construct their versions of events and how they manage to achieve particular effects through such versions. Thus, in closing this chapter, we are left with an emphasis on the use of language in social situations when studying remembering, a strong departure from the intense internal and mental memory focus of the IP approach.

Conclusion

In this chapter we have traced the development of psychology's investigation of our ability to remember. In this process you have been introduced to a large number of terms and ideas that has probably shifted the understanding of memory which you articulated at the beginning of this chapter. Our journey started with the information processing approach with its strong internal focus and emphasis on computer terms. Over a number of steps we then saw how the understanding of memory has shifted from that of a passive and internal store to a more dynamic and skilled phenomenon that is intimately tied up with both meaning and context. Finally, we completed our journey by showing how in recollecting, we can never arrive at a final true version of an event. Thus, the concept of memory lies distributed amongst these understandings. Memory is a field of study that is still as alive with debate and investigation as it was when psychology first became intrigued by our power to recollect more than a century ago.

18.3 MEMORY AND CONTEXT: CONTEXT-BASED ACCOUNTS OF DENTING THE DEAN'S CAR

A student is involved in a car accident with the Dean of Humanities. The following stories are given of the accident in different contexts:

To father.
I was driving behind the Dean when he suddenly hit the brakes. I couldn't stop in time and ran into the back of him. I wasn't driving up his rear but it was just so sudden! I just couldn't stop quickly enough.

To friends
I was really tired after working through the night to complete the psych essay. I didn't even know it was the Dean in front of me. If I did I would have stayed a mile away. Next thing all I see are red lights, and bang into the back of him! I shat myself! There I am, *moeg* [tired], just trying to get home and then 'boom'! It really made my day.

At the police station
Vehicle A was driving behind vehicle B down Church Street towards the Magistrates' Court. Vehicle B came to a stop. Vehicle A collided with vehicle B. Both vehicles were subsequently stationery.

Consider, is there one final true version of what happened?

Atkinson, R.C. & Shiffrin, R.M. (1968). Human memory: A proposed system and its control processes. In K.W. Spence & J.T. Spence (Eds.). *The Psychology of Learning and Motivation* (Vol. 2). London: Academic Press, pp. 89-105.

The Cambridge Dictionary of American English, http://www.dictionary.cambridge.org/results.asp.searchword=memory (accessed 4 March 2003).

Edwards, D. & Potter, J. (1992). *Discursive Psychology*. London: Sage Publications.

Edwards, D. & Potter, J. (1995). Remembering. In R. Harre & P. Stearns (Eds.). *Discursive Psychology in Practice*. London: Sage Publications, pp. 9-36.

Groome, D. (1999). *An Introduction to Cognitive Psychology: Processes and disorders*. London: Psychology Press.

Haberlandt, K. (1994). *Cognitive Psychology*. Boston: Allyn and Bacon.

Hammond, E.J. (1987). Memory. In G.A. Tyson (Ed.). *Introduction to Psychology: A South African perspective*. Johannesburg: Westro Educational Books, pp. 211-23.

Laboratory of Comparative Human Cognition (1983). Culture and cognitive development. In J.H. Flavell & E.M. Markman (Eds.). *Handbook of Child Psychology: Vol. III cognitive development*. New York: Wiley, pp. 295-356.

Lezak, M.D. (1995). *Neuropsychological Assessment* (3rd edition). New York: Oxford University Press.

Marcus, H.R. & Kitayama, S. (1991). Culture and the self: Implications for cognition, emotion and motivation. *Psychological Review*, 98(2):224-53.

Mistry, J. & Rogoff, B. (1994). Remembering in cultural context. In W.J. Lonner & R. Malpass (Eds.). *Psychology and Culture*. Boston: Allyn & Bacon, pp. 139-44.

Neisser, U. (1984). Interpreting Harry Bahrick's discovery: What confers immunity against forgetting? *Journal of Experimental Psychology*, *113*:32-5.

One Look Dictionary Search, www.onelook.com/?w=memory&ls=a (accessed 4 March 2003).

Psychological Corporation (1997). *Wechsler Adult Intelligence Scale. Third Edition Technical Manual*. San Antonio, Texas: The Psychological Corporation.

Reed, S.K. (1992). *Cognition: Theory and applications* (3rd edition). Pacific Grove, California: Brooks/Cole Publishing Company.

Shuttleworth-Jordan, A. (1997). Memory. In D.A. Louw & D.J.A. Edwards (Eds.). *Psychology: An introduction for students in southern Africa* (2nd edition). Johannesburg: Heinemann, pp. 275-320.

Multiple choice questions

1. According to the information processing (IP) approach, memory consists of three aspects. Which one of the following is not one of those aspects?
   a) retrieval
   b) storage
   c) input
   d) throughput

2. Which one of the following statements is false?
   a) the sensory register is part of Atkinson and Shiffrin's store model of memory
   b) the sensory register receives initial acoustic sensory input
   c) the sensory store recognises a stimulus and then passes it on to short-term memory
   d) the sensory store receives input from all sensory modalities

3. Working memory refers to
   a) the memory process that becomes possible once energy flow has been initiated through brain circuits
   b) a replacement of the passive store model of memory, where memory is understood as a more dynamic process
   c) that part of the memory store that remains intact after brain damage
   d) a model understood as consisting of three basic components: the sensory register, short-term memory and long-term memory

4. At a party, you are introduced to someone who looks a lot like Oprah Winfrey. Later, when trying to recall this person's name, all you can recall is Oprah's name. This experience is referred to as
   a) retroactive interference
   b) proactive interference
   c) schema interruption
   d) rapid forgetting

5. The more detailed and developed a schema is
   a) the greater the chance of proactive interference
   b) the easier the process of encoding and retaining information related to that schema
   c) the more difficult and slower the process of encoding and retaining information related to that schema
   d) the more you have a plan that takes into consideration all possible contingencies

6. According to Neisser (1984)
   a) memory is best thought of an ongoing record of events similar to a video tape recording
   b) memory can best be understood by studying it within natural contexts
   c) memory encoding is a highly accurate process where distortions are always indications of brain damage
   d) memory encoding is a highly accurate process where distortions are always indications of poor education

7. Some argue that many memory assessment tests are
   a) based on Western conceptualisations of memory
   b) prejudiced against people from non-Western cultural backgrounds
   c) biased towards particular types of memory skills
   d) all of the above

8. Edwards and Potter (1995) argue that
   a) Neisser makes an important contribution to improving the accuracy of laboratory based memory research
   b) Neisser's ecological approach to memory is removed from the context of the real world
   c) although possible, it is very difficult to attain a neutral and interpretation-free account of an event against which eyewitness accounts can be checked
   d) remembering cannot be separated from the social context in which it occurs

9. As a magistrate you are told about the same event by a person accused of stealing and the shop owner who witnessed the crime. It is important to realise that
   a) the person with the better education will be more accurate in their description
   b) the person with greater social status will be more accurate in their recollection of the event
   c) the accused will always provide a version of the event where he will try to portray himself as innocent
   d) the shop owner will provide a version of the event where he will more often than not portray him self as having objectively witnessed the event

10. Incidental learning refers to
    a) the learning of material where there was no conscious intention to do so
    b) the encoding of events during a motor vehicle accident
    c) the learning that takes place during conscious attempts to study a topic
    d) memories that one demonstrates without being aware of it

Short answer questions

1. What were the shortcomings with the notion of short-term memory (STM)? In what ways does its replacement, working memory, differ from STM?

2. You are trying to remember the name of an actor in a movie you saw last week but the only name that jumps to mind is the name of an actor you saw on television last night! What type of interference is this? What other type of interference is there? What would be an example of this type?

3. Construct a sentence that will allow you to remember the following series of numbers: 200419942010.
   What do we know about our ability to remember that allows me to give you such a task? Does your sentence tie up with a larger schema? Briefly detail the history of this schema in your life.

4. Mistry and Rogoff (1994) argue that we develop particular remembering skills within a specific cultural context. Reflecting on your formal and informal education, what types of information have been accentuated by your culture and society as important? What ways of (or skills for) memorising these forms of information have you been taught directly or indirectly?

5. Imagine that you fail all your exams at the end of this year. How would you share this fact with:
   • your parents, spouse or guardian;
   • your friends; and
   • a mentor?
   Reflect on the differences between these three accounts. What do these variations tell us about these relationships, the kind of society we live in, and the nature of recollection?

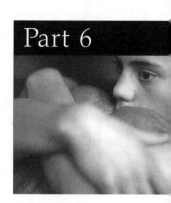

Part 6

Social Psychology

Garth Stevens

Social psychology has traditionally been conceptualised as a sub-discipline of psychology that deals with the manner in which individuals and groups interact as social beings within various contexts. This emphasis on human interaction is illustrated in the common-place contemporary definitions, which state that social psychology is the field of psychology that examines how people affect one another's behaviours, thoughts and feelings.

However, it is also partly the study of how human beings' behaviours are shaped by their social contexts, and how humans in turn interpret these social contexts and shape them. Given that humans are social beings, and that psychology is the study of human behaviour, it is safe to say that psychology is always social. Nevertheless, significant differences exist in defining this sub-discipline, which is constantly being transformed over time, and which can not be construed as a static and unitary or homogeneous field.

This part of the book does not favour a particular approach to social psychology, but engages specifically with some of the most pertinent social phenomena that influence, and are influenced by, human behaviour in the South African and global contexts. Rather than attempting to comprehensively review every facet of social psychology, the following chapters draw on significant findings and debates from experimental social psychology, political psychology, critical psychology, gender studies, peace psychology and public health. In so doing, this part of the book attempts to highlight the most salient forms of social organisation within contemporary social contexts and how they interface with human behaviour. It furthermore provides students with a useful introduction to the diverse areas of study and practice that can potentially constitute the field of social psychology.

In the first chapter, Swart focuses on groups. There is the recognition that humans are social beings, and that one of the primary ways in which this social nature is expressed, demonstrated and influenced, is through group behaviour. This chapter concentrates on some of the basic concepts associated with the study of groups, and outlines properties that are applicable to groups in general, reviews small group dynamics and processes and discusses various theories applicable to social groups.

Terre Blanche's chapter discusses poverty as a social psychological phenomenon. Despite the fact that this area has not traditionally been covered in social psychology, the chapter reveals that the pervasive impact of poverty on the lives and behaviours of ordinary people warrants such a focus. It reviews local and global statistics on poverty and shows how poverty is related to physical ill health. It discusses the dangers of attributing mental ill health to poverty, and details how poor people deal with the challenges of poverty individually and collectively. Finally, it discusses the psychological effects of consumer culture, the depletion of social capital and cultural imperialism on both poor and rich people.

The chapter by Stevens introduces ethnicity as a fluid, dynamic and unfixed social construct, and highlights the integral connectedness between the social and the psychological when examining the particular forms and expressions of ethnicity within different socio-historical contexts. This chapter explores some of the key social psychological mechanisms related to *Othering* (i.e. the process of defining the Self through the creation of an Other). In addition, it examines the relationship between the acquisition of attitudes and stereotypes, and their frequent expressions through social prejudice, discrimination and violence. However, the chapter importantly notes that ethnicity frequently intersects with dominant ideologies that promote a range of social asymmetries – most notably the ideologies of racism, nationalism, anti-Semitism and anti-Islamism. The chapter therefore acknowledges that ethnicity exists as an anthropological and sociological construct, but that through political and ideological processes, it is fundamentally based on, and re-inscribes, social asymmetries within given socio-historical contexts.

Having reviewed group behaviour as a process through which social organisation occurs, the chapter by Boonzaier and de la Rey examines gender and sex as a particular form of social organisation. This chapter reviews the main psychological theories that account for gender/sex differences, and explores key concepts in the study of gender such as the differences between 'sex' and 'gender', gender roles, stereotypes, socialisation, gender constancy and androgyny. In the second part of the chapter, there is a focus on gender in society by highlighting some of the challenges to gender equity and the ways in which the sources of gender inequality have been theorised.

In the penultimate chapter of this part, readers are introduced to the interrelated but distinct areas of violence and traumatic stress. Starting with some recent statistics of violence in South Africa and a discussion of the question of intentionality in defining violence, Higson-Smith looks briefly at some social psychological theory on violence before proposing a systemic model of violence and violence prevention over four levels: individual, small group, community and society. Finally, this chapter discusses integrated violence prevention strategies and interventions for survivors of violence. In so doing, the chapter not only identifies a practical response to this endemic, psychosocial priority in South Africa, but also highlights the potential role of psychology in bridging theory and practice as it attempts to contribute to improved health, equity and social well-being among populations.

The final chapter of this part, by Suffla, focuses almost entirely on the active role that psychology can potentially play in the context of peacemaking and peacebuilding. Unlike the preceding chapters, in which the focus is on forms of social organisation that impact on human behaviour, this chapter argues for a more critical conception of the role of psychology in building peace. It reviews the major assumptions underpinning the theory and practice of peace processes, and highlights the conceptual contours that differentiate the concepts of peacemaking and peacebuilding. The chapter concludes with illustrative examples derived from the global context to support and contextualise the theoretical discussion on peacemaking and peacebuilding.

19

Group Concepts, Processes and Dynamics

Tanya Swart

CHAPTER OBJECTIVES

After studying this chapter you should be able to:
- understand the reasons why individuals belong to groups, and the different ways in which groups have been defined
- locate the study of groups within the field of social psychology
- identify different types of groups that exist
- understand the features of small groups and some of the small group processes studied by social psychologists
- demonstrate a basic understanding of phenomena related to social groups, some of the earlier theories of intergroup relations and social identity theory.

Nosipho didn't really enjoy being in groups and tended to avoid them. Before coming to university she had spent her much of her time with just a few good friends. Being a bit of a loner, she was also quite used to her own company. She supposed it was shyness mostly that kept her away from big groups. But as she began to think about the social psychology of groups more deeply she wondered whether she had really managed to steer clear of groups as successfully as she imagined.

Nosipho might not have deliberately chosen to join clubs or teams but she certainly had been a part of her school whether she liked it or not – and sometimes she didn't! She was now of course also a member of her university. If someone saw her walking along the path that led to the campus as she did each morning, they would naturally assume that she was a learner. It was strange to think that others might see you as part of a group even when you weren't aware of it yourself. Sitting in the lecture hall, Nosipho looked around her she was suddenly aware that she was also a part of the psychology class. She was a member of a group right here and now! She didn't always feel like she quite fitted in with everybody – but even so here she was sitting quietly at a desk just like everyone else in the room. 'There were certainly some very effective group norms operating in the lecture hall', she acknowledged to herself. It was accepted that learners would sit and face the lecturer, write notes and not talk loudly amongst themselves. If one of the learners had suddenly got up and rushed towards the front of the room taking the lecturer's place, everyone would be most surprised. By accepting those group norms she was taking her place firmly in the group.

Nosipho mostly thought about herself as a separate individual, thinking her own private thoughts and making her own life plans. But it seemed clear to her now that the way she felt and behaved was being influenced far more by group membership than she realised. Her family was a kind of a group, a small one, but a group nonetheless. She saw herself as South African and that also made her a member of a very large kind of group – the nation. Most of the time she wasn't even thinking about these group memberships but it was true that she did identify with at least some elements. Like most of us though, Nosipho only became aware of her many group memberships when someone or something reminded her.

Introduction

Humans are social beings and one of the ways in which this social nature is expressed, demonstrated and influenced is through groups. Our participation in and interaction with various groups is an integral part of our daily lives. However, in order to truly understand the influence of groups on social life, it is necessary to examine groups more closely by looking at some of their fundamental qualities and dynamics. This chapter focuses on some of the basic concepts associated with the study of groups, and is intended to form an introductory understanding of group behaviour. The chapter outlines general group properties, concepts and processes that refer mainly to small social groups, and theories applicable to larger social groups.

For almost a century, social scientists have recognised the significance of groups in our lives (Worshel & Shebilske, 1994). Early experiments and observations from the late nineteenth century to early twentieth century suggested that groups influenced people and that this influence required further investigation. However, within psychology, Floyd Allport questioned this view, stating that primacy should by given to the study of individuals, not groups, and that groups were no more than a composite of the qualities of their individual members (Worschel & Shebilske, 1994). In contrast to this position, Solomon Asch later argued that groups were unique social organisms with properties and cannot be fully understood by studying individuals alone (Weiten, 1995). That is, as Gestalt psychology purports, 'the whole is more than the sum of its parts' (Weiten, 1995).

Over the past century the study of groups has expanded to such an extent that it is no longer the domain of any single branch of psychology (Worshel & Shebilske, 1994). Instead, groups are an important focal area in fields such as organisational psychology, developmental psychology, clinical psychology, cross-cultural psychology, community psychology and many others (Worshel & Shebilske, 1994). In addition, the study of groups is also a fundamental part of a number of other disciples in the social sciences, such as social anthropology, sociology and political science. However, this chapter introduces some of the basic understandings of groups from a social psychological perspective.

Reasons for group belonging

In order to understand group properties and dynamics, it is necessary to first look at some of the reasons why people belong to or form groups. Although groups are not always consciously formed, they function to fulfil many basic and intertwined human needs that cannot be satisfied by individuals alone (Bordens & Horowitz, 2002). These include biological, psychological, social, cultural and practical needs. For instance, groups fulfil our need for affiliation (Buunk, 2001), as well as for love and belonging (Maslow, 1954). Groups also play a large role in influencing individual self-esteem and in the development of the self-concept (Bordens & Horowitz, 2002). Furthermore, groups are an important source of social support, offer us information about the social world and ourselves and satisfy our need for social comparison (Festinger, 1954). Groups also provide a context in which individuals can pool their resources and solve problems more effectively collectively rather than individually (Bordens & Horowitz, 2002).

Group definitions

In everyday life, most people would refer to a group as a collection of people. However, various theorists have attempted to provide definitions of groups based on the presence of certain properties. Moghaddham (1998) distinguishes between definitions of groups that give salience to objective factors and those that give salience to subjective factors. An objective approach would be to consider an aggregate of individuals to be a group based on perceptions of common characteristics by an outsider. Ross (1968) refers to this type of group as a *statistical group*. A subjective approach would be to consider people to be a group when they perceive or categorise themselves as a group (e.g., Tajfel, 1978). Ross (1968) refers to this type of group as a *societal group*. Membership of a societal group does not necessarily imply interaction with other members, but membership nevertheless affects behaviour.

Brown (1988:2-3) asserts a definition that combines both subjective and objective dimensions: 'A group exists when two or more people define themselves as members of it and when its existence is recognised by at least one other'. Thus, according to this definition, a group exists when it is seen to exist both by its members and at least one outsider.

While group definitions based on objective and subjective factors do not necessarily imply interaction with other members of the group, this is the premise of what is referred to as a *social group* (Ross, 1968). By contrast, a *non-social group* exists when two or more people are present at the same time and place but are not interacting with each other (Aronson *et al.*, 1994). Within social psychology, the most important characteristics of social groups have been defined as interdependence among group members, interaction between them and mutual influence (Bordens & Horowitz, 2002; Forsyth, 1995). For instance, Forsyth (1995) defines a group as two or more interdependent individuals who influence one another through social interaction. Mutual influence arises out of the verbal or non-verbal information that members exchange (Bordens & Horowitz, 2002).

Overall, the various definitions highlight some of the complexities of groups and the variety of perspectives that have been taken to understand them. Examining some of the different types of groups that exist also assists in bringing greater understanding of this social phenomenon.

Types of social groups

There are many different ways of classifying groups. One of the simplest classifications involves the 'us' (the in-group) and 'them' (the out-group) typology. *In-groups* are groups to which people belong or think they belong, and *out-groups*, are those to which they do not belong or think they do not belong (Brown, 1998; Moghaddham, 1998). This classification of groups can be used for both small and large social groups.

Another useful distinction has been made between *primary groups*, *secondary groups* and *reference groups* (Moghaddham, 1998). Primary groups generally have a small membership and are characterised by intimate direct interactions, strong levels of group identification, strong affective ties between group members, multifaceted relationships and a long period of existence (Cooley, 1956). These groups are referred to as primary because of the role they have been conceptualised to play in personality development and primary socialisation (Cooley, 1956). The most common example of a primary group is the family. By contrast, in secondary groups there are few direct interactions, weak levels of identification with the group, weak affective ties

between group members, limited or functional relationships and a short period of existence (Moghaddam, 1998). An example of a secondary group could be a sports team or a university class. In this case, there may be individuals who have more long-standing relationships or more direct interactions in the group, but the group itself exists for more functional reasons and are relatively short-term in nature. A reference group is a group to which a person does not formally belong but with which she or he identifies (Moghaddham, 1998), or which he or she uses as a frame of reference (Appelgryn, 1991). That is, a reference group refers to any group which individuals use to guide and inform their values, attitudes, self-image and behaviours, but of which they do not have formal membership (Appelgryn, 1991). An example of a reference group could be an association, interest group or political group with which we identify, but do not formally belong as a member.

Figure 1 The family: A primary group

Small group characteristics

Social psychologists have attempted to understand small social groups by examining their characteristics. While social groups vary in many ways, they share certain common features that affect their functioning (Weiten, 1995). These regularities are said to reflect the group's *structure* or the stable underlying pattern of relationships among its members (Cartwright & Zander in Forsyth, 1995). Characteristics that social groups have in common are that most of them have a purpose for existing, norms about appropriate behaviour, a differential allocation of roles and responsibilities, a communication structure, differing levels of status and influence among members, a level of cohesiveness and attraction between members (Forsyth, 1990, 1995; Wilke & Wit, 2001). These characteristics are discussed further in the sections that follow.

Purpose

Social groups typically have a *purpose* or reason for existing, which may be implicit or explicit. According to Forsyth (1995), this purpose is generally *instrumental* (aimed at performing a task or achieving a goal) or *affiliative* (aimed at fulfilling the needs for support and interpersonal contact).

Norms

Members of small social groups usually develop *group norms* or shared expectations about the kinds of behaviours that are acceptable and are required by all group members. According to Bordens and Horowitz (2002:239), a norm is 'an unwritten social rule existing either on a wide cultural level or on a smaller, situation-specific level that suggests what is appropriate behaviour in a situation.' According to Tredoux (1991), group norms can be both prescriptive (recommend certain behaviours) and proscriptive (forbid certain behaviours).

Roles

Within a small social group, each individual member has a particular *role* or function – either formal or informal – that specifies the types of behaviour that are expected of him or her. There are many roles in groups, but most theorists draw a distinction between two basic types, *task roles* and *socio-emotional roles* (Forsyth, 1995). Task roles are those that focus on the attainment of group goals. Socio-emotional roles focus on the quality of the relationships among group members and include performing supportive, interpersonally-accommodative behaviours (Forsyth, 1995). One of the commonly identified group roles is that of the group leader. The role of the leader locates a person in a specific position of influence within the group that is separate from their role as individuals, and requires that they perform specific functions that advance the group towards it goals (Callan *et al.*, 1986).

Communication

Small groups usually have a particular pattern of communication that structures the flow of information between group members. This pattern is referred to as the group's *communication network* (Forsyth, 1995). The communication network will determine, for instance, who speaks, how often and to whom, and whether information flows through one person or through many individuals (Forsyth, 1995).

Status

Group members often have differing levels of *status* or prestige within a group (Forsyth, 1995). Status hierarchies occur in both formally and informally organised groups. Groups frequently confer status on exceptionally skilled individuals who contribute significantly to the group. However, qualities that have little relevance to the aims of a group, such as unrecognised prejudices, can also influence status within a group (Forsyth, 1995).

Socio-metric structure

In most small social groups, some group members are better liked than others are (Forsyth, 1995).

19.1 CROWD BEHAVIOUR

In examining the different functions of group norms in regulating intergroup behaviour, early theorists suggested that individuals acting in large groups may behave more aggressively or impulsively than when acting individually (Mummendey & Otten, 2001). In contemporary social psychology, this tendency is referred to as a process of *deindividuation*. Deindividuation is a large group phenomenon in which rational control and normative behaviour are weakened, resulting in a greater propensity to respond in an extreme manner and violate norms (Mummendey & Otten, 2001). Anonymity, diffusion of responsibility and a shortened time perspective have been identified as contributing towards this phenomenon (Mummendey & Otten, 2001). Deindividuation theory has previously been used to understand phenomena in South Africa's apartheid history such as necklacing. However, current perspectives on group processes recognise that deindividuation only partially accounts for such phenomena.

Patterns of liking and disliking form a group's *sociometric structure* (Doreian, 1986). This determines, for instance, which group members are most popular, which are neglected or rejected by the group, and which are average members who are liked by several others in the group (Coie *et al.*, Newcomb & Bukowski and Newcomb *et al.* in Forsyth, 1995).

Cohesiveness

A group's cohesiveness refers to the strength of the relationships linking the members to one another and to the group itself (Forsyth, 1995). Individuals in a cohesive group are proud to identify themselves as group members, and will defend the group against outside criticism (Forsyth, 1995). Group cohesiveness can be influenced by mutual attraction between group members (Levine & Moreland, 1990), propinquity, adherence to group norms and goal attainment (Bordens & Horowitz, 2002).

Small group influence

Several processes of small group influence have been identified and studied by social psychologists. In terms of decision-making, an area of interest has been investigating the effects of the presence of others on the nature of decisions reached. Group polarisation and groupthink are two important phenomena related to group decision-making:

- *Group polarisation* refers to the tendency for pre-existing individual opinions, ideas or positions to become more extreme or polarised following a group discussion (Bordens & Horowitz, 2002; Van Avermaet, 2001). This is seen to result from the process of normative or social comparison and persuasive arguments or informational influence (Bordens & Horowitz, 2002).
- *Groupthink* was first identified by Irving Janis and is a group process phenomenon that may lead to faulty decision-making by group members who are more concerned with reaching consensus than with carefully considering alternative courses of action (Bordens & Horowitz, 2002). Symptoms of groupthink are: the illusion of invulnerability, rationalisation, an unquestioned belief in the group's morality, a stereotyped view of the enemy, conformity pressures, self-censorship, the illusion of unanimity and the emergence of self-appointed mindguards (Bordens & Horowitz, 2002). Groupthink is likely to occur

when the group is highly cohesive, isolated from important sources of information, has a biased leader and is under decisional stress (Forsyth, 1995).

Social psychologists have also investigated group process related to performance. In some instances, groups have a positive influence on performance. A series of studies by Norman Triplett in 1898 verified a positive group performance phenomenon known as *social facilitation*, which occurs when there is improved individual task performance when working with others or in the presence of an audience (Forsyth, 1995). Zajonc (1965) found that social facilitation is more likely to occur when individuals perform tasks that are well learned, well rehearsed or instinctive. However, if individuals are required to perform tasks that are novel, complicated or are based on little prior experience, they are likely to perform better in the absence of others (Forsyth, 1995).

Groups may also have a negative effect on individual performance. *Social loafing* is a performance-inhibiting effect that involves relaxing individual effort based on the assumption that others will compensate (Bordens & Horowitz, 2002). Thus, some individuals will make less effort when working in a group than they would individually (Bordens & Horowitz, 2002). Social loafing is more likely to occur when completing everyday, repetitive tasks, and less likely when there are important tasks to complete (Williams & Karau in Bordens & Horowitz, 2002).

Figure 2 The group decision-making process

Social influence

Social psychologists explain social behaviour through examining various types of social influence. Social influence refers to the change in an individual's judgments, opinions and attitudes that occurs because of exposure to the judgments, opinions and attitudes of other individuals (Van Avermaet, 2001). Majority influence or *conformity* is one kind of social influence that involves modifying individual behaviour in response to real or imagined pressure from others. Deutsch and Gerrard (1955) identified two sources of influence that result in the pressure to conform: *informational social influence* and *normative social influence*. Informational social influence refers to the type of social influence that results from an individual's response to information provided by others (Bordens & Horowitz, 2002). According to Tredoux (1991), we are susceptible to informational social influence because we want to make accurate and informed judgments and opinions, and use other people's judgments to validate or evaluate our own. Normative social influence refers to social influence that results from an individual's response to pressure to conform to a norm (Bordens & Horowitz, 2002).

While there is compelling evidence of the power of majority influence on individual behaviour (Forsyth, 1995), some theorists such as Serge Moscovici and his colleagues (Moscovici, 1980, 1985; Moscovici & Lage, 1976; Moscovici & Nemeth, 1974) have been more concerned with investigating minority influence in groups. From these and other studies, certain conditions have been identified which facilitate minorities being able to influence the majority position in a group (Moghaddam, 1998). The central determinant of minority influence is that of *consistency* (Tredoux, 1991). Minorities are more likely to influence the majority if they maintain a firm and clear position on an issue, and are able to withstand pressures to conform (Van Avermaet, 2001). If so, they will be viewed as being confident in their judgments or opinions (Bordens & Horowitz, 2002). Another factor that has been found to affect minority influence is *rigidity* (Moghaddam, 1998). Minorities who are perceived as being consistent but rigid in their position are likely to have less group influence, while those that show flexibility are likely to have more influence on the majority (Bordens & Horowitz, 2002).

Another important type of social influence studied by social psychologists is the phenomenon of obedience. Obedience is a social influence process in which individual behaviour is modified in response to a command from an authority figure (Bordens & Horowitz, 2002).

Doise (1986) outlines four levels of analysis that assist social psychologists in taking the various dimensions of social influence into consideration. At the individual level, social behaviour is explained in terms of internal dispositions or processes, which include personality traits, emotions and cognitive

19.2 CLASSIC STUDIES IN CONFORMITY

Muzafer Sherif (1935) utilised the autokinetic effect, an optical illusion of movement of a single stationary point of light when viewed in the dark, to demonstrate the powers of social influence. Participants were placed alone or in small groups in a darkened room and presented with a small stationary light at a distance of 5 metres. When participants estimated the amount the light moved by themselves, their responses fluctuated around personal norms that differed between individuals. When participants gave their estimates in a group, the responses converged to form a group norm. Once established, adherence to the group norm persisted in subsequent individual trials indicating that individuals formed a joint frame of reference when with others that continued to affect their judgments in the absence of this form of influence.

Solomon Asch (1951) investigated whether the presence of others would influence individual judgments when group members held obviously incorrect viewpoints. Asch told groups with seven participants that he was investigating visual discrimination and tasked them with deciding which of three comparison lines was equal in length to a standard line over eighteen trials. The experimental group comprised only one true participant and six confederates. On each trial, the confederates unanimously offered a predetermined response. On six trials, this response was correct. On the remaining trials, they gave unanimous incorrect responses. The results revealed that individuals made errors consistent with the incorrect majority significantly more often when compared to their individual error rate.

In Stanley Milgram's (1963) study on obedience, each recruited participant was met by an experimenter and a confederate participant and told that the task they were to perform involved investigating the effects of punishment on learning. The participant was assigned the role of teacher and the confederate that of learner through a rigged selection procedure. They were taken to a room where the learner was strapped into a chair and fixed with electrodes. The experimenter explained that the learner would receive a painful but not permanently damaging electric shock for punishment. The teacher was led to an adjoining room, and given instructions on the learning task. The teacher communicated with the learner via an intercom system and was given a control panel for administering shocks ranging from 'slight' (15V) to 'severe' (450V) in 15V increments. The teacher was instructed to administer increased levels of electrical shock for every learning error. The apparatus appeared genuine and the teacher was given a sample shock to increase its believability.

Once the task commenced, the confederate made numerous deliberate errors to coerce the teacher into administering stronger shocks and acted accordingly. The experimenter insisted that the teacher continue whenever reservations were expressed and assumed all responsibility. Approximately two-thirds of the participants continued to the maximum shock level, and none stopped before 300V. The findings suggested that when given orders by a person seen to be a legitimate authority figure that will take responsibility for the actions, people may inflict harm on innocent individuals.

mechanisms. At the interpersonal or situational level, behaviour is understood as resulting from an interaction with other individuals or particular situational contexts. At the group or positional level, behaviour is explained in terms of group membership. The ideological level takes into account widely shared systems of ideas and social practices that perpetuate the domination of one group over another. This framework locates groups within a broader structure of power relations while simultaneously recognising the contributing influence of intra- and interpersonal factors.

Social groups and intergroup relations

Most of this chapter has focused on group concepts and processes that are usually applied to the understanding of small groups, but can also be identified in broader social groups. However, the field of social psychology has also focused on a larger array of phenomena related to broader social groups. Significant among these has been the development of theories aimed at explaining intergroup behaviour. According to Billig (1976), when we deal with intergroup relations, we are addressing the social fabric of our society. Intergroup behaviour refers to 'actions by members of one group towards members of another group' (Brown, 2001:480) and occurs when members of one group act towards another in terms of their group membership rather than for personal or idiosyncratic reasons (Brown, 2001). This section provides an overview of some of the most significant theories of intergroup behaviour, locating each within the framework provided by Doise (1986). It provides a particular focus on social identity theory, which has made the most significant advances in our understanding of the relationship between the individual, group and wider society (de la Rey, 1991).

Intergroup relations: Individual-level explanations

Freudian theory is one example of an individual level theory that has been applied to the understanding of intergroup behaviour. This approach is based on the extension of Freud's individual-level psychological concepts to the group context. From this perspective, the unconscious processes that drive individual behaviour are seen as the foundation for any group or intergroup behaviour (de la Rey, 1991; Moghaddam, 1998). Similarly located on the individual level, the *frustration-aggression theory* (Dollard et al., 1939) maintains that intergroup phenomena are based on displaced aggression arising from frustration that emerges when group goals are not attained (de la Rey, 1991). The frustration, which is most likely caused by an in-group member, induces aggression towards an out-group in order to preserve group cohesion (de la Rey, 1991).

Intergroup relations: Interpersonal-level explanations

Social exchange theory (Thibaut & Kelley, 1959) provides an economic model of relationships and suggests that people interact with others and evaluate relationships in terms of the rewards they offer and costs they entail (Bordens & Horowitz, 2002). Outcomes are decided by subtracting the costs from the rewards, and people tend to seek and maintain relationships that have positive and fair outcomes. Similarly, *equity theory* encompasses the same principles, but they are articulated more formally. Within this theory, contributions made to a relationship are referred to as inputs, while any benefits received are called outputs (Foster, 1993). Like social exchange theory, equity theory maintains that people assess relationships in terms of rewards and costs, but includes a focus on the perceived equity of the contributions in relationships (Hatfield *et al.* in Bordens & Horowitz, 2002). Equity occurs when the ratios of inputs and outputs are the same for both participants (Foster, 1993).

Intergroup relations: Positional-level explanations

Theories of intergroup relations at the positional or group level view intergroup behaviour as being a function of individuals acting in terms of their group membership. Sherif's (1966) *realistic conflict theory* focuses on the emergence and resolution of intergroup conflict (de la Rey, 1991). The theory asserts that group conflict results from incompatible goals or interests, or competition between groups over scarce resources. Social harmony is seen to result from co-operative activities and the achievement of goals that both groups desire but neither can achieve in the absence of assistance from the other group (Moghaddam, 1998). According to the *relative deprivation theory*, a sense of relative deprivation emerges when members of a disadvantaged group recognise that they are undervalued and have fewer social rewards than a preferred group (Bordens & Horowitz, 2002). This leads to social discontent and unrest (de la Rey, 1991), which motivates attempts at social change (Brown, 2001). *Resource mobilisation theory* conceptualises these intergroup dynamics from a materialist perspective. According to this theory, intergroup conflicts arise when those with resources mobilise and take collective action (Moghaddam, 1998).

Social identity theory (SIT) is another positional-level approach to the understanding of intergroup behaviour based on the premise that group membership is a fundamental component of identity (Foster,

19.4 THE DILEMMA OVER THE EXTENT OF INDIVIDUAL VERSUS GROUP INFLUENCE IN SOCIAL BEHAVIOUR

One of the tensions alluded to in this chapter within the field of social psychology is the extent to which individuals influence group behaviour and groups influence individual behaviour. Certain concepts that have been discussed, such as minority influence, clearly indicate the power of social minorities to exert social influence. The phenomenon of obedience similarly demonstrates both the power and danger of numerical minorities with social authority and power to exert social influence on individuals, often resulting in the individual feeling exempt from taking individual responsibility. This is particularly evident in the events of South Africa's apartheid history if we examine the ways in which the apartheid government sanctioned the massacre of Black South Africans in various townships over decades, and how armed military forces carried out instructions to fulfil this mandate.

However, other concepts discussed in the chapter indicate the profound effect of groups on individual behaviour, as is demonstrated through phenomena such as social facilitation, social loafing, deindividuation and conformity. Similarly, with regard to theories of intergroup relations, we see the same tension between those that maintain that individualistic factors determine the ways in which group members behave and those in which larger group or social factors determine the behaviour of individual members. The dilemma arises out of conflicting evidence regarding the salience of each. Social psychologists have attempted to resolve the dilemma by identifying specific contextual or situational features that contribute to the influence of the group over the individual or the individual over the group. However, the predicament is related to a more circular philosophical dilemma of whether individuals can exist without groups or groups without individuals. Given this impossibility, it remains a challenge to determine the nature of the relationship between individuals and groups, and the conditions which determine which has greater influence in a particular social context.

Figure 3 Crowds are social groups, open to the processes of deindividuation, minority influence, majority influence, social identity theory and ideology

to maintain and enhance self-esteem (Bordens & Horowitz, 2002). They also select group memberships based on their perceived success in meeting social challenges (Campbell & Robinson in Campbell, 1995).

Intergroup relations: Ideological-level explanations

The ideological level provides a different perspective on intergroup relations in that it refers to widespread complex belief systems that determine group behaviour. Foster (1993) emphasises the importance of understanding the relationship between the positional and ideological levels, by arguing that when people identify with a group they may take on the underlying ideology. Thus SIT could be seen to deal with both of these explanatory dimensions. However, similar to some of the other theories presented in this section, SIT has also been criticised on a number of levels for neglecting the broader social context, and because it is based primarily on the findings of experimental research it does not acknowledge the complexity of intergroup relations (Abrams in Bornman & Appelgryn, 1999). Also, it fails to account for ideological processes that create and maintain power relations of dominance and conditions of oppression (de la Rey, 1991; Foster, 1991; Stevens, 2001).

Conclusion

This chapter has attempted to present some of the basic concepts, process and dynamics in the study of group behaviour through examining both small and broader social groups. Although these concepts are presented as an introduction to a complex area of theorising, they nevertheless offer some of the foundations and tools that can be used to understand many historical and current social events, such as the abolition of apartheid in South Africa and the mass killings in Rwanda (Van Avermaet, 2001). Although the field of social psychology has developed over the years to include more complex theories of social influence and group behaviour, the basic concepts presented in this chapter have played an influential role in shaping our understanding of the ways in which individuals influence and are influenced by others.

1993). According to SIT, individuals internalise and integrate group membership as part of the social component of their self-concepts (Mokgatle & Schoeman, 1998). Social identity is defined as 'the individual's knowledge that he belongs to certain social groups, together with some emotional and value significance to him of group membership' (Tajfel, 1972:31), or 'that part of an individual's self-concept which derives from his knowledge of his membership to his social group' (Tajfel, 1981:255). Examples of this include defining identity in terms of group memberships related to language, race, culture gender, profession or religious affiliation.

Social identity formation is a process whereby the individual becomes part of a group and the group becomes part of the individual's self-concept. SIT proposes that individuals strive to achieve a positive social identity partially though their group membership, and will take action to remedy the situation if they perceive their social identity to be inadequate (Bordens & Horowitz, 2002; Moghaddam, 1998). Individuals are motivated to evaluate their own groups more favourably than other groups in order

Appelgryn, E.M. (1991). Social comparison and relative deprivation: Perceived justice and intergroup attitudes. In D. Foster & J. Louw-Potgieter (Eds.). *Social Psychology in South Africa*. Johannesburg: Lexicon, pp. 237-72.

Aronson, E., Wilson, T.D. & Akert, R.M. (1994). *Social Psychology: The heart and the mind*. New York: HarperCollins.

Asch, S.E. (1951). Effects of group pressure upon the modification and distortion of judgments. In H. Guetzkow (Ed.). *Groups, leadership, and men*. Pittsburgh, PA: Carnegie Press, pp. 177-90.

Billig, M. (1976). *Social Psychology and Intergroup Relations*. London: Academic Press.

Bordens, K.S. & Horowitz, I.A. (2002). *Social psychology* (2nd edition). London: Lawrence Erlbaum Associates.

Bornman, E. & Appelgryn, E.M. (1999). Predictors of ethnic identification in a transitionary South Africa. *South African Journal of Psychology*, 29(2):62-71.

Brown, R. (1988). *Group Processes: Dynamics within and between groups*. Oxford: Blackwell.

Brown, R. (2001). Intergroup relations. In M. Hewstone & W. Stroebe (Eds.). *Introduction to Social Psychology: A European perspective*. Oxford: Blackwell, pp. 479-518.

Buunk, B.P. (2001). Affiliation, attraction and close relationships. In M. Hewstone & W. Stroebe (Eds.). *Introduction to Social Psychology: A European perspective*. Oxford: Blackwell, pp. 371-402.

Callan, V., Gallois, C. & Noller, P. (1986). *Social Psychology*. Sydney: Harcourt Brace Jovanovich.

Campbell, C.M. (1995). The social identity of township youth: An extension of Social Identity Theory. *South African Journal of Psychology*, 25(3):150-9.

Cooley, C.H. (1956). *Social Organisation*. Glencoe: Free Press.

de la Rey, C. (1991). Intergroup relations: Theories and positions. In D. Foster & J. Louw-Potgieter (Eds.). *Social Psychology in South Africa*. Johannesburg: Lexicon, pp. 27-56.

Deutsch, M. & Gerrard, H.B. (1955). A study of normative and informational social influences upon individual judgement. *Journal of Abnormal and Social Psychology*, 51:629-36.

Doise, W. (1986). *Levels of Explanation in Social Psychology*. New York: Cambridge University Press.

Dollard, J., Doob, L.W., Miller, N.E., Mower, O.H. & Sears, R.R. (1939). *Frustration and Aggression*. New Haven: Yale University Press.

Doreian, P. (1986). Measuring relative standing in small groups and bounded social networks. *Social Psychology Quarterly*, 49:247-59.

Festinger, L. (1954). A theory of social comparison processes. *Human Relations*, 7:117-40.

Forsyth, D.R. (1990). *Group Dynamics* (2nd edition). Pacific Grove, CA: Brooks/Cole.

Forsyth, D.R. (1995). *Our Social World*. Pacific Grove: Brooks/Cole Publishing Company.

Foster, D. (1991). Introduction. In D. Foster & J. Louw-Potgieter (Eds.). *Social Psychology in South Africa*. Johannesburg: Lexicon, pp. 395-440.

Foster, D. (1993). Social psychology. In D.A. Louw & D.J.A Edwards (Eds.). *Psychology: An introduction for students in southern Africa*. Johannesburg: Lexicon, pp. 731-87.

Levine, J.M. & Moreland, R.L. (1990). Progress in small group research. *Annual Review of Psychology*, 41:585-634.

Maslow, A.H. (1954). *Motivation and Personality*. New York: Harper & Row.

Milgram, S. (1963). Behavioural study of obedience. *Journal of Abnormal and Social Psychology*, 67(4):371-8.

Moghaddam, F.M. (1998). *Social Psychology: Exploring universals across cultures*. New York: W.H. Freeman & Company.

Mokgatle, B.P. & Schoeman, J.B. (1998). Predictors of satisfaction with life: The role of racial identity, collective self-esteem and gender-role attitudes. *South African Journal of Psychology*, 28(1):28-35.

Moscovici, S. (1980). Toward a theory of conversion behaviour. In L. Berkowitz (Ed.). *Advances in experimental social psychology* (Vol. 13). New York: Academic Press, pp. 209-39.

Moscovici, S. (1985). Social influence and conformity. In G. Lindzey & E. Aronson (Eds.). *Handbook of Social Psychology* (3rd edition). Hillsdale, NJ: Erlbaum, pp. 347-412.

Moscovici, S. & Lage, E. (1976). Studies in social influence: III. Majority versus minority influence in a group. *European Journal of Social Psychology*, 6:149-74.

Moscovici, S. & Nemeth, C. (1974). Minority influence. In C. Nemeth (Ed.). *Social Psychology: Classic and contemporary integrations*. Chicago: Rand McNally.

Mummendey, A. & Otten, S. (2001). Aggressive behaviour. In M. Hewstone & W. Stroebe (Eds.). *Introduction to Social Psychology: A European perspective*. Oxford: Blackwell, pp. 315-40.

Ross, H.L. (1968). *Perspectives on the Social Order: Readings in Sociology* (2nd edition). New York: McGraw-Hill.

Sherif, M. (1935). *The Psychology of Social Norms*. New York: Harper.

Sherif, M. (1966). *Group Conflict and Co-operation*. London: Routledge & Kegan Paul.

Stevens, G. (2001). Critically reviewing academic discourses on race and racism in post-apartheid South Africa: Contributions from within the field of psychology. Paper presented at the conference on *International Perspectives on Race, Ethnicity and Intercultural Relations*, 18-22 April, Oxford, Mississippi.

Tajfel, H. (1972). Experiments in a vacuum. In J. Israel & H. Tajfel (Eds.). *The Context of Social Psychology*. London: Academic Press, pp. 69-119.

Tajfel, H. (1978). *Differentiation Between Social Groups*. London: Academic Press.

Tajfel, H. (1981). *Human Groups and Social Categories*. Cambridge: Cambridge University Press.

Thibaut, J.W. & Kelley, H.H. (1959). *The Social Psychology of Groups*. New York: Wiley.

Tredoux, C. (1991). Social influence II: Majorities and minorities. In D. Foster & J. Louw-Potgieter (Eds.). *Social Psychology in South Africa*. Johannesburg: Lexicon, pp. 395-440.

Van Avermaet, E. (2001). Social influence in small groups. In M. Hewstone & W. Stroebe (Eds.). *Introduction to Social Psychology: A European perspective*. Oxford: Blackwell, pp. 403-44.

Weiten, W. (1995). *Psychology: Themes and variations* (3rd edition). Pacific Grove: Brooks/Cole Publishing Company.

Wilke, H. & Wit, A. (2001). Group performance. In M. Hewstone & W. Stroebe (Eds.). *Introduction to Social Psychology: A European perspective*. Oxford: Blackwell, pp. 445-79.

Worshel, W. & Shebilske, W. (1994). *Psychology: Principles and applications* (5th edition). Engelwood Cliffs, New Jersey: Prentice-Hall.

Zajonc, R.B. (1965). Social facilitation. *Science*, 149:269-74.

Multiple choice questions

1. Which of the following types of groups represents an objective approach to defining groups?
   a) out-groups
   b) societal groups
   c) statistical groups
   d) social groups

2. A group's socio-metric structure refers to
   a) patterns of liking and disliking among group members
   b) the measurement of social influence by one group member on another
   c) patterns of social communication among group members
   d) the underlying social structure of a group

3. Which of the following terms is used to refer to majority influence?
   a) compliance
   b) obedience
   c) group polarisation
   d) conformity

4. Which of the following is not one of the levels of understanding social behaviour described by Doise (1986)?
   a) the social level
   b) the interpersonal level
   c) the individual level
   d) the ideological level

5. Minorities are more likely to influence the majority if they are
   a) rigid
   b) consistent and flexible
   c) consistent and rigid
   d) dominant

6. Social facilitation refers to
   a) a group process phenomenon that occurs when an individual facilitates social interaction
   b) a form of majority social influence
   c) a group phenomenon which occurs when an individual's task performance improves when working with others or in the presence of an audience
   d) a group process phenomenon which occurs when an individual's task performance improves group decision-making

7. Freudian theory and frustration aggression theory are theories used to understand intergroup behaviour at the
   a) positional level
   b) individual level
   c) interpersonal level
   d) ideological level

8. Social identity theory has been criticised for
   a) neglecting the broader social context and the complexity of inter-group relations
   b) being based primarily on the findings of experimental research
   c) failing to account for ideological processes that create and maintain power relations of dominance and conditions of oppression
   d) all of the above

9. Roles and norms are typical characteristics of
   a) statistical groups
   b) all groups
   c) non-social groups
   d) social groups

10. The social influence process in which individual behaviour is modified in response to a command from an authority figure is called
    a) obedience
    b) conformity
    c) minority influence
    d) deindividuation

Short answer questions

1. Explore your own identity through describing yourself according to the prompt: I am ... Identify which of these descriptors indicate your own internalisation of group membership, are subject to group influence or represent any of the various types of groups described in this chapter.

2. Collect one contemporary South African newspaper article that indicates or refers to the powers of group or social influence. Analyse and discuss the article.

3. In a courtroom scenario using a jury system, where a person's guilt or innocence is determined by a group of their peers, identify the types of group processes and social influence that may impact on decisions taken by a jury and explain the factors that contribute to the likelihood of each occurring.

4. Describe your own social identity by indicating those components of your identity that represent the internalisation of various types of group membership discussed in the chapter. Discuss how the group components of your identity may differ from

how you are perceived by others and how your social identity may influence your behaviour in relation to those with the same and different group memberships.

5. Select two theories of intergroup relations discussed in this chapter that are located in different levels of Doise's (1986) model and explain the ways in which each of these can be used to understand intergroup behaviour in relation to a contemporary or historical South African issue of your choice, reflecting on the strengths and weaknesses of each approach.

20

Poverty

Martin Terre Blanche

CHAPTER OBJECTIVES

After studying this chapter, you should be able to:
- describe global levels of poverty
- place South Africa relative to other countries in terms of levels of poverty and inequality
- describe the relationship between race, gender, the urban-rural divide and poverty
- list and describe the negative effects of poverty on physical health
- list and describe the effects of poverty on mental health in terms of the unique challenges poor people have to deal with
- explain why claiming that poverty always leads to mental ill health is problematic
- describe key elements of how people experience and respond to poverty as individuals and collectives
- list and describe some of the negative effects of consumer culture on both rich and poor people
- describe the depletion of social capital and the phenomenon of cultural imperialism as forms of impoverishment.

Nosipho couldn't decide if she had grown up rich or poor. If she compared herself to the film stars and millionaires she saw on TV, or even to people who lived in the smart White suburbs and drove big fancy cars, she supposed she would be considered poor. But when she compared her family to many of those who lived in the township, she felt that she had been quite well off. Her father had enjoyed a good job as a salesman and her mother worked part time as a nurse. They had always had enough to eat, buy nice clothes and even enough money to help out with relatives who were struggling financially.

Both her parents spoke about their experiences of having grown up in poor families. They had had to work very hard to give their children all the advantages they had experienced. Nosipho's Mom had told her how she had studied nursing in the day and worked at night as a cleaner to earn enough to cover her fees and board, and she still had to send money home to her family. Her father had given up his own dream of going to university because his family couldn't afford it. He had had to go

out to work instead. Nosipho felt very grateful that she didn't have to fight as hard to get what she wanted in her life. Everyone says that money doesn't buy happiness – but Nosipho knew that her life would have probably been a lot more difficult if her family had been very poor.

Nosipho had seen at close range how her uncle's family had been affected by his unemployment. He had lost his job at the brewery and couldn't find another for nearly two years. Nosipho had watched how demoralised and hopeless he and her aunt had begun to feel while he remained out of work. Her cousins had thanked her for her old clothes when they were given these, but Nosipho could see that they would have liked new clothes of their own. Nosipho's parents gave her aunt and uncle a lot of support, both financial and emotional, but she could see the difference in all of them when her uncle finally managed to get another job. While Nosipho didn't want to believe that money was so important, she could see that when you didn't have enough of it, it could change your whole outlook on life.

Introduction

This chapter discusses poverty as a social psychological phenomenon. It reviews local and global statistics on poverty and shows how poverty is related to physical ill health. It discusses the dangers of attributing mental ill health to poverty, and details how poor people deal with the challenges of poverty individually and collectively. Finally, it discusses the psychological effects of consumer culture, the depletion of social capital and cultural imperialism on both poor and rich people.

South Africa is classified as a middle income country, yet most South Africans are poor. This apparent contradiction is due to the fact that ours is a country of extreme inequality, with a small group of very wealthy people and a much larger group of poor people (May, 1998). Of the 44 million South Africans, about 8 million survive on less than a dollar a day (the internationally recognised poverty line) and 18 million on less than US$ 2 per day. Put differently, 37 per cent of South African households survive on less than R1 000 per month (Statistics South Africa, 2001).

Figure 1 Sol Plaatje

These are disturbing figures, but it is important to realise that they reflect not only the kind of country we are living in, but also – to a great extent – what the world as a whole is like at the beginning of the

20.1 HISTORY, POVERTY, CONTROVERSY

One of the largest and most influential social science research projects conducted in South Africa during the twentieth century was the Carnegie Commission on the 'poor White problem', which was launched in 1928 and resulted in government initiatives which greatly improved the conditions of poor White people – many of them Afrikaners impoverished as a result of the Anglo-Boer War.

Ironically, however, the majority of poor people in South Africa, then as now, were in fact Black. Their situation in the aftermath of the war was eloquently described by the first Secretary-General of the South African Native Congress (forerunner of the ANC), Sol Plaatje, in his 1916 book *Native Life in South Africa*. Plaatje was the first of many authors to trace the ways in which Black South Africans were systematically impoverished through legislation such as the Natives' Land Act (which reserved most of South Africa for White people) and apartheid-era measures such as job reservation (which prevented Black people from occupying many better-paying positions). Although the Carnegie Commission in the early 1980s launched a second enquiry which

focused on poverty in South Africa more broadly (Wilson & Ramphele, 1989) it is still, in the minds of many South African social scientists, associated with the earlier study which was concerned with White people only.

While in the post-apartheid era Black South Africans are no longer excluded from economic opportunities on the basis of race, it is clear that, as a group, Black people have been historically disadvantaged. This has led to the implementation of a series of strategies to economically empower Black people, the most controversial of which is the policy of affirmative action which entails giving preference to Black and female applicants over White men, provided the applicants have the necessary training and skills.

Some people argue that affirmative action is simply reverse discrimination. Others argue that affirmative action is needed at this point in our history to correct past injustices, and that in the long term, organisations will benefit from having a more diverse and representative workforce. What do you think?

twenty-first Century. Globally, as many as one in five people are poor and in some regions, such as sub-Saharan Africa, every second person is poor (World Bank, 2000). In South Africa, as elsewhere, poverty is very unevenly distributed – Black people are far more likely to be poor than White people; poverty is particularly severe in rural areas; and the poverty rate for female-headed households is much higher (60 per cent) than for male-headed households (31 per cent) (May, 1998).

20.2 THE GINI COEFFIECIENT

Countries and regions differ not only in terms of absolute poverty, but also in how unequally wealth is distributed. A commonly-used measure of income inequality is the GINI coefficient, which ranges from 0 (absolute equality) to 1 (absolute inequality). South Africa's GINI coefficient is 0.61, second only to Brazil, which at 0.63 has the world's highest GINI coefficient (SACP, 1999).

Shocking as they are, it has been argued (e.g., by Chossudovsky, 1998) that these sorts of figures represent an underestimate of the real extent of poverty because they rely on over-stringent criteria (such as the US$ 1 and 2 cut-offs) for classifying people as being poor.

Poverty is not limited to the so-called developing countries either. Even in supposedly wealthy countries such as the United States, there is a sizeable 'underclass' of poor people who do not have regular employment and who are dependent on ever-decreasing state grants (Lynn & McGeary, 1990; United States Census Bureau, 2001).

Why should psychologists, in South Africa and elsewhere, care about poverty? In this chapter we consider three ways in which the question of poverty is important to the study and practise of psychology. First, being poor has an impact on a person's physical and mental well-being. Second, being rich or poor (or somewhere in between) leads to people experiencing the world in very different ways and forming different kinds of social structures to try and improve their lives. Third, poverty is more than just an unfortunate condition from which some people happen to suffer – it is an important part of how the world is currently organised.

In the sections below we therefore look at poverty from an increasingly broader perspective: First,

how it affects individuals, then how people make collective sense of and respond to being rich or poor, and finally how poverty fits into the global economic and political landscape.

The negative effects of poverty

The fact that most South Africans are poor has an obvious and direct effect on their physical well-being. Poor people may have insufficient food, cannot afford to eat a varied diet (every tenth child in South Africa is malnourished), often work long hours, and usually do not have access to adequate heating, water and sanitation. As a consequence, they are more susceptible to contracting a variety of poverty-related diseases, including tuberculosis and AIDS. Being poor also exposes them, more so than rich people, to the risk of injury, through, for example, burns from open fires or paraffin stoves.

Figure 2 Living conditions in informal settlements place people at increased risk of contracting a variety of diseases and of suffering physical injury

The consequences of this can be seen in South Africa's high infant mortality rate of 45 per 1 000 live births (compared to 6 in the United Kingdom, for example), and low life expectancy of 48 years (compared to, for example, 78 in the United Kingdom) (World Health Organisation, 2003).

20.3 POVERTY, LIFE EXPECTANCY AND INFANT MORTALITY

Infant mortality (the number of children in every 1 000 who die before they reach the age of 5) and life expectancy (the average age at which people die) are frequently used indicators of a country's health status, and are strongly related to poverty and inequality.

While, as a general rule, poor countries have high infant mortality rates and low life expectancies, there are exceptions. For example, the infant mortality rate in Cuba (a much poorer country than South Africa) is only 7.39 and life expectancy is as high as 76.41 years. The reason for this is that Cuba's history as a socialist country has ensured that there is far less inequality than in South Africa. Its health care system has also been built up over a far longer period to cater for the primary health care needs of ordinary people, whereas in South Africa, health care facilities are still very much oriented towards those who can afford to pay for quality treatment.

In view of the clear evidence that poverty leads to physical ill health, it would seem to follow that being poor would also have a negative impact on mental health, and there is indeed a substantial body of literature on this issue (e.g., Barbarin & Richter, 1999; Duncan & Brooks-Gunn, 1997; McLeod & Shanahan, 1993). Some of this research has no qualms about claiming, for example, that low-income people are two to five times more likely to suffer from a diagnosable mental disorder than those of the highest income group (Bourdon *et al.*, 1994). However, in making claims about the relationship between poverty and mental ill health, we should be careful not to portray poor people as being somehow psychologically less developed than rich people. To say that a child is at risk of contracting a respiratory tract infection because she or he is growing up in conditions of poverty is a relatively neutral statement of fact; to claim that she or he is at risk of becoming emotionally disordered or intellectually stunted is not only far less well supported by research evidence but also more directly affects her or his dignity as a human being.

Rather than thinking in terms of poverty as having a direct causal effect on mental health, it is more productive to consider the unique psychological and other challenges that poverty presents people with and the opportunities that it takes away from them. For example, these are some of the challenges that children who grow up in environments of poverty face:

- Poor children are more at risk of physical disease and injury, and this may affect their intellectual performance. For example, poor children are more likely to have uncorrected hearing and visual problems and may be less able to concentrate due to an inadequate diet – all of which will affect their ability to learn in a formal school environment.
- Poor children are more likely to have to take on parental responsibilities at an early age, and may even have to act as the head of a household. While they develop caring and other skills in this process, they miss out on many other opportunities – especially socialising with their peers and schooling.
- Poor children typically grow up in relatively crowded environments. While, again, this pro-

20.4 THE KATHORUS STUDY

Context
Despite the fact that primary schooling is compulsory in South Africa, many children still do not attend school on a regular basis. According to the 1996 census, 8.5 per cent of children between the ages of 7 and 15 were not in school. The Wits Education and Health Policy Unit, Clacherty & Associates and Kathorus Enhanced Learning Initiative decided to try and establish how these children understand the reasons for their absenteeism.

Procedure
A 'life-story' approach was followed in which 200 school children from Kathorus were engaged in repeated conversations and participatory workshops. Each child's life story was documented and through careful interpretation of the stories, researchers tried to identify the causal factors at play.

Results and conclusion
Poverty was the most common theme in children's accounts of why they did not attend school (Chala, 2003). In many cases their families simply could not afford the costs of going to school, and felt unable to overcome the material obstacles. The researchers concluded that South African educational policies and practices should be changed so as to cater more effectively for children whose families have few material resources.

vides them with some unique opportunities for emotional and interpersonal growth, it can also entail considerable stress and may place them at greater risk of physical and sexual abuse.

- Poor children are more likely to witness or to be victims of crime and violence.
- Health services (including mental health services) are far less accessible to poor children – because either they cannot afford it and/or because they live in areas that have no or poorly-resourced clinics and other health facilities.

Thus, in summary, poverty and inequality have a negative effect on physical and mental health, but in the case of the latter the situation is far more complex and we should be careful not to stereotype poor people as 'mentally unhealthy'. One approach to emphasising the fact that poor people are not simply passive victims of their circumstances is the growing literature on resilience, which is defined as 'the ability to thrive, mature, and increase competence in the face of adverse circumstances' (Rouse, 1998:1). Resilient individuals often come from caring families and live in communities that, although poor, offer them opportunities for personal and social development (Rutter, 1995).

Figure 3 Levels of violent crime are higher in countries where there are large differences in income between rich and poor

The experience of poverty

Aliber (2001:13) notes that 'over the course of the past two decades, there has been increasing attention to the fact that poor people's experience of poverty involves a great deal more than inadequate income or consumption'. Poverty is not simply about being deprived of necessities such as food, medicine and clothing, but is often also about living in a situation of:

- hopelessness;
- uncertainty about the future; and
- alienation from 'mainstream' society.

Being poor is associated with *hopelessness* because people may feel themselves caught in a so-called 'poverty trap' with little prospect of ever escaping. Middle-class people like to think that people achieve things by their own efforts and that all that is therefore needed to get ahead in life is to be determined and to work hard. In reality, people rely to a very large extent on two things that are simply 'given' to them without their having had to put in any special effort, namely their network of relatives and friends, and their ability to present themselves (through subtle cues such as dress, accent and opinions) as being the sort of reliable, sophisticated person who can be trusted with a responsible job (and a large salary).

For example, most young people growing up in a poor Eastern Cape township simply do not have the right sort of network, nor will they ever have the opportunity to develop the kinds of self-presentation skills needed to enter into the formal economy. While they may be very strongly embedded in local social networks (via the church, family, friendship groups and so on), and highly skilled in presenting themselves within their immediate community, these things do not buy them access to the world that lies beyond the horizon of poverty. When this situation persists through several generations, with only the occasional exceptional individual finding a way out, people become resigned to the idea of always being poor and are said to be caught in a poverty trap. It would, however, be a mistake to depict all poor communities as trapped in a spiral of hopelessness, with only a few individuals emerging unscathed due to their greater resilience. Osher *et al.* (1999) have argued that resilience should in fact be viewed not as an individual characteristic, but as something that many poor communities and families have or can develop. Poor communities, for instance, often have extensive networks of mutual support which help families and individuals deal with and overcome difficult circumstances.

For many people, poverty is a state of *uncertainty about the future*. While everybody goes through life with a certain degree of anxiety about unforeseen events, poor people are particularly vulnerable in relation to economic 'shocks' such as losing a job, illness or becoming a victim of crime. Middle-class people are buffered against such economic risks (either directly through insurance or by the fact that they can appeal to their bank manager, friends or family if they get into financial difficulties), but poor people do not have the same safety nets and consequently have to live with greater levels of apprehension and uncertainty. Again, community structures such as church groups and mutual burial societies provide some poor communities with the resilience to deal with an uncertain future.

Perhaps not surprisingly, middle-class people usually believe in the justness of the system that allows them to achieve and maintain their position of relative wealth (Williamson, 1975). Although they may complain endlessly about 'the government' and wish that it would be more like governments in wealthy Western countries, they are basically satisfied that people get what they deserve. Poor people, on the other hand, often feel *alienated* from society, and can therefore be more fundamentally critical about the capitalist system as such, rather than simply about the performance of a particular government. While the vast majority of poor people are law-abiding citizens, for some the extent to which they have been alienated from the system (and the need for survival) takes the form of economic crimes such as theft and robbery. For other poor people, their sense of alienation places them in a better position to develop a critical theoretical understanding of how the system works. Karl Marx (1887) spoke of this ability as 'class consciousness' and considered it a necessary first step towards liberation. In a similar vein the radical educationist Paulo Freire (1971, 1973) argued that, through their first-hand experience, poor people are better able to develop critical consciousness and think theoretically about the relationship between individual lives and the ways in which wealth and power are distributed in a society.

The other side of the coin

It would seem obvious that the solution to poverty is simply to 'throw money at the problem', and to some extent this is indeed true. When governments collect taxes from the rich and spend it on health care, education and work-creation programmes for the poor, or when a country's economy grows and everybody becomes a little richer, people's lives do in fact improve in measurable ways.

However, simply being rich is not in itself a guarantee of physical and mental well-being. Between 1970 and 1999, the average American family's income increased by 16 per cent (adjusted for inflation), but the percentage of people who described themselves as 'very happy' fell from 36 to 29 per cent (LaBerre, 2003). There are at least three ways in which the process of wealth creation in the Western world, a process which South Africa and most other 'developing' countries are trying to emulate, can be seen as having led to psychological and social impoverishment.

First, most rich people do not *feel* particularly rich – they in fact often find themselves having to spend more money than they have and thus digging themselves into a 'debt trap' every bit as confining as a poverty trap. The reason for this apparently irrational behaviour is that they are in thrall to what has been called *consumer culture* (Shevchenko, 2002; Slater, 1997), which is the cultural fantasy that the solution to all life's problems is to buy more and more material things (Kasser, 2002). Consumer culture is a kind of psychological impoverishment in that it takes away from people their sense of what is important, of how to balance different aspects of their lives, and replaces it with a debilitating sense of never having enough.

Figure 4 South Africans are subject to a global culture of material consumption

Second, the Western model of wealth creation has led to impoverishment in that it has depleted what is known as *social capital* (Coleman, 1988; Putnam, 1995). Social capital is like physical capital in that it is a form of stored wealth, but rather than being stored in money or property, it is embedded in the networks, spaces and institutions (and in the sense of mutual trust) that make it possible for people to work together. Societies with a good 'stock' of social capital are more likely to have low crime figures, better health and higher educational achievement. Social capital can be seen in informal shared spaces such as 'the street' or 'the corner café' and in more formal spaces such as 'the church meeting', 'the school' or 'the election'. Putnam and others have shown how in developed countries (but especially in the United States) this kind of capital has declined in inverse proportion to the accumulation of physical capital. All over the world, spaces of sharing, debate and collaborative work (streets, schools, shopping districts, etc.) have been privatised, causing people to withdraw from participation in the processes which once made them feel part of society. In the United States very few people still bother to vote, while in the United Kingdom it is said that more people voted for the reality TV show *Big Brother* than in the national elections (epolitix, 2001).

Third, the kind of wealth creation that goes with Western capitalism has led to another kind of impoverishment known as *cultural imperialism*, which is the process whereby a stronger culture imposes its understandings and practices on weaker cultures. Cultural imperialism is not a modern phenomenon, but in the past it has never posed a serious threat to the rich diversity of the world's cultures. However, the twentieth and twenty-first century English-speaking countries in the West, particularly the United States, have achieved a level of global domination unparalleled in history. Euro-American culture has become so pervasive that other cultural practices have literally become unthinkable and undoable, or survive only by deliberately positioning themselves as strange and exotic (Said, 1978). The sterile suburbs and homogenised malls of South African cities, and the ways in which we market ourselves as an exotic tourist destination, bear testimony to the impoverishing effects of Euro-American cultural imperialism.

Conclusion: Always with us?

This chapter has tried to act as a reminder (for those who may need reminding) of the physical poverty in which most South Africans are trapped, but also tried to highlight the many ways in which poverty goes beyond simply not having enough money.

Perhaps it has also, as discussions about poverty often do, created the impression that 'the poor will always be with us'. Nothing could be further from the truth. The historically unprecedented wealth that has been created in developed countries, and in the wealthy enclaves of developing countries, has largely been at the expense of the poor and has been psychologically damaging to both rich and poor. However, it has also demonstrated that through technological innovation it has become possible to create sufficient wealth so as to eradicate poverty entirely. By applying these technologies in a more sustainable way, and by becoming more mindful of the processes of psychological and social impoverishment which have thus far accompanied capitalist wealth creation, the kind of modest utopia foreseen in the *Freedom Charter* remains within reach:

All people shall have the right to live where they choose, be decently housed, and to bring up their families in comfort and security (*The Freedom Charter*, Adopted at the Congress of the People, Kliptown, on 26 June 1955).

20.5 WHAT IS POVERTY?

'I used to think I was poor. Then they told me I wasn't poor, I was needy. Then they told me it was self-defeating to think of myself as needy, I was deprived. Then they told me deprived was a bad image, I was underprivileged. Then they told me underprivileged was overused, I was disadvantaged. I still don't have a dime. But I sure have a great vocabulary' (Jules Feiffer).

Aliber, M. (2001). *Study of the Incidence and Nature of Chronic Poverty and Development Policy in South Africa: An overview*. Pretoria: Southern African Regional Poverty Network.

Barbarin, O. & Richter, L.M. (1999). Adversity and psycho-social competence of South African children. *American Journal of Orthopsychiatry*, 69:319-27.

Bourdon, K.H., Rae, D.S., Narrow, W.E., Manderschild, R.W. & Regier, D.A. (1994). National prevalence and treatment of mental and addictive disorders. In R.W. Mandershild & A. Sonnenschein (Eds.). *Mental Health: United States*. Washington, DC: Center for Mental Health Services, pp. 22-51.

Chala, S. (2003). Poverty is the reason. *The Teacher*, 23 January.

Chossudovsky, M. (1998). Global Poverty in the Late 20th Century. *Journal of International Affairs*, 52(1):145-63.

Coleman, J.C. (1988). Social capital in the creation of human capital. *American Journal of Sociology*, 94:95-120.

Duncan, G.J. & Brooks-Gunn, J. (Eds.). (1997). *Consequences of Growing up Poor*. New York: Russell Sage Foundation.

epolitix (2001). *Big Brother outpolls party leaders*. http://www.epolitix.com/bos/epxrews/00000000B68C.htm (accessed 31 July 2001).

Freire, P. (1971). *Pedagogy of the Oppressed*. New York: Seabury Press.

Freire, P. (1973). *Education for Critical Consciousness*. New York: Seabury Press.

Kasser, T. (2002). *The High Price of Materialism*. Cambridge: MIT Press.

LaBerre, P. (2003). How to lead a rich life. *Fast Company*, 68:72.

Lynn, L.E. & McGeary, M.G.H. (Eds.). (1990). *Inner-city Poverty in the United States*. Washington, DC: National Academy Press.

Marx, K. (1887). *Capital. Volume 1*. Online version, http://csf.colorado.edu/psn/marx/Archive/1867-C1/ (accessed 15 June 2003).

May, J. (Ed.). (1998). *Poverty and Inequality in South Africa*. Report prepared for the Office of the Executive Deputy President and the Inter-ministerial Committee for Poverty and Inequality. Pretoria: Government Printer.

McLeod, J.D. & Shanahan, M.J. (1993). Poverty, parenting and children's mental health. *Sociological Review*, 58(3):351-66.

Osher, D., Kendziora, K.T., VanDenBerg, J., & Dennis, K. (1999). Beyond individual resilience. *Reaching Today's Youth*, 3(4):2-4.

Plaatje, S. (1916). *Native Life in South Africa, Before and Since the European War and the Boer Rebellion*, http://www.anc.org.za/books/nlife.html (accessed 15 June 2003).

Putnam, R.D. (1995). Bowling Alone: America's declining social capital. *Journal of Democracy*, 6(1):65-78.

Rouse, K.G. (1998). Resilience From Poverty and Stress. *Human Development & Family Life Bulletin*, 4(1):1-10.

Rutter, M. (1995). Psychosocial adversity: risk, resilience, and recovery. *Southern African Journal of Child & Adolescent Psychiatry*, 7(2):75-88.

SACP (South African Communist Party). (1999). *Discussion Document – Structure of the South African Economy: Challenges for transformation*. Presented at the SACP Special Strategy conference, 3 to 5 September, Johannesburg.

Said, E. (1978). *Orientalism*. New York: Pantheon Books.

Shevchenko, O. (2002). 'In Case of Fire Emergency': Consumption, security and the meaning of durables in a transforming society. *Journal of Consumer Culture*, 2(2):147-70.

Slater, D. (1997). *Consumer Culture and Modernity*. Cambridge: Polity Press.

Statistics South Africa (2001). *September 2000 Labour Force Survey*. Pretoria: Government Printer.

United States Census Bureau (2001). *Poverty in the United States*, http://www.census.gov/hhes/www/poverty01.html (accessed 15 June 2003).

Williamson, J.B. (1975). Beliefs about the rich, the poor, and the taxes they pay. *American Journal of Economics & Sociology*, 35:9-29.

Wilson, F. & Ramphele, M. (1989). *Uprooting Poverty in South Africa: Report for the 2nd Carnegie inquiry into poverty and development in South Africa*. Cape Town: David Philip.

World Bank. (2000). *Global Poverty Report*. Geneva: World Bank.

World Health Organisation (2003). *Country statistics*, http://www.who.int (accessed 15 June 2003).

Multiple choice questions

1. In terms of per capita income South Africa is classified as a
   a) lower income country
   b) lower-middle income country
   c) middle income country
   d) higher income country
2. Which of the following statements are incorrect?
   a) most Black people are poorer than White people
   b) most rural people are poorer than urban people
   c) poverty is rare in the developing world
   d) there are many poor people in the United States
3. Which of the following statements is correct?
   a) 1 in 2 children in South Africa is malnourished
   b) 1 in 3 children in South Africa is malnourished
   c) 1 in 5 children in South Africa is malnourished
   d) 1 in 10 children in South Africa is malnourished
4. Infant mortality and life expectancy in Cuba is
   a) very much lower than that in the United Kingdom
   b) slightly lower than that in the United Kingdom
   c) similar to that in the United Kingdom
   d) much higher than that in the United Kingdom
5. Which of the following statements is incorrect? We should be careful about claiming that poverty leads to mental ill health because
   a) there is no research to support this claim
   b) poor people are not psychologically inferior to rich ones
   c) such claims affect people's dignity as human beings
   d) it is more productive to consider how people experience and respond to conditions of poverty
6. Which of the following statements is true?
   a) poor children usually do not have many siblings
   b) poor children often have to act as parents
   c) poor children do not feel the effects of violence
   d) poor children are less resilient than rich children
7. Which of the following statements is incorrect? Middle-class people find it hard to understand the concept of 'poverty traps' because
   a) they believe that people get what they deserve
   b) they can rely on the help of other rich people
   c) they know how to present themselves to other rich people
   d) they are caught in a 'debt trap'
8. The following is more common among poor than rich people
   a) hopelessness about material circumstances
   b) belief in the justness of the economic system
   c) apprehension about future 'economic shocks'
   d) alienation from the rules of middle-class society
9. Which of the following is incorrect? Western capitalist wealth creation leads to psychological and social impoverishment in the following ways
   a) the rise of a consumer culture in which people believe that material things can buy happiness
   b) a steady increase in physical ill health even for those who can afford medical care
   c) the depletion of social capital so that people stop trusting one another and forget how to work together
   d) cultural imperialism in which people learn to devalue their own culture
10. Which of the following is correct?
    a) technology cannot be used to create wealth
    b) resilient people often come from caring families
    c) poverty cannot be eradicated
    d) poverty is limited to the 'developing world'

Short answer questions

1. Briefly explain why psychologists should care about poverty.
2. Why could it be problematic to claim that poverty has a negative impact on mental health?
3. Poor people often feel alienated from society. This has both positive and negative consequences. Explain.
4. In what ways are rich people mentally unhealthy?
5. What is social capital?

21

Ethnicity

Garth Stevens

CHAPTER OBJECTIVES

After studying this chapter you should be able to:
- define the concept of ethnicity
- understand related social psychological concepts and processes that facilitate the expression of ethnic identities
- define ideology and understand how it is transmitted and informs the content of ethnic identities in specific socio-historical contexts
- understand contemporary examples of ethnicity within this framework, by examining the relationship between expressions of ethnicity and the socio-historical contexts in which they occur.

Growing up, Nosipho had attended a racially mixed school, but outside of school hours she had little to do with families or children who weren't of her own ethnic group. Looking back, it was hardly surprising. Apartheid was no longer government policy, but all those years of forcing different ethnic groups to live separately had left a very deep mark on how she and most South Africans lived.

Nosipho had grown up in an area with only Black families. She didn't think of herself or her family as being racist, but it was just accepted that she wouldn't ask the White children home to her house. She wasn't concerned that mostly, they didn't invite her over either! Sometimes people in her neighbourhood would talk about 'the Whites', saying how different they were to themselves. She accepted this as a fact. But now at university, there seemed to be much more opportunity to get to know fellow-learners from a whole range of different ethnic groups. She had gone out a few times with a mixed group that included Whites as well as people from other ethnic groups. It was a real eye opener for her to see how much they had in common – much more than was different between them. While it was nice to feel more freedom to mix with whoever she wanted to, whatever 'race' they were, it was also awful to realise how much a political philosophy like apartheid could harm people's relationships with one another. It took simple differences like skin colour and exaggerated them. It made people believe that they were fundamentally different. When people didn't know one another it also made them suspicious – sometimes even afraid – of one another. Of course, in South Africa this kind of thinking had also been used as an excuse to divide up resources like jobs and land and housing unequally and to protect the interests of White people. With so many years of apartheid, it would take a long time to make society more equal and for people from different ethnic groups to learn to know and trust one another.

Introduction

This chapter introduces ethnicity as a dynamic and unfixed expression of individual and group identity. It suggests that forms and expressions of ethnicity are socially and historically determined in various contexts, and that these expressions often result in entrenching intergroup difference and inequality. Specifically, the chapter notes that as a form of group Othering (i.e. the process of defining *Self* as different and separate through the creation of an *Other*), ethnicity frequently overlaps with dominant ideologies that promote a range of social inequalities – most notably the ideologies of racism, nationalism, anti-Semitism and anti-Islamism in contemporary societies. It also identifies various psychological mechanisms and processes that are frequently associated with the expression of ethnicity, such as the acquisition of attitudes and stereotypes, their translation into prejudice, discrimination and violence, as well as intergroup differences and the establishment of intergroup hierarchies. In concluding, the chapter argues that through the influence of political and ideological processes, ethnic identities become based upon, and recreate social inequalities within different socio-historical contexts.

21.1 ETHNICITY AND VIOLENCE

From 1992-1995, approximately 200 000 Muslims, Croats and Serbs were killed in Bosnia's ethnic civil war (Burg & Shoup, 2000). During the same period, from April to June 1994, an estimated 800 000 'Tutsi' and moderate 'Hutus' were killed in just under 100 days in the Central African country of Rwanda (Nzongola-Ntalaja, 2001). More recently, in the United States of America, some US citizens, outraged at the hijacked-airliner attacks on the World Trade Centre on 11 September 2001, unleashed their own retaliatory strike – on American citizens of Arab descent, on legal immigrants, on Muslims and anyone else whose looks, speech, dress or names somehow fit Middle-East stereotypes (Telhami, 2002). Closer to home, on 27 February 1999, Andrew Babeile stabbed a fellow pupil, Christoffel Erasmus, in the neck with a pair of scissors. Babeile, a boy from the local township, had been surrounded by a group of White pupils outside the tuck shop. The assault was precipitated by the leader of this group, together with others, calling him a 'kaffir' ('Caught in the whirlwind of change', *Sunday Times*, 16 September 2001).

Ethnicity is both social and psychological

What is common to the above incidents is that they are all based on the presence of perceived 'ethnic' identities of Self and Other. While the severity of the overt consequences differs from incident to incident, in each instance there is a clear interface between social psychological processes such as attitudinal expression, the use of stereotypes, the presence of prejudice, the enactment of discrimination; and socio-historical conflicts that amplified existing intergroup differences and hierarchies and shaped the particular form of these deplorable acts.

In Bosnia, a declining economy provided a fertile ground for competing nationalist ideologies to emerge amongst the historically differentiated population of Croats, Serbs and Muslims, leading to secessionist movements for independence and disputes over land (Burg & Shoup, 2000). This involved the use of ethnic stereotypes, prejudice and discriminatory violence in a process of ethnic cleansing that was aimed at the creation of self-governing, ethnically pure, independent nation states.

In Rwanda, increasing civil strife between minority 'Tutsi' and majority 'Hutus' that had dated back to Belgian colonialism in the region, was fuelled when an aircraft carrying the 'Hutu' president of Rwanda was shot down by unknown forces, prompting the massacre of 'Tutsi' by government troops and civilian militia (Nzongola-Ntalaja, 2001). Once again, existing attitudes, stereotypes and prejudices regarding ethnic differences between these groups were utilised to incite the genocide in this regional conflict.

Figure 1 Mass graves depicting the ethnic genocide in Rwanda

Figure 2 Muslims may be subject to stereotypes

Figure 3 Ethnicity and race were used interchangeably during the apartheid era in South Africa

In the United States of America, longstanding tensions between several countries in the Middle East (many of them with predominantly Muslim populations) and the United States had emerged after decades of US military intervention in the Gulf region, implicit acceptance of Israeli domination of Palestinians, and the US-led wars in the Gulf. The events of 11 September 2001 crystallised these differences even further, resulting in several xenophobic attacks that relied on the stereotypical identification of Arab-Americans, Middle Eastern descendents and Muslims, and heightened fears among immigrant communities from the Middle East (Telhami, 2002).

Finally, in South Africa, political and constitutional reform after 1994 created the platform for 'racial' integration at all levels of society. However, 300 years of segregation and 46 years of institutionalised racism resulted in highly defined group identities that were bound to erupt into conflict under circumstances of integration, without meaningful interventions directed at reconciliation. Existing attitudes, stereotypes, prejudice and discrimination continue to influence and shape social behaviour, especially in situations of potential conflict (e.g., job competition between different social groups that were 'racially' segregated in the past and campaigning for political positions in certain regions of South Africa).

However, it should be noted that expression of ethnic identity does not always have overt acts of violence as its logical end-point. While in many instances the expression of ethnicity is integrally

Figure 4 Have ethnic identities been re-defined in post-apartheid South Africa?

linked to acts of discrimination and violence (e.g., Kollapen, 1999), this is not always the case.

Ethnicity is contested

The expression of ethnicity is also not fixed or consistent within social categories, as is evidenced in South Africa where identities are often varied (see Box 21.2). A further example can be found among immigrants from the Middle East, Arab descendants and Muslims in the United States of America after

11 September 2001. Many resisted the imposed identities placed on them by large sections of the American population, as being anti-American and religious fundamentalists. There was a clear attempt in many instances to separate political identity and religious identity, highlighting that their adherence to a particular religious faith did not imply a universal ethnic identity, a fundamentalist approach to religion, or anti-American political opinions and feelings (Telhami, 2002).

Said (in Bayoumi & Rubin, 2000:175-6) suggests that this type of stereotype is based on the idea that 'the West' is greater than, and has surpassed the stage of Christianity, its principal religion, [and] the world of Islam ... is still mired in religion, primitivity, and backwardness. Therefore, 'the West' is modern, greater than the sum of its parts, full of enriching contradictions ... [and] the world of Islam, on the other hand, is no more than 'Islam' ...

In the above illustration, it is clear that different forms, expressions and interpretations of ethnicity may operate simultaneously in relation to the same social group. One possible reason for the resistance to an imposed identity in the above example was to counter this simplistic and stereotypical overgeneralisation that Arab descendents, Middle Eastern populations and Muslims are all merely religious fanatics with malicious intentions against the West. In addition, it may also have served a defensive function and allowed this sector of the population to maintain group safety, and to enable its members to continue to function simultaneously as both Americans and Arab descendents, Middle Eastern immigrants and/or Muslims.

Ethnicity relies on socio-cultural symbols

The expression of ethnicity is also an unfixed social and psychological process that is linked to certain prominent socio-cultural symbols in any given context (Vail, 1989). For example, in contexts of social transition where cultural renewal or national pride takes root, the expression of ethnicity may be characterised by an emphasis on language, cultural rituals and symbols, and popular patriotic talk and emotion. This was evident among African-Americans 'returning to their African cultural roots' in the United States at the height of the Civil Rights

---

21.2 THE CHANGING AND CONTESTED NATURE OF IDENTITY

The imposed (and sometimes accepted) category of 'Coloured' during apartheid was resisted by many (but not all) in the 1970s in favour of the unifying Black Consciousness concept of 'Blackness', that referred to all people not classified as White (Ramphele, 1995). However, in post-apartheid South Africa, the understanding of 'Coloured' is once again being challenged and is often rejected by many as a racist label, interpreted by some as it was intended during apartheid, and still further understood by others as being related to an indigenous and cultural heritage associated with people of Khoi-San descent (Martin, 2001; Stevens, 1998). Moreover, despite the rejection of imposed ethnic and 'racial' identities during the anti-apartheid struggle, acceptance of the existence of distinct ethnic and 'racial' groups continues to be actively propagated by politicians, academics and ordinary people in post-apartheid South Africa (Stevens, 1998). Clearly, this form of identity expression is neither stable over time nor universally understood and accepted within the population.

Movement, and in Bosnia when national pride was actively encouraged through the use of historical claims to land and nationhood.

Ethnicity sustains social inequality in times of conflict

What is apparent is that in instances where social conflict is heightened between different social groups, ethnicity and its associated identities often become more formalised, (over)generalised, internalised and imposed, resulting in a rigidity in in-group/out-group boundaries and relationships. Ethnicity therefore frequently becomes the key factor to distinguish social groups from each other in such instances.

In this context, ethnicity is commonly politicised by those who are in disempowered positions as a rallying point around which to muster political support (e.g., minority political parties who campaign on an ethnic basis for votes), or alternatively, by those in a position of power to repress and suppress others (e.g., the former South African government's racial and ethnic categorisation of the population created deep divisions within disadvantaged com-

Figure 5 During the 1960s, many African-Americans 'returned' to traditional African dress codes as a symbol of their cultural renewal

Figure 6 World War Two holocaust survivors in an extermination camp

munities and helped to maintain apartheid). Under these conditions, ethnicity is invariably linked to unequal social relations through ideology (e.g., political doctrines advocating social inequality) and structural hierarchies (e.g., legislation favouring one group over another) within the social system (Riggins, 1997; Schalk, 2002).

Even though the expression of ethnicity may serve the function of social resistance for social minority groups at times, it ultimately only facilitates in-group cohesion. This form and expression of ethnicity is almost always dependent upon and associated with the recreation of social inequalities (e.g., the expression of ethnic identities among 'Hutus' and 'Tutsi' in Rwanda that were constructed and imposed during Belgian colonial rule, later became a rallying point for social resistance, but ultimately contributed to genocide after independence was attained).

Definitions of ethnicity

Even though there is no finality on a theoretical definition of ethnicity, there appears to be broad agreement that ethnicity as a concept refers to shared social elements such as language, religion, customs, traditions and history within a particular social group, which in some way contributes to the distinct identity of that group (Abercrombie *et al.*, 1984).

Barth (1969) also states that ethnicity is defined in terms of shared cultural values that are expressed in specific forms, makes up a field of communication and action, and has a membership that defines itself as such and is also viewed by others to be distinct from similar groups. In this sense, ethnicity becomes the group and intergroup expression of culture. Stated differently, culture refers to social information that humans require in order to interact (Thornton, 1988), and is comprised of collective symbols and learned aspects of society such as language, values, customs, belief systems, conventions and ideologies (Abercrombie *et al.*, 1984), but different groups have different levels of access to this information. The formation of ethnic groups is based partly on the group members' subjective interpretations and experiences of what cultural information they have access to, but also on the prevailing social conditions that either enhance or constrain such access to cultural information. Ethnicity is therefore the group and intergroup reflection of the diverse levels of access that we have to cultural information (Schalk, 2002).

Thompson (1990), however, emphasises that irrespective of the particular definition of ethnicity that is utilised, the meanings attached to it in different social contexts are in fact shaped by those contexts. He argues that it is important to note that ethnicity is therefore a socially and historically determined or constructed concept that may differ from one social environment to another. In this sense, he suggests that ethnicity is neither primordial nor essential in nature (i.e. that ethnicity is not a natural set of characteristics with which we are all born), but rather that our experiences of ethnicity are dependent on and influenced by the power relations, histories, levels of social conflict and inequalities operating in any society at a given point in time.

While this section of the chapter has not provided a single, all-encompassing definition of ethnicity, the selected definitions all support the ideas that ethnicity is certainly *both social and psychological, may be contested, relies on certain socio-cultural symbols in its expression, and may contribute to maintaining uneven social relationships.*

Definitions of related psychological concepts

Even though it is important not to seek comprehensive explanations for social phenomena such as ethnicity, purely at the individual and group levels of human interaction, it is useful to turn to the social psychological level to identify some of the key processes that facilitate the manifestation of ethnic identities. Several concepts will be addressed below in an attempt to generate a degree of clarity with regard to their definitions.

Ethnocentrism, group belonging and group identity

Much of the psychological literature has focused on the concept of ethnocentrism as a group process. Studies in group and intergroup behaviour have shown that the mere perception by individuals that they belong to a distinct social category or group, results in them enhancing the identity of the in-group at the expense of the out-group (Tajfel & Fraser, 1978). Ethnocentrism generally refers to this degree to which individuals perceive their own social group as being superior to others, while simultaneously harbouring feelings of negativity towards out-groups (Abercrombie *et al.*, 1984; Kolman, 1979). However, it is a common psychological process that occurs between social groups, and is characterised by a collective history/memory that results in a sense of uniqueness and superiority among members of the in-group as compared to members of the out-group (Cape Action League, 1987). Ethnocentrism is therefore a normal social psychological process that allows for the formation of ethnic groups, even though these groups will differ from one social and historical context to another (e.g., even though ethnocentrism operated in both Rwanda and Bosnia, social and historical conditions in Rwanda allowed for the formation of 'Hutu' and 'Tutsi' ethnic groups, while Serb and Croat ethnic groups were formed in Bosnia).

Attitudes

These normal group and intergroup processes often develop into more structured belief systems about both the in-group and the out-group. It is here that we deal with the construct of attitudes. Ajzen (1988) summarises the classical understanding of an attitude as a belief system that is essentially learned, is evaluative, can be deduced from both verbal and non-verbal behaviour, and forms a relatively stable part of the individual's disposition. The difficulty with this definition is that it isolates this concept from broader society, and transforms it into a product of the individual's mind.

Other writers have rather argued that attitudes must be viewed as part of the social, historical and cultural context out of which they emerge, and are in fact products of this context (e.g., Eiser & van der Plight, 1988). They have also argued that these belief systems are not merely expressed by individuals, but rather by entire social categories. They are therefore collective phenomena that reflect both positive and negative beliefs by and about, both the in- and out-group(s). They are also shifting, dependent upon these groups' status, power and perceived legitimacy within a society (Rattansi, 1992; Tajfel, 1981). Ethnic attitudes therefore act as a structured belief system that lays the foundations for different ethnic groups to be distinguished from each other (e.g., the commonly-held belief that Jews make good business people, have close family relationships, are fair-skinned, value education and are wealthy; while people of Indian descent are cunning business people, enjoy owning their own stores and have straight black hair).

Stereotypes

When attitudes become inaccurate (over)generalisations to entire perceived social categories or members of these categories, these are referred to as stereotypes. These may be either negative or positive attitudes, but have harmful consequences for three reasons:

- they take away our ability to treat each member of a group as an individual;
- they lead to narrow expectations of behaviour; and
- they lead us to make faulty attributions based on the (over)generalisation (Lahey, 1995).

Ethnic stereotypes are clusters of information that facilitate quick, overgeneralised and often inaccurate assessments of people, and therefore shape the manner in which we interact with them (e.g., the commonly-held belief that *all* African-Americans are good athletes and only enjoy rap music).

Prejudice

Building on the concept of attitudes, there appears to be general agreement that prejudice refers to a specific form of attitude – a negative attitude (Ashmore, 1970; Twitchin & Demuth, 1985). Aboud (1988) states that it is this negativity that ultimately defines prejudice, as the most salient characteristic of prejudice is its hateful quality, which is expressed towards the out-group. Dovideo and Gaertner (1986) also note that other than this aversive emotional component, this negative attitude is also based on irrational in-group beliefs about the out-group(s). This view is echoed by Rattansi (1992:25), who suggests that it is based on 'ignorance and faulty or incomplete knowledge', and that 'it is characterised by a tendency to stereotype' the out-group. Finally, Duncan (1993:47) argues that it is '... an antipathy based on a faulty and inflexible generalisation. It may be felt or expressed. It may be directed towards a [racial] group as a whole, or toward an individual because he is a member of that group'.

Based on the above, ethnic prejudice is often felt or expressed in relation to different ethnic groups in situations where social inequality or conflict is experienced between such groups. It is also in instances where prejudice is present, that ethnic discrimination and violence have a much greater potential to occur in any society.

Discrimination

While attitudes, stereotypes and prejudice may be seen operating through both verbal and non-verbal behaviour, they are fundamentally belief systems.

21.3 APPLYING SOCIAL PSYCHOLOGICAL CONCEPTS TO ETHNICITY

Each year, many African immigrants enter different countries in Europe. Simply because they are immigrants, they are often viewed and view themselves as a social group that is unique and different from Europeans. This common process through which different social groups are formed is referred to as ethnocentrism. When these different groups develop structured beliefs about themselves and each other (such as their differences in language, food, group behaviours, histories, etc.), these are referred to as attitudes, which may be both negative and positive. When these attitudes become overgeneralised to the point that all African immigrants are seen to be hard-working, but unskilled and unemployed, and all Europeans are seen to be highly skilled, wealthy, but lacking in compassion and understanding for less fortunate people, these beliefs can be characterised as stereotypes. However, when attitudes towards either of these groups are entirely negative, for example, when African immigrants are viewed as lazy, unintelligent criminals who are a drain on the country's resources, this is referred to as prejudice. Prejudice may be felt or expressed, but when it is translated into a social practice or action that diminishes a groups' status, social position, power or access to resources, it is referred to as discrimination. Discrimination can occur in the form of institutionalised social practices, such as the passing of legislation to prevent or minimise African immigrants from being employed in certain instances, or through everyday social practices, such as physical attacks on African immigrants to discourage them from settling in certain neighbourhoods.

The actual translation of these attitudes into overt social practices or acts that result in privilege, status and power for one social group at the expense of another, is known as discrimination. Discrimination is therefore the behavioural manifestation of these belief systems, and may or may not result in violence depending on the extent to which it is legitimised within the socio-historical context and the degree to which it is perceived to be socially desirable or undesirable (Stevens, 1997). Stated differently, ethnic discrimination refers to any social practice that may contribute to the unequal access to power or resources between different ethnic groups (e.g., not employing particular people because they are believed to be members of an untrustworthy ethnic group).

The relationship between the social and psychological

Ideology and its functions

This chapter has thus far argued that all forms of identity expression at an individual and group level (including ethnicity) are in some way influenced and shaped by the societies in which we live. But how does this process occur? One of the primary processes through which social meanings are given to ethnic identities is through ideology. While there are differing understandings of ideology (e.g., Althusser, 1971; Foster, 1991; Thompson, 1990), there are several core elements that characterise ideology (see Stevens, 1996).

Firstly, ideology is a system of beliefs that is reflected in all social practices that may be structural and/or discursive (i.e. these beliefs can be seen in the structures of society such as its laws, and may also be found in the ways that people talk). Racism, as a system of beliefs about the inferiority of Blacks and the superiority of Whites, could therefore be found in the laws of South Africa during apartheid, but was also seen in ways in which people spoke about the society.

Secondly, ideology often becomes widely accepted by humans in any society and allows them to function within those unequal social systems and to perpetuate that ideology (i.e. humans tend to take the system of beliefs as their own and then behave and speak in ways that support this ideology). In South Africa, many people believed in the superiority of Whites and the inferiority of Blacks, and so

behaved and spoke in ways that taught younger generations to believe in the same system of beliefs.

Finally, however, humans also have the capacity to act as active agents in the transformation of ideology as well as the development of alternative and opposing ideologies (i.e. not all humans accept the system of beliefs to be accurate and often generate alternatives to change or replace such a system of beliefs). The liberation movement in South Africa is a good example of how alternative systems of beliefs to apartheid were developed to promote democracy and equality.

Ideology, ethnicity and psychology

Ideologies such as racism, nationalism, anti-Semitism and anti-Islamism all contribute to the particular forms of ethnicity in specific societies, as they determine the most important social features around which ethnic identities are formed. In the case of racism, identities are structured around physical features; under the influence of nationalism, identities may be structured around who are citizens of a country and who are not; with regard to anti-Semitism, identities are determined by who is Jewish and who is not; and anti-Islamism helps define identities in terms of who is Muslim and who is not. In each of the above instances, it is important to note that these ideologies all help to create and maintain unequal social relationships, with one group having more access to power and resources at the expense of the other.

At a psychological level, present-day ideologies such as racism, nationalism, anti-Semitism and anti-Islamism also influence the specific forms and expressions of attitudes, stereotypes, prejudice and discriminatory practices in any society. These psychological processes are then likely to be arranged around social characteristics such as Blackness and Whiteness, citizenship or non-citizenship in a country, being Jewish, or being Muslim. Here again, the social meanings given to these psychological processes are likely to benefit one group at the expense of the other and also to perpetuate this inequality.

The 'racialisation' of ethnicity

The 'racialisation' of ethnicity involves using the notion of inherently different and unequal biological races to define ethnic in-groups and out-groups

(Miles, 1989). This process is extremely common and highlights the role of one of the most widespread ideologies that influences the expression of ethnicity in many societies – racism.

Defining racism

Most theorists agree that racism as an ideology has its origins in the changing economic systems that reach back from European expansion and slavery, through colonialism and imperialism, and presently, in the increased globalisation of trade (Banton, 1988; Foster, 1991; Leiman, 1993; Miles, 1989). The notion of inherently different and unequal biological races became central to racist ideology within these periods of economic development (Miles, 1989). Racism, as ideology, has been employed as a means to justify and rationalise the continued social oppression and economic exploitation of one social group by another – most notably, Blacks by Whites. The notion of 'race' has developed as a fundamental building block that sustains and justifies the existence of racism. In particular, it has been used in the process of racial categorisation, which is the '... delineation of group boundaries and of allocation of persons within those boundaries by primary reference to (supposedly) inherent and/or biological (usually phenotypical) characteristics' (Miles, 1989:74).

Racism is not only reflected in the social structures of societies (e.g., 1948 apartheid policy), but in less formalised social institutions (e.g., the family, religion, etc.), which continue to sustain and perpetuate it (Stevens, 1996).

While it is a system of beliefs about the superiority of some over others, it also minimises the potential conflict which could arise from these uneven social relations, by providing both the oppressed and oppressor with frameworks through which to understand the racist social order (Thompson, 1990). For example, if both Whites and Blacks believe that all Black people are lazy, unintelligent and criminals, and that all Whites are hard-working, intelligent and law-abiding, then this maintains and justifies the exploitation and maltreatment that many Blacks may experience, for both groups. Duncan (1993:31) suggests that this should be seen as a mechanism through which mental health is partly maintained under conditions of oppression, as it is a '... form of cognition which enables [us] to cope with these injustices and inequalities, and very importantly, to live with [ourselves]'.

The relationship between racism and ethnicity

As an ideology, racism influences the expression of ethnicity in several ways:

- Firstly, it informs the way in which ethnic groups are frequently defined (i.e. racial categories are often utilised to distinguish ethnic categories). In societies such as South Africa with a long history of racism, the racial categories of 'Coloured', 'White', 'Indian' and 'Black' became the same categories that were then utilised to define ethnic groups. What is then perceived to be ethnic difference is in fact based on racism.

- Secondly, the concepts of 'racial groups' and 'ethnic groups' become used interchangeably in these instances. Stated differently, ethnicity is often a synonym and euphemism for the notion of race. During apartheid (and even to some extent in South Africa today) it was the norm to utilise the ethnic label to refer to groups who had racial differences imposed upon them, rather than for groups who actually shared common socio-cultural elements. Sharp (1988:80) noted that this interchangeable use of race and ethnicity is applied politically by people who '... seek to form groups, and to differentiate one set of people from another, by appealing to the *idea* of ... cultural difference'. This involved a political attempt to invent distinctly separate ethnic identities, in order to strengthen the argument for distinctly separate races. Ethnic or cultural difference essentially came to mean racial difference, but was a more socially desirable way of stating this racist belief system. In addition, by suggesting that these differences were more than variations in physical features, and were in fact based on socio-cultural elements unique to certain groups, provided a further justification for segregating these groups (Giliomee & Schlemmer, 1989; Marks & Trapido, 1987). Ethnicity was therefore not only used as an interchangeable concept for race, but was used to support the argument for segregating people of different skin colour.

- Thirdly, ethnicity and ethnic groups start to take on the same meanings that are attributed to racial groups (i.e. some groups are defined as lazy, stupid, dirty, criminal, poor, ugly, etc., while others are viewed as hard-working, clever, law-abiding, wealthy, pretty, etc.). Within this process, some groups are accorded a higher social status, access to resources and access to power, at the expense of others. The result is that the inferior or superior position of people within such a society is seen to be because of their belonging to a specific ethnic group, and those who find themselves in a subordinate position are said to be there because of their ethnic deficits (Riggins, 1997). Ethnic hierarchies and oppression in such contexts are essentially racial hierarchies and oppression.

From the above, it can be argued that the 'racialisation' of ethnicity has the potential to create societies in which deep ethnic divisions may occur. In countries with a legacy of racial divisions, ethnic divisions would rely on the most prominent historical differences between groups of people, and these would be fundamentally based on the ideology of racism. Emerging ethnic identities are therefore likely to be identities that are race-based, and can result in further forms of racial separatism (Alexander, 1985).

The politicisation of ethnicity

While as an ideology, racism contributes to the particular expression of ethnicity in various societies, other contemporary political ideologies such as nationalism, anti-Semitism and anti-Islamism also inform the manner in which ethnicity is defined and articulated in other contexts. This process is referred to as the politicisation of ethnicity.

Anti-Islamism and ethnicity

Several writers have identified a long history of ideologies that have contributed to the subordination and domination of Muslims and the construction of this social category as a negative ethnic group. Miles (1989) notes that as early as the Crusades, Muslims were constructed as dark skinned, barbaric, violent, and sexually perverse 'Turks and Saracens' who followed a deviant religion. This was followed by European images of the 'Islamic threat' when Europe began to set its sights on the Middle East, North Africa and India for colonial conquest, and served to justify such conquest. Said (1981) suggests that there has been a longstanding attitude towards Islam within Western culture that stereotyped Muslims as oil suppliers, terrorists and bloodthirsty mobs. While these images have changed over time, it is also clear that after 11 September 2001, many of these images remain. Muslims are often characterised as religious zealots, violent, oppressive to women and anti-Christian. Such inaccurate and stereotypical overgeneralisations of all Arabs, Arab descendents, Middle Eastern communities and Muslims, are fundamental to the ethnic construction of this social group. They have clearly contributed to images of Muslims as a dangerous, secondary status ethnic group in contemporary society, and have provided the ideological justification for actions such as the US-led 'War on Terror' in Afghanistan, as well as the invasion of Iraq.

21.4 BLACK CONSCIOUSNESS: ETHNIC OR POLITICAL IDENTITY?

During the 1970s in South Africa, Black Consciousness emerged as the dominant political ideology opposing apartheid. While many have argued that this was a form of ethnic identity, others have argued that it was in fact a political identity. Black Consciousness drew on historical, linguistic and cultural heterogeneity (i.e. people with different languages, cultural practices and histories), but its defining element was that it attempted to bring together all those who were labeled 'other-than-White' in apartheid South Africa, under the banner of their common experiences as Blacks. The function was to unify a fragmented population who had similar experiences of oppression under apartheid, and was in fact a political defense against White racism. Unlike ethnic identity, which is based on the commonality of socio-cultural markers within a group, Black Consciousness was premised on the commonality of social, economic and political experiences of being 'other-than-White' in South Africa. In other words, rather than drawing on socio-cultural similarities to define a group (as is the case with ethnicity), Black Consciousness politically joined oppressed groups that had been artificially separated through apartheid-imposed racial or ethnic categories (Biko, 1978).

Anti-Semitism and ethnicity

Similarly, the ideologies of racism, anti-Semitism and nationalism in Germany partly accounted for the construction of Jews as an ethnic group that was responsible for Germany's poor domestic economy in the 1930s. The failing German economy paved the way for the emergence of heightened levels of nationalism, and together with the racist Nazi philosophy of creating a 'pure Aryan race', facilitated the genocidal killing of approximately six million Jews in extermination camps. Jews were constructed as economically exploitative, anti-Christian and 'racially' impure. This process also partly provided the ideological basis for the military expansion into Europe, Asia and Africa that was to become known as World War Two.

Figure 7 A popular representation, constructing Muslims as violent

21.5 ENTRENCHING ETHNIC STEREOTYPES IN THE WAR ON IRAQ

On the 20 March 2003, the US-led coalition of military forces initiated an invasion of Iraq to apparently disarm the military regime of Saddam Hussein of all weapons of mass destruction and to replace the current political leadership with a more 'democratic' form of governance. The speeches of President George W. Bush relied implicitly on negative stereotypes about the Muslim world as a threat to peace. Mr Bush declared that 'the tyrant will soon be gone ... All the decades of deceit and cruelty have now reached an end ... he [Saddam Hussein] will remain a deadly foe until the end ... Before the day of horror can come, before it is too late to act, this danger will be removed.' In response, President Saddam Hussein also relied on religious references and stereotypes, when he referred to the US-led coalition forces as 'American, English and Zionist invading aggressors' and predicted a 'holy war' that would defeat them ('As Baghdad empties, Hussein is defiant', *The New York Times*, 19 March 2003). While President Bush attempted to bolster support for military invasion by appealing to historically negative Western stereotypes of the Middle East, Islam and the Arab world, President Hussein appropriated this rhetoric to appeal for particular defensive support from the Arab world and Muslims internationally.

Figure 8 President George W. Bush of the USA

Figure 9 Former President Saddam Hussein of Iraq

Nationalism and ethnicity

More recently, examples of the relationship between nationalism and ethnicity can be found in both Rwanda and Bosnia. In Rwanda, Belgian colonialism had imposed artificial and separate ethnic identities on the 'Hutu' and 'Tutsi' populations and established the minority 'Tutsi' as a puppet elite. After independence, the legacy of this imposed ethnicity remained as the primary basis for social and political relationships in the country. The relationship between nationalism and ethnicity tends to emphasise the superiority of the 'true national' by creating a 'false national' (Balibar, 1990) or 'unwanted immigrant' (Van Dijk, 1997). As was the case

Figure 10 Former Yugoslav president, Slobodan Milosovic, frequently made reference to national pride and purity when inciting ethnic genocide

among Bosnian Serbs, Croats and Muslims, these ethnic identities became more rigidly defined within the context of national conflicts, ultimately contributing to the ethnic genocide in both countries.

Conclusion

This chapter has highlighted that ethnicity is not a set of natural features and characteristics with which we are born. Rather, these are socially determined. They become more pronounced under certain social conditions when ethnic features and characteristics are utilised as markers to identify, differentiate and unevenly structure groups in relation to each other (e.g., in times of conflict such as political elections, political mobilisation, war, etc.). In so doing, the social expression of ethnicity relies on certain social psychological processes, but the meanings attached to ethnicity and these related psychological processes are determined by the ideologies operating within the social context.

While some authors contend that ethnicity may act as a unifying force (e.g., Mazrui, 2001), history repeatedly shows that ethnic identities invariably rely on and recreate unequal social relations and result in further social divisions. Finally, as we consider how to promote more democratic and equal social relationships, it is apparent that we must move beyond the exclusive nature of ethnic identities to more inclusive social relationships that recognise our common humanity at a national, regional and global level.

REFERENCES

Abercrombie, N., Hill, S. & Turner, B.S. (1984). *Dictionary of Sociology*. Middlesex: Penguin Books.

Aboud, F. (1988). *Children and Prejudice*. New York: Basil Blackwell.

Ajzen, I. (1988). *Attitudes, Personality and Behaviour*. Milton Keynes: Open University Press.

Alexander, N. (1985). *Sow the Wind*. Johannesburg: Skotaville.

Althusser, L. (1971). *Lenin and Philosophy and Other Essays*. New York: Monthly Review Press.

Ashmore, R.D. (1970). Prejudice: Causes and cures. In B.E. Collins (Ed.). *Social Psychology: Social influence, attitude change, group processes, and prejudice*. Massachusetts: Addison-Wesley.

Balibar, E. (1990). Paradoxes of universality. In D.T. Goldberg (Ed.). *Anatomy of Racism*. Minneapolis: University of Minnesota Press.

Banton, M. (1988). *Racial Consciousness*. London: Longman.

Barth, F. (Ed.). (1969). *Ethnic Groups and Boundaries*. London: George Allen & Unwin.

Bayoumi, M. & Rubin, A. (2000). *The Edward Said Reader*. New York: Vintage Books.

Biko, S. (1978). *I Write What I Like*. London: Heinemann.

Burg, S.L. & Shoup, P.S. (2000). *The War in Bosnia-Herzegovina: Ethnic conflict and international intervention*. New York: M.E. Sharpe.

Cape Action League (CAL). (1987). *Introduction to 'Race' and Racism*. Salt River: CAL.

Dovideo, J.F. & Gaertner, S.L. (1986). *Prejudice, Discrimination, and Racism*. London: Academic Press.

Duncan, N. (1993). *Discourses on Racism*. Unpublished doctoral thesis. University of the Western Cape, Bellville.

Eiser, J.R. & van der Plight, J. (1988). *Attitudes and Decisions*. London: Routledge.

Foster, D. (1991). Social influence I: Ideology. In D. Foster & J. Louw-Potgieter (Eds.). *Social Psychology in South Africa*. Johannesburg. Lexicon Publishers.

Giliomee, H. & Schlemmer, L. (1989). *From Apartheid to Nation Building*. Cape Town: Oxford University Press.

Kollapan, J. (1999). *Xenophobia in South Africa: The challenge to forced migration*. Unpublished seminar, 7 October. Graduate School: University of the Witwatersrand.

Kolman, A.S. (1979). Family variables related to ethnocentrism in children: A literature review. *Ethnic Groups*, 2:93-107.

Lahey, B. (1995). *Psychology*. Madison: Brown and Benchmark.

Leiman, M. (1993). *The Political Economy of Racism*. London: Pluto Press.

Marks, S. & Trapido, S. (Eds.). (1987). *The Politics of Race, Class and Nationalism in Twentieth Century South Africa*. New York: Longman.

Martin, D.C. (2001). What's in the name 'Coloured'? In A. Segeye (Ed.). *Social Identities in the New South Africa. After Apartheid – volume I*. Cape Town: Kwela Books, pp. 249-68.

Mazrui, A.A. (2001). Shifting African identities: The boundaries of ethnicity and religion in Africa's experience. In S. Bekker, M. Dodds &

M. Khosa (Eds.). *Shifting African Identities*. Pretoria: HSRC, pp. 153-75.

Miles, R. (1989). *Racism*. London: Routledge.

Nzongola-Ntalaja, G. (2001). Ethnic identification in the Great Lakes region. In S. Bekker, M. Dodds & M. Khosa (Eds.). *Shifting African Identities*. Pretoria: HSRC, pp. 61-80.

Ramphele, M. (1995). *A Life*. Cape Town: David Phillip.

Rattansi, A. (1992). Changing the subject? Racism, culture and education. In J. Donald & A. Rattansi (Eds.). *'Race', Culture and Difference*. London: Sage Publications.

Riggins, S.H. (1997). The rhetoric of othering. In S.H. Riggins (Ed.). *The Language and Politics of Exclusion: Others in discourse*. Thousand Oaks, CA: Sage, pp. 1-30.

Said, E. (1981). *Covering Islam: How the media and the experts determine how we see the rest of the world*. London: Routledge & Kegan Paul.

Schalk, S. (2002). Ethnicity: Colonial legacy, ethnic and political manipulation as hindrance to democracy and nation-building in Africa. In N. Duncan, P.D. Gqola, M. Hofmeyer, T. Shefer, F. Malunga & M. Mashige (Eds.). *Discourses on Difference. Discourses on oppression*. Cape Town: CASAS, pp. 407-26.

Sharp, J. (1988). Ethnic group and nation: The apartheid vision in South Africa. In E. Boonzaaier & J. Sharp (Eds.). *South African Keywords: The uses and abuses of political concepts*. Cape Town: David Phillip.

Stevens, G. (1996). The *'Racialised' Discourses of a Group of Black Parents and Adolescents in a Western Cape Community*.

Unpublished Masters thesis. University of the Western Cape, Bellville.

Stevens, G. (1997). Understanding 'race' and racism: A return to traditional scholarship. *Psychology Resource Centre Occasional Publication Series*, University of the Western Cape, Bellville.

Stevens, G. (1998). 'Racialised' discourses: Understanding perceptions of threat in post-apartheid South Africa. *South African Journal of Psychology*, 28(4):204-14.

Tajfel. H. (1981). Social stereotypes and social groups. In J. Turner & H. Giles (Eds.). *Intergroup Behaviour*. Oxford: Blackwell.

Tajfel, H. & Fraser, C. (Eds.). (1978). *Introducing Social Psychology*. Middlesex: Penguin Books.

Telhami, S. (2002). Arab and Muslim America. A snapshot. *The Brookings Review*, 20(1):14-5.

Thompson, J.B. (1990). *Ideology and Modern Culture*. Cambridge: Polity Press.

Thornton, R. (1988). Culture: A contemporary definition. In E. Boonzaier & J. Sharp (Eds.). *South African Keywords: The uses and abuses of political concepts*. Cape Town: David Phillip.

Twitchin, J. & Demuth, C. (1985). *Multi-cultural Education: Views from the classroom*. London: BBC.

Vail, L. (Ed.). (1989). *The Creation of Tribalism in Southern Africa*. London: James Currey.

Van Dijk, T.A. (1997). Political discourse and racism: Describing others in Western parliaments. In S.H. Riggins (Ed.) *The Language and Politics of Exclusion: Others in discourse*. Thousand Oaks, CA: Sage, pp. 31-64.

Multiple choice questions

1. North-African immigrants in Europe frequently provide accounts of how they feel consciously excluded from mainstream social functioning and discriminated against because of their darker physical features, their cultural practices or religious beliefs. These experiences are most likely a result of
   a) the process of Othering that occurs in ethnicisation
   b) the process of Othering that occurs in racialisation
   c) a and b
   d) none of the above

2. The tendency to perceive our own social group as superior to others, while simultaneously harbouring negative feelings towards out-groups, is referred to as
   a) ethnicisation
   b) ethnocentrism
   c) discrimination
   d) racialisation

3. Negative attitudes toward an out-group are referred to as _____ and acting upon this belief to marginalise this group can be characterised as _____
   a) racism; discrimination
   b) stereotypes; racism
   c) prejudice; discrimination
   d) discrimination; prejudice

4. During apartheid, the overgeneralisation that all Blacks were unintelligent, unhygienic, etc. was an example of
   a) stereotyping
   b) nationalism
   c) discrimination
   d) ideology

5. The intersection between anti-Semitism and racism was in part responsible for the
   a) ethnic genocide in Rwanda between Hutus and Tutsi
   b) ethnic cleansing in Bosnia
   c) extermination of six million Jews in Nazi Germany
   d) massacre of Cambodians by the Khmer Rouge

6. While there is broad consensus around what constitutes ethnicity as a sociological and anthropological construct, its particular form and expression is
   a) linked to certain salient socio-cultural markers such as language, cultural practices, histories, etc.
   b) dependent upon the interface between social psychological processes (e.g., prejudice), and socio-historical factors (e.g., ideology)
   c) invariably linked to asymmetrical social relations
   d) all of the above

7. The contemporary negative constructions of Middle Eastern populations, the Arab world and Muslims are in part, linked to
   a) the historical connection between racist ideology and Islam, according to Miles (1989)
   b) Said's (1981) concept of Orientalism
   c) a and b
   d) none of the above

8. During apartheid, the racialisation of ethnicity occurred through
   a) the use of racial labels to refer to different religious groups
   b) the use of ethnic labels to refer to groups who had racial labels artificially imposed upon them
   c) the use of racial labels to refer to groups who adhered to different dress codes
   d) all of the above

9. Which of the following is/are not true? In both Rwanda and Bosnia, the ethnic cleansing that occurred was based on
   a) longstanding, historical divides in the population
   b) heightened social conflict that occurred prior to the genocide
   c) the strong emergence of nationalist ideologies
   d) the interface between Zionism and racism

10. Which of the following is/are not true? Ethnicity is
   a) primordial and essentialist in nature (i.e. a natural and fixed set of characteristics that we are all born with)
   b) socially constructed
   c) dependent on the level of access that we have to cultural information, according to Schalk (2002)
   d) b and c

Short answer questions

1. Referring to Box 21.2, to what degree do ethnic labels, groups and identities exist in post-apartheid South Africa? Compare these ethnic labels, groups and identities with racial labels that were utilised to differentiate the population during apartheid in

South Africa, looking specifically at the differences and similarities in meanings associated with these labels, groups and identities across the two historical contexts.

2. Imagine a fictitious situation in which different ethnic groups exist in a social context, but are also in conflict over land, mining rights, employment or political power. What are the potential strategies that could be employed to define Self and Other, as well as the potential strategies of marginalisation and control that could be employed within this situation, and relate them to South Africa's apartheid past.

3. Consult the library and conduct independent research from general texts, to examine ethnicity in the former Soviet Union, China or India. Investigate the historical basis for ethnic differentiation in these contexts, as well as the contemporary expressions thereof, and assess the degree to which ethnicity in these contexts operates differently to the examples in the text.

22

Sex and Gender in Society

Floretta Boonzaier & Cheryl de la Rey

CHAPTER OBJECTIVES

After studying this chapter you should be able to:
- identify the ways in which psychology has approached gender/sex differences
- construct accounts of gender development in childhood by discussing the basic tenets of each theory
- describe the basic principles of the various strands of feminist theory
- explain the differences between an essentialist and a social constructionist approach to gender
- understand the key concepts in the psychology of gender.

Nosipho saw herself as a feminist. She had grown up in quite a traditional household, where, even though her father had treated her mother with respect, if ever there was any difference of opinion, her father's decision was final. Her mother was a strong woman, but her father was definitely the 'head' of the family. Fortunately, her father was a kind and gentle man so this hadn't been the problem it might have been. But Nosipho had seen many families where the father bullied his wife and the children too. Everyone in her community knew of the families where the wife was being beaten by her husband – even if they didn't say it openly. When Nosipho and her mum discussed these kinds of things, they both got very angry on behalf of the women, but they felt helpless to be able to do anything about it. It seemed to Nosipho that many of the things that went wrong in families had to do with the way that men and women related to each other.

Nosipho had often tried to make sense of the problems she saw between men and women. Why did men seem so aggressive and why did women so often land up being treated badly? Nosipho had found herself wondering at various times about whether men and women were just too different from one another and, if they were, what had made them that way? Were they just born different or did their society and culture force them into these gender roles? There did seem to be some change, though. It seemed to Nosipho that the men in her generation seemed to be less afraid of showing their softer feelings and young women were often more assertive than their mothers had been. Perhaps things were improving.

Introduction

In this chapter we review the main psychological theories that account for gender/sex differences. Through our discussion of biological, psychoanalytic, social learning, cognitive-developmental, gender schema theories and social constructionism, we explore key concepts in the study of gender such as the differences between 'sex' and 'gender', gender roles, stereotypes, socialisation, gender constancy and androgyny. In the second part of the chapter, we focus on gender in society by highlighting some of the challenges to gender equity and the ways in which the sources of gender inequality have been theorised. We briefly outline liberal, radical, socialist/Marxist, Black and lesbian feminism. We end the chapter by showing how, despite earlier critiques, psychology has made a positive contribution to the study of gender.

The study of gender has not traditionally been included in psychology, and women's issues have not been the traditional and established focus of research, theory and practice. As a science, psychology has been criticised for being biased against women, emphasising and generalising from the experiences of men (mostly White, middle-class and heterosexual) to all of humanity. In response to such criticism, psychology as a discipline turned to the study of sex differences. Perhaps the most debated questions in this area of research are whether there are significant psychological differences between the sexes, and if so, what are the origins of these differences.

Sex difference research has focused on differences in sensory abilities, attention, verbal and spatial skills, cognitive styles, aggression and many other areas (Burr, 1998). Maccoby and Jacklin (1974) reviewed the evidence from studies that have focused on sex differences. They concluded that there are differences between females and males in only four areas, namely verbal, visual-spatial and mathematical abilities, and aggressiveness. Even though they found these areas of difference, Maccoby and Jacklin (1974) pointed out that the differences between men and women have been overstated and that similarities were frequently ignored.

Based on the assumption that there are real differences between the sexes, psychology has offered a number of theories accounting for the development of gender identity in children. The theories we discuss below include biological, psychoanalytic, social learning, cognitive-developmental, gender schema theories and the social constructionist approach to gender.

Biological accounts

Biological accounts argue that men and women are intrinsically different, and that masculinity and femininity follow from these biological differences (Macdonald, 1995) located in the genes, hormones or evolutionary factors. Biological factors are seen to produce gender differences in personality, such as aggressiveness in men or nurturance in women (Burr, 1998). This view has been labelled as essentialist. Essentialism refers to the belief in inherent, natural differences between women and men. It assumes that gender is inherent at birth and that gender traits are internal and unchanging (Bohan, 1997). Essentialist views place little emphasis on social, historical and cultural influences, and gender is assumed to be the same across time and location. Biological accounts of gender do not account for individual agency, choice and change. If we assume that men are inherently aggressive by virtue of their genetic make-up or evolutionary adaptation, why is it that only some men perpetrate acts of violence, and how do we combat problems such as male violence against women?

Psychoanalytic theory

Freud's psychoanalytic theory of personality and sexual development suggests that gender identity develops as a result of internal, unconscious conflicts in children. At the ages of three to five years, children develop an attraction to the opposite-sex parent. Freud suggested that boys experience an Oedipus complex, named after the Greek myth in which Oedipus kills his father and marries his mother. Girls experience a similar attraction to their fathers when they realise they do not possess a penis. Freud named this 'penis envy'. Both girls and boys experience conflict and anxiety over their attraction to the opposite-sex parent and their sexual competition with the same-sex parent. However, the conflict is resolved when they realise the risks of competing with the same-sex parent (Papalia & Olds, 1988) and they later come to identify with that parent and develop a gender identity and behaviour similar to the same-sex parent. Freud believed that the conflict was resolved differently for boys and girls. Boys are able to fully resolve the conflict, identify with their fathers and develop a strong superego (responsible for moral development). Girls, according to Freud, do not fully resolve the crisis and have a weaker identification with their mothers, resulting in a weaker superego and an inferiority complex (Stainton Rogers & Stainton Rogers, 2001).

As expected, Freud's views on women have been subjected to considerable criticism, particularly by feminist psychologists. His theory has also been critiqued for being essentialist and universalising about human sexual development (Chodorow, 1994), and for overlooking cultural, social and historical contingencies. As a result, theorists began to accord more attention to the social aspects of gender development.

Social learning theory

Social learning theory (Bandura, 1977) argues that attitudes and behaviours are learned from the surrounding environment. Theorists note that individuals acquire masculine and feminine characteristics and skills by role modelling significant others. The concept of socialisation was introduced to refer to the ways in which individuals learn gender-appropriate behaviour. It is a broad term which is generally used to describe the processes through which children learn the rules of behaviour and the systems of beliefs and values of the society in which they grow up. Socialising agents such as parents, family members, teachers, peers and the media convey repeated messages both verbally and through their actions. Through their exposure to these messages, children learn gender-appropriate behaviour patterns and attitudes.

Social learning occurs in complex ways. Adults communicate messages about gender both consciously and unconsciously. Babies, from the time of their birth, are treated differently depending upon their sex. The first question usually asked is: 'Is it a girl or a boy?' Conscious gendered messages conveyed by parents may include dressing children in different colours – blue for boys and pink for girls – and giving children sex-typed toys. At the unconscious level, parents also communicate differently with girls and boys. Burr (1998) cites research that shows that parents' and other family members' responses to children vary depending on their gender. For example, Walum (in Burr, 1998) found that baby girls' and boys' cries were interpreted differently – boys were assumed to cry to exercise their lungs, whereas girls' crying was interpreted as a sign of distress. Interpreting boys' mischievous behaviour, as 'natural' and expecting passive and constrained behaviour from girls is another example of an unconscious gendered message.

The stories children are told about princes and princesses, toys given to children and images of dolls and action heroes all convey messages about gender roles and stereotypes. Gender roles refer to the different tasks and responsibilities expected of men and women. The expectations that women care for children and that men are breadwinners are examples of gender roles. These roles frequently go unchallenged, and those who do challenge them are often criticised (for example, a mother who does not assume the role of primary caregiver may be labelled a 'bad mother/woman'). Gender roles and stereotypes form a network that shapes our behaviour in particular ways such as dress, language, style and sexuality.

Gender stereotypes refer to psychological traits and behavioural characteristics (often exaggerated) attributed to women and men by virtue of their group membership. Gender stereotypes are both descriptive (describing particular characteristics or

22.1 GENDER STEREOTYPES IN THE MEDIA

Furnham *et al.* (2001) examined the role of gender stereotypes in Zimbabwean television advertisements by analysing 110 advertisements. They found that women and men were frequently depicted in contrasting roles and settings. Men were more often portrayed as experts, professionals and product authorities. They were often represented in work or outdoors settings and were more likely to be associated with non-domestic products (cars or sports). Women were typically shown as consumers or product users, occupying roles such as wife or mother and commonly depicted with children. They were also more likely to be represented in dependent roles and shown in the home. Women were regularly associated with domestic products (body, food and home). Social learning theory suggests that we learn gender-appropriate behaviour through observation and role modelling. Therefore, gendered stereotyped messages would reinforce traditional gender roles and behaviour, particularly in children.

behaviours) and prescriptive (guiding the ways in which we act in particular situations) (Moghaddam, 1998). Our daily realities provide us with many examples of gender stereotypes, such as beliefs that women are emotional, passive and dependent, and that men are aggressive, strong and assertive. The stereotypical assumption that men are better drivers than women is also pervasive. Gender stereotypes are said to develop at a young age, and studies show how young children show preferences for gender-stereotyped toys (Serbin *et al.*, 2001). Visual preferences for gender-stereotyped toys (e.g., cars for boys and dolls for girls) emerge between 12 to 18 months of age and girls recognise that specific types of toys are associated with a particular gender.

Social learning theory has made significant advances to our understandings of gender, accounting for how individuals learn gender-appropriate behaviour and the norms and rules of their cultures. However, the theory has been critiqued for not acknowledging individual agency and for portraying individuals as passively responding to the socialising agents in the surrounding environment. In so doing, insufficient attention is accorded to children's cognitive processes and self-identification – issues that are addressed by the cognitive-developmental approaches to gender development.

Cognitive-developmental approaches

Cognitive-developmental approaches to gender, developed amongst others by Kohlberg (1966), are based on Piaget's stage theory of cognitive development. The approach suggests that children understand the world in terms of categories and use cognitive processes to acquire gender-related behaviour. Kohlberg argued that there are three aspects to the development of gender identity in children, namely gender labelling, gender knowledge and gender constancy. Gender labelling refers to the attribution of terms such as 'girl' and 'boy'. Gender knowledge refers to knowledge about the particular characteristics of females and males, and gender constancy is the recognition that gender does not change. Children's awareness of gender has been shown to become more complex with increasing age. Awareness of gender categories is typically displayed at about three years of age. Initially, gender is merely a label. For example, four-year-olds are likely to think that a person's gender has changed if

the person wears clothes associated with a different gender. By the age of six or seven, gender constancy is acquired and children recognise that gender has some level of consistency and stability – at this age they identify closely with and want to imitate their own gender. Cognitive-developmental theories focus on individual differences in development and pay scant attention to other factors, such as class or race. The theory also does not adequately account for why children choose gender as a primary category, rather than other categories such as religion or race.

Gender schema theory

The gender schema theory conceptualised by Sandra Bem (1981a) developed as a critique of the passive representations of children in the social learning approaches. It combines aspects of social/cultural learning with cognitive-developmental approaches. The theory suggests that gender identity and development arise from gender schematic processing. Schemata refer to the conceptual frameworks individuals use to make sense of the world around them. Children therefore develop conceptual schemata of masculinity and femininity through which they perceive the world and interpret their own and others' behaviour. Information used in the child's cognitive processing is mediated by the culture's definitions of masculinity and femininity.

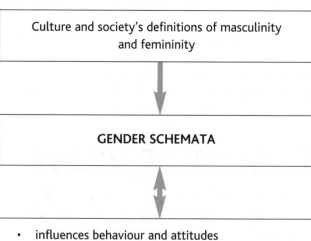

Figure 1 Gender schema theory

Gender schemata are crucial to the development of gender identity and constructions of self. They encompass assumptions about masculinity and femininity as well as appropriate behaviour and attitudes (Stainton Rogers & Stainton Rogers, 2001). Thus, like gender stereotypes they have a prescriptive element – guiding gender-appropriate behaviour. It is a common stereotype that men or boys express their anger more than women or girls. The social acceptability of this behaviour in men is related to male gender roles such as assertiveness and dominance. Stereotypes (and gender roles) are frequently internalised, and studies have found that girls typically suppress their anger more than boys or use gendered options for the expression of emotions (Cox *et al.*, 2000). Research has also shown that women in abusive relationships subscribe to gender stereotypical norms of the 'good woman' or the 'good wife' and conform to constructions of femininity as nurturing and caring (Boonzaier & de la Rey, 2003).

Psychologists have typically viewed sex difference as a fixed variable, dividing human beings into binary categories, such as male or female and masculine or feminine. The introduction of the concept of androgyny significantly challenged these assumptions. In the 1970s, Sandra Bem developed the Bem Sex-Role Inventory, which includes 20 stereotypically masculine, 20 stereotypically feminine and 20 neutral traits (Bem, 1981b). The inventory is used to test the degree to which women and men identify with these traits and score as either masculine, feminine, androgynous or undifferentiated. Androgyny is the term used to refer to individuals who show little difference between masculine and feminine scores, and denotes the integration of masculinity and femininity within an individual. Bem also proposed androgyny as a measure of psychological well-being since the androgynous individual's personality would include a balanced combination of masculine and feminine traits. The concept of androgyny, taken up by many feminist thinkers, was seen to liberate people from the restrictions of gender roles or behaviour. It also challenged traditional assumptions of the female-male dichotomy, allowing for individuals to possess traits associated with both genders (e.g., an individual could be both assertive and empathic). The male-female dichotomy has also been challenged by research that shows the existence of more than two sex categories, for example, hermaphrodites, transsexuals and transvestites (Moghaddam, 1998).

Bem's assertion that masculinity, femininity and androgyny are personality traits possessed by individuals has been subjected to much criticism (Burr, 1998). The typically masculine and feminine traits are gender stereotypical and rely on essentialist characteristics associated with particular genders. Some have also questioned the applicability of these characteristics to contemporary society. Although

	Social learning theory	Cognitive-developmental theory	Gender schema theory
Differences develop through:	Observation of role models and social influences	Stages of general cognitive development	Development of gender-specific schemata
Children:	Choose which models to imitate	Acquire and organise information about the social world	Use gender-specific schemata to make sense of the world
Gender development begins:	Usually during infancy as agents of socialisation have an impact	When child has the cognitive capacity (usually preschool years)	When child has the capacity to develop schemata (usually preschool years)
Gender development is complete:	Usually during adulthood but always subject to change	During late childhood or preadolescence	During late childhood
Girls and boys:	Often develop different gender knowledge and gender-related behaviours	Develop similar cognitive understandings of gender	Develop different schemata depending on the influences

Table 1 Social psychological theories of gender development

Source: Adapted from Brannon (1996)

gender schema theory incorporates the cultural definitions of masculinity and femininity, structural gender inequalities and cultural variations are overlooked.

The pervasive assumption about gender as a construct rooted in biological differences has been challenged by research that has shown that gender does not simply emerge from anatomy or hormones; instead, meanings of femininity and masculinity are created and recreated through the social order and social practices.

Social constructionism

A social constructionist approach suggests that gender differences, rather than being ascribed to biology, are constructed by the society in which we live and through our interactions with others. Rather than viewing masculinity and femininity as essential characteristics, this view posits that gender is constructed within particular social and historical contexts. Theorists point out that what it means to be

22.2 THE ESSENTIALIST/CONSTRUCTIONIST DEBATE

An area of theorising that has been characterised by much debate and controversy is the contestation between essentialist and constructionist views of gender. Essentialism is the belief in the 'true' essence of individuals. From a gendered perspective, the approach assumes that women and men are inherently different. Gender differences are prescribed at birth and are fixed throughout our lifespan. Essentialism espouses a belief in qualities such as aggression and nurturance as intrinsically male and female qualities, respectively (Burr, 1998). Biological differences are taken as the starting point for producing a variety of social and psychological consequences (attitudes, behaviours and social organisation).

Many psychologists reject essentialist assumptions, as they seem to excuse deviant male behaviour such as violence (Macdonald, 1995). Bohan (1997), in her discussion of essentialism and constructionism in feminist psychology, argues that essentialist theories have implications for the practice of feminist politics. For example, if we assume that women and men are essentially different in terms of their psychological make-up, it would be difficult to challenge inequality between the sexes. From an essentialist standpoint, differences between men and women are assumed to arise from biology or nature and would prescribe a 'natural' gender order where women are subordinate to men. From a different standpoint, Birke (in Macdonald, 1995) suggests feminist psychologists should not reject all aspects of biological essentialism. She suggests that psychologists should explore the effects of biological processes (such as menstruation and childbirth) on women's sense of gender identity. This approach encourages psychologists to look beyond childhood development in order to consider gender identity development as a lifelong, interactive

process (Macdonald, 1995).

Critiques of essentialism include challenges to the universalistic assumptions about 'women/woman' as a fixed category and to the lack of attention accorded to diversity amongst women and similarities between women and men (Bohan, 1997). Feminist debates on difference and equality (among women and between women and men) have called into question assumptions about a unitary female experience. As Flax (1990:56) asserts, any feminist standpoint will be partial and the category 'woman' does not exist 'except within a specific set of (already gendered) relations – to man and to many concrete and different women'. At this point, the social constructionist approach to gender enters the debate.

Theorists such as Crawford (1995) have identified the inherent biases in sex difference research and advocated the use of social constructionism as an alternative approach to gender relations. Gender is understood as socially constructed within particular cultural, social and historic contexts. We constantly 'do' gender (West & Zimmerman, 1991) because we are placed in gendered situations (or in contexts of gendered power relations) (Bohan, 1997). According to Shotter and Gergen (in Crawford, 1995) people develop their sense of self within prevailing discourses of power relations. Thus, we internalise gender norms and behave in gendered (or non-gendered) ways by either accepting or resisting those norms. This approach strengthens our theorising since diversity (arising from particular contexts) is acknowledged. The focus shifts from the individual to the social and the role of power in the construction of gender is examined (Bohan, 1997). Reflecting contemporary understandings of gender as a relational construction, this approach has gained ascendancy in feminist psychology.

male or female has changed over the centuries and is not the same in all cultural contexts. From a social constructionist perspective, gender is described as a system of relations operating at the individual, interpersonal and societal levels (Crawford, 1995). At the individual level, social constructionists analyse how particular definitions of femininity and masculinity are enacted and conform to or resist socially agreed upon standards. At the interpersonal level, gender affects how we relate to others, either male or female. And at the level of social structure, the role of power in the construction of gender is acknowledged (Crawford, 1995). We identify ourselves and are identifiable to others as feminine or masculine, as woman or man. In our society particular behaviours and codes of dress are understood as either masculine or feminine. But gender is not simply a characteristic or trait of individuals. It is embedded in an array of institutional arrangements and structures that constitute society.

From a social constructionist perspective, many studies have started to focus on what it means to be a man and issues that affect men's lives. An area of research entitled 'Men's Studies' or 'Critical Men's Studies' (Morrell, 2001) addresses issues of masculinity by critiquing male power and domination. Masculinity has been described as shifting, dynamic, socially constructed and contested (Morrell, 2001). Connell (1995) showed how all men do not equally benefit from male domination (patriarchy) and how certain forms of masculinity have become culturally dominant, depending on the norms and values of the surrounding culture. These forms of masculinity emphasised certain characteristics at particular social and historical moments. Traditionally, masculinity has been associated with aggressive, assertive and authoritarian ideals, and men have been defined as powerful, strong and aggressive. Violent behaviour is valorised as symbolic of masculinity and male authority (Dobash & Dobash, 1998). Within a patriarchal culture, men are socialised into keeping women subordinate through, for example, the use of violence. Thus, male violence is a reflection of male authority and domination over women. Studies address how men account for the perpetration of violence against their partners (Hearn, 1998) as well as the connections between masculinity and violence (Wood & Jewkes, 2001). Within this line of research, there appears to be some consensus that cultural or social contexts set the scene for men's violence against women and construct dominant forms of masculinity and femi-

ninity, which men and women draw upon in order to construct gendered identities.

Possibly the most common critique levelled at social constructionism is that it advocates a relativistic stance, in which there are multiple forms of truth/knowledge and no version is privileged over another. However, in suggesting this stance, social constructionism posits a particular form of knowledge itself. This 'form of knowledge' is based on relativism as a foundation and posits multiple forms of localised knowledge traditions. It has also been argued that this approach, through its focus on language, reduces the very real material conditions of human life into ideas and texts and therefore may obscure human suffering and oppression (Terre Blanche & Durrheim, 1999). Social constructionism should therefore not necessarily be seen as the only way to study gender in the social sciences. Different approaches should be deployed in order to addresses the variety of research questions in this diverse field of study.

22.3 MASCULINITY AND VIOLENCE

Wood and Jewkes (2001) explored how young men living in a township in the Eastern Cape spoke about perpetrating violence against female partners. They conducted in-depth interviews with young Xhosa-speaking men. Wood and Jewkes found that adolescent sexual relationships were characterised by violence, coercive sex and threats toward female partners. Young men's notions of 'successful masculinity' were partially defined in terms of their control over sexual relationships with women. In general, research participants constructed gender relations in patriarchal terms – with women constructed as sexually passive and men as sexually aggressive. Their talk also reflected compliance with the 'sexual double standard' – implying that it is acceptable for men to have multiple partners but completely unacceptable for women. Wood and Jewkes found connections between young men's talk about violence and predominant forms of masculinity available in the community, and in South Africa at large. They showed how culturally dominant (hegemonic) forms of masculinity are socially constructed and how young men draw upon these in their sexual relationships.

Gender in society

The issue of equality between men and women is one of the most debated social questions. Although women and men are equal in terms of South African law, women are still discriminated against in various sectors of society. Recent statistics gathered on women and men in South Africa, show marked differences in the quality of life of women and men, boys and girls as well as significant differences in terms of race and class (Budlender, Analysis and Statistical Consulting & Statistics South Africa, 2002). For example, the overall unemployment rate is higher for women than men. In 2001, 19 per cent of employed women earned R200 or less per month, compared to only 9 per cent of men. Twenty-three per cent of men, as opposed to only 14 per cent of women earned more than R4 500 per month.

Perhaps the most significant gender-related issue currently is violence against women. Forms of violence against women are multiple and include rape, sexual harassment and woman abuse, and are perpetrated mostly by men. Rape is an underreported crime in South Africa (as elsewhere). The reasons for underreporting often include shame, embarrassment and fear. In addition, women sometimes do not define their experiences of sexual coercion as rape, particularly when the perpetrator is an intimate partner (Boonzaier & de la Rey, 2003). Rape is more likely to occur in and around the home and to be perpetrated by someone known to the victim (Hirschowitz et al., 2000).

Women and girls may experience sexual harassment in a number of contexts, such as the workplace, educational institutions or in the home. Even schools are violent places for children, particularly girls. A recent study by Human Rights Watch (2001) found that South African schoolgirls are subjected to multiple forms of violence, such as sexual harassment, emotional abuse, verbal degradation and rape. These incidents were perpetrated by teachers, other learners, other school employees and strangers. In South Africa, estimates suggest that approximately 25 per cent of women are abused by their male partners (Jacobs & Suleman, 1999) and that a woman is killed by her partner every six days (Vetten, 1996). Other forms of gender violence, which are widespread, include femicide (the misogynistic killing of women), female genital mutilation and forced prostitution.

The World Health Organisation (cited in Jacobs & Suleman, 1999) estimates that violence against women is a greater cause of poor health than traffic accidents and malaria combined. Women suffer a range of physical injuries from violent attacks in the home and in public. Women who have been raped and those who experience sexual abuse are also at increased risk of contracting HIV/AIDS. Violence from intimate partners negatively affects women's mental health, with women experiencing anxiety, depression, suicide ideation or attempts, panic attacks, and other negative psychological and emotional consequences (Bollen et al., 1999). Overall, gender violence has a deleterious effect on women and girls' well-being and mental and physical health.

22.4 GENDERED NARRATIVES

Boonzaier and de la Rey (2003) explored how women constructed gender in their talk of violence. Their article reports on a narrative study conducted with 15 women who experienced violence from their partners in Mitchell's Plain, in the Western Cape. In their narratives of abuse, women constructed shifting gendered identities. At times, women's talk reflected compliance with hegemonic forms of femininity emphasising qualities such as caring, nurturance, submission and passivity. Women spoke about being a 'good wife/woman' by providing love, care and tenderness to soften their partners' hardness. Some women also took up gendered positions of the 'good wife' suggesting that they should remain sexually available to their husbands. At other times in their narratives, women resisted these stereotypical gendered constructions and spoke about their strength, determination and resistance. Women also constructed masculinity as powerful, dominant and authoritative while simultaneously being threatened by powerlessness, inferiority and emasculation. The study highlighted the shifting and contradictory nature of gendered identities, particularly in violent relationships.

As the current situation in South Africa testifies, men still exercise political, economic, personal and social power over women (Fedler & Tanzer, 2000). Several theories have been developed to explain the reasons for gender inequality. This body of knowledge is described as feminist theory. But, there is no single feminist theory. Instead, there are different strands of feminism that are each labelled according to its views on the sources of gender inequality. These strands of feminism are briefly explained below in order to properly locate the psychology of gender in its social, political and economic contexts (Burr, 1998).

Feminist theories

Liberal feminism asserts that women should be accorded the same rights as men and should enjoy equal status in all sectors of society. A significant achievement of liberal feminism is that it fought for the enfranchisement of women. The call for equal opportunities for women and men has been described as the defining feature of liberal feminism (Acker, 1994). However, a critique levelled at liberal feminist thought is that equality of opportunity is sought in a hierarchical society where resources are not equally available to all men based upon divisions of race or class.

Radical feminism posits male dominance or patriarchy as the primary reason for gender inequality and therefore focuses on the social system. The approach is marked by the assumption that the oppression of women is universal. On this point, radical feminism has been subjected to a great deal of criticism, as intersections of race, class and other differences amongst women are ignored. Thus, if a universal patriarchy is seen as the primary source of women's oppression, then Black and White women will be seen as being equally oppressed and the inequalities based upon race and class will be overlooked. The idea of a universalist concept of patriarchy was therefore criticised for ignoring societal and cultural differences (Whelehan, 1995).

Socialist/Marxist feminism is centred on the assertion that class and gender are significant sources of women's oppression. Socialist/Marxist feminists argue that capitalism is a central force in maintaining women's oppression. The approaches focus on the gendered division of labour and the value attached to 'women's work'.

Black feminism emerged both in response to the reluctance of feminism to address racism inside and outside its ranks, and the failure of Black consciousness groups to deal with gender issues. In the US, Black feminists confronted the women's movement for ignoring racism and failing to acknowledge differences among women as a group. The criticism was that the category 'women' was assumed to be synonymous with White women's experiences, with Black women regarded as the 'Other'. The perspective

that insisted that feminism could only be meaningful if it addresses racism became defined as Black feminism. Black feminists, however, were not the only group who felt excluded by mainstream feminism.

Lesbian feminists, too, struggled to gain visibility for their concerns. They identified sexual orientation as a factor in women's oppression. Lesbian feminism, based on a critique of heterosexuality contributed to the disruption of the notion of universal sisterhood, as it questioned the politics of heterosexual relationships.

As a result of the tensions around various groups of women – Black women, lesbians, working-class women – feeling excluded from mainstream feminism, in the 1980s a crisis in feminism was documented (Whelehan, 1995). The crisis compelled feminist theory to move away from the universalist tendencies of liberal, radical and socialist feminism towards the need to deal with differences amongst women as a group.

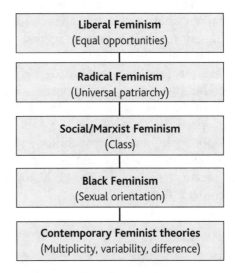

Figure 2 Feminist theories

In feminist theory today there has been agreement on the significance of new forms of theorising that move beyond a one dimensional focus on gender to include differences due to factors such as race and sexual orientation. At the same time, however, there is consensus on the need to address the inequalities which affect most women as women. Newer theories acknowledge multiplicity and variability in individual experience. For example, studies have focused on women's heterosexual desire and negotiation (Gavey, 1996; Shefer, 1999), women's aggression (Squire, 1998) and narratives of romantic love (Jackson, 2001).

A less popular, but emerging area of research is the theorising on masculinity that speaks directly to feminism and feminist issues. Morrell (2001) describes three categories of men's responses to gender change in South Africa, namely, defensive, accommodating and progressive strategies. In the first category men are invested in maintaining the traditional gender order and resist challenges by feminism and women's groups. In the second and third categories, men are challenging violent forms of masculinity and exploring new ways of being a man. As a result of continual challenges to masculinity and men's particular circumstances (e.g., unemployment), forms of masculinity are constantly shifting and contested.

Conclusion

To end this chapter, we return to the point made at the beginning, that psychology has traditionally been criticised for being biased against women. Psychology has also been critiqued for its individualistic bias, for ignoring the broader context in which gender identity and relationships develop. Illustrative of these critiques, we showed that to be able to properly understand gender, we must be prepared to look beyond psychology to other disciplines such as sociology and gender studies to properly locate it within the social, historical and political context (Burr, 1998).

In spite of the earlier critiques, psychology has made significant inroads in understanding gender. Social learning, cognitive-developmental and gender schema theories have each made unique contributions to our understandings of gender issues, particularly in childhood. The focus on women's issues from within psychology (the psychology of women) has also advanced our understanding of topics that have either been ignored or distorted. As an area of research, the psychology of women explores a wide range of psychological issues that concern women, such as menstruation, pregnancy, childbirth and menopause (Matlin, 1987). Theorists also explore topics that affect women almost exclusively, such as rape, woman abuse and other forms of gender violence. Areas that have traditionally been approached from a male point of view, such as achievement, work and sexuality, are also investigated (Matlin, 1987). There has also been a proliferation of critical studies on masculinity and issues relevant to men's lives, such as fathering, violence and relationships as well as interesting and emerging work on diverse forms of masculinity (Black, urban, working-class) and ways of being a man (see Morrell, 2001). Contemporary feminist psychologists acknowledge the need to transform psychology as a discipline by addressing its male bias, and many psychologists also acknowledge the need to shift away from traditional positivist research to research methods that are more able to account for variability of human experience and how we are affected by the social context.

REFERENCES

Acker, S. (1994). *Gendered Education: Sociological reflections on women, teaching and feminism*. Buckingham: Open University Press.

Bandura, A. (1977). *Social Learning Theory*. Englewood Cliffs: Prentice Hall.

Bem, S.L. (1981a). Gender schema theory: A cognitive account of sex-typing. *Psychological Review*, 88(4):354-64.

Bem, S.L. (1981b). *Bem Sex-role Inventory. Professional Manual*. Palo Alto: Consulting Psychologists Press, Inc.

Bohan, J.S. (1997). Regarding gender. Essentialism, constructionism and feminist psychology. In M.M. Gergen & S.N. Davis (Eds.). *Toward a New Psychology of Gender*. New York: Routledge, pp. 31-47.

Bollen, S., Artz, L., Vetten, L., & Louw, A. (1999). *Violence Against Women in Metropolitan South Africa: A study on impact and service delivery*. Institute for Security Studies monograph series, No. 41, www.iss.co.za (accessed 28 February 2003).

Boonzaier, F. & de la Rey, C. (2003). 'He,s a man and I,m a woman ...' Cultural constructions of masculinity and femininity in South African women,s narratives of violence. *Violence Against Women*, 9(8):1003-29.

Brannon, L. (1996). *Gender: psychological perspectives*. Boston: Allyn and Bacon.

Budlender, D., Analysis and Statistical Consulting & Statistics South Africa. (2002). *Women and Men in South Africa: Five years on*. Pretoria: Statistics South Africa.

Burr, V. (1998). *Gender and Social Psychology*. London: Routledge.

Chodorow, N.J. (1994). *Femininities, Masculinities, Sexualities. Freud and beyond*. Lexington: The University Press of Kentucky.

Connell, R.W. (1995). *Masculinities*. St Leonards, Australia: Allen & Unwin.

Cox, D.L., Stabb, S.D. & Hulgus, J.F. (2000). Anger and depression in girls and boys. A study of gender differences. *Psychology of Women Quarterly*, 24:110-12.

Crawford, M. (1995). *Talking Difference. On gender and language*. London: Sage.

Dobash, R.E. & Dobash, R.P. (1998). Violent men and violent contexts.

In R.E. Dobash & R.P. Dobash (Eds.). *Rethinking Violence Against Women*. Thousand Oaks: Sage, pp. 141-68.

Fedler, J. & Tanzer, Z. (2000). A world in denial. International perspectives of violence against women. In Y.J. Park & J. Fedler & Z. Dangor (Eds.). *Reclaiming Women's Spaces. New perspectives on violence against women and sheltering in South Africa*. Johannesburg: Nisaa Institute for Women's Development, pp. 17-46.

Flax, J. (1990). Postmodernism and gender relations in feminist theory. In L.J. Nicholson (Ed.). *Feminism/Postmodernism*. New York: Routledge, pp. 41-62.

Furnham, A., Pallangyo, A.E. & Gunter, B. (2001). Gender-role stereotyping in Zimbabwean television advertisements. *South African Journal of Psychology*, 31(2):21-9.

Gavey, N. (1996). Women's desire and sexual violence discourse. In S. Wilkinson (Ed.). *Feminist Social Psychologies. International perspectives*. Buckingham: Open University Press, pp. 51-65.

Hearn, J. (1998). *The Violences of Men*. London: Sage.

Hirschowitz, R., Worku, S. & Orkin, M. (2000). *Quantitative Research Findings on Rape in South Africa*. Pretoria: Statistics South Africa.

Human Rights Watch. (2001). *Scared at School: sexual violence against girls in South African schools*. New York: Human Rights Watch.

Jackson, S. (2001). Happily never after: Young women's stories of abuse in heterosexual love relationships. *Feminism & Psychology*, 11(3):305-21.

Jacobs, T. & Suleman, F. (1999). *Breaking the Silence: A profile of domestic violence in women attending a community health centre*. Health Systems Trust, www.hst.org.za/research/violence/ (accessed 5 October 2000).

Kohlberg, L. (1966). A cognitive-developmental analysis of children's sex-role concepts and attitudes. In E.E. Maccoby (Ed.). *The Development of Sex Differences*. Stanford: Stanford University Press, pp. 82-173.

Maccoby, E.E. & Jacklin, C.N. (1974). *The Psychology of Sex Differences*. Stanford: Stanford University Press.

Macdonald, M. (1995). *Representing Women. Myths of femininity in the popular media*. London: Edward Arnold.

Matlin, M.W. (1987). *The Psychology of Women*. New York: Holt, Rinehart and Winston, Inc.

Moghaddam, F.M. (1998). *Social Psychology. Exploring universals across cultures*. New York: W.H. Freeman and Company.

Morrell, R. (2001). Times of change: Men and masculinity in South Africa. In R. Morrell (Ed.). *Changing Men in Southern Africa*. Scottsville: University of Natal Press, pp. 3-37.

Papalia, D.E. & Olds, S.W. (1988). *Psychology* (2nd ed.). New York: McGraw-Hill.

Serbin, L.A., Poulin-Dubois, K.A., Colburne, M.G.S. & Eichstedt, J.A. (2001). Gender stereotyping in infancy: Visual preferences for and knowledge of gender-stereotyped toys in the second year. *International Journal of Behavioral Development*, 25(1):7-15.

Shefer, T. (1999). *Discourses of Heterosexual Subjectivity and Negotiation*. Unpublished Doctoral dissertation, University of the Western Cape, Bellville.

Squire, C. (1998). Women and men talk about aggression: An analysis of narrative genre. In K. Henwood & C. Griffin & A. Phoenix (Eds.). *Standpoints and Differences. Essays in the practice of feminist psychology*. London: Sage, pp. 65-90.

Stainton Rogers, W. & Stainton Rogers, R. (2001). *The Psychology of Gender and Sexuality*. Buckingham: Open University Press.

Terre Blanche, M. & Durrheim, K. (1999). Social constructionist methods. In M. Terre Blanche & K. Durrheim (Eds.). *Research in Practice. Applied methods for the social sciences*. Cape Town: University of Cape Town Press, pp. 147-72.

Vetten, L. (1996). 'Man shoots wife'. Intimate femicide in Gauteng South Africa. *Crime and Conflict*, 6(Winter), www.csvr.org.za/papers/papvet1.htm (accessed 27 February 2003).

West, C. & Zimmerman, D.H. (1991). Doing gender. In J. Lorber & S.A. Farrell (Eds.). *The Social Construction of Gender*. Newbury Park: Sage, pp. 13-37.

Whelehan, I. (1995). *Modern Feminist Thought: From the second wave to 'post feminism'*. New York: New York University Press.

Wood, K. & Jewkes, R. (2001). 'Dangerous' love. Reflections on violence among Xhosa township youth. In R. Morrell (Ed.). *Changing Men in Southern Africa*. Pietermaritzburg: University of Natal Press, pp. 317-36.

Multiple choice questions

1. 'Gender traits are internal, consistent and natural.' This quote is typical of which approach to gender?
   a) social constructionism
   b) essentialism
   c) naturalism
   d) none of the above

2. Freudian psychoanalytic theory argues that, in order to develop their gender and sexual identities, young children have to adequately resolve
   a) the sexual identity crisis
   b) penis envy
   c) the Oedipus complex
   d) the inferiority complex

3. Janet believes that, as a woman, it is her duty to do the grocery shopping, clean the home and take care of the children. Janet is adhering to strict
   a) gender bias
   b) gender labeling
   c) gender stereotypes
   d) gender roles

4. A two-year old boy who plays with cars and guns and shows aversion to playing with dolls illustrates early signs of
   a) gender role aversion
   b) gender stereotypical behaviour
   c) gender labelling
   d) gender modelling

5. Socialisation refers to
   a) the learning of feminine and masculine behaviour
   b) the learning of societal rules, norms and beliefs
   c) the internalisation of gendered messages conveyed by parents, peers, media and societal institutions
   d) all of the above

6. Gender labelling, gender constancy and gender knowledge are the underlying tenets of
   a) Bandura's social learning theory
   b) Piaget's cognitive-developmental approach
   c) Kohlberg's cognitive-developmental approach
   d) Bem's gender schema theory

7. When children recognise that a person's gender does not change when they wear clothing associated with the opposite sex, they are displaying an awareness of gender
   a) labelling
   b) knowledge
   c) constancy
   d) none of the above

8. Thandiwe's brother is attending a fancy dress party and is wearing a dress and a ribbon in his hair. As a result, Thandiwe thinks that he is no longer a boy or male. Thandiwe is likely to be how old?
   a) 3–4 years
   b) 5–7 years
   c) 1–2 years
   d) none of the above

9. Individuals who are undifferentiated with regard to masculine and feminine traits may be described as
   a) gender neutral
   b) asexual
   c) transsexual
   d) androgynous

10. The approach that views gender as comprised of individual behaviours and beliefs, interpersonal relations and social-structural power relations, is known as
    a) essentialism
    b) radical feminism
    c) social constructionism
    d) constructivism

11. The social movement that calls for equal opportunities for women and men is broadly defined as
    a) radical feminism
    b) socialist feminism
    c) liberal feminism
    d) Marxist feminism

12. Radical feminism views _____ as the primary source(s) of gender inequality
    a) sexism
    b) patriarchy
    c) discrimination
    d) all of the above

Short answer questions

1. Compare and contrast the defining features of each strand of feminist theory.

2. Discuss and compare the social-psychological theories that account for gender development in children.

3. What are the key features of Freud's approach to gender development? Discuss how Freud's approach has been critiqued.

4. Find a sample of 10 advertisements in a woman's magazine. Read the advertisements and look close-

ly at the pictures. Find examples of stereotypical portrayals of gender and answer the following questions:

- How are men and women depicted?
- What roles and responsibilities are assigned to men and women?
- What settings are women and men represented in?
- Which products are they associated with?

- Did you find evidence of challenges to traditional gender roles?
- Consider how these stereotypical depictions may reinforce traditional gender roles and behaviour.

5. Identify and describe the three central aspects of the cognitive-developmental approach to gender identity development in children. At which ages do children typically display the three processes?

23

Violence and Traumatic Stress

Craig Higson-Smith

CHAPTER OBJECTIVES

After studying this chapter you should be able to:
- give a definition of violence as well as a general overview of the breadth and depth of this field of study
- discuss violence as a public health problem using a systemic approach
- describe the consequences of violence, especially traumatic stress responses
- discuss and critique the range of violence prevention strategies in use, such as those used to assist individuals, families and communities affected by violence.

Like most South Africans, Nosipho was well aware of how violent a country she lived in. Under apartheid there was a long history of violent political repression and conflict. But instead of the improvement everyone had expected after 1994, it still seemed though that violence was one of the biggest threats people faced in their lives in South Africa.

Nosipho counted herself lucky that she had not been a victim of crime, but she had several friends and even some family members who had been mugged, robbed at gunpoint or threatened with violence. Quite recently, her cousin, a young man close to her own age, had been attacked by two knife-wielding men who had stopped him on his way home from the bus stop. She had seen him a few days after the incident, but when she asked about it, he had seemed reluctant to talk. 'It wasn't a big thing – they just took my wallet', he said. But Nosipho had been at home when her aunt visited the next day. Her aunt had told them how worried she was about her son. He had been very irritable since the mugging and didn't seem to want anyone around him. Nosipho's aunt described how he seemed to be shut off from everybody and had lost interest in his college work. As she listened Nosipho was convinced that, even while her cousin had tried to dismiss the mugging as unimportant, he had in fact been quite traumatised by his experience. Nosipho imagined what it might feel like to think you were about to be killed. Even if you survived physically unhurt, that brief moment of terror could have a lasting effect on the way you saw yourself and the world. The last time Nosipho had spoken to her cousin he had seemed more like his old self and seemed to have recovered from his ordeal. Nosipho wondered, though, if she would have been able to get over an experience like that so quickly.

While she had been concerned about her cousin, Nosipho also felt strongly that the problem of violence needed to be dealt with by the whole society, not just by each person who suffered its effects. She believed that people needed to start with children, teaching them that violence and aggression didn't solve their problems. Perhaps there were also things they could do in their local community to try to protect one another and strengthen themselves to fight violence. Even something as simple as campaigning for better lighting on the streets might make a difference, she thought. Some kind of neighbourhood watch might also discourage potential criminals. If people in the community started to work together they might be able to build a more peaceful place to live.

Introduction

This chapter introduces readers to the interrelated but distinct areas of violence and traumatic stress. It begins with some recent statistics of violence in South Africa and discusses the question of intention in defining violence. The chapter looks briefly at some social psychological theory on violence, and proposes a systemic model of violence and violence prevention over four levels: individual, small group, community and society. A focus on the individual effect of traumatic stress leads to a discussion of integrated violence prevention strategies and interventions to provide services to survivors of violence.

As South Africa enters the twenty-first century and tries to shake off its violent history, it carries with it an international reputation for violence. The violence of war, apartheid and armed struggle seems to have made way for terrible criminal, sexual and family violence. Violence remains a critical problem for our country, a problem that we must understand better if we are ever to be free of it.

In the *World Report on Violence and Health*, it is estimated that violence claimed the lives of 1.6 million people worldwide in the year 2000. Of these deaths, 91 per cent occurred in low- to middle-income countries. Men are more at risk of dying by violence than women, with males accounting for 77 per cent of homicide victims and over 60 per cent of deaths by suicide. Violent death is particularly common among adolescents and young adults, as is clearly illustrated by the following chart constructed out of the average African figures for violent death (Krug *et al.*, 2002).

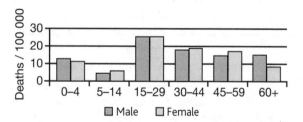

Figure 1 Deaths, by age, resulting from homicide in South Africa
Source: Krug *et al.*, 2002: 270

South Africa's National Injury Mortality Surveillance System (NIMSS) estimates that between 65 000 and 80 000 South Africans died as a result of non-natural causes in the year 2000. Once again, 80 per cent of victims were male, most commonly between 25 and 34 years of age. As illustrated in the chart below, acts of violence (i.e. homicide and suicide) account for more than half these deaths (Matzopoulos *et al.*, 2002).

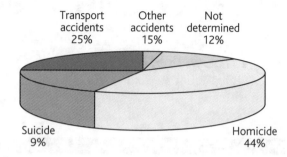

Figure 2 Non-natural deaths in South Africa in 2000
Source: Matzopoulus *et al.*, 2002, 18

And yet loss of life represents only a small part of the cost of violence to the world. In South Africa, at least 3.5 million people per annum require health care as a result of trauma (Peden & Butchart, 1999). The incidence and cost of non-fatal injuries is much more difficult to estimate, especially since many crimes such as rape, domestic assault and child abuse are seldom reported. Any attempt to understand the costs of violence to society must move beyond the costs associated with individual people, to the costs to families, communities and entire countries. In 1997, the Inter-American Development Bank sponsored studies on the economic costs of violence in several Latin American countries. The results show that health care expenses alone cost up to 1.5 per cent of these countries' gross domestic product (GDP), rising as high as 5 per cent of GDP in countries involved in ongoing conflicts (Buvinic *et al.* in Krug *et al.*, 2002). Clearly the costs of violence to society are very high, but do we really know what we mean by an act of violence?

What precisely is violence?

The question of how social scientists should define violence is a controversial one. The difficulty revolves around the idea of intention. To illustrate this problem, two definitions of violence are provided. One commonly used definition conceptualises violence as an act or situation that harms the health or well-being of oneself or others. It includes both attacks on a person's physical and psychological integrity and destructive acts that do not involve a direct relationship between victims and the institution, person or persons responsible for the harm (Bulhan, 1985).

According to this definition, any act that results in harm is essentially an act of violence. Sometimes this definition is considered too broad. For example, in the recently published *World Report on Violence and Health*, the World Health Organisation defines violence as:

> … the intentional use of physical force or power, threatened or actual, against oneself, another person, or against a group or community, that either results in or has a high likelihood of resulting in injury, death, psychological harm, maldevelopment or deprivation (Krug *et al.*, 2002:5).

Notice that while this definition still includes a broad spectrum of situations, it requires that the act must be intentional in order to be defined as violent.

To better understand the crucial difference between these two definitions, consider the following questions. If a person drives a motor vehicle while under the influence of alcohol and accidentally kills a pedestrian, has that person committed an act of violence? If a worker is hurt as a result of insufficient safety provisions at work, has the employer committed an act of violence? Finally, if a small child falls off a swing while her caregiver is not watching her, has that caregiver committed an act of violence?

These are difficult questions not only for social scientists but for many others, particularly people working within the criminal justice system. For the purposes of this chapter it is argued that where harm arises as a result of society's laws, regulations, and norms of due care being ignored, an act of violence has taken place, even when harm was not intended.

Types of violence

It is virtually impossible to define a complete taxonomy of the different forms of violence that have plagued human society throughout history. However, it is worth mentioning some broad categories.

Violence for material gain

Many acts of violence, such as muggings, armed robberies, hijackings and cash-in-transit heists are motivated by the desire for material gain. South Africa has extremely high levels of these kinds of violent crime.

Figure 3 Violence between township residents and the apartheid state

Domestic violence

Sadly, a great deal of violence occurs within families and homes, between people living close together. Whether such violence is the active abuse or neglect of children, battery of spouses or the abuse of elderly people, it is extremely destructive for families. Victims of domestic violence are often trapped within the abusive situation by social norms and economic pressures.

Sexual violence

Violence often takes on a sexual form. Whether in the form of rape, sexual assault, child sexual abuse, molestation, or sexual harassment in the workplace or other social arenas, sexual violence is responsible for very high levels of traumatic stress in society.

State and collective violence

State and collective violence has been a constant part of the past 200 years of South African history. Included in this history is the violence implicit in colonialism and apartheid from the wars between settlers and indigenous South Africans to the militarisation of South African society through conscription and the training of young people to fight in the liberation struggle, and acts of terror committed by both the apartheid regime and the liberation armies. Hate crimes and genocide are also examples of collective violence.

Self-directed violence

The final category is violence directed towards the self, most notably suicide and self-mutilation. Violence directed against the self is usually associated with great emotional pain and despair.

Theories of violence

Early theoretical approaches tried to suggest that people who commit acts of violence are somehow different from the majority of the population, because they are evil, disabled or sick. Although similar ideas guide the thinking of many people in the world today, these theories cannot explain the frequency of violence in our society, including the violence of wars and oppressive governments. Such approaches have resulted in people who committed acts of violence being executed, indefinitely imprisoned, having their brains operated upon, and being exiled, but have failed to reduce the incidence of violence in society.

Theories which acknowledge that the potential for violence exists within all people have a far greater chance of making a real contribution to violence prevention in the world. Socio-biological explanations of violence argue that human beings, like most other animals, have an innate capacity for violence. This capacity for violence enables human beings to hunt, to protect resources, and to respond to threat, all of which are fundamental to survival. Although an important starting point, such theories do not help social scientists to predict who will commit what act of violence and under what kind of circumstances. Without this information it is very difficult to prevent violence.

The emotional side of violence is also important. Work on the links between aggression and frustration provides some answers to this question. When a person becomes frustrated, they often feel angry and are ready for action. This combination is linked to acts of violence. The role of frustration is particularly important in finding ways to prevent crimes such as road- or air-rage. Nevertheless, people often feel angry or frustrated without becoming violent,

and many acts of violence are difficult to link to frustration.

Bandura's (1973) theory on social learning showed how violence, like many other human behaviours, is learned either through direct reinforcement or through modelling. Reinforcement occurs when particular behaviours are rewarded or punished. Depending upon his or her parents, a child may learn that punching his or her sibling either earns him or her the toy that he or she wanted, or his or her parents' anger. One outcome will increase the likelihood of violence in future, while the other will reduce it. Modelling happens when people learn from watching others. Thus a child who observes his or her parents solving conflicts with violence is more likely to use violence for problem solving later in life. This area of work has important implications for parenting as well as for discussions of television and film violence.

A further important component to understanding human violence is to recognise that people act differently when in groups as opposed to when they are alone. Early theories in this line argued that when in groups, people form mobs which are unthinking and by their very nature violent. Such theories discount the enormous complexity of human groups and are not helpful in preventing situations of violence. Work on obedience to authority, conformity, and shared responsibility goes a long way to explaining why groups tend to be more violent than individuals.

Of course, people always identify themselves as being part of different groups. We think of ourselves as belonging to a certain community or neighbourhood, ethnic group, religious denomination, language community, and so on. Social identity theory (Tajfel *et al.*, 1971) has produced a wealth of research that shows that group identity is very important to people, that people hold differing beliefs about their own and others' groups, and that under conditions of threat these group identities become stronger. So much of the conflict in the world today can be understood in terms of group conflicts.

23.2 VIOLENCE AND PREJUDICE

In 1996, Bar-tal and Labin (2001) repeatedly measured the attitudes of a sample of Israeli adolescents towards Palestinians, Jordanians and Arabs in general. An initial measurement was taken after a long period of peace, a second measurement was taken one day after two major terrorist attacks on Israelis by Palestinian extremists, and a third measurement was taken three months later. In the first measurement, Israeli adolescents held more positive attitudes towards Jordanians (Jordan was at peace with Israel at the time) and Arabs in general, than towards Palestinians. However, following the attacks, attitudes towards all three groups became more negative. This provides a clear demonstration of how violence and fear create greater difference between groups, even when those groups are not in conflict with each other.

Coming to grips with the effects of violence

Although we tend to think about violence in terms of its impact upon individual survivors, violence occurs at many levels. When a family member abuses all the other members of the family, this is an example of violence at the level of the small group, in this case, the family structure. Another example of small group violence happens in criminal gangs, where gang membership often depends on perpetrating violent acts such as rape. Violence can also occur at the level of the community. For example, when residents of a community victimise people of a particular group, violence occurs at the communi-

ty level. In South Africa in recent years, many non-South Africans have been labelled 'amakwerekwere' (a derogatory term meaning foreigner), and have been victimised. Finally, violence can occur at the level of society. The use of force by the apartheid government to systematically remove people from the land on which their families had lived for generations, is a clear example of violence at the level of society. Enforced conscription of young men to serve in armies is another form of violence at the level of society. There are therefore four broad levels at which violence can occur, namely the individual, small group, community and societal levels.

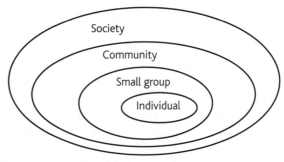

Figure 4 Ecological model of community

Violence at any level typically impacts upon other levels as well. For example, when a young man is conscripted into an army (societal level), he may well be exposed to violent acts that leave him emotionally compromised (individual level). Possibly he has become a very angry person who often drinks and becomes violent. Upon his return home, his emotional state impacts upon the family (small group level). Even single acts of violence at the individual level have ways of impacting upon many people's lives. For example, when a young child is sexually abused, members of the immediate family, possibly school friends and teachers, as well as police officers, social workers, prosecutors and magistrates, are also involved. If it is a high profile case which is discussed on television and radio news bulletins, millions of people may be exposed to that act of violence.

A framework that attempts to encompass the enormous complexity of a phenomenon such as violence that occurs at multiple, interconnected levels is called a systemic or ecological model. At times it is difficult to make sense of the way in which different acts of violence impact upon society at multiple levels. Broadly speaking, violence can be understood as being both fragmenting and disempowering at the same time.

Fragmentation refers to the breaking up or destruction of important linkages, and can occur at each level of society. For example, at an individual level, traumatic amnesia and dissociation are forms of fragmentation associated with exposure to violence. At the small group level, acts of violence often break up family structures, and result in people being expelled from other social groups. At community level, some forms of violence disrupt local services including workplaces, schools, religious institutions and so on. Finally, at societal level, many forms of collective violence lead to fragmentation of whole societies.

Disempowerment, in this model, refers to people's inability to fulfil their appropriate functions, personally, in their families, in their communities and in society more generally. For example, a child can be disempowered when he or she is injured and is therefore unable to interact with other people and the environment, and as a result does not develop to his or her full potential. The same is true of the frail grandparent who is unable to adequately care for the children left in her care while parents are at work, and the working adult who cannot earn a living as a result of injury or trauma.

Although it is important that social scientists strive to understand all the different effects of violence upon people and society, there is not room for such a comprehensive discussion. Instead, this chapter focuses on traumatic stress as one common result of exposure to violence at the individual level.

Traumatic stress

It is uncommon for a person to reach old age without having to endure moments of overwhelming fear, horror or helplessness. These events, where we literally face death, are usually deeply distressing, but also potentially life changing.

Although the causes of traumatic stress may be accidental, they are often not. Violence of different kinds is one of the most common causes of traumatic stress in human beings. While violence is a familiar and visible part of the world around us, traumatic stress is a phenomenon of the internal or psychological world, and is less directly observable. It is only through close examination of the behavioural changes in people who have recently survived a violent incident, and through survivors' expressions and descriptions of their feelings and thoughts, that traumatic stress can be understood.

Human beings, like other animals, have well developed mechanisms for surviving within a dangerous world. As a result, the majority of people endure traumatic experiences without any lasting psychological disturbance. Certainly these experiences are likely to cause a short period (usually four to six weeks) of emotional upset. During this time, the person may often feel anxious or afraid, and will spend a great deal of time going over the traumatic experience in his or her memory. Although often quite severe immediately after the event, these symptoms quickly become milder and less frequent as the person returns to normal functioning. During this time it is helpful for friends and family to ensure that the person feels safe, is assured that what they are experiencing is healthy and will pass, and knows that he or she is loved and supported by others.

A relatively small proportion of people do develop more lasting problems including post-traumatic stress disorder, acute stress disorder, or other psychological disorders. The number of people affected in this way varies substantially depending upon many variables, including the nature of the traumatic event and individuals' personal histories. For this group, the signs of traumatic stress do not reduce during the first four to six weeks following the event, and often become worse. In these cases it is likely that the person will require substantial psychological intervention by a traumatic stress specialist before he or she returns to previous levels of functioning.

Three broad categories of symptoms are associated with traumatic stress, namely re-experiencing, avoidance and arousal (Friedman, 2000). Re-experiencing symptoms are those in which associated thoughts, feelings, physiological responses and behaviours remain with the person long after the traumatic event is over. This may take the form of memories, intrusive images, nightmares or flashbacks. For example, a person who has been the victim of a mugging might find that he or she has persistent nightmares relating to the incident for many weeks thereafter. Similarly, a man who is recovering after a car hijacking incident might find that whenever he gets behind the wheel, he thinks constantly about the incident, feels his heart racing and notices that his palms become sweaty. Although the incident is in the past, his mind and body still react to the triggers associated with being in the driver's seat.

Avoidance symptoms are strategies people use to try and avoid the fear and pain caused by their ongoing re-experiencing of the event. Very often

Figure 5 Nervous driving thanks to a previous bad experience

people stay away from people, places and activities that remind them of the experience. It is also possible to avoid thinking about an event by blocking thoughts and constantly distracting oneself. People also block painful feelings, a strategy which is called numbing. For example, a bank employee whose life was threatened during a bank robbery might find it easier to stay away from work. A female rape survivor might pretend to herself and to the people around her that nothing happened in order to avoid the painful thoughts and feelings associated with the rape.

The arousal symptoms are closely related to our highly developed survival mechanisms. Following a traumatic experience people often find it very difficult to fall asleep and are easily woken, are often hyper-vigilant (constantly alert to danger), very jumpy and quick to anger. For example, a woman who experienced a vehicle hijacking might find that she constantly scans the roadside while stopped at traffic lights. A man who witnessed a shooting may find that he is extremely irritable for weeks after the event.

It is important to remember that all of these different symptoms of traumatic stress are signs that the person is working through a very difficult experience. They do not mean that there is something wrong with the person. However, in cases where the symptoms are not reducing or are getting worse, it is crucial that the person be encouraged to seek professional assistance urgently.

Violence prevention and peace-building

If the effects of violence are understood in terms of disempowerment and fragmentation, then it stands to reason that interventions to prevent violence and to assist individuals, families and communities to overcome their traumatic experiences resulting from violence, should be empowering and linking. This is illustrated in Figure 6.

The prevention of future violence is one of the most important ways in which psychologists and other social scientists can be of service to society. These interventions occur differently at all the levels of the ecological model.

Individual-level interventions

Violence prevention initiatives at the level of the individual include programmes aimed to teach children and young adults how to resolve conflicts non-violently (empowering), and helping children to identify protective places and adults in their community (linking).

23.3 VIOLENCE AND TRAUMA IN A STUDENT POPULATION

Hoffman's (2002) recent study of traumatic exposure and trauma symptoms in a South African tertiary education institution reveals the links between violence and trauma in a student population. Two hundred and forty-five students took part in the study and completed questionnaires designed to find out what traumatic experiences each student had been exposed to in the previous year, and how those experiences had impacted upon emotional functioning. More than two-thirds of the respondents reported one or more traumatic events in the previous year, with women reporting more events than men. The most frequent event was the death of a loved one, followed by negative changes to life circumstances and then witnessing serious injury or death. Intrusive thoughts and avoidance strategies were associated with many traumatic experiences, especially violent robbery and unwanted sexual activity.

Small group-level interventions

Family counselling aimed at helping families communicate more effectively can help to reduce domestic violence (empowering and linking) is one example of a small group intervention strategy to prevent violence. Other examples are helping youth gangs that survive by crime to find other ways to earn a living (mastery), and training teachers to identify and report child abuse responsibly (empowering).

Community-level interventions

Projects that bring together people who live in a particular area to establish a neighbourhood watch system (linking and empowering) are a community level intervention strategy, as are local awareness and public information campaigns.

Societal-level interventions

Intervention strategies that deepen the democratic process in a country (mastery) and encourage people to value diversity (linking) are some ways in which peace is built. Other examples of societal-level interventions are changes to the criminal justice system such as the provision of special courts for child victims of violence (empowerment) or projects to increase the co-operation between different agencies responsible for law enforcement (empowerment), and conflict resolution in times of conflict and war (linking).

Integrated strategies that operate at multiple levels are most likely to be successful. Thus, for example, an attempt to reduce the incidence of sexual vio-lence in a community would do well to start with an intensive awareness and information campaign. This might be accompanied by special training for local police officers and social workers to assist them to identify potential problems and respond effectively. Furthermore, an anger management support group and assistance for people with substance abuse problems would also be complimentary.

Assisting people and communities affected by violence

Despite our best efforts at prevention, there will always be individuals, families and communities whose lives have been disrupted by violence. Psychologists and other mental health activists have an important role to play in helping these people return to healthy social and psychological life.

Individual-level interventions

Many services are available in South Africa for individuals affected by violence. The majority of these services are run by counsellors whose main purpose is to reassure people that what they are feeling is normal, and to support them through the painful process of coming to terms with their traumatic experience. These counsellors are also equipped to recognise when a person needs more specialised assistance to deal with the event. In this case counsellors refer their clients on to trauma specialists who will use a range of trauma therapies, and possibly medication to assist the person.

Small group-level interventions

Group work depends on the principle that people are able to offer each other deep support and assistance during times of crisis. Support groups exist for various people including survivors of rape, child abuse and violent crime. Family therapy is another crucial form of intervention, particularly when children have been involved in traumatic experiences. By assisting families to function more effectively in times of crisis, mental health workers can have a great impact on the long-term well-being of children. Many other situations also lend themselves to group work. For example, where trauma occurs within a school or workplace, the most effective form of intervention might be to mobilise the care and support of others in the classroom or work team.

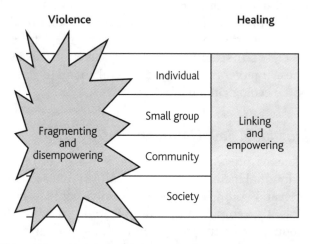

Figure 6 An approach to violence prevention

Wars and disasters often leave hundreds or thousands of people destitute and emotionally traumatised. It is common in such situations for the international community to mount large-scale humanitarian crisis response programmes, often along the lines described in this chapter. Many books and papers have been written describing massive psychosocial intervention programmes in Angola, Mozambique, Rwanda, Burundi, Ethiopia and Sudan. Of course such programmes are not restricted to Africa, with similar work happening in South America, Eastern Europe and South-East Asia. (See, for instance, Arcel *et al.*, 1995; Hastie, 1997; Higson-Smith, 2002; Strachan & Peters, 1997; Vassal-Adams, 1994.)

Common to many such programmes is the screening of large portions of the population for signs of post-traumatic stress disorder and other psychosocial problems, publication of self-help material, training of lay counsellors to offer care and support, as well as the establishment of various kinds of support groups and structures within communities. Such interventions are typically gratefully received by the intended beneficiaries. However, while the psychologists who design and implement these services are convinced of their usefulness, and often argue that without such intervention a return to healthy peaceful society would be impossible, there is seldom rigorous scientific evidence to support this argument.

Critics of these large scale intervention programmes argue that such work has very little benefit whatsoever, and in fact may even be damaging to individuals, families and the community at large (Summerfield, 1999). This argument is based on several important points:

Firstly, critics argue that such interventions are too short. International traumatic stress experts also spend too little time in the country with the crisis to understand the social and historical dynamics sufficiently to design effective interventions.

Secondly, they argue that such psychosocial interventions tend to be based on a very particular, Western understanding of people, community and mental health. What is generally understood to be healthy or unhealthy in the United States of America may not be appropriate when applied to people in rural Swaziland, or Chile. These attempts to identify people in need of psychosocial assistance might falsely identify people who are actually coping well, and miss many people who are not.

Thirdly, even if screening processes do correctly identify people with post-traumatic stress disorder or other severe psychosocial problems, these people often do not receive the care that they need. This is due to the fact that resources are typically very limited in humanitarian crises, especially once the need to supply medical treatment, housing and food is taken into account. It is of little use to provide people with a diagnosis if appropriate treatment cannot be offered as well.

Finally, critics argue that healthy communities have inbuilt mechanisms that protect the community and its members from the effects of disaster and warfare. It seems sensible to think that these mechanisms might be far more effective than those applied from outside the community. Moreover, by imposing an approach to healing that comes from beyond the boundaries of the community, it is likely that the intervention will damage the internal healing mechanisms that the community has relied upon for generations. This may well result in the intended beneficiaries being further compromised and left without any means of returning to healthy and stable community life.

And yet when crises do occur, it is very difficult for the international traumatic stress community to stand back and not try to offer any kind of assistance. Thus the challenge that many traumatic stress practitioners are struggling to meet, is to find ways of assisting in times of large scale crises which are based in the cultural, spiritual and historical context of the community in question, and which are effective and sustainable in the long term. Attempts to do this include advocacy work on the part of the international community to ensure that governments put some resources into ensuring that social and spiritual structures are protected and supported in times of crisis, channelling resources to local community-based organisations, providing appropriate capacity building for local healers, and building support groups within fragmented communities.

Community-level interventions

In some cases whole communities are affected by violence. This is particularly true in civil conflict situations, or following acts of terrorism. In these situations it is important to mobilise local community structures such as faith organisations, schools, youth clubs, sports teams as well as local media and business. Community activists can help people to pool their material and emotional resources in order to meet the challenge of trauma resulting from violence.

Societal-level interventions

Finally, interventions at the level of society are crucially important. The South African Truth and Reconciliation Commission gave people whose lives had been disrupted by violence an opportunity to have their suffering recognised. Similar interventions are required to provide appropriate services to veterans of South Africa's conflict-filled past, and to provide all victims of violence with the necessary support and care to take back control over their own lives and well-being.

Conclusion

Violence prevention and care for survivors of violence are not separate areas of work but are deeply interrelated. In a just society, healthy people can and do live together without violence. Violence prevention ensures that fewer people will be hurt by traumatic experiences, and healing the damage done by trauma plays an important role in preventing future violence.

Work in the fields of violence and traumatic stress represents some of the greatest health challenges to social scientists and mental health workers today. For this reason, the study of violence and traumatic stress is one of the most rapidly growing fields in social science and will continue to be so. For the individual practitioner, these areas of study offer difficult technical and emotional challenges, and yet they also offer an opportunity to interact with people in their least guarded moments. It is during these moments that the trauma specialist witnesses both the deep brutality and incredible nobility of the human species.

REFERENCES

Arcel, L.T., Folnegovic-Smalc, V., Kozaric-Kovacic, D. & Marusic, A. (1995). *Psycho-social Help to War Victims: Women refugees and their families from Bosnia and Herzegovina and Croatia*. Copenhagen: International Rehabilitation Council for Torture Victims.

Bandura, A. (1973). *Aggression: A social learning analysis*. Englewood Cliffs: Prentice-Hall.

Bar-Tal, D. & Labin, D. (2001). The effect of a major event on stereotyping: Terrorist attacks in Israel and Israeli adolescents' perceptions of Palestinians, Jordanians, and Arabs. *European Journal of Social Psychology*, 31:265-80.

Bulhan, H.A. (1985). *Frantz Fanon and the Psychology of Oppression*. New York: Plenum Press.

Friedman, M.J. (2000). *Post Traumatic Stress Disorder: The latest assessment and treatment strategies*. Kansas City: Compact Clinicals.

Hastie, R. (1997). *Disabled Children in a Society at War: A casebook from Bosnia*. Oxford: Oxfam GB.

Higson-Smith, C. (2002). *Supporting Communities Affected by Violence: A casebook from South Africa*. Oxford: Oxfam GB.

Hoffman, W.A. (2002). The incidence of traumatic events and trauma-associated symptoms/experiences amongst tertiary students. *South African Journal of Psychology*, 32(4):48-53.

Krug, E.G., Dahlberg, L.L., Mercy, J.A., Zwi, A.B. & Lozano, R. (Eds.). (2002). *World Report on Violence and Health*. Geneva: World Heath Organisation.

Matzopoulos, R., van Niekerk, A., Marais, S. & Donson, H. (2002). A profile of fatal injuries in South Africa: Towards a platform for safety promotion. *African Safety Promotion*, 1:16-22.

Milgram, S. (1974). *Obedience to Authority*. New York: Harper and Row.

Peden, M. & Butchart, A. (1999). Trauma and injury. In N. Crisp & A. Ntuli (Eds.). *1999 South African Health Review*. Durban: Health Systems Trust, pp. 331-4.

Strachan, P. & Peters, C. (1997). *Empowering Communities: A casebook from West Sudan*. Oxford: Oxfam GB.

Summerfield, D. (1999). A critique of seven assumptions behind psychosocial trauma programmes in war-affected areas. *Social Science and Medicine*, 48:1449-62.

Tajfel, H., Flamant, C., Billig, M.G. & Bundy, R.P. (1971). Social categorization and intergroup behaviour. *European Journal of Social Psychology*, 1:149-78.

Vassal-Adams, G. (1994). *Rwanda: An agenda for international action*. Oxford: Oxfam GB.

Multiple choice questions

1. According to Krug *et al.* (2002), what is the most common age range for death as a result of non-natural causes?
   a)   5 to 14 years
   b)   15 to 24 years
   c)   25 to 34 years
   d)   35 to 44 years

2. According to the Inter-American Development Bank, in countries involved in ongoing civil conflicts, the costs of health care following acts of violence is estimated to be as high as what percentage of gross domestic product?
   a)   0.5%
   b)   5%
   c)   15%
   d)   50%

3. According to the World Health Organisation's definition of violence, which of the following acts would not be considered violent?
   a)   a teacher spanking a naughty child
   b)   a parent spanking a naughty child
   c)   accidentally knocking a child over in the playground
   d)   knocking a child over in a playground fight

4. Which of the following is not a broad category of violence?
   a)   emotional violence
   b)   collective violence
   c)   self-directed violence
   d)   sexual violence

5. Milgram's (1974) experiment showed that
   a)   violent behaviour is learned from our parents
   b)   most people will hurt others if told to do so by an authority figure
   c)   violence inevitably damages our society
   d)   all of the above

6. What is the name given to models that present society as having multiple, hierarchically arranged levels?
   a)   scientific models
   b)   social learning theory models
   c)   social identity theory models
   d)   ecological models

7. Which of the following is not a category of symptoms associated with traumatic stress as described by Friedman (2000)?
   a)   avoidance symptoms
   b)   cognitive symptoms
   c)   arousal symptoms
   d)   intrusive symptoms

8. Which of the following is an avoidance symptom of traumatic stress as described by Friedman (2000)?
   a)   nightmares
   b)   sleeplessness
   c)   difficulty concentrating
   d)   not wanting to talk about the experience

9. According to Friedman (2000), how long does it typically take a healthy person to recover from a single traumatic experience?
   a)   four to six weeks
   b)   four to six months
   c)   four to six years
   d)   most people never recover from traumatic experiences

10. Under what circumstances would you recommend that a person who has survived robbery seek professional assistance?
    a)   everyone what has been robbed should seek professional assistance
    b)   only if they are unable to fall asleep on the night following the robbery
    c)   if they have no symptoms at all
    d)   if they have symptoms which are not going away or are getting worse

Short answer questions

1. Explain the essential difference between the two definitions of violence offered in the chapter? Provide an example that illustrates this difference.

2. List the five broad categories of violence mentioned in the chapter, and provide examples of each.

3. Describe a situation that you have witnessed or read about where a group of people have perpetrated an act of violence. Provide an explanation for this event based upon what you have read in this chapter about how people in groups behave.

4. Consider the case of a child being severely beaten at school. How do the concepts of 'disempowerment' and 'fragmentation' apply to this situation?

5. Based on the case described in question 4, outline an effective violence prevention intervention for this situation.

24

Peacemaking and Peacebuilding

Shahnaaz Suffla

CHAPTER OBJECTIVES

After studying this chapter you should be able to:
- define and describe in your own words the concepts of peacemaking and peacebuilding
- delineate the differences between peacemaking, peacekeeping and peacebuilding
- identify and elaborate on the major theoretical principles underlying these concepts
- present an argument for a culturally-centred approach to peacemaking and peacebuilding
- sketch a framework for action through which psychologists can contribute to peace processes.

Nosipho's first image of a psychologist had been of someone who worked only with individuals or sometimes small groups, helping them to deal with their emotional problems. It was very interesting to learn that psychologists could also play a role in building peaceful societies. Nosipho felt this was especially important in a country like South Africa, where violence and conflict had been so much a part of everyone's history.

Nosipho had only been a young child during the worst periods of political conflict. But even as a child she had been aware of the violence, the fear and anger around her. Her mother's brothers had been directly involved in the anti-apartheid struggle and one of them had left the country to join the ANC in exile. He had received military training in Tanzania, and her mother had only seen him again after many years when he returned to South Africa

after the first democratic elections. As Nosipho grew up she came to understand much more of the conflict and how it had affected not only her family, but almost everyone she knew. It was hard to discuss some of these things with White people, but as Nosipho began to develop better relationships with some White friends, they had been able to talk a little about their different experiences of living in South Africa. She had been surprised when a friend told her how traumatised her older brother had been after being sent out to keep 'control' in a township. She told Nosipho that she thought he had never really been the same again. All those years of war must have had an influence on everyone who was part of it. In South Africa, helping to build a peaceful country was probably one of the most important things for a psychologist to be involved in.

Introduction

Interest in peace as a distinct area of psychology began to increasingly emerge from about the 1980s onwards. Within the context of the complex and reconfiguring pattern of divisions and hostilities between and within different groups in the latter half of last century, the growing number of political and economic refugees across the world, the constant threat of nuclear warfare, and the increasing militarisation of societies, the field of psychology was compelled to critically review and reconceptualise its position towards, and treatment of, issues related to peace, conflict and violence (see Box 24.1).

Given that the discipline of psychology is explicitly concerned with the promotion of human well-being, the field was deemed to possess the necessary scholarly tools to address issues such as intergroup conflict, the behaviour of groups, social interactions between members of different groups, social identity and psychosocial healing, and thereby to have the capacity to prevent violence and promote peace. Contemporary psychology has since witnessed a range of theoretical developments on the psychosocial dimensions of peace, conflict and violence, which have effectively served to delineate and shape peace psychology as a field of research and practical intervention. Accordingly, peace psychology has been defined as seeking to develop theories and practices directed at the prevention and reduction of direct and structural violence, and the promotion of peacemaking and peace building (Christie *et al.*, 2001).

Against this backdrop, the current chapter seeks to examine the concepts of peacemaking and peace building, review the major assumptions underpinning the theory and practice of these peace processes, and highlight the conceptual contours that differentiate the two concepts. The chapter will draw from existing scholarship to sketch a framework for action for peace psychologists. The chapter will also include illustrative examples derived from the global context to support and contextualise the theoretical discussion of peacemaking and peace building.

Peacemaking

According to Christie *et al.* (2001), peacemaking is directed at reducing the occurrence and intensity of direct violence. Thus, peacemaking refers to the range of methods utilised to address direct, episodic

24.1 THE CONCEPTUALISATION OF PEACE PSYCHOLOGY

Historically, peace psychologists have not agreed on the inclusion of the issue of social justice in the conceptualisation of peace psychology. The early conceptual development of peace psychology was largely influenced by the intellectual milieu of the Cold War era and the hegemony of Euro-American psychology. The Cold War, which involved the United States and Soviet Union, involved a contest for global supremacy and military power. Against this backdrop, most American peace psychologists focused their attention on the prevention of nuclear war (see Christie *et al.*, 2001). Notions of structural violence and the requisite political and economic transformation of society were considered to divert from the dominant agenda of peace psychology, and therefore to be marginal to the field. Issues related to social reconstruction were considered to be primarily the domain of political scientists and politicians.

Consequently, scholarship on peace and war during this time remained limited at the levels of theoretical analysis, research and application. This conceptual positioning was supported by the historical role of organised professional psychology in South Africa. To this end, psychology in South Africa actively colluded with the ideology of racism prior to and during the apartheid era (see Suffla *et al.*, 2001). In contrast, groups of progressive psychologists in contexts such as Africa and Latin America increasingly challenged the status quo of mainstream psychology and, in particular, its exclusion of social transformation as a goal of psychology. Influenced by the ideas of scholars such as Frantz Fanon (see Fanon, 1967), the critiques of these groups offered substantial shape to the conception of liberation psychology, a form of peace psychology which centralises activism to promote social justice (see Dawes, 2001). The expansion of liberatory discourses within psychology, together with the shifting global and national landscape of conflict and violence, compelled peace psychology to reconceptualise its theoretical basis. Although still questioned by some, the current conceptualisation of peace psychology advances the distinction between direct violence and structural violence as conceptually and politically significant, thereby mainstreaming the principle of social justice.

violence. Direct violence refers to violence that harms the psychological or physical well-being of individuals or groups. Examples of direct violence include genocide, torture and sexual violence during armed conflicts. Peacemaking is commonly associated with the concept of peacekeeping, which evolved from the founding of United Nations (UN) missions to respond to conditions and environments of war across the world and to prevent the reoccurrence of war (Langholtz & Leentjies, 2001). For example, UN missions to Africa have included the deployment of UN personnel to countries such as Somalia, Rwanda and Angola to monitor the implementation of peace agreements, serve as a preventive military barrier between warring factions, assist in the co-ordination of humanitarian aid to relief workers and the civilian population, and allow for the safe return of refugees (Shawcross, 2001). While both peacemaking and peacekeeping refer to actions intended to lessen the probability of individuals and nations engaging in violence, peacemaking is recognised as a more positive approach to peace. Unlike peacekeeping, which generally relies on the presence of neutral forces to prevent or mitigate episodes of violence in contexts characterised by conflict and hostility, peacemaking advances methods to encourage positive and non-violent relations among adversaries. Thus, peacekeeping has traditionally concentrated on the management, rather than the resolution, of conflict.

Conflict resolution

To a large extent, the theory and practice of peacemaking is underpinned by the notion of conflict resolution. Conflict resolution is defined as a process which 'provides techniques to deal with disputes in a manner which is non-violent, avoids dominance or oppression by one party over the other, and, rather than exploiting one party, aims to meet the human needs of all' (Sanson & Bretherton, 2001:193). Articulated positively, the practice of conflict resolution seeks to employ knowledge of psychosocial processes to capitalise on the positive potential inherent in conflict and to minimise its destructive consequences (Sanson & Bretherton, 2001). This approach to conflict resolution is responsive to the values of peace, supports the utilisation of methods that promote dialogue, empathy and win-win consequences, and acknowledges the influence of the social context within which conflict is embedded.

Sanson and Bretherton (2001) have identified four basic principles which underlie most approaches to conflict resolution:
- The first principle emphasises that conflict resolution is supported by co-operation and not competition.
- The second assumption refers to the pursuit of integrative solutions through mediation and direct negotiation. That is, solutions are sought which converge to meet the needs of all groups.
- This focus on understanding and responding to the interests of all parties, also referred to as an interest-based approach to the resolution of conflict, represents the third principle. Central to the interest-based approach is the argument that knowledge is subjective in its construction, and that diverse views may therefore be equally legitimate.
- The final principle relates to the idea that both the conflict resolution process and its outcome are non-violent.

From a psychosocial perspective, the application of these principles includes involving an objective third party to act as mediator, active listening skills to ensure that the interests of both parties are heard, and acknowledging emotions and encouraging their responsible expression. Other strategies include the promotion of the use of 'I/We statements' to avoid criticism or blaming (e.g., 'I/We need ...' and 'I/We are concerned about ...'), and the use of brainstorming principles to generate creative solutions.

The reader is referred to the extensive literature that exists on conflict resolution theory and practice for a description of the various processes through which these four principles are typically applied. In general, this body of scholarship reveals a marked lack of responsiveness to the influence of the sociocultural context in conflict resolution processes. Much of the theory on conflict resolution has been developed in North America, thus reflecting a predominantly Westernised and monocultural perspective and prescription of responses to conflict.

The cultural context of peacemaking

The growing awareness of the need to integrate the ideas, practices and experiences of multiple cultures and contexts into existing knowledge on peacemaking has stimulated interesting and varied discourse on the cultural relativity of peacemaking knowledge and strategies. These contemporary viewpoints emphasise the idea that the meanings attributed to conflict and conflict resolution are embedded within the context of a specific culture. For example, in his analysis of the cultural context of peacemaking, Pederson (2001) observed that cultures outside of the Western milieu typically display a collectivistic approach to conflict resolution, with the accent placed on social cohesion, reciprocal role obligations and ritual and spirituality to symbolise peace settlements. In contrast, Western cultures characteristically attach less value to the significance of context, demonstrating an individualistic perspective which appreciates individual freedom, rights and autonomy, a controlling attitude to confrontation and the confidentiality of negotiations. The discussion on the different dimensions of peacemaking does not necessarily imply that any one approach is more effective than the other; instead, it cautions against cultural insularity and encourages the maintenance of cultural integrity in seeking solutions to conflict between groups.

The discourse on cultural sensitivity is also evidenced in the more recent literature on psychosocial interventions during times of conflict and post-conflict reconstruction. In reflecting on her experiences of trauma reduction work under war conditions in Bosnia, Agger (2001) stressed the critical value of incorporating indigenous healing methods into efforts directed at undermining the traumatising sequelae of conflict and violence. Likewise, in their work on demobilising and socially reintegrating former child soldiers in Angola after the 1992 to 1994 conflict, Wessells and Monteiro (2001) emphasised the inclusion of local communities and culture in the construction of a culturally-centred approach to healing.

In this respect, the National Peace Accord Trust in South Africa has adopted an innovative approach to addressing the social and emotional scars of militarised youth, which recognises the ineffectiveness of conventional counselling methods and instead draws together former enemies through a 'transformation trail' in the Drakensberg Mountains of KwaZulu-Natal (Schell-Faucon, 2001). Referred to as 'Wilderness Therapy', the project is directed at transforming trauma in the wilderness as a means of fostering individual and community healing. In the Bosnian case, psychosocial interventions included a traditional form of self-healing practiced by Bosnian women, that is, the establishment of knitting groups where coffee was served and the milieu provided for the telling and listening of trauma stories. The pro-

motion of mental health and human rights during the post-war reconstruction process in Bosnia included a focus on the psychological and social process of reconciliation within and between groups.

Similarly, Wessells and Monteiro (2001) encourage that the political, economic and social strategies typically implemented to facilitate the transition from violence to peace must necessarily include psychosocial interventions to interrupt cycles of violence and promote reconciliation, thereby calling into focus the role of psychologists in reconciliation and reconstruction in the aftermath of conflict.

Figure 1 Social psychological peace intervention: A woman and a child interact in a workshop

Reconciliation within the peace framework

Reconciliation, in conjunction with the concepts of truth, forgiveness and healing, is considered to be central to the psychological and spiritual dimensions of peacemaking. Reconciliation within the peace framework is argued to be premised on the process of rebuilding relationships, which is perceived to involve a willingness to acknowledge the truth and to offer and accept forgiveness (Lederach, 1997), and is frequently referenced in relation to truth commissions (Crawford, 2000; de la Rey, 2001; Lederach, 1997).

According to Crawford (2000), truth commissions attempt to heal the wounds of the past though the recognition of victims' pain, acknowledgement of wrongdoing by perpetrators and disclosure of the truth about past events. A recent example is the

South African Truth and Reconciliation Commission (TRC) (see Box 24.2). Among other things, the TRC was conceptualised to provide the opportunity for victims to publicly tell their stories of human rights abuses in a supportive context and to grant amnesty to perpetrators of human rights abuses who offered full disclosure about the crimes that they had committed, thereby promoting individual, community and national healing and reconciliation. Although the TRC is considered by many South Africans to have ultimately played a marginal role in the psychosocial, political, economic and social reconstruction process of South African society, some observers have suggested that through public truth-telling the TRC served as an adequately cathartic medium, particularly for Black South Africans (e.g., Knox & Quirck, 2000).

Many psychologists agree that reconciliation necessarily implies the expression of a range of painful emotions, including anger, grief and guilt (de la Rey, 2001). In this regard, psychologists provided support to some of the victims testifying at public hearings. Psychologists also provided testimony at special hearings on children, youth, women and the health sector, conducted assessments of some perpetrators, and to some extent have contributed to scholarly debate on the TRC and the issue of reconciliation.

When successful, peacemaking can contribute to the development of conditions necessary for the more challenging but imperative mission of building a peaceful society in which the structural configurations and cultural narratives are directed at promoting human security and well-being, and the reduction of inequality and oppression.

Peacebuilding

Peacebuilding seeks to mitigate structural violence, which refers to the social domination, political oppression and economic exploitation of individuals and groups (Montiel, 2001). Globalisation, resulting in vast inequality in wealth, and the coercive influence of militarization, are just some examples of structural violence in the twenty-first century. Given that factors such as excessive concentrations of political power and social privilege tend to contribute to conflict between groups, it is apparent that the effective redress of these inequalities implies the creation of local, regional and global conditions con-

ducive to social transformation. Peacebuilding is thus conceptualised as:

> Movement towards social justice which occurs when political structures become more inclusive by giving voice to those who have been marginalized in decisions that affect their well-being, and economic structures become transformed so that those who have been exploited gain greater access to material resources that satisfy their basic needs (Christie, 2001:277).

Peacebuilding initiatives are directed not only at structural reconstruction, but also the transformation of cultural discourses that maintain oppression and exploitation. Christie (2001) argues that in attending to the macro-level origins of violence, peace building provokes the development and execution of a critical consciousness that challenges the status quo. This position centralises the notion that a new social order must address peace not only as preventing or resolving conflict, but also in terms of pursuing social justice (see Table 1). Hence, while they appear to be theoretically discrete concepts, peacemaking and peace building are considered to represent an interlocking system of peace (Christie *et al.*, 2001).

Peacemaking	Peacebuilding
Addresses direct violence	Addresses structural violence
Focus on non-violent means	Focus on socially just ends
Prevention of violence	Promotion of social justice
Response to threat/ use of violence	Response to long-term structural inequalities

Table 1 Differences between peacemaking and peacebuilding
Source: Christie *et al.* (2001)

Transformatory discourses and practices

The most recent and comprehensive overview of scholarship on peacebuilding identifies the dominant themes emerging from the various conceptualisations and applications of peace building (Christie, 2001). These include: challenges to dominant cultural discourses, the honouring of multiple voices and co-construction of social change, adopting an activist agenda and the sustainable satisfaction of basic human needs. Challenges to dominant cultural discourses interrogate cultural discourses that sup-

port structural violence. For example, peace psychology has been criticised for lacking a gender perspective, and thereby marginalising the perspectives and contributions of women in peace building efforts (McKay & de la Rey, 2001). Despite salient evidence that demonstrates women's central role in the promotion of peace (see Box 24.3), the dominant gender discourses on peace and violence continue to position women as merely victims and survivors of violence (Suffla & Seedat, 2003). It is thus argued that peace psychology needs to balance the patriarchal assumptions that underpin its theory and practice by including women's perspectives at all levels of discourse, and by reversing the skewing influences of discourses of victimology. It is postulated that the critical development of conceptual frameworks that are inclusive of feminist, cultural and constructivist perspectives will offer peace psychology a much needed transformative vision, as well as a meaningful approach to conceptualising and researching the conjunction of the politics of peace and politics of gender.

The second theme foregrounds the idea that peace building involves multiple social actors, and that social change is co-constructed (see Box 24.3). With respect to knowledge production, for example, the objective systems of producing, transforming and applying the knowledge that operates in specific communities and societies are often marginalised in favour of a singular bias towards the creation of modern scientific knowledge (Le Grange, 2000). This reductionism of science, together with the dominance of mainstream Western knowledge traditions, has served to highlight the silences that have been imposed on cultures that engage different constructions and methods of peace and social justice, such as, the utilisation of the knowledge and methods of traditional healers to protect individuals and communities against violence and to promote peace. The preferred paradigm, however, honours multiple voices, acknowledges that knowledge is embedded in a system of social, cultural and economic representations, argues for the blending of scientific and indigenous knowledge technologies and encourages the mutual acknowledgement of the other as an active agent in the construction of social change.

This approach has both highlighted the hegemonic values embedded within mainstream Western psychology, as well as supported the argument for a psychology of liberation (Seedat, 1997). As a form of peace psychology, liberation psychology is concerned with issues of social empowerment, emancipation and transformation, and the needs of the

Peace building, as an expanded concept of peace, includes a focus on strengthening local level capacity as a critical shift towards building sustainable social, political and economic structures in post-conflict societies such as South Africa (MacLean, 1999). This motivation is underpinned by the contention that a more organic model of peace building that is characterised by participation and ownership of the process of social change is more likely to contribute to enduring peace (Lederach, 1997). An excellent example of local capacity development within the peacemaking-peace building nexus is the case of a group of Black women volunteers involved in peace and safety promotion work within a historically marginalised context in South Africa (Suffla & Seedat, 2003). Through their location within a Neighbourhood-Based Safety Promotion Programme, which is implemented by the University of South Africa's Institute for Social and Health Sciences, the women have adopted the principles of equality, peace and development as an organising framework for their violence prevention and peace promotion efforts. Their activities are enabled and reinforced through ongoing training, and are focused on environ-

mental upgrading, social development and support through a range of activity groups, home visitation, home-based after-care, and advocacy and lobbying. The Programme serves to nurture and promote local-level peace processes, thereby mainstreaming the contributions of one of the most marginalised groups in South Africa. Importantly, the participation of local peace agents accords value to the notion that social change is co-constructed. Research directed at examining the women's accounts of their involvement in peace promotion work indicated that they construct their contribution in the following ways:
- addressing the legacy of apartheid;
- building a culture of human rights;
- organic expression of historical roles; and
- individual and collective empowerment (Suffla & Seedat, 2003).

Research of this nature acknowledges the validity and range of the knowledge and perspectives of women, thereby challenging the dominant cultural narratives that unwittingly support structural violence.

politically and economically oppressed (Dawes, 2001). This positioning also embraces the third theme of peace building, that is, activism as an essential dimension to the pursuit of social justice and the process of social change. Dawes (2001) and Suffla *et al.* (2001) detail the activist agenda that informed the contributions of groups of progressive South African psychologists in response to the violence of apartheid prior to the transition to democracy in 1994. Primarily, the activism of these psychologists involved action aligned with efforts to dismantle apartheid, and to compel social transformation, such as calling attention to the psychological effects of human rights violations, and transferring psychological skills to lay helpers in order to enhance access of support services to victims and survivors of violence. (The reader is encouraged to peruse the following sources for a detailed description and discussion of the emergence of liberation psychology within the South African context: Dawes (2001), Nicholas and Cooper (1990), Seedat (1997) and Suffla *et al.* (2001).)

Finally, the notion of peacebuilding as the sustainable satisfaction of basic human needs is focal to many discussions on peacebuilding. Structural vio-

lence inevitably results in the deprivation of food, shelter, health care and other resources essential for normal human development and growth. This concern is strongly articulated in analyses of structural violence in relation to women and children. According to Montiel (2001:285), structural peace building therefore necessarily implies social arrangements wherein 'all groups have more equitable control over politico-economic resources needed to satisfy basic needs'. Various approaches have been proposed to ensure equal access to resources. From a psychological perspective, these have included empowerment-oriented interventions at the individual and family (e.g., skills training), community (e.g., advocacy and lobbying) and societal levels (e.g., development of co-operatives) (Webster & Perkins, 2001).

Analyses of peace and social justice inevitably elicit questions about the role of peace psychologists in building cultures of peace. The section to follow will provide a brief sketch of the actions that psychologists can employ to promote peace.

Figure 2 Endemic violence in South Africa

A framework for action

Psychologists can contribute to peace processes through multiple levels of engagement. These include peace education directed at the development of conflict resolution skills, psychosocial interventions to reduce conflict within families and communities, and the ongoing development of knowledge on the theory and practice of conflict, violence and peace. However, given the systemic connections between direct and structural violence, and therefore the argument that the sustainability of peace is ultimately contingent upon social change, psychologists can also contribute through participation in the public arena, accessing larger numbers of people, formulating social policy aimed at the institutionalisation of social justice and extending the level at which they can intervene (Wessells *et al.*, 2001).

Wessells *et al.* (2001) propose four venues for accomplishing the above:

- Firstly, they suggest that peace psychologists engage in sensitisation or consciousness-raising so as to contribute to agenda-setting and public dialogue. This can be effected through the utilisation and dissemination of psychological knowledge and skills, such as drawing attention to the psychosocial sequelae of human rights abuses through the mass media.
- The second venue is through offering expertise on issues of social justice and peace. Consultation services could include a focus on training, education, research, programme design and evaluation and human rights monitoring.
- Thirdly, they argue that peace psychologists should see themselves as activists. Projects of activism would necessarily consider issues of non-violence, empowerment and mobilisation, critical discourse at multiple levels, and the construction of psychological organisations committed to mobilising for peace.
- Finally, peace psychology is considered to have an influential role to play with respect to public policy. Peace psychologists could intervene at this level through conducting policy research to inform policy development, offering psychologically informed critiques of existing policies, mobilising public opposition to damaging policies, monitoring policies, and advocating for policies based on sound psychological knowledge.

In effect, such a framework for action translates into a position which constructs peace as a political process, and rejects the notion of neutrality at the levels of both science (see Box 24.4) and practice.

24.4 RESEARCH ON KNOWLEDGE PRODUCTION WITHIN PSYCHOLOGICAL SCIENCE

A number of recent scholarly contributions on knowledge production within South African psychology have critiqued the notion of neutrality within psychological science. For example, Duncan (2001) examined how, and the extent to which, South African psychologists supported the ideology of racism through their academic contributions prior to and during the apartheid era. The study, which was conducted between 1990 and 1993, analysed all the articles on racism and racism-related topics published in 22 South African journals and monograph collections since their origination to the end of the 1980s. Findings indicated that only 48 articles of the 1 980 scrutinised contained a focus on racism related issues. Duncan's findings also suggested that none of these explicitly addressed racism as a form of structural violence. Of the themes that emerged from the texts that were analysed, the theme on 'the representation of Blacks' represented Blacks as destructive. This theme appeared to best illustrate the argument that knowledge production within South African psychology historically sanctioned and perpetuated the ideology of racism.

Conclusion

In summary, this chapter described the dominant assumptions and discourses associated with the concepts of peacemaking and peace building, and illustrated that these two dimensions of peace work operate jointly to form an interconnected system of peace. That is, efforts to mitigate and resolve conflict are inextricably linked to the process of transforming unjust social conditions into more equitable and peaceful structures. This discussion revealed a number of important caveats in relation to peace psychology. These include the caution against cultural insularity and the resultant marginalisation of voices and knowledge located outside the dominant paradigm, the universal application of dominant values and traditions, the polarisation of different knowledge systems, and the inattentiveness to the contextual dimensions of peace processes. In concluding with a brief scrutiny of how psychologists can contribute to peacemaking and peacebuilding, the chapter argued for a more critical conception of the role of psychology in building peace.

As we begin to advance through the twenty-first century, we continue to be confronted by warfare,

Figure 3 African collective peace initiatives may be political or non-partisan

atrocities against women and children, ethnic conflict and severely oppressive social structures. The trajectory of psychology is therefore obliged to continue to interrogate and expand its orientation and scope of justice. The pursuit of social justice and the quest for human security, particularly as it relates to the African context, should in fact be a central concern and responsibility of psychology in Africa and invoke our best commitment, vision and passion for crafting enduring peace.

REFERENCES

Agger, I. (2001). Reducing trauma during ethno-political conflict: A personal account of psycho-social work under war conditions in Bosnia. In D.J. Christie, R.V. Wagner & D.D. Winter (Eds.). *Peace, Conflict and Violence: Peace psychology for the 21st century*. New Jersey: Prentice Hall, pp. 240-50.

Christie, D.J. (2001). Peacebuilding: Approaches to social justice. In D.J. Christie, R.V. Wagner & D.D. Winter (Eds.). *Peace, Conflict and Violence: Peace psychology for the 21st century*. New Jersey: Prentice Hall, pp. 277-81.

Christie, D.J., Wagner, R.V. & Winter, D.D. (2001). *Peace, Conflict and Violence: Peace psychology for the 21st century*. New Jersey: Prentice Hall.

Crawford, N.C. (2000). The passion of world politics: Propositions on emotions and emotional relationships. *International Security*, 24(4):116-56.

Dawes, A. (2001). Psychologies for liberation: Views from elsewhere. In D.J. Christie, R.V. Wagner & D.D. Winter (Eds.). *Peace, Conflict and Violence: Peace psychology for the 21st century*. New Jersey: Prentice Hall, pp. 295-306.

de la Rey, C. (2001). Reconciliation in divided societies. In D.J. Christie, R.V. Wagner & D.D. Winter (Eds.). *Peace, Conflict and Violence: Peace psychology for the 21st century*. New Jersey: Prentice Hall, pp. 251-61.

Duncan. N. (2001). Dislodging the sub-tests: An analysis of a corpus articles on racism produced by South African psychologists. In N. Duncan, A. van Niekerk, C. de la Rey & M. Seedat (Eds.). *Race,*

Racism, Knowledge Production and Psychology in South Africa. New York: Nova Science Publishers, pp. 125-52.

Fanon, F. (1967). *Black Skin, White Masks*. New York: Grove Press.

Foster, D. (2000). The Truth and Reconciliation Commission and understanding perpetrators. *South African Journal of Psychology*, 30(1):2-13.

Foster, D. & Nicholas, L. (2000). Cognitive dissonance, de Kock and odd psychological testimony. *South African Journal of Psychology*, 30(1):37-40.

Hamber, B. (1995). Do Sleeping Dogs Lie? The psychological implications of the Truth and Reconciliation Commission in South Africa. Paper presented at the *Centre for the Study of Violence and Reconciliation, Seminar No. 5*, Johannesburg.

James, W. & van der Vijver, L. (2001). *After the TRC: Reflections on truth and reconciliation*. Athens, Ohio: Ohio University Press.

Knox. C. & Quirk, P. (2000). *Peace Building in Northern Ireland, Israel and South Africa*. New York: St. Martin's Press.

Langholtz, H.J. & Leentjies, P. (2001). U.N. Peacekeeping: Confronting the psychological environment of war in the twenty-first century. In D.J. Christie, R.V. Wagner & D.D. Winter (Eds.). *Peace, Conflict and Violence: Peace psychology for the 21st century*. New Jersey: Prentice Hall, pp. 173-82.

Lederach, J.P. (1997). *Building Peace: Sustainable reconciliation in divided societies*. Washington, DC: United States Institute of Peace.

Le Grange, L. (2000). Is there a 'space' for enabling disparate knowledge traditions to work together? Challenges for science (education) in an African context. *South African Journal of Education*, 20(2):114-7.

MacLean, S. (1999). Peacebuilding and the new regionalism in southern Africa. *Third World Quarterly*, 20(5):943-57.

McKay, S. & de la Rey, C. (2001). Women's meanings of peacebuilding in post-apartheid South Africa. *Peace & Conflict: Journal of Peace Psychology*, 7(3):227-42.

Montiel, C.J. (2001). Towards a psychology of structural peacebuilding. In D.J. Christie, R.V. Wagner & D.D. Winter (Eds.). *Peace, Conflict and Violence: Peace psychology for the 21st century*. New Jersey: Prentice Hall, pp. 282-94.

Nicholas, L.J. & Cooper, S. (Eds.). (1990). *Psychology and Apartheid*. Johannesburg: Vision/Madiba Publication.

Pederson, P.B. (2001). The cultural context of peacemaking. In D.J. Christie, R.V. Wagner & D.D. Winter (Eds.). *Peace, Conflict and Violence: Peace psychology for the 21st century*. New Jersey: Prentice Hall, pp. 183-92.

Sanson, A. & Bretherton, D. (2001). Conflict resolution: Theoretical and practical issues. In D.J. Christie, R.V. Wagner & D.D. Winter (Eds.). *Peace, Conflict and Violence: Peace psychology for the 21st century*. New Jersey: Prentice Hall, pp. 193-209.

Schell-Faucon, S. (2001). *Journey Into the Inner Self and Encounters with the Other: Transformation trails with militarized youth of opposing groups*. Unpublished manuscript, Department of Science of Education/Adult Education, University of Cologne, Germany.

Seedat, M. (1997). The quest for liberatory psychology. *South African Journal of Psychology*, 27:261-70.

Shawcross, W. (2001). *Deliver us from Evil: Warlords and peacekeepers in a world of endless conflict*. London: Bloomsbury Publishing.

Suffla, S., Stevens, G. & Seedat, M. (2001). Mirror reflections: The evolution of organized professional psychology in South Africa. In N. Duncan, A. van Niekerk, C. de la Rey and M. Seedat (Eds.). *Race, Racism, Knowledge Production and Psychology in South Africa*. New York: Nova Science Publishers, pp. 27-36.

Suffla, S. & Seedat, M. (2003). *Towards Building Cultures of Peace: The role of women in safety promotion and violence prevention*. Unpublished manuscript, University of the Western Cape, Bellville & ISHS, University of South Africa, Johannesburg.

Webster, L. & Perkins, D.D. (2001). Redressing structural violence against children: Empowerment-based interventions and research. In D.J. Christie, R.V. Wagner & D.D. Winter (Eds.). *Peace, Conflict and Violence: Peace psychology for the 21st century*. New Jersey: Prentice Hall, pp. 330-40.

Wessells, M. & Monteiro, C. (2001). Psychosocial intervention and post-war reconstruction in Angola: Interweaving Western and traditional approaches. In D.J. Christie, R.V. Wagner & D.D. Winter (Eds.). *Peace, Conflict and Violence: Peace psychology for the 21st century*. New Jersey: Prentice Hall, pp. 262-75.

Wessells. M, Schwebel, M. & Anderson, A. (2001). Psychologists making a difference in the public arena: Building cultures of peace. In D.J. Christie, R.V. Wagner & D.D. Winter (Eds.). *Peace, Conflict and Violence: Peace psychology for the 21st century*. New Jersey: Prentice Hall, pp. 350-62.

Multiple choice questions

1. Peace psychology is aimed at the
   a) reduction of direct and structural violence
   b) conflict resolution
   c) promotion of social justice
   d) all of the above
2. Peacekeeping activities relate to
   a) United Nations truth commissions
   b) monitoring of peace agreements
   c) humanitarian relief
   d) b & c
3. The core principles of conflict resolution include
   a) empathy and unconditional positive regard
   b) psychosocial resolution
   c) collaboration
   d) 'I/We' statements
4. The idea of cultural relativity emphasises the following
   a) multiple contexts
   b) dominant discourses
   c) collectivistic approach
   d) reciprocity
5. Truth commissions are directed at
   a) conflict resolution
   b) psychosocial healing
   c) peacekeeping
   d) all of the above
6. The dominant themes underlying the application of peace building include
   a) reconciliation
   b) mediation
   c) activism
   d) satisfaction of psychosocial needs
7. The focus on women's contributions to peace processes is important because
   a) peace psychology always acknowledges women
   b) women are peacemakers by nature
   c) more women than men practice traditional healing
   d) none of the above
8. Liberation psychology is concerned with
   a) human security
   b) indigenous knowledge systems
   c) social justice
   d) all of the above
9. The following represent psychosocial approaches to the sustainable satisfaction of basic human needs
   a) skills training
   b) lobbying for equal access to resources
   c) funding
   d) a & b
10. The participation of peace psychologists in the public arena involves the following
    a) conflict resolution skills training
    b) policy research
    c) psychotherapeutic intervention
    d) none of the above

Short answer questions

1. What is peace psychology and what are some of the issues that it aims to address?
2. You are a peace psychologist, and have been selected to mediate between two warring factions in South Africa. The dispute appears to be related to the ownership of land. Describe your strategy and provide a rationale for your plan of action.
3. Discuss the role of peace psychologists in the pursuit of social justice in the African context.
4. Present your opinion of the form that the peace process could take in contexts currently embroiled in conflict (e.g., Arab-Israeli conflict in the Middle East; India-Pakistan conflict over Kashmir).
5. Your task is to support the contributions of South African women to national peace processes. How will you do this?

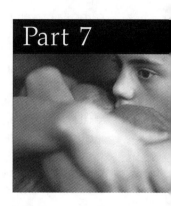

Part 7

Educational Psychology

Elias Mpofu

The four chapters in this part of the book all deal with different psychological aspects of education, with special reference to the sub-Saharan, African context. The significance of this set of chapters is that they provide a broad-based introduction to the goals, processes and outcomes of education that are of interest to policy makers, educators, learners and ordinary citizens in Africa. Education in Africa, as in many societies around the world, is perceived as a vehicle for development and change. For that reason, what happens (or does not happen) in educational provision is of interest to many.

The chapters in this part present a selection of themes that inform the psychology of education in modern Africa. Specifically, five broad themes are explored: educational values, diversity in education, educational processes, educational outcomes and special needs in education.

Mpofu's first chapter explores the multiple meanings and contexts of the terms 'teaching' and 'learning'. The objective of the chapter is to enable the reader to appreciate the ordinariness of teaching and learning. At the same time, the chapter draws from a rich body of both African and international literature on the essence of teaching and learning and implications for education. Among the many observations made is that the goals of teaching and learning are unique to the learning context and objectives. The diverse ways of understanding learning and some key principles of learning and their relevance to teaching and learning are also examined.

The chapter by Nsamenang addresses the multi-layered cultural heritage of African education systems, particularly traditional African and Western systems. Nsamenang regards participatory education as a cornerstone of the traditional African cultural heritage, in the sense that it is used by parents, siblings and peers across Africa. He observes that participatory education may be lacking in many modern African schools that teach Western values and present these as finished products that learners need to assimilate uncritically. According to Nsamenang, there is a potential that the discontinuities in the experience of school and community by African learners can be detrimental to the quality of their learning.

Engelbrecht's chapter presents and contrasts two types of curriculum models, namely, the prescriptive and participatory models. The prescriptive model is premised on the assumption that formally qualified curriculum 'experts' know what should be taught in schools and how and when the teaching should occur. Engelbrecht notes that curricula that are based on the prescriptive model lack the potential for change and innovation. As a consequence, curricula based on the prescriptive model may be less suited to meeting the educational needs of a changing society. Engelbrecht also discusses the participatory model in curricula development. The participatory approach to curriculum development involves all the stakeholders in education (e.g., teachers, parents and learners) and is likely to yield educational experiences that are relevant to the needs of the community.

The final chapter in this part, by Mpofu, focuses on strategies for learners with special educational needs in inclusive or ordinary settings. The point is made that, historically, learners with special educational needs were educated in the same settings as other learners (e.g., in the family and community) and that for many such learners in sub-Saharan Africa, inclusive education remains the only alternative. The chapter explores the cultural meanings that influence educational opportunities for African learners with special needs, both from the viewpoint of their cultures of origin and the cultures of practice of the professionals from whom these learners receive services.

Space limitations constrained both the selection and scope of the themes presented in this part. An important theme that could have been explored by all the authors of this part is that of the unintended (or hidden) curriculum that greatly shapes what teachers and schools teach or what learners actually learn. The official curriculum only partially overlaps with the hidden curriculum to which learners are exposed, as teachers select from and interpret the official curriculum, and learners make sense of the multiple experiences that comprise their education. In the chapter on inclusive education, the role of assessment in legitimating disability status, and inclusive education options for learners with special needs could have been explored more fully. The assignment of special need status is a relatively subjective process, except perhaps for extreme cases. Many African learners may not regard themselves as having special needs, until after assessment. As will become clear, the role of assessment in the social construction of special needs is manifestly important for a more complete understanding of the special needs of African learners and the design of appropriate interventions.

25

The Intersection of Traditional African Education with School Learning

Bame Nsamenang

CHAPTER OBJECTIVES

After studying this chapter you should be able to:
- explain the nature and process of traditional African education
- describe how traditional African education fits with the concept of 'the school of life'
- specify the role of the family, especially that of the parents and older siblings, in participatory learning and school learning
- identify at least three areas of possible conflict or tension between traditional African education and formal education, and two strengths and weaknesses of each system of education
- identify at least three psychological principles embedded in traditional African education and demonstrate how each could apply in school learning in an African society
- justify why it is necessary to make education culturally relevant in African countries.

Nosipho's parents had believed strongly in the value of education. They had helped her with her school work and encouraged her to apply for university. 'A university education will let you do anything you want to do', they always told her. She knew that her parents regretted that they hadn't had the opportunity to go to university themselves. Her grandparents on both sides had been poor and apartheid had made it difficult for her parents to actualise their educational aspirations. But thinking about different kinds of education and what African education could offer made Nosipho suddenly question whether in fact her parents had missed out on so much. While they hadn't had her opportunities in formal education, they had had other important kinds of education growing up in tight-knit communities in the rural areas of South Africa.

Nosipho's father would often sit with the family and nostalgically recall what life had been like when he was a child. He attended the local village school where he did well, but the best times for him were accompanying his own father when he went around to the nearby villages to sell the produce they had grown on their small farm. Nosipho's father always said he had learned so much about people, about marketing and even about economics as he helped out on these trips. He worked as a salesman now and he often said, only half joking, that he had had the best training of any of the employees at the company he worked for. As she thought about it, Nosipho wondered whether in fact her own schooling and university education taught people as well as her father had been taught. Learning in classrooms and from books taught a particular kind of thinking – but sometimes it was hard see how it fitted with real life. Perhaps there were many different ways of learning effectively.

Introduction

In Africa today, both traditional African and foreign ways of thinking and educating children are available and useful, though they sometimes produce conflict situations. In this way, present-day Africa has elements of several cultures co-existing in what Mazrui (1986) has called a 'triple heritage'. It is a triple inheritance because it comes from three sources, namely Arabic-Islamic influences, Western-Christian legacies or Westernisation and deep-seated African educational traditions (Nsamenang, 2003). The main objective of this chapter is to sketch the current state of traditional or indigenous African education and to briefly describe how it coexists with other world systems of education, particularly schooling. In doing so, the chapter attempts to identify some principles of learning and teaching relevant to African settings. It is hoped that the chapter can serve as a challenge to African learners and scholars to rethink their educational and other heritages and how they can inspire appropriate, innovative curricular reforms in education in their countries.

An overview of systems of education

Education is a specific form of enculturation and socialisation, and is partly provided through formal schooling (Nsamenang, 2002) or instructed learning (Tomasello *et al.*, 1993). Formal, formalised or institutional education is in contrast, but also complementary to participatory or societal learning. In other words, teaching and learning are not restricted to schools; they occur in and outside the school (Desforges, 1995; Chapter 28, this volume). Thus, 'schooling is only one small part of how a culture inducts the young into its canonical ways' (Bruner, 1996:ix).

Educational reform as adjustment to change and need

Education is a process that seeks to prepare children for the responsibilities of life or a call to a specific duty. At the same time, it must prepare citizens to cope with local and global change. In fact, all educational systems must cope with, and adjust to change. The need to make education relevant leads to ongoing revisions of educational curricula. According to Cookson *et al.* (1992), educational reform is an ongoing process that really has no end. It is a change process, and change is an important aspect of human life. Africa has made attempts to reform the systems of education it inherited from European colonisers. Unfortunately, the reforms have tended to be incomplete, so that some inconsistency with African cultures and economic and ecological realities prevails.

History and structure of systems of education

Human beings in all cultures throughout the world seek to pass on what they learn and have inherited to their younger generations. This is meant to ensure that their offspring and culture survive and do not become extinct (Reagan, 2000). As previously noted, the history of African education that is being taught today focuses almost entirely on Western education in Africa rather than African education. It neglects other educational traditions that inform the African worldview, like those of Asia and the local African traditions.

In general terms, we can fit the existing systems of education into two basic models of teaching and learning (Nsamenang, 2003). One model is the didactic or instructional framework, and the other is the participatory model. In Western societies education is organised so that children can learn from adults, especially teachers. Teachers instruct learners

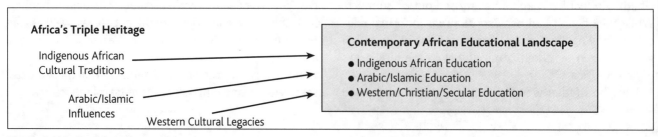

Figure 1 Africa's triple heritage

Figure 2 Tradition and science

and stimulate their cognition in well-organised institutions such as schools. Cognition here refers to mental activities like reasoning and thinking, among many others. Schools, for example, provide instruction to learners under controlled conditions (with teacher, subject matter and objectives). However, with traditional Africa education, children are encouraged to observe and learn from their involvement in the life of the family and the cultural and economic activities going on around them. This is often done without formal instruction but with the encouragement and support of parents and peers (Nsamenang, 2002).

The instructional and participatory models carry implications for the process of teaching and learning, and more importantly, for the generation or creation and control of knowledge. With the instructional or didactic model, teachers tend to control or 'own' knowledge. In the participatory model, learners actively co-create and co-control knowledge with their teachers. Knowledge is rarely an object nor 'property' which one person (e.g., the teacher or parent) possesses (Freire, 1970). It exists to be discovered. As regards the developing individual or child, he or she produces knowledge from interaction with other people, objects (e.g., the task that has

to be learned) and the environment. The participatory model sees learners not as 'empty vessels', but as agents or partners who are active in the process of learning. They actively acquire, interact and generate and share knowledge (Nsamenang, 2002, 2003).

25.1 HOW DO WE APPROPRIATELY DEFINE EDUCATION?

Education, as deliberate teaching or preparation of the young, is a specific form of enculturation and socialisation, widely referred to as schooling. It has been characterised as instructed learning (Tomasello *et al.*, 1993), school learning, formalised or institutional education that is often contrasted with participatory learning, home learning, and societal or non-formalised education. Teaching and learning are not the monopoly of schools; they occur in and out of school throughout life. In some cultures, learning is organised primarily through didactic instruction in schools, with considerable cognitive stimulation. In African family traditions, children are guided and encouraged to observe and participate in ongoing cultural and economic activities that emphasise socially distributed norms (Nsamenang & Lamb, 1995). African schools tend to give the impression that African homes are culturally deficient dungeons to be escaped from or obstacles to overcome (Serpell, 1993). Thus, the role of the school is to help Africans overcome their 'backwardness'. This deficit model fails to realise that the education so far imparted in Africa generally has had limited to no relevance to the life paths of Africans (Nsamenang, 2002:85).

Indigenous African education

Education, culture and stages of human development

Education in African traditions is part and parcel of the culture. It is built on the daily routines and activities of the family and community. Like education everywhere, it is organised in conformity to the stages of life (Moumouni, 1968). Traditional African education does not divide domains of knowledge, such as agriculture, economics, arts, science, etc. Instead, it integrates knowledge about all aspects of life into a single curriculum. The curriculum is arranged in sequence to fit into different milestones

Figure 3 The whole made up of parts: Education may be like a puzzle

of development that the culture perceives or recognises. In other words, what is taught or what children are made to learn fits their abilities and successive stages of development. This implies that a child may be 'mature' in chronological age but immature in some abilities (Nsamenang, 1992). In psychology, such children are called late developers because the emergence of their abilities fails to match, or lags behind their chronological age and the social expectations for that age.

The gradual, stage-like nature of African educational thought and practices follows from the principle that since we cannot teach or learn everything at once, the tasks and activities to be taught and learned have to be arranged in sequential order within the curriculum as well as across the stages of development. This permits teaching and learning to be systematic. Another principle is that children are born with a disposition to become competent, to learn to relate to other human beings, and to regulate their behaviour and activities. Guided by these two principles, among others, the aim of African education is to progressively connect children to their cultural heritage, ways of life and the continuation of their family and community.

Africans tend to think of child development in terms of a garden metaphor, a *seed*. Just as the seed germinates and grows into a mature plant, the individual matures in a progressive manner and gradually acquires knowledge (growing in wisdom) and a sense of personal identity (or self-identity). Whereas a seed is nursed or cultivated into maturity in an African garden of mixed crops, the child is reared in a dense social network in which several members share roles in childcare and family duties (Nsamenang, 2002). Erny (1968) described this view of child development in Africa as a 'becoming'. In this sense, becoming an adult is a gradual process. The assessment of how well a child is maturing or 'becoming' an adult is based on how he or she is fulfilling the social roles expected of him or her. It equally depends on the extent to which the child is integrated into his or her family and community. Mead (1972:154) captured how the child progressively establishes his or her self-identity in the following words: 'The self has a character, which is different from the physiological organism. The self is something, which has a development; it is not initially there at birth but arises in the process of social experience and activity.'

At each successive stage of life, the child faces and must achieve developmental tasks. Each task is defined by the culture according to important points in growing up and patterns of participating in the life of the people at those points. This perhaps explains why education is organised to gradually introduce children to different roles and responsibilities at various stages of development. The education guides and directs children to participate in useful cultural and economic activities at designated or

Figure 4 Nurturing and growing

recognised stages. We may regard such education as 'cultivation' into and through 'pivot' roles that mark different 'stations' of an individual's social development (Nsamenang & Lamb, 1995).

Through such participation, children master their language and the rules of their culture. They do so by practicing with proverbs, mental arithmetic, dilemma tales, legends, etc. By the end of adolescence, a normally developing boy or girl is expected to complete his or her social, intellectual, moral and practical training. Although such a young person or emerging adult may begin to assume responsibility in the world of adults, he or she does not automatically attain adult status. A full adult status is synonymous with being married and becoming a parent (Nsamenang, 1992).

25.2 SOCIAL CLASS, FAMILY VALUES AND PEER INFLUENCE

Ali is a twelve-year-old Abakwa boy. Abakwa is a residential area in Bamenda, Cameroon, where lower-class families live. Suh is an eleven-year-old boy who lives at Bamenda Upstation, a residential quarter for the middle- and upper-class families in Bamenda. Ali treks daily to and from school, but Suh is chauffeur-driven to and from school. Unknown to their parents, Ali and Suh are good friends; they have been planning to attend the same secondary school and had to figure out how each would convince his parents. While Suh's parents disqualified his intended school as cheap and of low quality, Ali's parents discouraged him from it because they could not afford to pay for his education in it. Both families became furious when each discovered the influence of the other family's child over their son.

Describe a friendship you know that transverses social or cultural boundaries. What qualities make for a good friendship in your community? How can we make the effect of such influence positive and constructive? How typical or unusual are these experiences among African teenagers? Discuss them in the light of your own knowledge or experiences.

The family: The foundation of education

The composition and function of the normal family varies throughout Africa. The most common type of African family is the extended family. But the number of single-parent families and other forms of family is increasing. The family, the child and the family environment interact and influence each other. The family context or atmosphere determines what is normal and what facilitates or impairs child development. This is a particularly important point because the foundation of child development is laid in the family long before the child is born. In addition, the family unit sets the pace and sustains children's learning of their culture (Tomasello *et al.*, 1993), as well as prepares them for entry into school. It is the family that prepares children to acquire skills in interpersonal processes, communication and mental abilities. It is equally through the family that children expand their horizons and growing sense of identity and life purpose.

In other words, children's search for understanding, competence and 'the right ways' of the world begin in the family with their parents, long before they meet non-family members in the neighbourhood and/or at school. The family constitutes a secure base on which children build the confidence needed to relate to others and the world beyond the family. It is within the family that children learn the social, linguistic cognitive and other prerequisites for cultural living (Nsamenang, 1992).

As the first educators of children, parents are therefore the source of primary knowledge and values for children's head start (or take-off) in life, espe-

Figure 5 The 'active' family: Parents and children working together

cially their transition into and adjustment at school. A firm foundation for school learning is laid in the security of the home, long before the child enters school. Parents can play a crucial role in orienting their child to life in general and the motive to achieve in particular. Different parents and families possess different capacities to prepare their children adequately for school and to motivate them to achieve at school and in life (Serpell, 1993).

The role of parents in fostering children's development is three-fold (Nsamenang, 2001):

- to guide children to understand and accept the appropriate adult identity and models toward which they are being socialised;
- to communicate standards of valued behaviour and virtue; and
- to prime or sensitise children to acceptable values, rules and standards of the family and society, and to ensure their acquisition.

Parents have differing capacities to perform these roles.

25.3 PARTICIPATORY LEARNING IN A KENYAN ETHNIC CULTURE

From a very early age, Kikuyu children are taught their cultural history and values through lullabies and stories. Apart from this, learning occurs by means of observation and modelling, and children engage in numerous activities such as wrestling, fighting, herding animals and household chores. During adolescence both boys and girls are initiated by circumcision, which is considered a very important step in the development of a Kikuyu child. A Kikuyu who is not initiated experiences difficulty adjusting to his or her environment, since he or she is looked down on and is not allowed to marry or to own property (Mwamwenda, 1990).

Socialisation of responsible intelligence

In African societies, children are socialised according to values and norms that foster support for one another from an early age (Weisner, 1997). This is a highly cherished moral quality that is relatively ignored in the curricula of most schools in Africa (Serpell, 1993). Africans tend to use social competence to assess how responsible or 'intelligent' a child is (see Mundy-Castle, 1975). In fact, African parents use evidence that a child has the ability to give and receive social support, and notice and attend to the needs of others as markers of mental and general development (Weisner, 1997). In conformity to this principle, Serpell (1993:64) clarified that:

> Adults presumably keep some mental tally of the proportion of errands that a given child performs adequately, and this serves as an index of how 'tumikila' (responsible) the child is. In the short term this attribute is used to choose which child to send on another such errand; in the longer term it feeds into an assessment of that child's expertise and responsibility.

In order to train children in responsibility, parents and caregivers allocate chores and send them on errands (Nsamenang & Lamb, 1995). Such errands include, but are not limited to, cleaning duties, fetching objects, purchasing items and delivering messages to neighbours. Child work inculcates prosocial values and the acquisition of cognitive, socioeconomic and other competencies and productive skills. Above all, it promotes social integration. The moral lessons and skills children have to learn are not separate, but are part and parcel of social interactions, cultural life and economic activities and daily routines (Nsamenang, 1992, 2002). Children are not instructed but discover these values and skills in the process of participation.

Figure 6 Child as caregiver and domestic helper

Yula, a 10-year-old schoolgirl in Grade 4, attends school in Kimbo, Cameroon, with two younger brothers in Grades 2 and 1. Her unmarried mother runs a roadside eating-house. After dismissal from school the three kids join their mother at the food kiosk. After having had something to eat, Yula helps her mother in the marketplace, while the young ones play around, but sometimes help, whenever necessary and appropriate, depending on what task has to be accomplished. Yula helps her mother to bring items home and to prepare the food to sell the next day. It is only from about 9 pm that Yula studies or completes her assign-ments; yet, she is one of the high achievers in her class.

What does this vignette contain about the edu-cational circumstances of schoolchildren among low-income Africans? One theme that this vignette invokes is 'motivated achievement'. Discuss the different dimensions of this theme and how each play out in the life of a young person you know well. Is the African child, like Yula, who may be 'usefully' socialised through participatory learning:
- Socially responsible?
- Responsibly intelligent?
- Participating in child labour?

The role of the peer group and children's creative spirit

From toddlerhood, typical African children begin to distance themselves from their parents, and they increasingly come under the influence of the peer group. During peer group activities children often act as *father* and *mother*. Elder peers or siblings rather than the parents or other adults readily correct, supervise and mentor them. As children rehearse and enact the roles of adult models, they use the peer culture to re-address and resolve the confu-sions and uncertainties that arise in their interac-tions with parents (Nsamenang & Lamb, 1995). The free spirit of the peer culture challenges children to address and resolve conflicts, take others' perspec-tives into account and notice the needs of others. They also learn how to plan and organise activities and collaborate. In so doing, children integrate adult models into their own worlds. When their contribu-tions are accepted they see themselves as significant social partners. Thus, children do not passively accommodate adult worlds. They are active and cre-ative social producers of new forms of knowledge and modes of functioning. In the process of such cre-ativity and functioning, children become emotional-ly mature, gain leadership skills, learn how to han-dle crises and gain social and mental competence (Nsamenang & Lamb, 1995). The motivation inher-ent in the peer culture may be more acceptable and stimulating to children than the opportunities pre-pared for them by parents.

A primary goal of this chapter is to develop the stance that people develop as participants in cultur-al communities. Their development can be under-stood only in light of the cultural practices and cir-cumstances of their communities – which also change.

To date, the study of human development has been based largely on research and theory coming from upper-income communities in Europe and North America. Such research and theory often have been assumed to generalise to all people. Indeed, many researchers make conclusions from work done in a single group in overly general terms, claiming that 'the child does such-and-so' rather than 'these children did such-and-such'.

For example, a great deal of research has attempted to determine at what age we should expect 'the child' to be capable of certain skills. For the most part, the claims have been generic regard-ing the age at which children enter a stage or should be capable of a certain skill.

A cultural approach notes that different commu-nities may expect children to engage in activities at vastly different times in childhood, and may regard 'timetables' of development in other communities as surprising or even dangerous. Consider these questions of when children can begin to do certain things, and reports of cultural variations in when they do:

- When does children's intellectual development permit them to be responsible for others?
- When can they be trusted to take care of an infant?

In upper-income US families, children are often not regarded as capable of caring for themselves or tending to another child until perhaps age 10 (or later in some regions). In the UK, it is an offence to leave a child under age 14 years without adult supervision (Subbotsky, 1995). However, in many other communities around the world, children begin to take on responsibility for tending to other children at ages 5 to 7 years (Rogoff *et al.*, 1975), and in some places even younger children begin to assume this responsibility. For example, among the Kwara'ae of Oceania, three-year-olds are skilled workers in the gardens and households, excellent caregivers of their younger siblings and accomplished at social interaction. Although young children also have time to play, many of the functions of play seem to be met by work. For both adults and children, work is accompanied by singing, joking, verbal play, and entertaining conversation. Instead of playing with dolls, children care for real babies. In addition to working in the family gardens, young children have their own garden plots. The latter may seem like play, but by three or four years of age many children are taking produce they have grown themselves to the market to sell, thereby making a significant and valued contribution to the family income (Watson-Gegeo in Rogoff, 2003:3-4). (See also Rogoff (1990).)

Due to the lack of commercial toys, African children are usually encouraged to create their own playthings using local materials (Nsamenang & Lamb, 1995). Such creations express remarkable ingenuity, and their recognition as 'products' enhances self-esteem and fosters children's cognitive and creative abilities. It also teaches abstract and spatial thinking and how to plan and organise work, measure objects and co-ordinate materials (Segall *et al.*, 1999). In actual fact, the rich traditions of African arts evolved through participatory learning.

Figure 7 Peer group activity

The mismatch between school and some aspects of African educational traditions

Generally, education in sub-Saharan Africa does not really take into consideration the 'subject matter: the theories and concepts through which the owners of the culture see their cultural world' (Anyawu, 1975:149). That is, the education of African children does not incorporate traditional African mentalities and wisdom. The school instead gives the impression that African cultures are backward and obstacles to learning and modernity (Serpell, 1993). Accordingly, the school should help Africa to overcome its backwardness. The view that traditional African education is backward is a deficit model of education and misrepresents African values (Serpell, 1993). Although many African children attend school, the average African school rarely teaches the economic activities of farming that most Africans value. Thus, it is doubtful just how well 'modern' schools train the average African child to function in his or her community.

The school promotes values of individual achievement, personal ambition and competition (Oyserman, 1993). This is contrary to those of traditional African education, which reinforce family, cooperation and sharing, among others (see Nsamenang, 1992, 2002). As a result, graduates from most African schools experience difficulty participating in the application of local knowledge. In fact, highly educated Africans or those with graduate degrees from colleges and universities may be poorly informed about their communities and countries.

25.6 TENSION BETWEEN THE SCHOOL AND INDIGENOUS REALITIES

Fanla's father, Mr Nkeng, cooks for a local college. Every day he sets out to work in the early hours of the morning. Mr Nkeng frequently alerts his son of his impoverished life circumstances, which he wants his son to escape. Consequently, his primary goal was to inculcate the spirit of hard work and the achievement motive as insurance against failure. To ascertain success at the entrance examination into the secondary school, he organised additional coaching for his son. Unfortunately, Fanla was a truant. Thus, Mr Nkeng received the news of his son having gone fishing a few days prior to the entrance exam instead of preparing for it at school with utter disbelief. Mr Nkeng was exasperated when his son, who is quite intelligent, mustered the courage to question the wisdom of education when his struggles through school might not fetch him a job. Fanla further infuriated his father by intimating that he was more serviceable to the family than his elder brother, Tomla, an unemployed university graduate and liability to the family. Fanla felt a sense of responsibility and achievement in feeding the family and earning some income for it from fishing, while Tomla increasingly dips into frustration.

Identify and critically discuss or debate the issues raised and lessons that emerge from your understanding of this vignette in the light of your country or an African country or society of your choice.

Inappropriate education and unemployment

The unemployment of school leavers and graduates is a growing problem because school learning is unsuitable for the needs of Africa's largely agrarian economies and job markets. For example, school children learn little or nothing about farming even though over 70 per cent of the people are engaged in peasant agriculture (Nsamenang, 1992). African countries thus face a cruel paradox of spending large portions of their national budgets on education, which only churns out increasing numbers of educated but unemployed graduates (or graduates who are illiterate about the values and means of the local community). These educated youth cannot even fend for themselves. This confirms Bruner's (1996:ix) view that the school may 'be at odds with a culture's other ways of inducting the young into the requirements of communal living'. One source of the high rate of school dropouts may be the perceived value of the school. The school evokes limited interest and hope in African learners (Nsamenang, 2002). Another hypothesis is that the pressure and anxiety generated by the 'diploma syndrome' exacerbates dropout and failure rates in African education systems (Serpell, 1993). The uninteresting nature of school curricula or their lack of relevance to addressing community needs may demotivate many learners.

Social integration of children

Whereas indigenous African educational traditions endeavour to connect children to their local contexts and activities of daily life, the school tends to separate and distance them. Schooling separates children from parents and family. As such, it increases peer influence and the generation gap. It also limits children's availability and contribution to the family welfare and economy (Nsamenang, 2002). Many of the children who drop out of school are increasingly participating in street commerce in sprawling African cities.

Figure 8 The child in the community

The mismatch between what the school teaches and the daily life of most Africans poses the challenge whether African youth are acquiring the right skills and values to catch up with changing technologies. How can we incorporate and merge truly African ideas, issues and practices (Serpell, 1992) with webs of change? How can we bring the local and the global together into comprehensive curricula that can stimulate confidence, creativity and ensure progress and sustainable development in the twenty-first century?

Conclusion

African educational thought and practices, along with a variety of foreign educational legacies, are available to most African children today. The challenge facing Africans is to explore, understand and channel their educational heritages to creative and useful purposes. This education is fitted into the developmental pathways and traditions African children follow as they participate in the cultural life and economic activities of the family and community. These differ from the Western traditions of education, which, through institutional schooling, are now given priority in spite of their lack of accurate fit with the participatory learning within African families and communities. As a result, 'modern' education in Africa produces dilemmas and paradoxes. It equally conflicts with some aspects of the indigenous systems, especially the value placed on agriculture as the mainstay of African livelihoods. We need to study this confusing state of education in order to extract lessons and useful principles inherent in Africa's participatory model of learning. One such lesson is to derive educational content from the familiar local context, as it is an integral part of the global community and to creatively integrate learning into productive skills. The lessons can then feed into relevant curricula designed to propel Africa into the technologies and sustainable development of the Third Millennium. We should challenge every African, particularly learners and scholars, to contribute to this important, liberatory project!

Anyawu, K.C. (1975). African religion as an experienced reality. Africa: Thought and Practice. *Journal of the Philosophical and Sociological Association of Kenya*, 2(2):145-57.

Bruner, J. (1996). *The Culture of Education*. Cambridge, MA: Harvard University Press.

Cookson, P.W., Sadovnik, A.R., & Semel, S.F. (1992). Introduction. In P.W., Cookson, A.R., Sadovnik & S.F. Semel (Eds.). *International Handbook of Educational Reform*. New York: Greenwood Press, pp. 1-7.

Desforges, C. (1995). Learning out of school. In C. Desforges (Ed.). *Introduction to Teaching: Psychological perspectives*. Oxford: Blackwell, pp. 93-112.

Erny, P. (1968). *L'Enfant dans la Pensée Traditionnelle de l'Afrique Noire* (The Child in Traditional African Thought). Paris: Le livre Africain.

Freire, P. (1970). *The Pedagogy of the Oppressed*. New York: Seabury.

Mazrui, A.A. (1986). *The Africans*. New York: Praeger.

Mead, G.H. (1972). *Mind, Self and Society*. Chicago: University of Chicago Press.

Moumouni, A. (1968). *Education in Africa*. New York: Praeger.

Mundy-Castle, A.C. (1975). Social and technological intelligence in Western and non-Western cultures. In Pilowsky (Ed.). *Cultures in Collision*. Adelaide: Australian National Association for Mental Health, pp. 344-8.

Mwamwenda, T.S. (1990). *Educational Psychology*: An African perspective. Durban: Butterworths.

Nsamenang, A.B. (1992). *Human Development in Cultural Context: A third world perspective*. Newbury Park, CA: Sage.

Nsamenang, A.B. (2001). Indigenous view on human development: A West African perspective. In N.J. Smelser & P.B. Baltes (Eds.). *International Encyclopedia of the Social and Behavioral Sciences*. Oxford: Elsevier, pp. 7297-9.

Nsamenang, A.B. (2002). Adolescence in Sub-Saharan Africa: An image constructed from Africa's triple inheritance. In B.B. Brown, R.W. Reed & T.S. Saraswathi (Eds.). *The World's Youth: Adolescence in eight regions of the globe*. London: Cambridge University Press, pp. 61-104.

Nsamenang, A.B. (2003). Conceptualizing human and education at the interface of external cultural influences. In T.S. Saraswathi (Ed.). *Cross-cultural Perspectives in Human Development: Theory, research, and applications*. New Delhi: Sage India, pp. 213-35.

Nsamenang, A.B. & Lamb, M.E. (1995). The force of beliefs: How the parental values of the Nso of Northwest Cameroon shape children's progress toward adult models. *Journal of Applied Developmental Psychology*, 16:613-27.

Oyserman, D. (1993). Who influences identity? Adolescent identity and delinquency in interpersonal context. *Child Psychiatry & Human Development*, 23(3):203-14.

Reagan, T. (2000). *Non-western Educational Traditions: Alternative approaches to educational thought and practice*. Mahwah, NJ: Erlbaum.

Rogoff, B., Sellers, M.J., Pirotta, S., Fox, N. & White, S.H. (1975). Age of assignment of roles and responsibilities to children: A cross-cultural survey. *Human Development*, 18:353-69.

Rogoff, B. (1990). *Apprenticeship in Thinking: Cognitive development in social context*. Oxford: Oxford University Press.

Rogoff, B. (2003). *The Cultural Nature of Human Development*. Oxford, Oxford University Press.

Segall, M.H., Dasen, P.R., Berry, J.W. & Poortinga, Y.H. (1999). *Human Behavior in Global Perspective*. Boston: Allyn & Bacon.

Serpell, R. (1992, April). *Afrocentrism: What contribution to science of developmental psychology?* Paper presented at the First ISSBD Regional Workshop on the theme Child Development and National Development in Africa. Yaounde, Cameroon.

Serpell, R. (1993). *The Significance of Schooling: Life-journeys in an African society*. Cambridge: Cambridge University Press.

Subbotsky, E. (1995). The development of pragmatic and non-pragmatic motivation. *Human Development*, 38:217-34.

Tomasello, M., Kruger, A.C. & Ratner, H.H. (1993). Cultural learning. *Behavioral & Brain Sciences*, 16:405-552.

Weisner, T.S. (1997). Support for children and the African family crisis. In T.S. Weisner, C. Bradley & C.P. Kilbride (Eds.). *African Families and the Crisis of Social Change*. Westport, CT: Bergin & Garvey, pp. 20-44.

Multiple choice questions

1. Ali Mazrui used the concept 'triple heritage' to refer to the fact that the cultural character of contemporary Africa can be more appropriately described as consisting of
   a) a tripartite inheritance of three cultural realities
   b) biological heritage and historical and cultural inheritances
   c) indigenous cultures and two imported cultural legacies

2. As explained in this chapter, which of the following statements is more accurate?
   a) teaching occurs everywhere, both in and out of school
   b) there is no instruction in traditional African education
   c) if you want to teach an African child, put him/her into school

3. The idea of the 'school of life' refers more accurately to
   a) a school, which teaches about how to progress through the stages of life.
   b) participatory learning organised according to each stage of life.
   c) teaching and learning activities organised as life long activities.

4. One fundamental difference between school learning and leaning within African family traditions is
   a) learners are under the authoritarian control of parents and adults
   b) learners receive knowledge from expert teachers or instructors
   c) learners have freedom to generate knowledge in their own way

5. The model of education into which education in African family traditions fits is the
   a) deficiency model
   b) didactic model
   c) participatory model

6. Which of the following statements most accurately reflects traditional African education?
   a) it is built on daily routines and social and economic activities
   b) it divides domains of human knowledge into traditional patterns
   c) it fails to recognise science, changing technologies and cognition

7. A key assumption (and principle of traditional African education) is that
   a) children are passive and simply have to learn to adjust to societal requirements
   b) learners possess a natural disposition to acquire culture and become competent
   c) parents know their children well and have responsibility to train and raise them

8. African parents tend to think of child development in terms of a garden metaphor. This implies that
   a) children are like African gardens for training purpose in families
   b) the African child learns at an early age to work in the garden
   c) the child is like a seed sown or a plant cultivated in a garden

9. African parents assess a child's intelligence by considering
   a) a child's level of mental development
   b) a child's level of school achievement
   c) a child's level of social responsibility

10. Jerome Bruner says the school may be 'at odds with a culture's other ways' of preparing young people for life. This position implies that
    a) schooling is unnecessary for Africa's agrarian lifestyles and economies
    b) school curricula are not always relevant to the needs of Africa's economies
    c) African countries face the paradox of education and unemployment

Short answer questions

1. What is the primary factor that differentiates the world's systems of education? Identify and discuss the different systems of education available in your ethnic group or country.

2. Does Africa really have educational thought and practices? Explain your answer.

3. What are some of the strengths and weaknesses of indigenous African education, if any? How can we sustain and improve on the strengths and eliminate or work on the weaknesses?

4. Identify and describe three strategies or methods of indigenous education in your cultural community.

5. Identify and explain:
   • three principles of learning; and
   • three pedagogic principles operative within indigenous education.

Curriculum Development

Petra Engelbrecht

After studying this chapter you should be able to:
- define each of the following terms: curriculum, curriculum development and outcomes-based education (OBE)
- explain the relationship between a curriculum and its context
- identify and describe two approaches to curriculum development
- critique Tyler's model of curriculum design and development from a social constructivist perspective
- examine OBE to determine the extent to which it draws from other models of curriculum design that you have studied in this chapter
- compare OBE with the historical approach (i.e. pre-democracy) to curriculum design in South Africa
- evaluate the extent to which OBE is an improvement over the previous curricula practices in South Africa.

As she started to discover more about how psychologists thought about education Nosipho found herself thinking back on her own learning at school. Her high school had, like many others, adopted an 'outcomes'-based approach to education. Although, she hadn't given much thought at the time to the way she was taught, she could see now that the teachers at her school had given quite a lot of encouragement to the learners' own involvement in their learning.

While they had still had conventional exams and tests at Nosipho's high school the teachers also put a lot of emphasis on what they called 'project work'. Some of Nosipho's best learning experiences had been when the class was allowed to do group or individual projects – especially when they had been allowed to choose the topic. In this kind of work she found she was able to get really excited about learning and felt that the ideas she was creating really 'belonged' to her. She also felt that she was being allowed to explore something that really interested her. Nosipho also found that whenever a teacher encouraged class participation and discussion, she grew more enthusi-

astic about the subject – even if it hadn't been something she had started off having an interest in.

There were some classes, though, that didn't inspire Nosipho in the same way. The approach to learning seemed sometimes to depend on the particular teacher and whether they were comfortable with learners sharing their opinions in class. Some teachers seemed to prefer to be 'in charge' and simply told the learners what to do. Nosipho found that when she just had to listen to a teacher reading information out of the text book she grew bored and sometimes switched off and drifted into a daydream. For her, the kind of learning that worked was learning that made her feel that she could be involved, that her ideas and thoughts mattered and that she also had something to contribute to other people's learning. As she listened to her lecturer presenting the day's material on psychology, Nosipho wondered whether there were ways that university education could be changed to allow learners more opportunities to participate in their own learning.

Introduction

It is universally recognised that the main objective of an education system in a democratic society is to provide quality education for all learners so that they will be able to reach their full potential and meaningfully contribute to, or participate in that society throughout their lives. The responsibility of the education system to develop and sustain such learning is premised on the recognition that education is a fundamental right, which extends equally to all learners (Department of National Education, 1997a).

Essentially, creating equal and inclusive opportunities for effective learning means that the range of differences or diversity between all learners should be taken into account when these opportunities are planned and implemented. The question that we are concerned with in this chapter is how the curriculum can be responsive to the needs of all learners in order to provide them with the opportunity to participate fully in the learning process.

The purpose of this chapter is therefore to familiarise you with:

- the concepts, 'curriculum' and 'curriculum development'; and
- curriculum transformation in the recent past as well as a case study of transformative curriculum development in South Africa since 1994.

Curriculum and curriculum development

Before we look at a definition of 'curriculum' it is important to note that definitions of concepts are always influenced by the contexts in which they are used. By taking the context into consideration, information is seen in a new light, and becomes more understandable. In education, there are many contexts (e.g., local communities and wider contexts, such as national and international communities) that may shape experiences and problems. The relationship between smaller contexts (e.g., local communities) and larger contexts (provincial or national contexts) is based on the interdependence of the contexts and comprises the whole (Engelbrecht, 1999). For instance, the context within which the concept 'curriculum' is defined can reveal the existing principles and practices regarding our understanding of the nature of knowledge. It can also simultaneously provide information on curriculum shortcomings

and be an impetus for the development of more suitable principles and practices. However, since contexts differ significantly, it is difficult to have a generally accepted definition of 'curriculum'.

The word, *'curro'* (I run) is of Latin origin and refers to a race or the track on which athletes competed. A notable feature of this meaning is that it emphasises the role of the individual as he or she participates. It seems an appropriate analogy for the education process in which teachers plan educational experiences and learners (as a group and as individuals) proceed to reach certain objectives (e.g., completing high school or graduating from university) (Carl, 2002; Eisner, 1990).

To most people who are not professional educators, 'curriculum' has a narrow focus: it indicates either the specific subjects or courses learners need to pass to obtain a qualification or the selected content of a single subject. For professional educators, on the other hand, the meaning can be wider and can include everything that takes place within a school, including subject matter, content, behavioural objectives, interpersonal relationships, as well as the learning experiences of both learners and teachers. The concept 'curriculum' can therefore have a broad or narrow meaning, depending on the context within which it is used.

For the purpose of this chapter, a broader definition of curriculum is suggested. It includes:

- objectives or outcomes to be achieved;
- planned and incidental learning experiences (including a sequence of activities) for learners within a physical context, social climate or ethos; and
- the involvement of teachers, parents, learners, and significant others (e.g., peers) in contributing to the learning content and processes.

This position on curriculum also recognises that no curriculum teaches itself and that how teachers, parents and communities interpret and implement the curriculum is crucial (Eisner, 1990).

As in the case of curriculum, different interpretations can be given to 'curriculum development' and will depend on the context within which it is defined. For the purpose of this chapter, 'curriculum development' is regarded as an umbrella concept for improving or changing learning opportunities, and as a process that is responsive to the socio-cultural context. It is also a vehicle by means of which teachers plan learning opportunities and learners construct new knowledge.

Changing approaches to curriculum development

In the continuous struggle to make curricula more effective, curriculum experts reflect on its various aspects and provide systematic analyses of ongoing curriculum development efforts. Approaches to curriculum development are strongly influenced by various socio-cultural contexts as well as different views on teaching and learning. Two views on learning that have strongly influenced approaches to curriculum development are behaviourism and socio-constructivism. The philosophy of behaviourism has, for example, influenced traditional approaches to curriculum development. It has a strong psychological bias, focusing on observable human behaviour. Learning is seen as a passive process: learners passively receive knowledge and teachers rely on overt reactions (behaviour) from learners to show that 'learning' is taking place (e.g., learners repeating or regurgitating newly presented information). Socio-constructivism, on the other hand, is a belief that knowledge is created or 'constructed' by active efforts to make meaning and by learners' interactions with other people and with things in order to do so (Seifert, 1999). In other words, learners do not passively absorb information; they actively co-construct knowledge as they make meaning of their contexts.

The more traditional approaches to curriculum development (e.g., behaviourism) are essentially prescriptive and exclusive, in the sense that each one resembles a well-defined structure. These approaches are linear, strongly structured and with a strong emphasis on teaching rather than learning. Furthermore, teaching and learning are based on the assumptions that:
- only that which can be observed through the human senses represents true knowledge (positivism);
- every phenomenon has a specific, logical and predictable cause (determinism);
- the whole can be better understood by studying the parts (reductionism); and
- there is always a direct and linear relationship between any structure and its function.

A curriculum, based on these assumptions, assumes that learners are passive recipients and not creators of knowledge, spectators who even in their most creative moments can only discover that which already exists, with teachers as the source of knowledge.

A well-known approach to curriculum development based on more traditional approaches is that of Tyler (1949) who built his approach around the following four fundamental questions:
- *Aims and objectives*: What educational purposes should the educational institution (e.g., the school) seek to attain?
- *Context*: What educational experiences can be provided that are likely to attain these purposes?
- *Methods*: How can these educational experiences be effectively organised?
- *Evaluation*: How can we determine whether the envisaged educational purposes are being attained?

This approach regards curriculum development as an overarching, timeless and unchanging process in which systematic and purposeful planning by experts features strongly, from the design stage to evaluation.

A chief criticism of this approach has been that it is strongly prescriptive and de-contextualised, in the sense that the people who are involved with the day-to-day implementation of the curriculum (teachers and learners) are effectively disempowered in terms of active involvement in the teaching and learning process (Jacobs, 1999; Schreuder et al., 2002).

Significant changes in curriculum development occurred in the later half of the previous century. Moving away from a view of curriculum as prescriptive and linear, new approaches were more democratic, descriptive, critical and transformative in nature. Instead of focusing exclusively on how things 'should' be done, the focus was now on what was actually happening in schools. Emphasising a socio-constructivist view of learning, learning was increasingly seen as a social process, and curriculum knowledge and knowledge about curriculum, as socially constructed by learners, teachers, other school personnel, parents and researchers, amongst others. Schwab (1973) was a strong supporter of alternative approaches to curriculum development. He suggested that external experts cannot understand educational situations in formal settings and that the school itself should be at the centre of curriculum development. He identified four points in education at which interaction occurs and around which discussion should occur: teacher, learner, subject matter and the milieu or culture of each school. According to this approach, teachers should be treated as people who can think for themselves and who exhibit a willingness to share their curriculum experiences with colleagues, learners and parents. Subject matter should be interesting and exciting and should reflect on inequities caused by discrimination on all levels (e.g., gender, race, disability and class). Learners, as active learners, should gain knowledge that meets their diverse needs and the specific context of each school should be taken into account in the curriculum of that school on a continuous basis (Eisner, 1994; Jacobs, 1999; Schreuder *et al.* 2002; Schubert, 1986; Schwab, 1973).

Why is it necessary to transform a curriculum?

Broadly speaking, governments or communities may embark on changing and transforming curricula in order to reflect changing political contexts (e.g., building a more democratic social order and new teaching and learning models and their application to the curriculum). One example of an approach for transforming the curriculum which became popular in the 1980s and 1990s is outcomes-based education (OBE). OBE is based on an integration of the traditional and newer approaches to curriculum development. It emphasises an outcomes-defined curriculum in which learners are active participants in the learning process and in which they acquire skills to deal with new challenges in a global society. Therefore, OBE represents a shift in emphasis from teaching to learning (Spady, 1994). It is based on the belief that all learners can learn and succeed and that schools control the conditions of success, with learners' success being seen as the responsibility of the teacher.

The curriculum development process in OBE focuses on the following components:

- *Situation analysis*. To design an effective curriculum it is imperative to explore the context in which it is to take place and find out whether the curriculum is compatible with the context. This includes analysing the relevant factors inside and outside the school or classroom. Outside factors would include factors such as political and social reform, as well as the needs and expectations of the country, which may affect decisions about the form, and structure of the curriculum. Factors within schools and classrooms include learners' age, diverse abilities and needs, available facilities or resources, as well as teacher values, beliefs and strengths.

- *Outcomes*. Outcomes are indicators of learning that occur at the end of a significant set of learning experiences and direct the selection and organisation of learning content. Outcomes also determine the teaching and assessment strategies that are adopted.
- *Learning content*. What is to be taught, that is, the learning content and material, is an essential consideration in the OBE curriculum. There is a need for a careful selection of content, particularly regarding its suitability for specific groups of learners in specific contexts. This will enable learners to take ownership of the curriculum content.
- *Teaching strategy*. This component determines the nature of the learning opportunities (i.e. the methods, procedures, activities and techniques) aimed at helping learners learn. It also involves setting high standards of teaching and learning (Schwarz & Cavener, 1994).
- *Assessment* consists of a series of tasks to obtain information about a learner's competence on an ongoing basis. The primary assessment technique for OBE is continuous assessment with the help of tests and examinations. Learners are also expected to engage in self-assessment, peer assessment, and the compilation of learning portfolios (Jacobs & Chalufu, 2000).

Box 26.1 contains a description of a curriculum development process in South Africa associated with the institutionalisation of democracy. It illustrates the competing interests in curriculum innovation at a national, community and school level.

The implementation of a new national curriculum for the twenty-first century was introduced in 1997 (Department of National Education, 1997b). The following rationale for an OBE approach was provided: to phase in a new transformed curriculum based on the ideal of life long learning and essentially to effect a shift from a content-based curriculum to an outcomes-based curriculum (initially also known as Curriculum 2005 within schools). In this instance, 'outcomes' specifically refers to the specification of what learners should be able to do at the end of a learning experience, and 'based' means to define, direct, focus and determine what is done in relation to the results to be achieved at the end of the learning experience.

To a certain extent, Table 1 below reflects the key differences between the traditional, rigid content-based approach and the current, more flexible outcomes-based approach to curriculum design.

	Historical approach	Outcome-based education
The learner	Passive learners	Active learners
Assessment	Graded, exam-driven; exclusionary	Continuous assessment; learners are assessed on an on-going basis
Role of teacher	The teacher is central and is textbook bound	The teacher is seen as facilitator; the teacher constantly uses group work and team work
Curriculum framework	The syllabus is seen as fixed and non-negotiable	Learning programmes are seen as guides that allow teachers to be innovative and creative in designing programmes
	The emphasis is on what the teacher hopes to achieve	There is an emphasis on outcomes, i.e. on what the learner becomes and understands
Time and learner pacing	Content is placed into rigid time-frames	Flexible time-frames allow learners to work at their own pace

Table 1 Comparison of the historical and OBE approaches to curriculum design

26.1 TRANSFORMING A NEW CURRICULUM IN SOUTH AFRICA: A COMPLEX PROCESS

Until 1994, South African education was characterised by a uniformly rigid and predictable curriculum policy. While core curricula were regularly devised for all schools based on a school subjects or contents-based approach, these curricula were introduced into schools with vastly different race-based resource contexts. Many disadvantaged communities did not have well trained teachers or proper facilities. Inevitably, the curricula prescribed by the central authority, with its emphasis on apartheid-based academic content, resulted in deeply divided communities, excluding vast numbers of South African citizens from an equitable education. Learners and teachers had little control over the learning and teaching process. Furthermore, teachers, parents and communities had little power in determining curriculum content and school policy.

The dominant and exclusive curriculum of the apartheid education system was increasingly questioned and vehemently debated. In the period following the release of Nelson Mandela, various stakeholders began to express the need for the transformation of the school system, and more specifically, of curricula,

in order to redress the prevailing inequalities in the South African context (Jacobs & Chalufu: 2000; Jansen, 1999; Kraak, 1999).

In an effort to fundamentally transform the South African education system and create equal opportunities for learners with diverse needs in the post-apartheid education system, the government initiated several transformative policies, including curriculum-related reforms. These reforms included attempts to eliminate racially offensive and outdated content in the curriculum, the introduction of continuous assessment in schools, and the implementation of an outcomes-based approach to education and training (OBE) (Jansen, 1998).

Visit the archives of local major newspapers in your community to read articles that debated curriculum transformation for a new South Africa in the 1990s. How would you have stated your position if you had the opportunity to contribute to this debate? What is your current view of the quality of the debate that ensued and its likely impact on the final curriculum innovation by the post-Apartheid South African government?

In a critical analysis of the underpinnings of OBE as it is implemented in South Africa, it becomes clear that various approaches to curriculum development are integrated. The focus on visible, measurable and specifically formulated outcomes has strong roots in traditional approaches. The focus on the role of teachers as facilitators of knowledge and not as authoritarian sources of knowledge and power, and learners as active participants in the learning process, acknowledges the emphasis on learning as a social process, as discussed earlier.

Implementing OBE has resulted in conflicting responses. There are those who see OBE as a far-reaching initiative to transform the curriculum (particularly in relation to the role of the learner and the teacher), providing opportunities for all learners to take part in the learning process. Others see it as idealistic and problematic for a range of reasons, including the following: Although teachers were represented on some of the planning committees, most teachers, parents and learners were not actively engaged in the development of the new curriculum, and individual school contexts were not taken into account. The result was that teachers and parents experienced it as top-down in a way that strongly resembled the imposition of apartheid curricula. Although the government did provide in-service training opportunities, resources were totally inadequate and training opportunities minimal. This resulted in scaled-down plans for implementation (Geyser, 2000; Jacobs, 1999; Jansen, 1998).

How is the process of curriculum transformation described here similar to, or different from the previous approach?

Transforming a curriculum requires continuous interaction between vision and conditions on the ground, creating detailed planning and engagement and taking the complexity of school contexts into account. OBE in South Africa has started with given procedures developed by outsiders (see Box 26.2) reminiscent of the more traditional approaches to curriculum development, rather than with the concerns, needs and commitments expressed by teachers, learners and parents in specific contexts, as advocated by transformative approaches.

Conclusion

Developing curricula which afford inclusive opportunities for effective learning in a diverse community is a complex process. The purpose of this chapter was to give a broad overview of curriculum development and the important role that different contexts and views on learning and teaching play in transforming curricula. Equal and effective opportunities for learning in a curriculum are only possible if the range of differences or diversity within contexts and between individuals is taken into account. The South African case study served as an example of how implementing a transformed curriculum can be complicated if it is not underpinned by an understanding and acknowledgement of the specific concerns and needs of all involved in the learning context.

Figure 1 How do these learners feel about OBE?

Carl, A.E. (2002). *Teacher Empowerment Through Curriculum Development: Theory into practice* (2nd edition). Lansdowne: Juta.

Department of National Education. (1997a). *Quality Education for All: Overcoming barriers to learning and development.* Report of the NCSNET & NCESS Commission. Pretoria: Government Printers.

Department of National Education. (1997b). *Foundation Phase: Policy document (Grades 1-3).* Pretoria: Government Printers.

Engelbrecht, P. (1999). A theoretical framework for inclusive education. In P. Engelbrecht, L. Green, S. Naicker & L. Engelbrecht (Eds.). *Inclusive Education in Action in South Africa.* Pretoria: Van Schaik, pp. 3-11.

Eisner, E.W. (1990). Creative curriculum development and practice. *Journal of Curriculum & Supervision,* 6(1):62-74.

Eisner, E.W. (1994). *The Educational Imagination: On the design and evaluation of school programs.* New York: MacMillan.

Geyser, H. (2000). OBE: A critical perspective. In T. Mda & S. Mothata (Eds.). *Critical Issues in South African Education After 1994.* Landsdowne: Juta, pp. 21-41.

Jacobs, M. (1999). Curriculum. In E. Lemmer (Ed.). *Contemporary Education: Global issues and trends.* Sandton: Heinemann Higher and Further Education, pp. 96-126.

Jacobs, M. & Chalufu, N. (2000). Curriculum design. In M. Jacobs, N. Grawe & N. Vakalisa (Eds.). *Teaching-Learning Dynamics.* Sandton: Heinemann Higher and Further Education, pp. 91-131.

Jansen, J. (1998). Curriculum reform in South Africa: A critical analysis of outcomes-based education (1). *Cambridge Journal of Education,* 28(3):321-32.

Jansen, J. (1999). Why outcomes-based education will fail: An elaboration. In J. Jansen & P. Christie (Eds.). *Changing Curriculum: Studies on OBE in South Africa.* Landsdowne: Juta, pp. 145-56.

Kraak, A. (1999). Competing education & training policy discourses: A 'systemic' versus 'unit standards' framework. In J. Jansen & P. Christie (Eds.). *Changing Curriculum: Studies on OBE in South Africa.* Landsdowne: Juta, pp. 21-58.

Schreuder, D.R, Reddy, C.P.S. & Blanckenberg, J.M. (2002). *Curriculum Enquiry and Development.* Stellenbosch: University of Stellenbosch.

Schubert, W.H. (1986). *Curriculum: Perspective, paradigm and possibility.* New York: MacMillan.

Schwab, J.J. (1973). The practical: Translating into curriculum. *School Review,* 81:501-22.

Schwarz, G. & Cavener, L.A. (1994). Outcome-based education and curriculum change: Advocacy, practice and critique. *Journal of Curriculum and Supervision,* 9(4):326-35.

Seifert, K.L. (1999). *Constructing a Psychology of Teaching and Learning.* New York: Houghton Mifflin.

Spady, W.G. (1994). *Outcomes-based Education. Critical issues and answers.* Arlington: The American Association of School Administrators.

Tyler, R.W. (1949). *Basic Principles of Curriculum and Instruction.* Chicago: University of Chicago Press.

Multiple choice questions

1. Curriculum refers to
   a) books, syllabi and examinations
   b) whatever the Department of Education pre-scribes
   c) formal and informal teaching and learning experiences
   d) 'running' towards an educational goal
2. The major difference between behaviourist and socio-constructivist approaches to learning is that the former is more
   a) prescriptive
   b) educational
   c) sophisticated
   d) enriching
3. Which pair is best matched?
   a) active learners; behaviourist
   b) learners as enquirers; socio-constructivist
   c) teacher controlled; socio-constructivist
   d) learner controlled; behaviourist
4. Tyler (1949) proposed a model of curriculum design that was
   a) South African
   b) supportive of apartheid
   c) universal
   d) a-theoretical (not based on theory)
5. Curriculum transformation in the new South Africa was necessitated by the
   a) release of Nelson Mandela from imprisonment
   b) creation of new education administrative provinces
   c) fact that teachers had to retrain for democracy
   d) changed context of education in post-apartheid South Africa
6. The approach to education currently used by the Department of Education is called
   a) the Tyler model
   b) socio-constructivist
   c) outcomes-based education (OBE)

   d) education for democracy
7. Critics of OBE have considered it a(n)
   a) imposition
   b) inconvenience
   c) European model
   d) African model
8. Outcomes-based education makes both ___ and ___ accountable for educational achievement
   a) syllabi; books
   b) curriculum; teachers
   c) learners; teachers
   d) parents; syllabi
9. Assessment under OBE is primarily through_____ and _____
   a) portfolios; unforeseen examinations
   b) mock examinations; summative assessment
   c) participatory learning; continuous assessment
   d) self-examination; democracy
10. Which of the elements in curriculum transforma-tion reflects an interest in the context of the cur-riculum?
    a) learning content
    b) outcomes
    c) teaching strategy
    d) situation analysis

Short answer questions

1. What is the role of context in defining curriculum and curriculum development?
2. How would you define curriculum in your own con-text?
3. Compare a behaviourist and a socio-constructivist approach to learning.
4. Briefly discuss more traditional approaches to cur-riculum development. How effective are these approaches as vehicles for educational change?
5. Discuss outcomes-based education as an effort to transform curriculum in the South African context.

Teaching and Learning

Elias Mpofu

CHAPTER OBJECTIVES

After studying this chapter you should be able to:
- list and describe four principles of learning
- distinguish between: class teaching from everyday teaching; teaching and learning; teaching and instruction; and teaching and education
- show how teaching is both an everyday activity and also a specialised activity
- examine the role of feedback in learning
- relate the distribution of practice to the nature of the learning task and expected learning outcome
- critique theories of extrinsic and intrinsic motivation with reference to research.

Like most learners, Nosipho had been much more aware of what she was supposed to be learning rather than how she was learning or even if she was learning. As she thought about it, though, she realised that learning was much more complicated than just sitting in a lecture and taking notes. There were times that Nosipho sat in a lecture and came out hardly able to remember anything that had been spoken about. Fortunately there were other times that things just made sense, when she hardly felt like she was concentrating, but came out of a lecture with a much deeper understanding of the subject. When that happened it was hard to explain what exactly had happened – she just felt that she saw things differently, like something had fitted together in her mind.

Nosipho supposed that she learned better when the material was interesting for her. It wasn't just the subject matter, though. Nosipho most enjoyed learning when she was able to participate more. Although she was shy, she liked tutorials where she was able to give her opinion and listen to people discuss their ideas. Probably, best of all though, Nosipho enjoyed reading. She read books on psychology but she also found that she learnt a lot about psychology from novels. Of course she also learned about psychology from observing other people – and herself! Nosipho had thought about learning as something that happened specifically at school or university, but there was also a great deal of learning that took place outside these settings.

Introduction

Many people take teaching and learning for granted in the sense that they assume they know what these terms mean. There are numerous reasons why people hold this assumption. Among the reasons for assuming an understanding of teaching and learning is the fact that teaching and learning are ongoing processes in human life. For example, there are teaching and learning opportunities from peer and family interactions. There are also significant opportunities to learn by observing others, and also to teach oneself through planned and unplanned experiences. Planned teaching and learning opportunities include goal-oriented learning that is designed to achieve a particular outcome (e.g., a particular skill). Unplanned teaching and learning activities occur in the activities of everyday life and are no less important than planned activities. In fact, the way an individual manages the activities of everyday life greatly depends on informal learning (Sternberg, 1999). Moreover, one person's activities of everyday life are another person's planned teaching or learning activities. This adds to both the ordinariness and uniqueness of teaching and learning. In modern societies, schools are set up for the purposes of facilitating teaching and learning in a more formal sense, although a lot of informal learning occurs within the school environment.

This chapter presents a discussion on teaching and learning. It defines teaching and shows how it is associated with instruction, education and learning. The chapter also provides alternative views of learning and describes some of the key principles of learning.

Teaching

School teaching is unique in that it involves at least four elements: the teacher, the learner, the goal of teaching and the subject matter through which the goal of teaching is realised (Mpofu, 1994). The teacher is often an adult who has professional training and experience, is aware of the goals of teaching, and can and is willing to teach. The pupil or learner, on the other hand, has the potential to learn and is expected to want to learn (Brophy, 1998). In broad terms, the goal of teaching is to expose the learner to reality so that the learner can interact effectively with the environment. In school teaching, subject matter is the principal tool through which teachers help learners interact with and construct reality. Therefore, school teaching refers to those systematic activities by means of which the teacher helps the learner to learn how to do certain things that will help the latter cope with and improve his or her environment. The major goal of teaching is to enhance problem-solving skills in learners (Biggs, 1991; Joyce et al., 2000; Nickerson, 1994).

Self-teaching can result in significant learning. For example, children learn important information about things in their environment through self-initiated activities. Many people learn a lot from reading literature of various kinds, watching television, taking part in various social situations (or hearing others talk about them), interacting with the physical environment, and so on. The lessons that emerge from these informal learning situations are not any less concrete and useful than those that result from direct teaching. For the class teacher, direct teaching does not preclude the possibility of self-teaching by the learners. This is because learners can achieve their own learning objectives in addition to those set by the teacher.

Two terms that tend to be used interchangeably with teaching are instruction and education. The reason why these terms may be associated with teaching is that the practices of educating and instructing often occur within teaching. However, teaching can be distinguished from both instruction and education.

Teaching and instruction

Instruction comprises those events, activities or objects that influence a human being's learning (Gagne & Briggs, 1983; Martinez, 2001; Renzulli & Dai, 2001). Such events or activities can be internal to the individual (e.g., prior knowledge and learning readiness). They may also be external to the individual (e.g., the opportunity to learn and the curriculum structure). People can teach themselves important things (self-instruction) because they perceive such learning to be important. There are also many instances in which people learn from others.

Teaching involves, within its realm, an instructional component. Teachers ordinarily give instructions to their classes on a variety of issues, such as:
- the correct handling and use of learning aids, as well as the procedure for their collection, distribution and storage;
- the expected course of an activity and its goals;
- the required class organisation for an activity; and

Learners have their idiosyncratic interpretations of school tasks and experiences. These interpretations and experiences are often unintended by the teachers or curriculum.

Study

Mpofu and Watkins (1997) investigated academic self-esteem in Black and White Zimbabwean adolescents. The learners attended multiracial schools and were taught by White or Black teachers.

Results

Black learners taught by White teachers had lower self-reported reading self-esteem than their White classmates. There was no difference in reading self-esteem between Black and White learners taught by Black teachers.

Conclusion

Race influenced students' self-perceptions as readers.

Consider some possible explanations for the findings of this study.

• the change of class organisation from one activity or lesson to the next.

Instruction, in this case, refers to the teacher's organisational tools for learner learning. Learners can also be said to have received instruction in a subject. In this regard, emphasis is on the transmission of blocks of knowledge and facts to the learner. Subject matter, rather than the learner and his or her unique learning needs, is central to this kind of instruction. This kind of knowledge transmission is not recommended for class teaching, as it does not lead to learning (Sharratt, 1995).

As will be discussed, learning involves the active re-organisation of, and interaction with materials under specific supportive conditions. These materials may be concrete objects and/or ideas. Certain instructions may well accompany how the materials are to be manipulated (as under guided discovery learning) and can be distinguished from instruction in the sense of filling up the learner with information. Instruction, in the sense of events, activities or objects that facilitate human learning is broader than teaching. This is so because although the teacher may create and/or manipulate some events, activities or objects in order to influence learning, some of these have instructional value independent of the teacher. From this viewpoint, then, teaching is 'one form of instruction, albeit a signally important one' (Gagne & Briggs, 1983:3).

Figure 1 Ordinary classroom teaching and learning activity

Teaching and education

Education is a life long process by which people or communities learn about themselves and effective ways of interacting with their environment (Bruner, 1996; Martinez, 2000; Serpell, 1991). The cultural products that a people or community produces are indicators of a people or community's view of education. Cultural products can be in the form of materials and/or ideas. Schools are centres of education to the extent that what they teach is consistent with the cultural values of the community of which they are a part. In societies that are experiencing rapid socio-cultural transformation (such as those in sub-Saharan Africa or the developing world), the education that the school gives could be at variance with the core values of certain communities. For example, superior achievement by children on tasks that were highly valued by Zambian Chewa villagers (e.g., clay moulding) did not correspond to achievement on school tasks (e.g., pen and pencil tasks) (Serpell, 1991). Similarly, Kenyan Luo children who had a superior knowledge of traditional herbs used to treat a variety of ailments among that people did not achieve at a similar level on school tasks (Sternberg et al., 2001). The Luo of Kenya regarded school education as separate from that relevant to village life (Grigorenko et al., 2001). At the same time, schools

Figure 2 Learners often have to perform important family and community tasks, such as helping to run the family business

can be vehicles for cultural development in that they can be pivotal to changing a society towards different or more enabling values (see Chapter 26, this volume; Grossen, 2000; Serpell, 1991). School education is valued by many African communities for its instrumental value in creating economic opportunities in the formal, industrial employment sector (Grigorenko *et al.*, 2001; Mpofu, 2004; Serpell, 1991). Teaching is only one of many ways by which people learn, and schools are one of many locations for teaching and learning. Teaching for education happens both in schools and in the community (e.g., Grigorenko *et al.*, 2001; Serpell, 1991; Chapters 25 and 28, this volume). Thus, teaching can be a source of education alongside many other educative experiences that inform how a person or community lives.

Learning

Many definitions of learning have been proposed (e.g., Bandura, 1986; Biggs, 1991; Richards & Combs, 1992; Rogers & Freiberg, 1994). The diverse ways in which learning is regarded can be reduced to three major approaches, namely the humanistic, behavioural and information processing approaches.

Humanistic approaches

Views of learning that emphasise the inner being are collectively referred to as the humanistic (or phenome-

nological) approaches. From a humanistic perspective (e.g., Richards & Combs, 1992; Rogers, 1994), learning is considered as mostly concerned with inner changes in the individual that reflect new ways of self-perception and perceiving the environment. The subjective aspects of learning (e.g., beliefs, will (known technically as conation) and personal meaning) are more central to the humanistic or phenomenological approaches to learning than the objective aspects (learning schedules or prescribed curricula and common objectives). True or significant learning, from a humanistic perspective, refers to the processes by means of which a person seeks to meet his or her needs as subjectively defined and to a level that is personally satisfying. Therefore, the act of learning, from a humanistic perspective, is self-directed.

A basic assumption of the humanistic approaches to learning is that people are naturally disposed to seek and engage in growth-enhancing experiences (Rogers, 1994). For that reason, each learner is an expert at selecting experiences that are enriching to the self or that add to personal growth. A school, for example, would best be regarded as a community of learner experts, in the sense that each person who is a member of the school community has in him- or herself the ability to identify, create or participate in self-enhancing learning experiences (Brown, 1998; Rogers & Freiberg, 1994). Prescribed curricula, learning sequences and formal testing are perceived by humanistic educationists as external impositions on learners. They are considered to have the disadvantage of psychologically separating learners from being in touch with their inner selves so that they become less capable of participating in self-directed learning.

From a humanistic perspective, the outcomes of learning include:

- a greater understanding of the self as a person;
- a greater contact with own feelings, respect for self and others; and
- a heightened capacity to select growth-enhancing experiences.

These learning outcomes are perceived as a means for a person to become more of what he or she has the potential to be, rather than an end in itself (Rogers, 1994). In other words, educators with a humanistic approach would perceive the processes and products of learning as mutually constituting each other.

Behaviourist approaches

Proponents of the behaviourist approaches (e.g., Skinner, 1968) define learning as a relatively permanent change in behaviour (or behaviour potentiality) as a result of reinforced practice. The notion that learning can result in behavioural potentiality derives from the assumption that learning makes it likely that a class of behaviours associated with a certain learning experience will occur. The potential that learning will translate into behaviour may also depend on the situation that cues the behaviour for which prior learning is relevant. The notion that learning is reinforced behaviour distinguishes it from behavioural changes that may be due to momentary states such as fatigue or illness. The belief that learning is achieved through practice and with reinforcement is a hallmark of the behavioural approaches to learning.

In contrast to the humanistic approaches, behaviourist approaches to learning regard the learning process to be determined by objective factors that are true to most animate organisms (e.g., birds, cats, monkeys and humans); the need to control rewards in the environment being one such factor. For that reason, behaviourist approaches to learning consider it to be a scientific (or law-governed) process in that it is predictable under certain conditions (e.g., with knowledge of a person's needs and his or her environment). With the behaviourist approaches, it is possible to derive hierarchies of learning outcomes that would apply to all learners and against which individual achievement can be measured. Consistent with the view that learning is knowable or an entity that occurs in relation to specified objectives, the behaviourist approaches to learning support the use of prescribed syllabi, learning content, and tests of mastery that are similar for most learners.

Schools are centres of learning, and are mandated by national or provincial governments to provide an education that is consistent with national developmental goals (e.g., Chapter 26, this volume; Watson, 2002). The requirement that schools teach skills for national development directs the approaches to learning that schools adopt away from humanistic and towards behaviourist approaches (Mpofu, 1994; Richards & Combs, 1992). There are practical reasons why schools may have a bias towards behaviourally-oriented learning. A major reason is that today's technological world makes societies that know more of how to do certain things more 'successfully' than those that know less (Martinez, 2001). The fact that many developing countries have less access to tools of information management (also called the digital divide) speaks to the fact that many modern societies value technological 'know-how' rather than matters of internal self-exploration. It follows from this observation that what one knows and can do is a prized educational outcome by the standards of today's world. Thus, school learning retains a decidedly behaviourist, rather than humanistic bias, although most communities would endorse a humanistic educational philosophy.

Information processing approaches

In their various forms, the information processing approaches explain learning in terms of the mental activities that are used to achieve learning. Biggs (1991, 2001) proposed an information processing model for learning that appears to have wide applicability. According to Biggs, approaches to learning can be understood in terms of surface and deep level learning strategies, as well as the motives for achieving or learning (see Table 1 below). Surface level approaches to learning aim at getting the 'right answer' at the cost of understanding. Deep level approaches to learning are relevant to grasping the underlying meanings of learning experiences. Research has documented that learners will handle learning tasks differently, depending on their perceptions of the anticipated outcomes of learning. For example, Omokhodion (1989) reported widespread surface level learning amongst a sample of Nigerian urban school children that thought that getting the correct answer at any cost was the basic goal of

Discussion highlight

Most governments in Africa are grappling with how to equalize learning opportunity for students. They expect students with the same learning potential to achieve similarly, regardless of the school the students attend. However, the results of learning are mediated by many factors, including the way learning outcomes are assessed, and students' expectation for learning.

Types of learning Outcomes

The results of learning can be described in quantitative terms (how much is learned), qualitative terms (how well it is learned), and institutional terms (e.g., the marks obtained). Depending on the marking or assessment system used and the classroom climate, learners may adopt deep or surface level approaches to learning (Campbell *et al.*, 2001; Mpofu & Oakland, 2001). For

example, Campbell *et al.* (2001) reported a greater use of surface learning approaches in classes that were teacher directed. The particular learning approach that a learner will adopt will, to an extent, depend on how he or she interprets the requirements for successful learning in a particular learning environment.

Lesson

Learners continuously map their learning strategy and efforts onto expectations for learning that are communicated to them. Thus, students attending relatively poorly resourced schools can achieve at higher levels than those in materially better-off schools.

Dilemma

A higher education budget does not necessarily translate into high achieving schools or students.

---

learning. South African and Zimbabwean adolescents used more deep level approaches than surface approaches (Mpofu & Oakland, 2001; Watkins *et al.*, 1994; Watkins & Mboya, 1997), and to a greater extent than same-age Australian, Kenyan and Nigerian adolescents (Watkins *et al.*, 1994; Watkins & Mboya, 1997).

To date, no single theory is universally accepted as adequate in describing the learning process (Ormrod, 1999). However, there is some consensus on the usefulness of certain principles of learning in facilitating learning.

Principles of learning

Some of the key principles for facilitating learning are related to knowledge of results, motivation, distribution of practice, transfer of learning and perception. Each of these is discussed next.

Knowledge of results

Learning is facilitated if the learner has some way of knowing how well he or she is doing in terms of the goals of learning (Ryan & Pintrich, 1998; Wolters *et al.*, 1996). Information that helps a learner assess his or her progress in terms of the goal of learning is called feedback. In this regard, learning is more efficient when feedback is immediate rather than delayed. Immediate feedback is that which follows closely upon the rele-

vant performance, whereas delayed feedback is further removed from the performance in terms of time.

A distinction can be made between intrinsic and extrinsic feedback. Intrinsic feedback is that which depends on bodily sensations. For instance, successful completion of most physical activities rests on the ability of the individual to sense correct posture and movement for the required action (e.g., manual writing draws on intrinsic feedback). Extrinsic feedback is that which emanates from sources external to the individual. Extrinsic feedback can be broken down into direct (or primary) and indirect (or secondary) feedback. Direct or primary feedback occurs when the individual directly observes the result of his or her own action. An example of an activity that utilises primary feedback is learning to throw the javelin. That action requires a specific body and arm swing for a successful throw. In this situation, the feedback is built into the behaviour (correct bodily orientation for the throw), which in itself is an intermediate goal in learning to throw the javelin. Indirect or secondary feedback comes from an external source (e.g., a person or gadget) that approves (or disapproves) of the correctness of a response to a particular task. An example typical of classroom learning is the teacher's approval of the result of learning (e.g., 'that's correct'). Effective teachers often capitalise on the principle of feedback in learning by offering more immediate rather than delayed feedback, involving learners in direct investigation and using structured learning experiences that allow for self-teaching and learning (Mpofu, 1994).

Motivation

As previously noted, learning outcomes are affected by the learner's willingness to learn (Brophy, 1998). Learners who are well disposed toward playing certain learner roles (such as paying attention, actively participating in learning situations, etc.) are said to be well motivated. Two types of motivation have been identified: intrinsic and extrinsic motivation (see Brophy, 1998; Cameron, 2001; Deci *et al.*, 1999; Ryan & Deci, 2000).

Intrinsic motivation is that which is inherent to the learning task. Certain tasks interest learners enough to inspire them to undertake the tasks without reference to an end other than the enjoyment of those tasks. Extrinsic motivation, on the other hand, is that which is independent of the learner's natural interest in the task. It is when the learner sees in the accomplishment of the learning task, a desired state of affairs such as social approval, prestige, and so on. Class teachers are often encouraged to create an inviting learning atmosphere so that learners are intrinsically motivated (Brophy, 1998; Martinez, 2001). Certain characteristics of the materials teachers use with learners are designed toward complexity or to induce a sense of surprise or novelty – qualities that enhance intrinsic motivation in students.

Intrinsic motivation is important for developing in learners a healthy attitude of inquiry and curiosity for sustained learning (see Box 27.3).

To date, there is no clear answer to the question of how intrinsic and extrinsic motivation used in combination would affect learning (Cameron 2001; Deci *et al.*, 1999, 2001). From a common sense perspective, the relationship between extrinsic and intrinsic motivation may seem obviously additive. For example, it makes sense to think that high praise of a learner by the teacher combined with interesting and challenging work should result in optimum learning. However, research findings on the effect of extrinsic motivation on intrinsic motivation have been inconclusive. On the one hand, an additive relationship between extrinsic motivation and intrinsic motivation on task performance could not be confirmed (Deci *et al.*, 1999, 2001). According to Deci and others, extrinsic reinforcement seemed to result in less willingness by children to perform tasks that they naturally enjoyed doing. Their research findings seemed to support the view that when extrinsic motivation is tied to performance, intrinsic motivation suffers. On the other hand, Cameron (2001), Cameron and Pierce (1994), Scott and Miller (1985) and Dickinson (1989) found support for an additive effect between extrinsic rewards and intrinsic motivation on task performance. They observed that the subtractive effects of extrinsic rewards on intrinsic motivation are temporary and

Approach	Description
Surface approach	
Surface motivation	Motivation is utilitarian; the main aim of learning is to gain qualifications at the minimum allowable standard
Surface strategy	The learning strategy is to produce the bare essentials using rote learning
Deep approach	
Deep motivation	Here motivation is an interest in the subject and its related areas
Deep strategy	Here the strategy is to understand what is to be learned through inter-relating ideas and reading widely
Achieving approach	
Achievement motivation	Here motivation is to obtain highest possible grades
Achievement strategy	The strategy is highly organised and designed to achieve high marks by being a 'model' student (e.g., doing additional readings on a topic)

Table 1 Biggs' student approaches to learning
Source: Mpofu & Oakland (2001)

Question
What is the effect on learning of combining extrinsic rewards with doing an interesting task?

Hypothesis
Providing rewards for interesting work should result in higher task performance.

Study
Leeper *et al.* (1973) had young children perform a number of interesting activities, one of which involved drawing with a felt tip pen. Some of the children were reinforced for the activity by being given a 'good player' certificate.

Results
Children who were rewarded for drawing using a felt tip pen drew less frequently than the children who were not rewarded for the activity.

Conclusion
Extrinsic reinforcement for an interesting task resulted in less willingness to perform the task. When extrinsic motivation is tied to performance, intrinsic motivation suffers.

Figure 3 A learner deeply engaged in a learning task

that extrinsic rewards enhance natural interest in a task.

Several explanations have been advanced for these contradictory effects. Deci *et al.* (1999) proposed as an explanation a cognitive evaluation theory which departs from the assumption that people want to feel in control of their behaviour. In this regard, extrinsic motivation makes people feel that their behaviour is being controlled by external forces, while intrinsic motivation makes people feel that they are in control of their behaviour. According to Deci *et al.* (1999), a combination of extrinsic and intrinsic rewards could be subtractive and yield a more diminished overall motivation than would be the case if either were used singly. They speculated that extrinsic rewards for naturally interesting tasks lowered an individual's sense of control over their learning.

The subtractive effect of extrinsic rewards on intrinsic motivation has also been explained in terms of the over-justification theory (Leeper *et al.*, 1973). Briefly, Leeper *et al.* (1973) argued that an inherently motivating task justifies itself to the

performer by reason of its built-in interest. To offer external rewards for performing such a task would over-justify the task and reduce the intrinsic desire to do it.

Reiss and Sushunsky (1976) offered a third explanation called the competing response hypothesis. Their view was that extrinsic rewards reduced intrinsic motivation by generating responses that interfere with the original activity.

Regardless of the different explanations for the effect of extrinsic and intrinsic rewards on task performance, there can be no over-emphasising the fact that motivation is an important determinant of learning.

Distribution of practice

Learning outcomes are also affected by the scheduling of learning sessions over time. Distributed practice and massed practice are two ways of learning. Distributed practice sessions are those that allow for breaks within the learning period, whereas massed practice sessions do not allow for breaks. To date, the research has been inconclusive as regards to how practice sessions interact with certain task characteristics to produce specific learning outcomes (Dempster, 1989; Dempster & Farris, 1990; Hertenstein, 2001; Kanfer *et al.*, 1994; Perruchet, 1989; Sims, 1998). The effect of spacing on learning seems to be mediated by the characteristics of the learning tasks as well as those of the learners. For example, massed practice was more effective than spaced practice in promoting goal-oriented learning (Kanfer *et al.*, 1994; Hertenstein, 2001). Spaced practice was more effective than massed practice for long-term learning and with varied ways of information presentation (e.g., repetition, alternative format and periodic testing) (Dempster, 1989; Dempster & Farris, 1990). Spaced practice was comparable to massed practice with incidental and intentional learning involving unfamiliar content (Perruchet, 1989).

Three points seem apparent with regard to the effects of massed and spaced practice on task performance. One is that coherent segments of learning content presented over a period of time should be more readily learned than disjointed material (Dempster, 1996). Another is that task segments can be learned more efficiently with massed as compared to spaced practice. Finally, interspersing learning with short breaks may carry the advantages of both massed and spaced practice, and result in more learning than would be the case with either type of practice.

Transfer of learning

Learning is most beneficial when it can support both current and future learning. It must also be useful for solving problems in contexts other than the ones in which the learning occurred. The ability to use specific learning in various contexts relates to the transfer of learning (Singley & Anderson, 1989).

A distinction has been made between lateral and vertical transfer (Lee, 1980; Robertson, 2001; Vrey, 1979). Lateral transfer refers to those instances when a learner uses knowledge gained in one context to solve problems in another similar context (Robertson, 2001). An example of lateral transfer is the use of 'probability theory' by a student to estimate the chances that a certain section of content in a school subject will have more questions in an examination than other sections. Vertical transfer relates to the supportive abilities that a learner needs to have mastered before he or she can cope with more advanced work of a similar nature (Lee, 1980; Vrey, 1979). Most school mathematics and language courses are best learned with vertical transfer.

The transfer of learning is not an automatic process. It depends, amongst other things, on the manner of learning and the teaching methods used to support learning (Singley & Anderson, 1989). Lateral transfer is facilitated by a teaching approach that emphasises the integration of subjects so that ideas common to a number of subjects are identified and reconciled. Vertical transfer, on the other hand, is helped by the logical breakdown and presentation of content. According to Vrey (1979:309), transfer is facilitated when the teacher assists the learners to become 'personally involved in the act of learning and to experience … relationships with the subject matter meaningfully'. The meanings thus assigned, grouped, and consolidated by the learner are available for transfer to new situations that call for their application.

Perception

In simple terms, perception refers to how we make meaning out of the sensory impressions around us (Anderson, 2000). Studies on perception have determined certain laws or principles relevant to how humans mentally organise the things, objects or events they observe. Amongst the principles of perceptual organisation that have been proposed are those of figure and ground, proximity, similarity, closure, continuity and symmetry (see Chapter 10, this volume). People tend to see things against a background (both literally and figuratively). What a person considers important is his or her figure, and this will be closely scrutinised; that which is relatively unimportant is the (back)ground. The principle of proximity refers to the fact that events, objects or ideas that are presented together tend to be perceived as related. The events, objects or ideas that are close in presentation or occurrence may also be perceived as more similar than they actually are. If perceived as repeating, the events, objects or ideas may be perceived as continuous, even though they may be discontinuous or random. The tendency to perceive continuity also inclines individuals to see things as constituting identifiable wholes or entities (the principle of closure). There is also a tendency by individuals to search for symmetry or a balance. In a nutshell, human perception is inclined towards simplifying complex material through a process of discerning redundancies or similarities.

Perception is important for learning in a number of ways. Firstly, learning should be organised for meaning. In this connection, teachers can make use of relevant learner experience as the basis for learning. For example, the background that a learner brings to the learning process gives him or her a unique perspective for understanding a situation or problem. Failure to take adequate account of the learner's background to an issue will impair learning success. However, one learner's background may be another learner's figure so that learners may reach different conclusions from what appears to be the same information. Secondly, in presenting learning content, teachers can assist learners achieve insight by making use of comparisons so that concepts or ideas that are related or similar can be interlinked or differentiated (discriminated) from those that are not related. Thirdly, teachers can also aim at achieving the most efficient learning path for tasks by seeking the essence of the learning task. Attending to perceptual aspects of the teaching-learning situation is an important consideration.

Conclusion

Teaching, instruction and education have been briefly described and compared. Although they are closely related, they are distinguishable one from the other. Teaching is only a part of education and instruction. Education subsumes teaching, learning and instruction.

Teaching and learning are activities so closely associated with each other that they might imply the other. It is not unreasonable to think that one objective of teaching is to influence (if not cause) learning and that learning is a direct result of teaching. Whereas teaching should result in learning, not all teaching results in learning. Some teaching may fail to influence learning due to:

- the incompatibility between the teaching style of the teacher and the learning style of the learner (styles are preferences in the use of abilities) (Renzulli & Dai, 2001);
- the teacher's failure to accurately estimate the learner's potential in a given area in relation to the learner's pre-existing experiences and the competencies on which the new learning is to be built;
- the teacher's failure to utilise methods and media appropriate to the learning task and/or for the learner in terms of variables, like the age and environment of the learner;
- the teacher's insensitivity to developing difficulties during the course of teaching, leading to the failure to offer timely intervention; or
- problems of motivation – it might be that the teacher is unwilling to teach and/or the learner is unwilling to learn.

Where the management of teaching or learning materials and activities match learner characteristics (such as learning style, age and experience), learning is expected to result. As previously discussed, it is possible for learning to occur without direct teaching. Teachers can use problem solving and other approaches to create conditions that would aid the learners to be efficient self-teachers. At the end of the day, teachers want to produce learners who are self-reliant and original in thought and action, or who are educated.

Anderson, J.R. (2000). *Cognitive Psychology and its Implications* (5th edition). New York, NY: Worth Publishers.

Bandura, A. (1986). *The Social Foundations of Thought and Action: A social cognitive theory*. Englewood Cliffs, NJ: Prentice Hall.

Biggs, J.B. (1991). *Teaching and Learning: The view from cognitive psychology*. Hawthorne, Australia: The Australian Council of Educational Research.

Biggs, J. (2001). Enhancing learning: A matter of style or approach? In R.J. Sternberg (Ed.). *Perspectives on Thinking, Learning and Cognitive Styles*. Mahwah, NJ: Lawrence Erlbaum, pp. 73-106.

Brophy, J. (1998). *Motivating Students to Learn*. Boston, MA: McGraw Hill.

Brown, R.A. (1998). 'Where do you people get your ideas from?' Negotiating zones of collaborative learning within an upper primary classroom. In B. Baker, M. Tucker & C. Ng (Eds.). *Education's New Timespace: Visions from the present*. Brisbane: Post Pressed, pp. 107-12.

Bruner, J. (1996). *The Culture of Education*. Cambridge, MA: Harvard University Press.

Cameron, J. (2001). Negative effects of reward on intrinsic motivation – A limited phenomenon: Comment on Deci, Koestner, and Ryan (2001). *Review of Educational Research, 71*:29-42.

Cameron, J. & Pierce, W.D. (1994). Reinforcement, reward, and intrinsic motivation: A meta-analysis. *Review of Educational Research, 64*:363-423.

Campbell, J., Smith, D., Boulton-Lewis, G., Brownlee, J., Burnett, P.C., Carrington, S. & Purdie, N. (2001). Student's perceptions of teaching and learning: The influence of students' approaches to learning and teachers' approaches to teaching. *Teachers & Teaching: Theory & Practice, 7*:173-87.

Deci, E.L., Koestner, R. & Ryan, R.M. (1999). A meta-analytic review of experiments examining the effects of rewards of extrinsic rewards on intrinsic motivation. *Psychological Bulletin, 125*:627-68.

Deci, E.L., Koestner, R. & Ryan, R.M. (2001). Extrinsic rewards and intrinsic motivation in education: Reconsidered once again. *Review of Educational Research, 71*:1-27.

Dempster, F.N. (1989). Spacing effects and their implications for theory and practice. *Educational Psychology Review, 1*:309-30.

Dempster, F.N. (1996). Distributing and managing the conditions of encoding and practice. In E.L. Bjork & R.A. Bjork (Eds.). *Memory. Handbook of perception and cognition*. San Diego, CA: Academic Press, pp. 317-44.

Dempster, F.N. & Farris, R. (1990). The spacing effect: Research and practice. *Journal of Research & Development in Education, 23*:97-101.

Dickinson, A.M. (1989). The detrimental effects of extrinsic reinforcement on 'intrinsic motivation'. *Behavior Analyst, 12*:1-15.

Gagne, R.M. & Briggs, L.J. (1983). *Principles of Instructional Design*. New York, NY: Holt, Rinehart & Winston.

Grigorenko, E.L., Geissler, P.W., Prince, R., Okatcha, F., Nokes, C., Kenny, D.A., Bundy, D.A. & Sternberg, R.J. (2001). The organization of Luo conceptions of intelligence: A study of implicit theories in a Kenyan village. *International Journal of Behavioral Development, 25*:367-78.

Grossen, M. (2000). Institutional framings in thinking, learning and teaching. In H. Cowie, & G. van der Aalsvoort (Eds.). *Social Interaction in Learning and Instruction: The meaning of discourse for the construction of knowledge. Advances in Learning and Instruction Series*. Amsterdam, Netherlands: Pergamon/Elsevier Science, pp. 21-34.

Hertenstein, E.J. (2001). Goal orientation ad practice condition as predictors of training results. *Human Resource Development Quarterly, 12*:403-19.

Joyce, B., Weil, M. & Calhoun, E. (2000). *Models of Teaching*. Boston, MA: Allyn & Bacon.

Kanfer, R., Ackerman, P.L., Murtha, T.C., Dugdale, B. & Nelson, L. (1994). Goal setting, conditions of practice, and task performance: A resource allocation perspective. *Journal of Applied Psychology, 79*:826-35.

Lee, H. (1980). The effects of review questions and review passages on transfer skills. *Journal of Educational Research, 73*:330-35.

Leeper, M.R., Green, D. & Nisbett, R.E. (1973). Undermining children's intrinsic motivation with extrinsic rewards: A test of the overjustification hypothesis. *Journal of Personality & Social Psychology, 28*:129-37.

Martinez, M.E. (2000). *Education as the Cultivation of Intelligence*. Mahwah, NJ: Lawrence Erlbaum.

Martinez, P.M. (2001). *The Psychology of Teaching and Learning: A three-step approach*. New York, NY: Continuum.

Mpofu, E. (1994). *Towards Successful Teaching*. Harare, Zimbabwe: Books For Africa Publishing House.

Mpofu, E. (2004). Being intelligent with Zimbabweans: A historical and contemporary view. In R.J. Sternberg (Ed.). *International Handbook of the Psychology of Human Intelligence*. Cambridge, MA: Cambridge University Press, pp. 364-90.

Mpofu, E. & Oakland, T. (2001). Predicting school achievement in African school settings using Bigg's Learning Process Questionnaire. *South African Journal of Psychology, 31*:20-8.

Mpofu, E. & Watkins, D. (1997). Self-concept and social acceptance in African multiracial schools: A test of the insulation, subjective culture and bicultural competence hypotheses. *Cross-Cultural Research, 31*:331-55.

Nickerson, R.S. (1994). The teaching of thinking and problem solving. In R.J. Sternberg (Ed.). *Thinking and Problem Solving: Handbook of perception and cognition*. San Diego, CA: Academic Press, pp. 409-49.

Omokhodion, J.O. (1989). Classroom observed: The hidden curriculum in Lagos, Nigeria. *International Journal of Education Development, 9*:99-110.

Ormrod, J.E. (1999). *Human Learning* (3rd edition). Upper Saddle River, NJ: Prentice Hall.

Perruchet, P. (1989). The effect of spaced practice on explicit and implicit memory. *British Journal of Psychology, 80*:113-30.

Reiss, A. & Sushunsky, L.W. (1976). The competing response hypothesis of decreased play effects: A reply to Leeper and Green. *Journal of Personality & Social Psychology, 33*:233-44.

Renzulli, J. & Dai, D.Y. (2001). Abilities, interests, and styles as aptitudes for learning: A person-situation interaction perspective. In R.J. Sternberg (Ed.). *Perspectives on Thinking, Learning and Cognitive Styles*. Mahwah, NJ: Lawrence Erlbaum, pp. 26-46.

Richards, A.C. & Combs, A.W. (1992). Education and the humanistic challenge. *Humanistic Psychologist, 20*:327-88.

Robertson, S.I. (2001). *Problem Solving*. Philadelphia, PA: Psychology Press.

Rogers, C. (1994). *Freedom to Learn for the '80s*. Columbus, OH: Merrill.

Rogers, C.R. & Freiberg, H.J. (1994). *Freedom to Learn* (3rd edition). New York: Merrill/Macmillan.

Ryan, A. & Pintrich, P.R. (1998). Achievement and social motivational influences on help seeking in the classroom. In S.A. Karabenick (Ed.). *Strategic Help-seeking: Implications for learning and teaching*. Mahwah, NJ: Lawrence Erlbaum, pp. 117-39.

Ryan, R.M. & Deci, E.L. (2000). Self-determination theory and the facilitation of intrinsic motivation, social development, and well-being. *American Psychologist, 55*:68-78.

Scott, J.R. & Miller, L.K. (1985). Intrinsic motivation and the overjustification effect: A failure to replicate. *Journal of Genetic Psychology, 146*:469-76.

Serpell, R. (1991). Wanzelu ndani? A Chewa perspective on child development and intelligence. In Serpell, R. (ed.). *The Significance of*

Schooling: Life-journeys in an African society. Cambridge: Cambridge University Press, pp. 24-71.

Sharratt, P. (1995). Is educational psychology alive and well in the new South Africa? *South African Journal of Psychology,* 25:211-16.

Sims, R.R. (1998). *Reinventing Training and Development.* Westport, CT: Quorum Books.

Singley, M.K. & Anderson, J.R. (1989). *The Transfer of Cognitive Skill.* Cambridge, MA: Harvard University Press.

Skinner, B.F. (1968). *The Technology of Teaching.* Englewood Cliffs: Prenctice Hall.

Sternberg, R.J. (1999). The theory of successful intelligence. *Review of General Psychology,* 3:292-375.

Sternberg, R.J., Nokes, C., Geissler, P.W., Prince, R., Okatcha, F., Bundy, D.A. & Grigorenko, E.L. (2001). The relationship between academic and practical intelligence: A case study in Kenya. *Intelligence,* 29:401-18.

Vrey, J.D. (1979). *The Self-actualizing Educand.* Pretoria, South Africa: University of South Africa.

Watkins, D., Akande, A. & Mpofu, E. (1994). Student approaches to learning: Some African data. *Ife Psychologia,* 2:1-18.

Watkins, D. & Mboya, M. (1997). Assessing learning processes of Black South African students. *Journal of Psychology,* 131:632-40.

Watson, P. (2002). The role and integration of learning outcomes into the educational process. *Active Learning in Higher Education,* 3:205-219.

Wolters, C., Yu, S. & Pintrich, P.R. (1996). The relation between goal orientation and students' motivational beliefs and self-regulated learning. *Learning & Individual Differences,* 8:211-38.

Multiple choice questions

1. _____ learning is closer to that which happens through everyday activities
   a) planned
   b) incidental
   c) instructional
   d) behavioural

2. Significant learning is associated with
   a) insight
   b) coaching
   c) practice
   d) knowledge

3. Education implies
   a) schooling and learning
   b) training and instruction
   c) prescription and experience
   d) teaching and learning

4. The humanistic approaches to learning place a higher value on
   a) subject matter
   b) self-knowledge
   c) practice effects
   d) observable behaviour

5. Prescribed syllabi and objectives are consistent with the _____ approach to learning
   a) behaviourist
   b) humanistic
   c) information processing
   d) experiential

6. The _____ learning strategy encourages the linking of ideas and wide reading
   a) surface
   a) achieving
   a) deep
   a) motivation

7. Research suggests that a combination of intrinsic and extrinsic motivation may have a(n) ____ effect on task performance
   a) subtractive
   b) additive
   c) cumulative
   d) neutral

8. Extrinsic rewards for interesting work may interfere with performance by
   a) interfering with an on-going activity
   b) taking away a person's sense of control
   c) reducing natural interest in a task and making the performance appear less worthwhile
   d) all of the above

9. The research on the effects of massed versus spaced practice on learning suggests that
   a) task characteristics make a difference
   b) both forms of practice are equivalent across tasks
   c) massed practice is superior to spaced practice
   d) massed practice is superior with less experienced learners

10. Transfer of learning is when learning is applied to _____contexts or situations
    a) other
    b) structured
    c) simpler
    d) familiar

Short answer questions

1. Briefly explain what you understand by each of the following:
   • teaching
   • learning
   • education
   • instruction

2. Describe any two theories of learning, and show how each of them may be relevant to ways of learning in your community.

3. Discuss any three principles of learning. Explain their relevance to teaching and learning.

4. 'A combination of extrinsic and intrinsic motivation should result in the most effective learning'. Discuss this statement with reference to:
   • Your own motivation preferences or practices;
   • Your view of the motivational preferences of someone you know well; and
   • Your view of motivation preferences of members of your community of origin.

5. Distinguish between vertical and lateral transfer. With reference to the particular learning content from a subject of your own choice, show how to teach for both kinds of transfer.

28

Learning through Inclusive Education

Elias Mpofu

CHAPTER OBJECTIVES

After studying this chapter you should be able to:
- list the conditions that cause disabilities in learners
- describe the phenomenon of stigma and its impact on the individual and others
- explain the relative lack of involvement by African governments in the education of learners with disabilities
- set own criteria for inclusive education and show how that would apply to people with a difference of your choice
- define each of the following: inclusive education, disability, functional integration and community-based rehabilitation
- discuss the challenges and opportunities of inclusive education for: learners with disabilities in sub-Saharan Africa and in your own community; and for different others in your community
- evaluate the relevance of the cultural background of a learner to his or her experience of inclusive education in the family, at school and in the community.

Nosipho knew many people with disabilities in the township where she lived. There were people who were blind, hearing impaired, who had mental disabilities and many who were unable to walk, often because of injuries. These things were just a part of normal life. In spite of this, though, at Nosipho's school there had been very few learners with disabilities. Some of the children with disabilities in her neighbourhood went to 'special schools', but some of them didn't attend school at all and, if they were lucky, were taught a little reading and writing by their families. Sometimes they were treated by others as though they were stupid, but Nosipho knew this wasn't the case.

As she thought about it, Nosipho realised that there were many things about her school which would have made it difficult, if not impossible, for pupils with disabilities to attend. Almost every classroom had to be entered via stairs and there were no lifts or ramps for people with wheelchairs. The classrooms were also often overcrowded and the teachers were impatient with anyone who needed extra help of any kind. At university there were much better facilities for learners with disabilities, the buildings were better designed and there were other kinds of learning help like readers and notetakers available for learners who needed this. As Nosipho saw how learners with disabilities succeeded at university, she felt sad about how many children with disabilities in her neighbourhood had not been able to get proper schooling and had not been able to develop their full potential.

Introduction

Learners with disabilities are diverse in their characteristics. They may have a developmental disability (e.g., autism, Attention Deficit Hyperactive Disorder (ADHD), Down's Syndrome, Fragile X, learning disability) or an acquired disability (e.g., Fetal Alcohol Syndrome or disabilities resulting from physical trauma like burns, amputations and childhood diseases). Some disabilities are both developmental and acquired (e.g., mental retardation, visual impairment and hearing impairment). Learners with disabilities may have sensory disabilities (e.g., blindness or visual impairment and deafness or hearing impairment) or physical disabilities (e.g., disabilities resulting in impaired mobility), or they may have multiple disabilities (e.g., deafness with blindness or mental retardation with mental illness). In general, they experience significant limitations in carrying out the ordinary activities of daily life and for reasons associated with having a disability. They are also less well accepted by society and peers, and stigmatised because of their disability-related difference.

Social stigma and disability

Goffman (1963) described the social rejection of different others in terms of stigmatisation. Stigmatised persons are seen by society as possessing 'an attribute that is deeply discrediting' (Goffman, 1963:3), and they are considered as less than fully human because of it. The attribute associated with the stigma could be physical (e.g., visible disability, skin colour and dress code), social (e.g., religious affiliation and social class) or geographical-cultural (e.g., area of origin). However, the more visible the attribute, the more stigma it generates for the beholder, and the greater the disruption it can cause to social relationships or social acceptance.

Stigma can apply to an individual, a group, or persons who associate with a particular person or group. Goffman (1963:30) coined the term 'courtesy stigma', which refers to the spread of stigmatisation effects from the stigmatised individual to his or her connections. Thus, social stigma can severely constrain opportunities for social participation for both the stigmatised and their associates (e.g., peers and family).

Learners with disabilities experience significant social stigma by society. For example, a survey by the author (Mpofu, 1999) on the social acceptance of Zimbabwean primary school learners with disabilities attending ordinary schools in that country revealed that learners with disabilities were twice as likely to be ascribed negative behavioural characteristics by their classmates (e.g., being lazy, dishonest and dirty) than peers without disabilities. Barnatt and Kabzems (1992) found that about 53 per cent of a sample of Zimbabwean teachers would not accept a learner with a sensory disability in their class. Research carried out in North America showed that:

- non-disabled people were more anxious, uncertain and uncomfortable interacting with people with physical disabilities as compared to those without physical disabilities (Kilbury, 1995); and
- interactions with people with physical disabilities tended to be shorter and less genuine in content (Karnilowicz *et al.*, 1994; Kleck *et al.*, 1966).

Regarding learners with disabilities, the effect of the disability-related stigma by society is to lower their overall quality of life through society's denial of their essential humanity. In communities where programmes to counter prejudice towards learners with disabilities are not put in place, the social and occupational life chances of learners with disabilities are severely curtailed and their human rights are likely to be violated.

Current practices in the education of learners with disabilities in sub-Saharan Africa and worldwide emphasise their inclusion in ordinary schools and exposure to regular educational opportunities (Chimedza *et al.*, 2000). Learning through inclusive education has been regarded as a way of enhancing the life chances of individuals with disabilities as well as helping society acquire more positive attitudes towards people with disabilities.

Inclusive education for learners with disabilities: Definition and background

Inclusive education has been defined as the 'placement of a child with disabilities in a general education classroom with supplemental supports and adaptations that allow the child to benefit from that placement' (Coots *et al.*, 1998:317). Inclusive educational practices include:

- encouraging the participation of every child in ordinary school life to the optimum, while retaining the services special education can provide;

- welcoming every learner into the regular classroom; and
- a commitment by all persons in a school to share the responsibility and privilege of working with different others (e.g., learners with disabilities) (Smith & Hilton, 1997).

Historically, inclusive education has been considered an alternative to the school segregation of learners with disabilities. The association of inclusive education with schooling was encouraged by legislation and reports on educational reform from North America and the United Kingdom. Examples of disability-related educational legislation and reports are *US Public Law 92-142: Education for All Handicapped Children of 1975* and the *Warnock Report* (United Kingdom) of the early 1980s. However, the association of inclusive education and schooling is neither necessary nor inevitable. Equating inclusive education with schooling is limited in that such a perspective fails to take into account that education is more than schooling. For instance, the author has elsewhere defined education as those life long activities or experiences that enable a person to meaningfully take part and contribute to the cultural life of his or her community (Mpofu 1994). Similarly, Gottlieb *et al.* (1991:70) defined education as:

> Any endeavor involving the attainment of cognitive, affective and behavioral improvement. [Education] leads to new and improved skills in any aspect of human growth and development … regardless of degree of handicap, the end product of education and implicitly the objective of education, is to equip all children with the behavioral repertoire that will enable them to participate … in mainstream society.

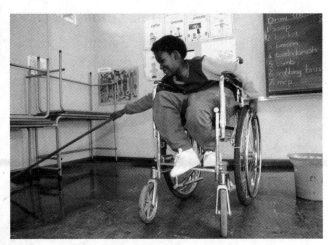

Figure 1 Learner with a disability

Thus, education implies the acquisition and application of knowledge, skills, and abilities for successful community participation. Examples of educative experiences include schooling, family life, peer relationships, consumption of goods and services, employment and production of cultural products (e.g., ideas and goods) (see Chapter 25, this volume).

The presumed benefits of inclusive education for learners with disabilities include that they will achieve at a higher level due to the higher demands and expectations of ordinary educational opportunities. Learners with disabilities would also benefit from exposure to learners without disabilities who would model higher-level adaptive skills. The social acceptance of learners with disabilities by peers is expected to increase through contact with a greater number of classmates without disabilities. Learners without disabilities are also expected to benefit from learning how to work with different others, such as learners with disabilities. The actual benefits of inclusive education to individuals with disabilities depend on the level of support that inclusiveness has at the classroom, school and community levels, individual learner characteristics (e.g., behaviours and emotional control) and family resources (e.g., the amount of parental support for the learner's efforts at school).

From the foregoing, it should be apparent that to view inclusive education only as an alternative schooling arrangement for learners with disabilities is misleading. Inclusive education is realised in a variety of contexts, and certainly is not the preserve of schools or those in charge of schools. In this chapter, inclusive education is considered as the involvement of individuals in normative or age-appropriate and culturally valid activities or experiences in the family, school and community. Family, school and community are contexts for inclusive education. Therefore, this discussion will consider the inclusive education of learners with disabilities with reference to family, school and community.

In previous discussion, inclusive education was regarded as the processes and contexts within which individuals with disabilities acquire competencies for community living. The cultural contexts of the individuals determine the relevant competencies that should be the goal of learning or education. Specific cultural contexts also determine what constitutes a disability and the specific experiences of the individual considered to have a disability. Therefore, a discussion on the inclusive education of learners with disabilities in sub-Saharan Africa must

Conceptions of disability in sub-Saharan Africa

Sub-Saharan Africa is the geographical region that incorporates the countries that lie south of the Sahara desert. This sub-region of the African continent has a rich cultural heritage, both indigenous or traditional and modern. The majority of the 650 million citizens of this sub-region hold indigenous traditional, cultural worldviews. The minority of citizens subscribe to modern, scientific worldviews as a result of the African continent's colonial heritage and modernisation. Thus, conceptions of disability in this sub-region also tend to be dualistic: traditional and modern. For example, indigenous traditional societies of sub-Saharan Africa regard a disability as 'a limitation in social role functions resulting from physical, sensory or emotional abnormalities and is of spiritual origin' (Mpofu & Harley, 2002:27). Thus, a majority of languages indigenous to sub-Saharan Africa have the suffix, '-lema' or '-rema' (i.e. become heavy, fail, or experience difficulty) in words that refer to disability (Burch, 1989; Devlieger, 1998). The implicit meaning of the suffix is that having a disability makes an individual incapable of many roles. Moreover, in a majority of sub-Saharan Bantu languages, the word 'lema' or 'rema' is prefixed by the object or animal-referent 'ki-', 'chi-' or 'isi-' (for 'it') as in 'kilema' (e.g., in Luba, Sanga, Songye languages: Angola, Congo, Zambia), 'chirema' (Shona language: Mozambique, Zimbabwe) or 'isilima' (Ndebele/Nguni: Malawi, South Africa, Tanzania, Zimbabwe) or the human-referent 'mu-', as in 'mulema' (e.g., in Kiluba, Kisanga, Songye languages). Therefore, the sub-Saharan African languages consider a person with a disability as somewhere between a human being and an animal (Devlieger, 1998).

At the same time, many communities of sub-Saharan Africa accept people with disabilities (Ingstad, 1995; Mpofu, 2000a). Indeed, people with certain disabilities are revered. For example, a person with sight in one eye is regarded as more perceptive that those with both eyes, whereas some behaviours that may be considered psychiatric by Western medical practice (e.g., hearing voices) may be regarded as special gifts (Gobodo, 1995). A common saying among indigenous people of sub-Saharan Africa is that 'a disabled person has his way of doing things', which attests to the fact that while a person with a disability may do things differently, he or she is not necessarily viewed as deficient as a result of this (Mpofu, 2000b).

Modern African views of disability are largely influenced by the continent's Western European colonial heritage and modernisation (Mpofu, 2000b). For example, a modern Zimbabwean definition of disability is that it is a 'physical, mental or sensory [condition] which gives rise to physical, cultural or social barriers inhibiting [an individual] from participating at an equal level with other members of society in activities, undertakings or fields of employment that are open to other members of society' (Government of Zimbabwe, *Disabled Persons Act*, 1994:51).

These parallel conceptions of disability (i.e. traditional and modern) among the communities of sub-Saharan Africa influence the nature and extent of inclusive education for people with disabilities. For example, practices in school-based inclusive education for learners with disabilities in sub-Saharan Africa are based on modern conceptions of disability. Community-based inclusive education programmes may draw from both modern and traditional views of disability. Families of African learners with disabilities may subscribe to traditionalist or modern views of disability or hold both traditional and modern views of disability and inclusiveness (Mpofu, 2000b; Piachaud, 1994).

Inclusive education for learners with disabilities in sub-Saharan Africa

School-based inclusive education

Inclusive education is the most common educational option for learners with disabilities in sub-Saharan Africa (Chimedza *et al.*, 2000; Mpofu *et al.*, 1997; Peresuh *et al.*, 1997; Serpell *et al.*, 1993). For example, a survey on educational practices with people with disabilities in 12 sub-Saharan African countries by Mpofu *et al.* (1997) established that inclusive education was the major educational strategy for individuals with disabilities in sub-Saharan Africa. The survey by Mpofu and others covered Botswana, Ethiopia, Eritrea, Kenya, Lesotho, Malawi, Namibia, Swaziland, Tanzania, Uganda, Zambia and Zimbabwe.

School-based inclusive education services in East and Southern Africa generally follow a functional integration model in which children with disabilities attend class part-time to full-time with their non-disabled peers and receive support from a full-time specialist (i.e. resource room) teacher (Charema & Peresuh, 1997; Chimedza *et al.*, 2000; Peresuh *et al.*, 1997). Resource rooms are classrooms equipped with learning materials that are helpful in meeting the unique learning needs of learners with disabilities (e.g., Braille machines, talking clocks and books). Specialist teachers maintain the resource room, provide intensive individualised instruction to children with disabilities, and work closely with mainstream teachers in planning and effecting integration strategies for children with disabilities. Specialist teachers are trained in teaching learners with particular disability types (e.g., blindness, deafness and mental retardation). A functional integration model is generally preferred for learners with moderate to mild sensory (e.g., hearing and visual), physical, and cognitive handicaps. With a few exceptions, most integration units for the visually handicapped and hearing-impaired are residential, whereas those for children with moderate to mild physical and cognitive handicaps are non-residential. Learners with the more severe disabilities (e.g., severe mental retardation and deafness with blindness) generally attend rehabilitation centres. These facilities are typically residential in nature, and provide more specialised resources than the ordinary integration units (e.g., medicine, occupational, and physio- and speech therapy).

Compared to current needs and potential demand, school-based inclusive education facilities in sub-Saharan Africa are severely limited in number and resources. For example, less than 1 per cent of the approximately 6 million children with disabilities in sub-Saharan Africa who are of school-going age attend school (Chimedza *et al.*, 2000). Prejudice by teachers and peers against learners with disabilities may lower the educational opportunities available to the latter (Barnatt & Kabzems, 1992; Kisanji,

Figure 2 Learners with disabilities in a segregated classroom setting

28.1 CASE STUDY

Mavende (not real name), a boy of 8 years of age, was referred for assessment by a rural primary school in Zimbabwe so that he could be appropriately placed for education. The headmaster reported that Mavende had a 'perpetual running nose and salivates on his shirt ... looks afraid under very calm conditions ... has not developed writing or clear speaking skills and tends to isolate himself'. Mavende had been in Grade 1 for two years at the time of his assessment.

According to the headmaster's report, Mavende's parents were peasant farmers. Both of them had acquired a basic education up to Grade 7. Mavende was their first-born of three children. The other two siblings did not present any unusual problems. Mavende's mother informed me that they had seen a number of medical doctors in connection with Mavende's condition. On the day of psychological assessment, the records on doctor consultations were not available. However, Mavende's mother reported that a doctor at the local town had put him on some kind of medication. According to the mother, the medication tended to make Mavende so forgetful that they discontinued the medication without consulting the doctor.

The results of psychological assessment showed that Mavende had very poor adaptive skills as compared to children of a similar age in his locality. For example, Mavende could not initiate and maintain age appropriate peer relations, had poor self-care habits and manifested poor school adjustment. However, Mavende had good listening and hearing abilities and could follow simple instructions. The author (Mpofu) diagnosed Mavende as having mental retardation (intellectual disability) and recommended that he attend a residential school for learners with mental retardation.

1995; Mpofu, 1999). For instance, teachers and classmates may consider a learner with a disability to be incapable of important school or classroom roles or activities (e.g., the role of school or class prefect), which may lower the learner's social acceptance (Mpofu, 1999).

Community-based inclusive education

Learners with disabilities from most of sub-Saharan Africa live in villages or integrated community settings (Kisanji, 1997). To an extent, their participation in local schools is an extension of the activities in their communities.

A tiny minority of learners with disabilities are participants of community-based rehabilitation (CBR) programmes that are provided by non-governmental organisations (NGOs). NGO-led CBRs are the exception rather than the rule in sub-Saharan Africa. These rehabilitation programmes utilise experts in the local community (e.g., village health workers, district social welfare workers, NGOs, rehabilitation technicians and school teachers) to help train the children with disabilities and their families in community living skills. They typically make use of manualised training programmes (e.g., for self-help skills) with a strong behavioural component (e.g., task analysis, reinforcement and successive approximation) (Mariga & McConkey, 1987; Serpell, 1988).

The CBRs currently in place in sub-Saharan Africa tend to fail due to in-built logistical problems. For instance:

> The Local Supervisor (with a few weeks' training) tries to find a family Trainer (who gets a few hours' orientation), while the main fount of wisdom is a manual. In most parts of the developing world there is no tradition of reading, assimilating and referring back to the printed word. Even if as many as 30% of the adult population is 'literate', less than a quarter of them are likely to have the habit of reading (Miles, 1986:112).

In addition, family members of a child with a disability may be expecting a cure much like that for regular physical ailments and may not follow through with treatment regimens that take away time and effort from their established daily routines on the promise of positive outcomes months later. For instance, medical doctors, who often have no training in psychosocial rehabilitation, may tell a family member 'nothing can be done about the child'. Such misinformation may be accepted uncritically by the family, and handicap any future efforts at improving adaptive functioning. Alternatively, medical doctors may, with good intentions, prescribe medication and fail to put in place measures to ensure treatment compliance or follow-up (e.g., involving the village health worker, local clinic or school administration in helping and encouraging the family to comply with treatment or seek timely review). The case described in Box 28.2 by Mpofu (2000a) is illustrative.

28.2 CASE STUDY: DILEMMA

Tendai was six years old, living with her mother who was a peasant farmer. She had a mild right-sided hemiplegia, mild mental retardation, and epilepsy; otherwise she was a bright and likeable child who made good social contact. Her mother was concerned that Tendai was not going to school, so we, and the clinic staff, talked to her mother who eventually talked to the headmaster and Tendai went to school accompanied by her brothers. One day she had a fit on the way to school. Everybody ran away from her. There was great concern and she stopped going to school. Her mother was very upset but when we suggested going to mediate with the headmaster, explain about epilepsy and try to get her back to school, her mother disagreed and did not want to follow this up. It became clear that the mother was responding to the community stigma. If she had continued sending Tendai to school, she would have become stigmatised and isolated. There seemed no solution in the short time we had to work with this family, but there was a need to reflect on how far we should push other people to become champions of the rights we believe in and to wonder whether change in social systems always requires sacrificial lambs (Piachaud, 1994:385).

The case of Mavende (Box 28.1) suggests that his parents may not have received any counselling from the medical doctor with regard to the condition for which medication was prescribed, the probable side effects, and the need for review or available support in the immediate community. Such shortcomings in health service delivery put at risk millions of learners with disabilities in sub-Saharan Africa. The decision to place Mavende at a residential school for learners with mental retardation was one of several possibilities. A recommendation for a specific educational placement should take into account the best interests of the learner and should also be acceptable to the family.

It was noted previously that the majority of learners with disabilities in sub-Saharan Africa are integrated into the ordinary activities of citizens of their villages or communities. However, there could be rural-urban differences in the community participation of learners with disabilities. For instance, learners with disabilities in rural areas may be seen by more of their classmates (who are often fellow villagers and/or relatives) in socially valued social roles (e.g., livestock-tending, home-keeping and child-care) than those in urban areas. This positive visibility may raise the overall social acceptance of learners with disabilities in rural as compared to urban areas (Mpofu, 1999). Learners with disabilities in urban settings may not be seen performing similar roles by the majority of their peers who may come from other parts of the city, or are in homes that are fenced in. Thus, learners with physical disabilities in urban areas may experience more community segregation or lower levels of inclusive education. Opportunities for community-based inclusive education may also be lower for older and female learners with disabilities. This is because of the greater restrictions on social participation by females among the majority of communities in sub-Saharan Africa (Bukumunhe, 1992; Mpofu, 1983) and widespread prejudice against older people with disabilities (Mpofu, 1999).

Many of the learners with disabilities in sub-Saharan Africa learn skills that are useful in their communities, and they may still achieve the equally important skills taught by the formal school system that are necessary for participation in modern economies (e.g., reading, writing, arithmetic and technology). However, as previously observed, regrettably few of them have access to formal schooling.

Challenges to inclusive education of learners with disabilities in sub-Saharan Africa

There are numerous challenges to the provision of inclusive education to learners with disabilities in sub-Saharan Africa. Among the leading barriers to inclusive education are a lack of commitment to the needs of learners with disabilities by national governments and cultural prejudice by service providers against people with disabilities. Problems due to limited resources at the disposal of national governments, and prejudice by the wider society have already been acknowledged and will not be repeated here.

Lack of commitment by national governments

Apart from lofty public pronouncements, African policy makers have rarely been able to translate their philosophical belief in the right of every child to education into legislation that directly addresses the educational needs of learners with disabilities. Donor agencies have generally carried the education programmes for learners with disabilities (special education) in all the countries in sub-Saharan Africa. There is a real possibility that many of the programmes currently in operation will collapse with the termination of support by international donor agencies in particular (Mpofu *et al.*, 1997). Among the reasons for the apparent neglect of school-based inclusive education by national governments in sub-Saharan Africa include:

- poor resource allocation priorities, which at the same time cause avoidable disabilities in millions of African children (Marfo, 1986);
- the legacy from the colonial period that special education was charity work done by missionaries and donor agencies and did not require substantial government resource commitment (Charlton, 1993);
- ignorance on the part of learners with disabilities and their families of their right to a quality education (Mpofu, 2000a); and
- young and inexperienced disability pressure groups that are still at the experimental stage of political action may lack a coherent action plan to translate disability rights ideology into legislation (Chimedza & Peters, 1999; Eleweke, 1999).

Only one country in the entire sub-Saharan region has disability legislation (i.e. Zimbabwe). Several (e.g., Nigeria, South Africa and Uganda) have *affirmative policies* for people with disabilities and other minorities. Non-discrimination policies are also enshrined in the constitutions and education Acts of several countries in sub-Saharan Africa and, by implication, apply to people with disabilities. Although affirmative action policies and constitutional protections for minorities are important to equalising opportunities for people with disabilities, they may not increase opportunities for people with disabilities as would disability legislation. Ideally, disability legislation should commit national governments to fund programmes covered by the legislation (e.g., education, rehabilitation, vocational training and employment of people with disabilities), and to enforce compliance with the legislation. However, disability legislation without commitment to action does not necessarily guarantee that people with disabilities will have access to education and other services. For example, although the Zimbabwe government enacted the *Disabled Persons Act* in 1994, the Act does not commit the Zimbabwe Government to inclusive education in any concrete way.

Cultural prejudice by service providers

Some inclusive education service providers have claimed that African communities hide children with disabilities from social agencies such as schools, thereby making them unreachable for life skills education or wider community participation (Fryers, 1986). However, these allegations have tended to be made by persons from outside the communities in which the children with disabilities live (Ingstad, 1995). Outsiders often do not consider that many communities in sub-Saharan Africa consider a disability to be a family matter that does not concern outsiders. For that reason, families are rather protective of members with a disability and will need time

to build a level of trust with inclusive education service providers (e.g., schools and NGOs). Furthermore, parents of learners with disabilities who are not in school may be acting rationally in that they may have genuine concerns about the physical safety of their child on the way to and from school and within school. Consider the case example by Piachaud (1994) regarding a Zimbabwean child who could be regarded as having mental retardation, detailed in Box 28.2.

There are numerous issues of learner and family neglect and disempowerment that are raised by this case study. Firstly, when integrating Tendai at the local school, there was no community education by the school about the particular disability that Tendai had, which could have eased Tendai's return to school after the incident. In that regard, Tendai's mother's refusal for her to return to school was a rational decision. Secondly, there also was no education of Tendai's fellow learners and peers about epilepsy and its management (hence their running away in fear). Thirdly, the school administration could have taken steps to re-establish contact with Tendai's family with a view of encouraging her school attendance and putting in place a seizure management programme in liaison with the local clinic and Tendai's family. It is very likely that Tendai's peers would have reported the incident to their teachers. However, some schools in Africa do not see themselves as having educational responsibilities towards children with a disability status.

28.3 CASE STUDY

Nompumelelo was a 10-year-old girl with spastic quadriplegia. At the time of identification by the Department of Education, she had no previous schooling experience. She was from a poor working-class family. Her father worked for a meat packaging family in the local town. The family stayed in a makeshift home in an informal settlement in the town.

Apart from that Nompumelelo had not previously been enrolled with the local school. She needed a wheelchair for mobility. The Ministry of Health and Child Welfare subsequently provided a wheelchair gratis to Nompumelelo's family upon the recommendation of the Education Department. Among the reasons for granting a free wheelchair to Nompumelelo was to facilitate her school attendance as well as improve her quality of life as a person living with a disability.

It turned out that Nompumelelo's school attendance subsequently was erratic and with many unexplained absences. Investigation by the Department of Social Welfare revealed that her father had taken over the wheelchair for himself and was using it as his house chair. Apparently, the father, who ordinary sat on a traditional three-legged wooded stool of about 30 centimetres in height, would not accept Nompumelelo sitting higher than him. Culturally, the mother and children were all to sit at a height lower than that of the father. That seating order reinforced the father's authority over the family. The coming of the wheelchair upset the seating order and symbolically threatened the father's authority. For that reason, Nompumelelo was dispossessed of her wheelchair and could not even use it to attend school.

Research question: Are learners with physical disabilities less socially accepted by peers as compared to those without a physical disability?

Study

Mpofu (1999) collected social acceptance data on 235 adolescents with physical disabilities and 231 adolescents without a disability. The social acceptance data were from 8 009 classmates without disabilities and the learners with physical disabilities themselves.

Results

Learners with and without physical disabilities had similar social acceptance ratings. However, learners with disabilities were twice as likely to be nominated for negative behaviours (e.g., unreliable and lazy) as compared to peers without disabilities.

Conclusion

Learners with physical disabilities were as socially accepted as peers without a physical disability. Having a visible disability made it more likely that a negative behavioural trait would be ascribed. The sources of the negative attributions were unclear.

The culture of the family of the learner with a disability may not always be in the best interests of the learner. The case study in box 28.3 illustrates an instance of conflict between culture and inclusive education opportunities available to children with disabilities.

Subsequent counselling of the father by the Department of Education resulted in Nompumelelo regaining the use of the wheelchair for schooling. It remained unclear as to who sat on the wheelchair in the evenings. Nompumelelo would not talk for fear of reprisal by the father. A pragmatic solution to Nompumelelo's risk of the dispossession of her wheelchair by the father was to buy him a low-cost chair with a higher seat elevation than Nompumelelo's wheelchair. That arrangement could have allayed any anxiety in her father about the seating and associated authority hierarchies within the family.

Conclusion

Learners with disabilities may have a variety of physical, sensory and behavioural or emotional conditions that significantly limit their participation in most everyday activities. Inclusive education, which includes life skills education for learners with disabilities that is provided in ordinary family, school, and community settings, has the potential to enhance the participation of learners with disabilities in the community. Many learners with disabilities in sub-Saharan Africa participate in the activities of their communities to the extent permitted by the support of their families and caregivers. A tiny minority of learners with disabilities in the sub-region attend school or participate in community-based inclusive education programmes that are provided by NGOs. National governments in sub-Saharan Africa could be more involved with the inclusive education effort. Social prejudice against people with disabilities and cultural prejudice by inclusive education providers are significant barriers to the education of learners with disabilities in sub-Saharan Africa. Family culture may be both a resource and a hindrance to the inclusive education of learners with disabilities.

Barnatt, S.N. & Kabzems, V. (1992). Zimbabwean teachers attitudes towards the integration of pupils with disabilities into regular classrooms. *International Journal of Disability, Development & Education*, 39:135-46.

Bukumunhe, R.B. (1992). I will definitely go. In D. Driedger & S. Gray (Eds.). *Imprinting our Image: An international anthology by women with disabilities.* Canada: Gynergy Books, pp. 74-9.

Burch, D.J. (1989). *Kuoma Rupandi (The parts are dry): Ideas and practices about disability in a Shona ward. Research report 36.* Leinden: African Studies Center.

Charema, J. & Peresuh, M. (1997). Support services for special needs educational needs: Proposed models for countries South of the Sahara. *African Journal of Special Needs Education*, 1:76-83.

Charlton, J.I. (1993). Development and disability: Voices from the periphery-Zimbabwe. In B.L. Mallory, J.I. Charlton, R.W. Nicholls & K. Marfo (Eds.). *Traditional and Changing Views of Disability in Developing Societies: Causes, consequences, cautions.* Durham, NH: The National Institute of Disability Research, pp. 41-70.

Chimedza, R., Mpofu, E. & Oakland, T.R. (2000). Special education in East and Southern Africa: An overview. In C.R. Reynolds & E. Fletcher-Janzen (Ed.). *Encyclopedia of Special Education.* New York: John Wiley & Sons, pp. 1678-86.

Chimedza, R. & Peters, S. (1999). Disabled people's quest for social justice in Zimbabwe. In F. Armstrong & L. Barton (Eds.). *Disability, Human Rights and Education.* Buckingham: Open University Press, pp. 7-23.

Coots, J.J., Bishop, K.D. & Grenot-Scheyer, M. (1998). Supporting elementary age learners with significant disabilities in general education classrooms: Personal perspectives on inclusion. *Education & Training in Mental Retardation & Developmental Disabilities*, 33:317-30.

Devlieger, P.J. (1998). Physical 'dsability' in Bantu languages: Understanding the relativity of classification and meaning. *International Journal of Rehabilitation Research*, 21:63-70.

Eleweke, C.J. (1999). The need for mandatory legislation to enhance services to people with disabilities in Nigeria. *Disability & Society*, 14:227-37.

Fryers, T. (1986). Screening for developmental disabilities in developing countries: Problems and perspectives. In K. Marfo, S. Walker & B. Charles (Eds.). *Childhood Disability in Developing Countries: Issues in habilitation and special education.* New York: Praeger, pp. 27-40.

Gobodo, P. (1995). Notions about culture in understanding Black psychopathology: Are we trying to raise the dead? *South African Journal of Psychology*, 20:93-8.

Goffman, E. (1963). *Stigma: Notes on the management of spoiled identity.* Englewood Cliffs, New Jersey: Prentice Hall.

Gottlieb, J., Alter, M. & Gottlieb, B.W. (1991). Mainstreaming mentally retarded children. In J.L. Matson & J.A. Mulick (Eds.). *Handbook of Mental Retardation* (2nd edition). New York: Pergamon Press, pp. 63-73.

Government of Zimbabwe. (1994). *Disabled Persons Act.* Harare: Government Printer.

Ingstad, B. (1995). Mpho ya Modimo – A gift from God: Perspectives on 'attitudes' toward disabled. In S.R. Whyte & B. Ingstad (Eds.). *Disability and Culture.* Berkeley: University of California Press, pp. 246-65.

Karnilowicz, W., Sparrow, W.A. & Shinkfield, A.J. (1994). High school learners' attitudes toward performing social behaviors with mentally retarded and physically disabled peers. *Journal of Social Behavior & Personality*, 9:65-80.

Kilbury, R.F. (1995). *The Effects of Gender and the Presence of Physical Disability on the Personal Space Given Individuals.* Doctoral dissertation, Southern Illinois University at Carbondale, Dissertation Abstracts, AAC 9516023.

Kisanji, J. (1995). Interface between culture and disability in the Tanzania context: Part 1. *International Journal of Disability, Development & Education*, 42:93-108.

Kisanji, J. (1997). The relevance of indigenous customary education principles in the education of special needs education policy. *African Journal of Special Needs Education*, 1:59-74.

Kleck, R., Ono, H. & Hastorf, A.H. (1966). The effects of physical deviance upon face-to-face interaction. *Human Relations*, 19:425-36.

Mariga, L. & McConkey, R. (1987). Home-based learning programmes for mentally handicapped people in rural Zimbabwe. *International Journal of Rehabilitation Research*, 10:175-83.

Marfo, K. (1986). Confronting childhood disability in the developing countries. In K. Marfo, S. Walker & B. Charles (Eds.). *Childhood Disability in Developing Countries: Issues in habilitation and special education.* New York: Praeger, pp. 3-26.

Miles, M. (1986). Misplanning for disabilities in Asia. In K. Marfo, S. Walker & B. Charles (Eds.). *Childhood Disability in Developing Countries: Issues in habilitation and special education.* New York: Praeger, pp. 101-28.

Mpofu, E. (1994). *Towards Successful Teaching.* Harare, Zimbabwe: Books for Africa Publishing House.

Mpofu, E. (1999). *Social Acceptance of Zimbabwean Early Adolescents with Physical Disabilities.* Ann Abhor, Michigan: UMI.

Mpofu, E. (2000a). *Educational Considerations for Learners Who Are Mentally Challenged/Retarded.* Harare: Zimbabwe Open University.

Mpofu, E. (2000b). Rehabilitation in international perspective: A Zimbabwean experience. *Disability & Rehabilitation*, 23:481-89.

Mpofu, E., Zindi, F., Oakaland, T. & Peresuh, M. (1997). School psychological practices in East and Southern Africa. *Journal of Special Education*, 31:387-402.

Mpofu, E. & Harley, D.A. (2002). Disability and rehabilitation in Zimbabwe: Lessons and implications for rehabilitation practice in the US. *Journal of Rehabilitation*, 68(4):26-33.

Mpofu, E, & Herbert, J.T. (2002). *Enhancing Learner Experience with Disabilities Through Interactive Web-based Video Clips and Multimedia Instructional Delivery.* Department of Counselor Education, Counseling Psychology and Rehabilitation Services, Penn State University.

Mpofu, J.M.M. (1983). *Some Observable Sources of Women's Subordination in Zimbabwe.* Harare: University of Zimbabwe Centre for Applied Social Sciences.

Piachaud, J. (1994). Strengths and difficulties in developing countries: The case of Zimbabwe. In N. Bouras (Ed.). *Mental Health in Mental Retardation.* Cambridge, UK: Cambridge University Press, pp. 382-92.

Peresuh, M., Adenigba, S.A. & Ogonda, G. (1997). Perspectives on special needs education in Nigeria, Kenya and Zimbabwe. *African Journal of Special Needs Education*, 2:9-15.

Serpell, R. (1988). Childhood and disability in cross-cultural context: Assessment and information needs for effective services. In P.R. Dasen, J.W. Berry & N. Sartorius (Eds.). *Health and Cross-cultural Psychology: Towards applications.* London: Sage, pp. 257-80.

Serpell, R., Mariga, L. & Harvey, K. (1993). Mental retardation in African countries: Conceptualization, services, and research. *International Review of Research in Mental Retardation*, 19:1-34.

Smith, J.D. & Hilton, A. (1997). The preparation and training of the educational community for inclusion of learners with developmental disabilities: The MRDD position. *Education & Training in Mental Retardation and Developmental Disabilities*, 32:3-10.

Multiple choice questions

1. _____ is a developmental disability and _____ an acquired disability
   a) Down's syndrome; fetal alcohol syndrome
   b) burns; learning disability
   c) fetal alcohol syndrome; Down's syndrome
   d) learning disability; attention deficit hyperactive disorder

2. Courtesy stigma is due to the _____ of stigma from one individual to his or her associates
   a) decrease
   b) spread
   c) elimination
   d) removal

3. Inclusive education is for
   a) people with a disability
   b) people with handicaps
   c) the poor and crippled
   d) schooling with the disabled

4. Disabilities are variously defined
   a) within and between societies
   b) because of stigma
   c) when they occur in learners
   d) due to a lack of resources

5. Which is a type of integrated educational setting?
   a) functional
   b) locational
   c) residential
   d) specialist

6. _____ is the most natural type of inclusive education
   a) school-based education
   b) community-based education
   c) resource room placement
   d) a residential hospital

7. Inclusive education is more successful when people have _____ with regard to how best to meet their educational needs
   a) routines
   b) prescriptions
   c) choices
   d) wishes

8. A barrier to inclusive education with learners with disabilities in sub-Saharan Africa is the decreasing
   a) presence of the donor community
   b) preparedness of the schools
   c) respect for culture
   d) disability stigma

9. Disability pressure groups in sub-Saharan can best be described as
   a) emerging
   b) experienced
   c) established
   d) influential

Short answer questions

1. Identify the various types of disabilities that learners may present with. Describe the characteristics of such a disability in a person you know. Interview this individual about the characteristics of his or her disability. Compare your description of that specific disability with that of the person you interviewed. Explain any differences of description.

2. Interview an individual with a disability to learn of his or her experiences in relation to the disability. Identify and describe instances of stigmatisation of that individual. How may similar kinds of stigmatisation apply to different others (e.g., in terms of race, religion and gender)?

3. What do you understand by the term, 'inclusive education'? How does this construct apply to education about and with different others? What has been your experience with inclusive education with regard to:
   • learners with disabilities; and
   • others who may be different?

4. Consider the cases of Mavende, Tendai and Nompumelelo. In each case:
   • identify the barriers to inclusive education; and
   • suggest ways in which inclusive education could better be achieved.

5. Describe the status of inclusive education in your community. Explain any successes and failures.

Part 8

Occupations

Gideon de Bruin

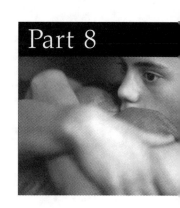

The chapters in this section focus on two important human activities, namely work and sport. In Chapter 29, the focus is on career choice in late adolescence and early adulthood. De Bruin and van Niekerk describe a simple six dimensional model (attributable to John Holland) that can be used to describe work environments *and* people's vocational personalities. The authors emphasise that people are more likely to experience job satisfaction and produce quality work when their personalities match the characteristics and requirements of the working environment. Chapter 29 also describes Social Cognitive Career Theory, which holds that people's beliefs about their abilities have a strong influence on the career choices that they make. The theory provides useful guidelines for enhancing people's beliefs about their abilities. The world of work is becoming increasingly complex and less predictable, and in this regard the chapter proposes that an attitude of 'positive undecidedness', which is characterised by a readiness to react on opportunities, may be beneficial in a time where old jobs are disappearing, new ones are emerging, job changes become common and entrepreneurship is rewarded.

Chapter 30 addresses the exciting field of sport psychology, which is fast growing in popularity as an applied and research area in psychology. Whitton highlights the interplay between academic and applied sport psychology and shows how psychological techniques may be used to enhance sport performance and recovery after injury. An important question is whether elite sports people differ from other sportspeople in terms of personality, and Whitton discusses this issue in some depth. The chapter also highlights the role of sport in mental health, with a focus on the psychological benefits of involvement and participation in sport. In addition, Chapter 30 examines the role of learning and the implications thereof for coaching and practice. In closing, the chapter comments on the role of sport psychology in contemporary South Africa.

29

Career Choice and Development in Adolescence and Early Adulthood

Gideon de Bruin & Leon van Niekerk

CHAPTER OBJECTIVES

After studying this chapter you should be able to:
- understand the difference between an occupation and a career
- know what person X environment fit is, and how it impacts on job satisfaction
- understand the basic principles of Holland's theory of vocational types
- name and describe the six vocational personality types according to Holland
- name and describe the six working environments according to Holland
- explain the interaction between the six vocational types according to the hexagonal model of vocational interests
- define congruence and consistency in the context of career development theories
- define self-efficacy expectations and outcome expectations, and explain how they influence career development decisions
- name and describe the four sources of self-efficacy expectations
- relate person X environment theories and social cognitive theories of career development to your own ideas about career development
- explain how person X environment theories and social cognitive theories of career development fit into the South African context.

While Nosipho had always been interested in people, she had not at first known that she would like to be a psychologist. She hadn't known any psychologists in her neighbourhood, and it was only when she went to high school that she found out that it was possible to turn her interest in people into a career. Although Nosipho was usually quite modest about her capabilities, she did feel that she had a good ability to understand people. Although sometimes a little shy, she knew she was a good listener and had been told by her friends that she was easy to talk to.

In choosing a career, Nosipho hoped she would be able to do something that would be fulfilling and also something that fitted with her as a person. She knew she didn't have the right kind of personality to go into a career in business or even into something like advertising. These jobs, she felt, needed a more forceful and extroverted person, while she tended to be quiet and more thoughtful. She had wondered though about whether she should develop her interest in psychology to become a clinical psychologist or counsellor. On the other hand, she might enjoy just learning more about people, as a researcher. She was doing quite well at university so far and she certainly enjoyed reading, learning and discovering new knowledge – perhaps she should be a university lecturer.

Sometimes, though, it was hard for Nosipho to picture herself in these kinds of jobs – as a psychologist, a researcher, a university lecturer – partly because she didn't know many people from her community who did work like this. She had discovered that there were, in fact, very few Black psychologists in the country. In spite of this though, she felt it was important that she find the career that was right for her.

Introduction

The aim of this chapter is to provide an introduction to the field of career development in adolescence and early adulthood. The focus falls on two theories of career choice and development, namely person X environment theory (Holland, 1997), and social cognitive career theory (Lent *et al.*, 1996). Both theories are internationally popular and are widely used and researched in the South African context.

To set the context for the rest of the chapter, it is necessary to explain what is meant by the concepts 'career' and 'occupation'. The concept 'occupation' refers to a position of employment, such as a psychologist, engineer or farmer. In turn, the concept 'career' may be defined as the sequence of occupations, jobs and positions that a person may hold throughout his or her working life (Super *et al.*, 1957). Hence career refers to a developmental process rather than a particular job or occupation.

Career psychologists aim to answer questions such as the following: Why do some individuals appear to be happier and more satisfied in their working environments than others? How do individuals choose certain occupations above others? Why do some workers deliver satisfactory work and others not?

Person X environment theory

Some psychologists believe that the answer to these questions lies in the degree of fit between an individual's characteristics, on the one hand, and the characteristics of the work environment, on the other hand. Psychologists sharing this viewpoint are often called person X environment psychologists (e.g., Holland, 1997; Lofquist & Dawis, 1991) because of their focus on the interaction between an individual and his or her environment. Person X environment career psychologists believe that people seek out environments that correspond with their personalities, interests, values and abilities. If they achieve such correspondence or congruence, chances are that they will be happy and satisfied and that they will have the skills to provide quality work. If, however, there is a lack of correspondence or congruence, people are more likely to be dissatisfied and to provide work of lesser quality (Holland, 1997; Lofquist & Dawis, 1991).

In the paragraphs that follow one important person X environment theory of vocational choice and adjustment, namely the theory of John Holland

(1997), will be examined more closely. Holland (1997) believes that an individual's choice of work may be viewed as an expression of his or her personality. From this perspective, the way that people view themselves is reflected in the work that they do. Holland essentially views personality and vocational interests as synonyms. Although there are potentially a very large number of vocational interests, Holland has argued that they may be summarised in terms of six broad vocational interest or personality types, namely Realistic (R), Investigative (I), Artistic (A), Social (S), Enterprising (E) and Conventional (C). The acronym R-I-A-S-E-C is used to refer to these six types and the model they represent. Interestingly, Holland postulated that we may describe people and work environments in terms of these six types. Each of the six vocational personality types will be briefly described below:

- *Realistic type (R)*: Realistic people like technical, mechanical and practical work environments. They enjoy working with their hands, building and fixing things and being outdoors.
- *Investigative type (I)*: Investigative people like scientific and mathematical activities. They enjoy fields such as physics, chemistry and biology.
- *Artistic type (A)*: Artistic people enjoy the fine and performing arts. They like poetry, painting, drama, music and dance.
- *Social type (S)*: Social people like educating and helping other people improve the quality of their lives. They seek out the company of others and wish to make a difference in the lives of other people.
- *Enterprising (E)*: Enterprising people like to influence other people and seek out positions of leadership. They like environments that allow them to do this, such as business and law.
- *Conventional (C)*: Conventional people prefer structured working environments. They enjoy clerical activities and work with office machines, such as computers.

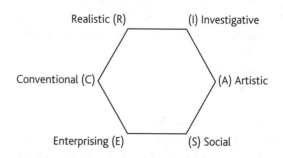

Figure 1 Holland's (1997) hexagonal model of vocational personalities and work environments

Holland (1997) specifies that the six vocational personality types can be spatially represented as a hexagonal ordering of the R-I-A-S-E-C types (see Figure 1), and that the distances between types on the hexagon reflects the strength of their relations. Adjacent types, such as Social and Enterprising, are most alike, whereas opposite types, such as Artistic and Conventional, are most unlike. Alternate types on the hexagon, such as Realistic and Artistic, are somewhat unlike. An individual may be described in terms of his or her resemblance to these six vocational personality types. To this end, Holland suggests that people be described in terms of the three types that correspond best with them. For instance, someone may be described as Social, Enterprising and Artistic (SEA). The order of the three types reflects how well each of them describes the person. In our SEA example, the individual is best described by the Social type, followed by the Enterprising type, and then the Artistic type.

As pointed out earlier, Holland (1997) also argues that work environments may be described in terms of the six vocational personality types:

- *Realistic environment*: This environment promotes technical skills through the need for orderly and systematic use of tools and machinery. Engineers, farmers, foresters, motor mechanics, electricians and plumbers occupy realistic environments.
- *Investigative environment*: Investigative personality types tend to dominate this environment, where scientific skills are promoted through the symbolic, systematic, and creative investigation of physical, biological and cultural phenomena. Natural and social scientists and researchers occupy investigative environments.
- *Artistic environment*: Artistic skills such as creative thinking and freedom of expression are promoted in this environment through unplanned and unstructured activities. Performing and fine artists, writers, and musicians occupy artistic environments.
- *Social environment*: This environment lends itself to congeniality, where people who want to make a difference in other's lives, by educating, helping and caring for them, develop social skills. Teachers, nurses, social workers, and preachers occupy social environments.
- *Enterprising environment*: A highly competitive atmosphere could well be a feature of this environment, where Enterprising types set out to obtain leadership positions in order to influence people. Business people, lawyers and politicians occupy enterprising environments.

- *Conventional environment*: This environment is characterised by the systematic and orderly manipulation of data (such as record-keeping), and workers are expected to conform to set demands. Conventional skills, such as administration and computational skills are promoted in this environment. Accountants, secretaries, typists and clerks occupy conventional environments.

Just as people are best described by a combination of three vocational personality types, environments are classified in the same way.

The most important aspect of Holland's theory is that people seek out work-related environments that match or correspond with their work-related personalities. Hence, we would expect, for instance, a Social type person to be drawn to a Social type environment. Such correspondence, or in Holland's terminology *congruence*, will allow people to express their interests and to find satisfaction in the tasks they do. Similarly, if congruence is achieved the working environment will be satisfied with the individual, because he or she brings characteristics to the working environment that are needed and valued. Holland predicts that the greater the amount of congruence, the greater the degree of satisfaction that an individual will experience. The relations between congruence and job satisfaction are depicted in Figure 2.

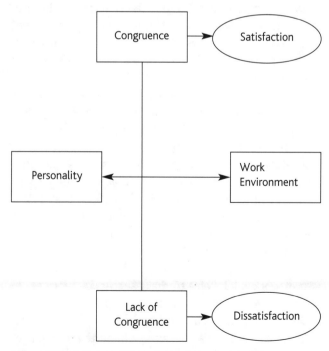

Figure 2 The influence of congruence between people's personalities and their working environment on job satisfaction

Much research has focused on the relationships between congruence and important outcomes such as job satisfaction and employee turnover (see Gottfredson & Holland, 1990; Meir *et al.*, 1995). It appears that workers whose personality types are congruent with the working environment experience more job satisfaction and are less likely to resign from their jobs. This relationship is not perfect, however, and some people may be satisfied with their jobs even if the congruence between their personality types and the environment is less than ideal. Moreover, it is important to note that neither people nor working environments are static. Individuals develop constantly, often as a result of the environment wherein they function, and may in turn introduce changes to the work environment. Similarly, environments develop and change, often as a result of the individuals who inhabit them. It is clear that the interaction between individuals and their environments is dynamic and that person X environment fit is constantly negotiated and evaluated.

On the basis of the hexagonal ordering of the R-I-A-S-E-C types Holland also postulates that an individual who, for instance, corresponds most closely with, for example, the Enterprising type, will be likely to also correspond with the Social and Conventional types (which are adjacent to the Enterprising type on the hexagon). This individual would also be unlikely to correspond with the Investigative type, which lies opposite the Enterprising type on the hexagon. People whose interest types lie adjacent to each other are said to demonstrate *consistency* in their interest profiles. Such people are likely to find it easier to associate and integrate their personalities, interests and values with the working environment than individuals who have low consistency regarding their interests (Holland, 1997).

Although Holland's theory is widely accepted and has been validated in many different countries, we may ask whether it is universally applicable in the South African context (du Toit & de Bruin, 2002). For instance, an important assumption of Holland's theory is that individuals have the freedom to choose an occupation. This assumption clearly does not hold in contexts such as South Africa, where jobs are scarce and many people do not have skills that are valued or

29.1 ARE USA MODELS USEFUL IN SOUTH AFRICA?

Should South African psychologists discard existing career theories and models that were developed in the USA? Are those theories of limited value in understanding and influencing the career related behaviour of South Africans? Should psychologists rather attempt to develop indigenous career theories that explicitly address local issues and problems. Or would this lead to a reinvention of the wheel?

These issues have been heavily debated in the last decade (e.g., du Toit & de Bruin, 2002; Naicker, 1994; Stead, 1996; Stead & Watson, 1999). Proponents of the indigenous theories approach argue that theories developed in the US, such as Holland's (1997) person X environment theory and Lent *et al.'s* (1996) social cognitive theory are based on assumptions that do not hold in the South African context (see Akhurst & Mkhize, 1999). These assumptions include:
- that work is freely available;
- that individuals who know themselves and the world of work will be able to make successful choices;
- that everybody has access to educational opportunities of equal quality; and
- that the individual is the most important role player in the career decision-making process.

Western theories fall short because in South Africa work is not freely available and there are huge historical imbalances in access to educational opportunities, with Whites often having access to better opportunities than their Black counterparts (Naicker, 1994). Furthermore, Western theories overemphasise the role of the individual in the career decision-making process. In collectivist African societies important decisions are often made within a broader family context.

On the other hand, it may be unwise to summarily discard the existing body of career knowledge. Western theories may contain aspects that are relevant in the South African context. For instance, the social cognitive approach's emphasis on learning experiences in career development appears to be universally applicable. Similarly, we might argue that it is universally desirable to be interested in your work (because of the sense of enjoyment and meaningfulness that it may provide) and therefore an exploration of an individual's interests may remain a valid activity. The challenge to career psychologists lies in developing new theories that uniquely address the South African context, while capitalising on the wealth of knowledge that have been accumulated in Western countries.

needed in the contemporary technology-driven work place. Furthermore, it is not clear whether Holland's hexagonal representation of the structure of interests and occupations corresponds to the way that South Africans perceive the world of work. Research by du Toit and de Bruin (2002) suggests that Black South Africans' patterns of vocational interests are not well represented by Holland's hexagon. However, more research in this regard needs to be done.

29.2 DECIDING ON A CAREER, CHOOSING AN OCCUPATION

It may be 'unhealthy' to be too decided too quickly. This is especially true in a world that is characterised by fast and unpredictable changes in the workplace. Individuals may become so focused on entering a particular occupational field that they don't notice other opportunities or learning experiences. Recently, some career psychologists have advocated a position called 'positive uncertainty' (Gelatt, 1989) or 'planned happenstance' (Mitchell *et al.*, 1999), which emphasises the role of uncertainty and chance factors in career decision-making. Individuals might capitalise on some uncertainty by being ready to identify and embrace unexpected opportunities. This is most likely to happen if an individual is optimistic, curious, persistent, flexible, and willing to take risks (Mitchell *et al.*, 1999).

Social cognitive theory of career development

One of the most interesting contemporary theories of career development is the social cognitive career theory (Lent *et al.*, 1996) that developed out of Albert Bandura's (1986) general social cognitive theory. The aspect of Bandura's work that has received the most attention in the career domain is the concept of *self-efficacy expectations*. Bandura explained that individuals with positive beliefs in their ability to accomplish a particular task are likely to be more successful in the task than those individuals who doubt their ability. Individuals who believe that they can be successful are said to have positive or high self-efficacy expectations regarding the task, whereas individuals who doubt their ability to be successful are said to have negative or low self-efficacy expec-

tations regarding the task. Note that self-efficacy expectations are task-specific – we may have high expectations of success for one particular task, but low expectations of success for another. Hence, it is not appropriate to refer to general self-efficacy expectations as though referring to personality traits.

Self-efficacy expectations can be distinguished from outcome expectations. The latter refers to expectations regarding the results of behaviour. Self-efficacy expectations are related to the question: Can I do it? In contrast, outcome expectations are related to the question: If I do it will I like the outcome(s)? Bandura (1986) pointed out that individuals may view the outcomes of behaviour as desirable, but refrain from performing the behaviour because they don't believe they can be successful in performing the behaviour. In the career domain, people may view the outcomes of being in a particular occupation as very attractive, but if they doubt their ability to successfully perform the tasks of that occupation, they will be unlikely to enter or pursue goals in that occupation.

The concept of self-efficacy expectations was first applied to the career development field by Betz and Hackett (1981), who pointed out that men had more positive self-efficacy expectations regarding a broader range of occupations than women. Specifically, women had low self-efficacy expectations for occupations that were traditionally dominated by men, such as engineering and management. The result of this was that many women did not consider or aspire to careers in several potentially rewarding occupational fields. Rottinghaus *et al.* (2003a) recently reported that college men have higher self-efficacy expectations than women for technical, mathematical, mechanical and scientific activities. In contrast, women have higher self-efficacy for activities related to cultural sensitivity and teamwork.

When applied to career development and choice, we would expect individuals to choose careers or occupational fields in which they believe they will be successful and where they have positive outcome expectations. Similarly, we would expect individuals to avoid careers or occupational fields in which they believe they will be unsuccessful and where they have negative outcome expectations.

How do self-efficacy expectations develop, and how is this related to the development of occupational preferences? Bandura distinguished between four main sources of self-efficacy information. In descending order of importance, these are:

Social learning and social cognitive approaches may overemphasise the role of learning in the development of interests. Behavioural genetic studies suggest that interests are at least partly influenced by genetic factors (Gottfredson, 1999). Betsworth *et al.* (1994) reported that genetic factors accounted for between 40 and 50 per cent of the variance in interest measures. Genes may influence an individual's exposure and sensitivity to environments, which in turn may influence his or her learning opportunities. It is clear that both genetic and environmental factors need to be taken into account in understanding the development of interests.

- *Personal performance accomplishments*: Personal performance accomplishments refer to direct success experiences when confronted with a task. We would expect individuals who experience success in the accomplishment of a task to develop positive self-efficacy expectations for the particular task, while individuals who experience failure will develop negative self-efficacy expectations. Bandura (1986) posited that personal performance accomplishments are the most powerful source of self-efficacy expectations. Within the career context we might expect individuals to approach and develop interests in activities where they experience success and to avoid activities where they experience failure. For instance, if an individual is successful in subjects such as mathematics and science, he or she will be more likely to develop positive self-efficacy expectations with regard to those subjects and to eventually develop an interest in them.
- *Vicarious learning*: Vicarious learning refers to learning that takes place through observation of other people's behaviour. When an individual observes another person achieving success in a particular task, it may enhance his or her beliefs about suc-

cessfully completing the task. Similarly, an individual's beliefs about achieving success in the task may be lowered if he or she observes another person failing. This is especially likely to be true if the person who is observed is perceived to be similar to the observer. In the context of career development, we might expect individuals to develop positive self-efficacy expectations for career-related activities where they observe others, whom they perceive to be similar to them, to be successful. When self-efficacy expectations increase, the individual will be more willing to attempt tasks that are related to the occupation and in that way interest in the task may increase.

- *Physiological arousal*: Bandura (1986) views physiological arousal and anxiety as an important source of self-efficacy information. The more anxious and physiologically aroused we become when confronted by a task, the lower our self-efficacy expectations become. Many people, for instance, become anxious when confronted with mathematical tasks, which leads to weak performance on such tasks. The reduced performance and the anxiety result in lowered self-efficacy expectations regarding mathematics and the avoidance of mathematical tasks. As a result, individuals with mathematics-related anxiety may not develop interests in mathematically-related tasks and occupations and will not pursue mathematically-related goals.
- *Verbal persuasion*: Verbal persuasion is the last and weakest source of self-efficacy information to be discussed. The self-efficacy expectations of individuals regarding a particular task may be enhanced through verbal encouragement by parents, teachers or peers. The effect thereof is likely to be less powerful than direct success experiences or the observation of appropriate role models. Figure 3 provides a simplified graphical model of how different sources of self-efficacy information might impact on mathematics self-efficacy and interests.

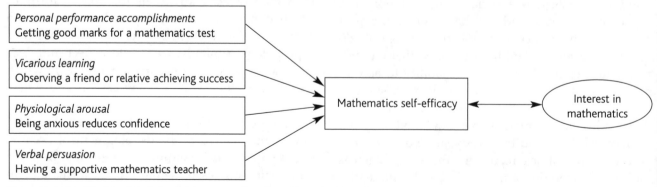

Figure 3 A simplified model of the development of mathematics self-efficacy and interests

The above discussion may suggest a one-directional causal relationship between self-efficacy expectations and vocational interests and goals, where individuals with high self-efficacy expectations in a particular vocational area will be more likely to pursue goals and to develop interests in that area. Recent research, however, shows that self-efficacy expectations and interests have a reciprocal relationship (Chartrand *et al.*, 2002; Rottinghaus *et al.*, 2003b). Individuals with strong interests in a particular area are more likely to attempt tasks in that area and to experience success.

One of the strengths of the social cognitive approach to career psychology is that it highlights the role of demographic and individual difference variables in the career choice process. Variables such as gender, socio-economic status, race and ethnicity interact with background and contextual variables to influence people's learning experiences. For instance, a boy from a poor rural area in South Africa may have fewer opportunities to be exposed to modern dance lessons than a girl from an affluent area in a major city. Hence, the boy from the rural area will be less likely to develop self-efficacy expectations and an interest in modern dance.

Conclusion

Lent *et al.* (1996) have emphasised that background and contextual variables may serve as perceived barriers in the career choice process. In the South African context, poverty, the lack of educational opportunities and appropriate role models, high unemployment rates, and poor proficiency in English, are often perceived to be career-related barriers (de Bruin, 1999; Subich, 1996). These barriers need to be taken into account when trying to describe and understand the career-related behaviour of South Africans. From this perspective we can easily see that Holland's person X environment fit theory is potentially limited in the South African context. In societies with high unemployment rates it is often more important for an individual to obtain any work than it is to obtain work that fits his or her personality type. Put differently, survival is more important than satisfaction. Hence, salient theoretical aspects of Holland's theory, such as congruence and consistency may be ignored when individuals make career-related decisions in conditions of poverty and high unemployment. This does not render the concepts of congruence and consistency completely irrelevant – even in conditions of high unemployment we would expect an individual who does find work to be more satisfied if the work corresponds with his or her personality type. Holland's theory may be especially helpful in describing and understanding the career-related choices and behaviour of individuals who have access to a reasonable education and who perceive that they can make choices regarding particular occupational fields.

Social cognitive theory is useful because of its emphasis on environmental factors in the development of vocational interests and career-related goals. The theory emphasises the role of learning in career development and provides guidelines for enhancing or developing vocational interests. For instance, it is often said that South Africa needs more students with an interest in mathematical and technology-related fields. Social cognitive theory helps us to understand that if schools have limited laboratories, poorly trained teachers and a lack of appropriate role models with whom learners can identify, then it will be difficult to produce learners with mathematical and technology-related interests and goals. This has important educational policy implications.

29.4 SITUATIONAL FACTORS AND CAREER CHOICE

Contextual approaches to career theory and practice have recently gained popularity (see Young *et al.*, 2002). Specifically, social constructionist meta-theories take a critical stance toward established ideas in career psychology by emphasising the role of history, culture, and language in the understanding of career. Social constructionist theorists and practitioners focus explicitly on career choice and development as a socially constructed rather than an individually constructed phenomenon. This raises interesting questions about the importance of individual agency in the career choice process. Are social, cultural and historical processes so powerful that they negate freedom and choice on the part of the individual?

Akhurst, J. & Mkhize, N.J. (1999). Career education in South Africa. In G.B. Stead & M.B. Watson (Eds.). *Career Psychology in the South African Context.* Pretoria: Van Schaik, pp. 163-179.

Bandura, A.L. (1986). *Social Foundations of Thought and Behaviour: A social cognitive theory.* Englewood-Cliffs, NJ: Prentice-Hall.

Betsworth, D.G., Bouchard, T.J., Jr., Cooper, C.R., Grotevant, H.D., Hansen, J.C., Scarr, S. & Weinberg, R.A. (1994). Genetic and environmental influences on vocational interests assessed using adoptive and biological families and twins reared apart and together. *Journal of Vocational Behavior,* 44:263-78.

Betz, N.E. & Hackett, G. (1981). The relationship of career related self-efficacy expectations to perceived career options in college women and men. *Journal of Counseling Psychology,* 28:399-410.

Chartrand, J.M., Borgen, F.H., Betz, N.E. & Donnay, D. (2002). Using the Strong Interest Inventory and the Skills Confidence Inventory to explain career goals. *Journal of Career Assessment,* 10:169-89.

De Bruin, G.P. (1999). Social cognitive career theory as an explanatory model for career counselling in South Africa. In G.B. Stead & M.B. Watson (Eds.). *Career Psychology in the South African Context.* Pretoria: Van Schaik, pp. 91-102.

Du Toit, R. & de Bruin, G.P. (2002). The structural validity of Holland's R-I-A-S-E-C model of vocational personality types for young black South African men and women. *Journal of Career Assessment,* 10:62-77.

Gelatt, H.B. (1989). Positive uncertainty: A new decision making framework for counselling. *Journal of Counseling Psychology,* 36:252-56.

Gottfredson, G.D. & Holland, J.L. (1990). A longitudinal study of the influence of congruence: Job satisfaction, competency utilization, and counter productive behavior. *Journal of Counseling Psychology,* 37:389-98.

Gottfredson, L.S. (1999). The nature and nurture of vocational interests. In M.L. Savickas & A.R. Spokane (Eds.). *Vocational Interests: Meaning, measurement, and counseling use.* Palo Alto, CA: Davies-Black.

Holland, J.L. (1997). *Making Vocational Choices: A theory of vocational personalities and work environments* (3rd edition). Odessa, FL: Psychological Assessment Resources.

Lent, R.W., Brown, S.D., & Hackett, G. (1996). Career development from a social cognitive perspective. In D. Brown, L. Brooks & Associates (Eds.). *Career Choice and Development* (3rd edition). San Francisco, CA: Jossey-Bass, pp. 373-421.

Lofquist, L.H. & Dawis, R.V. (1991). *Essentials of PersonXenvironment Correspondence Counseling.* Minneapolis, MN: University of Minnesota Press.

Meir, E.I., Melamed, S. & Dinur, C. (1995). The benefits of congruence. *Career Development Quarterly,* 43:257-66.

Mitchell, K.E., Levin, A.S. & Krumboltz, J.D. (1999). Planned happenstance: Constructing unexpected career opportunities. *Journal of Counseling & Development,* 77:115-24.

Naicker, A. (1994). The psychosocial context of career counselling in South African schools. *South African Journal of Psychology,* 24:27-34.

Rottinghaus, P.J., Betz, N.E. & Borgen, F.H. (2003a). Validity of parallel measures of vocational interests and confidence. *Journal of Career Assessment,* 11:355-78.

Rottinghaus, P.J., Larson, L.M. & Borgen, F.H. (2003b). The relation of self-efficacy and interests: A meta-analysis of 60 samples. *Journal of Vocational Behavior,* 62:221-36.

Stead, G.B. (1996). Career development of black South African adolescents: A developmental-contextual perspective. *Journal of Counseling & Development,* 74:270-75.

Stead, G.B. & Watson, M.B. (1999). Indigenisation of career psychology in South Africa. In G.B. Stead & M.B. Watson (Eds.). *Career Psychology in the South African Context.* Pretoria: Van Schaik, pp. 214-25.

Subich, L.M. (1996). Addressing diversity in the process of career assessment. In M.L. Savickas & W.B. Walsh (Eds.). *Handbook of Career Counseling Theory and Practice.* Palo Alto, CA: Davies Black, pp. 277-90.

Super, D.E., Crites, J.O., Hummel, R.C., Moser, H.P., Overstreet, P.L. & Warnath, C.F. (1957). *Vocational Development: A framework for research.* New York: Teachers College Press.

Young, R.A., Valach, L. & Collin, A. (2002). A contextualist explanation of career. In D. Brown, L. Brooks & Associates (Eds.). *Career Choice and Development* (4th edition). San Francisco, CA: Jossey-Bass, pp. 206-52.

Multiple choice questions

1. Which one of the following does Bandura regard as the most important source of self-efficacy information regarding a particular task?
   a) observing someone else achieve success
   b) reducing anxiety
   c) achieving success in the task
   d) encouragement from parents and teachers

2. Which one of the following is false?
   a) people seek out environments that match their personalities
   b) the better the match between a person and his or her job environment, the better the chance that he or she will be satisfied
   c) people will stay in a job if their personalities match the job environment
   d) people and environments influence each other

3. Which one of the following is false?
   a) Western theories of career choice and development are of no value in an African context
   b) Western theories of career choice and development are based on some assumptions that do not necessarily hold in an African context
   c) aspects of Western theories of career choice and development may shed light on career choice and development in an African context
   d) the assumptions on which career choice and development theories are based are irrelevant in the evaluation of such theories

4. Choose the correct option below. Contextual approaches to career choice and development place more emphasis on
   a) abilities
   b) interests
   c) self-efficacy expectations
   d) history, culture and language

5. In a rapidly changing world it is desirable to adopt a position of 'planned happenstance' or 'positive uncertainty'. Which one of the following is not a characteristic of these positions?
   a) conformity
   b) optimism
   c) curiosity
   d) willingness to take risks

6. Which one of the following is not characteristic of the social-learning approach to career choice and development?
   a) emphasis on genetic factors

   b) emphasis on the environment
   c) emphasis on learning
   d) emphasis on role models

7. Choose the incorrect option below. Congruence between an individual's personality and the work environment is likely to lead to
   a) job satisfaction
   b) job turnover
   c) job performance
   d) job retention

8. Below, four individuals are described in terms of their strongest preferences for Holland's personality types. Which one of these individuals shows the greatest degree of consistency in his or her preferences?
   a) SIR
   b) SAC
   c) SAE
   d) SEI

9. Which of the following personality types is most similar to the Social type?
   a) Investigative
   b) Enterprising
   c) Realistic
   d) Conventional

10. Choose the correct option below. A point of criticism against the social cognitive career theory from a behavioural genetic perspective is that it
    a) acknowledges the role of the environment
    b) neglects the role of the environment
    c) emphasises the interaction between person and environment
    c) overemphasises the role of the environment

Short answer questions

1. Explain how congruence between an individual's personality and his or her working environment can influence their degree of job satisfaction. Refer to Holland's model of vocational personality types and working environments.

2. Explain why Holland's theory does not necessarily work in the South African context, making reference to socio-economic factors such as poverty, unemployment and skills availability. Provide examples where possible.

3. Discuss the role of self-efficacy expectations and outcome expectations in the development of career interests. How do they differ and which of them

are likely to be more powerful in determining whether a person will perform a behaviour?

4. Explain how self-efficacy expectations might influence the development of vocational interests.

5. Explain how background and contextual variables could influence the development of self-efficacy expectations with special reference to the South African context. Focus on the five sources of self-efficacy information in formulating your answer.

30

Sport Psychology

Greig Whitton

CHAPTER OBJECTIVES

After studying this chapter the learner should be able to:
- identify the purpose and contribution of sport psychology
- distinguish between academic and applied sport psychology
- describe the broad scope of sport psychology with reference to specific 'sub-fields'
- identify critical, unique factors that impact on sport psychology in South Africa.

Introduction

Where did 'Baby' Jake Matlala find the confidence to challenge so many larger opponents? Are the Proteas mentally weaker than their Australian counterparts? What impact has Penny Haynes, as an inspirational role model, had on the motivation of young South African swimmers? Would Bafana Bafana have more team spirit if only locally-based players were selected? These are just some of the questions that sport psychologists try to answer.

The nature and purpose of sport psychology

Sport psychology is the study of the impact that psychological phenomena have on sport participation and performance (and vice versa) as well as the practical application of that knowledge (Weinberg & Gould, 2003). Traditionally, the scope of sport psychology has extended beyond sport to encompass physical activity more broadly. However, the emergence of health and exercise psychology as specialised fields has resulted in a blurring of boundaries, which is evident even today in sport psychology books, journals and education programmes. This chapter shall focus on sport psychology primarily in the context of sport, which might be defined as serious competition between participants engaged in an institutionalised physical activity with formalised rules and regulations (Nixon, 1984).

Both in theory and practice, sport psychology bridges the broader fields of kinesiology or sport science and psychology. Historically, there has been considerable debate (and even territorial conflict) as to whether sport psychology is a sub-discipline of sport science or psychology (Feltz & Kontos, 2002). However, training in *both* fields is a prerequisite for all-round sport psychology competence.

Sport psychologists involve themselves in three inter-related activities: research, education and practice. A distinction is often made between academic sport psychology (education and theoretical research) and applied sport psychology (practice and applied research) (Feltz & Kontos, 2002). Through their activities, sport psychologists make an important contribution towards:

- elite athletic performance (e.g., exceeding limits by developing untapped psychological potential);
- sport as business (e.g., enhancing franchise profitability via superior competitive success);
- sport as politics (e.g., developing the ambassadorial quality of international sporting icons); and
- spectator interest (e.g., reducing hooliganism and fan violence) (LeUnes & Nation, 2002).

Sport psychologists are usually certified by non-statutory organisations, like the Association for the Advancement of Applied Sport Psychology (AAASP), which set training standards and issue codes of conduct. Although certification with a professional body isn't always necessary, licensure (a legal process) is non-negotiable since 'psychologist' is a legally defined title. Of course, it is perfectly feasible to practise sport psychology by adopting a professional title that excludes the term 'psychologist' (e.g., 'Certified Consultant – AAASP', as issued by AAASP to those applicants who meet their stringent criteria) (LeUnes & Nation, 2002).

Despite the explosion of professional opportunities that has accompanied sport psychology's growing popularity, most sport psychologists make a living in academic settings and only consult on a part-time basis (LeUnes & Nation, 2002). Unfortunately, the image of applied sport psychology is still marred by charlatan practice as well as misconceptions about what professional sport psychologists actually do (in my own experience I have regularly had to reassure clients that I won't be hypnotising them or analysing their early childhood!). The glamorous vision of working exclusively with famous, world-class athletes is more fantasy than reality, and budding sport psychologists need to cultivate diligence, patience, self-belief and entrepreneurialism if they wish to work exclusively in an applied setting.

Current trends and possible future developments in sport psychology include:

- Integrating academic and applied sport psychology (e.g., the long-standing division between academic and applied sport psychology journals has recently been bridged by *Psychology of Sport and Exercise*, a journal that reflects academic and applied research).
- Encouraging a cross-disciplinary approach instead of maintaining traditional multi-disciplinary methods (i.e. collaborating with other kinesiology and psychology specialists instead of working in isolation).
- Applying sport psychology to non-sport sectors (e.g., youth life-skills and corporate productivity).
- Developing a broader conceptual framework through innovative approaches towards understanding psychological phenomena in sport (e.g.,

the escalation of qualitative research in sport psychology) (Feltz & Kontos, 2002; Weinberg & Gould, 2003).

Sport psychology in action: Academic research and applied practice

Motivation, 'mental toughness' and 'big match temperament' are concepts that are often erroneously thought to be synonymous with sport psychology. In truth, sport psychology goes far beyond 'psyching' athletes up! Figure 1 identifies some of the many issues that sport psychology addresses as well as its overlap with other disciplines. Categorising these issues into sub-fields is entirely arbitrary since, in reality, research and applied practice often cross different 'sub-fields'. Furthermore, there is very little consensus amongst sport psychology publications with respect to organising the field's body of knowledge. Nevertheless, these categories do provide a useful framework for seeing the sport psychology 'big picture'.

Performance enhancement: Arousal and anxiety

For decades, performance enhancement (i.e. improving athletic performance by using psychological skills) has been the cornerstone of sport psychology. To date, many introductory sport psychology publications still devote more attention to performance enhancement than any other 'sub-field' (see Table 1). Another common term for performance enhancement is Psychological Skills Training (PST) (Weinberg & Gould, 2003).

Figure 1 The field of sport psychology

Despite the dual impact of physical and mental attributes on performance, the emphasis in athletic training remains very much on physical preparation – even at an elite level (Weinberg & Gould, 2003). Ironically, when PST is embraced it is often mistakenly believed to be an elixir that can magically solve all problems and guarantee success. If only that were true! In reality, training of any kind (psychological or physical) can only maximise the chances of competitive success by optimising individual and team performance. Another common misconception is that PST is only for elite athletes. Actually, PST can benefit any sportsperson, of any age, participating at any level in any sport.

Although PST programmes will differ from one team or individual to the next, there are several core attributes underpinning consistent elite performance and well-established skills for developing these attributes (see Table 1).

Core attributes	Core skills
Composure	Arousal regulation
Confidence	Self-talk
Motivation and commitment	Goal setting and vision building
Concentration	Focus cues
Mental preparedness	Imagery
Team cohesion	Communication

Table 1 Core attributes and skills underpinning consistent elite performance

Arousal regulation is one of the most important of these skills because of an extremely common, and potentially debilitating, athletic experience: anxiety. It is very important to distinguish between anxiety and arousal since the two are often used interchangeably. Arousal is a broad continuum of physiological and psychological activation or energy. Anxiety, however, is a specific form of arousal: a negative emotional state characterised by worry, nervousness and physiological arousal or activation (Cashmore, 2002).

A distinction is often made between state anxiety (which is situation-specific and ever-changing) and trait anxiety (which is a relatively stable predisposition to experience state anxiety in a wide variety of situations). More recently, a second distinction has been made between cognitive anxiety (i.e. worry

and nervousness) and somatic anxiety (i.e. physiological arousal symptoms like an elevated heart rate, muscular tension, etc.) (Gould *et al.*, 2002).

Anxiety is usually the result of how we perceive the demands of a particular situation as well as how we perceive our ability to meet those demands (Weinberg & Gould, 2003). For example, while competing in an evenly-matched game of tennis, one player might be worried about losing and, as a result, experience high levels of anxiety. The other player, however, might be excited by the challenge and thrill of competing against someone of equal ability and, as a result, experience excitement instead of anxiety.

Not surprisingly, an enormous amount of research has been devoted to how arousal and anxiety affect performance. The first model, Drive theo-

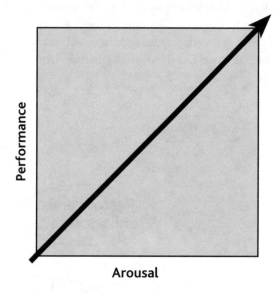

Figure 2 Drive theory

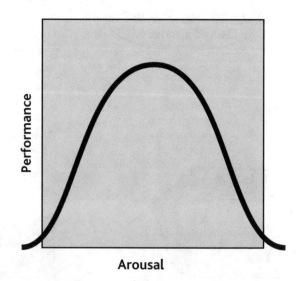

Figure 3 The Inverted U theory

ry, proposes a positive linear relationship between arousal and performance (Spence & Spence, 1966). According to this theory, the more 'psyched up' an athlete is, the better she or he will perform. Drive theory has long since faded into the annals of sport psychology history and currently receives little, if any, support. However, it did pave the way for future theories, the most enduring of which has been the Inverted U model.

According to the Inverted U theory, performance will increase with arousal to an optimal point – thereafter, performance will deteriorate as arousal continues to increase (Hebb, 1955). This model has received considerable support for many decades, but has been heavily criticised more recently (e.g., for failing to take into account individual differences). Despite this criticism, and in spite of its flaws, the Inverted U model still enjoys support for its simplicity and intuitive appeal. Until more advanced theories are conclusively validated, the Inverted U model will prevail. Future academic activity in this field will most likely involve testing more complex theories, researching the impact of individual variables

(personality, effort, self-confidence, etc.) and improving methodologies for evaluating arousal and performance (Gould *et al.*, 2002; Woodman & Hardy, 2001).

Regardless of the precise relationship between arousal and performance, too much anxiety can be debilitative by increasing muscular tension (thus, compromising co-ordination) and impairing attention (Weinberg & Gould, 2003). On the other hand, arousal can also bolster motivation and effort – particularly in the case of a highly confident athlete (Woodman & Hardy, 2001). Thus, regulating anxiety is a common goal for sport psychologists and usually involves a combination of several strategies:

- Identifying sensations and emotions that characterise optimal arousal so that individual athletes can better recognise when they are under- or over-aroused. This may also include evaluating anxiety and arousal levels using physiological measures (e.g., a heart rate monitor) and/or psychological instruments (e.g., the Competitive State Anxiety Inventory). A combination of both is often recommended to overcome their respec-

30.1 NEW DEVELOPMENTS, NEW DISAGREEMENTS

As already suggested, there are a number of competing theories in sport psychology. The relationship between arousal, anxiety and performance reflects this theme particularly well. In recent years, several new theories have been proposed as advances on, or alternatives to, the Inverted U model. Three of the most developed of these theories are presented here to illustrate how sport psychologists sometimes disagree:

- *Individualised Zones of Optimal Functioning (IZOF) theory*: The IZOF model is essentially an extension of the Inverted U theory in two important ways: firstly, it hypothesises that the inverted U will differ from one individual to the next as different athletes approach optimal performance at different locations along the inverted U curve. Secondly, the IZOF model proposes that optimal performance is associated with a zone of arousal rather than a single point – thus, athletic performance improves as athletes approach and enter their individualised zone of optimal arousal. Since its development, the IZOF theory has received considerable support; however, it has also been criticised for failing to identify the variables that account for individual difference (Hanin, 1980; Woodman & Hardy, 2001).

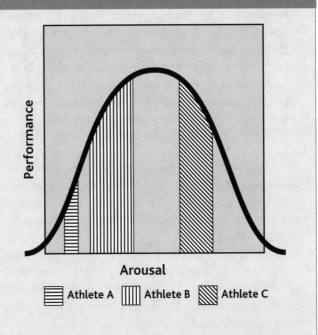

Athlete A   Athlete B   Athlete C

- *Multidimensional Anxiety Theory (MAT)*: MAT was developed in response to the distinction between cognitive and somatic anxiety. It hypothesises that cognitive anxiety shares a negative linear relationship with performance (i.e. performance decreases as cognitive anxiety increases) whereas somatic anxiety influences performance in the same way as the Inverted U model (i.e. somatic anxiety improves performance to an optimal point after which further somatic anxiety reduces performance) (Burton, 1988). However, MAT has not received much support (Landers & Arent, 2001a) and has been superseded by Catastrophe theory.

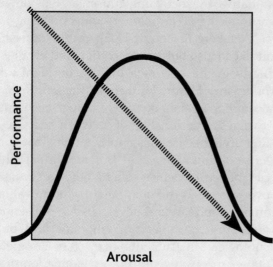

Arousal

- *Catastrophe theory*: Catastrophe theory is arguably the most complex anxiety-performance theory to date and is an extension of MAT. According to Catastrophe theory, somatic anxiety increases performance as per the Inverted U model if cognitive anxiety is low. If cognitive anxiety increases, then performance will increase further to an optimal point – thereafter, any further arousal will precipitate rapid performance deterioration (i.e. a catastrophe). Catastrophe theory has received some support but it is a difficult theory to test (Hardy, 1990).

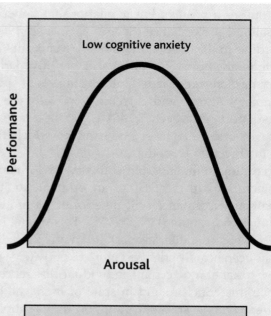

Low cognitive anxiety

Arousal

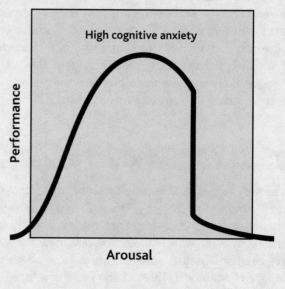

High cognitive anxiety

Arousal

tive weaknesses (e.g., physiological measures don't reflect whether one is anxious or excited; and, psychological instruments aren't always completed accurately or honestly!) (LeUnes & Nation, 2002).

- Educating athletes and coaches about the performance implications of being under- or over-aroused in order to dispel any misconceptions (such as the more 'psyched up' we are the better we will perform).
- Tailoring individual coaching strategies (e.g., de-emphasising event importance for athletes with high trait anxiety).
- Developing skills for regulating arousal and reducing anxiety (Weinberg & Gould, 2003).

A wide variety of techniques are available for reducing arousal (Weinberg & Gould, 2003). Arguably the most popular of these is Progressive Muscular Relaxation (PMR), which involves tensing and releasing muscle groups. PMR is particularly useful for developing an awareness of tense and relaxed states. Another powerful technique for developing arousal awareness and control is biofeedback. This involves observing the (usually electronic) monitoring of our autonomic functioning (heart rate, skin temperature, etc.) and learning how to exercise conscious self-regulation.

Probably the simplest relaxation technique is controlled breathing (consciously maintaining a smooth, deep breathing rhythm). A somewhat similar technique, rarely used today, is Autogenic Training. Essentially light self-hypnosis, Autogenic Training is designed to regulate specific physiological sensations (particularly warmth and heaviness of the muscles).

With such a smorgasbord of skills available, choosing which one(s) to use can be difficult. Athletes are often advised to select skills that match the nature of their anxiety (i.e. cognitive or somatic anxiety) (Williams & Harris, 2001). Thus, PMR or biofeedback might be used for a pounding heart and tense muscles, whereas Benson's Relaxation Response might be more appropriate in the case of worry and doubt.

Clinical sport psychology: Injury onset and recovery

Figure 4 The effects of physical athletic injury are often more than simply physical

While the emphasis in sport psychology may still be on performance enhancement, athletes can experience mental and emotional difficulties like anyone else. During the 1980s and 1990s, mental health began to receive increasing attention in sport psychology (Andersen, 2001). In many ways the division between performance enhancement and mental health reflects the divide between sport psychologists from a psychology background and those from a kinesiology background.

One of the consequences of sport psychology's dramatic growth has been a trend towards specialisation, with some sport psychologists choosing to specialise in counselling and/or clinical issues. A specialised clinical sport psychologist is usually preferable to a 'general' clinical or counselling psychologist because there are a number of mental health issues specific to sport. These include:

- *Identity absorption*: Athletes who prioritise sport to the point where it becomes the 'be all and end all' of their lives may experience a severe identity crisis if they are unable to participate (e.g., due to injury).
- *Eating disorders*: The root causes of anorexia and bulimia for athletes might differ from the general population.
- *Anger management*: Many sports (particularly contact sports) encourage aggressive behaviour which can spill over into non-sport settings.
- *Relationship difficulties*: Athletes are often away from their social networks for extended periods of time which can precipitate loneliness, depression and infidelity (Andersen, 2001).

Unfortunately, the boundary between performance enhancement and counselling is not always clear (Andersen, 2001). Sometimes performance enhancement can compromise mental health (e.g., imagery that may accidentally remind an athlete of a traumatic experience), and in extreme situations a choice may have to be made between the two (e.g., a gymnast with an eating disorder who is able to perform extremely well due to her low body weight). Conditions that might prompt referral include:

- a debilitative experience that transcends sport participation (e.g., an anxiety disorder – like social phobia – as opposed to a sport-specific anxiety experience);
- unusual and/or maladaptive emotional reactions (e.g., severe depression or aggression);
- failure of traditional sport psychology interventions (e.g., inability of relaxation techniques to reduce acute competitive anxiety); and
- issues raised by an athlete that are not performance related (e.g., relationship problems) (Andersen, 2001).

One of the most common athletic experiences that can lead to a person requiring counselling is injury (see Table 2). While injury may sometimes be perceived in a positive light (e.g., as an opportunity to focus on other areas of our life), it can also be seen as a disaster and provoke emotional distress, confidence loss and even identity crisis (Weinberg & Gould, 2003). Psychosocial factors are estimated to influence as much as 18 per cent of time lost due to injury (Smith *et al.*, 2000), and the stress associated with injury (e.g., fear of re-injury) can actually increase the likelihood of further injury due to heightened muscular tension and impaired awareness (Williams *et al.*, 2001).

Much of the sport psychology research into athletic injury has attempted to understand the psychological processes associated with injury onset. Early research focused on personality predispositions to injury but produced inconsistent results (interestingly, there has been a recent resurgence in personality research indicating that optimism, self-esteem, hardiness and anxiety may well play a role) (Weinberg & Gould, 2003). The most comprehensive model to date builds on the link between stress and injury vulnerability by proposing that several core factors (personality, history of stress and coping resources) mediate stress and, as a result, influence the likelihood of injury (Andersen & Williams, 1988).

A second important area of study has focused on psychological responses to athletic injury. Early models proposed a stage process whereby injured athletes passed through different stages characterised by distinct psychological responses. The most famous of these is the Kübler-Ross Grief Model that was adapted from counselling psychology (Williams *et al.*, 2001). However, these stage-based models have failed to garner empirical support and are criticised for being too rigid. More recent models, like that by Wiese-Bjornstal and colleagues, emphasise flexibility and a holistic perspective that integrates cognitive, emotional and behavioural variables (Udry & Andersen, 2002).

In an applied setting, the four primary goals of a clinical sport psychologist dealing with injury onset and recovery include:

- reducing the likelihood of injury onset;
- dealing with injury-related emotional distress;
- accelerating injury recovery time; and
- assisting in a return to full participation (see Table 2).

The relationship between stress and injury vulnerability implies that stress reduction is a viable strategy for reducing the likelihood of injury onset (Williams *et al.*, 2001). Thus, many of the relaxation skills discussed in the performance enhancement section are relevant for this purpose. When injury occurs it is obviously critical to support the athlete

Goal	Strategies
Reduce likelihood of injury onset by reducing stress	Relaxation skills
Deal with injury-related emotional distress	Support Education Recovery goals
Accelerate recovery time	Recovery goals Imagery Self-talk Relaxation skills
Assist in returning to full participation	Cognitive-restructuring

Table 2 Injury-related goals and strategies for clinical or counselling sport psychologists

and accurately educate him or her about the nature of the injury and the rehabilitation process (Weinberg & Gould, 2003). Once the athlete has come to terms with any emotional distress, it is imperative to set recovery goals immediately in order to accelerate recovery time.

Although it may sound far-fetched, the power of the mind to accelerate physical healing has been demonstrated in recent studies (Cupal & Brewer, 2001; Ievleva & Orlick, 1991). In these studies, athletes set recovery goals, practised healing imagery (i.e. creating vivid mental images of the injury healing) and used positive self-talk (e.g., replacing negative thoughts like 'my injury will never heal properly' with positive ones like 'every day I am getting better and better'). Relaxation skills can also enhance recovery by reducing rehabilitation pain (Weinberg & Gould, 2003).

When an athlete is preparing for a return to full participation, the clinical sport psychologist can play an important role in re-structuring any negative beliefs, expectations or attitudes (e.g., fear of re-injury or worry about performance ability). Self-talk and imagery are useful skills for accomplishing this by contributing to the shift from negative cognitions to constructive ones (e.g., visualising a successful return will bolster positive beliefs and expectations) (Weinberg & Gould, 2003).

Testing and assessment: Personality

Just as in most other fields of psychology, psychological evaluation is a time-honoured practice in sport psychology. Personality testing in particular

Figure 5 Testing the athletic personality can guide training

has lured sport psychologists for decades with the ambition of accurately identifying young sporting talent, selecting athletes for competition, developing training programmes and predicting success on the basis of personality profiling (LeUnes & Nation, 2002). The enormous volume of research devoted to personality in sport is highlighted by Fisher (1984) who located more than 1 000 studies.

Much of the personality research in sport psychology has been guided by developments in psychology more broadly. In both cases there has been very little consensus in attempting to define personality. For the purposes of this chapter, personality shall be considered the sum of characteristics that make us unique, including core variables that reflect who we really are (values, attitudes, interests, beliefs, etc.), typical responses (e.g., general optimism) and role-specific responses (e.g., an aggressive attitude when driving) (Weinberg & Gould, 2003).

The attention paid to personality in psychology has produced a wide variety of theoretical approaches. Those that have been most frequently applied in sport psychology include dispositional, interactionist and social cognitive approaches (Vealey, 2002). Much of the early personality research in sport involved dispositional theories which propose that personality is a collection of traits that are relatively consistent over time and across different situations. These studies focused mostly on profiling different athlete subgroups (e.g., athletes participating in different sports), identifying the relationship between traits and sport behaviour (e.g., attempting to predict success on the basis of certain qualities), as well as the impact of sport activity on traits.

Interactionist theories developed, in part, as a reaction to dispositional theories and contend that personality traits interact with situational factors to produce personality states that are temporary and which shift from one situation to the next (Weinberg & Gould, 2003). Studies involving state theories have focused mostly on the relationship between performance and our mental or emotional state. The IZOF model discussed earlier is an example of such research.

The next major shift was from global personality to specific, personality-relevant constructs (Auweele *et al.*, 2001). An important factor influencing this shift was the appreciation that personality is more complex than a neat list of descriptive qualities and that it interacts with core constructs like self-efficacy and perceived control. Social cognitive theories have been integral to this shift, and studies that have applied these theories include research into sport behaviour (e.g., persistence), differences between athlete subgroups (e.g., successful and less successful athletes), the impact of participation on personality, as well as stress and coping (Vealey, 2002). Although social cognitive theories have been dominant for the last two decades, it is debatable just how much of the research in this area is truly 'personality research' and how much is 'personality-related research'.

The conclusions that can be drawn from this vast body of research are not comforting for applied sport psychologists who favour personality profiling (Vealey, 2002). Firstly, no distinguishable 'athlete personality' has been shown to exist, no consistent trait personality differences between athlete sub-groups have been shown to exist, and no personality differences between successful and less successful athletes have been shown to exist (although successful athletes do differ from less successful athletes with respect to regulating personality variables like anxiety). Secondly, while sport psychology interventions can enhance performance and coping, they are less effective in altering personality variables. Finally, sport participation has not been found to enhance socially valued personality traits (in fact, it can actually encourage rivalrous, anti-social behaviour) and physical activity in general has little impact on personality traits (although it can enhance self-concept and reduce undesirable emotional states).

The most significant implication of these findings for applied sport psychologists is that personality testing for selection purposes is unsubstantiated and ethically questionable (Vealey, 2002). However, this does not mean that personality testing should never be conducted. On the contrary, insight into an athlete's personality can provide a valuable guide for customising

Although sport participation may not encourage valued personality traits, its impact on mental health makes it a viable alternative to traditional therapy interventions (Weinberg & Gould, 2003). The influence of physical activity on mental health is a major focus of health and exercise psychology. However, given that sport is a popular means of being physically active it is worth reviewing some of the core findings here.

Until recently, the possibility of physical activity benefiting mental health was considered with caution due to mostly inconsistent and methodologically flawed research (Landers & Arent, 2001b). However, the quality of research since the 1990s (especially the completion of large-scale epidemiological investigations, experimental studies and meta-reviews) has inspired a shift from caution to optimism.

Arguably the most significant mental health benefit of physical activity (and certainly the one that has received the most attention) is the reduction of anxiety and depression. Although a causal relationship has still to be conclusively established (i.e. we can't say for certain that physical activity directly reduces anxiety or depression) a relationship between physical activity and reduced anxiety or depression has nevertheless been validated which, in most cases, is comparable to other treatments such as psychotherapy (Landers & Arent, 2001b). This is notable not only in light of the worldwide prevalence of these disorders, but also with respect to their impact on quality of life and vulnerability to chronic medical conditions like cardiovascular heart disease, cancer and asthma (to name but a few) (Dishman & Buckworth, 2001).

The correlational relationship between physical activity and mood goes beyond reducing undesirable emotions (like depression and anxiety) – it also extends to enhancing positive mood (e.g., vitality and pleasantness). Support also exists for correlational relationships between physical activity and personality-related constructs (particularly elevated self-esteem and coping ability) as well as physical activity and cognitive functioning (e.g., memory and reaction time) (Weinberg & Gould, 2003). Although these relationships have not been as extensively studied as anxiety and depression, the research to date is encouraging in its support and will likely prompt future investigation (Landers & Arent, 2001b).

A variety of theories have been developed to explain how physical activity might influence mental health (Dishman & Buckworth, 2001; Weinberg & Gould, 2003). Physiological theories propose that elevated blood flow in the brain, the release of neurotransmitters (like endorphins), increased oxygen delivery to the brain, reduced muscular tension, and elevated body temperature might be responsible. Other psychological theories have suggested that perceived control, enhanced competency, social interaction, distraction from worries and fun are accountable. Unfortunately, many of these theories (including the popular endorphin hypothesis) have received mixed support at best (Landers & Arent, 2001b).

In general, regular low-moderate intensity exercise lasting at least 30 minutes has been associated with the most significant benefits (Weinberg & Gould, 2003). Although these criteria might exclude certain sports, this does not mean that such sports will not yield mental health benefits. It is also important to bear in mind some of the mental health dangers associated with exercise (Weinberg & Gould, 2003). These include negative exercise addiction (exercising to the detriment of our health, career, and/or relationships), burnout and eating disorders. Fortunately, these can be avoided with moderation and a balanced lifestyle.

psychological training (e.g., an athlete with high trait anxiety would likely benefit from relaxation training) (Weinberg & Gould, 2003). When personality testing is conducted, strict procedures need to be followed:

- personality testing must only be conducted by those who are licensed to do so and who are competent in using the relevant inventories in a sport context;
- those being assessed must be told why they are being evaluated, how the data will be interpreted and for what purpose the findings will be used;
- the confidentiality of the information regarding those being assessed must be ensured;
- clinical tests should be avoided in favour of sport-specific instruments; and
- personality inventories should not be relied on as the only assessment tool. Other processes (e.g., interviews and observations) should be included for comparison and validation (Vealey, 2002; Weinberg & Gould, 2003).

For many years personality research and testing have been considered 'dead', partially as a reaction

	Present stimulus	Remove stimulus
Positive stimulus	Positive reinforcement Example: awarding food vouchers or money for scoring a goal	Extinction Example: no longer paying attention to disruptive, attention-seeking behaviour
Aversive stimulus	Punishment Example: verbally humiliating an athlete for missing a tackle	Negative reinforcement Example: allowing an athlete who follows instructions to sit out of a gruelling training exercise

Table 3 Operant learning in sport

to the disappointment of failing to find distinct personality profiles that could accurately predict success or validate selection. However, a future revival is possible, especially as sport psychologists pay more attention to qualitative assessment methodologies (interviews, observation, etc.), shift their attention from deterministic models (i.e. predicting behaviour) to probability models (i.e. calculating the probability of different behaviours), narrow their focus to specific personality elements (e.g., anxiety and self-efficacy) and work with small (sometimes individual) case studies instead of attempting to sample large groups (Auweele *et al.*, 2001; Vealey, 2002; Weinberg & Gould, 2003).

Learning and skills development: Practice and coaching

Natural ability is rarely sufficient for a person to be successful in sport – skills development is nearly always equally important (if not more so!) Of course, learning and skill development goes far beyond sport psychology – it is a major component of psychology in general and integral to the field of motor control. In sport, practice structure and coach-

ing style are two of the most important learning processes.

Learning involves three phases: cognitive, associative and autonomous (Cashmore, 2002). The cognitive phase is characterised by an intellectual understanding of the skill to be performed and ought to be accompanied by a demonstration of the skill as well as specific feedback following practice. The associative phase involves practising the skill until it can be reproduced accurately and consistently. During this phase attention is not as tightly focused as in the cognitive phase and there is an increased environmental and strategic awareness which makes it possible to place greater emphasis on anticipation, selective attention and strategy. Finally, the autonomous phase is defined by skill mastery and automaticity (performing the skill 'on auto-pilot'). At this stage the priority training goals are motivation and skill maintenance, since any further significant technical improvement will be near-impossible (Fischman & Oxendine, 2001).

Fundamental principles of learning (like those described above; see also Table 3) have been carefully researched to determine the optimal conditions for practising sport skills and maximising technical development. In general, practice ought to include

Dimension	Format	Example (using soccer)
Sequence Random vs blocked	Random: intersperse different skills Blocked: practise skills sequentially	Random: rotate passing, tackling and shooting exercises Blocked: practise passing exhaustively – then move on to tackling or shooting
Context Variable vs constant	Variable: practise skills under different conditions Constant: practise skills under the same conditions	Variable: practise shooting with one, two or three defenders present Constant: practise shooting with only one defender present
Cohesion Whole vs part	Whole: practise skills in their entirety Part: practise skill segments independently	Whole: practise heading at goal as an entire sequence Part: practise running into space, timing the jump, and directing the header separately

Table 4 Multidimensional practice structuring

well-defined, challenging tasks, accurate feedback, freedom to correct errors and motivation to improve (Fischman & Oxendine, 2001). Practice can be structured around three dimensions: sequence (random versus blocked), context (variable versus constant) and cohesion (whole versus part) (see Table 4).

Random practice (interspersing different skills) has been found to be more beneficial than blocked practice (exhaustively completing skills sequentially). This is likely due to the elaborate mental processing that random practice demands (Fischman & Oxendine, 2001). Similarly, variable practice (practising the same skills under different conditions) has been found to be superior to constant practice (practising the same skills under the same conditions) – probably as a result of the diverse responses that variable practice generates. Deciding on whether to use whole practice (practising skills in their entirety) or part practice (practising skill segments separately) depends on the complexity of the skill, leaner ability, and the degree of similarity between individual skill segments and their completion within the skill as a whole.

As highlighted earlier, feedback is a critical component of the learning process and a powerful means of reinforcing sport behaviours like passing and shooting. Behavioural reinforcement is an area of psychology unto itself, and has been extensively researched and applied in sport psychology for the purpose of skills development. Arguably the most frequently used behavioural reinforcement process in sport is operant learning, whereby the consequences of behaviour influence the likelihood of the behaviour being repeated (Smith, 2001). This usually takes the form of punishment or positive reinforcement, with both of these strategies involving the presentation of a consequence (aversive in the case of punishment; positive in the case of positive reinforcement). However, operant learning can also involve removing consequences, be they aversive (negative reinforcement) or positive (extinction) (see Table 4).

Feedback is a reward because it taps into intrinsic motivational factors like pride and a sense of achievement. For example, being told that you improved your technique and successfully eliminated an important error would probably inspire a sense of pride and accomplishment – positive feelings that would reinforce the likelihood that you would continue to perform the technique correctly.

Traditionally, many sport coaches have relied on punishment as a means of improving performance through eliminating errors and other undesired behaviour. This is unfortunate because punishment:

- relies on fear and pain (which can result in unhappiness, frustration and/or depression severe enough to provoke even more undesirable behaviour);
- highlights what is not desired rather than what is desired; and
- indirectly encourages strategies like lying and cheating (to avoid being punished) (Matlin, 1999).

Due to these flaws, punishment often fails to achieve desirable, long-term behaviour change (although it can be successfully applied when critical, short-term change is needed). Thus, positive reinforcement is a preferred alternative, and can be optimised by systematically:

- identifying, and clearly defining, the desired behaviours;
- selecting the rewards that will have maximum reinforcing impact for each individual athlete;
- strategically linking the rewards to the desired behaviours such that they are customised for each individual athlete (it is important to reward processes (e.g., making a good pass) rather than outcomes (e.g., winning) since rewarding outcomes can indirectly reinforce undesirable behaviour (e.g., cheating));
- recording the behaviour of the athletes; and
- providing feedback to the athletes and presenting rewards as appropriate (Smith, 2001; Weinberg & Gould, 2003).

Initially, rewards should be consistently presented whenever the desired behaviour is produced. Over time, however, reinforcement needs to be gradually phased out to ensure that the athlete is intrinsically motivated and not dependant on the coach for extrinsic (i.e. external) reinforcement.

Sport psychology and the social world: Masculinity

Traditionally, sport psychologists have tended to focus on group dynamics, team cohesion, leadership, spectator effects and aggression when investigating social processes in sport. Very little attention is ever paid to gender. Some might argue that gender crosses over into sociology territory, however, sport psychologists regularly investigate issues that overlap with other fields (like motor learning).

Figure 6 Mainstream sport: A man's world?

Others contend that psychology is the study of *individual* behaviour, thoughts and feelings – yet it is impossible to fully understand individuals outside their social context. A more convincing explanation is that sport psychology's neglect of gender reflects the field of psychology more broadly and, unfortunately, the place of women in sport and in sport psychology (Gill, 2002).

If you think gender is not important in sport, consider the following questions:
• What are the nicknames of the South African *female* rugby, soccer and cricket teams?
• How many *female* South African athletes can you name who are currently competing in any sport?
• How many *women* do you know of who are involved in sports coaching, administration, refereeing or commentating anywhere in the world?

How would your answers compare if the questions were re-phrased to focus on men, rather than women? The obvious counter-response is that male athletes receive more attention (and thus are better known) because they are faster and stronger than their female counterparts. But why does sport have to revolve around speed and strength? Why can't it be about creativity, skill or fun? In truth, many modern sports were developed for the express purpose of preparing young men for their future social, political and occupational positions (Kidd, 1987). Thus, many sports were designed as an exclusively male domain that discouraged, prohibited and disadvantaged female participation (Kidd, 1987). This defensive opposition to female participation still operates today.

Gender theory and research have moved away from the notion of 'sex roles' (i.e. the assumption that biological differences determine social behaviour) towards an emphasis on the social construction of gender (Beal, 1996). Hence, the concept of 'doing gender' – a term which acknowledges that gender is an active process of social construction rather than a passively acquired quality or state (West & Zimmerman, 1987). Gender is also not a black and white distinction between 'masculine' and 'feminine' – it is a two dimensional continuum that includes androgynous and undifferentiated orientations (Gill, 2002).

	Low femininity	High femininity
Low masculinity	Undifferentiated	Feminine
High masculinity	Masculine	Androgynous

Table 5 Gender orientation

The concept of masculinity is broad, and each culture will have a masculine ideal that will not encompass the experiences of all men equally but will affect all men nonetheless through the social expectations associated with the ideal (Beal, 1996). From this develops the concept of 'masculinities' rather than 'masculinity' – the use of the plural recognises that there is no universal set of socially-expected masculine qualities (Carrigan *et al.*, 1987). Different masculinities stand in complex relations of dominance and subordination to each other (Anderson, 1999). Hegemonic masculinity is a term used to label the most powerful, culturally idealised masculinity at any given time (Connell, 1990).

It is important to bear in mind that sport is not monolithic: gender is created and resisted differently in different sports (Anderson, 1999). It is hypothesised that new sports, emphasising less dominance-oriented movements and encouraging an egalitarian ethos, will produce more pro-social masculinities (Prain, 1998; Wheaton, 2000). However, most studies on sport and masculinity have involved mainstream sports (like football, basketball and rugby) that have a history of excluding, or separating, women. Little research has been conducted on alternative or emerging sports (Anderson, 1999). Nevertheless, even these traditional, mainstream sports are capable of promoting more pro-social masculinities if the vocabularies, images, and values associated with them are reconstructed in accord with healthier, pro-social values (Coakley, 2001).

If alternative, progressive masculinities are to be constructed through sport, then it makes sense to target the youngest athlete populations possible. Physical education classes for school pupils are prime targets for such interventions because they are domains that often encourage dominance-oriented masculinities (Humberstone, 1990). However, by encouraging (not degrading) pupils and selecting activities that allow all pupils (boys and girls) to excel, physical educators can foster experiences and gender relations founded on collaboration, responsibility and support rather than aggression, competition and individualism.

Conclusion: Contemporary sport psychology in South Africa

Sport psychology has yet to fully establish itself in South Africa, and faces several critical challenges before it can do so. Arguably the greatest of these is licensure: the title 'sport psychologist' does not, in fact, have any legal existence in South Africa. In other words, you cannot legally refer to yourself as a sport psychologist, irrespective of your training or experience. Only a few specialised titles are legally acknowledged (e.g., clinical and research psychologist), and even these may disappear soon with the introduction of a new licensing process that will recognise only the term 'psychologist'.

This problem is compounded by the absence of a sound professional association, with efforts to establish one thus far not meeting with much support from sport psychologists themselves (Schomer, 1998). Without a South African equivalent of the American Association of Applied Sport Psychologists (AAASP), ethical standards or accreditation guidelines. Furthermore, they have no code of conduct, professional identity or common vision. Of even greater concern is that practitioners calling themselves 'sport psychologists' may actually have very little specialised sport psychology training (and, in some cases, no psychological training at all). Thus, with neither a licensing process that legally confers the specialised title 'sport psychologist', nor a professional body that accredits and regulates sport psychologists, athletes and coaches have no way of distinguishing between qualified sport psychologists and incompetent fraudsters!

A third challenge is the extreme difficulty involved with training to become a qualified 'sport psychologist'. Most South African educational institutions do not offer specialised sport psychology curricula, and those programmes that do exist are usually inadequate – especially with respect to practical experience. Consequently, it is suspected that

---

30.3 BEYOND MEN ... BEYOND GENDER

The importance of gender issues in sport was highlighted by a recent Sport and Recreation South Africa report that explicitly set the following objectives:

- ensuring that gender sensitive policies are integrated into sport and recreation structures;
- collating statistical information on the number of women involved in sport and recreation structures; and
- reviving WASSA (Women and Sport South Africa) to manage the sport and recreation needs of women.

Unfortunately, these objectives have enjoyed limited translation into practice. The report goes on to highlight only a few instances where any sort of significant action was taken (e.g., organising exposure for a campaign addressing violence against women at the PSL Coca-Cola Cup Final, and launching women's rugby to coincide with National Women's Day).

The lack of serious action is all the more deplorable given that accurate research, highlighting gender disparities in South African sport, has been available for many years. A comprehensive survey of women's participation in South African sport identified that:

- even though women comprise more than half of the national population, only 21 per cent of them participate in sport compared to 40 per cent of men;
- only 9 per cent of women who are involved in sport are serious competitors compared to 15 per cent of men;
- the most popular sports for women are netball, aerobics, tennis, road running, swimming and squash (none of which receive any kind of significant media exposure); and

- some of the most significant obstacles to being involved in sport (as perceived by women) include a lack of facilities, discrimination against female participants, low self-confidence, not knowing where to begin, a lack of role models and an absence of media coverage for female athletes.

At the same time, it is also important to recognise that gender is not developed in isolation – age, social class, sexual orientation and race support and inhibit opportunities to exhibit masculine and feminine qualities (Anderson, 1999). In South Africa, it goes without saying that racial issues are deeply ingrained and permeate all social institutions. Sport is, arguably, the most visible of these institutions. A recent colloquium on racism in sport, involving a number of national sport federations, set the following objectives:
- confronting and condemning racism;
- setting up infrastructures in disadvantaged areas;
- providing opportunities for, and visible access to, participation in sport for all South Africans; and
- setting targets for national and provincial representation.

Increasing the sport participation of marginalised groups (particularly Black, female and disabled South Africans) was also a headline objective of Sport and Recreation South Africa's most recent strategic plan. However, much like the issue of gender disparity, the talk and strategising that surrounds racial disparity in South African sport has not always been translated into significant, practical action. One of the most controversial examples of this is the decision taken by the United Cricket Board to abolish racial quotas despite failing to reach appropriate transformation targets (as determined by an accurate demographic analysis) or to sufficiently develop players of colour at a provincial level (Ministerial committee of inquiry into transformation in cricket, 2002).

Another controversial example is the decision taken by the South African Rugby Football Union and the African National Congress (ANC) to retain the springbok as the symbol of the national rugby team. During apartheid, the springbok was a potent symbol of racial

segregation and the ANC's attempt to confer new values upon it has only alienated the majority of its Black constituency while offending conservative Whites (Booth, 1998). The euphoria of the 1995 Rugby World Cup has long since died and it is notable that while the springbok endures, 'amabokoboko' and 'shosholoza' (two powerful symbols reflecting the national unity that the 1995 Rugby World Cup catalysed) have not.

Even more damning is the fact that, just like gender disparity, an awareness of racial disparity in South African sport is nothing new. Almost 10 years ago sport administrators highlighted the need to increase non-racial participation in sport and ensure that opportunities for, and access to, sport participation were available to all (Western Cape Department of Sport and Recreation, 1995). That these same needs are still being set as objectives today is indicative of a failure to successfully address racial disparity.

Clearly a comprehensive approach involving all stakeholders in South African sport (athletes, coaches, administrators, government, media, sponsors, etc.) is required to reverse the problems of gender and racial disparity. Sport psychologists can contribute to this process in several ways by:
- raising awareness about opportunities for marginalised groups to be involved in sport – be it as a social participant, serious competitor, coach, manager, commentator, referee or sports writer;
- educating marginalised groups about the practical processes associated with the above opportunities;
- developing the confidence and motivation of marginalised groups to be involved in sport;
- celebrating female and Black sporting champions (both past and present), and develop their influence as role models; and
- developing talented female and Black athletes who can command respect and status through sheer ability and success to the point where they can serve as powerful icons (like Steffi Graf, Anika Sorenstan, Tiger Woods and Muhammed Ali).

See www.srsa.gov.za and the linked documents and reports (especially www.srsa.gov.za/strategicframework.asp and www.srsa.gov.za/sportsrecreation.asp).

many practising 'sport psychologists' in South Africa hold clinical, counselling or research psychology degrees, with little (if any) academic exposure to sport psychology and/or kinesiology. However, this assumption cannot be verified due to the absence of a regulatory professional association.

Even when the above challenges are surmounted, 'sport psychologists' still face the difficulty of convincing sport managers and coaches that they can add value. There are still many misconceptions about what sport psychology entails as well as a conservative tendency to reject progressive

Figure 7 Sport and athletes in the new South Africa

approaches to athletic training in favour of familiar, 'tried and tested' methods. It is hoped that these trends will reverse as the media exposure that sport psychology increasingly receives provides 'sport psychologists' with opportunities to explain their profession and demonstrate their value.

Beyond these challenges, there are several other issues specific to South Africa that impact on sport psychology research and practice:

• *Cultural diversity*: It goes without saying that South African society is blessed with rich cultural variety.

However, while diversity can yield considerable benefits (e.g., innovative problem solving through alternative perspectives), it can also encourage stereotyping and discrimination. In any field of psychology (indeed, in any profession) it is critically important to respect the cultures of others and appreciate that behaviour, emotion, thought and interpersonal styles are powerfully influenced by our culture. This is especially relevant for sport psychology since sport is, arguably, the one South African social institution where different cultures

---

30.4 SPORT AND THE NATION

The importance of sport far exceeds competitive success! By transcending socio-demographic boundaries sport can have a significant impact on:

• international relations (e.g., building national friendships via globally televised sporting events like the 2003 Cricket World Cup that was staged in South Africa);

• national image (e.g., the professional and personal conduct of icons like South Africa's Ernie Els);

• nation building (e.g., building community bridges through national pride like the celebrations that swept South Africa following the success of the Springboks at the locally-hosted 1995 Rugby World Cup); and

• the economy (e.g., it is estimated that sport makes up 1.9 per cent of South Africa's GDP by directly contributing R11 billion and creating employment for 47 000 people).

Sport psychology can play a valuable role in the context of these benefits by contributing to the sport and recreation priorities explicitly set out by South Africa's national sport authorities. Some of these priorities that lend themselves to the input from sport psychologists include:

• motivating communities to develop active lifestyles (e.g., structuring community exercise programmes such that they maximise adherence);

• identifying and develop athletic talent (e.g., profiling talented young athletes and identifying development needs – like the ability to reduce competitive anxiety); and

• preparing elite athletes by designing high performance programmes (e.g., ensuring that South Africa's sportsmen and women are mentally and emotionally prepared).

See www.srsa.gov.za especially www.srsa.gov.za/strategicframework.asp.

intersect more frequently than any other. Thus, it is essential that sport psychologists actively familiarise themselves with the cultures of those with whom they work lest they isolate themselves from cultures other than their own or implement inappropriate interventions.

- *Language*: Sport psychologists must ensure that they can communicate clearly with their clients and that they respect those languages in which they are not proficient. It is critical to identify any irreconcilable language differences prior to implementing interventions, and if any such differences do exist then the client(s) ought to be referred to a sport psychologist proficient in the relevant language(s). Translation should only be considered as a last resort since it can necessitate extra time, compromise confidentiality and modify the intended meaning of the information that is presented.

- *Socio-economic heterogeneity*: South African society is characterised by a diverse spectrum of socio-economic environments. This heterogeneity can create logistical challenges for athletes and coaches, like transport difficulties or an inability to afford sport psychology services. Sport psychologists obviously need to be mindful of these difficulties – by ignoring them it is easy to become inaccessible and elitist. Socio-economic differences don't only apply to individuals – they extend to sports themselves. Rugby and cricket have traditionally been South Africa's wealthiest sports and enjoy well-established infrastructures. Other sports have fewer resources, and sport psychologists need to be logistically flexible (e.g., by adopting a sliding fee scale) if they wish to develop a diverse practice.

REFERENCES

Andersen, M.B. (2001). When to refer athletes for counselling or psychotherapy. In J. Williams (Ed.). *Applied Sport Psychology: Personal growth to peak performance*. Mountain View, CA: Mayfield, pp. 401-12.

Andersen, M.B. & Williams, J.M. (1988). A model of stress and athletic injury: Prediction and prevention. *Journal of Sport & Exercise Psychology*, 10:294-306.

Anderson, K.L. (1999). Snowboarding: The construction of gender in an emerging sport. *Journal of Sport & Social Issues*, 23(1):55-79.

Auweele, Y.V., Nys, K., Rzewnicki, R. & van Mele, V. (2001). Personality and the athlete. In R. Singer, H. Hausenblas & C. Janelle (Eds.). *Handbook of Sport Psychology*. New York: John Wiley & Sons, pp. 239-68.

Beal, B. (1996). Alternative masculinity and its effects on gender relations in the sub-culture of snowboarding. *Journal of Sport Behaviour*, 19(3):204-20.

Booth, D. (1998). *The Race Game: Sport and politics in South Africa*. London: Frank Cass.

Burton, D. (1988). Do anxious swimmers swim slower? Reexamining the elusive anxiety-performance relationship. *Journal of Sport & Exercise Psychology*, 10:45-61.

Carrigan, T., Connell, B. & Lee, J. (1987). Hard and heavy: Toward a new sociology of masculinity. In M. Kaufman (Ed.). *Beyond Patriarchy: Essays by men on pleasure, power, and change*. Toronto: Oxford University Press, pp. 139-94.

Cashmore, E. (2002). *Sport Psychology: The key concepts*. London: Routledge.

Coakley, J. (2001). *Sport in Society: Issues and controversies*. New York: McGraw-Hill.

Connell, R.W. (1990). An iron-man: The body and some contradictions of hegemonic masculinity. In M.A. Messner & D.F. Sabo (Eds.). *Sport, Men and the Gender Order: Critical feminist perspectives*. Champaign, IL: Human Kinetics, pp. 83-95.

Cupal, D.D. & Brewer, B.W. (2001). Effects of relaxation guided imagery, reinjury anxiety, and pain following anterior cruciate ligament reconstruction. *Rehabilitation Psychology*, 46(1):28-43.

DePauw, K.P. & Gavron, S. (1995). *Disability and Sport*. Champaign, IL: Human Kinetics.

Dishman, R.K. & Buckworth, J. (2001). Exercise therapy. In J. Williams (Ed.). *Applied Sport Psychology: Personal growth to peak performance*. Mountain View, CA: Mayfield.

Feltz, D.L. & Kontos, A.P. (2002). The nature of sport psychology. In T. Horn (Ed.). *Advances in Sport Psychology*. Champaign, IL: Human Kinetics, pp. 3-20.

Fischman, M.G. & Oxendine, J.B. (2001). Motor skill learning for effective coaching and performance. In J. Williams (Ed.). *Applied Sport Psychology: Personal growth to peak performance*. Mountain View, CA: Mayfield, pp. 13-21.

Fisher, A.C. (1984). New directions in sport personality research. In J.M. Silva & R.S. Weinberg (Eds.). *Psychological Foundations of Sport*. Champaign, IL: Human Kinetics, pp. 70-80.

Gill, D.L. (2002). Gender and sport behaviour. In T. Horn (Ed.). *Advances in Sport Psychology*. Champaign, IL: Human Kinetics, pp. 355-76.

Gould, D., Greenleaf, C. & Krane, V. (2002). Arousal-anxiety and sport behaviour. In T. Horn (Ed.). *Advances in Sport Psychology*. Champaign, IL: Human Kinetics, pp. 207-41.

Hanin, Y.I. (1980). A study of anxiety in sports. In W.F. Straub (Ed.). *Sport Psychology: An analysis of athlete behaviour*. Ithaca, NY: Mouvement, pp. 236-49.

Hanrahan, S.J. (1998). Practical considerations for working with athletes with disabilities. *The Sport Psychologist*, 12(3):346-57.

Hanrahan, S.J., Grove, J.R. & Lockwood, R.J. (1990). Psychological skills training for the blind athlete: A pilot program. *Adapted Physical Activity Quarterly*, 7(2):143-55.

Hardy, L. (1990). A catastrophe model of performance in sport. In G. Jones & L. Hardy (Eds.). Stress and Performance in Sport. Chichester, England: Wiley, pp. 81-106.

Hebb, D.O. (1955). Drives in the C.N.S. (conceptual nervous system). *Psychological Review*, 62:243-54.

Humberstone, B. (1990). Warriors or wimps? Creating alternative forms of physical education. In M.A. Messner & D.F. Sabo (Eds.). *Sport, Men and the Gender Order: Critical feminist perspectives*. Champaign, IL: Human Kinetics, pp. 201-10.

Ievleva, L. & Orlick, T. (1991). Mental links to enhanced healing. *Sport Psychologist*, 5(1):25-40.

Kidd, B. (1987). Sports and masculinity. In M. Kaufman (Ed.). *Beyond Patriarchy: Essays by men on pleasure, power, and change*. Toronto: Oxford University Press, pp. 250-65.

Landers, D.M. & Arent, S.M. (2001a). Arousal-performance relationships. In J. Williams (Ed.). *Applied Sport Psychology: Personal growth to peak performance*. Mountain View, CA: Mayfield, pp. 206-28.

Landers, D.M. & Arent, S.M. (2001b). Physical activity and mental health. In R. Singer, H. Hausenblas & C. Janelle (Eds.). *Handbook of Sport Psychology*. New York: Wiley & Sons, pp. 740-65.

LeUnes, A. & Nation, J.R. (2002). *Sport Psychology: An introduction*. Belmont, CA: Wadsworth Thomson Learning.

Matlin, M.W. (1999). *Psychology*. Fort Worth, TX: Harcourt Brace College Publishers.

Ministerial committee of inquiry into transformation in cricket (2002). *Transformation in Cricket*.

Nixon, H.L. (1984). *Sport and the American Dream*. New York: Leisure Press.

Prain, V. (1998). 'Playing the man' and changing masculinities. In C. Hickey, L. Fitzclarence & R. Matthews (Eds.). *Where the Boys Are: Masculinity, sport and education*. Victoria, Australia: Deakin Centre for Education and Change, pp. 55-66.

Schomer, H. (1998). Letter to the editor. *Sport Psychology Bulletin*, 11:3.

Sherill, C., Gilstrap, T., Richir, K., Gench, B. & Hinson, M. (1988). Use of the personal orientation inventory with disabled athletes. *Perceptual & Motor Skills*, 80(5):740-44.

Smith, R.E., Ptacek, J.T. & Patterson, E. (2000). Moderator effects of cognitive and somatic anxiety on the relation between life stress and physical injuries. *Anxiety, Stress & Coping*, 13:269-88.

Smith, R.E. (2001). Positive reinforcement, performance feedback, and performance enhancement. In J. Williams (Ed.). *Applied Sport Psychology: Personal growth to peak performance*. Mountain View, CA: Mayfield, pp. 29-38.

Spence, J.T. & Spence, K.W. (1966). The motivational components of manifest anxiety: Drive and drive stimuli. In C.D. Speilberger (Ed.). *Anxiety and Behavior*. New York: Academic Press, pp. 291-326.

Udry, E. & Andersen, M.B. (2002). Athletic injury and sport behaviour. In T. Horn (Ed.). *Advances in Sport Psychology*. Champaign, IL: Human Kinetics, pp. 529-54

Vealey, R.S. (2002). Personality and sport behaviour. In T. Horn (Ed.). *Advances in Sport Psychology*. Champaign, IL: Human Kinetics, pp. 43-82.

Weinberg, R.S. & Gould, D. (2003). *Foundations of Sport and Exercise Psychology* (3rd edition). Champaign, IL: Human Kinetics.

Western Cape Department of Sport and Recreation (1995). *Executive summary of draft rainbow paper on sport and recreation*.

West, C. & Zimmerman, D.H. (1987). Doing gender. *Gender & Society*, 1:121-51.

Wheaton, B. (2000). 'New lads'? Masculinities and the 'new sport' participant. *Men & Masculinities*, 2(4):434-56.

Williams, J.M. & Harris, D.V. (2001). Relaxation and energizing techniques for regulation of arousal. In J. Williams (Ed.). *Applied Sport Psychology: Personal growth to peak performance*. Mountain View, CA: Mayfield, pp. 229-46.

Williams, J.M., Rotella, R.J. & Schozer, C.B. (2001). Injury risk and rehabilitation: Psychological considerations. In J. Williams (Ed.). *Applied Sport Psychology: Personal growth to peak performance*. Mountain View, CA: Mayfield, pp. 456-71.

Williams, J.M. & Straub, W.F. (2001). Sport psychology: Past, present and future. In J. Williams (Ed.). *Applied Sport Psychology: Personal growth to peak performance*. Mountain View, CA: Mayfield, pp. 1-12.

Woodman, T. & Hardy, L. (2001). Stress and anxiety. In R. Singer, H. Hausenblas & C. Janelle (Eds.). *Handbook of Sport Psychology*. New York: Wiley & Sons, pp. 290-318.

Multiple choice questions

1. Worry, apprehension and nervousness are characteristics of
   a) arousal
   b) cognitive anxiety
   c) somatic anxiety
   d) static anxiety
2. According to the Inverted U model
   a) as arousal increases so performance improves
   b) as arousal increases so performance deteriorates
   c) somatic and cognitive anxiety influence performance in different ways
   d) as arousal increases so performance improves to an optimal point – thereafter, it deteriorates
3. Progressive Muscular Relaxation involves
   a) tensing and releasing different muscles
   b) controlling our breathing
   c) light self-hypnosis
   d) using electronic monitoring of muscular tension to develop arousal awareness and control
4. Athletes should not be referred to a clinical sport psychologist if
   a) they experience unusual and/or maladaptive emotional reactions like severe depression
   b) traditional sport psychology interventions prove ineffective
   c) they raise issues that are non-performance related
   d) they are going through a performance slump
5. Personality research in sport indicates that
   a) sport psychology interventions are an effective means of changing personality traits
   b) different sports produce different personalities
   c) sport participation can encourage anti-social personality qualities
   d) personality profiling can be used to predict success
6. Which of the following forms of exercise would likely have the most positive impact on our mood?
   a) walking
   b) weight training
   c) aerobics
   c) spinning (intense cycling)
7. A coach who is working with an athlete in the autonomous phase of learning should prioritise
   a) motivation and skill maintenance
   b) intellectual understanding
   c) team work and personal conduct
   d) strategic and environmental awareness
8. Telling an athlete, who is misbehaving to impress his team mates, to sit by himself away from the rest of the team is an example of
   a) punishment
   b) negative reinforcement
   c) classical conditioning
   d) extinction
9. Punishment should only be used when
   a) the coach is frustrated or angry with the team
   b) the team isn't winning
   c) critical, short-term behaviour change is needed
   d) the team is preparing for an important match
10. 'Doing gender' implies that
    a) gender is an active process of social construction
    b) different cultures have different gender ideals
    c) gender is biologically determined
    d) gender includes androgynous and undifferentiated orientations – not just masculinity and femininity

Short answer questions

1. What contributions do sport psychologists have to offer to sport?
2. Identify five of the core attributes that underpin consistent elite athletic performance.
3. How might a clinical sport psychologist assist an athlete who is recovering from injury?
4. What are some of the problems associated with hegemonic masculinity in sport?
5. How can sport psychologists correct gender and racial disparities in South African sport?

Part 9

Psychology and Health

Inge Petersen

Health psychology is one of the fastest growing areas of psychology world-wide, and with good reason. With the increase in chronic, degenerative illnesses and behaviour-related illness such as cancer, HIV/AIDS and substance abuse, it has become clear that it is no longer sufficient to think of health and illness only in terms of the functioning and malfunctioning of the body. There has been an increasing awareness of the links between psychological, social and cultural factors with the biochemistry and physiology of the body. Health psychology, through understanding the mind-body relationship and how this relationship influences why people become ill, how they respond to treatment and how they stay well contributes to improving health in many different ways. Health psychologists are concerned with the prevention and treatment of illness and disability, the promotion and maintenance of good health, coping and adapting to illness and disability and improving health care service delivery.

Scientific evidence from behavioural medicine has shown that there is a strong connection between mental and physical health. Thoughts, feelings and behaviours are now known to have a major impact on health. For example, people who are depressed are more likely to develop heart disease. Conversely, it is also realised that physical health influences mental health and well-being. People with persistent pain have, for instance, been shown to be four times more likely to have an anxiety or depressive disorder than those without pain.

Mental and physical health mutually influence one another in two fundamental ways: through the biochemical and physiological systems such as the endocrine and immune systems and/or through health behaviour. When people are anxious or depressed, their endocrine and immune systems may be compromised, thus increasing their susceptibility to physical illness. It is known, for instance, that stress is related to the development of the common cold. This relationship is explored in greater detail in Pillay's chapter on stress. Furthermore, as demonstrated in the chapter on nutrition, certain micronutrients, such as iodine, are essential to healthy cognitive development, with nutritional intake also being influenced by psychological and societal factors. Moreover, as illustrated in the chapter on HIV/AIDS, tuberculosis and parasitic infections, the disease process or parasitic infection itself can often impact on cognitive functioning.

Health behaviour, which refers to activities such as diet, exercise and sexual practices also plays an important role in shaping a person's health status. Health behaviour is an important influence on non-communicable diseases or health problems such as cardiovascular disease, cancers, injury, and substance abuse, but also plays an important role in the spread and control of infectious diseases, such as HIV/AIDS, tuberculosis, and parasitic infections.

Health behaviour has been found to be related to a number of psychosocial influences. A person's attitudes, beliefs and mental well-being have been found to play a major role in determining their health behaviour, be it engaging in high risk behaviour, their health-seeking behaviour or adherence to treatment. It has been found, for instance, that young people with depression are more likely to engage in high risk behaviour compared to those with no depressive disorder. In addition, health behaviour is influenced by interpersonal factors such as role modelling the behaviour of parents and peers, as well as by environmental and societal influences such as poverty and socio-cultural norms. These relationships are explored in greater detail in Govender and Petersen's chapter in this part on risk and risk behaviour.

Health psychology has contributed to the understanding of a wide variety of health conditions and behaviours. In this part, we also focus on issues which are of particular concern in sub-Saharan Africa: nutrition and under-nutrition, substance abuse, HIV/AIDS, tuberculosis (TB) and parasitic infections such as malaria and bilharzia.

Given that the field of health psychology is very broad, it is not possible in the scope of a text such as this to cover all aspects of the field. The chapters focusing on particular health issues are therefore designed to introduce the reader to different aspects of how the principles of health psychology can be applied:

- The chapter by Meyers and Bhana introduces substance abuse as an area in which psychologists can play an important role in the prevention of health problems. Prevention of disorder and health promotion at individual and broader social levels are core activities of health psychologists, and the field of substance abuse is one in which psychologists have been very active. Though it is certainly true that substance abuse affects development and psychological functioning, consideration of these issues is not a key concern of this chapter.

- The chapter by Richter and Norris on nutrition emphasises the impact that physical health can have on mental and social development. The important role that certain micronutrients and a healthy diet play in cognitive and psychosocial development is emphasised. The chapter also shows how psychological factors can affect nutritional status – as in the case of eating disorders such as anorexia nervosa.

- The chapter on HIV/AIDS, tuberculosis and parasitic infections demonstrates how, when we consider these complex conditions, we need to think about them simultaneously at a range of levels. We emphasise in this chapter the role played by psychology in the prevention, treatment and control of these conditions, and also consider some of the psychological and social consequences of the spread of these conditions. While there are many infectious diseases, HIV/AIDS, tuberculosis and parasitic infections are focused on, given that collectively these diseases contribute massively to death rates in the developing world, in spite of the fact that we know a great deal about how to prevent the conditions or to contain their impact.

Given that health and illness is understood as a product of the interaction of biological, psychological and social factors, medical and psychological strategies need to be accompanied by interventions at the community and societal levels, which address cultural and socio-economic barriers to health. Poverty as well as socio-cultural norms fuel many of the health problems covered by these chapters. Without addressing these issues as well, health promoting behavioural change interventions as strategies for prevention will be severely compromised, and at times a fruitless exercise. Learners are encouraged, when thinking about how psychology can be helpful in the health field, to think beyond the boundaries of this part of the book. The insights of Part 6 (Social Psychology) and Part 10 (Mental Health) should prove especially useful.

31

Understanding Risk and Risk Behaviour

Kay Govender & Inge Petersen

CHAPTER OBJECTIVES

After studying this chapter you should be able to:
- demonstrate an ecological-systems understanding of the concept of risk, risky behaviour and resilience
- demonstrate a theoretical understanding of key mechanisms or concepts that can be used to enable behaviour change in the promotion of mental health and well-being.

Nosipho had always been a fairly cautious person who tried to weigh up her options carefully before she took a risk of any kind. She didn't drink or smoke, and she tried to live a healthy life and to take care of her physical well-being. Sometimes, though, when she read articles in magazines and newspapers about the many different risks that might affect her health, Nosipho was just left feeling anxious. There seemed to be so much information and so many confusing rules about how to keep safe and fit these days. Reading this kind of material also sometimes left Nosipho feeling a bit guilty, as though if she got sick, it was her own fault for not taking proper care of herself. Having so much information about health and risk sometimes didn't feel helpful at all.

In spite of this information overload, Nosipho did believe that it was important for people to have accurate information about some of the serious health risks they faced and what they could do to avoid the problems. HIV/AIDS was a good example of a disease that could be prevented if people knew the risks and took better care of themselves. Nosipho knew, though, that a lot of her friends didn't really take the risk of HIV seriously. They knew all the facts, but they seemed to believe it could only happen to other people. She remembered one of her friends saying that she didn't have to worry because she didn't go out with the 'kind of people who had AIDS'. Nosipho knew this was nonsense. Anyone could get AIDS if they had sex without a condom! Nosipho had heard that some of the young men on campus would talk about how they didn't believe in condoms. They said that a condom wasn't 'manly' and they weren't afraid of anything. It must be very hard for their girlfriends to persuade them to use condoms – even when they were aware of the risks, Nosipho thought.

Introduction: What do we mean by risk and risk behaviour?

Smoking cigarettes, drinking large quantities of alcohol, overeating and having unsafe sex are a few of the common high-risk behaviours that people engage in. HIV/AIDS is the most prominent risk-related illness that confronts South African society. Infection with HIV can, however, be prevented largely by the adoption of safe sexual practices. This is clearly illustrated by the dramatic decrease in HIV infections in the gay community in San Francisco in the 1980s as a result of HIV/AIDS risk reduction programmes promoting condom use (Catania *et al.*, 1991).

Figure 1 The riskiest behaviour can be as simple as smoking, drinking too much alcohol and overeating

But there has been considerable resistance to the use of condoms in South Africa, particularly in 'intimate' or 'primary' heterosexual relationships because individuals are being challenged to negotiate its use where intimacy, trust and love are at issue (Wood & Foster, 1995). Therefore, managing safe sexual relationships can be a fragile process characterised by contradiction and anxiety, involving, at once, practices of risk reduction and risk opportunity.

In this sense we are often told that we live in a 'risk society' (a term coined by Ulrich Beck (1992)) in which experts increasingly disagree about what is dangerous and what should be considered risky behaviour, and how we should manage risk. Such disagreements have also interfered with combating HIV/AIDS, notably the conflicting discourses on the cause, treatment and behavioural management of the HIV/AIDS pandemic.

In the face of increasing fragmentation, and mistrust of expert systems to which people turn for advice, there is a heightened awareness of the physical and social dangers that we are exposed to in everyday life. The effect of this is that risk management strategies like negotiating safe sex, managing our diet or exposure to harmful substances are increasingly placing individuals as ultimately responsible for monitoring and managing the risk in their lives (Rhodes & Cusick, 2000). The 'dumping' of risk by expert systems into individual responsibilities, wherein individuals bear the anxieties of risk decision-making can, however, be problematic in situations where people do not have the freedom to control their lives. For example, it has been found that gender inequality and economic dependence render women less likely to be able to control whether they have safe sex or not (Jewkes *et al.*, 2003). Vulnerability to risk behaviour is determined by a number of risk factors at the biological, psychological and social levels. In this regard it is useful to distinguish between risk factors and risk behaviours.

In this chapter we explore why people sometimes behave in ways that can be perceived as harmful or risky to their mental and physical health. An ecological-systems approach (Brofenbrenner, 1986) understands vulnerability to high risk behaviour as being influenced by multiple contexts which can be broadly categorised into four levels of influence, namely the individual level, interpersonal level, community level and societal level. The interdependence of systems is visible in the permeable boundaries that separate one system from another.

Different perspectives at these four levels also provide strategies for reducing vulnerability to high risk behaviour and promoting healthy behaviour. These strategies can generally be split into person-centred and situation-centred interventions. Person-centred interventions work with individuals and groups to promote health protective behaviour which is also termed a resilience enhancing process. Situation-centred interventions are focused on creating more protective environments which enable individuals and groups to practice healthy behaviour.

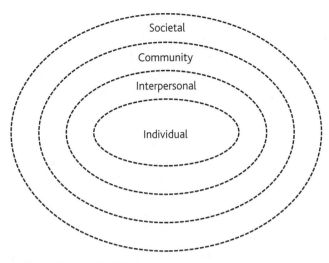

Figure 2 Four levels of influence

The individual level

The cognitive (mental) perspective is commonly used at the individual level for understanding risky behaviour. It is concerned with understanding individual characteristics that influence behaviour, such as knowledge, attitudes and beliefs. This perspective has a number of well known models that try to understand why individuals engage in risky behaviour that may be harmful to their physical and mental well-being. These include the Stages of Change Model (Prochaska & DiClemente, 1984), the Theory of Reasoned Action (Fishbein & Middlestadt, 1989) and the Health Belief Model (Becker, 1986).

The Health Belief Model (HBM) was one of the first models that adapted theory from the behavioural sciences to understand health problems, and remains one of the most widely recognised conceptual frameworks of health behaviour. The HBM focuses on five constructs that influence how a person will act in a given situation. Before a person engages in any behaviour he or she will consider the health risk of the situation in terms of the following concepts, which account for a person's 'readiness to act':

- *perceived susceptibility* or our opinion of the chances of getting the condition;
- *perceived severity* or our opinion of how serious a condition and its consequences are;
- *perceived benefits* or our opinion of the efficacy of the recommended action to reduce risk or seriousness of impact;
- *perceived barriers* or our opinion of the tangible and psychological costs of the advised action; and
- *self-efficacy* or our confidence in being able to successfully perform a behaviour.

While the cognitive perspective has been valuable in quantifying risk, it has been criticised for being too individualistic and assuming that people make 'rational' decisions. Most adolescents and some adults do not, however, approach risk-taking from a logical perspective that acknowledges that emotional and interpersonal factors, as well as economic and power relations in society, play an important role in

Figure 3 Unsafe sex is a high-risk behaviour

determining risk behaviour (Airhihenbuwa & Obregon, 2000).

The interpersonal level

This level is concerned with interaction between cognitive and interpersonal factors that influence behaviour. By interpersonal, we mean the nature of our interaction with other people in our social world. The Social Cognitive Model plays an important role in understanding behaviour at this level. The cornerstone of this model is the 'reciprocal determinism' between thought, behaviour and environment (Bandura, 1986). Rather than focusing on the automatic shaping of behaviour by environmental forces, this approach emphasises the importance of intervening thought processes (information acquisition, storage and retrieval) and self-efficacy in the performance of a behaviour. The Social Cognitive Model maintains that behaviour is determined by *expectancies* and *incentives*. Cognitive expectations are the beliefs about the likely results of an action in terms of rewards or punishments. Incentives or perceived rewards encourage a particular behaviour and are known as *positive reinforcements*. Negative reinforcement or *punishment* discourages a particular behaviour. Most learning occurs through *observational learning* or modelling, where people are likely to perform the behaviour they observe, particularly if the model is similar to themselves in age, gender or race, and when the behaviour results in a desirable social, psychological or material consequence. Furthermore, status persons, such as sports and music celebrities have been found to exert a stronger influence on behaviour than low status individuals (Bennet &

Murphy, 1997). In addition to outcome expectations that a certain behaviour will produce a given outcome based on observational learning is, however, *self-efficacy* expectancy, which refers to a person's conviction that they can perform a particular behaviour successfully.

The concepts used in the Social Cognitive Model have been applied to a recent study in KwaZulu-Natal which explored young women's understanding of risk for HIV/AIDS and teen pregnancy (see Box 31.3).

While individual and interpersonal factors are often taken into consideration in understanding

31.3 PEER GROUP EMPIRICAL STUDY

Procedure
This qualitative study used peer group discussions with school going girls in the rural Hlabisa district of KwaZulu-Natal.

Results
Access to money and gifts played an important role in young women's decisions to have sex with men. Risky sex was often driven by a desire for status and acquisition of luxuries, which young girls in poor communities could not afford. As one girl participant stated about her older boyfriend who was a taxi driver: 'He is quite old, but it doesn't matter, If he's right and has got the style, (wears fancy designer label clothes) it is okay, after all love has no age.' Clearly these girls were entering into sexual relationships with older and economically well off men because of the *expectant positive rewards* of material wealth and status. Girls were *modelling* the sexual behaviour of their peer group. Girls were *punished* by being beaten up or abandoned if they refused sex. On the other hand, some girl participants indicated that they would delay their sexual debut until they were adults. These girls obviously had a different role model for success. They demonstrated high levels of *self-efficacy* in practicing abstinence from sex during their teens. The *expectant outcome* of abstaining from sex was that they would not contract AIDS or be burdened with the role of being teen mothers during their school years.

Conclusion
People model certain behaviours because of perceived expectant material and psychological rewards (Harrison *et al.*, 2001).

high risk behaviour, the role of broader issues occurring at a community and societal level is often neglected. Mary Douglas in her influential work *Purity and Danger* is particularly critical of the dominant individualistic and interpersonal approaches taken by psychological researchers in risk perception research because of their focus on processes of cognition and individual choice. The cognitive model in particular has treated risk as an 'objective fact' independent of society. This modern, scientific understanding of risk has departed completely from the Middle Ages or pre-modern understanding, which viewed danger as a result of fate or *fortuna*, with risk excluding the idea of human responsibility and being perceived in terms of events beyond our control, for example, a storm, flood or epidemic (Giddens, 1990).

The community level

Whittaker and Hart (1996) note that people's social location is integral to the ways in which they conceptualise and deal with risk. Rather than responding as autonomous agents to the risks they perceive, people act as members of social networks. These networks mediate the capacity of these individuals to respond to high risk situations.

In this regard, community social networks can act as a protective factor. This protective factor has been widely termed as *social capital*, which means that membership of a social group or network secures certain benefits for an individual (Putnam, 1995). These benefits can be *relational and/or material*. Trust and reciprocity between members allow group members to draw favours, share socio-economic resources, circulate privileged information, and gain better access to opportunities (Portes, 1998). Communities with high levels of social capital are also better able to resist disruptive forces. They are more likely to identify external threats as a group problem and a threat to the survival of the group. Marginalised groups, as collectives, can sometimes mobilise effectively to pressure decision makers to address their concerns.

Public policies, such as that of apartheid, which enhance socio-economic inequities as well as disrupt the personal, domestic and community social networks of poor communities, render such communities particularly vulnerable to the development of high risk behaviours (Wallace, 1991). This occurs through a variety of interrelated mechanisms associated with a failure to socialise adolescents properly as well as compromising social controls which are used in most communities to minimise negative influences such as early sexual debut, teenage and/or unwanted pregnancy, sexual abuse, alcohol and drug abuse and criminal violence. A recent study in an informal settlement in KwaZulu-Natal, found that girls and women felt particularly vulnerable to sexual abuse given the lack of supportive community networks and controls in place to protect them (Petersen *et al.*, 2003).

In order to build relational ties, health promoters may promote *self-help* organisations, which promote a sense of community and empowerment of group members through sharing common problems and mutually giving and receiving help (Rappaport, 1985).

The societal level

Perspectives at this level take into consideration the broader role played by society in determining risk, and can be broadly categorised into the cultural and structural materialist approaches.

Cultural perspectives

Douglas (1985) contends that our cultural value systems are always brought to bear in the ways we judge risk or danger. So when people engage in activities they know to be labelled as 'risky', for example, having condom-less sex when unsure of the HIV status of a sexual partner, this behaviour cannot only be attributed to a poor understanding of the dangers of contracting HIV/AIDS through unprotected sex. For instance, in the face of high knowledge about HIV transmission, students have been found to report that they still engage in risky sexual practices (Petersen *et al.*, 2001). This is attributed to strong cultural beliefs that condom-less or 'flesh to flesh' sex is more pleasurable, a notion that is reinforced within a social system of shared conventions and cultural expectations of appropriate and acceptable sexual behaviour and what constitutes risk. Douglas (1985), in emphasising the cultural relativity of judgements about risks, also notes that there are differences between groups within the same culture in terms of what is considered a risk and how acceptable it is thought to be.

An illustration of how cultural beliefs become influential to understanding HIV/AIDS is provided in a study in Box 31.4. This investigation was

Procedure

A qualitative study using in-depth interview.

Results

The Shona people believe that a man who has sex with another man's wife will get a fatal disease called Runyoka. A married man places this permanent curse on his wife so that he can punish any other man who has an illicit sexual relationship with her. This affliction will only strike the guilty man and not the offending wife or her husband. Further, Runyoka is also believed to strike a man who breaks sexual taboos by having sex with a woman who is menstruating or has miscarried. A significant proportion of respondents (22 per cent) in this study believed that AIDS and Runyoka were the same disease.

Conclusion

The implications for sexual risk are obvious. Men may think that they will not get HIV if they have multiple partners, providing that they do not have sex with married women and adhere to the sexual taboos (Scott & Mercer, 1994).

conducted among the Shona people of south eastern Zimbabwe.

Structuralist perspectives

The structural and materialist critique of traditional cognitive and social learning theories is based on Marx's theory of material inequities and power imbalances in capitalist societies (Miliband, 1969). Beck (1992) suggests that significant sectors of society are more affected than others by the distribution and growth of risks, and that these differences are structured through inequalities such as class and position. At this level risk is much more pervasive than at the community or cultural level because systems of governance are at issue. The disadvantaged have fewer opportunities to avoid risks because of their lack of economic and political resources compared with the advantaged.

Lasch (1994) argues that a socially and economically privileged person has the resources to be more thoughtful of his or her actions with the purpose of changing behaviour. Social class, gender, ethnicity and position in the life course are important structuring factors that may not allow some people the

opportunity to have as much control over their actions as other people. We have to ask: How much of an opportunity does a young single mother have to consider her behaviour which may be putting her at risk for HIV, when her promiscuous boyfriend is her only source of income? Just how much freedom from structural poverty does this ghetto mother have to self-construct her own 'life narrative'?

In order to address power relations at a structural level, health promoters may facilitate empowerment of groups to challenge structures through two processes: *conscientisation* (Freire, 1970) and *social action* (Wallerstein, 1992). The first process enables members to develop skills to critically analyse their problems and to recognise the roles they may take in changing their social conditions. The second process of social action promotes participation of people in community efforts towards a common goal like improved quality of life, social justice and political efficacy.

The recent confrontation between the South Africa government and the Treatment Action Campaign (TAC) on the issue of provision of anti-retroviral therapy to People Living With AIDS (PLWAS), is illustrative of social action. The TAC's effective defiance campaign through public demonstrations, consciousness-raising activities and legal action has been effective in empowering PLWAS to pressure government to make anti-retroviral therapy more accessible to HIV positive people ('AIDS Drugs For All', *Mail & Guardian*, 11 October 2002).

Figure 4 Addressing social risk may require social action and protest

Conclusion

While the different levels of influence on risk behaviour have been explored separately, a fundamental principle of the ecological-systems approach is that there is a reciprocal relationship between the individual, interpersonal, community and societal levels of influence. Any intervention aimed at behaviour change should thus ideally address the influences maintaining the high risk behaviour at each level. Table 1 provides a risk-resilience matrix of examples of the different levels of influence, the theories or models covered, behaviour change mechanisms and how this is actioned at the intervention stage.

LEVEL	THEORY	BEHAVIOUR CHANGE MECHANISMS	TYPE OF INTERVENTION
Individual	Health Belief	Knowledge	Education
		Perceived susceptibility	Personalise circumstances of risk if low
	Model	Perceived severity	Specify consequences or conditions of risk
		Perceived benefits	Define action to take: how, where, when; clarify positive effects to be expected
		Perceived barriers	Reduce barriers through reassurance, assistance and incentives
		Self-efficacy	Provide training to increase confidence in performing a desired behaviour
Interpersonal	Social Cognitive	Reciprocal determinism	Focus on individual (cognitive) and peer group (social) to change the environment
		Expectations	Include information about the likely results of a behaviour
	Model	Modelling	Positive identity role models to emulate
		Reinforcement	Provide incentives, rewards, praise and self-reward
		Self-efficacy	Provide training to increase confidence in performing action
Community	Community Theory	Empowerment through mutual self-help organisations	Multisectoral development initiatives, self-help organisations
Societal	Cultural Theory	Understanding the mediating role of cultural beliefs in perceiving risk	Re-negotiate cultural beliefs that promotes high-risk behaviour at a collective level, while being sensitive to people's value systems
	Structural Theory	Conscientisation and social action	Community mobilisation, public awareness, demonstrations, protests marches, legal action. Leading to policy change, political, economic and legal reforms, resource allocation to disadvantaged or marginalised sectors and or societies

Table 1 The risk/resilience matrix

Airhihenbuwa, C. & Obregon, R. (2000). A critical assessment of theories/models used in health communication for HIV/AIDS. *Journal of Health Communication*, 5:5-15.

Bandura, A. (1986). *Social Foundations of Thoughts and Actions*. Englewood Cliffs, NJ: Prentice Hall.

Beck, U. (1992). From industrial society to the risk society. *Theory, Culture & Society*, 9:97-123.

Bennet, P. & Murphy, S. (1997). Cognitive mediators of health related behaviours. In P. Bennet & S. Murphy (Eds.). *Psychology and Health Promotion*. Buchingham: Open University Press, pp. 2-44.

Becker, M. (1986). The tyranny of health promotion. *Public Health Review*, 14:15-23.

Brofenbrenner, U. (1986). Ecology on the family as a context for human development. Research Perspectives. *Developmental Psychology*, 22:723-42.

Catania, J.A., Coates, T.J., Stall, R. & Bye, L. (1991). Changes in condom use among homosexual men in San Francisco. *Health Psychology*, 10:109-99.

Douglas, M. (1969). *Purity and Danger: An analysis of concepts of pollution and taboo*. London: Routledge.

Douglas, M. (1985). Risk acceptability according to the social sciences. *Social Sciences & Medicine*, 34(6):675-85.

Fishbein, M. & Middlestadt, S.E. (1989). A theory of reasoned action. Using the theory of reasoned action as a framework for understanding and changing AIDS-related behaviours. In V.M. Mays, G.W. Albee & S.F. Schneider (Eds.). *Primary Prevention of AIDS: Psychological approaches*. Newbury Park: Sage, pp. 93-110.

Freire, P. (1970). *Pedagogy of the Oppressed*. New York: Seabury Press.

Giddens, A. (1990). *The Consequences of Modernity*. Cambridge: Polity Press.

Harrison, A., Xaba, N., Kunene, P. & Ntuli, N. (2001). Understanding young women's risk for HIV/AIDS: Adolescent sexuality and vulnerability in rural KwaZulu-Natal. *Society in Transition*, 32(1):69-78.

Jewkes, R., Levin, J. & Penn-Kekana, L. (2003). Gender inequalities, intimate partner violence and HIV preventive practices: findings of a South African cross-sectional study. *Social Science & Medicine*, 56:125-34.

Lasch, S. (1994). *Economics of Signs and Space*. London: Sage.

Miliband, R. (1969). *The State in Capitalist Society*. London: Weidenfeld & Nicolson.

Petersen, I., Bhagwanjee., A. & Makhaba, L. (2001). Understanding HIV transmission dynamics in a university student population in South Africa: A qualitative systemic approach. *Journal of Psychology in Africa*, 11:144-64.

Petersen, I., Bhagwanjee, A., Bhana, A. & Mzimela, F. (2003). Urban regeneration in the era of HIV/AIDS. The case of Cato Manor. Paper presented at the *Urban Reconstruction and Cato Manor: Reflections on International Best Practice* conference. International Convention Centre, Durban, 22-24 January 2003.

Portes, A. (1998). Social capital: Its origins and applications in modern sociology. *Annual Review of Sociology*, 24(1):1-24.

Prochaska, J.O. & DiClemente, C.C. (1984). Stages and processes of self change of smoking: Toward an integrative model. *Journal of Consulting & Clinical Psychology*, 51:390-5.

Putnam, R.D. (1995). Bowling alone: America's declining social capital. *Journal of Democracy*, 6:65-78.

Rappaport, J. (1985). The power of empowerment language. *Social Policy*, 53:596-602.

Rhodes, T. & Cusick, L. (2000). Love and intimacy in relationship risk management: HIV positive people and their sexual partners. *Sociology of Health & Illness*, 22:1-26.

Scott, S.J. & Mercer, M.A. (1994). Understanding cultural obstacles to HIV/AIDS prevention in Africa. *AIDS Education & Prevention*, 6(1):81-9.

Wallace, R. (1991). Social disintegration and the spread of AIDS: Thresholds for propagation along 'sociogeographic' networks. *Social Science & Medicine*, 33(10):1155-62.

Wallerstein, N. (1992) Powerlessness, empowerment and health: implications for health promotion programs. *American Journal of Health Promotion*, 6:197-205.

Whittaker, D. & Hart, G. (1996) Research note. Managing risks: The social organisation of indoor sex work. *Sociology of Health & Illness*, 18(3):399-414.

Wood, C. & Foster, D. (1995). 'Being the type of lover ...' Gender-differentiated reasons for non-use of condoms by sexually active heterosexual students. *Psychology in Society*, 20:13-35.

Yun, H., Govender, K. & Mody, B. (2001). Factoring poverty and culture into HIV/AIDS campaigns: Empirical support for audience segmentation. *The International Journal for Communication Studies*, 64 (1):1-32.

Multiple choice questions

1. Risk factors refer to
   a) bio-psychosocial behaviours or environments that increase susceptibility to a specific disease or illness
   b) bio-psychosocial behaviours or environments that decrease susceptibility to a specific disease or illness
   c) both a and b
   d) none of the above

2. Risk behaviour refers to specific forms of behaviour which are proven to be
   a) associated with increased susceptibility to protective factors
   b) associated with increased susceptibility to a specific disease or ill-health
   c) associated with decreased susceptibility to a specific disease or ill-health
   d) both a and b

3. Vulnerability is defined as
   a) susceptibility to positive outcomes under conditions of resilience
   b) susceptibility to positive outcomes under conditions of risk
   c) susceptibility to negative outcomes under conditions of risk
   d) susceptibility to negative outcomes under conditions of resilience

4. Protective factors are those influences that
   a) limit the likelihood of high risk behaviour
   b) reduce the likelihood of non-risky behaviour
   c) reduce the likelihood of risk factors
   d) none of the above

5. Locate the appropriate categorisation
   a) individual (Heath Belief Model), interpersonal (Social Cognitive Model), community (Social Capital Model), societal (Cultural Model)
   b) individual (Heath Belief Model), interpersonal (Social Cognitive Model), community (Cultural Model), societal (Social Capital Model)
   c) individual (Social Cognitive Model), interpersonal (Heath Belief Model), community (Cultural Model), societal (Social Capital Model)
   d) none of the above

6. Perceived susceptibility is
   a) my opinion of your chance of getting a disease or illness
   b) my opinion of my chance of getting a disease or illness
   c) my opinion of other people's chances of getting a disease or illness
   d) other people's opinion of my chance of getting a disease or illness

7. Which statement is associated with the concept of perceived benefit?
   a) using a condom will protect me from contracting HIV/AIDS
   b) I feel confident in using a condom
   c) I find it difficult to talk to my sexual partner about using a condom
   d) I currently use a condom

8. Which statement is associated with the concept of positive reinforcement?
   a) young girls have sex because they fear being beaten by their older boyfriends
   b) young girls abstain from sex because they fear punishment from their parents
   c) young girls have sex with older men because of money
   d) none of the above

9. Social capital refers to
   a) membership of a social group or network secures certain benefits for the member
   b) membership of a social group or network marginalises the member from certain benefits
   c) membership of a social group or network allow the member to act more independently
   d) none of the above

10. Conscientisation means
    a) the action towards a common goal
    b) ability to think critically about one's circumstances
    c) a and b
    d) none of the above

Short answer questions

1. What are risk factors and risk behaviours?
2. What are protective factors?
3. What do resilience enhancing interventions attempt to do?
4. What are the main criticisms of the models of understanding risk behaviour at the individual and interpersonal levels?
5. Why is it important to consider culture in understanding risk behaviour?

32

Stress

Basil Pillay

CHAPTER OBJECTIVES

After studying this chapter you should be able to:
- define stress
- understand the psychophysiology of stress
- understand the relationship between stress and illness
- be familiar with stress reduction methods.

Nosipho and her friends often used the word 'stress' to describe what they were feeling when things were getting them down in some way or other. But, although she had used it so often in conversation, Nosipho hadn't given a great deal of thought to what it really meant. But as she learned about the concept in her psychology course, she was able to identify more clearly the ways that the mind and body reacted to demanding circumstances.

Nosipho found exams difficult and would get very nervous in the weeks before they started. On the day of the actual exam she often had sweaty palms and would feel her heart beating faster. Sometimes she even had difficulty breathing, but if she deliberately tried to slow her breathing down, this seemed to help a little. In between exams she felt less panic, but still felt tense and irritable. She would often end the day with a headache and a stiff neck and shoulders. By the end of the exam period she would feel exhausted, almost like she had run a marathon. Then, just as she should be celebrating that the exams were all over, Nosipho would inevitably come down with a cold or flu. It always seemed so unfair!

Nosipho wished that she didn't react so badly to exams. Most other people worried about them a little, but they seemed to be able to place them in some kind of emotional perspective. Nosipho wondered what it was about her that made her especially vulnerable to this particular stressful experience. On the other hand, she had friends who got stressed over issues to which she hardly paid any attention. One friend said she found new relationships very stressful while another found driving home from university in the rush hour traffic left her feeling on edge and irritable. Nosipho knew, of course, that some people also had much more serious issues that caused stress in their lives. There were people who worried about whether they had the money to feed their children or had to think of how to look after a family member who was very ill. If she looked around her it seemed that many people had to deal with a great deal of stress and pressure in their daily lives and Nosipho wondered what sorts of long term effects this might have on how they felt both emotionally and physically.

Introduction

Stress has become synonymous with modern living and lifestyle. In fact, it is probably one of the most frequently used words in daily conversations. Even if not directly expressed it is often alluded to by phrases such as 'chill out', 'relax' or 'take it easy'. Everyone has sometimes, if not often, experienced the negative feelings associated with everyday pressures, deadlines, disappointments, losses and disruptions. The effects of stress directly affect our functioning and are responsible for many of the problems that we experience: health, occupational, relationships and accidents. The concept has become increasingly popular, as can be seen from the burgeoning attention the subject receives in popular magazines and on radio and television. There has also been a phenomenal increase in the availability of self-help books and workshops to assist both lay people and professionals understand, cope, manage and prevent this growing problem. No wonder stress has been as dubbed the 'millennium malady'.

The term 'stress' has been used to describe a variety of negative feelings and reactions that accompany threatening or challenging situations. Generally, stress is a set of physiological, psychological and behavioural reactions that serves an adaptive function (Franken, 1994). Hans Selye (1982) points out that few people define the concept of stress in the same way or even bother to attempt a clear-cut definition. According to him, an important aspect of stress is that a wide variety of dissimilar situations are capable of producing the stress response such as fatigue, effort, pain, fear, and even success. This has led to several definitions of stress, each of which highlights different aspects of stress. Traditionally, stress research involved the body's reaction to stressors and the cognitive processes that influence the perception of stress. According to this definition, stress refers to physiological and psychological responses or reactions to certain situations, events or sets of circumstances that require an extraordinary response. These stressors may be demanding life events (e.g., death, job loss, divorce or a motor vehicle accident), chronic situations (e.g., unemployment, poverty or illness) or catastrophic events (e.g., hijackings, assault, rape, floods or fires).

Another approach to defining stress has been to focus on the relationship or interaction between the individual and environment that places excessive demands on the individual's resources (Lazarus & Folkman, 1984). According to this view, known as the Transaction Theory of stress, the cognitive appraisal of stress is a two-part process which involves a primary appraisal and a secondary appraisal by the individual. *Primary appraisal* involves the evaluation of an event as stressful. If the event is appraised as stressful, it is then evaluated as a harm or loss, a threat, or a challenge. A harm or loss refers to an injury or damage that has already taken place. A threat refers to something that could produce harm or loss. A challenge refers to the potential for growth, mastery, or some form of gain. These categories are based mostly on the individual's prior experiences and learning. Also, each of these categories generates different emotional responses. Harm or loss stressors can elicit anger, disgust, sadness or disappointment. Threatening stressors can produce anxiety, and challenging stressors can produce excitement. This theory helps to integrate both the motivational aspects of stress and the varying emotions that are associated with the experience of stress.

Secondary appraisal occurs after the assessment of the event is regarded as a threat or a challenge. During secondary appraisal, the individual now evaluates his or her coping resources and options. In order for an event to be appraised as a stressor, it must be personally relevant and there must be a perceived mismatch between the demands of a situation and our resources to cope with it.

A more comprehensive model that brings together the various approaches on stress is the bio-psychosocial model of stress (Bernard & Krupat, 1994). This model of stress involves three components:

- *External component*: The external component involves environmental events that precede the recognition of stress and can elicit a stress response. These are a variety of psychosocial stimuli that are either physiologically or psychologically threatening, commonly referred to as stressors.
- *Internal component*: The internal component of stress involves the psycho-physiological reactions to stress.
- *Interaction between the external and internal components*: The interaction between the external and internal components involves the individual's cognitive processes. In other words, this is the transaction theoretical view of stress.

However, not all stress reactions are negative. A certain amount of stress is essential to our health and performance. There is a strong correlation between stress and performance (See the stress curve in Figure 1).

Insufficient stress results in boredom and lack of stimulation. The optimal level of stress, called *eustress* or 'healthy stress', is necessary for optimal functioning, health and performance. Too much stress is referred to as *distress* and results in ill health, poor performance and dysfunctional behaviour.

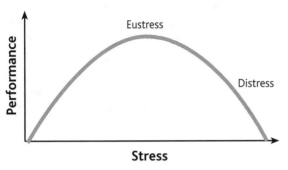

Figure 1 The stress curve

Stress can be acute, intermittent or chronic:

- *Acute stress (short-term stress)* is the reaction to an immediate threat, and results in the fight-or-flight response. It often involves a tangible threat that is readily identified as a stressor. The threat can be any situation, even those we are unaware of or falsely experienced as a danger. Under most circumstances, once the acute threat has passed, the fight-or-flight response becomes inactivated and levels of stress hormones return to normal. They are stressors of relatively short duration and are generally not considered to be a health risk because they are limited by time.

- *Intermittent stress* refers to responses to stressors that vary in duration, alternating between periods of stress and calm. If viewed as a challenge, it may improve our physiological resistance to stress by causing repeated, periodic increases in sympathetic arousal which conditions the body to better withstand subsequent stressors (resulting in 'physiological toughening' (Dienstbier, 1989)).

- *Chronic stress (long-term stress)* is typical of modern life which poses on-going stressful situations that are not short-lived, and the fight-flight reaction has to be suppressed. This results in stress that is chronic. Common chronic stressors include: on-going highly pressured work, long-term relationship problems, loneliness, and persistent financial worries. These stressors are of relatively longer duration and can pose a serious health risk due to their prolonged activation of the body's stress response. Chronic stressors are not readily identified as stressors because they are often ambiguous and intangible. Being part of modern life, they may be taken for granted and can therefore pose a serious health risk if they are not recognised and appropriately managed.

32.1 DOES STRESS EXIST?

This is a strange question to ask given that were have talked so much about stress in this chapter. However, not all people believe that stress exists. Some believe that researchers, in trying to study the phenomenon had to invent or devise a word, as an 'abstract linguistic device', to represent or explain hundreds of specific problems and difficulties which do really exist and which affect us from time to time.

What do you think? Having read the chapter thus far do you think that stress exists? Have you ever experienced stress?

As already mentioned, stress is associated with or linked to ill-health. When we consider mental illness it is implicitly believed that either stress significantly underlies or stressors trigger such illnesses. One example of a mental disorder that we frequently encounter in our country, because of the high levels of trauma, and strongly linked to stress is Post-traumatic Stress Disorder (PTSD).

In PTSD the person develops characteristic symptoms following exposure to an extreme traumatic stressor involving direct personal experience of an event or events that involve actual or threatened death or serious injury, or a threat to the physical integrity of oneself or others and in which the response to the traumatic event involves intense fear, helplessness, or horror (American Psychological Association, 2000).

The symptoms of PTSD are:

- The re-experiencing of the traumatic event, persistently in at least one of the following ways: Recurrent and intrusive distressing recollections of the event, including images, thoughts, or perceptions; recurrent distressing dreams of the event; acting or feeling as if the traumatic event were recurring (this includes a sense of reliving the experience, illusions, hallucinations, and dissociative flashback episodes, including those that occur on awakening or when intoxicated); intense psychological distress at exposure to internal or external cues that symbolise or resemble an aspect of the traumatic event; and physiological reactivity upon exposure to internal or external cues that symbolise or resemble an aspect of the traumatic event.

- The persistent avoidance of stimuli associated with the trauma and numbing of general responsiveness (not present before the trauma), as indicated by at least three of the following: efforts to avoid thoughts, feelings, or conversations associated with the trauma; efforts to avoid activities, places, or people that arouse recollections of the trauma; inability to recall an important aspect of the trauma; markedly diminished interest or participation in significant activities; feeling of detachment or estrangement from others; restricted range of affect (e.g., being unable to have loving feelings); and a sense of a foreshortened future (e.g., not expecting to have a career, marriage, children, or a normal life span).

- Persistent symptoms of increased arousal (not present before the trauma), as indicated by at least two of the following: difficulty falling or staying asleep; irritability or outbursts of anger; difficulty concentrating; hypervigilance; and exaggerated startle response (American Psychological Association, 2000).

Psycho-physiology of stress

Whenever there is a perceived threat the body reacts immediately in a sequence of psycho-physiological responses called the fight-or-flight response. This response is irrespective of whether the stressor is an actual threat (being held at gunpoint), being startled (balloon burst) or a new experience (roller coaster ride). The body automatically responds to the situation. Several systems and sub-systems get into action to deal with the threat. These involve the autonomic nervous system and endocrine system which together produce the response pattern referred to as the fight-or-flight response.

The autonomic nervous system

The autonomic nervous system is divided into two separate but interdependent systems – the *sympathetic* and *parasympathetic systems*, which generally have opposing functions. The sympathetic system is responsible for the arousal or 'stimulated' state while the parasympathetic system brings the body back to its rested state (Figures 3 and 4). The sympathetic system acts as a unit and is responsible for arousing neural and glandular function. This arousal involves an increase in heart rate, dilation of arteries of skeletal and heart vessels, constriction of arteries of the skin and digestive organs and activation of certain endocrine glands. The parasympathetic system acts relatively specifically and selectively in its activation of organs and is primarily concerned with the vegetative functions. It participates in digestion and serves to conserve and protect bodily resources (Ross & Wilson, 1985).

The endocrine system

The sympathetic system works in close association with the endocrine system. This interaction is import in understanding how psychological events are translated into physiological reactions. The endocrine system is made up of the following glands: pituitary, thyroid, parathyroids, islets of Langerhans, adrenal and gonads (Figure 4). The endocrine system is slow acting and controls body function and activity through chemicals called hormones. These hormones are secreted by the various endocrine glands into the blood stream, roving throughout the body and acting in various ways on different sites in the body (Ross & Wilson, 1985).

The hypothalamus through neuronal and secretary pathways is connected to the pituitary gland which controls the rest of the endocrine system. The hypothalamus signals to the pituitary gland to secrete two important hormones, namely adrenocorticotropic (ACTH) and thyrotropic (TTH). The ACTH acts on the adrenal glands producing adrenalin (epinephrine) and noradrenalin (norepinephrine). Adrenalin is sometimes referred to as the 'fear hormone', while noradrenalin as the 'anger hormone'. Here we see how a psychological factor plays a role in how the adrenal gland responds. Adrenalin interacts with organ receptor cells to increase heart rate and blood pressure and instruct the liver to release extra sugar. ACTH stimulates the outer layer of the adrenal glands (adrenal cortex) resulting in the release of corticosteroids which are important in metabolic processes and in the release of glucose from the liver.

The TTH acts on the thyroid to produce thyroxine which stimulates metabolism. High levels of thyrox-

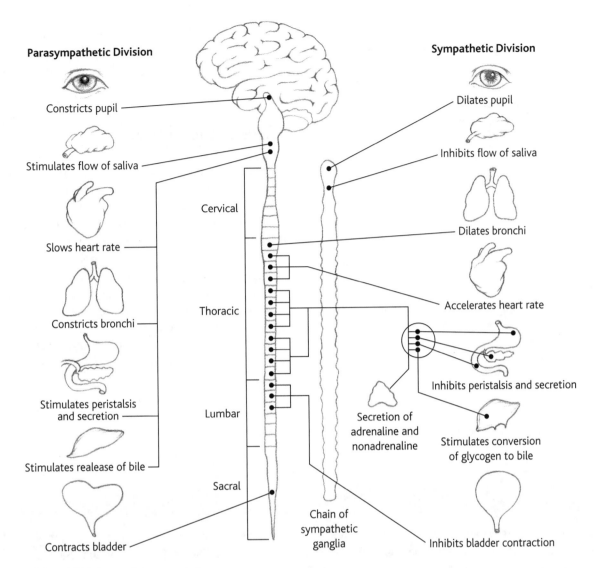

Parasympathetic Division

Constricts pupil

Stimulates flow of saliva

Slows heart rate

Constricts bronchi

Stimulates peristalsis and secretion

Stimulates realease of bile

Contracts bladder

Cervical

Thoracic

Lumbar

Sacral

Sympathetic Division

Dilates pupil

Inhibits flow of saliva

Dilates bronchi

Accelerates heart rate

Inhibits peristalsis and secretion

Secretion of adrenaline and nonadrenaline

Stimulates conversion of glycogen to bile

Chain of sympathetic ganglia

Inhibits bladder contraction

Figure 2 Functions of the autonomic nervous system
Source: Atkinson *et al.* (1987)

ine produce symptoms such as increased sweating, nervousness, shakiness, chronic fatigue and insomnia. However prolonged, the high level of hormones may disrupt homeostasis, harming internal organs and leaving the organism vulnerable to disease. ACTH also signals other organs to release hormones which are responsible for the body's adjustment and response to emergency situations. These play a major role in the body's immune responses. The most negative results of stress are its effects on the body's immune system. When the immune system is compromised the body is susceptible to infections and illness.

General Adaptation Syndrome (GAS)

The general reaction to stress is viewed as a set of reactions that mobilize the organism's resources to deal with an impending threat. Selye (1985) noted

that a person who is subjected to prolonged stress goes through three phases:

- *Alarm reaction*: is equivalent to the fight-or-flight response and includes the various psycho-physiological responses to a stressor.
- *Stage of resistance*: is a continued state of arousal. If the stressful situation is prolonged, the high level of hormones during this phase may damage internal organs, making the organism vulnerable to disease. Selye (1985) has noted that, in humans, many of the diseases precipitated or caused by stress occur in the resistance stage and he refers to these as 'diseases of adaptation'. These diseases of adaptation include headaches, insomnia, high blood pressure, and cardiovascular and kidney diseases. In general, the central nervous system and hormonal responses aid adaptation.

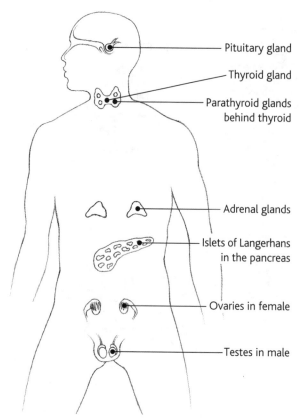

Figure 3 Location of the endocrine glands in the body
Source: Ross & Wilson (1985)

- *Exhaustion stage*: occurs after prolonged resistance. During this stage, the body's energy reserves are finally exhausted and breakdown occurs.

Stress and illness

There is compelling evidence that an inability to adapt to stress is associated with a number of mental and physical illnesses. Experimental and clinical evidence implicates stress as a major predisposing factor in depression and other severe psychiatric disorders (Leonard, 2002). The repeated release of stress hormones produces hyperactivity in the hypothalamus-pituitary-adrenal axis and disrupts normal levels of serotonin, the nerve chemical that is critical for feelings of well-being. Low serotonin levels are associated with depression (Lee *et al.*, 2002; Paykel, 2002). Stress has significant effects on the brain, particularly on memory, concentration and learning. Although some memory loss occurs with age, stress may play an even more important role than aging in this process.

32.3 MEASURING STRESS?

Stress is such a fashionable topic that we often find popular magazines include a questionnaire that readers may complete to measure their level of stress. Another device is the 'Biodot'. The biodot, available from book stores and retail outlets, is like a miniature thermometer that can measure the change in temperature at the surface of the skin. There is a correlation between stress and temperature change, the amount of temperature change depends on the stressor or problem and how you react to stress. If you would like to experiment visit the Timothy Lowenstein website (www.cliving.org/stress.htm) to learn more about biodots.

Are these reliable stress measures? These popular measures, although interesting, are not accurate ways to measure or 'diagnose' stress. These tests do not have the rigorous standards required of psychological tests. To accurately 'diagnose' stress a suitably trained health professional would usually take a comprehensive clinical history, undertake a mental status examination and may use one or more stress measures. Stress measurements fall into two categories: Checklists and biofeedback measures. Sometimes laboratory tests are done to

establish immune functioning. There are a number of stress checklists or inventories that have been used in research to measure stress. One of the popular checklists is the Holmes and Rahe (1967) Life Events Questionnaire. This questionnaire focuses on major life changes and weights them according to severity. Here is an example of the first 10 items and the weight assigned to each life event:

- Death of spouse   = 100
- Divorce   = 73
- Marital separation   = 65
- Jail term   = 63
- Death of close family member   = 63
- Personal injury or illness   = 53
- Marriage   = 50
- Fired at work   = 47
- Marital reconciliation   = 45
- Retirement   = 45

A checklist, the Stress Symptom Checklist recently developed by Schlebusch (in press), for the South African context, measures non-pathological stress by individuals responses on physical, psychological and behavioural reactions. Why don't you complete the Stress Symptom Checklist to see how many stress reactions you endorse.

THE STRESS SYMPTOM CHECKLIST

Name: _____

Make a ✔ if you experience the symptom often (i.e. at least once a week or more), and a – if you experience it sometimes (i.e. less than weekly, but at least monthly).

Do you experience:

PHYSICAL REACTIONS					
unusual tiredness		high blood pressure		unexplained nausea	
apathy/lack of enthusiasm		sexual problems		frequent indigestion	
breathlessness for no reason		unexplained headaches\pain		erratic bowel function	
feelings that your appearance has altered for the worse		feeling faint or unusually weak for no reason		excessive perspiration for no reason	
difficulty in relaxing		muscle tension		dizzy spells for no reason	
disturbing dreams/nightmares		feeling physically unwell		feeling tight-chested for no reason	

PSYCHOLOGICAL REACTIONS					
feelings of helplessness		feelings of disliking yourself		feelings that you are a failure	
feelings of depression		being afraid of disease		feeling you can't cope	
feelings that no one understands you		an increase in complaints about what happens to you		feelings that other people dislike you	
feelings of general anxiousness		low self-esteem/low opinion of yourself		feelings of confusion	
phobias (irrational fears)		feelings of being gossiped about		feelings of concern mainly for yourself	
awkward feelings when close to others		being over self-critical		feelings of frequent criticism	
feelings that you have failed in your role as a parent, spouse, child employee, employer		feelings that no one wants to work with you		feelings that you have been neglected or let down	
panicky feelings		feeling tense and keyed-up		feelings of loneliness and no one to talk to	
being upset by disease in others		persistent guilt		a lack of self-confidence	

BEHAVIOURAL REACTIONS					
memory loss/ forgetfulness		difficulty in making up your mind		disinterest in other people	
poor long-term planning		difficulty in showing/expressing your true feelings		suppressed or unexpressed anger	
poor concentration		worrying		fearfulness	
inconsistency		social withdrawal		poor decision-making	
inability to meet deadlines		making unnecessary mistakes		unco-operative relationships	
poor time management		the need to regularly work late		feeling disgruntled/moody/irritable	

procrastination	poor work quality	emotional outbursts	
the need to constantly take work home	difficulty in completing one task before rushing on to the next	greater use of alcohol, caffeine, nicotine, medicines to cope	
poor problem-solving skills	the need to cancel leave	fidgeting/ restlessness	
accident-proneness	nailbiting	unpredictability	
low interest in work	an excessive appetite	a loss o f appetite	
a drop in personal standards	engaging in frequent criticism of others	the need to cry for no reason	
increased aggressiveness	frantic bursts of energy	tics/nervous habits	
lack of interest in life	little sense of humour	sleep disturbances	

Rate the PRESENT INTENSITY of your stress somewhere along the scale below. Choose any number between lowest intensity (1) to highest intensity (10). Circle only one number along the scale below:

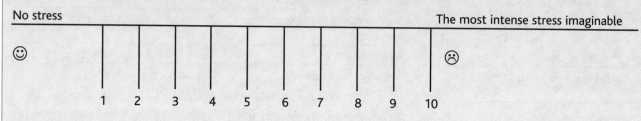

No stress · · · · · · · · · The most intense stress imaginable

1 2 3 4 5 6 7 8 9 10

Biofeedback involves using electronic instrumentation to obtain information about specific non-voluntary patho-physiological patterns (e.g., brain activity, blood pressure, muscle tension and heart rate) and training people to develop voluntary control to change these patterns in order to reduce or eliminate symptoms.

Stress has also been implicated in heart disease. The activation of the sympathetic nervous system affects many organs which negatively affect the heart in several ways. These include: the constriction of arteries posing a risk for blocking blood flow to the heart; the blood becoming stickier (possibly in preparation of potential injury) increasing the likelihood of an artery-clogging or blood clot; the release of fat into the bloodstream, raising blood-cholesterol levels; altering the heart rhythms and posing a risk for serious arrythmias in people with existing heart rhythm disturbances; and sudden increases in blood pressure which may, over time, develop injuries in the inner lining of blood vessels. Damage to the vascular system also increases the likelihood of stroke.

Chronic stress compromises the immune response and increases the risk for infections. Not only is one more vulnerable to infections but stress can exacerbate the symptoms. Some research has found that HIV-infected men with high stress levels progress more rapidly to AIDS when compared to those with lower stress levels. This is true of infections generally (Wootton & Sparber, 2001).

Stress has also been linked to gastrointestinal problems, such as Irritable Bowel Syndrome and peptic ulcers. In Crohn's disease or ulcerative colitis, stress is associated with symptom flare-ups. Other illnesses associated with stress include muscular and joint pain, headaches, sexual and reproductive dysfunction, skin disorders and allergies (Rice, 1998).

Stress reduction

There are a number of practical things that we can do to reduce stress, based on theory and research on stress. Firstly, a sound knowledge of stress helps us recognise and identify sources of stress. Secondly, healthy lifestyle changes should be considered, which include: regular exercise, a healthy diet (rich in a variety of whole grains, vegetables and fruits, low in fat and avoidance of excessive alcohol, caffeine and tobacco), restructuring priorities, increasing leisure and developing good social networks. A third aspect is engaging in healthy psychological behaviours such as discussing and expressing feelings of anger and frustration, being optimistic and keeping a balanced perspective on life. A fourth consideration is learning a relaxation technique. Relaxation lowers blood pressure, respiration, and pulse rates, releases muscle tension, and eases emotional strains. A combination of progressive relaxation and imagery seems most beneficial. If such changes do not contain the stress then professional help should be sought. Cognitive-behavioural therapy is probably the most effect psychological treatment for stress and stress-related illnesses.

Given the vast research on stress, it still appears to be predominantly a Western notion. For example, the lack of an equivalent term in African languages makes the understanding of this concept in these cultures difficult. Generally, the words used among African language speakers to describe stress are words employed to refer to broad or general negative emotional problems, depression, abuse, etc. Among younger African people the hybrid word 'istress' is being increasing used. Socio-cultural contexts certainly influence stress reaction and perception (Ahmad-Nia, 2002; Cuellar, 2002). Not only a better understanding of how various social and cultural structures influence and shape the individual's experience of stress is needed, but research should also focus on what events are perceived as stressful, what coping strategies are acceptable to use in a particular society and what is the acceptable way to assist. These issues pose serious questions in the understanding, recognition and management of stress in multicultural contexts.

Conclusion

Like Nosipho, we soon learn that 'stress' is more than a 'buzzword'. Stress, as we have discovered, is difficult to define because of the variety of meanings and connotations that are ascribed to the concept. While traditionally, stress research involved the body's reaction to stressors and the cognitive processes that influence the perception of stress, theories such as the transaction theory of stress and bio-psychosocial model of stress are more comprehensive in their approach and allow a better understanding of stress. Stress has important implications for human health and functioning. Therefore there is a growing concern that the pressures of modern living and burgeoning future developments will severely impact on our health and burden of disease. Based on theory and research, there are a number of practical things that can be employed to reduce stress. These include: gaining a sound knowledge of stress, adopting healthy lifestyle changes, engaging in healthy psychological behaviours, learning a relaxation technique and knowing when to seek professional help and advice.

REFERENCES

American Psychological Association. (2000). *Diagnostic and Statistical Manual of Mental Disorders* (DSM-IV-TR) (4th edition). Washington, DC: American Psychological Association.

Ahmad-Nia S. (2002). Women's work and health in Iran: A comparison of working and non-working mothers. *Social Science & Medicine*, 54(5):753-65.

Atkinson, R.L., Atkinson, R.C., Smith, E.E. & Hilgard, E.R. (1987). *Introduction to Psychology* (9th edition). New York: Harcourt Brace College Publishers.

Bernard, L.C. & Krupat, E. (1994). *Health Psychology: Biopsychosocial factors in health and illness*. New York: Harcourt Brace College Publishers.

Cuellar, N.G. (2002). A comparison of African-American and Caucasian-American female caregivers of rural, post-stroke, bed-bound older adults. *Journal of Gerontological Nursing*, 28(1):36-45.

Dienstbier, R.A. (1989). Arousal and physiological toughness: Implications for mental and physical health. *Psychological Review*, 96:84-100.

Franken, R.E. (1994). *Human Motivation* (3rd edition). Belmont, CA: Brooks/Cole Publishing.

Holmes, T.H. & Rahe, R.H. (1967). The social readjustment rating scale. *Psychosomatic Medicine*, 11:212-18.

Lazarus, R.S. & Folkman, S. (1984). *Stress, Appraisal and Coping*. New York: Guilford.

Lee, A.L., Ogle, W.O. & Sapolsky, R.M. (2002). Stress and depression: Possible links to neuron death in the hippocampus. *Bipolar Disord*, 4:117-28.

Leonard, B.E. (2002). Stress, norepinephrine and depression. *Acta Neuropsychiatrica*, 14:173-80.

Paykel, E.S. (2002) Which depressions are related to life stress? *Acta Neuropsychiatrica*, 14:167-72.

Rice, P.L. (1998). *Health Psychology*. New York: Brooks/Cole Publishing.

Ross, J.S. & Wilson, K.J. (1985). *Foundations of Anatomy and Physiology* (5th edition). London: Churchill Livingstone Edinbourgh.

Schlebusch, L. (in press). The development of a stress symptom checklist. *South African Journal of Psychology*.

Selye, H. (1982). History and present status of the stress concept. In L. Goldberger & S. Breznitz (Eds.). *Handbook of Stress: Theoretical and clinical aspects*. New York: The Free Press.

Selye, H. (1985). History and present status of the stress concept. In A. Monat & R.S. Lazarus (Eds.). *Stress and Coping* (2nd edition). New York: Columbia University Press.

Wootton, J.C. & Sparber, A. (2001). Surveys of complementary and alternative medicine: Part III – Use of alternative and complementary therapies for HIV/AIDS. *Journal of Alternative & Complementary Medicine*, 7(4):371-7.

Multiple choice questions

1. Stress may be seen as
   a) a variety of negative feelings and reactions that accompany threatening or challenging situations
   b) a set of physiological, psychological and behavioural reactions that serves an adaptive function
   c) the body's reaction to stressors and the cognitive processes that influence the perception of stress
   d) all of the above

2. Stressors may be
   a) demanding life events (e.g., death, job loss, divorce or motor vehicle accident)
   b) chronic situations (e.g., unemployment, poverty, illness)
   c) catastrophic events (e.g., hijackings, assault, rape, floods or fires)
   d) all of the above

3. Transaction theory of stress focuses on
   a) the relationship or interaction between the individual and environment that places excessive demands on the individual's resources
   b) the cognitive appraisal of stress
   c) both a and b
   d) interpersonal dynamics

5. Cognitive appraisal involves
   a) the evaluation of an event as stressful and an assessment of the coping resources and options
   b) rational assessment of a situation that may or may not be stressful
   c) secondary appraisal
   d) primary appraisal

6. The bio-psychosocial model of stress
   a) is a comprehensive model of stress
   b) involves three components: an external component, an internal component, and the interaction between the external and internal components
   c) involves the interaction between the external and internal components
   d) both a and b

7. Stress can be
   a) acute in that it is the reaction to an immediate threat, and results in the fight-or-flight response

   b) intermittent, namely a response to stressors that vary in duration, alternating between periods of stress and calm
   c) chronic which is typical of modern life which poses on-going stressful situations
   d) all of the above

8. The fight-or-flight response involves
   a) the body delayed reaction to psycho-physiological responses
   b) the body's automatic response to a situation
   c) the autonomic nervous system and endocrine system which together produce a response pattern
   d) b and c

9. Adrenocorticotropi (ACTH)
   a) is not an hormone
   b) is secreted by the pituitary gland
   c) stimulates the outer layer of the adrenal glands (adrenal cortex) resulting in the release of corticosteroids which are important in metabolic processes and in the release of glucose from the liver
   d) b and c

10. The General Adaptation Syndrome (GAS) refers to
    a) a set of reactions that mobilise the organism's resources to deal with an impending threat
    b) the alarm reaction, the stage of resistance and exhaustion
    c) a and b
    d) the fight-or-flight response and includes the various psycho-physiological responses to a stressor

11. Experimental and clinical evidence implicates stress as a factor in
    a) depression and other severe psychiatric disorders
    b) brain function, particularly on memory, concentration and learning
    c) heart disease and/or infection
    d) all of the above

Short answer questions

1. What is stress?
2. Explain the different categories of stress.
3. What is post-traumatic stress disorder?
4. How does stress impact on a person's health and functioning?

33

Understanding Substance Abuse

Bronwyn Myers & Arvin Bhana

CHAPTER OBJECTIVES

After studying this chapter you should be able to:
- understand the meaning of substance abuse
- demonstrate an understanding of the concept of continuum of problem severity, prevention and substance abuse
- show familiarity with multiple theories of the causes of substance use disorders
- explain and discuss risk, vulnerability, resilience and protective factors with regard to substance abuse
- outline how the risk, vulnerability, resilience and protective factors operate at multiple levels of influence, namely individual, interpersonal and environmental levels.

Nosipho had grown up in a household where nobody drank alcohol but, like most South Africans, she had already learned a great deal about drugs and alcohol by the time she was a teenager. Many of the kids at school drank beer on the weekends, and Nosipho had been told by her friends that it was really easy to buy drugs out on the street or even inside the grounds of her high school, if you wanted. Nosipho's school teachers spoke to them quite a lot about the dangers of drugs, but she knew that most of the class didn't take their warnings seriously. Some of the kids at school hadn't seemed to be affected very much by their drinking or even by taking drugs. Others, she could see as they got older, seemed to just get worse and worse. There was one boy who had been in her class who she knew had been smoking 'white pipes', a mixture of dagga and mandrax. He dropped out of school before the end of Grade 10, even though he had been one of the brightest kids in the class before he started smoking. She sometimes saw him sitting around on the side of the road with a group of young men who seemed to do little other than drink and smoke. 'What was it', Nosipho wondered, 'that turned some people into addicts?'

Since Nosipho had come to university she had also noticed how much drinking was regarded as a normal part of campus life. She would often overhear other learners talking about how much they had had to drink the previous night and everyone would laugh as they held their heads complaining of a 'hangover'. Most social activities on campus seemed to involve drinking and sometimes she felt a bit left out, like she was the only sober person there! Because drinking was such a normal part of many people's lives it was hard to know when it became a problem.

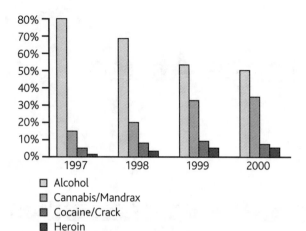

Figure 1 Alcohol and drug abuse in Cape Town using specialist treatment data (1997-2000)
Source: Parry *et al.*, 2001

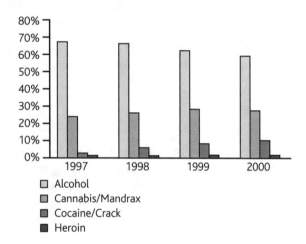

Figure 2 Alcohol and drug abuse in Durban using specialist treatment data (1997-2000)
Source: Parry *et al.*, 2001

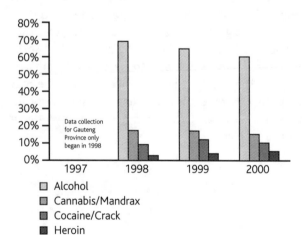

Figure 3 Alcohol and drug abuse in Gauteng using specialist treatment data (1998-2000). Data collection for Gauteng province only began in 1998
Source: Parry *et al.*, 2001

Introduction

Alcohol and drug use have been variously labelled in everyday usage and the professional literature. 'Alcoholism', 'alcohol dependence', and 'drug addiction' are some of the terms commonly used. The term 'substance use' is currently used to cover the broad spectrum of alcohol and drug dependence. It is useful to distinguish misuse from abuse and dependence:

- *Substance misuse* refers to a pattern of substance use that results in some adverse consequences, which are not recurrent (e.g., a single 'driving while intoxicated' charge).
- *Substance abuse* refers to a maladaptive pattern of substance use that manifests recurrently and has significant negative consequences. These consequences may include a failure to fulfil social roles, recurrent legal, social and interpersonal problems (American Psychiatric Association, 1994).
- *Substance dependence* refers to a cluster of cognitive, behavioural and physiological symptoms indicating that a person continues to use a substance despite significant substance-related problems. There is a pattern of repeated use that often results in tolerance, withdrawal and compulsive drug taking behaviour (American Psychiatric Association, 1994).

Conceptual understandings of substance dependence

Historically, conceptual understandings of substance dependence have been dominated by categorical thinking that viewed substance dependence as either present or absent (Miller, 1996). Researchers have since argued that substance use behaviour occurs on *a continuum of problem severity*. That is, substance use behaviour ranges from non-problematic (recreational) use, through misuse, to substance abuse and finally substance dependence (Institute of Medicine, 1990).

Different stages of problem severity require different types of interventions (Figure 4). The more severe the problem, the less likely a person is able to return to non-problematic use. For such individuals, the primary goal of treatment should be abstinence. In contrast, the less severe the problem, the more likely the person is able to maintain non-problematic use. For these individuals, a goal of treatment could be controlled use.

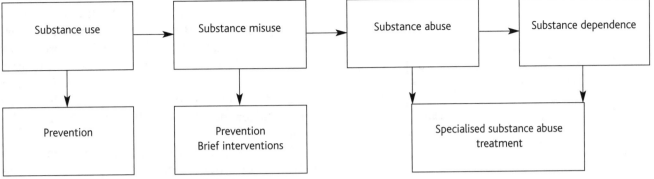

Figure 4 The continuum of substance use behaviour

Understanding the causes of substance use disorders

Numerous theories have tried to identify the causes of substance use disorders. Some theories have examined *intra-personal* factors that may lead to the development of substance use disorders. Other theories have identified *interpersonal* factors that play a role in the formation of substance use disorders. The role of *environmental* factors in the etiology of substance use disorders has also been explored. To date, no single cause has been able to fully explain the development of substance use disorders. It is now widely recognised that substance use disorders have multiple causes.

33.1 THE CAUSES OF DISORDERS

Intra-personal factors
Those factors that are located within the individual such as biological or psychological causes.

Interpersonal factors
Those factors that are located between individuals such as peer influence and social learning experiences.

Environmental factors
Those factors that are located within a particular environment such as a culture of drug use, high availability of alcohol in a particular community.

The risk and resilience approach to substance use disorders among adolescents

It is generally recognised that initiation of use of alcohol and drugs occurs at about the onset of adolescence. The recognition that there are multiple factors that place an adolescent at risk for developing a substance use disorder led to the adoption of a risk factor approach (see Chapter 31 for definitions of risk, vulnerability, resilience and protective factors) to understanding substance use among adolescents (De Wit & Silverman, 1995). This approach assumes that substance use disorders have a number of causes (Newcomb *et al.*, 1987), and that as the number of risk factors increases, the risk of an individual developing a substance use disorder also increases (Cosden, 2001).

Risk of developing a substance use disorder, however, is mediated by *protective factors* that provide adolescents with the *resilience* to withstand the pressures of living in a risky environment (Cosden, 2001; De Wit & Silverman, 1995). Risk and protective factors are thus seen as two conceptually distinct dimensions that together form part of the larger construct of *vulnerability* to substance use (Cosden, 2001; Weinberg, 2001). The greater the number of risk factors in relation to protective factors, the greater the likelihood that a person will engage in substance use behaviour (Weinberg, 2001). *Risk factors* thus tend to predict the increased likelihood of vulnerability to substance use. In contrast, protective factors predict a decreased likelihood of vulnerability to substance use. It should be noted that protective factors act to buffer the probability of drug use occurring only in high risk environments (Amaro *et al.*, 2001; Weinberg, 2001).

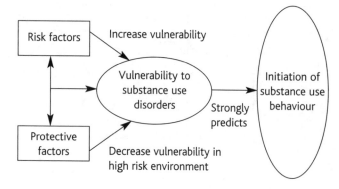

Figure 5 A vulnerability model of substance use disorders

Individual, interpersonal and environmental etiological factors

As mentioned, researchers have identified multiple sets of risk and protective factors that operate at the level of the individual, at the level of interpersonal functioning, and at the level of the environment (Amaro *et al.*, 2001). The following sub-sections examine factors implicated in the development of substance use disorders for each level of functioning.

Factors located at the level of the individual

Biological factors

The possibility of a genetic predisposition to developing alcohol and other drug (AOD) problems has been widely investigated through the use of family, adoption and twin studies. A recent review of controlled family studies reported that the risk for developing alcohol dependence was three times greater among first degree relatives of alcoholics than controls, and the risk for developing drug dependence was two times greater among first degree relatives of alcoholics than controls (Merikangas & Avenevdi, 2000).

A review of adoption studies also reported that individuals whose biological parents were alcoholics were two-and-a-half times more likely to develop alcohol-related problems, regardless of their home environment, than control subjects (Merikangas, 1990). Later adoption studies also reported that children whose biological parents were substance dependent were more likely than controls to develop a substance use disorder (Cadoret *et al.*, 1996).

Twin studies have compared monozygotic (MZ,

identical) twins and dizyogtic (DZ, fraternal) twins to establish the extent to which substance use disorders are hereditary. Heath *et al.* (1997) reported that two-thirds of the risk for developing alcohol-related problems was genetically mediated, with the remainder of the risk being determined by environmental factors not shared by the two members of the twin pair. Kendler and Prescott's (in Weinberg, 2001) study of MZ and DZ twins found heritability for substance dependence of up to 80 per cent in some populations. There appears to be significantly greater heritability for substance dependence than for substance abuse, and significantly greater heritability for substance abuse than for non-problematic use (Merikangas & Avenevdi, 2000).

Genetic linkage studies have also provided evidence of a genetic predisposition to alcohol use disorders. The isolation of specific genes that influence susceptibility to alcohol use disorders may help in identifying people at great risk for developing a substance use disorder (Bierut *et al.*, 2000).

There seem to be two major neurological processes that contribute to the development of substance dependence. Occurring together, *reinforcement and neuroadaptation* seem to underlie both the acute response to AODs and the establishment of long-term tolerance, craving and withdrawal characteristic of substance dependence. Some of these neuroadaptive changes may be permanent (Koob & Lemoal, 1997). The extended amygdala in the basal forebrain region appears to play an important role in the reinforcing activities of AODs.

33.2 REINFORCEMENT AND NEUROADAPTATION

Reinforcement
Reinforcement refers to the presence of a rewarding stimulus or the relief of an unpleasant sensation that increases the probability of a particular behavioural response (such as AOD use).

Neuroadaptation
Neuroadaptation refers to the compensatory adjustment the brain makes in an attempt to continue normal functioning despite the presence of AODs.

Psychological factors

A number of personality traits have been identified as risk factors for substance use disorders.

Individuals with high levels of novelty and sensation seeking seem to be at risk for the development of substance use disorders (Wills *et al.*, 1994). People with high levels of disinhibition, characterised by low levels of behaviour control and high levels of impulsivity also appear to be at risk for substance use disorders (Amaro *et al.*, 2001; Griffin *et al.*, 2000; Weinberg, 2001). Other personality factors associated with the initiation of AOD use are an external locus of control (Amaro *et al.*, 2001) and a low self-esteem (Amaro *et al.*, 2001).

Deficits in psychosocial skills have also been identified as key determinants in the initiation of AOD use. In particular, poor coping, peer refusal, and weak communication skills have been linked to drug use (Amaro *et al.*, 2001). Deficits in neuropsychological functioning, especially deficits in executive functions, also seem to be risk factors for substance abuse. Impoverished self-regulation is thought to be the core deficit in executive functioning that places a person at risk for substance use disorders (Weinberg, 2001).

Psychiatric disorders also contribute to the development of substance use disorders. Conduct disorder and anti-social behaviour have been strongly associated with the development of substance use disorders (Amaro *et al.*, 2001; Assanangkornchai *et al.*, 2002). Depression and anxiety disorders have also been strongly linked to the initiation of AOD use (Amaro *et al.*, 2001; Merikangas & Avenevdi, 2000). For women, post-traumatic stress disorder (due to childhood abuse or intimate partner violence) is a significant predictor of substance use disorders (Saloman *et al.*, 2002).

A number of psychological characteristics that reduce the risk of AOD use in adolescents have been identified. These include autonomy, social competence, problem solving ability, intelligence, and high levels of religiosity, self-esteem, affect regulation, and conventionality (Wills *et al.*, 2001).

and marital discord) has also been associated with adolescent drug use. In contrast, positive role models tend to buffer the risk of adolescent drug use (Wills & Pierce, 1996; Wills *et al.*, 2001).

The attachment and control aspects of the parent-adolescent relationship have also been associated with adolescent drug use. In terms of attachment, parental displays of affection and identification with the parent (Morojele & Brook, 2001) have been associated with reduced involvement with AODs. A family environment with strong family ties and high levels of social support has also been associated with lower levels of AOD involvement (Amaro *et al.*, 2001; Weinberg, 2001). In contrast, parental absences and poor parental monitoring have been associated with greater drug use (Weinberg, 2001). In terms of control, parental permissiveness and the use of authoritarian disciplinary practices have been associated with greater drug use (Morojele & Brook, 2001). Similarly, inadequate and inconsistent *family management practices* have been associated with greater involvement with AODs. In contrast, adolescents with high perceptions of family sanctions against drug use tend to be buffered against drug use (Weinberg, 2001). For example, a study of 826 adolescents revealed that family rules and parental monitoring provided a significant buffer against substance use (Stewart, 2002).

Peer factors

Peer-related variables, especially hanging out with friends after school, close involvement with drug-using peers and peer pressure are powerful predictors of adolescent drug use (Weinberg, 2001; Wills & Pierce, 1996). In general, the possibility of an adolescent engaging in AOD use increases as the extent to which the adolescent is embedded in a substance-using peer context increases (Hussang, 2002). In contrast, low pressure to use drugs by peers and low involvement with substance-using peers are some

Factors located at the level of interpersonal functioning

Family factors

Family drug use has often been associated with adolescent drug use (Wills & Pierce, 1996). Family dysfunction (due to a family history of criminal behaviour, negative family life events, parent-child conflict

> ### 33.3 PEER FACTORS
>
> Peer pressure is a common reason given by South African adolescents for AOD use and misuse. Ziervogel *et al.* (1997) reported that peer and parental influences (especially peer approval) were given as reasons for initiating AOD use among male adolescents in the Cape Peninsula.

protective factors that reduce the risk of AOD use (Hussang, 2002).

Factors located at the level of the environment

Mainstream institutions

The degree of attachment to mainstream institutions (e.g., schools and religious organisations) is a significant predictor of AOD use among adolescents (Amaro *et al.*, 2001). In terms of attachment, school drop out, poor school attendance (Amaro *et al.*, 2001), school failure, low levels of educational achievement, low levels of educational aspirations (Morojele & Brook, 2001), and low investment in academic institutions (Hawkins *et al.*, 2002) are significantly associated with increased involvement in AOD use. In contrast, academic achievement, high levels of educational aspirations (Morojele & Brook, 2001), and frequent school and church attendance and greater influence of religious and cultural background (Amaro *et al.*, 2001) appear to operate as protective factors that buffer the risk of AOD use.

Cultural factors

Ethnic minorities often face a number of stressors such as being witness to or a victim of violence, lower educational attainment, lower income, the inability to secure employment, and the daily experiences of discrimination. These discriminatory experiences and cultural victimisation appear to act as indirect risk factors that increase stress levels and therefore the likelihood of AOD use (Amaro *et al.*, 2001). Rapid acculturation is also an indirect risk factor for AOD use. Rapid cultural changes are not only stressful but also affect the extent to which peer norms influence substance use. Peer influence tends to become more pronounced as levels of acculturation increase, placing an adolescent at greater risk for AOD use.

Occupational factors

In South Africa, certain occupational factors have also contributed to high levels of alcohol misuse. In the farming areas of the Western Cape, the 'dop' or 'tot system' (where farm workers received alcohol as part payment of their wages) has been a significant contributing factor to high levels of alcohol dependence among these communities (London, 2000; Parry *et al.*,

2002a). The mining industry has also contributed to high levels of alcohol misuse. Kew (1994) reported that various features of miners' lifestyles encouraged alcohol misuse, especially the living conditions. Many migrant miners lived in same sex hostels where the only place to socialise was the local liquor outlet, where alcohol was available on credit.

Availability and accessibility

The lack of appropriate law enforcement and the availability and accessibility of AODs in particular communities also places adolescents at risk for substance use disorders (Wills & Pierce, 1996). According to the public health model, vulnerability to substance use disorders is only expressed when the host (the individual) is exposed to the agent (i.e. the alcohol or drugs) (Merikangas & Avenevdi, 2000). In other words, accessibility to and the availability of AODs in a particular community may enhance or protect against vulnerability for developing substance use disorders.

33.4 AVAILABILITY OF AODs IN SOUTH AFRICA

Since 1994, accessibility and availability of AODs has increased in South Africa. This is due in part to socio-political changes that have made South Africa an attractive new market for drug merchants. These changes include relaxed border controls, poorly resourced law enforcement agencies, increased international travel, good transport and banking facilities, and the country's relative affluence in the region. South Africa's geographic location also makes it a convenient transhipment point for drugs to Europe and the US (Parry *et al.*, 2002b).

Poverty has also been a contributing factor to AOD use as micro-enterprises have developed around the production and distribution of AODs. These informal sales provide many with an income and play a significant role in the economy (Parry *et*

Implications of the risk factor approach for the prevention of substance use disorders

The public health model for the prevention of disease and disorders involves assessing the epidemiology of a disorder in the target population, identifying the risk factors associated with the problem, applying interventions known to reduce the risk and enhance the protective factors that buffer against the effects of the risk factors, and monitoring the impact of the intervention on the incidence and prevalence of the target disorder (Hawkins *et al.*, 2002). This model recognises that there is no single, optimal strategy for reducing the health, social and economic burden associated with AOD misuse. Instead, this model emphasises the importance of designing and implementing interventions aimed at addressing the problem on multiple levels.

Reviews of prevention research indicate that risk and protective factors should be the primary target for prevention interventions and that the *risk-reduction protection-enhancement model* is the best available framework for preventing AOD problems in adolescence (Hawkins *et al.*, 2002). However, in South Africa, few community-wide prevention interventions aimed at reducing risk and enhancing protective factors for substance abuse have been implemented. Of those implemented, none have been systematically evaluated.

So far research has shown that interventions that reduce multiple risk factors in the individual and environment hold promise for preventing AOD use among adolescents. For example, experimental evaluations of school prevention programmes that taught social competence and established norms against substance abuse reported a reduction in favourable attitudes towards substance use and a reduction in the prevalence of substance use in the school population (Botvin, 1995).

Many of the effective substance abuse prevention programmes have focused on preventing or delaying the start of AOD use in early adolescence as early use has been shown to increase the risk of later substance abuse and dependence (Hawkins *et al.*, 2002). Studies of these interventions have reported almost an immediate effect in preventing early initiation of use, and a more prolonged effect in preventing the use of substances in later adolescence (Hawkins *et al.*, 2002). These results suggest that focusing on risk or protective factors in early adolescence is a viable approach for preventing later AOD abuse and dependence (Hawkins *et al.*, 2002).

However, prevention programmes often fail when implemented in communities as few communities have the resources to address all the potential risk factors and few programmes encourage communities to prioritise the most pressing needs of local populations (Hawkins *et al.*, 2002). Recent researchers have

recognised the need to identify risk and protective factors of the greatest relevance to a local community and select and implement effective evidence-based prevention strategies that matched to these priority factors. One effective programme that incorporates these prevention principles is the Communities That Care programme (CTC) (Hawkins *et al.*, 2002).

The Social Development Model (SDM) underpins the CTC programme. The SDM describes processes that lead to the strengthening of social ties between youth and adults in the community, the explicit expression of healthy beliefs and clear standards for behaviour across developmental periods. These are important protective factors that motivate healthy behaviour in both the developing child and in the community (Hawkins *et al.*, 2002). SDM provides the underlying theory for promoting healthy youth development in CTC's prevention model. SDM also acts as a guide for mobilising the community to implement an effective prevention strategy by creating opportunities for all members of a community to learn about prevention techniques, creating a shared community vision for positive youth development, developing prevention skills within the community, developing a strategic action plan for the community, and suggesting appropriate recognition activities for community participants (Hawkins *et al.*, 2002). As strategies for change are more likely to produce observable effects when the prioritised risk and protective factors are addressed in a number of socialisation domains, communities are encouraged to select interventions that affect risk/protective factors in both the family, school, community, and peer domains. There is therefore a clear and consistent behaviour norm expressed for youth (Hawkins *et al.*, 2002).

The CTC approach trains community members to collect data on risk and protective factors at the local level. Communities then select prevention services that focus on the geographic area displaying the highest risk. In this targeted area the most prominent risk factors are identified and prioritised for preventive action. Prevention interventions, with demonstrable effectiveness in addressing these priority factors, are then selected for implementation. Decision-making is thus based on local epidemiological data on risk, protection and substance use outcomes. This programme facilitates the implementation of a strategic intervention programme tailored to the unique risk profile of each community (Hawkins *et al.*, 2002). Existing evaluations have shown that the CTC programme is effectively imple-

33.5 SOCIAL DEVELOPMENT MODEL (SDM)

SDM builds on social control and social learning theory. SDM argues that bonding to prosocial groups and clear norms against anti-social behaviour behaviour act as protective factors that inhibit the development of substance use behaviour.

Bonding consists of attachment and commitment to the family, school, community and positive peers as well as a belief in the shared value of these social units. As prosocial bonding increases, adolescents are less likely to violate the norms for the behaviour of the group. Clear norms thus provide behavioural guidelines for people bonded to the group.

SDM argues that bonding is created when people are given opportunities to become involved or make a contribution to the social unit, when they have the skills to take advantage of these opportunities, and when they are recognised for their contribution. SDM thus assumes that interventions that involve opportunity, skill and recognition are likely to improve bonding to prosocial groups, the adoption of healthy beliefs, and clear standards for behaviour.

---

mented with communities successfully implementing evidence-based strategies to prevent AOD use, and with these interventions resulting in lasting change among adolescents. In terms of effectiveness, this model has not yet been compared to other approaches to AOD prevention (Hawkins *et al.*, 2002).

Conclusion

Alcohol and drug use can be lead to misuse, abuse and dependence. No single factor completely accounts for AOD use problems. The vulnerability model that examines both risk and protective factors and which includes psychosocial, environmental and genetic factors allows intervention to occur at multiple levels. Primary, secondary and tertiary prevention efforts need to match the available resources and relevance of risk and protective factors in community settings.

REFERENCES

Amaro, H., Blake, S.M., Schwarz, P.M. & Flinchbaugh, L.J. (2001). Developing theory-based substance abuse prevention programmes for young girls. *Journal of Early Adolescence*, 21(3):256-96.

American Psychiatric Association. (1994). *Diagnostic and Statistical Manual of Mental Disorders* (4th edition). Washington DC: American Psychiatric Association.

Assanangkornchai, S., Geater, A.F., Saunders, J.B. & McNeil, D.R. (2002). Effects of paternal drinking, conduct disorder and childhood home environment on the development of alcohol use disorders in a Thai population. *Addiction*, 97(2):217-26.

Bierut, L.J., Schuckit, MA., Hesselbrock, V. & Reich, T. (2000). Co-occurring risk factors for alcohol dependence and habitual smoking. *Alcohol Research & Health*, 24:233-42.

Botvin, G.J. (1995). Principles of prevention. In R.H. Coombs & D. Zedonis (Eds.). *Handbook of Drug Abuse Prevention: A comprehensive strategy to prevent the abuse of alcohol and other drugs*. Boston: Allyn & Bacon, pp. 19-44.

Cadoret, R.J., Yates, W.R., Troughton, E., Spencer, T., Woodworth, G. & Stewart, M.A. (1996). Adoption study demonstrating two genetic pathways to drug abuse. *Archives of General Psychiatry*, 52:42-52.

Cosden, M. (2001). Risk and resilience for substance abuse among adolescents and adults with learning disabilities. *Journal of Learning Disabilities*, 34:352-59.

De Wit, D.J. & Silverman, G. (1995). The construction of risk and resilience factor indices for describing adolescent alcohol and other drug use. *Journal of Drug Issues*, 23(4):837-64.

Griffin, K.W., Botvin, G.J., Epstein, J.A., Doyle, M.M. & Diaz, T. (2000). Psychosocial and behavioural factors in early adolescence as predictors of heavy drinking among high school seniors. *Journal of Studies on Alcohol*, 61(4):603-6.

Hawkins, J.D., Catalano, R.F. & Arthur, M.W. (2002). Promoting science-based prevention in communities. *Addictive Behavior*, 27:952-76.

Heath, A.C., Bucholz, K.K., Madden, P.A., *et al.* (1997). Genetic and environmental contributions to alcohol dependence risk in a national twin sample: Consistency of findings in women and men. *Psychological Medicine*, 27:1381-96.

Hussang, A.M. (2002). Differentiating peer contexts and risk for adolescent substance use. *Journal of Youth & Adolescence*, 31(3):207-20.

Institute of Medicine. (1990). *Broadening the Base of Treatment for Alcohol Problems*. Washington DC: National Academy Press.

Kew, G. (1994). A descriptive study of alcohol consumption patterns on a South African gold mine. MRC *Urbanisation & Health Newsletter*, 21:39-42.

Koob, G.F. & Lemoal, M. (1997). Drug abuse: Hedonic homeostatic dysregulation. *Science*, 278(5353):52-8.

London, L. (2000). Alcohol consumption amongst South African farm sity of marijuana and other illicit drug use among adult initiators. *The Journal of Genetic Psychology*, 162(4):430-50.

Merikangas, K.R. (1990). Comorbidity for anxiety and depression. Review of family and genetic studies. In J.D. Master & C.R. Cloninger (Eds.). *Comorbidity of Mood and Anxiety Disorders*. Washington DC: American Psychiatric Press, pp. 331-48.

Merikangas, K.R. & Avenevdi, S. (2000). Implications of genetic epidemiology for the prevention of substance use disorders. *Addictive Behavior*, 25:807-20.

Miller, W. (1996). What is a relapse? 50 ways to leave the wagon. *Addiction*, 91:S15-27.

Morojele, N.K. & Brook, J.S. (2001). Adolescent precursors of the intensity of marijuana and other illicit drug use among adult initiators. *The Journal of Genetic Psychology*, 162(4):430-50.

Newcomb, M.D., Maddahian, E., Skager, R. & Bentler, P.M. (1987). Substance abuse and psychosocial risk factors among teenagers: Associations with sex, age, ethnicity and types of school. American *Journal of Drug & Alcohol Abuse*, 13:413-33.

Parry, C.D.H., Pluddenamm, A., Bhana, A., Matthysen, S., Potgeiter, H. & Gerber, W. (2001). *SACENDU Research Brief*, 4(11):1-19.

Parry, C.D.H., Bhana, A., Myers, B., Pluddemann, A., Flisher, A.J., Peden, M. & Morojele, N.K. (2002a). Alcohol use in South Africa: Findings from the South African Community Epidemiology Network on Drug Use (SACENDU) Project. *Journal of Studies on Alcohol*, 63:430-35.

Parry, C.D.H., Bhana, A., Pluddemann, A., Myers, B., Siegfried, N., Morojele, N.K., Flisher, A.J. & Kozel, N. (2002b). The South African Community Epidemiology Network on Drug Use: Description, findings and policy implications. *Addiction*, 97:969-76.

Saloman, A., Bassuk, S.S. & Huntington, N. (2002). Relationship between intimate partner violence and the use of addictive substances in poor and homeless single women. *Violence Against Women*, 8(7):785-815.

Stewart, C. (2002). Family factors of low-income African-American youth associated with substance use: An exploratory analysis. *Journal of Ethnicity in Substance Abuse*, 1(1):97-111.

Weinberg, N.Z. (2001). Risk factors for adolescent substance abuse. *Journal of Learning Disabilities*, 34:343-52.

Wills, T.A. (1994). Self-esteem and perceived control in adolscent substance use: Comparative tests in concurrent and prospective analyses. *Psychology of Addictive Behaviours*, 8:223-34.

Wills, T.A. & Pierce, J.P. (1996). Large scale environmental risk factors for substance use. *American Behavioral Scientist*, 39:808-23.

Wills, TA., Sandy, J.M., Yaeger, A. & Shinar, O. (2001). Family risk factor and adolescent substance use: Moderating effect for temperament dimensions. *Developmental Psychology*, 37(3):283-97.

Ziervogel, C.F., Ahmed, N., Flisher, A.J. & Robertson, B.A. (1997). Adolescent alcohol misuse. A qualitative investigation. *International Quarterly of Community Health Education*, 17:25-41.

Multiple choice questions

1. Substance abuse refers to
   a) adverse consequences following binge drinking
   b) recurrent maladaptive substance use that has significant negative consequences
   c) compulsive drug taking
   d) being in an intoxicated state

2. Substance dependence refers to
   a) non-recurrent substance use that has significant negative consequences
   b) being in an intoxicated state
   c) a pattern of repeated use resulting in tolerance, withdrawal and compulsive drug taking
   d) a cluster of cognitive and behavioural symptoms

3. Substance use behaviour is clinically best understood as
   a) either present or absent
   b) non-problematic or problematic
   c) misuse or substance dependence
   d) a continuum of problem-severity

4. Research has shown that the more severe the substance use problem
   a) the less likely the person is able to return to non-problematic use
   b) the more likely the person is able to return to non-problematic use
   c) the more likely the person is able to maintain non-problematic use
   d) the more likely controlled use is indicated

5. Substance use is best treated through
   a) specialised substance abuse treatment
   b) brief intervention
   c) prevention
   d) all of the above

6. Theories of the etiology of substance use disorders include
   a) interpersonal, environmental and cultural factors
   b) intra-personal, biological and environmental factors
   c) intra-personal, personality traits and biological factors
   d) intra-personal, interpersonal and environmental factors

7. The risk factor approach to substance use among adolescents assumes that
   a) as the number of risk factors increases, the development of a substance use disorder decreases
   b) as the number of risk factors increases, the number of protective factors decreases
   c) as the number of risk factors increases, the number of protective factors increases
   d) as the number of risk factors increases, the number of resilient factors decreases

8. Vulnerability to substance use refers to the ratio of
   a) weak to strong personality traits
   b) strong protective factors to strong resilient factors
   c) risk factors to protective factors
   d) resilient factors to protective factors

9. Family studies indicate that the risk for developing alcohol dependence is
   a) three times greater among first degree relatives
   b) two times greater among fraternal twins
   c) five times greater among identical twins
   d) all of the above

10. The following psychological factors have been identified as risk factors for substance use
    a) external locus of control
    b) low self-esteem
    c) sensation seeking
    d) all of the above

Short answer questions

1. Distinguish between substance misuse, abuse and dependence.

2. Match the type of intervention with the level of substance abuse behaviour:
   a) substance abuse   a) prevention, brief interventions
   b) substance dependence   b) prevention
   c) substance misuse   c) specialised substance abuse treatment
   d) substance use   d) prevention

3. What is meant by a 'risk factor approach' to understanding substance use?

4. Explain vulnerability, protective factors and resilience in substance use.

5. How do twin studies help explain genetic influences in substance use disorders?

6. What parent-adolescent relationships factors are involved in measuring risk for substance abuse?

7. How does the *Social Development Model* explain risk and protective factors in substance abuse?

34

Nutrition

Linda Richter & Shane Norris

CHAPTER OBJECTIVES

After studying this chapter you should be able to:
- demonstrate that both under- and over-nutrition are problems in many parts of the world due to food shortages and aspirations to thinness, on the one hand, and dietary transitions and fast food consumption, on the other hand
- argue that growth patterns and nutritional effects are determined very early in life, importantly in the pre-natal period, so that later nutrition affects an already primed physiological system
- show that important changes in growth and nutrition occur during puberty and the adolescent growth spurt, as a result both of physiological demands as well as psychosocially determined changes in activity levels, eating patterns and self-concept related to size and shape
- demonstrate that the nutrition of older people is an important part of continuing health and longevity
- understand how HIV/AIDS, which affects millions of people, directly impacts on the immune system, and how nutritional interventions can help to maintain the health and prolong the life of infected individuals.

Nosipho was aware of how many young women of her age worried about their weight. Diets and dieting was often one of the main topics of conversation during breaks between lectures. Magazines and newspapers were full of pictures of thin models and it was hard not to compare yourself with them. There had been quite a number of girls in her class at school who seemed to take their concern with weight to extreme lengths. Quite a few had developed eating disorders of one kind or another, some becoming frighteningly thin and others vomiting their food up in the toilet after lunch. There was so much pressure on women to have perfect bodies. Nosipho also sometimes worried about gaining weight herself, although she didn't believe in dieting. She rather tried to just eat healthily and exercise when she could.

Nosipho found it strange to think of how so many people worried about staying thin, while there were even more people in southern Africa who were not getting enough to eat. Having enough food was something she and most of her friends just took for granted. It was very hard to even imagine what it must be like to be hungry all the time or to worry about your children going without food, but Nosipho knew this was a reality for many people. In her own neighbourhood, young children would come to the door to ask for food and Nosipho's mother would always try to give them something, knowing sometimes that it might be the only meal they would have. Nosipho wondered what it was like for a child to try and learn, play or even sleep with an empty stomach.

Introduction

Food and water are basic constituents of life and thus necessary, in sufficient quality and quantity, for people at all ages and in all conditions. The nature and amount of food consumed by people has an important effect on physical health and mental health. Too little or too much food, or food too low or too high in specific constituents (iron or zinc, for example), can cause dramatic changes in immune function, energy levels, attention, cognitive acuity, mood and emotional reactivity (Mason *et al.*, 2001). The nutritional sciences have developed norms for required food intake under normal conditions, expressed as Recommended Dietary Intakes (RDI). Special feeding regimens are required during illness and recuperation, including recovery from periods of extreme under-nutrition.

However, the influence of food on psychological functions and mental health is not unidirectional. Existing or developing states of health and mental health also affect what and how much food people select to eat. Children and adults who have had little to eat for a long time lose their appetite, and may even refuse food when it becomes available. Similarly, abnormal eating patterns, such as anorexia, bulimia and binging, are associated with disturbed mood states and psychopathology (Harris, 1991).

Under- and over-nutrition

Both extreme under-nutrition and over-nutrition are serious global problems. It is a matter of shame for the whole world that half the people in sub-Saharan Africa live on less than US $1 a day (United Nations Development Programme, 2002). This is extreme income poverty, some features of which are hunger, starvation and dramatically increased mortality in comparison to people living in developed countries. For example, the lifetime chance of a person dying during pregnancy or childbirth is 1 in 13 in southern Africa, compared to 1 in 4 085 in Europe and the United States. It is of concern to local and international agencies that malnutrition among children in southern Africa has worsened during the last decade as a result of increased poverty associated with political conflicts and climatic disasters (United Nations Children's Fund, 2002). However, some improvements have been achieved with respect to micronutrients (see Box 34.1).

34.1 IMPACT OF MICRONUTRIENT DEFICIENCY

'... two of the micronutrients identified at the World Summit for Children as key to preventing 'hidden hunger' – vitamin A and iodine – have been success stories of the 1990s. The lack of vitamin A can lead to blindness and make children more susceptible to illness, but can be prevented by fortification of food or the distribution of capsules as part of immunization campaigns. Between 1996 and 1999, the number of countries with 70 per cent or higher coverage in vitamin A rose from 11 to 43. Iodine deficiency, meanwhile, which is the main cause of preventable mental retardation, is most easily addressed through the simple process of iodizing salt. The goal of virtually eliminating iodine deficiency disorders has not been met, but the percentage of people in developing countries consuming iodized salt has gone up from under 20 per cent to around 72 per cent. Given this progress, the elimination of iodine deficiency disorders by 2005 looks to be a realistic prospect, though it will require both effort and commitment, since there are still 37 countries where less than half of the households consume iodized salt' (United Nations Children's Fund, 2002:15).

In a recent national study of close to 3 000 children, a team of South African researchers found that 1 in 10 children were underweight for their age, and 1 in 5 were stunted, that is, with diminished height-for-age. Children between one and three years of age were worst affected, as were children living in rural areas and, ironically, children living on commercial farms. By contrast, 1 in 13 children in formal urban areas were overweight, and this number was higher (1 in 8 children) among the children of women with comparatively higher levels of education (Labadarios, 2000).

In developed countries, particularly the USA, as well as in some developing countries, public health concern has grown around the increasing population-wide trend in obesity (over-nutrition) among children and adolescents (Kain *et al.*, 1998). Between the early 1960s and 1990s, the prevalence of obesity in the US almost tripled in girls between 6 and 11 years of age. Similarly, both overweight and obesity in adolescent girls aged 12 to 17 years has also increased markedly. The rise in children and adolescents of non-insulin-dependent diabetes, traditionally viewed as an adult-onset condition, is believed to be a consequence of the currently high prevalence of obesity in American youth (Kimm *et al.*, 2001). In South Africa, a similar trend in obesity is emerging, with 7 per cent of preschool children being overweight, as defined by a weight-for-height more than two standard deviations of the National Center for Health Statistics (USA) and the World Health Organisation reference tables (de Onis & Blossner, 2000). The 1998 South African Demographic and Health Survey (Medical Research Council, 1998) found that 57 per cent of women and 29 per cent of men were overweight or obese. The obesity epidemic in South Africa, particularly noticeable among adult females, is due to rural-urban migration and transition to a more Western lifestyle, with reduced physical activity and increasing availability of energy-dense foods, as found in many fast-food types (Puoane *et al.*, 2002).

34.2 MOVE FOR HEALTH

One of the World Health Organisation initiatives is 'move for health'. Physical activity among children and adolescents is being encouraged, not only for its benefit in weight management, but also as a crucial element of a healthy lifestyle that reduces the risk of developing diabetes and cardiovascular disease.

Although balanced nutrition is important throughout the life span, its effects on psychological functioning and mental health are most discernible during periods of rapid growth. Adequate intake of nutrients is critical for growth and differentiation in physical stature and the elaboration of physiological capacity and function. Very rapid growth occurs during the prenatal period, during infancy and later, in the early teen years, during the pubertal growth spurt. Although these three periods are dealt with in more detail below, it should be noted that there are several other discernible periods of major physiological growth, re-alignment or decline, during which time nutrition has very important effects on emotions, cognitive capacity and mental health. These are: the growth spurt and bone mineralisation that occurs in early adulthood sometime between 16 and 24 years, menopause in women which occurs between 45 and 55 years of age and old age.

Prenatal development and birth weight

Virtually explosive growth occurs during the prenatal period. In the 270-odd days' duration of a normal pregnancy, the fertilised egg, barely visible to the naked eye, grows to a baby with an average 3.3kg weight and 105cm length. At around 4 months gestational age, the foetus grows at roughly 1.5cm per day. With such rapid growth, adequate nutrition is critical. Nutrition has two main effects on the foetus. Together with other influences on the baby, nutrition affects birth weight, and certain nutritional components act as teratogens – or environmental influences that can disrupt prenatal development.

A woman needs a balanced diet during her pregnancy, as well as sufficient food to gain the requisite weight to support a foetus (between 12 and 18kg). The foetal brain grows especially rapidly during this period, and diminished nutritional intake can severely affect cognitive and emotional develop-

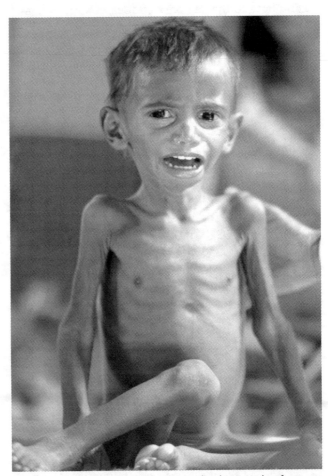

Figure 1 The under-nourished infant is disadvantaged as far as growth is concerned

ment. Distressing real-life experiments on the effects of maternal malnutrition occurred during the World War Two famine in parts of Europe. During this time, there was a significant increase in abortions, still births, developmental abnormalities and perinatal mortality, especially if women experienced food shortages in the early stages of pregnancy. Under-nutrition later in pregnancy tended to be associated with foetal growth retardation and low birth weight (Antonov, 1947).

Birth weight is a proxy for the quality of the intrauterine environment, and is a strong predictor of both physical and psychological development during the preschool years (Aylward *et al.*, 1989; Richter & Griesel, 1994). There is an inverse correlation between birth weight and mortality, and congenital abnormalities occur more frequently in chil-

dren with birth weights below 2.5kgs (called low birth weight or LBW) and below 1.5kgs (called very low birth weight or VLBW). About 10 per cent of South African babies are born with low birth weight (Richardson, 1986). LBW babies have more respiratory problems, seizures and other neurological problems, and later show a higher prevalence of hyperactivity. In general, parents of LBW babies find them more labile in their response to caregiving (Crnic *et al.*, 1983).

Infancy and early childhood

Apart from prenatal development, growth during the first two years occurs at a more rapid pace than at any other time of life. The emergence of complex neural networks that occur with brain development in early life enable the acquisition of motor, communicative, cognitive and social skills that are the essential building blocks of psychosocial development. Birth weight, infant feeding, illness and postnatal increases in height and weight very strongly affect neuropsychological development (Barbarin & Richter, 2001).

The five most common causes of child deaths in the world are malaria, measles, pneumonia, diarrhoea and under-nutrition. Because under-nutrition increases the likelihood that a child will succumb to the effects of disease, under-nutrition is believed to account for about 70 per cent of all under-5 mortalities in developing countries.

Malnutrition has a variety of negative effects on young children. It reduces energy, activity and attention levels, and distorts exploration and social interaction. Malnourished children tend to cling to their caregivers and eschew opportunities to manipulate objects. Over time this is likely to negatively affect cognitive development and social adjustment (Richter, 1993; Richter & Griesel, 1994).

Infants and young children do not simply eat what's put in their mouths, offered to them on a spoon, or placed in front of them in a bowl. Feeding needs to occur in the context of an affectionate and stable relationship, and children need to be fed or encouraged to feed by someone who is responsive to their state, mood and tempo. Controlling for levels of poverty, malnutrition occurs more frequently in households that are disorganised, in which there has been a change of caregivers, and in which caregivers fail to express affection towards the child (Galler *et al.*, 1984).

34.3 CONTROVERSY: THE BARKER HYPOTHESIS

In recent years, evidence has accumulated in support of a hypothesis that intrauterine experiences can contribute to the adult risk of diseases such as obesity, hypertension, ischaemic heart disease and glucose intolerance. It is suggested that the lower the birth weight of a child, the greater the risk of adult obesity, hypertension and diabetes (Barker, 1998). The hypothesised cause is a priming of the absorption patterns of the physiological system in response to deprivation. Studies have demonstrated that instead of a straightforward linear relationship between birth weight and adult obesity, the relationship is curvilinear (J- or U-shaped). This means that a higher prevalence of obesity is seen amongst people who had the lowest and highest birth weights (Fall *et al.*, 1995). Data from the 1958 British birth cohort study found that maternal weight, or maternal Body Mass Index (BMI) during pregnancy, largely explains the association between child birth weight and later BMI. Heavier mothers have heavier babies who tend to become heavier adults, regardless of birth weight. From this evidence, maternal weight may be the more important risk variable for obesity in the child than low birth weight (Parsons *et al.*, 2001). Maternal nutrition during pregnancy (adequate dietary intake), health (blood pressure, weight) and environmental exposures (e.g., lead, alcohol and tobacco) can have consequences for the unborn child, by affecting the child's birth weight and, in turn, adult risk of chronic diseases of lifestyle.

The strong link between psychosocial care and nutrition is illustrated in a disorder called non-organic failure-to-thrive (NOFTT), or growth retardation with no clear organic aetiology. The syndrome may include, apart from growth deficits, diminished physical activity, depressed cognitive performance, decreased immunologic resistance and long-term behavioral problems and developmental delays (Black & Dubowitz, 1991). NOFTT infants and young children appear emaciated and listless, with diminished vocalisations, minimal smiling, little cuddliness, and they are unusually watchful. The syndrome was first described in institutionalised infants who experienced little contact with caregivers, and it occurs in a very large number of poor children in developing countries, even if the children are not diagnosed with moderate to severe malnutrition (Guedeney, 1995). The problems of NOFTT become particularly severe when they are superimposed on the health and development problems of children growing up in poverty.

Interventions consisting of compensatory nutrition and psychosocial stimulation for young children show very positive benefits (World Health Organisation, 1999). Interventions at later ages, for example, through schools, are also important. In September 1994, the Primary School Nutrition Programme (PSNP) was launched in South Africa as a Presidential Lead Project of the Reconstruction and Development Programme. The purpose of the PSNP was to contribute to the improvement of education quality by enhancing primary school pupils' learning capacity (by alleviating hunger), school attendance and punctuality, and to contribute to general health and development. There is both sound conceptual and empirical evidence linking school performance and nutrition. Pollitt (1994), for example, argued that poor nutrition and concurrent illnesses interfere with the schooling of children in low-income countries, and that educational interventions have to include children's health issues, including chronic protein-energy malnutrition, iron-deficiency anaemia, iodine deficiency and intestinal infections. A causal link between under-nutrition and cognitive performance among South African samples is suggested by several reviews (Richter & Griesel, 1994). To date, however, there has only been one attempt to assess the benefits of the school feeding programme, with ambiguous results. School feeding was associated with greater attention in class and less distractible behaviour, but there was no clear link with improved school performance (Richter et al., 1997).

34.4 BIRTH TO TWENTY STUDY

Birth to Twenty (Bt20) is the largest and longest running birth cohort study of child health and development in South Africa, and has been tracking more than 3 000 children born in Johannesburg-Soweto during a 7-week period in 1990. Mean birth weights of the Bt20 children were less than American norms (National Center for Health Statistics, 2001) and girls weighed significantly more than boys. The percentage of low birth weight children of normal gestation age (about 7 per cent) was similar to that of developed countries. Growth in weight exceeded that of the National Center for Health Statistics reference standards during the first 6 months of life, a trend that is attributed to almost universal breastfeeding among African mothers. However, after 6 months, weight began to fall below the norms. Poor weaning foods, infections and low levels of stimulation are believed to account for the characteristic drop off in weight seen amongst preschool children in developing countries. By two years of age, 22 per cent of Bt20 children were stunted (lower than expected height-for-age) and 7 per cent were wasted (very much less than expected weight). Catch-up growth occurred between 4 and 5 years resulting in a reduction in the prevalence of stunting and wasting to 5 per cent and 1 per cent, respectively, at 5 years of age (Cameron et al., 1998).

For more information about Birth to Twenty, go to www.wits.ac.za/birthto20.

See also Chapter 5, this volume.

The pubertal growth spurt and adolescence

During puberty, the primary sexual organs mature and very rapid increases in height occur. Amongst girls, this growth spurt takes place sometime between 9 and 15 years; it happens a bit later amongst boys (between 10 and 16 years). These changes are triggered by hormones, but are also affected by environmental factors, most particularly nutrition (Marshall & Tanner, 1970). The tallest and heaviest girls start to menstruate the earliest. The age of menarche, or menstruation, is becoming progressively earlier all over the world, a change associated with improved nutrition among girls. In the early 1800s in the US and Europe, menarche occurred at around 17 years of age, whereas the mean age of starting to menstruate is now 12 to 13 years. Similar trends have been demonstrated in South Africa (Cameron, 1993).

Adolescence is considered to be a nutritionally vulnerable phase for several reasons. First, there is an increased demand for macronutrients (carbohydrate, fat and protein) and micronutrients (e.g., iron, calcium and vitamin A) to meet the dramatic increase in physical growth and cognitive development. Second, the frequent changes in lifestyle and food habits of adolescents affect their nutrient intake. The shift in attitudes and perceptions around foods and body esteem may result in pathological eating behaviour, and environmental influences (family, peers and media) may impact on dietary practices. Third, there are special nutrient needs associated with participation in sports, adolescent pregnancy, development of an eating disorder, excessive dieting and use of alcohol and drugs (Spear, 1996).

Several facets of eating behaviour are different or more pronounced during adolescence: missing meals (especially breakfast), snacking, eating fast foods, high consumption of soft drinks and the start of alcohol intake. The danger is that habits that are started during adolescence are often continued into adulthood and may ultimately contribute to a number of debilitating diseases (Spear, 1996). In early adolescence, young people tend to be preoccupied with body image, they trust and respect adults, are anxious about peer relationships and are ambivalent about autonomy. The nutritional implications are that these adolescents tend to be willing to try to do things to improve their body image. In middle adolescence, teens are greatly influenced by the peer group, tend to be mistrustful of adults, value independence, and experience significant cognitive developments. During this stage, the adolescent may engage in altered dietary habits, alcohol intake, smoking and dieting. In late adolescence, the teenager is likely to have established a body image, be oriented toward the future, independent and developing intimacy and permanent relationships. Adolescents in this stage are more open to improving their overall health but may have already developed unhealthy eating practices and activity patterns (Massey-Strokes, 2002).

Both over-nutrition (obesity) and under-nutrition (dieting and anorexia) are seen among adolescents, and both are associated with mental health problems, most notably anxiety and depression, as well as difficulties in social relations. Obesity is a complex medical disorder that is affected by genetics and the environment. Environmental factors that contribute

34.5 SOUTH AFRICAN FOOD-BASED DIETARY GUIDELINES

- enjoy a variety of foods;
- be active;
- make starchy foods the basis of most meals;
- eat plenty of vegetables and fruit every day;
- eat dry beans, peas, lentils and soya regularly;
- chicken, fish, milk, meat or eggs could be eaten daily;
- eat fats sparingly;
- drink lots of clean, safe water;
- if you drink alcohol, drink sensibly; and
- use salt sparingly.

to adolescent obesity include high caloric intake (diets high in saturated fat and sugar) and sedentary behaviour. Youth learn these unhealthy behaviours from parents and other influential role models (Daee *et al.*, 2002). The South African Department of Health has adopted the South African Food-based Dietary Guidelines to encourage responsible eating habits, ensuring that all macro- and micronutrient requirements are meet. There are serious negative consequences to dieting, and consequently, controlled health-promoting behaviour such as increased fruit and vegetable intake, lowered fat intake, and more exercise, should be encouraged for overweight and obese adolescents.

Over one-third of American adolescent females engage in at least one episode of harmful weight loss practice (such as chronic dieting, excessive exercise, self-induced vomiting and abuse of laxatives, diet

Figure 2 What would these individuals' dietary and nutritional intake be like?

medications and water pills) (Massey-Strokes, 2002). The mean age of onset of anorexia nervosa in the US is approximately 17 years of age, and some evidence suggests that there are bimodal peaks around 14 and 18 years of age (American Psychiatric Association, 1994). Adolescent weight-loss behaviour is associated with anaemia (iron deficiency), poor calcium intake (which may lead to a relatively low peak bone mass and risk of osteoporosis in later life), growth stunting, poor body image, decreased immune function, menstrual cycle disruptions and even death (Daee *et al.*, 2002).

34.6 IMPACT OF WESTERN SOCIO-CULTURAL INFLUENCES ON NUTRITION

It has been suggested that one of the strongest socio-cultural factors influencing girls and women today is the Western beauty ideal, in which fatness is stigmatised and thinness praised. Worldwide media exposure focusing on mainstream cultural values is a powerful force in shaping public perceptions regarding the value of thinness and, hence, contributing to the rise in eating disorders in non-Westernised populations. Among the changes taking place in South Africa as a result of acculturation is what is considered to be acceptable body size and shape. Recent findings suggest that the prevalence of abnormal eating attitudes is equally common in South African schoolgirls from different ethnic backgrounds. However, White girls still exhibit greater body image concerns and dissatisfaction than mixed race or Black girls (Caradas *et al.*, 2001). Given current trends, the prevalence of eating disorders pathology is expected to increase significantly among Black South Africans.

Young athletes are particularly vulnerable to nutritional misinformation and unsafe practices that promise enhanced performance. Pressures to achieve optimal performance and muscle mass encourage athletes, particularly adolescent males, to experiment with supplements and ergogenic aids (muscle fuels and steroids) in order to achieve the 'competitive edge' and muscle gain, and which may affect health and growth. Adequate fluid intake and prevention of dehydration are critical for younger athletes. In fact, heat illness ranks second to head injury as a cause of reported non-cardiac causes of death in adolescent athletes (Steen, 1996).

Nutrition at older ages

Nutrition interacts with the ageing process in numerous ways, and the risk of nutrition-related health problems increases in later life, either as a result of impaired food intake or reduced nutrient utilisation. The most important physiological change occurring in gastrointestinal function with ageing is the atrophy of the stomach mucosa which results in less acid and pepsin secretion and, ultimately, reduction in the bioavailability of calcium, iron, folate and vitamin B12 (Evans & Campbell, 1993). Calcium needs are higher in post-menopausal women to protect against osteoporosis as their oestrogen levels have dropped resulting in greater bone loss. Overall, older adults need to ensure that they obtain similar intakes as younger adults for most vitamins and minerals, but usually lower energy-dense foods due to the reduction in total energy needs. Therefore, a nutrient-dense diet is a high priority for older people. Nutrient deficiencies in older adults can exacerbate both physiological and cognitive deterioration.

34.7 CONTRIBUTIONS TO NUTRITIONAL PROBLEMS IN OLDER PEOPLE

Physical factors:
- reduced absorptive and metabolic capacities of macro-and micronutrients;
- chronic diseases;
- alteration in taste and smell perception;
- poor appetite;
- poor dental health;
- difficulty in swallowing;
- lack of exercise; and
- physical disability.

Psychosocial factors:
- depression;
- loneliness;
- memory loss;
- social isolation;
- bereavement;
- loss of interest in cooking; and
- dementia.

Socio-economic factors:
- lack of transport and shopping difficulties;
- low income; and
- inadequate cooking or storage facilities.

Nutrition in HIV infection

It is estimated that 38 million people are infected with HIV around the world, of which two million are children under the age of 15 years. HIV/AIDS affects nutrition directly and indirectly. The direct effects result from physiological reactions related to the disease. The indirect effects are caused by poverty and malnutrition as AIDS cuts a swathe through impoverished communities, depleting the reserves of breadwinners and subsistence activities. It is also caused by the inability of AIDS-sick individuals to eat because of the pain of oral thrush and/or lack of appetite due to generalized illness.

Common complications of HIV infection and AIDS are malnutrition, lactose intolerance, fat malabsorption and AIDS-related anorexia (Kotler, 1998). In children with HIV, it is important to maintain good nutrition as this helps their immune systems to continue functioning while their bodies are growing. As children have young immune systems and small protein reserves, they are at greater risk for immune suppression and, therefore, they are dependent on good nutrition management and tolerable anti-retroviral treatment to minimise disease progression and promote survival (Fontana et al., 1999; Nerad et al., 2003).

Deficiencies in macro- and micronutrients occur in HIV-infected patients as nutrients are used faster by the body to fight the infection and repair the damage caused by the virus and other infections, poor absorption of nutrients as a result of intestinal infections and diarrhoea, and loss of appetite, fatigue, nausea and vomiting. These nutrient deficiencies further strain the immune system and other physiological systems as nutrients provide the building blocks for both the body's physical structure (cells, tissue and organs) and its function. Studies have shown that in both HIV-infected children and adults, deficiencies in zinc, selenium, copper, and vitamins C, E, B6 and B12 (all of which are important for an intact immune response) are common (Nerad et al., 2003). Nutritional counselling, careful food preparation and sanitation, oral nutritional supplementation and regular resistance exercise programmes have been shown to be effective in influencing health outcomes in HIV-infected patients (Rabeneck et al., 1998; Roubenoff et al., 1999).

Nutritional assessment and support of the HIV-infected child:

- A dietician should be consulted as soon as possible after diagnosis.
- Detailed diet history (food frequency and/or 24 hour recall) and supplement use should be taken to determine macro- and micronutrient intake. Special attention to food intolerances, feeding skills and developmental milestones should be noted in developing an appropriate eating plan. Nutritional counselling includes meal pattern planning, hygienic food preparation, ensuring good oral intake of food and liquids and strategies to cope with diarrhoea and malabsorption.
- Drug-nutrient interactions should be monitored and adjustments made to medications contributing to poor nutritional intake.
- Anthropometric assessments (height, weight, height-for-age, weight-for-age, weight-for-height, head circumference and body fat percentage) should be tracked over time to ensure that growth is optimal and to note any subtle changes in fat and lean muscle stores. The definition for AIDS Wasting Syndrome is 10 per cent body weight loss which, among paediatric patients, could be as little as 1kg.
- Laboratory biochemical tests to assess nutritional status, and liver, immune and renal functioning are necessary to manage the sick child.

Challenges facing developing countries:
- HIV medical nutrition therapy requires specialized knowledge of nutrition, especially in relation to HIV disease, medications, complications, and sensitivity to the infected and affected populations served. The number of qualified medical nutrition therapy providers is completely inadequate in developing countries.
- In the face of this, increased effort needs to be made to educate primary health care providers around nutrition and nutritional counselling.
- Restricted government funding, resources, facilities and medication.

Nutritional counselling for HIV-infected children and adults should be a key strategy to help HIV and AIDS patients fight the virus, protect the functioning of their bodies, improve their quality of life and manage co-infections. Nutritional counselling should be integrated into public awareness campaigns.

Conclusion

The human condition is determined by mental and physical factors that are inextricably linked together. Nutrition is a key aspect of physical health and can contribute to mental and physical ill-health; in the same way, poor nutrition may also result from mental and physical ill-health. Because of their dual economies and split urban-rural development, developing countries, including South Africa, are showing an increase in nutrition and lifestyle-related diseases in the context of continuing high levels of disease associated with poverty. Most psychological and mental health problems associated with nutrition are preventable and/or can be remedied with appropriate intervention. Preventive measures to reduce diet-related disease should begin early in life; however, improvements in diets, eating habits and physical activity can benefit health regardless of age. Poverty, underdevelopment and poor education are significant barriers to good nutrition in resource-poor environments.

REFERENCES

American Psychiatric Association. (1994). *Diagnostic and Statistical Manual of Mental Disorders (DSM-IV)* (4th edition). Washington DC: American Psychiatric Association.

Antonov, A. (1947). Children born during the siege of Leningrad in 1942. *Journal of Pediatrics*, 30:250-59.

Aylward, G.P. Pfeiffer, S., Wright, A. & Verhulst, S. (1989). Outcome studies of low birth weight infants published in the last decade: A meta-analysis. *Journal of Pediatrics*, 115:515-20.

Barbarin, O. & Richter, L. (2001). *Mandela's Children: Growing up in post-Apartheid South Africa*. New York: Routledge.

Barker D.J.P. (1998). *Mother, Babies and Health in Later Life*. Edinburgh: Churchill Livingstone.

Black, M. & Dubowitz, H. (1991). Failure to thrive: Lessons from animal models and developing countries. *Journal of Development & Behavioral Pediatrics*, 2:259-67.

Cameron, N. (1993). Assessment of growth and maturation during adolescence. *Hormone Research*, 39:9-17.

Cameron, N., De Wet, T., Ellsion, G.T. & Bogin, B. (1998). Growth in height and weight of South African urban infants from birth to five years: The Birth to Ten study. *American Journal of Human Biology*, 10:495-504.

Caradas, A.A., Lambert, E.V. & Charlton, K.E. (2001). An ethnic comparison of eating attitudes and associated body image concerns in adolescent South African schoolgirls. *Journal of Human Nutrition & Diet*, 14:111-20.

Crnic, K., Ragozin, A., Greenberg, M., Robinson, N. & Basham, R. (1983). Social interaction and developmental competence of preterm and full-term infants during the first year of life. *Child Development*, 54:1199-210.

Daee, A., Robinson, P., Lawson, M., Turpin, J.A., Gregory, B. & Tobias, J.D. (2002). Psychologic and physiologic effects of dieting in adolescents. *South Medical Journal*, 95:1032-41.

de Onis, M. & Blossner, M. (2000). Prevalence and trends of overweight among preschool children in developing countries. *American Journal of Clinical Nutrition*, 72:1032-39.

Evans, W.J. & Campbell, W.W. (1993). Sarcopenia and age-related changes in body composition and functional capacity. *Journal of Nutrition*, 123:465-8.

Fall, C.H. Osmond, C., Barker, D.J., Clark, P.M., Hales, C.N. & Stirling, Y. (1995). Fetal and infant growth and cardiovascular risk factors in women. *British Medical Journal*, 310:428-32.

Fontana, M., Zuin, G. & Plebani, A. (1999). Body composition in HIV-infected children: Relation with disease progression and survival. *American Journal of Clinical Nutrition*, 69:1282-6.

Galler, J., Ricciuti, H., Crawford, M. & Kucharski, L. (1984). The role of the mother-infant interaction in eating disorders. In J. Galler (Ed.). *Nutrition and Behaviour* (Volume 5). New York: Plenum Press, pp. 73-158.

Guedeney, A. (1995). Kwashiorkor, depression and attachment disorders. *The Lancet*, 346:1293.

Harris, R. (1991). Anorexia nervosa and bulimia nervosa in female adolescents. *Nutrition Today*: 30-4.

Kain, J., Vio, F. & Albala, C. (1998). Childhood nutrition in Chile: From deficit to excess. *Nutrition Research*, 18:1825-37.

Kimm, S.Y.S., Barton, B.A., Obarzanek, E., McMahon, R.P., Sabry, Z.I., Waclawiw, M.A., Schreiber, G.B., Morrison, J.A., Similo, S. & Daniels, S.R. (2001). Racial divergence in adiposity during adolescence: The NHLBI growth and health study. *Paediatrics*, 107:34-9.

Kotler, D.P. (1998). Nutritional management of patients with AIDS-related anorexia. *Seminal Gastrointestinal Disease*, 9(4):189-99.

Labadarios, D. (Ed). (2000). *The National Food Consumption Survey (NFCS): Children aged 1 to 9 years, South Africa 1999*. Stellenbosch: Department of Health, Directorate Nutrition.

Marshall, W. & Tanner, J. (1970). Variations in the pattern of pubertal changes in boys. *Archives of Diseases in Childhood*, 45:12-23.

Mason, J., Lotfi, M., Dalmiya, N., Sethuraman, K. & Deitchler, M. (2001). *The Micronutrient Report: Current progress and trends in the control of vitamin A, iodine and iron deficiencies*. Ottawa: The Micronutrient Initiative.

Massey-Strokes, M. (2002). Adolescent nutrition. *Clearing House*, 75:286-92.

Medical Research Council. (1998). *South African Demographic and Health Survey*. Cape Town: Medical Research Council.

National Center for Health Statistics. (2001). www.cdc.gov/nchs/

Nerad, J., Romeyn, M., Silverman, E., Allen-Reid, J., Dieterich, D., Merchant, J., Pelletier, V.A., Tinnerello, D. & Fenton, M. (2003). General nutrition management in patients infected with human immunodeficiency virus. *Clinical Infectious Diseases*, 36(S2):S52-62.

Parsons, T.J., Power, C., Logan, S. & Summerbell, C.D. (2001). Childhood predictors of adult obesity: A systematic review. *International Journal of Obesity*, 23:(S)1-107.

Pollitt, E. (1994). Poverty and child development: Relevance of research in developing countries to the United States. *Child Development*, 65:283-95.

Puoane, T., Steyn, K., Bradshaw, D., Laubscher, R., Fourie, J., Lambert, V. & Mbananga, N. (2002). Obesity in South African: The South African Demographic and Health Survey. *Obesity Research*, 10:1038-48.

Rabeneck, L., Palmer, A., Knowles, J.B., Seidehamel, R.J., Harris, C.L., Merkel, K.L., Risser, J.M. & Akrarawi, S.S. (1998). A randomized controlled trial evaluating nutrition counseling with and without oral supplemenations in malnourished HIV-infected patients. *Journal of the American Dietetics Association*, 98(4):434-8.

Richardson, B. (1986). Low birth weight and health in the preschool years – letter. *South African Medical Journal*, 69:411.

Richter, L.M. (1993). Protein-energy malnutrition and the psychological development of young children. *South African Journal of Clinical Nutrition*, 6:28-32.

Richter, L. & Griesel, L. (1994). Malnutrition, low birth weight and related influences on psychological development. In A. Dawes & D. Donald (Eds.). *Childhood and Adversity in South Africa: Psychological perspectives from South African research*. Cape Town: David Philip, pp. 66-91.

Richter, L., Rose, C. & Griesel, R. (1997). Cognitive and behavioural effects of a school breakfast. *South African Journal of Clinical Nutrition*, 87:93-100.

Roubenhoff, R., McDermott, A. & Weiss, L. (1999). Short-term progressive resistance training increases strength and lean body mass in adults infected with human immunodeficiency virus. *AIDS*, 13:231-9.

Spear, B.A. (1996). Adolescent growth and development. In V.I. Rickert (Ed.). *Adolescent Nutrition: Assessment and management*. New York: Chapman and Hall, pp. 100-28.

Steen, S.N. (1996). Timely statement of the American Dietetic Association: Nutrition guidance for adolescent athletes in organised sport. *Journal of American Dietetic Association*, 96:610.

United Nations Children's Fund. (2002). *State of the World's Children, 2002*. New York: United Nations Children's Fund.

United Nations Development Programme. (2002). *State of the World Population, 2002. People, Poverty and Possibilities: Making development work for the poor*. New York: United Nations Development Programme.

World Health Organisation. (1999). *A Critical Link: Intervention for physical growth and psychological development*. World Health Organisation: Geneva.

Multiple choice questions

1. Which two micronutrients were identified by the World Health Organisation as key to preventing 'hidden hunger'?
   a) Vitamin C and zinc
   b) Vitamin D and calcium
   c) Vitamin A and iodine
   d) Vitamin E and Vitamin A
2. What is the Barker hypothesis?
   a) environmental exposure, particularly nutrition, within the first year of life after birth is critical in determining an individual's risk of developing mental illness
   b) poor maternal health and nutrition during pregnancy can programme the foetus' physiology in a way that can contribute to the risk of diseases such as obesity
   c) a baby born with low birth weight is not at risk for developing hypertension and diabetes
   d) maternal smoking during pregnancy does not alter the physiological programming and growth of the foetus
3. Two of the five most common causes of child deaths in the world are?
   a) HIV/AIDS and measles
   b) malaria and over-nutrition
   c) pneumonia and malnutrition
   d) measles and chicken pox
4. Adolescence is considered to be a nutritionally vulnerable phase for several reasons such as?
   a) increased demand for macronutrients (carbohydrate, fat, protein) and micronutrients (e.g., iron, calcium, vitamin A) to meet the dramatic increase in physical growth and cognitive development
   b) the shift in attitudes and perceptions around foods and body esteem may result in pathological eating behaviour, and environmental influences (e.g., family, peers, medical may impact on dietary practices)
   c) special nutrient needs associated with participation in sports, adolescent pregnancy, development of an eating disorder, excessive dieting, and use of alcohol and drugs
   d) all of the above
5. Which is not a South African food-based dietary guideline?
   a) eat fats daily (25% of dietary food intake)
   b) make starchy foods the basis of most meals
   c) chicken, fish, milk, meat or eggs should be eaten daily
   d) eat dry beans, peas, lentils and soya regularly
6. The obesity epidemic in South Africa affects which group particularly?
   a) young men in their teens
   b) adult women
   c) young women in their teens
   d) adult men
7. Congenital abnormalities occur more frequently in infants born in which birth weight category?
   a) more than 4 000 grams
   b) more than 3 000 grams
   c) less than 3 500 grams
   d) less than 2 500 grams
8. Children with NOFTT were first diagnosed in?
   a) concentration and refugee camps
   b) orphanages
   c) poor homes with working parents
   d) day care centers
9. The drop off in weight among toddlers seen in developing countries is not due to?
   a) excessive outdoor play
   b) poor weaning foods
   c) infection
   d) low levels of stimulation
10. Which of the following are not common nutritional complications of HIV infection and AIDS?
    a) lactose intolerance
    b) gluten intolerance
    c) fat malabsorption
    d) AIDS-related anorexia

Short answer questions

1. What food groups have been associated with hyperactivity in children?
2. What are the common micronutrient deficiencies in children, and what food groups are important to prevent them?
3. What is the common micronutrient deficiency associated with injuries in older women, and what food groups are important to prevent it?
4. What psychological and physiological dangers are associated with dieting?
5. What social and psychological factors are associated with early or late menarche?

35

HIV/AIDS, Tuberculosis and Parasites

Inge Petersen, Arvin Bhana, Jane Kvalsvig, Sheldon Allen &
Leslie Swartz

CHAPTER OBJECTIVES

After studying this chapter you should be able to:
- demonstrate a basic understanding of the spread of HIV/AIDS, tuberculosis (TB) and parasites, and associated risk factors
- understand how these medical conditions are spread
- appreciate the social and psychological factors that contribute to high levels of these diseases
- understand the role psychologists can play in curbing these diseases
- show an understanding of the ways in which these diseases impact on mental health and human development.

Nosipho was aware, like most young South Africans, that she was living through a pandemic. Information on HIV/AIDS and how it was spread had been given to her while she was at school, and there were often pamphlets and information provided about it on campus. At first, she did not believe that HIV/AIDS could be as serious as something like malaria, which she knew affected many people living near the Mozambique border, where her aunt lived. She also could not believe it could cause as much trouble as tuberculosis (TB) which was quite common in her community. More recently, though, she began to realise the impact it was having on people's lives. More and more often she saw and heard about people in her local community who were ill or dying. In many cases no-one would say outright what was wrong, but Nosipho and everyone else knew that it was AIDS that was killing them. There seemed to be more and more people dying of TB as well, and she had heard that people who had HIV were more likely to get TB and to die from it. It seemed that mainly young people were dying – whether from TB or from other complications of HIV/AIDS – and quite often it was parents who left their children to be taken in by neighbours, friends and elderly relatives.

Nosipho felt it was really important that everyone understood, right from an early age, how the disease was transmitted and what they could do to protect themselves and other people from getting it. She knew about the importance of safe sex and condom use. Sometimes, though, when she chatted to girlfriends, they spoke about how hard it could be to persuade their partners that they should use a condom. Some of her friends said they sometimes were just too embarrassed to raise the subject, but then they worried afterwards that they could have caught the disease. A few of her friends had already been tested for HIV/AIDS, and fortunately their test results had come back negative. At university, very few people admitted openly that they had AIDS, but Nosipho assumed that there must be a fair number who were infected. Because it was possible to have no signs of illness and still be infected, there were also probably many more people in her immediate environment who had the virus and didn't even know that they had it. These days in South Africa HIV/AIDS was an inevitable part of life and even though she didn't want to think about it, she knew that it was important that she did.

Introduction

According to the Global Fund, HIV/AIDS, tuberculosis and malaria (a parasitic infection) collectively account for 6 million deaths annually (Global Fund, 2004), with the majority of these occurring in the developing world. In Africa, in 2002, 54 per cent of all deaths were due to infectious and parasitic diseases, whereas in the world as a whole in the same year, only about 20 per cent of deaths were due to these causes. Similarly, a widely accepted measure of disablement due to illness or injury – what is known as Disability Adjusted Life Years, or DALYs – shows that 53 per cent of all disablement in Africa in 2002 was a result of infectious diseases and parasites, as opposed to 24 per cent world-wide. More than 10 per cent of disability in Africa in 2002, as measured by DALYs, was due to malaria, and almost 20 per cent to HIV (as opposed to 2 per cent and 6 per cent world-wide, respectively) (figures for deaths and disability computed from statistics compiled by the World Health Organisation, 2004).

Infections and parasites, therefore, have a devastating impact on families, communities and economies around the world, but particularly in developing countries. These diseases and parasites act immediately on the body; they weaken the immune system, they attack and damage healthy lungs and they compromise the integrity of vital blood. There is little doubt that these diseases also have a profound psychological effect on those unfortunate enough to be infected with them and on the nation as a whole.

The irony is that many of the conditions which disproportionately affect poorer countries and regions of the world (and Africa in particular) are wholly curable or preventable. There is no cure for HIV/AIDS, for example, but we know precisely what kinds of behaviour lead to the spread of the pandemic, and how people can avoid becoming infected. In the case of TB, there are well established biomedical cures. Similarly, we know how to prevent malaria and bilharzia, and, in general, how to cure those infected with parasites. Biomedical science has made enormous strides in providing us with the means to contain all these conditions, but they continue to spread. Why? This is because, as we shall see in this chapter, social, political, economic and personal factors contribute to the spread of these conditions. If HIV/AIDS, TB and parasites are to be effectively controlled, reduced, or even altogether eradicated, an all-encompassing approach is imperative: biomedicine needs to work closely with psychology and social science.

In this chapter we examine the bio-psychosocial influences that promote and maintain the HIV/AIDS pandemic, the TB epidemic and parasitic infection, with an emphasis on the social psychological influ-

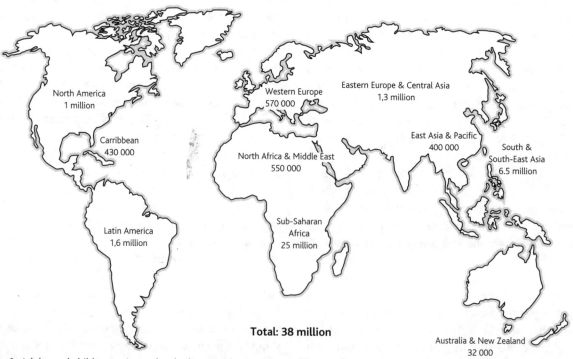

Figure 1 Adults and children estimated to be living with HIV/AIDS as of the end of 2003
Source: UNAIDS (2004)

ences, as well as the contributions that psychology can make to prevention and control of these infectious diseases. We also examine how these diseases and parasites impact on the mental health of those infected.

The HIV/AIDS pandemic

Extent of the problem

HIV/AIDS is a devastating pandemic. Since it was first identified in 1980, twenty million people worldwide have already died of AIDS, with 38 million people currently living with HIV (UNAIDS, 2004). Across the globe, everyday 12 000 adults and 2 000 children are infected with HIV. Frighteningly, at least 95 per cent of these new infections occur in developing countries, with more than 50 per cent affecting women and young children (Lamptey *et al.*, 2002). Without a co-ordinated and substantial response to the pandemic, it is projected that worldwide there will be 45 million new HIV infections by 2010 (Goliber, 2002).

Sub-Saharan Africa has the most infected people, as depicted in Figure 1, with 16 countries in this region having more than 10 per cent of their population of reproductive age infected (World Health Organisation, 2002b). More people die of AIDS-related illness in sub-Saharan Africa than of any other cause.

In 2002, 5 million South Africans were infected with AIDS, which is the highest absolute number of infections of any country in the world. It is estimated that infection rates in the South African population will peak at between 7 to 8 million, with a total of between 5 and 6 million people who will probably die as a result of HIV/AIDS by 2010 (Desmond & Gow, 2002). In 2002, South Africa's child mortality rate was 97 deaths per 1 000 children. Without AIDS it would have been 61 deaths per 1 000.

The transmission and course of HIV/AIDS

The HI virus is transmitted through unsafe vaginal, anal or oral sex with an infected person; and/or, from mother to child, mostly during childbirth but also by fluid transmission in the womb, or through breastfeeding; and/or through direct contact with infected blood or blood products such as needle-stick injuries, unsterilised needles or blades or through sharing needles during intravenous drug use. The most common method of transmission in sub-Saharan Africa is through heterosexual intercourse, with the most significant biomedical factor

driving the AIDS pandemic being the high prevalence of sexually transmitted infections (STIs) (Barnett & Whiteside, 2002; Desmond & Gow, 2002).

On entering the body, the HI virus reproduces by integrating its genetic instructions into the white blood cells of the human host and attacks the body's immune system, thus rendering the human host vulnerable to opportunistic infections, such as pneumonia, meningitis, cancers and tuberculosis (TB) (Barnett & Whiteside, 2002). As the HI virus attacks the body's immune system slowly over time, newly infected individuals will not know they are infected unless they have an HIV test. A person who is HIV-positive will pass through a relatively asymptomatic or HIV-well stage (without symptoms), which may last from 3 to 7 years, to a symptomatic HIV-ill stage, which lasts from 12 to 18 months during which the person may suffer weight loss and bouts of illness from opportunistic infections, to finally having full-blown AIDS (characterised by a variety of persistent and debilitating infections and health problems such as persistent diarrhoea, oral and/or vaginal candida (thrush), severe mental deterioration and persistent respiratory infections).

Common opportunistic infections associated with HIV/AIDS include TB (discussed below), which accounts for about one third of AIDS deaths in sub-Saharan Africa (Lamptey *et al.*, 2002). Given the length of the HIV-well or asymptomatic stage, unless tested for HIV, the majority of those infected will not know they are infected. A consequence is that the disease spreads like wildfire as infected people, who do not know their status, continue to have unsafe sex.

Bio-psychosocial influences that increase vulnerability to HIV/AIDS

In a nutshell, we all are vulnerable, but in sub-Saharan Africa certain biological, cultural and socio-economic conditions render women of child-bearing age, and especially those who live in informal settlements, where there is a mix of poverty and social dislocation, more vulnerable to contracting HIV/AIDS (Lamptey *et al.*, 2002; Shishana & Simbayi, 2002). During unprotected vaginal intercourse, a women's risk of becoming infected is up to four times higher than that of a man's risk of infection. In addition to this biological vulnerability, unequal gendered power relations at a socio-cultural level limit a woman's ability to negotiate or control sexual interaction, especially with older men

(Lamptey *et al.*, 2002; LeClerc-Madlala, 2001). Furthermore, in South Africa, women's and girls' vulnerability to infection is also increased by a culture of physical and sexual violence, which is so common that it has come to be perceived as normative and largely accepted (Wood *et al.*, 1997). Inserting poverty and social dislocation into this mix compounds women's risk of infection. At a structural level, poor job prospects due to women's relative lack of education and training combined with the burden of domestic work, child bearing and child care, has increased the number of women living in poverty (see Chapter 22, this volume). It has also increased their dependence on men, reducing their ability to negotiate safe sex and increasing their vulnerability to being sexually exploited, with many young women having resorted to 'transactional sex' – exchanging sex for money or other goods in order to survive (Campbell & MacPhail, 2002; LeClerc-Madlala, 2001). Women living in informal settlements are particularly vulnerable given that social capital is likely to be low, with inhabitants being drawn from a variety of disparate communities. As discussed in the chapter on risk and risk behaviour (Chapter 31, this volume), social capital is a key resource used by poorer communities to cope with the stressors of poverty through sharing of socio-economic resources and networks.

Furthermore, youth in these communities, while being vulnerable to HIV infection because of their propensity to engage in high risk behaviours anyway, are particularly vulnerable because conventional role models (such as employed parents) and symbols of self-worth (such as the prospect of being gainfully employed) are minimal.

Contributions of psychology to the prevention and control of HIV/AIDS

Without a cure or vaccination, and given that the most common means of transmission of the virus in sub-Saharan Africa is through heterosexual intercourse, reducing high risk sexual behaviour remains the principal strategy for curbing the pandemic. Psychology thus has an important role to play in providing health-promoting behavioural change strategies at the individual and interpersonal levels. Efforts have largely concentrated on promoting the ABC (abstinence, being faithful and monogamous, 'condomising') model of prevention, which encourages abstinence or not engaging in sex, particularly

Figure 2 Conditions of poverty and poor hygiene increase vulnerability to HIV/AIDS

amongst the youth, as well as promoting safe sexual practices amongst the sexually active.

Given the multiple levels of influence that render people vulnerable to HIV infection, it is important, however, that prevention efforts adopt an ecologically systemic understanding of risk described in Chapter 31, ensuring interventions occur at all levels: individual, interpersonal, community and societal.

A large number of prevention efforts have focused on empowering women, and to some extent men, at the individual level with respect to improving knowledge on HIV transmission, promoting health enhancing attitudes and improving skills to negotiate and practice safe sex. These efforts need to be accompanied by interventions at the interpersonal, community and socio-cultural levels. Of importance at the interpersonal level is the need to promote protective peer or social norms that enable behaviour change towards safe sexual practices, particularly for males in Africa where the socio-cultural norm associates masculinity with multiple partners. The need for interventions at this level is highlighted by the evaluation of a risk reduction curriculum for tertiary level students at one tertiary institution in South Africa described in Box 35.1.

The Stepping Stones sexual health programme implemented in The Gambia in Africa described in Box 35.2, provides an example of a community based intervention at the individual, interpersonal and community levels, which was found to be suc-

Procedure

In the experimental condition, tertiary students were exposed to a participatory group-based risk reduction curriculum over a number of sessions cohering around three dominant themes: knowledge of HIV/AIDS, awareness and skills building. Knowledge sessions included understanding the epidemiology of HIV/AIDS, modes of HIV transmission (including myths and conceptions) and biological factors that underpin the progression of AIDS in a person infected with HIV. Awareness sessions focused not only on understanding risky sexual behaviour but also on developing a critical consciousness about gender roles and the impact of gender roles on risky sexual behaviour. The skills building exercises attempted to enhance relationship building and sexual communication, negotiation and condom use. In the control condition, students were exposed to a series of lectures on HIV/AIDS, which largely focused on knowledge of HIV/AIDS. Evaluation used a pre- and post-test knowledge, attitude and practices (KAP) survey questionnaire, followed up by qualitative interviews with participants.

Results

The findings showed an improvement in both the experimental and control conditions on knowledge of HIV/AIDS, with the experimental condition producing a significant improvement on awareness of the role of social influences on sexual behaviour. No significant change in behaviour was found for either group (Bhagwanjee et al., 2002). The qualitative interviews revealed that while students exposed to the experimental condition felt empowered by the programme, behaviour change was difficult given the peer norms that prevailed on campus, which promoted high risk sexual behaviour (Mahintso, 2003).

Conclusion

To be successful, interventions targeting behaviour change at the individual level need to be accompanied by interventions aimed at creating peer norms that are enabling and supportive of behaviour change.

---

cessful at altering sexual norms and creating a health enabling community context that is supportive of behaviour change.

Furthermore, given the role of poverty, gender inequality and social dislocation in increasing vulnerability to infection, behaviour change strategies cannot be separated from structural interventions at a societal level, which are focused on poverty alleviation, multi-sectoral development and building a more egalitarian society.

In addition, HIV transmission is integrally related to treatment and care of those infected and affected by HIV of which health-promoting counselling plays a central role. Voluntary counselling and testing (VCT), prevention of mother to child transmission (PMCT) and managing sexually transmitted infections (STIs) are all regarded as prevention interventions, as their primary function is to reduce transmission of HIV (Geffen et al., 2003). Anti-retroviral treatment (ART), which refers to medication

---

Procedure

Stepping Stones, a participatory STI/HIV prevention workshop programme based on empowerment techniques, was administered to both male and female peer groups in the experimental condition, which comprised two villages. The control condition comprised two adjacent matched villages. The workshops covered relationship skills, including assertiveness training , as well as information on sexually transmitted infections and condom practice sessions. Pre and post intervention evaluation adopted multiple methods including a knowledge, attitude and practices (KAP) survey, in-depth interviews and focus group discussions.

Results

Three primary areas of change were identified in the experimental condition: increased risk awareness, condom use and dialogue within marriage. Norms were reported to have changed and trust between partners increased. Social cohesion on issues of sexual health were reported to have increased, with these topics being discussed in public for the first time.

Conclusion

Peer group interventions at a community level can be used to collectively challenge group norms and create a community context that is enabling and supportive of behaviour change (Paine et al., 2002).

that slows down the rate at which the HIV multiplies in the body and therefore allows HIV infected people to stay healthy for longer, also plays a role in prevention. It can lower viral loads, and the availability of such treatment should hopefully encourage people to go for VCT. It is very important for people to know their status. It has been found that VCT encourages behavioural change towards safer sexual practices (UNAIDS, 2001), with people who are negative being motivated to practice safe sex in order to stay negative. Secondly, with counselling, those who are positive are encouraged to practice safe sex in order to prevent infecting others as well as re-infecting themselves.

Johnson and Dorrington (2002) estimate that over 2.5 million new infections and approximately 3 million deaths could be avoided in South Africa between 2002 and 2015 if treatment with anti-retroviral therapy was provided to those infected in addition to prevention and treatment of opportunistic infections.

The impact of HIV/AIDS on mental health

Studies show that people who are infected with HIV are at greater risk of developing a mental disorder than those who are not infected with the disease (Desjarlais *et al.*, 1995). This occurs at two levels. Firstly, the stress of knowing your positive status, which in the absence of a cure is often regarded as a death sentence, together with the stigma that accompanies the illness, may trigger an acute stress reaction, depression and/or anxiety. Desjarlais *et al.* (1995) report that individuals who are HIV positive have a higher suicide rate than HIV negative individuals. Secondly, mental disorders may also result as a complication of HIV infection. People in the final stages of infection may suffer from dementia, delirium and psychotic disorders as brain cells are destroyed by the virus as well as by opportunistic infections, such as meningitis (Desjarlais *et al.*, 1995).

Furthermore, having family members infected with HIV is likely to impact on the psychological well-being of the rest of the family as a consequence of stigma and premature death. The psychological effects on children orphaned by AIDS, while under researched, is likely to be substantial (World Health Organisation, 2002a). UNICEF (2002) notes that the trauma and hardship associated with the loss of parents cannot be overstated. Grief over the death of a parent, fear of the future, separation from siblings, and distress about worsening economic circumstances and HIV/AIDS-related discrimination and isolation often results in depression and anxiety.

The TB epidemic

Extent of the problem

The statistics on tuberculosis (TB) are shocking. Someone in the world is newly infected with TB every single second, with nearly one per cent of the world's population being newly infected with TB each year. Overall, one-third of the world's population is currently infected with the TB bacillus. Five to ten per cent of people who are infected with TB (but who are not infected with HIV) become sick or infectious at some time during their life. TB kills about 2 million people each year (including persons infected with HIV). More than 8 million people become sick with TB each year. About 2 million TB cases per year occur in sub-Saharan Africa. This number is rising rapidly as a result of the HIV/AIDS pandemic. Around 3 million TB cases per year occur in south-east Asia. Over 250 000 TB cases per year occur in Eastern Europe (World Health Organisation, 2002b:1).

TB is a disease which hits hardest in poorer countries, and there is an enormous burden in Africa and south-east Asia in particular. Figure 3 shows the World Health Organisation's estimate of incidence (the number of new cases) of TB in 2001. The countries which have the fastest growth of TB (those shaded dark blue and dark grey on the map) also tend to be the poorest countries (in Africa, Latin America and Asia). According to the World Health Organisation (2003a:109), South Africa has the seventh highest number of TB cases of any country in the world. In South Africa, as elsewhere, the HIV pandemic is a major factor in making the TB epidemic worse.

The transmission and course of TB

Formerly termed the 'white plague', 'consumption' and 'phthisis' (meaning 'to waste away') (Whalen & Semba, 2001), TB is a contagious disease, which spreads through the air. When a person infected with pulmonary TB (i.e. TB of the lung, the most common form of TB) sneezes, spits, talks or coughs, that person releases TB germs, known as bacilli, into the air. Only a small number of bacilli need to be inhaled for a new infection to occur. However, people infected

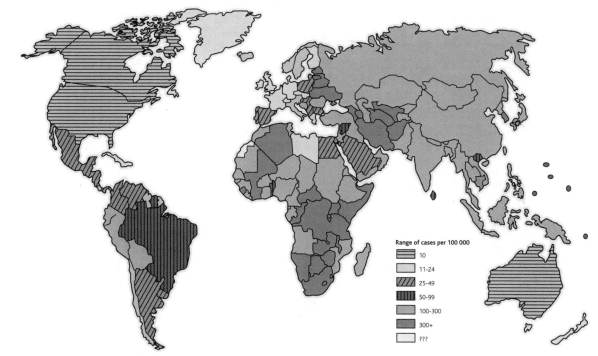

Figure 3 Estimate of rates of new cases of TB in 2001
Source: World Health Organisation (2003b)

Range of cases per 100 000
- 10
- 11-24
- 25-49
- 50-99
- 100-300
- 300+
- ???

with TB will not necessarily become ill. The immune system protects the body against TB, and the bacilli can lie dormant in the body for years. When a person has a weakened immune system, this increases the chance of becoming ill (World Health Organisation, 2002b:1). Figure 4 shows a simplified description and picture of how pulmonary TB develops.

There are drugs that can cure TB, the best known being isoniazid and rifampicin. In order for the drugs to work, however, they have to be taken regularly for a long period of time (six to eight months). If people take the drugs for a short time and then stop, or take the drugs irregularly, strains of TB develop that are resistant to those drugs. There are now increasing rates of multi-drug resistant TB (MDR-TB), which is defined as TB that does not respond to either isoniazid and rifampicin. These drug-resistant strains of TB can be spread to other people. This means that if for any reason a person does not fully complete the required drug treatment for TB, this can have very serious consequences both for the person and for others, through the spread of drug-resistant TB (World Health Organisation, 2002b:2).

Bio-psychosocial influences that increase vulnerability to TB

The poor, regardless of gender, sex, age, race, and people who are HIV positive or who have AIDS, are extremely vulnerable to TB. The reasons for the rapid spread of TB in poor countries are complex. Health providers have largely attributed the current spread to poor patient adherence to treatment, while others take a broader view by looking at the way that factors such as migration, HIV and poorly managed health care services contribute to the rise in TB (World Health Organisation, 2002b).

The World Health Organisation attributes the rise in tuberculosis over recent times to:
- The increased impact of HIV, which fuels TB infections by weakening the immune system and accelarating the spread of both diseases.
- Poorly managed TB programmes, which have lead to the development of multi-drug resistant TB.
- Greater migration and displacement of people related to global trade, war and poverty.

It is clear that although TB is a physical problem, which is well understood medically, the factors that contribute to its continuing spread are economic, social and psychological. These factors operate at a range of levels.

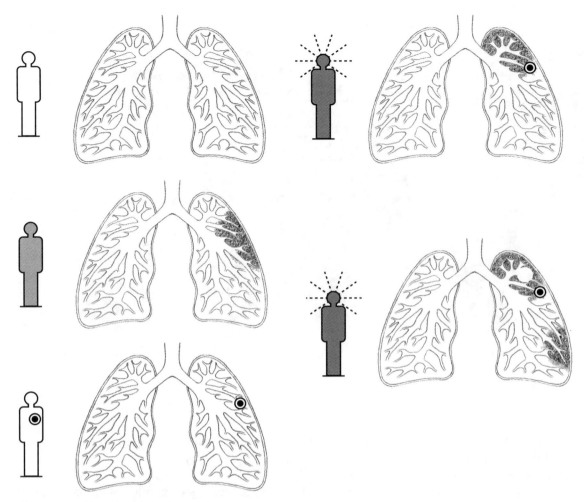

Figure 4 How pulmonary TB develops
Source: Canadian Lung Association (2003)

Poor people are exposed to unhealthy working and living conditions, and often are poorly nourished. These factors make them easy prey for TB (Packard, 1989). Poverty not only increases the chances of becoming infected with TB and developing the disease, it also limits the likelihood that medical treatment will be accessed and utilised successfully (Farmer, 1997).

In South Africa, poverty and TB have been divided unequally along racial lines. The result is that disadvantaged groups, particularly African or Black workers, have been hardest hit by the disease (Packard, 1991). Periods of economic recession during the last century created a shortage of employment, and this also contributed to the development of overcrowded peri-urban slums with poor and ever-deteriorating living conditions (Metcalf, 1991). There are still disparities in the TB incidence and mortality rates of different racial groups in South Africa, largely because these racial or socio-economic inequalities have not changed significantly.

Migration is another force that has promoted the spread of TB throughout history (Metcalf, 1991). Urbanisation, economic instability, industrialisation and colonisation together with civil unrest, war and natural disasters have increased migration and displacement (Gandy & Zumla, 2002). South Africa has been a good illustration of the contribution of these factors, and in the age of globalisation, the so-called developing world remains a good illustration of TB's link to the movement of people, whether they move by force or by free choice.

Thus, from a global perspective, factors like urbanisation and overcrowding that historically helped TB to spread in Europe and elsewhere, are fuelling the epidemic in low-income countries today (Saraiya & Binkin, 2000). People are far more mobile than ever before, moving between countries and within countries to seek refuge from civil unrest, political asylum, employment or study, for example. Migration makes accessing health care and adhering to long-term treatment particularly difficult. These migrant populations tend to have higher rates of infection and spread TB as they move (World Health Organisation, 2003b).

Contributions of psychology to the prevention and control of TB

A cure for TB has been available for more than 50 years. Adherence is essential if the TB treatment is to be successful, but it presents particular challenges to both patients and health providers. The treatment process for this stigmatised disease is long, and involves 6 to 8 months of taking large amounts of drugs for 3 to 5 days a week. The range of recommended drugs can have a variety of unpleasant side effects, such as rashes, stomach pain, hepatitis, nausea, deafness and visual impairment. After two months of treatment, patients begin to feel well again and tend to stop taking their treatment. This non-adherence is perhaps the greatest barrier to progress in TB control, and it is in improving treatment adherence that psychology can play a role in the control of the disease, and in slowing the development of multi-drug resistant (MDR) TB, the treatment of which is far more expensive than the treatment of TB in its usual forms. The prevention of MDR-TB is a very serious challenge, since the spread of MDR-TB can lead ultimately to an incurable epidemic.

In order to improve worldwide TB control, the World Health Organisation (2003c:1-2) recommends a strategy for detection and cure of TB. It is known as DOTS. DOTS comprises five elements:

- *Government commitment* to sustained TB control activities.
- *Case detection by sputum smear microscopy* among symptomatic patients self-reporting to health services.
- *Standardised treatment regimen of six to eight months* for at least all sputum smear positive cases, with directly observed therapy or treatment (DOT) for at least the initial two months.
- *A regular, uninterrupted supply of all essential anti-TB drugs.*
- *A standardised recording and reporting system* that allows assessment of treatment results for each patient and of the TB control programme performance overall.

If we examine these guidelines, we can see that though there are technical requirements in combating the TB epidemic (such as the supply of the correct drugs), psychological and behavioural factors are also key. At the heart of the DOTS approach is the commitment to directly observed treatment, whereby the patient is observed taking the medication for at least a portion of the treatment period. The reason for the DOT approach is simple: health providers are seriously concerned about adherence to medication, and look for ways to ensure that this adherence occurs. If a person is watched five days a week for six to eight months taking medication, the argument goes, then this is the best way that we can be sure they are indeed taking the medication. But things are not so simple, for at least three reasons. First, when researchers have examined whether DOT works better than other methods, there does not seem to be conclusive evidence that this is so (Volmink *et al.*, 2000). Second, it has been pointed out that in different countries and contexts, what people mean by DOT differs greatly (Macq *et al.*, 2003). Third, it has been argued that the process of directly observed treatment can create a situation in which the health provider treats the person with TB as a 'case' of infection rather than as a person who has their own feelings and views. The patient may even be seen as a 'bad person' who is spreading disease, and who may be treated disrespectfully by staff (van der Walt & Swartz, 2002). Paradoxically, this can lead patients to avoid coming for treatment, and to their rebelling against the DOT regime. The DOT debate is a complex one and will not be discussed in detail here, but at the heart of the debate is the question of how best to understand and contribute to increasing patient adherence to treatment.

Psychology can play an important role in the control of the TB epidemic through understanding and developing behavioural strategies to increase treatment adherence. It is important to emphasise, though, that the adherence challenge – which is a world-wide challenge to health care (see Jaret, 2001; Vermeire *et al.*, 2001; World Health Organisation, 2001) – cannot be addressed by addressing patient behaviour alone. On the contrary, adherence needs to be addressed at the health provider level as well. Each of these levels will be considered in turn.

Interventions aimed at assisting patients to adhere to treatment include:
- ensuring that educational materials are produced appropriately for patients' contexts and literacy levels;
- labelling drugs clearly and packaging them conveniently for patients;
- motivating patients to complete treatment, including providing rewards for treatment completion;
- reminding patients regularly to take their medication – it is easy to forget to take medication if it has to be taken for a long time and the patient does not feel ill;

- helping patients develop self-monitoring skills and confidence so that they more easily take charge of their treatment;
- providing group support for patients so patients do not feel isolated and have others to talk to;
- supporting family members who in turn support the ongoing treatment; and
- helping patients cope with the stigma and social isolation that the disease may lead to in their communities, and educating communities about TB and the importance of social support.

Interventions aimed at assisting health care providers to create an environment conducive to adherence include:

- assisting providers to think about adherence from the patient's point of view, and not to assume that all patients will lie about adherence;
- helping providers share power with patients in health consultations, creating an atmosphere in which patients will be able to discuss their adherence difficulties openly, and hence to solve them;
- improving providers' understanding of health behaviour and human motivation;
- improving providers' communication skills, appropriate to their working context;
- supporting providers and their managers in dealing with their work, so that providers can focus on the needs of the patients and not be distracted by work-related and personal concerns; and
- understanding the social and cultural context of the health care system, and working to ensure that the system as a whole is accessible and respectful of patient rights and needs.

While there are psychological factors in adherence to TB treatment pertaining to the relationship and communication between health providers and TB patients, there are also broader social, cultural and economic issues that underlie the attitudes, experiences and beliefs held by patients, their family members, friends and the community about the particular illness and its treatment (Vermeire *et al.*, 2001). In fact, to date, almost 200 different variables have been used to try to account for poor adherence, with little or no success (Vermeire *et al.*, 2001). According to a recent review, the characteristics of the disease, the nature of the referral process, the type of clinical setting, the therapeutic regimen and patient demographics do not seem to play a decisive role (Vermeire *et al.*, 2001). The presence of psychiatric disorders, features of the treatment (e.g., duration, number of medications, their cost and the frequency

of doses) and the degree of disability, however, appear to be closely linked to adherence.

The impact of TB on mental health

Like any other debilitating condition, TB can affect people's ability to learn, to concentrate, and to accomplish the tasks that are required of them daily. In rare cases, furthermore, TB can lead to brain conditions which have neuropsychological consequences. The most common mental health impact of TB, however, is probably that which arises from social and economic factors.

Because it is a disease of poverty, TB has for a long time carried a stigma, and many people have felt ashamed of having TB. With the advent of the AIDS pandemic, this stigma is further complicated because often people think that TB-infected individuals are HIV positive or have AIDS. The internalisation of these associations can be psychologically damaging for the TB patient. Much like HIV/AIDS, and equally negative, psychologically speaking, can be the effect of suffering a chronic illness while already marginalised and down-trodden.

Also, the long duration of medication, the sheer volume of medication and the cost of medication can also have profound psychological effects. Work may be disrupted (and patients may even lose their jobs) because of the need to attend treatment regularly, and where work is scarce and income small, this can have devastating effects on the mental health of the patient and the family. The long course of illness itself can be emotionally draining. The patient might wonder whether he or she is ever meant to be well, if he or she can ever conquer a condition for which so much treatment is needed, and if he or she can afford the treatment (particularly at a cost to others or at the sacrifice of other expenses).

More broadly, the ongoing TB epidemic can contribute to demoralisation in families and communities, and can impact on productivity and entrepreneurship. Given that TB is in fact curable, it is all the more urgent that psychologists redouble their efforts at containing the epidemic.

Parasites

Extent of the problem

Millions of children especially in sub-Saharan Africa are prey to common species of parasites, and often harbour several different parasite species simultaneously. Parasites live off others, deriving food and shelter from their hosts. These parasites include intestinal worms, malaria and bilharzia. Malaria and bilharzia are the main killers, and form the focus of attention in this section.

Malaria is the number one killer. The incidence of malaria escalated significantly in the 1990s, with 90 per cent of the cases being in Africa. The disease kills more than 2 million people a year, the majority of them children in sub-Saharan Africa. This situation has been attributed to drug resistance and to unreliable health systems in many southern African countries.

Bilharzia is even more widespread than malaria, and has been successfully controlled in many parts of the world, notably China, Japan, Brazil, Egypt and Morocco, but not in sub-Saharan Africa (Engels *et al.*, 2002). There are a number of possible explanations for the lack of control in sub-Saharan African countries: deteriorating socio-economic conditions, loss of diagnostic potential and the presence of more extreme health problems like HIV/AIDS and TB. Bilharzia tends to occur intensively over focal areas, so the total number of cases in a country may not be high, but some areas may have pockets of very high intensity infections.

35.3 THE MAIN KILLERS: MALARIA AND BILHARZIA

Malaria

Plasmodium falciparum is one of four species of malaria, but is the main killer. All malaria is transmitted by the *Anopheles* mosquito, as it moves from one human host to another. The malaria parasites (sporozoites) find their way to the liver within minutes of the mosquito biting a host. In the liver they divide rapidly over the course of about a week, forming thousands of merozoites, which burst out of the liver and into the bloodstream, where they invade red blood cells, contributing to anaemia. This situation develops rapidly, and if unchecked, the inability to deliver oxygen to the body's vital organs can result in death. There are two other ways in which the parasite can damage the host. Firstly, the mobilisation of chemical agents called cytokines which form part of the host's immune response may cause damage to host cells if present in excess. Secondly, a process called 'sequestration' involves the withdrawal of the infected red blood cells into small blood vessels. This compromises blood flow and delivery of oxygen to tissues, thereby causing damage. Usually the disease is limited either by treatment or by the host's immune system, but in some cases it threatens life, as in the well known cerebral malaria where the patient goes into a coma and often has convulsions (Marsh, 2002).

Repeated infections are a fact of life for people living in malaria-endemic areas, and over time they acquire the mechanisms that can kill the parasite or limit its replication. Another important mechanism develops which limits the body's own immune response so that the excessive cytokine action is no longer a feature of the infection.

Bilharzia

Schistosoma haematobium and *Schistosoma mansoni* are the two main species of bilharzias affecting humans in southern Africa. All bilharzias are transmitted by water and contaminated water is maintained through infected people urinating in the water. The eggs of the parasite hatch and develop to cercariae in water snails. These are shed into the water and penetrate the skin of people in the water.

The World Health Organisation advises member countries to control bilharzia through the primary health care system, and their expert committees have designed strategies for high burden communities and high risk individuals and simple, affordable assessment tools (Montresor *et al.*, 1998; Montresor *et al.*, 1999). On the positive side, Praziqantel, the drug of choice, has dropped in price significantly over the last decade, and control can be effected through the delivery of regular chemotherapy (probably only once a year) to primary school children at school. A comparison of spontaneous activity levels before and after treatment with Praziqantel has shown that activity increases after treatment (Kvalsvig, 1986), and so does physical fitness (Stephenson, 1989).

The intensity of infection (which is usually measured in terms of egg output in urine or faeces) is thought to give an indication of the handicap imposed by the parasite or the morbidity. The eggs may lodge and calcify anywhere in the body and cause damage in this way, and the loss of blood in the urine or stools which is characteristic of more intense infections may contribute to anaemia.

Transmission and course of parasitic infections

Parasites are well known to scientists: their life cycles have been identified, and there are tried and tested methods of prevention and treatment. Even malaria, the number one killer, is curable if adequately and promptly treated.

There are some similarities between the different species of parasites and the way in which they exploit their human hosts.

Bio-psychosocial influences which increase vulnerability to parasitic infections

Anyone who is exposed to parasites may contract parasitic infections. However, parasites thrive in conditions of poor nutrition and poor hygiene, where water and sanitation services are inadequate, where preventive services are weak, where treatment is difficult to obtain, where the physical environment is hot and/or humid, and where poverty and destitution are widespread. As is already clear, anyone with a compromised immune system or chronic illness (HIV/AIDS and/or TB) and living in such conditions is particularly vulnerable to parasites.

In the case of malaria, children who have not yet developed this immunity are at greater risk of severe disease and death, as are pregnant women and non-immune travellers. The latter group includes tourists, refugees and migrant labourers. In the case of schistosomiasis (bilharzia), children who play in rivers (usually those from about 8 to 14 years of age) are the most likely to acquire the infection. Children are also more likely than adults to suffer serious effects from parasitic infections, mainly because they have special nutritional needs for growth and cognitive development, and if nutrients are not present in sufficient amounts at the proper time, the course of development is disrupted.

The role of psychology in the prevention and control of parasitic infections

In theory, prevention of parasitic infection should not be too difficult. People can adopt behaviours that prevent the parasites from reaching them, their immune systems can mount defensive action and medical science has provided effective treatments to kill intruders.

However, in practice, a range of factors (much like those outlined, above, in the case of TB infec-

tion) compromise effective prevention of parasitic diseases. Psychology can play a role in the development of behaviour change strategies. With regard to prevention, in the case of malaria, getting people to 'cover up' at night as well as use mosquito nets and insecticide sprays is important. In the case of bilharzia, prevention requires that people living in infected areas stop urinating in the local dams, lakes or rivers as well as avoid swimming in contaminated water, and have regular medical check-ups at the local clinic. As with HIV/AIDS and TB, these behaviour change strategies are likely to be mediated by socio-economic factors. In some instances, 'covering up', may not be practical, sprays may be too expensive and not bathing in contaminated water may be impractical because of constraints on water supply and transport or logistics. Psychology can also play an important role in the control of parasitic infections through developing an understanding of treatment-seeking behaviour and treatment adherence, and developing behavioural strategies to increase people's access and completion of effective treatment. In the case of malaria in sub-Saharan Africa, it has been found, for instance, that people often self-treat, delay in seeking treatment from a health facility and, as is the case with TB, stop taking medications when they feel better (Williams & Jones, 2004).

The impact of parasites on mental health

The effect of parasites on children and pregnant women is particularly devastating. While physical and bodily damage may occur, psychological damage is common-place. If not fatal, cerebral malaria may cause severe and sometimes permanent structural damage to the brain and the nervous system. Both malaria and bilharzia, furthermore, considerably weaken and fatigue the body. Psychologically, there can be little doubt that parasites affect cognitive development and socialisation of children. Being 'run-down' and/or bedridden translates into being absent from school, being unable to take part in formative social interactions and events and in being excluded from 'normality' as far as the lives of children are concerned.

From a psychologist's point of view, the difficulty of assessing the impact of the parasites on the development of thinking skills in children is considerable. Developmental psychology is concerned with changes over time. When children in endemic communities start to move around at between one and two years of age, their exposure to infective agents

The case of Bahati Kazungu shows how devastating the effects of cerebral malaria can be, although less than 5 per cent children who survive will have such a severe outcome. Bahati was 2 years old when he fell ill with malaria. He lived a two hour bus journey away from the nearest hospital, and by the time he and his mother arrived, he had suffered three different attacks of seizures, and was in deep coma. He remained in coma for four days. At admission Bahati was found to have a high number of *Plasmodium falciparum* parasites in his blood. After he arrived in hospital he had no more seizures, but he had severe respiratory problems, and his blood sugar fell to a low level. When Bahati came out of coma the doctors thought that he was on the slow road to recovery. Unfortunately within days Bahati fell back into coma, a relatively uncommon pattern of illness which is referred to as bi-phasic. The prognosis is poor, but Bahati survived. He came out of this second coma alive, but not unscathed. He was discharged with severe and global impairments, and developed epilepsy. When he was followed up five years later he was found to still be under regular medication. At seven years old Bahati remained with severe cognitive impairments. He was unable to speak, and to wash and dress. He could do less for himself than he had been able to do before his illness. His family is close, and share the twenty four hour care that he needs. His younger cousins try to include him in their play, and his older siblings to train him to feed himself. Bahati is able to walk, pick up objects, and stay close to his family. Bahati will remain totally dependent upon them (personal communication, P. Holding, Kilifi, Kenya).

the brain become fully functional. There is some evidence that nutritional deficits such as iron deficiency (see Chapter 34, this volume) caused by parasites can slow myelination (Roncagliolo *et al.*, 1998). Other ways in which the parasites may affect development is by affecting the energy available to the child, or by the action of the immune system itself. Cytokines are known to have receptors in the brain, and there is considerable evidence that infections can cause sleep disturbances and other behavioural changes. From a developmental perspective, the damage to psychological functioning caused by parasitic infection is likely to be linked to the time of acquisition of the infection, its intensity and duration.

It has to be said that the evidence linking parasite infections to cognitive deficits is difficult to come by. Not many studies have attempted the difficult task of apportioning blame to parasites in contexts, which are fraught with other risk factors for development (such as poverty and poor nutrition). The evidence is mounting, however, and a recent pilot study tracking school-based control of bilharzia (as well as other parasites) in endemic areas showed that there was an association between grade repetition and high parasite load (Kvalsvig *et al.*, 2001). Age, height-for-age and intensity of parasitic infection were all significant predictors of performance on a scholastic task. Older children, better nourished pupils and/or pupils with lower parasite loads scored higher on the test.

Conclusion

As has been illustrated, there are multiple influences at the biological, psychological and social levels which increase vulnerability to the transmission of infectious diseases and parasites. Furthermore, these diseases in turn impact at all these levels as well. In addition to the obvious biophysical effects, at a social level they help to perpetuate poverty. They restrict economic growth – there are medical costs of treatment and prevention, educational costs for interrupted and delayed schooling, financial costs due to job losses and difficulty finding employment if infected with HIV/AIDS, TB, or a parasite. Furthermore, those who are ill need to be looked after and cared for, and they are frequently socially marginalised. There are also, of course, psychological costs – those who are ill may have to bare

increases dramatically. During the period from one to six, the increased risk of infection by both malaria and bilharzia coincides with a period when the child rapidly acquires skills in different domains and at different times. A developmental perspective alerts us to the fact that these skills are built on the foundations of what has preceded them (Piaget, 1973). Motor development precedes and facilitates the development of language and social skills, which involve the exchange of ideas and viewpoints and enable the formation of concepts.

Underlying the development of these observable skills is the process of myelination in the brain which facilitates new mental skills as new areas of

the brunt of prejudice, they may feel inferior, depressed, be riddled with self-doubt and/or self-pity. They may feel that they are an unforgivable burden, and hence experience guilt. They may experience anxiety. Their growth and development may be stunted and arrested, thereby affecting their identity and sense of self. Those who look after and care for the ill may also suffer psychologically in the face of tragic suffering, pain and even trauma.

Table 1 provides a schematic summary of just some of the activities which psychologists can undertake in making a contribution both to curbing the spread of infectious and parasitic disease and to limiting the negative effects of these diseases on communities and nations.

Psychologists are already making important contributions, as we have seen, but much remains to be done. An important strength of psychology, in this regard, is that the discipline as a whole is committed to the evaluation of our efforts, and to requiring evidence that our interventions work. The pandemics and epidemics with which we are confronted are too serious for us to take on face value that what we do about them works, and psychology as a science requires that we measure the impacts (good and bad) of what we do, and that we learn lessons both about successes and failures.

Health-related activity	Example of how psychology can contribute
Prevention of infection	Design and evaluation of prevention programmes
Reducing stigma	Design and evaluation of community-based programmes to reduce stigma
Treatment support	Devising approaches to treatment which fit easily into patients' lives and which do not alienate patients
Community-based care	Supporting family members and other carers in dealing with disablement, losses, and care of people who are ill, and those affected by illness and deaths in their family and social groups
Support to health care personnel	Training front-line health care personnel on psychological issues; providing support for patient-centred care
Advocacy for resources	Documenting the cognitive and mental health impact of parasitic infections, and bringing the social cost of these infections to the attention of authorities
Health care innovation	Exploring and evaluating new ways in which health care can be delivered, taking into account different social, economic, and cultural contexts
Making health a community-wide issue	Working with community-based structures (such as civic, women's and men's organisations) to put health issues on their agenda for social change and development

Table 1 Some examples of how psychology can contribute to the control of infectious and parasitic diseases

Barnett, T. & Whiteside, A. (2002). *AIDS in the 21st Century. Disease and Globalization*. New York: MacMillan.

Bhagwanjee, A., Bhana, A. & Petersen, I. (2002). The development and evaluation of an HIV/AIDS risk reduction programme for tertiary level learners. *SAHARA (Social Aspects of HIV/AIDS Research Alliance) Conference*, Pretoria, 1-4 September 2002.

Campbell, C. & MacPhail, C. (2002). Peer education, gender and the development of critical consciousness: participatory HIV prevention by South African youth. *Social Science & Medicine*, 55:331-45.

Canadian Lung Association (2003). *How pulmonary TB develops*, www.lung.ca/tb/abouttb/pulmonary/ (accessed 8 December 2003).

Desjarlais, R., Eisenberg, L., Good, B. & Kleinman, A. (1995). *World Mental Health: Problems and priorities in low-income countries*. New York: Oxford.

Desmond, C. & Gow, J. (2002). The current and future impact of the HIV/AIDS epidemic on South Africa's children. In G.A. Cornia (Ed.). *AIDS, Public Policy and Child Well-being*, www.unicef-icdc.org/webif/publications (accessed 20 March 2003).

Engels, D. Chitsulo, L., Montresor, A. & Savioli, L. (2002). The global epidemiological situation of schistosomiasis and new approaches to control and research. *Acta Tropica*, 82:139-46.

Farmer, P. (1997). Social scientists and the new tuberculosis. *Social Science & Medicine*, 44(3):347-58.

Gandy, M. & Zumla, A. (2002). The resurgence of disease: Social and historical perspectives on the 'new' tuberculosis. *Social Science & Medicine*, 55(3):385-96.

Geffen, N., Nattrass, N. & Raubenheimer, C. (2003). *The Cost of HIV Prevention and Treatment Interventions in South Africa*. Cape Town: Centre for Social Science Research, University of Cape Town.

Global Fund. (2004). www.theglobalfund.org (accessed 20 May 2004).

Goliber, T. (2002). *Background to the HIV/AIDS epidemic in sub-Saharan Africa*, www.prb.org/background (accessed 3 January 2003).

Jaret, P. (2001) 10 ways to improve patient compliance, www.hippocrates.com/FebruaryMarch2001/02features/02feat_compliance.htm (accessed 18 February 2002).

Johnson, L.J. & Dorrington, R.E. (2002). The demographic and epidemiological impact of HIV/AIDS treatment and prevention programmes: An evaluation based on the ASSA2000 model. *Paper presented the 2002 Demographic Association of Southern Africa conference*.

Kvalsvig, J. (1986). The effects of Schistosomiasis haematobium on the activity of school children. *Journal of Tropical Medicine & Hygiene*, 89:85-90.

Kvalsvig, J.D., Appleton, C.C., Archer C., Mthethwa, P., Memela, C., Mpanza, J.T., Mweni, S.L., Ngcoya, M., Nkomokazi, J. & Qotyana, P. (2001). *The KwaZulu-Natal Parasite Control Programme*, 1998-2000. Pietermaritzburg: KwaZulu-Natal Department of Health.

Lamptey, P., Wigley, M., Carr, D. & Collymore, Y. (2002). Facing the HIV/AIDS pandemic. *Population Bulletin*, 57(3):3-28.

LeClerc-Madlala, S (2001). Demonising women in the era of AIDs: On the relationship between cultural constructions of both HIV/AIDS and femininity. *Society in Transition*, 32(1):38-46.

Macq, J. C., Theobald, S., Dick, J. & Dembele, M. (2003). An exploration of the concept of directly observed treatment (DOT) for tuberculosis patients: from a uniform to a customised approach. *International Journal of Tuberculosis and Lung Disease*, 7:103-9.

Mahintsho, Z. (2003). *Process Evaluation of a Manualised AIDS Risk Reduction Programme Piloted on University Students*. Unpublished Masters dissertation, University of Durban-Westville, Durban.

Marsh, K. (2002). Research directions in malaria. *Welcome News Supplement*, 6:4-6.

Metcalf, C. A. (1991). A history of tuberculosis. In H.M. Coovadia & S.R. Benatar (Eds.). *A Century of Tuberculosis: South African perspectives*. Cape Town: Oxford University Press, pp. 1-31.

Montresor, A., Crompton, D.W.T., Hall, A., Bundy, D.A.P. & Savioli, L. (1998). *Guidelines for the Evaluation of Soil-transmitted Helminthiasis and Schistosomiasis at Community Level*. WHO/CTD/SIP/98.1. Geneva: World Health Organisation.

Montresor, A., Gyorkos, T.W., Crompton, D.W.T., Bundy, D.A.P. & Savioli, L. (1999). Monitoring Helminth Control Programmes: *Guidelines for monitoring the impact of control programmes aimed at reducing morbidity caused by soil-transmitted helminths and schistosomes, with particular reference to school-age children*. WHO/CDS/CPC/SIP/99.3. Geneva: World Health Organisation.

Packard, R.M. (1989). *White Plague, Black Labour: Tuberculosis and the political economy of health and disease in South Africa*. Pietermaritzburg: University of Natal Press.

Packard, R.M. (1991). Holding back the tide: TB control efforts in South Africa. In H.M. Coovadia & S.R. Benatar (Eds.). *A Century of Tuberculosis: South African perspectives*. Cape Town: Oxford University Press, pp. 42-97.

Paine, K., Hart, G., Jawo, M., Ceesay, S., Jallow, M., Morison, L., Walraven, G., McAdam, K. & Shaw, M. (2002). 'Before we were sleeping, now we are awake': Preliminary evaluation of the Stepping Stones sexual health programme in Gambia. *African Journal of AIDS Research*, 1:41-52.

Piaget, J. (1973) *The Child's Conception of the World*. St Albans: Paladin.

Roncagliolo, M., Garrido, M., Walter, T., Periano, P. & Lozoff, B. (1998). Evidence of altered central nervous system development in infants with iron deficiency anemia at 6 mo: Delayed maturation of the auditory brainstem responses. *American Journal of Clinical Nutrition*, 68:683-90.

Saraiya, M. & Binkin, N.J. (2000). Tuberculosis among immigrants. In L.B. Reichman & E.S. Hershfield (Eds.). *Tuberculosis: A comprehensive international approach* (2nd edition). New York: Marcel Dekker, pp. 661-92.

Shishana, O. & Simbayi, S. (2002). *Nelson Mandela/HSRC study of HIV/AIDS. South African National Prevalence Study. Behavioural Risks and Mass Media. Household Survey*. Cape Town: Human Sciences Research Council Publishers.

Stephenson, L.S. (1989). Urinary schistosomiasis and malnutrition. *Clinical Nutrition*, 8:356-64.

UNAIDS. (2001). *Report on the Global AIDS Epidemic*. Geneva: UNAIDS.

UNICEF. (2002). *Children on the Brink 2002: A joint report on orphan estimates and programme strategies*. Geneva: UNAIDS.

Van der Walt, H. & Swartz, L. (2002). Task orientated nursing in a tuberculosis control programme in South Africa: Where does it come from and what keeps it going? *Social Science & Medicine*, 54:1001-9.

Vermeire, E., Hearnshaw, H., Van Royen, P. & Denekens, J. (2001). Patient adherence to treatment: Three decades of research. A comprehensive review. *Journal of Clinical Pharmacy and Therapeutics*, 26(5):331-42.

Volmink, J., Matchaba, P. & Garner, P. (2000). Directly observed therapy and treatment adherence. *The Lancet*, 355:1345-50.

Whalen C. & Semba, R.D. (2001). Tuberculosis. In R.D. Semba & M.W. Bloem (Eds.). *Nutrition and Health in Developing Countries*. Totowa, NJ: Humana Press, pp. 209-35.

Williams, H.A. & Jones, C.O. (2004). A critical review of behavioural issues related to malaria control in sub-Saharan Africa: What contributions have social scientists made? *Social Science & Medicine*, 59:501-23.

Wood, K., Jewkes, R. & Maforah, F. (1997). The violence connection in reproductive health: Teenage accounts of sexual relationships in Khayelitsha. *Urbanisation & Health Newsletter*, 3:21-4.

World Health Organisation (2001). *Adherence to Long-term Therapies: Policy for action*. Geneva: World Health Organisation.

World Health Organisation (2002a). *The World Health Report 2001. Mental Health: Understanding new hope*. Geneva: World Health Organisation.

World Health Organisation (2002b). *Tuberculosis: Fact Sheet No. 104, Revised August 2002*, www.who.int/mediacentre/factsheets/who104/en/ (accessed 8 December 2003).

World Health Organisation (2003a). *Global tuberculosis control report. Country profile: South Africa*, www.who.int/gtb/publications/globrep/pdf/country_profiles/zaf.pdf (accessed 8 December 2003).

World Health Organisation (2003b). *World maps (Annex 5 to the Global tuberculosis control report)*, www.who.int/gtb/publications/globrep/pdf/annex_5.pdf (accessed 8 December 2003).

World Health Organisation (2003c). *What is DOTS?* www.who.int/gtb/gtb/dots/whatisdots.htm (accessed 8 December 2003).

World Health Organisation (2004). Estimates by WHO region: Mortality and DALY, www3.who.int/whosis/menu.cfm?path=evidense,burden_estimates, burden_estimates_2002,burden_estimates_2002_Region&language= english (accessed 25 May 2004).

Multiple choice questions

1. Psychology can contribute to the prevention and control of HIV/AIDS, TB and malaria through providing
   a) behaviour change strategies
   b) researching the impact of these diseases on mental health and cognitive functioning
   c) VCT
   d) all of the above
2. The most common method of transmission of HIV in Africa is through
   a) homosexual intercourse
   b) mother to child transmission
   c) sharing of needles during intravenous drug use
   d) heterosexual intercourse
3. Women and girls are more vulnerable to HIV infection because they
   a) are biologically more vulnerable
   b) are less able to negotiate sexual interaction because of economic and gendered power relations
   c) are vulnerable to sexual violence
   d) all of the above
4. Most efforts at HIV prevention in South Africa have focused on
   a) behaviour change
   b) reducing poverty
   c) promoting more equal gender power relations
   d) promoting greater social cohesion
5. Increasing self-efficacy with regard to negotiating safe sex is an example of an intervention at the
   a) community level
   b) individual level
   c) interpersonal level
   d) societal level
6. Parasites are definitively described as
   a) vermin
   b) organisms which obtain their nutrition and shelter from other organisms
   c) organisms which cause disease
   d) plagues
7. What are the problems in mapping out the harmful effects of parasites on human development?
   a) we do not know how parasites reproduce themselves
   b) parasites occur in contexts where there are a number of other risk factors
   c) we do not know how to treat parasite infections
   d) we do not know how people get infected with parasites
8. Tuberculosis can affect psychological functioning through
   a) leading to illness and people being off work and school
   b) people being marginalized from their social groups because of stigma
   c) in rare cases, affecting brain functioning
   d) all of the above
9. Adherence to treatment of an illness can best be enhanced by
   a) making sure that all patients are completely under control of health personnel
   b) supporting both patients and staff to make informed health care decisions
   c) allowing patients to make whatever health care decisions they see as best
   d) recognising that medical approaches to dealing with diseases do not work
10. The fact that there is such a strong association between poverty and vulnerability to many infectious diseases means that
    a) we need to focus more on poverty issues than on health issues
    b) it is always useless to treat poor people for infectious diseases
    c) we need health care strategies which focus both on medical and on broader psychosocial issues
    d) medical personnel do not understand the true causes of disease

Short answer questions

1. What are the different ways in which HIV/AIDS impacts on mental health?
2. What are the risk factors, which make women of child-bearing age particularly vulnerable to HIV infection?
3. What are examples of HIV/AIDS preventions interventions at the individual level and interpersonal levels?
4. Suggest and discuss pathways by which a parasitic infection can affect a child's relationship with her family and caregivers.
5. You have been asked by a community health centre to assist them in lowering the rates of TB in their health district. Outline the areas you would consider focusing on in planning help of this kind.

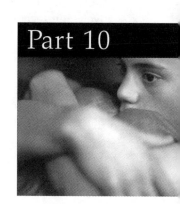

Part 10

Mental Health

Tony Naidoo

As a discipline and profession, psychology has spawned a range of theories and interventions directed at making a difference (hopefully positive!) in the lives of individuals, groups, communities and in the broader society. The four chapters in this closing part of the book provide examples of unique and yet divergent ways in which psychological knowledge, skills and practice have been, and are, utilised to address specific needs that psychologists regularly deal with in their work domain.

Cartwright's chapter on psychopathology deals specifically with mental health problems bearing in mind that these often have an integral relationship with physical health problems. This chapter provides an introduction to psychopathology, providing an overview of different ways of understanding psychopathology, examining how mental health problems have been understood historically, and detailing current perspectives and the contemporary classification of mental health problems.

One primary skill that psychologists have is being able to conduct or engage in psychotherapy with a client or patient or with a group. While a myriad of psychotherapeutic approaches exist and new ones will continue to be developed, Africa's chapter on psychotherapies describes three dominant approaches to working therapeutically with an individual. This chapter illustrates some of the core features underlying the theoretical notions and intervention techniques and objectives of each approach.

While Africa's chapter illustrates how the psychologist actively engages in promoting the mental health of individuals (and Cartwright's chapter helps contextualise this), the chapter by Naidoo, van Wyk and Carolissen highlights the need for broadening the focus of psychology to making a difference at community level as well. Whereas psychotherapy focuses on curative or restorative goals with individuals, community mental health initiatives have a wider agenda seeking to promote and enhance the health and well-being of individuals, groups and communities, and to engage in the prevention of social problems that undermine mental health. A useful model for conceptualising mental health interventions is provided, indicating various strategic roles that psychologists can play in making a difference in the communities in which they work.

In treating or managing the mental health of individuals with psychiatric illnesses, medication is often indicated as part of the psychological intervention process. Mpofu's chapter provides an overview of psychopharmacological interventions, describing the use of psychoactive drugs to treat the symptoms of psychiatric illness. The mechanisms of action of psychoactive drugs, their classification, uses and effects are described in a relatively non-technical way.

In their divergent foci, the four final chapters delineate not only different ways that psychologists (and indeed psychology) can make a difference in the lives of individuals and communities, but also intimate different theoretical paradigms, functions and roles that psychology (and psychologists) can play in making a difference in and to society.

36

Psychopathology

Duncan Cartwright

CHAPTER OBJECTIVES

After studying this chapter you should be able to:
- explain how abnormal behaviour has been defined using the criteria of statistical deviance, maladaptiveness and personal distress
- describe broader political and socio-cultural factors that influence our perceptions of abnormality and normality
- briefly review the history of mental illness as it has evolved through a number of eras
- describe the classification of mental illness, particularly the use of the Diagnostic and Statistical Manual of Mental Disorders
- review some of the current models of psychopathology
- understand the use of the bio-psychosocial model and the diathesis-stress model as multidimensional approaches to understanding psychopathology
- outline two forms of psychopathology (post-traumatic stress disorder and schizophrenia) relevant to the South African context.

When Nosipho first started to read about all the symptoms of different psychological disorders she felt a little nervous, wondering whether she could be diagnosed with some of the conditions described. She was relieved when she talked to some of her friends and found that they had been having similar thoughts. It was also quite reassuring as she began to realise that many people did have some slight symptoms of psychopathology and it was only when these were severe or caused problems in their lives that you could begin to diagnose a 'disorder'. Nosipho, like many people, had grown up hearing about 'crazies'. People would sometimes talk about this or that person who was mad, sometimes making a joke about them or saying how dangerous they were. After a while there would be rumours that they had been sent away to the rural areas to be 'cured' – or worse that they had gone to a mental hospital and wouldn't be seen for a long time. These things had always seemed rather strange and frightening to Nosipho.

Things changed, though, when one of her cousins had developed a psychological disorder. Thandi, who was then 24, had just had her first child. Nosipho and her family watched as Thandi became more and more withdrawn, and she refused after a while to even look after her own child. Eventually she just stayed in her room most of the days and wouldn't to talk to anyone. Sometimes they would hear her in her room talking to herself as though there were other people in there with her – when they knew she was alone. Finally, her husband had taken Thandi to the clinic where she had been given some medication for what they said was post-natal depression. As she began to recover, Thandi had spoken to Nosipho about how awful she had felt during the time of her depression. She said everything had seemed hopeless and pointless. She just couldn't make herself care about anything – even her own child. She had just wanted to die. Most frighteningly for her, she had started to hear voices telling her to kill herself. She could see now that the voices weren't real but at the time they had felt that way. Listening to her Nosipho realised psychological disorders looked very different from the inside than from the outside.

Introduction: What do we mean by psychopathology?

The term 'psychopathology' is derived from the words 'psyche', meaning mind or soul, and 'pathology', meaning disease or illness. In essence, then, the term may be understood as referring to the study of 'mind illnesses' or psychological disorders. But how do we define what should be called illness or pathology of the mind? In order to make a decision about what should be termed a psychological disorder, we first need to establish defining criteria that separate such disorders from normal behaviour.

Statistical deviance

One way of defining psychopathology is to use statistical norms of behaviour and experience to determine what is 'normal'. Here, anything that falls far from the norm would be deemed 'abnormal'. From this point of view relatively rare behaviours, like violence, public nudity or hallucinations (e.g., hearing voices that do not exist in reality) are seen as abnormal or as a sign of mental illness. The problem with this definition, however, is that the norm or what is considered 'normal' behaviour would depend on our cultural or social perspective. For instance, hearing voices and some forms of public nudity, the 'abnormal' behaviours just mentioned, are considered normal in many African cultures and play an important role in giving cultural meaning to particular life events. Furthermore, what might be considered 'normal' may not always be considered healthy or appropriate behaviour. Racist attitudes are often the norm in many societies, but it would be incorrect to view these as correct or normal. In other words, abnormality and statistical deviance cannot always be equated, and the context in which the individual lives needs consideration. Taking this into account, a more accurate way of understanding deviance is the extent to which cultural norms or ideological perspectives are breached.

Even within a particular cultural context, equating deviance with abnormality is problematic. It is problematic because such a criterion fails to distinguish between positive and negative behaviours that deviate from the norm. For example, deviations from the norm may be due to characteristics like eccentricity, genius or some form of outstanding achievement. These could hardly be viewed as abnormal or pathological.

Maladaptiveness

The extent to which certain behaviours or experiences are maladaptive to self or others is also used as a means of defining psychopathology. Here, behaviours that appear to prevent the individual from adapting or adjusting for the good of the individual or group are defined as abnormal. The maladaptive criterion is based on the assumption that individuals should change and adapt for the good of the self and to ensure the survival of the individual and the broader community. Common signs of psychopathology like suicide, depression and fatigue would fit this criterion in that they stand in the way of the individual's personal growth and actualisation.

In a similar way to the criterion of statistical deviance, maladativeness is also relative to the particular cultural perspective within which it is being examined. Many West African countries, for instance, still partake in female circumcision ceremonies, a practice viewed by many as abnormal and barbaric. However, from within some of these cultures such practices are viewed as adaptive and are practiced for the purpose of instilling cultural beliefs

Figure 1 Ideological determinations: Some forms of public nudity are considered normal in many African cultures

about sexual reproduction and sexuality in their people. In other words, it is not viewed as abnormal by many individuals within that culture.

One of the main problems with criteria like statistical deviance and maladaptiveness is that they attempt to assess abnormality from a position outside of the individual's own experience of the apparent problem. This has lead to many researchers turning to considering the criterion of personal distress as an indicator of psychopathology.

Personal distress

Suffering often accompanies psychological disorders. In cases where anxiety and depression are the prominent symptoms, the individual often struggles with unbearable negative thoughts about themselves and their world. The criterion of personal distress being associated with what constitutes a psychological disorder fits well in these cases. But once again there are exceptions. Individuals who suffer from Anti-social Personality Disorder (APD) often do not feel appropriate forms of distress and are more likely to find pleasure in inflicting pain on others. Although individuals with APD are more likely to be violent and abusive in the their relationships with others, if we only applied the criterion of personal distress to such cases they would not be viewed as being abnormal. This would clearly be incorrect.

Figure 2 Personal distress is in some instances an appropriate and healthy response

Personal distress, as a criterion of abnormality, also implies that all personal distress is inappropriate or unhealthy. This is clearly not the case. Distress is often a normal response to difficult or dangerous situations. For example, we would expect an individual to endure an immense amount of personal distress if he or she were to lose a loved one. This, however, is clearly a healthy response to the situation where distress is an important part of bereavement and the mourning process.

As has been shown in using the criterion of statistical deviance, maladaptiveness and personal distress, there is no clear-cut answer to the problem of what is normal and what is not. This is an ongoing problem in the field of psychology, and is reflected in how the boundaries of what constitutes normality have shifted throughout history. Homosexuality, for instance, up until relatively recently, used to be a diagnosable mental disorder. The diagnosis, however, was subsequently (in 1973) no longer regarded as a diagnosable disorder because there was no clear link to be found between mental disorders, abnormality and homosexuality. Broader political and socio-cultural forces have also been shown to have an important impact on how we view mental disorders. We shall return to this when we consider current perspectives on psychopathology.

36.1 SOME MYTHS ABOUT MENTAL ILLNESS

Myth	Fact
Abnormal bahaviour is odd and bizarre	The behaviour of mental patients is most often indistinguishable from that of 'normal' persons
Mental patients are unpredictable and dangerous	A typical mental patient is no more dangerous than a 'normal'
Mental disorders are caused by fundamental mental deficiencies and hence are shameworthy	Everyone shares the potential for becoming disordered and behaving abnormally
Abnormal and normal behaviour are different in kind	Few if any abnormal behaviours are unique to mental patients. Abnormality usually occurs when there is a poor fit between behaviour and the situation in which it is enacted

Aim
To explore attitudes towards psychology, psychiatry and mental illness.

Method
Stones used a self-report questionnaire survey. He conducted his study on a large sample of university students as well as on smaller groups of health-care professionals, patients and the general public.

Findings
Some of the main findings of this study included the following:
- the extent of the individual's knowledge of mental illness and the degree of contact with mental-health professionals significantly influenced their perception of mental illness;
- members of the public were found to be more optimistic about the efficacy of psychological treatment than psychologists; and
- although psychologists and other health-care professionals were viewed positively, the general public still preferred to consult a friend rather than a psychologist in times of personal distress.

Conclusion
Attitudes towards mental illness and its treatment are influenced by knowledge and understanding of mental illness and treatment (Stones, 1996).

History of mental illness: A brief sketch

Our current understanding and treatment of psychopathology has emerged from a long history that has undergone many developments and changes. The history of our relationship with mental illness might be understood as evolving through a number of eras.

The early era

There is evidence dating as far back as 5000 BC that indicates that problems with madness and insanity have always been a part of the human condition (Porter, 2002). Some of the skulls discovered from this era have holes burrowed into the cranial region indicating that primitive man attempted to rid himself of mental disturbance using this method. Presumably, by boring a hole in the patient's skull, the evil spirits causing the mental disturbance could be driven out. Such a practice has been termed *trephining*. The dominant understanding of mental illness during this period was informed by a belief that individuals who became psychologically disturbed were possessed by evil supernatural forces. There are no signs at this early point in history that human beings were able to act out of free will or personal choice. As Porter (2002:13) puts it: 'Living and conduct ... were seen as being at the mercy of external, supernatural forces. Only once mankind began to develop a sense of consciousness and awareness about reason and personal choice did this dominant ideology begin to change.'

The ancient era

The first evidence of a shift to a *naturalistic view* of mental illness can be found in the work of a Greek physician named Hippocrates (460-377 BC). His work illustrates that the ancient Greeks began to adopt a view that physical disease was the cause of mental illness. Hippocrates believed that psychological disorders where the result of imbalances in four essential fluids or humors in the body: blood, phlegm, yellow bile and black bile. For example, he believed that a disproportionate amount of black bile would cause melancholia (a form of depression). He prescribed naturalistic remedies to heal these kinds of problems, such as recommending solitude, changing the individual's diet or abstinence from sexual activity. Although Hippocrates' understanding of mental illness was later found to be incorrect, his findings marked the rudimentary beginnings of the biomedical approach to understanding psychopathology that emerged centuries later. For this reason he is often referred to as the father of modern medicine.

After the fall of the Roman Empire and during the Middle Ages, the naturalistic approach to understanding mental disorder gained little favour, and religion dominated all explanations of psychopathol-

Figure 3 Hippocrates: The father of modern biomedicine

ogy. There was a return to earlier supernatural explanations of mental illness, which now emerged from more organised forms of religious doctrine. From this point of view mental illness was seen as a punishment for sins committed, or as a form of demonic possession. The church became the main vehicle through which such 'possessions' could be exorcised.

During this period Europe began to witness extensive witch hunts. Individuals appearing to go against the Christian faith were accused of being possessed by the devil and were thought to have various supernatural powers that could cause great harm to others. It is well known that many mentally ill people of this era were thought to be possessed by demons and were severely punished or killed as a result.

Although the birth of the asylum came later in our history, formal segregation of mentally disturbed individuals began in the late Middle Ages where the church, supposedly out of charity, began locking up the so-called insane. The best-known institution for the insane was established in the religious house of St Mary of Bethlehem (well known as 'Bedlam', a term that has come to connote confusion, disorder and chaos) in London late in the fourteenth century (Porter, 2002).

The Renaissance era

During the Renaissance (1400-1600), patients who were psychologically ill began to be treated more humanely, and ideas related to witchcraft were more openly challenged. Johann Weyer (1515-1588), a German physician, argued that such individuals were not possessed by the devil but were mentally unstable and could not be held responsible for their actions. Later, in 1584, Reginald Scot published *Discovery of Witchcraft* in which he argued that so-called 'possessions' were medical illnesses not visitations from evil spirits. With this, understanding began to shift from the idea that mental disorders were caused by demonic possession to the idea that such disturbances were illnesses. This lead to people being treated more as if they were in need of help and care for such problems.

The asylum era

Although scientific understanding of mental illness began to increase, the institutionalisation of the mentally ill was also on the increase in the sixteenth century. Patients were housed in asylums that became well known for their inhumane treatment of

Figure 4 Even today, witchcraft is shunned and problematised – or made the subject of film and literature, such as in the movie *The Witches of Eastwick*

Figure 5 The asylum

Figure 6 The treatment of many mental patients has changed with the emergence of humanitarian reforms

mental patients. Common treatments included restraining patients for long periods of time, placing them in dark cells and subjecting them to torture-like treatments. Inmates were often subjected to electric shocks, bleeding in order to rid the body of 'dangerous' fluids, powerful drugs, and starvation.

Late in the eighteenth century, these kinds of treatments were gradually challenged with the emergence of *humanitarian reforms* across the Western world. In France, Pinel (1745-1826) put forward the revolutionary idea that mental patients needed to be treated with kindness and consideration if they were to recover. He argued that their chains should be removed and they should be moved out of the dungeons where they had been incarcerated and placed in sunny rooms, be permitted to do exercise and partake in other constructive activities. Similarly, in England, Tuke established a country retreat in which patients could rest peacefully and work in a caring and supportive atmosphere. Such interventions had a profound effect on patients whose conditions had only worsened after the brutal treatment they had received in asylums. Many of them were reported to have completely recovered from their mental illnesses once they were treated in a humanitarian fashion. The changes that followed revolutionised the way mental illness was treated during this time. Patients were treated with care and understanding, and gradually trained nurses and other professionals were introduced to help in the treatment of mental patients.

The scientific era

Towards the end of the nineteenth century, scientific discoveries related to mental disturbance began to increase. Central to this breakthrough was the discovery that General Paresis (syphilis of the brain), a disease that caused paralysis and insanity, had a biological cause and could be successfully treated. This fuelled the search for other biological causes that may be associated with mental illness and formed the foundation of modern-day psychiatry. We shall return to some of the more recent findings in this area when we look more closely at the biomedical model later in the chapter.

Many other developments have occurred during this era in an attempt to identify, understand and treat different forms of psychopathology. Mental disorders were now largely understood to be medical illnesses that could be identified through their signs and symptoms. In 1883, Kraepelin observed that certain symptoms occurred with specific types of mental disease. From this he developed a classification system for a number of disorders, most notably dementia praecox (known today as schizophrenia) and manic-depressive psychosis (known today as bipolar affective disorder). Kraepelin's views about classification were revolutionary and served as a precursor to the Diagnostic and Statistical Manual of Mental Disorders that is currently used to make a diagnosis.

The scientific era has also been characterised by the development of many different psychological theories and treatments. In the late nineteenth century, Sigmund Freud devised a means of treating patients who suffered from hysterical and neurotic conditions based on his theory that psychopathology is largely caused by the repression of forbidden wishes or instinctual drives. He called this approach Psychoanalysis. In the 1950s, behaviourism emerged in reaction to psychoanalysis and its claims that psychopathology had its genesis in psychological conflict caused by instinctual drives. Based on the work of influential theorists like Skinner and Pavlov, behaviourists believed that we could better understand psychopathology by observing how abnormal behaviour is learned and reinforced by the external environment. Behaviour therapy thus sought to change the factors in the environment that tended to reinforce maladaptive behaviours. Many other forms of psychological treatments have emerged in the past fifty years, all of them claiming to have a better understanding of the human condition and abnormal behaviour. Existential psychotherapy, primal therapy, cognitive behaviour therapy, gestalt psychotherapy, logotherapy, and neurolinguistic programming are but a few of the treatments developed in this era.

The different approaches that have emerged have given rise to a number of controversies in the study and treatment of abnormal behaviour. Over the years there has been a great deal of conflict about which treatments are more effective, and this has often led to some treatments being favoured over others without a clear explanation given as to why one treatment modality is favoured over another. Often the treatment method chosen simply depends

Figure 9 Pavlov: Pavlov's dogs have long provided the most famous example of conditioning

on the therapist's chosen theoretical orientation. The choice of different treatment modalities remains an ongoing debate in psychology and a great deal of *outcome research* is still being compiled to consider if indeed some treatments are more effective than others.

The introduction of psychotropic (mood-influencing) drugs in the 1950s has also been heralded as an important landmark in the history of mental illness. Drugs like lithium, chlorpromazine and imipramine were hailed as miracle drugs because, for the first time, symptoms associated with mania, psychosis and depression could be controlled through the use of medication. This made it possible for many patients to leave or altogether avoid having to be hospitalised in psychiatric institutions. Many were able to maintain normal productive lives under continuing medication. In this way, psychopharmacological treatment was able to provide a cost-effective way of managing patients without having to resort to lengthy stays in psychiatric hospitals.

The postmodern era

Currently, the status of applied psychology appears to be shifting away from adopting a single theoretical or disciplinary approach for understanding, managing and treating psychological problems.

Anti-psychiatry was coined by David Cooper in 1967, and is generally associated with phenomenological philosophers like Thomas Szasz, Gregory Bateson and R.D. Laing. It is a socio-political movement which rejects the methodologies, medical practices and underlying assumptions of psychiatry (Cooper, 1967).

A key understanding of 'anti-psychiatry' is that mental illness is a myth (Szasz, 1972). The argument is that illness is a physical concept and therefore cannot be applied to psychological disorder without any sign of physical pathology. The anti-psychiatry movement argues that doctors tend to view the mentally ill as blameless victims of brain disease and the structural and physiological basis for mental illness is assumed to have been demonstrated (Double, 1992). This has led, they argue, to the inhumane treatment of patients where they are treated as though they are objects or things (Johnstone, 2000).

In opposing the medical psychiatric view, anti-psychiatry holds an anti-authoritarian position that argues against the use of psychiatric diagnosis, drug and electro-convulsive treatments and involuntary hospitalisation.

As a political force, anti-psychiatry waned during the 1970s. However, due to the growing use and abuse of psychiatric drugs in the general population, anti-psychiatry is currently experiencing a resurgence as a human rights watchdog.

There is a growing awareness that our understanding of psychopathology is always *context-dependent*, and it is this that needs to be addressed first and foremost. It is important to note, for instance, that even this brief historical account of mental illness is not free of a particular context and is largely a history told from a Western perspective, a perspective that dominates much of our thinking in this field.

The individual's context and perspective, emerging from factors like cultural heritage, socio-economic status, racial grouping and so forth, are important considerations in determining what kinds of treatment might best work in a given situation. Such an approach is essentially *multidimensional* and draws on the strengths of many different models of psychopathology in a way that best helps the patient. In other words, although differences between approaches are acknowledged, this is not viewed as a reason why some approaches cannot be used alongside others. Such an approach is especial-

ly useful in the South African context given the important role that culturally-derived understandings of mental illness may play in being able to help a patient. From this perspective, a patient may be diagnosed and medicated for a mental disorder while at the same time be encouraged to consult an indigenous healer, with neither needing to take priority over the other. We shall return to this kind of approach in considering some forms of psychopathology that are specifically relevant to the South African context.

Classification of mental illness

The mostly widely used classification system can be found in the Diagnostic and Statistical Manual (DSM) of Mental Disorders (Fourth Edition) (American Psychiatric Association, 1994). The classification system has been under development since 1952, and has undergone a number of changes since its inception. Its essential purpose is to help clinicians identify and diagnose mental illness.

The DSM approach is derived from the biomedical model, where signs and symptoms are grouped together to identify an underlying pathological cause or syndrome. In this way the DSM approach attempts to create a taxonomy (an organised system of categories) for mental disorders. There are a number of important reasons why the classification of mental disorders is necessary. They are as follows:

- classification helps psychologists establish a professional language that ensures that they are communicating about the same categories of mental illness;
- classification is an essential first step towards research, discussion and treatment of the commonly identified categories of mental illness;
- similarly, if commonalities in types of illness are established through classification, so too can the causes of such problems be shared; and
- classification also makes it possible to perform statistical analyses on groups of disorders in order to establish the epidemiology of the diagnosis.

The DSM-IV evaluates an individual's behaviour on five axes. Each axis explores a different dimension of the person's problem:
- Axis 1: Clinical psychiatric syndromes like depression, schizophrenia, dementia.

- Axis 2: Pervasive maladaptive personality problems or mental retardation in children.
- Axis 3: Medical disorders that may be present.
- Axis 4: Severity of psychosocial stressors. Here a six-point rating scale is used to assess the severity of psychosocial stressors that the individual is currently experiencing (see Box 36.4).
- Axis 5: Level of adaptive functioning or what is termed the global assessment of functioning; recent degree of coping with current circumstances. (A score that indicates how well the individual is coping is obtained from Box 36.5).

36.4 RATING THE SEVERITY OF PSYCHOSOCIAL STRESSORS

Rating code	Severity	Example
1	none	no apparent psychosocial stressors evident
2	mild	broke up with boyfriend; left baby alone; family arguments
3	moderate	marital separation; loss of job; serious financial problems
4	severe	divorce; birth of child; unemployment
5	extreme	diagnosis of serious illness; death of spouse; victim of violence or rape
6	catastrophic	death of child; suicide of loved one; taken hostage

36.5 GLOBAL ASSESSMENT OF FUNCTIONING

Code	Level of functioning
100–91	superior function in a wide range of activities
90–81	absent or minimal symptoms (e.g., mild anxiety before an exam)
80–71	transient, expectable symptoms present (e.g., anger after a family argument)
70–61	some mild symptoms and some impairment in social and occupational functioning (e.g., depressed mood or poor appetite)
60–51	moderate symptoms; moderate difficulty with social or occupational functioning (e.g., panic attacks, feeling of anxiety)
50–41	serious symptoms (e.g., suicidal)
40–31	some impairment in reality testing (e.g., speech is sometimes illogical)
30–21	behaviour is influenced by delusions and hallucinations (e.g., inappropriate behaviour in responding to hallucinations) or inability to function in most areas
20–11	some danger of hurting self and others (e.g., suicidal intention without thoughts of death)
10–1	persistent danger of hurting others (e.g., recurrent violence)

The DSM-IV system has been criticised for a number of reasons that are important to consider:

- *Descriptive emphasis*: The DSM system only describes disorders and does not explain why they might occur.
- *Biomedical emphasis*: In a quest to ensure that the study of psychopathology is seen to be scientific, the DSM-IV classifies psychopathology in a similar way as the medical profession diagnoses and classifies diseases and medical problems. In most cases, a medical diagnosis is dependent on some physical abnormality in the body that serves as confirmation of the illness. To use a medical example, dizziness, fatigue, anxiety, high blood pressure are symptoms that can be used to diagnose hypertension (the underlying pathology or medical illness) in a patient. The question remains however: Can such an approach be used in diagnosing psychopathology? Some researchers have challenged this view based on the argument that many forms of psychopathology do not have an underlying physical cause (Hook & Eagle, 2002; Parker et al., 1995; Szasz, 1972). They argue that the DSM approach is erroneous because in most cases mental illness is not caused by 'brain diseases' and cannot be located in some biological abnormality.
- *Individualistic approach*: The DSM system adopts an individualistic approach whereby the syndrome is assumed to only exist as an isolated problem in the patient. The group or family context is not given priority when the diagnosis is being considered.
- *Cultural bias*: The DSM system is criticised for creating diagnostic categories that have a Western cultural perspective. For example, anorexia nervosa, a disorder characterised by the restricted

Aim

Rosenhan conducted a famous study that attempted to explore the validity of psychiatric diagnoses.

Method

A form of participant observation was used in the study whereby eight psychologically healthy individuals were admitted to different psychiatric units after claiming to have been 'hearing voices'. No other symptoms or problems were discussed. After gaining admission all subjects acted their normal selves and no longer claimed to be hearing voices.

Findings

Once the admission to the hospital had taken place, Rosenhan found that no matter what these individuals did, they where perceived as being psychological ill by the staff in the hospital.

Conclusion

The validity of making a psychiatric diagnosis is questionable as the staff in the hospital failed to distinguish between healthy individuals and those who where genuinely mentally ill (Rosenhan, 1973).

Diagnosis	Main defining symptom
Mental retardation	Sub-average intellectual functioning (IQ below 70)
Autistic disorder	Severely impaired development in social interaction and communication
Pica	Persistent eating of non-nutritive substances
Dementia	Disturbance of consciousness and cognitive ability
Substance abuse	Maladaptive pattern of substance (e.g., alcohol) abuse
Bipolar I disorder	Manic and depressive mood swings
Panic disorder	Recurrent unexpected panic attacks
Obsessive-compulsive disorder	Persistent presence of obsessive-compulsive thoughts and behaviours (e.g., hand-washing)
Conversion disorder	Motor or sensory impairment that appears to have a psychological cause (e.g., paralysis of the hand)
Factitious disorder	Intentional production of symptoms in order to assume the 'sick role'
Dissociative identity disorder	The presence of two or more distinct identities in one person
Male orgasmic disorder	Delay or absence of orgasm following sexual excitement
Primary insomnia	Difficulty initiating or maintaining sleep
Adjustment disorder	The development of symptoms in relation to a particular stressor
Narcissistic personality disorder	Grandiose sense of self-importance

intake of food and excessive weight loss, is primarily a Western phenomenon. Although the DSM refers to such disorders as *culture-bound syndromes*, culture is still viewed as a second influence in the emergence of such disorders and the DSM is still criticised for not giving enough emphasis to the role of cultural beliefs and their relationship to mental illness.

- *Concerns about validity and reliability*: Concerns have been raised about the validity of the DSM-IV system. In other words, does it measure what it claims to measure. If a psychologist makes a diagnosis of Schizophrenia using the criteria set out in the manual, how sure are we that the patient actually has Schizophrenia. The reliability of the DSM-IV system has also been questioned. Reliability refers to whether a diagnosis would remain constant if the same patient was independently assessed by a number of psychologists. A number of studies have found that the reliability of some diagnostic categories in the manual is limited (Bertelsen, 2002; Campbell, 1999).
- *Labelling*: A diagnosis does not describe the person, but only a set of behaviours associated with the person's problem. This has lead to a great deal of controversy in psychology, as classification systems are often blamed for causing the clinician to lose sight of the person behind the diagnosis. In practice this often has grave consequences as it

leads to stigmatisation of the individual where the diagnosis (or label) given creates a number of negative preconceptions and expectations in the patient and in others. Such preconceptions and expectations often have a negative impact on the person's identity and well-being. To return to Rosenhan's (1973) study, cited earlier, he found that when normal individuals were given a psychiatric diagnosis most subsequent behaviours were interpreted as being 'abnormal'. This was largely because the hospital staff were responding to how the person had been 'labelled' or diagnosed and could no longer respond to them as ordinary human beings.

Current perspectives on psychopathology

The biomedical perspective

The *biomedical model* claims that all mental illnesses have a biological cause. Other factors such as social pressures, type of parenting, or additional environmental factors are viewed as secondary in the precipitation of mental disorders. Biological abnormalities are understood to occur mainly in three different areas:

- *Genetic predisposition*: We inherit our genetic predisposition from our parents. Genes, or chemical units, are arranged in a specific order along chromosomes and they are responsible for determining things like the physical appearance (hair and eye colour, race, etc.) and the sex of an individual. Most of us have 46 chromosomes. Some researchers have found that abnormalities in genetic makeup can predispose some individuals to particular mental illnesses. Much of the research in this area has been done on twins because they have the same genetic makeup in common. It has been found, for instance, that *monozygotic twins* who share a mother with a mental disorder (twins with the same genetic makeup) have a greater likelihood of both developing mental illness. However, this is not the case with twins who do not share the same genetic makeup (*dizygotic twins*). Evidence that genetic predisposition plays a role in the development of mental illnesses has been demonstrated with disorders like Schizophrenia (Gottessman, 1991),

depression (McGuffin & Katz, 1993) and alcoholism (McGue, 1993). We shall return to some of these disorders later in the chapter.

- *Abnormal functioning of neurotransmitters*: Neurotransmitters are chemical substances in the brain responsible for the communication of nerve impulses among the brain cells. An increase or decrease in certain neurotransmitters, like dopamine and serotonin, has been found to be associated with a number of psychiatric illnesses.
- *Structural abnormalities in the brain*: Structural abnormalities occurring in the brain have also been associated with various disorders. It has been well established that different parts of the brain perform different functions related to the individual's behaviour. For instance, it has been found that the limbic system serves to regulate emotional reactions like fear, aggression and sexual expression. Damage caused to this part of the brain would thus have serious consequences for the individual's ability to control emotions. Structural abnormalities in the brain may be caused by genetic disorders, birth abnormalities, drug-related brain damage or physical injury.

The psychodynamic approach

Contemporary psychodynamic approaches are derived from Sigmund Freud's development of *psychoanalysis*. Those who work from a psychoanalytic point of view believe that the way we relate to ourselves and others is largely influenced by internal forces that exist outside of consciousness. Freud believed that sexual and aggressive instincts and associated thoughts and feelings become repressed and unconscious once they are perceived to be forbidden by society. Although such thoughts and feelings are forced into the unconscious, Freud believed that they were still able to exercise partial control over the individual by expressing themselves through symptoms. He viewed the formation of psychological symptoms as a compromise between the expression of forbidden wishes and their total repression.

Freud viewed the personality as being divided into three parts. The *ego, superego* and the *id*. He used the term ego to refer to the part of the mind that attempts to control the expression of instincts and drives (what he referred to as the id). The superego, on the other hand, represents a person's conscience and the ability to distinguish between right and wrong. Freud believed that the formation of these mental structures was strongly influenced by early childhood experiences and the quality of the child's relationship with his or her parents. From this perspective, psychopathology occurs for two main reasons. Firstly, psychological disorders emerge when *conflict* between the instinctual forces (the id), the superego and the ego gives rise to distressing symptoms. Secondly, mental disorders emerge when *deficiencies* in the ego retard the individual's ability to repress instinctual drives. In both cases the individual makes use of psychological *defense mechanisms* in an attempt to ward off excessive psychological pain and repressed fears (see Box 36.8).

In contemporary psychodynamic thinking the above still remain the most important causes of psychopathology. However, contemporary approaches also emphasise the importance of *internalised object relations* in the development of the personality. Internal objects are essentially *mental representations* that are formed when significant others (or external objects) are 'internalised' by the individual, adding to the nature of the personality. Object relation theorists believe that early relationships, particularly with the mother, shape the personality and set the foundation for other relationships in the person's life. Early trauma or deprivation is also understood to be a key factor in the development of psychopathology. In this way, contemporary psychodynamic approaches, like the object relations approach, emphasise the role that emotional relationships and the surrounding environment play in the formation of the personality. Less emphasis in placed here on the role of instinctual drives typical of the Freudian approach.

The cognitive behaviour perspective

Central to the cognitive behaviour perspective is the idea that cognitions, or learned ways of thinking, directly impact on the individual's emotions and behaviours. Cognitive therapists believe that irrational beliefs and automatic thoughts are principally responsible for the development of psychopathology (Beck, 1972; Ellis, 1995; Glasser, 1984).

Aaron Beck (1976), a leading cognitive psychologist, showed how this worked in cases of depression. He believed that negative automatic thoughts like 'I am not a good person' or 'I am not a good student' set up a negative cycle of thought, emotion and

---

36.8 EXAMPLES OF PSYCHOLOGICAL DEFENCE MECHANISMS

Displacement

One way to avoid the risk associated with feeling unpleasant emotions is to displace them, or put them somewhere other than where they belong. A learner may, for example, be angry with a lecturer for a poor mark he or she has received but cannot express it, so goes home and gets angry with his or her mother instead.

Sublimation

The healthy redirection of an emotion. For example, the learner in the previous example may chose to direct more energy into his or her studies rather than getting angry with his or her mother.

Projection

Projection is something we all do. It is the act of taking something of ourselves and placing it outside of us, on to others; sometimes we project positive and sometimes negative aspects of ourselves. Sometimes we project things we don't want to acknowledge about ourselves (for example, 'I have not made a mistake, it is you who is critical of me and everything I do').

Intellectualisation

Intellectualisation involves removing the emotion from emotional experiences, and discussing painful events in detached, uncaring, sterile ways. Individuals may understand all the words that describe feelings, but have no idea what they really feel.

Denial

The refusal to acknowledge what has happened, is happening, or will happen (for instance, 'my wife is not having an affair' – when in reality she is).

Repression/Suppression

Repression involves putting painful thoughts and memories out of our minds and forgetting them.

Reaction-Formation

When we have a reaction that is too painful or threatening to feel (such as intense hate for someone with power over us), we turn it into the opposite (intense liking for that person). An example would be behaving very badly towards someone because you really like them.

behaviour in the individual. After accepting such distorted thoughts he or she would look for ways to confirm such thoughts through adopting negative behaviours (like not learning for a test or behaving badly in class) that, in turn, would impact on the individual's emotions, making him or her feel more depressed. This sets up a vicious cycle as the more depressed the individual feels the more negatively he or she thinks of him- or herself. According to Beck (1976), depressed persons display distorted negative thoughts about the self, the world and the future. He called this the *cognitive triad* of depression.

The community psychology perspective

Community psychology is most interested in understanding psychopathology from within the context of the community. As Ahmed and Pretorious-Heuchert (2001:19) state: 'This means that community psychology regards whole communities, and not only individuals, as possible clients. There is an awareness of the interaction between individuals and their environments, in terms of causing and alleviating problems.' The emphasis here lies on the importance of the social, political and cultural context in understanding, identifying and treating psychological problems.

- *Political context*: The discipline of community psychology largely developed out of a need to challenge oppressive forces in society (Seedat *et al.*, 2001). For this reason community psychologists are sensitive to the fact that socio-political factors impact on our mental health. Apartheid rule in South Africa, for instance, clearly had a tremendous impact on the way that members of the oppressed Black population of this country perceived themselves. Racist attitudes and policies depicting Blacks as stupid, lazy, and primitive caused many to think negatively of themselves and identify themselves as inferior to the White population.
- *Social context*: Community psychologists argue that social factors need to be considered if we are to fully understand the development of psychological problems. This would include factors like the socio-economic status of the community, access to resources and the nature of social interaction within the community. All such factors impact on the mental health of the individual. From this perspective, problems like violence and sexual abuse can-

not be understood unless the social context of the community is also considered.
- *Cultural context*: The community psychology perspective emphasises the fact that an individual's actions always take place with a cultural context. How an individual experiences distress or makes sense of psychological problems is dependent on deeply ingrained cultural beliefs and practices. Therefore how we understand various psychological symptoms is often dependent on a particular cultural perspective. For example, in Zulu and Xhosa-speaking communities 'ukuthwasa' is a psychological state associated with an ancestral calling to become an indigenous healer. Individuals afflicted with this condition endure states of emotional turmoil, hear voices (of the ancestors calling the individual to become an indigenous healer) and experience bouts of depression and mania. Although such symptoms share similarities with those used to diagnose mental illness in Western diagnostic systems, it would be incorrect to make use of such a diagnosis without having a full understanding of the cultural meaning of such symptoms.

36.9 FOUR MYTHS ABOUT MENTAL ILLNESS IN NON-WESTERN COUNTRIES

- Mental illness does not exist in developing countries.
- Mental illness is not recognised as pathological in non-Western communities.
- Mental illness is accepted in non-Western communities in an unstigmatised manner.
- All mental disorders can be cured by indigenous healers (Swartz, 1998).

This should not be taken to mean that mental illness does not exist in non-Western communities. A number of studies, using epidemiological research, have indicated that psychiatric disorders do exist in non-Western communities (e.g., Asuni *et al.*, 1994; Swartz, 1998).

Understanding how mental illness is experienced and treated by different cultures is also inextricably linked to concerns about access to treatment. We know, for instance, that indigenous healers from within a particular community are able to reach communities in ways that Western forms of medicine cannot (Swartz, 1998). As well as helping patients gain better access to treatment, community psychologists also concern themselves with the *prevention* of mental illness (and other social problems) by facilitating social change and empowerment in the community.

Integrating perspectives: The bio-psychosocial approach and the diathesis-stress model

The above perspectives are often used in an integrated way to gain a fuller understanding of psychopathology and its precipitating causes. Two approaches are particularly useful in this regard: The diathesis-stress model and the bio-psychosocial approach. The diathesis-stress model was first introduced by Meehl (1962). He suggested that some people inherit or develop predispositions (diathesis) to psychopathology. Although this is the case, mental disorders will not emerge until environmental stressors or biological stressors become intense enough to convert predispositions into actual psychological disorders. In a similar way, the bio-psychosocial approach attempts to integrate biological, psychological and social factors to gain a better understanding of why mental disorders occur.

Psychopathology: Some relevant disorders in South Africa

As we have seen, there are many categories of psychological illness. In the following section two common mental disorders will be discussed.

Post-traumatic stress disorder (PTSD)

Given the high rate of crime and violence in South Africa, post-traumatic stress disorder has become one of the most frequently diagnosed forms of psychopathology.

Case illustration

One evening Uzail, a 28 year old man, was driving home from work when he was held up at gun point by two men standing at a traffic light. They ordered

---

36.10 MENTAL RETARDATION: A BIO-PSYCHOSOCIAL APPROACH

The bio-psychosocial approach claims that a number of interactive factors play a role in mental retardation:

Biological factors
Biological factors are important in understanding mental retardation but are not, on their own, sufficient to explain the causes of the disorder:
- The majority of cases of mental retardation are genetically transmitted.
- Many structural abnormalities in the brain are responsible for severe forms of mental retardation. These abnormalities can be caused by disease, injury or prenatal factors.

Psychological factors
Psychological factors interact with biological vulnerabilities to influence the development of accompanying disorders:
- Depression frequently accompanies mental retardation. Depression often occurs due to a sense of frustration about an inability to perform certain tasks and/or a sense of alienation from mainstream society.
- Other psychological disorders, like oppositional defiant disorder or conduct disorder, may occur once the individual realises his or her limitations

Social factors
Biological and psychological factors operate with a particular social context:
- Environmental factors associated with poverty play an important role in the etiology of mental retardation. Limited access to health care facilities during pregnancy, poor nutrition during pregnancy and increased risk to physical injury, are all preventable factors that may cause mental retardation.
- Support within the community can help successfully support and care for mentally retarded persons.
- Educational programmes can be used to inform communities about the problems associated with mental retardation.

him to given them his wallet and threatened to kill him if he made a wrong move. Both men sat in the car and ordered Uzail to drive to a nearby neighbourhood. Uzail was persistently threatened with his life while he drove them to their requested location before they set him free. After the event Uzail was markedly anxious, he was unable to sleep, and kept feeling that his attackers would return. For two months following the event he often had nightmares about the event and experienced 'flash thoughts' that made him feel like the events of the crime were constantly being repeated. He also could not tolerate driving in a car, and found that he had grown increasingly angry, hyperactive and irritable since the crime. After consulting a psychologist he was diagnosed with post-traumatic stress disorder.

Discussion

Post-traumatic stress disorder occurs when a person experiences or witnesses a situation that involves threat of or actual death, which leads to the following symptoms:

- *Distressing re-experiencing of the event*: The traumatic experience is persistently re-experienced after the event through:
  - mental flashbacks to the scene;
  - recurrent distressing dreams;
  - recurrent and intrusive thoughts of the event; and
  - hypersensitivity to cues that may be associated with the event.
- *Avoidance and emotional numbing*: The trauma event causes a great deal of anxiety in the patient leading to a persistent avoidance of anything that might be associated with the event. It also causes a 'psychic numbing' in the individual's general responsiveness to his or her current surroundings.
- *Increased arousal*: Patients suffering from PTSD also display symptoms of increased arousal such as difficulties falling asleep, irritability and exaggerated startle responses.

The above symptoms need to persist for at least one month after the event before post-traumatic stress disorder is diagnosed. The epidemiology of PTSD varies depending on occurrence of traumatic situations. Given the high rate of crime and violence in South Africa at present, the prevalence rate of PTSD in the general population is thought to be well above most international norms.

Etiology

The major factors in the etiology of the disorder are the stressor, the social environment in which the trauma took place, the character traits of the individual and the biological vulnerability of the victim. The intensity of traumatic reactions appears to be dependent on the suddenness of the threat, its duration and the amount of fear associated with the event. In general, it has been found that young children and the elderly have greater difficulty in coping with traumatic events and are thus at greater risk of developing PTSD.

Biological theorists have found that patients with a vulnerability to anxiety are at greater risk of developing PTSD. They have also found that patients with PSTD show an increased risk of catecholamine (stress hormones that prepare the body for and emergency) while re-experiencing trauma.

Psychodynamic psychologists take the view that traumatic events reactivate unresolved conflicts from early childhood. In an attempt to cope with the trauma the ego constantly repeats the distressing events associated with the trauma in an attempt to master them and reduce the level of anxiety experienced by the victim.

The symptoms of PTSD can fluctuate over time and are more apparent during periods of stress. It is estimated that approximately 30 per cent of patients recover, 60 per cent continue to experience mild anxiety symptoms associated with the trauma, and 10 per cent remain unchanged and may even become worse (Kaplan & Sadock, 1998).

Schizophrenia

Schizophrenia shares a number of symptoms with some indigenous forms of 'illness' in South Africa like 'ukuthwasa' (ancestral calling) and 'amafufunyana' (spirit possession). This has led to a lot of debate around whether to understand the presenting symptoms from within the context of the indigenous healing system (where traditional healers like 'Inyangas' and 'Isangomas' would be used) or from the perspective of the biomedical model where it would be diagnosed as schizophrenia. In appears that the answer lies in being able to make use of the strengths of both models.

Schizophrenia is a condition characterised by disorganised and fragmented emotions, behaviours and cognitions. One of the most common misper-

36.11 XHOSA-SPEAKING SCHIZOPHRENIC PATIENTS' EXPERIENCES OF THEIR CONDITION: PSYCHOSIS AND 'AMAFUFUNYANA'

Aim
The study explores Xhosa-speaking patients' experiences of their condition.

Method
Using open-ended interviews 10 patients were asked to describe their experience of their condition as well as its treatment. They were also asked to talk about their views on what had caused their condition (i.e. its etiology).

Findings
Although the patients described their illness in terms related to traditional conceptions (in this case 'amafufunyana') of mental distress, they preferred to used psychiatric services rather than consult with a traditional healer.

Conclusion
The separation of psychosis and 'amafufunyana' as distinct categories is a false distinction. This is because patients employ psychiatric, religious and traditional understandings in a complex way that does not warrant this separation in the treatment of such disorders (Lund & Swartz, 1998).

ceptions about schizophrenia is that it refers to people with a split personality. 'Split personality' is a disorder usually called dissociative identity disorder and refers to a condition in which an individual develops two or more separate identities or ego states. Each identity exists separately and has its own set of emotional and behavioural characteristics. However, this phenomenon does not occur in schizophrenia. Schizophrenics suffer from a mental disorder that is more correctly characterised by the splitting of emotions and thoughts.

Case illustration

Sibusiso, a 23 year old student, was referred to a psychologist by his mother after he claimed that she was poisoning his food. His appearance was unkempt and he appeared agitated when he walked into the psychologist's consulting rooms. He sat down and began to speak to the psychologist in a very incomprehensible manner. For example, he began by singing the psychologist a song. He claimed that 'a man in the radio' had told him to sing the song every time he saw a psychologist. He then went on to explain why he had come to the consultation: 'I need to see you because there are aliens on the roof of my house. They come down every night. I see them, they want me to say bad things.' Sibusiso appeared emotionless and unresponsive to the psychologist's questions. After a while his speech became more and more disorganised and there seemed to be no way of following what he was saying: 'did you know that feet ate meat' he said, 'and time is mine and crime is bad too? During the session Sibusiso often got up excitedly from his chair and sat down again without any explanation.

On contacting the mother the psychologist learned that Sibusiso had been unable to carry on with his studies and had taken to locking himself in his room for long periods of time claiming that 'the aliens were going to get him'. She also complained that he was not able to carry out basic chores at home and stopped contacting his friends. Prior to these changes in his behaviour, Sibusiso was successful in his studies and kept regular contact with a number of his friends.

Discussion

As the above case shows, the schizophrenic condition is characterised by gross distortions of reality testing leaving such individuals feeling disorientated and fragmented, a condition most commonly called *psychosis*. Schizophrenic symptoms can be divided into two categories: positive and negative symptoms. Positive symptoms refer to the presence of behaviours and feelings normally not present, while negative symptoms refer to the absence of behaviours and feelings usually present in a normal individual. The most common symptoms associated with schizophrenia are listed below. Many of these can be observed in the above case illustration.

Positive symptoms
- *Delusions*: Fixed ideas or false beliefs that do not have any foundation in reality (Sibusiso thought his mother was poisoning his food).
- *Hallucinations*: False sensory perceptions that occur in the absence of a related sensory stimulus (seeing aliens or other visions, hearing voices, claiming that the radio was giving him a command).
- *Catatonic behaviour*: Marked motor abnormalities such as bizarre postures, purposeless repetitive

movements and extreme degree of unawareness (Sibusiso got up from his chair in a repetitive way).

- *Disorganised behaviour*: Inability to persist in goal-direct activity. Grossly inappropriate behaviours in public (singing songs to his psychologist, inability to follow a line of questioning, not being able to perform basic tasks).
- *Disorganised speech*: Speech is incomprehensible and only remotely related to subject under discussion (Sibusiso's speech was clearly disorganised and incoherent).

Negative symptoms

- *Alogia*: A speech disturbance in which the individual talks very little and gives brief empty replies to questions (Sibusiso did not display this symptom).
- *Flat Affect*: The lack of emotional responsiveness in gesture, facial expression or tone of voice (Sibusiso appeared emotionless in his responses to the therapist).
- *Avolition*. A negative symptom that involves the inability to begin and sustain goal-directed activity (Sibusiso did not appear to be able to perform everyday activities).

For a diagnosis of schizophrenia to be made, continuous signs of disturbance need to persist for at least six months.

Schizophrenia affects 1 per cent of the population, and usually begins before age 25 and persists throughout life. It is found among all social classes and there is no difference in the prevalence rates of the disorder between males and females. Approximately 20 per cent of schizophrenics are able to lead relatively normal lives, 20 per cent continue to experience moderate symptoms, while 40 to 60 per cent remain severely impaired by the illness for the rest of their lives (Kaplan & Sadock, 1998). Unlike psychological problems like depression, schizophrenic patients often do not return to their previous level of functioning once a psychotic breakdown has occurred. There is usually some deterioration in cognitive and behaviour abilities even after the positive symptoms of schizophrenia have subsided.

Etiology

The etiology of schizophrenia is not known. One of the most convincing biological theories of schizophrenia relates to the levels of the neurotransmitter dopamine at receptor cites in the brain. The *dopamine hypothesis* claims that excessive levels of dopamine cause schizophrenic-like symptoms. Anti-psychotic medications, which serve to inhibit the level of dopamine in the brain, lend support to this hypothesis as psychotic symptoms are markedly reduced by such medications (Gao & Goldman-Rakic, 2003; Koh *et al.*, 2003; Weiner, 2003).

Genetic predisposition is also believed to render an individual vulnerable to developing schizophrenia. It has been found that monozygotic twins of a schizophrenic patient have a 47 per cent chance of developing schizophrenia, while dizygotic twins only have a 12 per cent chance of developing the illness.

Many psychological theories have been put forward in an attempt to understand schizophrenia. Some psychoanalytic theorists believe that schizophrenia is caused by a defect in the rudimentary functions of the ego giving rise to intense hostility and anger which in turn distorts the child's ability to relate to others around him or her. This leads to a personality organisation that is very vulnerable to stressful situations. Learning and cognitive behaviour theorists, on the other hand, believe that schizophrenia develops from learning irrational reactions and distorted ways of thinking from emotionally disturbed parents.

Conclusion

This chapter has introduced some of the main concepts, arguments and theories that have been used to understand mental illness or psychopathology. Abnormal behaviour has been defined using the criteria of statistical deviance, maladaptiveness and personal distress. In addition to these criteria, it has been argued that broader political, socio-cultural and historical factors are important in understanding the nature of normality or abnormality.

The complexities of classifying mental illness using the Diagnostic and Statistical Manual of Mental Disorders were then considered in terms of its constructive use and limitations. Classification, however, is not able to offer explanations as to why various psychological problems occur. For this reason various theories of mental illness were considered. It was suggested that the bio-psychosocial model and the diathesis-stress model offer us broad theoretical frameworks that allow a number of different perspectives to be used to illuminate the multidimensional nature of psychopathology. Finally, two common forms of psychopathology found in South Africa were explored using brief case examples.

Ahmed, R. & Pretorious-Heuchert, J.W. (2001). Notions of social change in community psychology: Issues and challenges. In M. Seedat, N. Duncan & S. Lazarus (Eds.). *Community Psychology: Theory, method and practice*. London: Oxford University Press, pp. 63-81.

American Psychiatric Association. (1994). *Diagnostic and Statistical Manual of Mental Disorders* (4th edition). Washington DC: American Psychiatric Association.

Asuni, T., Schoenberg, F. & Swift, C. (1994). *Mental Health and Disease in Africa*. Ibadan: Spectrum Books.

Beck, A. (1976). *Cognitive Therapy and the Emotional Disorders*. New York: International University Press.

Beck, A. (1972). *Depression: Causes and treatment*. Philadelphia: University of Pennsylvania Press.

Bertelsen, A. (2002). Schizophrenia and related disorders: Experience with current diagnostic systems. *Psychopathology*, 35:89-93.

Campbell, T.W. (1999). Challenging the evidentiary reliability of DSM-IV. *American Journal of Forensic Psychology*, 17(1):47-68.

Cooper, D. (1967). *Psychiatry and Anti-psychiatry*. London: Tavistock Publications.

Double, D.B. (1992). *Understanding schizophrenia*. BMJ, 305:775-6.

Ellis, A. (1995). Changing rational-emotive therapy into rational-emotive behaviour therapy. *Journal of Rational Emotive & Cognitive-Behaviour Therapy*, 13:85-90.

Gao, W.J. & Goldman-Rakic, P.S. (2003). Selective modulation of excitatory and inhibitory microcircuits by dopamine. *Proc Natl Acad Sci*, 100:2836-41.

Glasser, W. (1984). *Take Effective Control of Your Life*. New York: Harper Collins.

Gottessman, I.I. (1991). *Schizophrenia Genesis: The origins of madness*. New York: Freeman.

Hook, D. & Eagle, G. (Eds.). (2002). *Psychopathology and Social Prejudice*. Lansdowne: University of Cape Town Press.

Johnstone, L. (2000). *Users and Abusers of Psychiatry: A critical look at psychiatric practice* (2nd edition). London: Routledge.

Kaplan, H.I. & Sadock, B.J. (1998). *Clinical Psychiatry*. London: Williams & Wilkims.

Koh, P.O., Bergson, C., Undie, A.S., Goldman-Rakic, P.S. & Lidow, M.S. (2003). Up-regulation of the D1 Dopamine receptor-interacting protein, Calcyon, in patients with schizophrenia. *Arch Gen Psychiatry*, 60(3):311-9.

Lund, C. & Swartz, L. (1998). Xhosa-speaking schizophrenic patients' experience of their condition: psychosis and *amafufunyana*. *South African Journal of Psychology*, 28(2):62-70.

McGue, M. (1993). From proteins to cognitions: The behaviour genetics of alcoholism. In R. Plomin & G.E. McClearn (Eds.). *Nature, Nurture and Psychology*. Washington DC: American Psychological Association, pp. 245-68.

McGuffin, P. & Katz, R. (1993). Genes, adversity, and depression. In R. Plomin & G.E. McClearn (Eds.). *Nature, Nurture and Psychology*. Washington DC: American Psychological Association.

Meehl. (1962). Schizotaxia, schizotypy, schizophrenia. *American Psychologist*, 60:117-74.

Parker, I., Georgaca, E., Harper, D., Mcclaughlin, T. & Stowell-Smith, M. (1995). *Deconstructing Psychopathology*. London: Sage publications.

Porter, R. (2002). *Madness: A brief history*. London: Oxford University Press.

Rosenhan, D.L. (1973). On being sane in insane places. *Science*, 179:250-8.

Seedat, M., Duncan, N. & Lazarus, S. (Eds.). (2001). *Community Psychology: Theory, method and practice*. London: Oxford University Press.

Stones, C.R. (1996). Attitudes toward psychology, psychiatry and mental illness in the central Eastern Cape of South Africa. *South African Journal of Psychology*, 26(4):221-5.

Swartz, L. (1998). *Culture and Mental Health: A southern African view*. Cape Town: Oxford University Press.

Szasz, T.S. (1972). *The Myth of Mental Illness*. Paladin: London.

Weiner, I. (2003). The 'two-headed' latent inhibition model of schizophrenia: Modeling positive and negative symptoms and their treatment. *Psychopharmacology*, 25:235-49.

Multiple choice questions

1. According to the criteria of statistical deviance, a behaviour is abnormal when it
   a) deviates from previous family patterns
   b) deviates from the norm of a specified social or cultural group
   c) deviates from maladaptiveness
   d) deviates from personal distress
2. Hippocrates (460–377 BC) adopted a naturalistic approach to understanding mental illness. He believed that
   a) mental illness was primarily caused by natural spirits
   b) mental illness could be cured by nature
   c) mental illness was caused by imbalances in the natural fluids of the body
   d) mental illness resulted from the fusion of blood, phlegm, yellow bile, and black bile
3. Axis 4 of the DSM-IV system evaluates
   a) psychiatric illness
   b) severity of psychosocial stressors
   c) global assessment of functioning
   d) general stressors
4. The DSM-IV approach has been criticised for
   a) establishing a professional language that does not ensure better communication about the same categories of mental illness
   b) being too complex in its approach
   c) being too biomedical in emphasis
   d) establishing a bio-psychosocial approach
5. Reginald Scot claimed that
   a) so-called 'spirit possessions' were medical illnesses not visitations from evil spirits
   b) so-called 'medical illnesses' were spirit possessions and were not the result of biological disease
   c) general paresis was the main cause of mental illness during the 1800s
   d) the classification of dementia praecox was the main why medical science was able to explain 'spirit possession'
6. Genetic predisposition appears to explain some of the reasons why some individuals display mental illness while others do not. This is most clearly observed in studies that show that
   a) abnormal DNA cannot cause mental illness
   b) monozygotic twins of a mentally ill mother have a greater likelihood of developing mental illness relative to the general population
   c) dizygotic twins of a mentally ill mother have a greater likelihood of developing mental illness relative to the general population
   d) dopamine can cause mental illness
7. From a psychoanalytic perspective psychopathology occurs when
   a) conflict between instinctual forces, the superego and the ego gives rise to distressing symptoms
   b) deficiences in the ego retard the individual's ability to repress instinctual drives
   c) instinctual drives take over the superego
   d) both (a) and (c)
8. Researchers have found that patients with PSTD show an increased risk of _____ while re-experiencing trauma
   a) dopamine
   b) anxiety
   c) catecholamine
   d) both (a) and (d)
9. Delusions can be best defined as
   a) distortions in thinking
   b) fixed ideas or false beliefs that do not have any foundation in reality
   c) fixed distortions in perceptual activity
   d) fixed ideas and beliefs that are found in schizophrenia
10. Studies show that ____ of patients diagnosed with PTSD will continue to experience mild anxiety symptoms associated with the precipitating trauma
    a) 50%   b) 10%   c) 60%   d) 20%

Short answer questions

1. Choose a behaviour that you consider abnormal. Using the criterion of maladaptiveness, statistical deviance and personal distress, consider which criterion best fits the chosen behaviour.
2. Why do we need a classification system? What are the main limitations of the DSM system?
3. How do community psychologists understand psychopathology? Use an example to illustrate your answer.
4. List and describe, using your own words, four of psychological defences used to understand psychopathology. Use your own examples to explain how these defences occur.
5. How do positive symptoms of schizophrenia differ from negative ones? List and describe the positive symptoms of schizophrenia.

Psychotherapies

Adelene Africa

After studying this chapter you should be able to:
- describe what psychotherapy is
- distinguish between and explain the central ideas of the three core psychotherapeutic approaches, namely psychoanalytic psychotherapy, cognitive therapy and person-centred therapy
- differentiate between the therapeutic techniques and procedures employed by each approach
- describe how each approach can be applied in a case of psychological distress
- describe the role that indigenous therapies can play in promoting psychological well-being.

When Nosipho used to think about psychotherapy she imagined a person lying on a couch while a grey haired man sits on chair behind him or her, taking notes. This was the way that therapy was often shown in cartoons and movies. Amongst her friends it was often just something to joke about: 'He needs a bit of therapy', they might say about some young man who was being irritating.

Nosipho's ideas about therapy and therapists had changed though when she first started university. In those first few months she had felt terribly lonely and very afraid of everything. She got to the point where she would wake up in the morning with a stomach ache and a feeling of dread at having to go to her lectures. She went to see one of the doctors at the Student Health Clinic who, instead of just giving her something for her stomach pain as she had expected, told her she was suffering from anxiety and referred her to the one of the psychologists at the Clinic. Although she hadn't really wanted to go at first, looking back, it was one of the best things that she could have done.

The psychologist she saw was a lovely, gentle woman who had seemed so easy to talk to. Nosipho found herself telling her everything she was feeling and in one session, where she had felt very bad, she sat and cried and cried. Somehow talking about the problem – and even crying – made her feel better. While the psychologist didn't really give advice, she did help Nosipho feel that her problems were manageable. She seemed to be able to ask questions and say things that not only sounded like she understood what Nosipho was feeling, but also helped her see things in a new light. Somehow, after a session, Nosipho didn't feel quite so stuck and she began to feel that she would be able to cope with the new demands of university. Nosipho had only gone for six sessions, but in the end had felt much better than she had when she started. Even though she knew it had helped it was hard for Nosipho to pin down exactly what it was about the therapy that had made her feel better. She was curious to find out more about how therapy worked.

Introduction

The best way to introduce this chapter is by way of an example. Carefully examine the following case study:

Themba is an 18-year-old first year university learner who lives in residence. He has been experiencing difficulty in sleeping and has not had an appetite for several days. He feels lethargic and does not have any energy to play soccer, which used to be his favourite sport. He describes his mood as being 'down in the dumps' and indicates that there are times when he feels very sad. He has not been coping with his academic work and has not been able to meet his essay deadlines. He has not been attending lectures as he has difficulty concentrating and feels that he is not learning anything. He has experienced similar bouts of depression being 'down in the dumps' before and cannot understand why he feels this way, as he does not seem to have any serious problems that may cause him distress. He does not know where all these unpleasant feelings stem from and feels that his current experience is worse than previous ones. He has tried talking about his situation to his best friend, Sipho, but it has not made him feel any better. He is thinking about leaving university as he feels that there is no point in pursuing his studies.

Themba is clearly experiencing psychological distress and has tried to deal with it by talking to a friend. However, this has not helped and he appears to be feeling worse than on previous occasions. What other sources of help or support can Themba seek? Can psychological intervention assist him in dealing with his problems? What is psychotherapy and what are the various approaches that are available? These are some of the questions that we will address in this chapter.

What is psychotherapy?

The term psychotherapy conjures up pictures of 'mentally ill' people who seek 'treatment' from psychologists and/or psychiatrists. However, as we will see, this stereotype is limiting as it does not allow us to consider the role that psychotherapy can play in helping people who do not suffer from serious psychopathology. Corey (1996) defines psychotherapy as an 'engagement' between two individuals, namely the therapist and the client, who are focused on bringing about change within the client via the therapeutic relationship. This definition does not specify any particular psychotherapeutic techniques and, therefore, aptly describes the essence of individual models of psychotherapy. It is important to note that there are other models of psychotherapy for groups as well as psychological interventions that are aimed at communities (see Chapter 39, this volume). However, in this chapter we will be focusing specifically on individual psychotherapy.

There are numerous psychotherapeutic approaches which advocate various ways in which change can be brought about within the client. Karasu (1986), in reviewing models of psychological intervention, indicated that there are more than 400 models of psychotherapy that are currently in use. However, we will limit our discussion to a few of the dominant models of individual psychotherapy, which will give us some idea as to the diversity in theory and practice. Mcleod (1993) identifies three 'core' psychotherapeutic approaches that illustrate differences in the way in which emotions, behaviour and psychological distress are conceptualised. These are psychoanalytic psychotherapy, cognitive-behavioural therapy and person-centred therapy (see Table 1). Corey's (1996) discussion of various models of individual therapy also categorises the approaches according to their emphases on either analytic processes (e.g., psychoanalytic psychotherapy), problem-solving (e.g., cognitive therapy), or the primacy of the therapeutic relationship (e.g., person-centred therapy). For this reason, we will focus on an example from each of the core approaches to illustrate each of these theoretical orientations.

Psychoanalytic psychotherapy

Analytic or psychodynamic approaches, which are the derivatives of traditional psychoanalysis, are largely concerned with helping the client to gain insight into the underlying causes of emotional difficulties in order to bring about changes within personality and behaviour. These approaches are rooted in the psychoanalytic model, which was developed by Sigmund Freud. Psychoanalysis is largely regarded as the foundation for other models of psychotherapy and has had a major influence on the development of these models. Despite the decrease in dominance of psychoanalysis in recent years, several psychodynamic approaches, which are influential within the therapeutic arena, have developed

	Psychoanalytic psychotherapy	Cognitive therapy	Person-centred therapy
Key ideas	Unconscious conflicts are the root of psychological distress	Cognitive distortions (faulty thinking) result in psychological distress	Incongruence between self-concept and reality result in psychological distress
Goals of therapy	• Gain insight into childhood roots of distress • Resolve unconscious conflicts • Personality change	• Change negative thinking • Develop realistic ways of perceiving the world	• Develop congruence between self-concept and reality • Acceptance of self • Personal growth • Self-actualisation
Therapeutic techniques	• Free association • Interpretation • Dream analysis • Transference	• Psycho-education • Thought stopping • Recording negative automatic thoughts • Homework tasks	• Core conditions • Congruence • Unconditional positive regard • Accurate empathy

Table 1 Three core approaches to psychotherapy

from it (Ursano & Silberman in Weiten, 2001). For this reason it is useful for us to consider the central ideas within this therapeutic approach.

Psychoanalysis is concerned with uncovering the factors that motivate behaviour, and Freud believed that the roots of psychological distress lie within the unconscious. The resolution of distress depends on uncovering the meaning of symptoms, as well as the influence of repressed thoughts and feelings on a person's psychological well-being (Eagle & Wolitzky, 1992). Before we consider the various elements of this therapy we need to briefly look at some of the key concepts of psychoanalytic theory so as to better understand its practice.

Key ideas

Freud was primarily concerned with treating people who had anxiety disorders, and therefore his theory focused on trying to understand the roots of those disorders, which were termed neuroses. According to the psychoanalytic model, neuroses such as phobias, panic disorders and other anxiety disorders, are caused by unconscious conflicts stemming from early childhood. People rely on various defence mechanisms to cope with the anxiety arising from these conflicts. For example, if a young man is unable to accept that his mother is senile, he may deny this and rationalise her odd behaviour as being eccentric. He employs the defence mechanisms of denial and rationalisation to cope with the anxiety which his mother's illness causes him. Defence

mechanisms have adaptive value as they help people to cope with anxiety caused by these repressed thoughts and feelings (see Figure 1). However, Freud believed that these defence mechanisms can become self-defeating when people become too reliant on them (Eagle & Wolitzky, 1992).

The key aim of psychoanalytic therapy is, therefore, to make the unconscious conflicts conscious so that people can gain insight into the childhood origins of their problems. However, insight alone does not lead to the resolution of psychological distress. Another task of therapy is to help the client to confront old patterns of behaving in order to effect change. Given the nature of the theory underlying this approach, it can be understood why traditional psychoanalytic psychotherapy is not time-limited. It usually takes a few years of therapy to help the client uncover and explore the material in his or her unconscious material (Corey, 1996). Hence this type of therapy is long-term and relies on several techniques to achieve its aims.

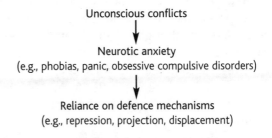

Figure 1 The psychoanalytic view of psychological distress

Therapeutic techniques and procedures

Given that the unconscious cannot be accessed directly, the therapist has to infer the content of unconscious conflicts from the client's thoughts, feelings and behaviour. This is done by using some of the following techniques and procedures:

Free association

In free association the client spontaneously expresses whatever comes to mind. She or he reports any thoughts or feelings without censoring them, regardless of how silly, trivial or embarrassing they might be. These associations are believed to be important indicators of the unconscious material which has been repressed. The therapist is then able to analyse and interpret these thoughts and feelings to help the client to identify the unconscious roots of their distress (Saretsky in Corey, 1996).

Interpretation

One of the key roles of the therapist is to interpret the material that the client brings to the therapeutic situation. Thus, when the client free-associates, the therapist strives to explain the hidden meaning of these thoughts and feelings. Similarly, the therapist also analyses the client's dreams in an attempt to explain their symbolic meaning. While interpretation is central to the analytic process, the therapist does not routinely interpret everything that the client brings to therapy. The interpretation has to be appropriately timed so that the client is able to tolerate its content. Thus, the therapist gently offers interpretations progressively so as not to overwhelm the client (Saretsky in Corey, 1996).

Dream analysis

Another way in which unconscious material is accessed, is through dream analysis. The therapist interprets the symbolic content of the client's dreams, thus giving him or her insight into unresolved conflicts. Freud viewed dreams as being the 'royal road to the unconscious' because they allow for the expression of unconscious wishes, needs and conflicts. As some thoughts, feelings and needs may be too unacceptable to be consciously expressed, they are repressed in the unconscious and find symbolic expression in the symbolic form of dreams. Thus, the therapist distinguishes between the manifest content, which is the actual content of the dream, and the latent content, which consists of the repressed material that underlies it. It is the latent content which has to be interpreted and shared with the client (Saretsky in Corey, 1996).

Resistance

Even though the therapist endeavours to time the interpretations appropriately, this does not mean that the client is always open to receiving them. There are times when the client offers resistance to the uncovering of unconscious material. Resistance is a key concept in psychoanalysis, and refers to any unconscious defensive strategy that may hinder the process of therapy. It serves the purpose of protecting the client from overwhelming anxiety that may arise if she or he becomes aware of repressed feelings (Saretsky in Corey, 1996). Resistance is manifested in various ways such as arriving late or missing sessions, an unwillingness to relate certain thoughts and feelings during free association, or acting with hostility towards the therapist (Corey, 1996). Essentially the therapist helps the client to understand and work with his or her resistance to gain insight into the purpose that it serves. Therefore, the nature of the therapeutic relationship between client and therapist is of paramount importance.

Transference

The therapeutic relationship itself provides a useful tool for helping the client to uncover unconscious material. Transference is an essential element of this relationship and occurs when the client unconsciously relates to the therapist in ways that are similar to significant relationships in his or her life (Saretsky in Corey, 1996). Thus, as the therapy progresses the therapist is able to observe the impact of early childhood relationships by the way in which the client relates to him or her within the therapeutic situation. For example, if the client related to his or her parent in a passive, dependent manner, this way of relating may be reproduced in therapy. Thus, transference provides a powerful tool for understanding the impact of the client's early childhood on his or her current functioning. However, how the therapist reacts to this (countertransference) is also important for the process of therapy. Thus transference provides a powerful tool for understanding the impact of the client's early childhood on his or her current functioning.

The psychoanalytic therapist and Themba

As we have discussed, the process of psychoanalytic psychotherapy relies on various techniques to help the client uncover unconscious material, which will eventually lead to change. How can this type of therapy help Themba?

Themba's history of depression would be understood in terms of repressed childhood difficulties that are now impacting on his current functioning. Thus, within the therapeutic situation the focus will be on uncovering the material which he has repressed. By delving into his past, Themba may discover the source of his current distress. Perhaps he fears failure because his parents have often ridiculed him. He may have internalised these experiences, which may lead to anger and guilt whenever he is unable to meet expectations. These feelings could therefore be the root cause of his depression. In order to make these connections, the therapist will encourage Themba to explore his past by using the various techniques such as free association, interpretation and dream analysis described above. The therapist therefore listens to the content of what he has to say and explains the symbolic meaning of these thoughts and feelings.

A central focus will be on encouraging the development of the transference relationship between Themba and the therapist. Themba may come to view the therapist as a parent who has high expectations of him. He may react by arriving late for appointments or acting with hostility within the therapeutic situation. The therapist needs to be aware of this and her or his reaction to Themba's behaviour. By appropriately interpreting the transference relationship, the therapist will help Themba to eventually gain insight into the origins of his depression and of his fear of failure.

Cognitive-behaviour therapy (cognitive therapy)

Whereas psychoanalytic psychotherapy is primarily concerned with helping the client to gain insight into unconscious motives, cognitive-behaviour therapy is more action-oriented, focusing on the conscious motivation of behaviour. While the identification of the causes of behaviour is important, this does not form the focus of the therapy. Instead, the intervention is aimed at how the relationship between thoughts, feelings and behaviour gives rise to psychological distress (Dryden & Feltham, 1995). We will consider Beck's (1976) model of cognitive therapy as an example of the cognitive behavioural approach.

Key ideas

Aaron Beck's (1976) cognitive therapy highlights the impact that the client's thinking has on his or her feelings and behaviour. According to Beck, psychological distress is caused by the way in which people interpret events in their lives. Thus, the way in which they view and understand the world impacts on their feelings and behaviour (see Figure 2). The aim of therapy is to help the client to become attuned to the 'internal dialogue', which refers to those negative automatic thoughts that accompany certain feelings and behaviours. By identifying these thoughts, the client is able to judge the appropriateness of the dialogue and, if necessary, change the way that situations are perceived.

Cognitive distortions (faulty thinking)
(e.g., arbitrary inferences, selective abstraction, overgeneralisation)

↓

Psychological distress
(e.g., depression)

Figure 2 The cognitive therapeutic view of psychological distress

Cognitive distortions and the roots of psychological distress

Beck (1976) argues that psychological distress is caused by 'cognitive distortions' that occur when the client makes errors in reasoning. Thus, the client makes faulty assumptions about him- or herself and the world. There are several types of distortions in thinking which lead to emotional difficulties (Beck *et al.*, 1979). These include arbitrary inferences, magnification and personalisation. To illustrate the 'cognitive distortions' outlined by Beck *et al.* (1979), we will use the example of a social work learner who has sought professional help because she is experiencing emotional difficulties as a result of the academic demands of her course.

Arbitrary inferences
Arbitrary inferences occur when the client draws conclusions about herself and the world without any supporting evidence in objective reality. For example, the client may believe that she will not suc-

ceed at university because she is incapable of achieving anything. Selective abstraction occurs when the client draws conclusions based on a specific detail of an event while ignoring any other disconfirming information. For example, she may only focus on her failures while ignoring those occasions when she has been successful.

Overgeneralisation

Overgeneralisation occurs when the client holds extreme ideas as a result of an isolated incident and applies this to other situations. For example, if she has experienced difficulty in understanding a prescribed reading for one course, then she may conclude that she is not at all suited to academic study.

Magnification and minimisation

Magnification and minimisation occur when the client perceives a situation either in an exaggerated or understated manner. For example, if the client has experienced difficulties in her one of her counselling practicals, she may consider herself incapable of eventually practicing as a social worker. In this way the situation is magnified.

Personalisation

Personalisation occurs when the client relates external events to herself even when there is no logical reason to make this connection. For example, if the tutor refuses to supply the class with additional information for an assignment, she may interpret this as the tutor's dislike of her.

Labelling and mislabelling

Labelling and mislabelling occur when the client defines herself in terms of her shortcomings. For example, if the client has failed a test, she may believe that she is worthless.

Polarised thinking

Polarised thinking involves thinking and interpreting situations in extremes. Consequently, the client may think in all-or-nothing terms. For example, she may perceive herself as either a brilliant learner or a complete academic failure.

The cognitive distortions outlined above provide us with some indication of how faulty interpretations of situations can lead to psychological distress. How, then, does the cognitive therapist help the client to change distorted thinking?

Therapeutic techniques and procedures

The techniques employed by the cognitive therapist are psycho-educational, which means that therapy is viewed as a learning process. Not only does the clients gain insight into the negative automatic thoughts that underlie their feelings and behaviour, but they learn new ways of perceiving and interpreting situations (Corey, 1996).

Therapeutic techniques are essentially task-oriented and the client is encouraged to actively monitor those thoughts that accompany psychological distress. Thus, in recording those situations where negative automatic thoughts occur, the client is able to see both the content and context of those thoughts. The therapist also challenges these thoughts by asking the client to provide evidence for the beliefs that she or he has about him- or herself. In order to address the cognitive distortions that cause distress, the therapist helps the client to explore them. The client is encouraged to replace negative ways of viewing the world with more positive ones. In addition, he or she is encouraged to perceive him- or herself as more competent and capable. The therapist may assign homework tasks, which will enable the testing of beliefs in real-life situations. In this way, faulty thinking is also challenged. Homework also serves the purpose of teaching the client new skills, such as relaxation methods and social skills (Beck *et al.*, 1979).

Cognitive therapy is aimed at helping the client to actively deal with psychological distress. The therapist is directive and actively encourages the client to change the way situations are interpreted. This therapy is therefore time-limited as it has a specific problem-solving focus (Beck, 1976). Thus, while the psychoanalytic therapist views the client's symptoms as indicative of underlying conflicts, the cognitive therapist views faulty thinking as the problem. This approach to therapy therefore advocates that it is more important to actively identify and change maladaptive thoughts and beliefs than to merely understand what causes them.

The cognitive therapist and Themba

Beck's (1976) approach was originally developed as treatment for depression, and therefore we can briefly consider how the cognitive therapist could help Themba.

Themba's depression can be understood as being triggered by the negative view that he has of himself. He blames his experiences at university on personal shortcomings and is unable to consider alternative explanations for events. He also interprets all his experiences in a negative manner and as such selectively abstracts from situations to support the views that he has about himself. Themba's gloomy vision of the future also serves to deepen his depression, as he does not allow himself to have any positive thoughts about it. In addition, the physical symptoms that he is experiencing also serve to heighten his negative self-perceptions.

To be able to help Themba, the therapist will challenge his negative thoughts by asking him to provide evidence for these beliefs. Thus he may be asked to list reasons why he views himself in this way. He may also be asked to provide evidence to dispute this view of himself. In doing so the therapist aims to show Themba that it is his distorted perceptions and not reality itself, which is the cause of his depression. One of the aims of therapy may be to encourage Themba to stay at university by helping him to deal with those thoughts and feelings that prevent him from pursuing his studies. To encourage him to become more active and to counter his lethargy, homework tasks may be assigned that include setting up an activity schedule that requires him to perform certain tasks. Themba also feels overwhelmed by the demands of his course and often this feeling is exaggerated. As a result, he reacts by not doing anything. The therapist may help him to prioritise tasks and to break down his work into manageable units. In this way, he may feel some sense of mastery and be able to see how the magnification of his feelings leads to distorted perceptions about his abilities.

Person-centred therapy

Corey's (1996) definition of psychotherapy emphasises the importance of the therapeutic relationship in bringing about change within the client. While the importance of the relationship is emphasised in both the psychoanalytic and cognitive approaches, particular techniques are key factors in helping clients to bring about change in their lives. The person-centred approach advocated by Carl Rogers (1951) departs from this focus on theory and technique. This approach emphasises the centrality of the personal qualities of the therapist

and the quality of the therapeutic relationship in helping the client to change. This approach is rooted in humanistic philosophy, which believes that each person has the potential to self-actualise (i.e. to express their unique self), given the proper environment. Thus, the central aim of person-centred therapy is to help the client to achieve his or her potential by providing a supportive emotional therapeutic climate.

Key ideas

The humanistic philosophy within which this approach is located advocates a positive view of human nature. The belief is that the client possesses the inherent capacity to become psychologically healthy when the correct emotional climate is provided. The therapeutic relationship is viewed as providing the client with the mechanism to achieve this goal (Rogers, 1951). An important aspect of this approach is that the client and not the therapist directs the process of therapy. Rogers rejects the notion of the therapist as expert. Instead, he argues that the client is the expert on his or her distress and should therefore be the one to direct the process of healing.

Rogers' (1951) conception of the causes of psychological distress differs from the two approaches discussed previously. He argues that distress is caused by 'incongruence', which is the discrepancy between the client's self-perception and reality. Anxiety arises when the client is confronted with feedback from objective reality, which is at odds with the self-concept. The client then employs defence mechanisms in order to protect the self from this anxiety (see Figure 3). Rogers views these defences as maladaptive because they protect the client's distorted self-concept. He believes that a supportive environment can help the client to address this incongruence.

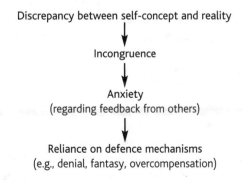

Figure 3 The person-centred view of psychological distress

Consider the example of the social work learner who is struggling academically. If she believes that she is a resilient person who is coping well with the demands of her studies, negative feedback from others as well as the reality of her poor marks may result in anxiety. She may rely on defence mechanisms or she may distort reality to deal with the anxiety. This will result in her being unable to actualise and achieve her potential. Within a person-centred approach this learner will be helped to achieve a self-concept that is more realistic so that she is able to appreciate herself. The therapeutic situation will enable her to explore and integrate various feelings that she has previously been unable to acknowledge.

Therapeutic techniques and procedures

As mentioned earlier, the person-centred approach does not emphasise the centrality of techniques in helping clients to change. Instead, the focus is on providing a therapeutic climate that will enable clients to express their sense of self. Thus the primary responsibility for healing and change is placed on the client. However, Rogers (1961) avers that there are certain 'core conditions' within the therapeutic relationship which are 'necessary and sufficient' for the client to change, namely congruence, unconditional positive regard and accurate empathy.

The 'core conditions' for therapeutic change

Congruence
Congruence refers to the genuineness that the therapist expresses in the relationship. Thus the therapist has to be authentic in his or her reactions to the client. There must be a genuine acknowledgement of feeling regarding the client in order to enhance honest communication. The therapist may need to express certain feelings in an attempt to be authentic, but this does not mean that the client's feelings are pushed aside. Congruence implies that the therapist is willing to confront his or her feelings so as to provide the client with a positive, growth-enhancing experience.

Unconditional positive regard
Unconditional positive regard refers to the therapist's unconditional acceptance of the client as a person. This means that the therapist is non-judgemental in caring for the client even when she or he disapproves of the client's behaviour. The central concern is for the client as a human being, regardless of the thoughts, feelings and behaviour that are expressed within the therapeutic situation.

Accurate empathy
Accurate empathy refers to understanding the client's thoughts and feelings from the client's perspective. This requires that the therapist must share the client's subjective experience so that his or her understanding can be reflected back to the client. When the therapist accurately empathises with the client, the probability of change is greatly enhanced.

Empathy is more than a reflection of those thoughts and feelings that are obvious to the client. When the therapist is accurately attuned she or he is able to reflect those feelings that underlie the content. Thus the client gains insight into the roots of the incongruity between her or his self-concept and reality. By accurately acknowledging these feelings, the therapist helps the client to resolve the incongruity and effect constructive change.

Rogers (1961) believes that a supportive therapeutic relationship which contains the above three elements is fundamental in helping the client to change. The 'techniques' that will help the client to better understand her or his feelings, are listening, reflecting and providing clarification.

Given the relationship orientation of this approach, how can the person-centred therapist help Themba?

The person-centred therapist and Themba

In terms of the person-centred approach, Themba's personal distress is seen as being due to the incongruence between his self-concept and reality. Through the process of therapy Themba may come to realise that his perception of himself as a conscientious learner is at odds with his lecturers' perception of him. They may perceive him as someone who does not apply himself to his studies because he procrastinates and often misses deadlines. As a result, he does not achieve good marks in his courses. Themba feels threatened and anxious when confronted with this feedback from his lecturers. He responds by avoiding his studies and withdrawing into himself. In this way he does not have to face the reality of his poor academic performance. The incongruence between Themba's self-concept and the feedback from his lecturers is at the heart of his current distress. He realises that a problem exists and that he needs to explore options for change. The person-centred framework provides Themba with an opportunity to explore these feelings. The therapist provides a warm and caring environment within which he feels free to express these feelings. The therapist listens intently to his thoughts and feelings and clarifies and reflects these back to him. By being genuine and accepting him unconditionally, the therapist creates a climate that will encourage Themba to examine his sense of self. Essentially, the therapist aims to provide Themba with a safe experience, which will increase his confidence in his abilities to discover an alternative way of being. Ultimately, he will be empowered to take responsibility for directing the course of his life.

37.1 HOW DO WE ASSESS THE EFFECTIVENESS OF PSYCHOTHERAPY?

Our discussion has centred on three therapeutic approaches but as we have seen, there are more than 400 types of therapy that are currently being practiced (Karasu, 1986). How do we assess the effectiveness of these approaches? Seligman (1995) says that there are two ways in which researchers have tried to measure the outcomes of psychotherapy, namely efficacy studies and effectiveness studies. The former is more popular and has been the primary manner in which researchers have evaluated the outcomes of certain types of psychological intervention. Efficacy studies are conducted in an experimental situation where participants are randomly assigned to experimental (treatment) and control conditions so as to assess if a particular type of therapy is effective in treating a particular disorder. The experimental group is required to subscribe to the therapy for a set number of sessions and the treatment is short-term and time-limited as researchers want to establish whether a particular intervention actually works. In these studies only participants with one diagnosis are allowed because multiple diagnoses militate against the assessment of the effectiveness of the therapy for a particular disorder (Seligman, 1995). Thus, if there is an improvement in the psychological well-being of the experimental group, then it is concluded that the therapy works and it is given greater legitimacy. Seligman (1995) says that efficacy studies have become the 'gold standard' by which the utility of therapies is assessed. While there is value in using this method to assess the usefulness of therapies for the treatment of certain disorders, we can see that it becomes problematic when we try to assess the outcomes of long-term therapies such as psychoanalysis. As we have discussed, efficacy studies typically evaluate therapies such as cognitive therapy, which are time-limited. It would be extremely difficult to assess psychoanalysis in this manner, as this type of therapy is dependent on the uncovering of unconscious material – a process that cannot be confined to a limited number of sessions. In addition, the analytic process may result in many issues being raised in therapy and consequently more than one diagnosis may be made.

Does this mean that we are unable to assess the utility of psychoanalysis or are there other means by which we can achieve this? Seligman (1995) suggests that effectiveness studies may well provide the solution to this dilemma. These studies essentially employ a survey method, thus asking respondents to report on their actual experiences in therapy. Seligman (1995) refers to the *Consumer Reports* study, which was published in the United States of America in 1995. This study surveyed the experiences of several thousand people with regard to their experiences in therapy. The questions ranged from details regarding the type of therapy engaged in and the competence of the therapist, to the reasons for terminating the therapy. The study concluded that people benefited from psychotherapeutic intervention and that long-term therapy was more effective than short-term interventions. Seligman (1995) argues that this survey method allows us to gain a clearer view of the effectiveness of a wide range of therapies. However there are methodological flaws associated with this type of research. Amongst others, there were no control groups to compare this sample with, this method relies on the participants' self-reports, which are highly subjective, and participants were asked to retrospectively report on their emotional states. Thus the study was not without problems. However, Seligman (1995) argues that the positive features of this method should be used in conjunction with those of the efficacy method, as this will provide the best way in which to provide scientific validation for the effectiveness of psychotherapy.

The effectiveness of psychotherapy

Our discussion has thus far focused on how these three approaches may be used to alleviate Themba's psychological distress. A pertinent question at this point may be whether these approaches are effective in achieving this aim. The issue that faces the advocates of various types of therapy is whether or not psychotherapy actually works. Is psychotherapy the 'talking cure' that Freud intended it to be, and if so, how does one measure if the client has been 'cured'? This dilemma has been a bone of contention for many therapists as they try to establish the validity of their therapies. Numerous efforts have been made to empirically prove that certain therapies are indeed effective, and in some instances researchers have tried to prove that some therapies are superior to others. However, as we will see, this is a complex issue, and to date, most studies have focused on evaluating therapies within an experimental context, which militates against the inclusion of a wide range of therapies.

Lambert and Bergin (1994), in assessing the effectiveness of psychotherapy, conclude that there are minimal differences in the outcomes of the various models. Research has shown that while some psychological difficulties are more amenable to certain types of therapy, it is difficult to say which approach is most effective. Essentially, the indications are that some form of therapy is better than no therapy at all.

The role of indigenous therapies in an African context

Cross-cultural issues in therapy

Our discussion thus far has focused on the psychotherapeutic approaches that form the core of Western psychological models of intervention. We have applied these approaches to a case study of Themba who is a young, Black, South African male so as to see how each approach can alleviate his distress. However, we have not considered the impact of culture (i.e. ethnic or racial background) on Themba's interaction with the various therapists. This may create the impression that culture is not important and that Western modes of intervention are readily transportable to any socio-cultural con-text. An important aspect of therapeutic intervention is the acknowledgement of the impact of the cultural framework of both client and therapist. The client's experience of the problem is coloured by her or his cultural experience. Similarly, the therapist's cultural background influences her or his interaction with the client and therefore she or he needs to be cognisant of this (Corey, 1996).

Not only does culture provide the context within which to understand the individual, there are other factors such as gender and class, which also need to be considered. An acknowledgement of the impact of culture, class and gender enables the therapist to gain a holistic view of the client and militates against the therapist making undue assumptions of the client and her or his problem. Pedersen (1994) argues that psychotherapists have two choices, namely to address the issue of culture or to ignore it. However, regardless of the choice that is made, culture (and gender and class) will impact on the interaction between client and counsellor. These considerations have led to the development of theories and techniques for multicultural or cross-cultural therapies, and represent attempts by mainstream psychotherapeutic models to become more applicable to non-Western settings (Corey, 1996; Pedersen, 1994). However, it is important to note that while cultural issues may be taken into account, the central ideas of these models remain the same.

Indigenous therapies

The attempts at adapting mainstream models of intervention so as to be applicable to non-Western cultures do not imply that these models are the best or only way of helping people. Western notions of psychological distress and the concomitant modes of helping, reflect Western ideas and values that may not always be suitable for other cultural contexts (Peltzer, 1995). There are other forms of non-professional intervention which people turn to in times of distress. Of concern to us, are the 'folk sector healers' who are non-professional healers who use a variety of techniques such as rituals, herbal remedies, symbolic healing and spiritualism to help clients in distress (Kleinman, 1980).

Swartz (1998) identifies two types of folk healing in use in southern Africa, namely, 'indigenous healing' and 'religious healing'. In the former, there is diversity in terms of the type of healing offered and the contexts within which they occur. For example, in indigenous healing in KwaZulu Natal, a distinction is made between an 'isangoma' (diviner) and an 'inyanga' (doctor). The 'inyanga' is a dispenser of herbal remedies, while the 'isangoma' is a person who has been chosen by the ancestors to become a healer (Ngubane in Swartz, 1998). The way in which distress is conceptualised and treated will depend on the healer's orientation.

In indigenous healing, psychological distress is attributed to disturbances in the physical (nature), social (family and other relationships) and supernatural (bewitchment, spirit possession) realms (Swartz, 1998). For example, Themba's emotional state and his failure to achieve may be seen to have been caused by a curse placed on him by a jealous neighbour who is envious of his university studies. His distress is not viewed as having internal roots. Instead, it is something that has been thrust upon him by external forces. Themba may seek help from an indigenous healer in order to establish how to deal with his 'misfortune'. The intervention may require the use of herbal remedies or rituals to alleviate his distress.

Religious healing is the second type of healing which falls within the folk sector. Swartz (1998) says that the 'African independent churches' employ a mixture of Christian beliefs and practices and indigenous healing. In some churches there is a significant emphasis on elements such as spirit possession, while others emphasise charismatic Christian aspects. This type of healing appeals to many people as it provides spiritual solutions to their problems.

Swartz (1998) also states that folk sector healing often occurs within a communal setting. Thus the distress and healing is shared with others. This approach differs from the individualised Western dyadic models which were discussed earlier in the chapter. Folk sector healing reflects certain values which are cherished in African cultures.

Conclusion

We have focused on three core approaches to helping patients alleviate their psychological distress. In our discussion we have explored some of the key ideas that underpin these models and have examined the therapeutic techniques that are employed in the respective approaches. The benefits of psychotherapeutic intervention have been briefly highlighted. In addition, we have considered the role of indigenous therapies in alleviating psychological distress.

As we have seen, these three models have been conceptualised within particular Western contexts and seek to address problems of living within these environments. While models of psychotherapy have utility in addressing the psychological needs of individuals, these individual models may be limited in meeting the large-scale mental health needs of the country. In addition, we need to ask ourselves whether Western models of psychological distress and therapeutic intervention can and should be transposed onto the African context. We cannot uncritically accept these notions even if individual psychotherapy represents one of the core competencies in which psychologists are trained. The search for theory and practice that takes account of our particular socio-political and economic context is one that challenges mental health practitioners in South Africa today. As a result, psychologists are redefining the parameters of therapy so as to make it more socially relevant and accessible to people. (See Chapter 39 for a discussion of other approaches within a community mental health approach.)

REFERENCES

Beck, A. (1976). *Cognitive Therapy and the Emotional Disorders.* Harmondsworth: Penguin.

Beck A.Y., Rush, A.G., Shaw, B.F. & Emery, G. (1979). *Cognitive Therapy of Depression.* New York: Guilford.

Corey, G. (1996). *Theory and Practice of Counselling and Psychotherapy* (5th edition). Pacific Grove: Brooks/Cole.

Dryden, W. & Feltham, C. (1995). *Counselling and Psychotherapy. A consumer's guide.* London: Sheldon Press.

Eagle, M.N. & Wolitzky, D.L. (1992). Psychoanalytic theories of psychotherapy. In D.K. Freedheim (Ed.). *History of Psychotherapy: A century of change.* Washington DC: American Psychological Association.

Karasu, T.B. (1986). The specificity versus non-specificity dilemma: Toward identifying therapeutic change agents. *American Journal of Psychiatry,* 14(3):687-95.

Kleinman, A. (1980). *Clients and Healers in the Context of Culture.* Berkeley: University of California Press.

Lambert, M.J. & Bergin, A.E. (1994). The effectiveness of psychotherapy.

In A.E. Bergin & S.L. Garfield (Eds.). *Handbook of Psychotherapy and Behaviour Change* (4th edition). New York: Wiley.

Mcleod, J. (1993). *An Introduction to Counselling.* Buckingham: Open University Press.

Pedersen, P. (1994). *A Handbook for Developing Multicultural Awareness* (2nd edition). Alexandria, VA: American Counseling Association.

Peltzer, K. (1995). *Psychology and Health in African Cultures: Examples of ethno-psychotherapeutic practice.* Frankfurt: IKO-Verlag fur Interkulturelle Kommunikation.

Rogers, C. (1951). *Client-centred Therapy.* Boston: Houghton Mifflin.

Rogers, C. (1961). *On Becoming a Person.* Boston: Houghton Mifflin.

Seligman, M.E.P. (1995). The effectiveness of psychotherapy: The Consumer Reports study. *American Psychologist,* 50:965-74.

Swartz, L. (1998). *Culture and Mental Health.* Cape Town: Oxford University Press.

Weiten, W. (2001). *Psychology: Themes and variations* (5th edition). Stanford: Wadsworth.

Multiple choice questions

1. Thabo experiences his therapist as authoritative and emotionally distant and in many ways their relationship mirrors the relationship which he had with his father. This is an example of
    a) resistance
    b) projection
    c) transference
    d) countertransference

2. Free association is a psychoanalytic technique in which the client
    a) makes connections between the conscious and unconscious
    b) spontaneously talks about whatever comes to mind
    c) feels free to question the therapist on personal matters
    d) censors the thoughts and feelings which are shared with the therapist

3. Since talking about the death of his mother, Simpiwe consistently arrives late for sessions with his therapist. This is an example of
    a) denial
    b) grief
    c) resistance
    d) countertransference

4. Psychological distress is caused by the way in which people interpret events in their lives. This understanding underpins the _____ approach to psychotherapy.
    a) psychoanalytic
    b) cognitive-behavioural
    c) person-centred
    d) cognitive

5. Carol believes that she is a complete failure because she failed a maths test at school. Her belief is held in spite of the good marks which she attains in her other subjects. This belief is an example of
    a) personalisation
    b) selective abstraction
    c) magnification
    d) minimisation

6. When the client is taught new ways of perceiving and interpreting situations in order to bring about change, this approach is seen as
    a) dynamic
    b) psychoeducational
    c) empathic
    d) homework

7. Jim tells the therapist that he has committed a crime and feels guilty about it and she responds by saying that she does not judge him even though she does not agree with what he has done. This caring, non-judgemental attitude expressed by the therapist toward the client is called
    a) acceptance
    b) empathy
    c) unconditional positive regard
    d) congruence

8. The discrepancy between a person's self-concept and reality is what Rogers calls
    a) psychological distress
    b) anxiety
    c) incongruence
    d) genuineness

9. There are certain 'core conditions' in the therapeutic relationship which are _____ for the client to change
    a) necessary and sufficient
    b) fundamentally important
    c) equally necessary
    d) therapeutically important

10. Non-professional healers who use rituals, herbal remedies and symbolic healing fall within the _____ framework as opposed to a Western psychotherapeutic framework.
    a) lay counselling
    b) indigenous healing
    c) religious healing
    d) spiritual healing

Short answer questions

1. Discuss any three of the following therapeutic techniques used in psychoanalytic psychotherapy:
    a) free association;
    b) interpretation;
    c) dream analysis; and
    d) transference.

2. Explain what a cognitive distortion is and define and give examples of the following:
    a) overgeneralisation;
    b) personalisation; and
    c) labelling

3. How does the person-centred approach conceptualise psychological distress? Illustrate your answer by means of a diagram.

4. Name and describe the 'core conditions' that are necessary and sufficient for the client to change.

5. What are 'folk-sector healers' and how do they differ from psychotherapists trained in Western models?

38

Psychopharmacology

Elias Mpofu

CHAPTER OBJECTIVES

After studying this chapter you should be able to:

- define each of the following: psychoactive drugs, psychopharmacology, neurotransmitter, drug potency and effective dose
- describe the processes by which a psychoactive drug acts on a receptor site
- explain the psychopharmacological actions of any three drugs in terms of the neurotransmitters that they mimic or potentiate
- distinguish between drug potency and drug dosage, on the one hand, and types of drug tolerance, on the other
- relate drug efficacy to the method of administration
- classify: specific drugs in terms of their major uses and alternative uses, neurotransmitters in terms of their excitatory (arousal) and inhibitory functions, and drugs in terms of their main and side-effect profiles
- compare alternative drug classification systems with regard to their practical usefulness
- explain the development of drug tolerance and dependency
- with reference to specific psychiatric conditions, show how the biochemical theory behind their causation relates to the selection of specific psychoactive agents for treatment.

Introduction

Psychoactive drugs are substances that achieve their effect by altering or modulating mood, thoughts and behaviour. Their use in the management of mental health is referred to as psychopharmacology. As psychopharmacological interventions, psychoactive drugs are typically used to treat the symptoms of psychiatric illness. They also serve a prophylactic function such as when they are used to prevent the onset or recurrence of a symptom or the development of symptoms (e.g., when used to ameliorate the side effects of another drug that a person may be taking concurrently) (Eckler & Fair, 1996). The treatment of psychiatric illness with psychoactive drugs is premised on the fact that all behaviour has a neuropsychological basis or that neurophysiology has a primary role in the mediation of specific maladaptive behaviours (Mpofu, 2002; Mpofu & Conyers, 2003).

Neurophysiological predisposition to a mental health condition could translate into a mental illness in adverse environmental conditions, and in some people rather than others (Antonovsky, 1993). The interaction between the environment and a pre-existing neurophysiological predisposition to the experience of a mental illness is important to an understanding of the origins of mental illness and its treatment. It is the subject of discussion in Part 3 of this volume and will not be pursued further in this chapter.

This chapter presents a non-technical account on the mechanisms of action of psychoactive drugs, their classification, uses and effects. Specific attention is paid to the neurochemistry of psychoactive drugs, and dose response issues. As far as possible, illustrative examples from commonly used drugs or substances are cited.

The mechanisms of action of psychoactive drugs

Mechanisms of action refer to the particular process by which an agent (e.g., a drug) achieves its effects. Neurons are structures of the nervous system that are involved in the transmission of messages throughout the nervous system (see Chapter 9, this volume). The messages are in the form of electrical impulses or signals. Each neuron comprises a cell body, dendrites and an axon. Axons carry nerve impulses to adjacent cells and dendrites receive the impulses. Between each axon and a dendrite is a space called a synaptic cleft. In transmitting nerve impulses, axons release chemicals called neurotransmitters that help with the conductance of the nerve impulse across the synapse to the next neuron. In this connection, a psychoactive agent may achieve its effects by: 1) facilitating or inhibiting the actions of a neurotransmitter receptor site, and 2) regulating neurotransmitter availability in the synaptic cleft (Ebadi, 1997; McCormick, 1998; Oslon, 2001).

Receptor site activity in nerve impulse conduction

Receptor sites on which the molecules of a psychoactive drug attach or bind are on a cell membrane or within the cell. The cell membranes comprise of chains of proteins and a fat barrier. The protein chains and fat barriers are permeable to some drugs and not to others. In general, a drug must be fat soluble (i.e. dissolve in oil) to penetrate a cell membrane or be available for binding to the proteins of the cell membrane (Hucho, 1993; McCormick, 1998; Moss & Henley, 2002). However, cell membranes also contain small pores that allow water-soluble drugs to permeate the cells. Thus, cell membranes regulate the transfer of drugs from the outside of a cell (e.g., intestines into blood stream) and inside of a cell into the general circulation. In general, drugs can achieve their expected effects on the neurons on five sites: presynaptic, within the presynaptic terminal membrane, synaptic cleft, post-synaptic membrane and post-synaptic neuron (see Figure 1).

Proteins in the cell membrane have binding sites for particular neurotransmitters (ligands). Changes in the structure of the protein accompany the binding of drug molecules and translate into a signal that is passed on to the intracellular side of the cell membrane. Specifically, when a drug molecule occupies a receptor site, it activates (agonist action) or inhibits (antagonist action) that receptor site. In other words, it facilitates or blocks the actions of a neurotransmitter, leading to the expected treatment effect and associated side effects. Drug molecules can also indirectly enhance or inhibit signal transmission by a receptor site by impacting on other cellular events that are associated with signal transmission or reception. For example, psychoactive agents can effect signal transmission indirectly by facilitating or inhibiting the functions of an enzyme or DNA molecule involved in an action (Eckler & Fair, 1996; Hucho, 1993; McCormick, 1998; Powis & Bunn, 1995).

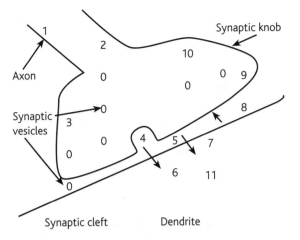

Legend

1. Presynaptic transmission of nerve impulse
2. Arrival of nerve impulse at nerve terminal
3. Neurotransmitter storage or carrier units
4. Release of transmitter from synaptic vesicle into synaptic cleft with stimulation by nerve impulse
5. Diffusion of neurotransmitter across synaptic cleft
6. Stimulation of post-synaptic receptors by neurotransmitter
7. Post-synaptic release of neurotransmitter back into the synaptic cleft
8. Destruction of some of the neurotransmitter by enzymes in the synaptic cleft
9. Reuptake of some of the neurotransmitter back into the pre-synaptic nerve terminal
10. Available neurotransmitter for storage in pre-synaptic vesicles and synaptic release with nerve impulse stimulation
11. Post-synaptic action with nerve impulse conduction

Figure 1 A simplified sequence of neurotransmitter action

Psychoactive drugs vary in their capacity to bind on receptor sites for which they are designed (Ariano, 1998; Hucho, 1993; Oslon, 2001). The more potent drugs, or those that achieve the most therapeutic effect, have the best fit with the specific receptor site. Drug molecules that are a partial match to the receptor site for which they are intended may have lower therapeutic effects as compared to those with a better fit. To a great extent, the strength of a drug molecule attachment is positively proportional to the degree of fit between the drug molecule and the drug-specific receptor site. A single neurotransmitter typically has multiple receptor sites (McCormick, 1998; Murphy *et al.*, 1998), which adds to the complexity of predicting the actions of a psychoactive agent on a receptor site.

From the foregoing, it should be apparent that agonist or antagonist actions of a psychoactive agent rest primarily on the fact that receptor sites are selective to certain drug molecules, or that drug molecules bind only to particular receptor sites. The strength of a drug attachment to a receptor site determines its therapeutic effectiveness. Ultimately, the chemical structure of the drug is the underlying factor that determines its localisation to specific receptors, the interaction of the drug and the specific receptors, and the associated effects.

Neurotransmitter types and actions

Over 40 neurotransmitters have been identified (Cohen, 1988; Moller, 2003; Webster, 2001). Some of the neurotransmitters function as primary neurotransmitters in that they are directly involved in the neuron signal transmission. Others modulate the transmission of primary transmitters or alter the responsiveness of post-synaptic neurons. For example, a neurotransmitter with a modulatory role can be involved in speeding up or slowing down the availability of a neurotransmitter in the synaptic cleft. The specific functions of the majority of neurotransmitters that have been identified are unknown.

Four classes of neurotransmitters have received significant research attention: catecholamines, acetylcholine, amino acids and opioid peptides. Catecholines comprise epinephrine (Epi), norepeniphrine (NE), dopamine (DA) and serotonin (5-hydroxytryptamine or 5-HT). Of these, only NE, DA and 5-HT are found in the brain. The individual catecholamines tend to be concentrated in various areas of the brain, and to impact the brain's functioning in different ways. For instance, NE has greater availability in the cerebral cortex, limbic system (i.e. amygdala, the hippocampus, mammillary bodies), hypothalamus, and the cerebellum. It is involved with orienting responses like alerting and focusing as well as the experience of hunger, thirst and emotion. NE activity is also involved in the experience of feelings of reward, sexual arousal, and regulation of blood pressure. 5-HT's major areas of concentration in the brain include the upper brain stem, pons, and the medulla oblongata. Its functions include the regulation of sleep and wakefulness, mood, feeding and sexual activity and temperature. In general, the functions of NE and 5-HT are different in that NE has excitatory behavioural functions, whereas those of 5-HT tend to be inhibitory. DA is available in large quantities from the basal ganglia (particularly the substantia nigra), frontal cortex, the limbic system, and the midbrain. Dopamine cell bodies are involved in the regulation of thought processes and integration of emotions. The availability of dopamine in the midbrain area is associated with the enhancement of reward centres of the brain (e.g., the nucleus accumbens, ventral tegmental area and the limbic system). Drugs that mimic dopaminergic or norepinephinergic reactions on the reward systems of the brain tend to be compulsively abused (e.g., nicotine and cocaine).

Acetycholine (Ach) is available in both the central and the peripheral nervous system. It has higher concentrations in the caudate nucleus, brain stem, spinal cord and cerebral cortex. Ach secreting neurons are active in behavioural excitation, learning, and memory formation and retrieval. Two groups of amino acids have neurotransmitter functions: glutamine, and aspartic acid, on the one hand, and (i.e. gamma-aminobutyric acid or GABA) and glycine, on the other. Glutamine and aspartic acid have behavioural excitatory functions, whereas GABA and glycine have inhibitory functions. GABA receptors are found in virtually all cell bodies of the brain. For that reason, GABA is the main inhibitor of neurotransmission in the brain (Julien, 1996; Levine *et al.*, 2000).

Factors influencing drug response

Apart from the chemical basis of the actions of drugs on particular receptor sites, the effect of a psychoactive agent also depends on its potency, efficacy, dose as well as the method administration. Each of these is briefly discussed in the next section.

Drug potency, efficacy and dose

The potency of a drug is the *absolute amount* of the drug that is required to achieve a desired effect. Its efficacy is the *maximum effect* that is possible with the drug. The dose is the *quantity of volume* of the drug that is administered. The effective dose (ED) is that which has been determined to produce the desired effect in a majority of people and with the least possible side effects (Ebadi, 1997; Eckler & Fair, 1996; Janicak *et al.*, 1997). However, the ED for individuals may vary within certain limits. This variation may be due to the differences in the genetic make up of individuals as well as their previous experience with the same or a different class of drugs, and their age. For example, people with experience with repeated use of a certain type of drug may need to take higher doses of the drug to achieve the same effect as those with less exposure to the drug (Eckler & Fair, 1996; Evans *et al.*, 1992;

MacDermott & Deglin, 1994). There is also significant variability in drug absorption and metabolism among younger and older people as compared to the general population (Janicak *et al.*, 1997). The effective dose for these special populations is less well established.

Highly potent drugs tend to achieve the desired effects at lower dosages than less potent drugs (Eckler & Fair, 1996; MacDermott & Deglin, 1994; Turley, 1999). At high dosages, the more potent drugs are toxic and can lead to significant organ damage or death. With highly potent drugs, the absolute increase in dosage necessary to reach toxicity is very small. For that reason, highly potent drugs need to be used with a high degree of medical care or supervision. The efficacy of a drug depends on its chemical structure rather than the dosage level (Julien, 1996; Kalant & Roschlau, 1998). For example, morphine, which is an analgesic (pain reliever) will achieve its effect on pain at lower doses than aspirin. Similarly, amphetamine, a stimulant, achieves effects superior to caffeine at a much lower dosage.

About six methods of drug administration are in common use: oral (by mouth), rectal (through the rectum), intravenous (injected directly into the blood stream), subcutaneous (injected under the skin), intramuscular (injected into the skeletal muscle) and mucous membrane (under the tongue or nasal inhalation). These methods are appropriate for different drugs, although some psychoactive drugs can be administered using alternative methods. For the purposes of this discussion, the effectiveness of an orally administered drug depends, in part, on its ability to survive intestinal gastric acids. Intravenously administered drugs are the least susceptible to loss of availability due to method of administration. The advantages and disadvantages of alternative methods of drug administration will not be considered here. Suffice to say that the level of drug available in a person (and hence influencing neurotransmitter activity) partly depends on the method of administration.

Drug classification, uses and effects

Psychoactive drugs are classifiable by various criteria: mechanism of action, potency, efficacy, side effects and chemical structure. For instance, drugs can be regarded as high or low in potency, efficacy, or side effects in treating a particular condition. Ideally, psychoactive drugs should be classified by their mechanisms of action since the reason for their actions would be explainable theoretically (Racagni & Nicoletta, 1999). A theory about why and how a particular drug achieves a particular action would be useful in the design of better or more effective psychoactive drugs for specific purposes. Unfortunately, little is currently known about the receptor site actions of particular psychoactive agents, and how these actions vary among individuals and health conditions (Julien, 1996; Levine *et al.*, 2000; Murphy *et al.*, 1998). Further to that, psychoactive drugs with the same presumed mechanisms of action can have different behavioural effects, whereas those with theoretically different mechanisms of action can be similar in behavioural effects. Classification of psychoactive drug by chemical structure is also problematic for the reason that psychoactive drugs with different chemical structures may have similar neurophysiological effects.

The reality that psychoactive agent classifications based on a drug's presumed mechanisms of action or chemical structure are not valid for predicting drug physiological-behavioural effects has supported the practice of classifying psychoactive drugs by their behavioural effects. The classification of psychoactive agents by their characteristic behavioural effects is also justified pragmatically by the fact that it is the observable alterations in behaviour that are often sought by those who use psychoactive agents (Mpofu, 2002). Moreover, classification by behavioural effects is reliable for identifying clusters of drugs with a similar behavioural presentation, even if the presumed mechanisms of action or chemical structures are different.

In the next section, the uses and effects of four main classes of psychoactive drugs are briefly discussed: central nervous system depressants, psychostimulants, anti-depressants and anti-psychotics.

Central nervous system (CNS) depressants

Alternative names for drugs commonly referred to as CNS depressants are sedatives, tranquilisers, anxiolytics and hypnotics. The drugs in this class share the common characteristic of depressing psychomotor behaviour. That is, they diminish environmental awareness and responsiveness. They are useful for relieving anxiety, inducing sleep, unconsciousness and coma. They are also used as anti-convulsants. The effects of CNS depressants are additive in that use of one CNS depressant (e.g., alcohol) together or subsequent to another CNS depressant (e.g., barbiturates) results in more severe behavioural depres-

38.1 NEUROTRANSMITTERS ARE NOT ENTIRELY UNDERSTOOD

The apparently counterintuitive observations in the previous paragraph attest to the fact that neurotransmitter activity is complex and the factors influencing incompletely understood. For instance, a particular neurotransmitter is involved in multiple activities (e.g., behavioural arousal, temperature regulation, and so on) so that its response to a psychoactive agent represents the intended effects of the psychoactive agent as well as interactions involving other activities in which that neurotransmitter is involved. Similarly, a specific psychoactive agent (e.g., aspirin) may achieve a variety of actions (e.g., pain, temperature and inflammation control) through its inhibitory actions on a receptor site that interacts with an enzyme (or enzymes) involved in tissue inflammation. The fact that a single psychoactive drug or receptor action is involved in multiple effects is central to an appreciation of the use of psychopharmacology in the treatment of mental health conditions. As previously discussed, differences in dosage levels can alter behavioural presentation even by the same psychoactive agent. Subsequent discussion on drug tolerance by individuals will highlight the fact that repeated exposure to a psychoactive drug may alter the physiological environment for the drug so that its effects may be different from those that would be expected on the basis of the theory on the drug's mechanisms of action or its chemical composition.

sion. Use of a CNS depressant may also have an additive effect on a person's pre-existing mental state. For example, a person with mental fatigue is likely to experience a higher level of psychomotor retardation with the ingestion of a CNS depressant, such as alcohol.

Benzodiazepines and barbiturates are among the CNS depressants with a long history in the treatment of anxiety, panic attacks and phobias (Brody *et al.*, 1998; Katzung, 2001; Turley, 1999). They are also effective in treating alcohol dependence in that they ameliorate withdrawal symptoms (Julien, 1996). Benzodiazepines, also referred to as minor tranquilisers, are not effective in treating major psychosis (Lido, 2000; Turley, 1999). However, their use has also been associated with higher suicide rate among users, respiratory compromise, and ataxia (staggering) (Julien, 1996). Barbiturates have a high risk for inducing drug dependence or compulsive abuse (Julien, 1996; Lane & Reed, 1992). Buspirone is a newer type of CNS depressant with a lower risk profile and the drug of choice in the treatment of anxiety and panic disorders (Maxmen & Ward, 1995). It does not seem to be effective with people who were previously on a benzodiazepine (Julien, 1996).

CNS depressants achieve behavioural inhibition by enhancing gamm-aminobutyric acid (GABA) receptor activity in the cerebral cortex, hippocampus, cerebellum and brain stem and the spinal cord (Evans *et al.*, 1992; Hucho, 1993). Depressant drug effects on specific brain structures are associated with particular behavioural responses. For example, the sedative-hypnotic effects of CNS depressants are thought to arise from their effect on GABA receptors in the cerebral cortex. The anti-convulsant effects of the benzodiazepines may be a result of their effect on GABA receptors in the cerebellum and the hipoccampus whereas their muscle relaxant effects seem to emanate from their effect on GABA receptors located in the cerebellum, brain stem and spinal cord (Cohen, 1988; Hucho,1993). Benzodiazepines are thought to have anti-convulsant effects through raising the seizure-triggering threshold of the hippocampus (Julien, 1996).

Psychostimulants

Psychostimulants are used to increase mental alertness, increase motor activity or reduce fatigue, relieve boredom and enhance task performance (Turley, 1999). At lower doses, they raise the heart rate and blood pressure, cause the pupils to dilate and increase the flow of blood to the muscles. They also suppress the appetite through their action on serotonin neurons.

Caffeine and nicotine are among the most widely used non-prescription psychostimulant drugs. Amphetamines and amphetamine derivatives such as methylphenidate or Ritalin and Pemoline (Cylert) are prescription psychostimulants that are widely used with people with a variety of disorders of attention, as well as obesity (through appetite suppression) (Julien, 1996). Cocaine is currently an illicit drug in most countries, although a cocaine derivative is medically used as a local anesthetic (Brody *et al.*, 1998; Julien, 1996).

Psychostimulants carry the risk of compulsive abuse because of the dopamine-induced reinforcement (MacDermott & Deglin, 1994; Turley, 1999). For example, repeated use of amphetamines appears to have the effect of suppressing the dopamine releasing neurons so that the experience of a high energy level becomes possible through the

use of psychostimulants. The memory of having achieved a high with the drug reinforces dependency on the drug. A vicious circle of drug use and withdrawal symptoms ensues. At higher doses, psychostimulants may cause anxiety, insomnia, irritability, hypertension, sexual dysfunction, and a variety of psychotic behaviours (e.g., paranoia and persecutory fears).

Psychostimulants seem to achieve their effect by impacting on the behavioural activation and inhibition functions of the hypothalamic-pituitary-adrenal (HPA) axis involved in the regulation of emotions or impulses (Brody *et al.*, 1998; Eckler & Fair, 1996; Hucho, 1993). Specifically, psychostimulants appear to enhance a feeling of euphoria or being upbeat and energetic by enhancing the release of the biological amine adrenalin, which drives the fight-or-flight response in humans and other mammals. They increase adrenaline levels by augmenting the actions of dopamine and norepinephrine receptors in the lateral hypothalamus that are involved in modulating levels of adrenaline. The augmentation of dopamine and norepinephrine is achieved by prolonging the synaptic activity of dopamine and norepinephrine through delaying the re-uptake of these neurotransmitters back into the presynaptic nerve terminals. The enhancement of dopamine neurotransmission also indirectly augments the activities of serotonin neurons, which are involved in creating a sense of satiety.

Anti-depressants

Anti-depressants are used to elevate mood, increase physical activity, improve appetite and sleep patterns in people with mood disorders, particularly major depression (Lane & Reed, 1992; Turley, 1999). People with major depression experience profound sadness, pessimism, diminished energy, mental fatigue, and helplessness and lack of sleep, which cannot be explained by their objective circumstances. Those with sadness due to apparent cause tend not to show signs of psychosis, and are not candidates for treatment with anti-depressants.

People with major depression can be treated with a variety of anti-depressants. The anti-depressants fall into three broad classes: Tricyclic anti-depressants (TCAs), serotonin-specific re-uptake inhibitors (SSRIs), and monoamine oxidase inhibitors (MAOs) (Lane & Reed, 1992; Julien, 1996). They also respond to electroconvulsive shock and psychotherapy in combination with psychopharmacological treat-

The biochemical causes of major depression are incompletely understood (Racagni & Nicoletta, 1999). A widely accepted explanation for the occurrence of major depression is that it is caused by abnormally low levels of the neurotransmitters norepinephrine, serotonin and dopamine (Evans *et al.*, 1992; Racagni & Nicoletta, 1999). This depletion may be due to the activities of an enzyme that metabolises the neurotransmitters. Diminished neurotransmitter availability may also be due to post-synaptic neuron hypersentivity leading to abnormally high conductivity of the neurotransmitter across the synapse (Julien, 1996). A third possibility is that synaptic neurotransmitter insufficiency may be due to rapid re-uptake of the neurotransmitters back into the pre-synaptic vesicles (Brody *et al.*, 1998; Hucho, 1993; Julien, 1996).

A complication with the diminished availability of neurotransmitter hypothesis is the observation that a there is a significant time lag between the biochemical effect (e.g., increase in synaptic neurotransmitter availability) and the change in mood that is being sought (i.e. elevation in mood) (Brody *et al.*, 1998; Turley, 1999). With some anti-depressants (e.g., paxil), the time lag between observing a biochemical response and a clinically significant change in behaviour can be as much as two weeks (Maxmen & Ward, 1995). Some psychoactive drugs that cause augmentation of synaptic neurotransmitters (e.g., cocaine) do not have anti-depressant effects. These observations have cast doubt on the adequacy of the synaptic neurotransmitter deficiency hypothesis. Nonetheless, the contradiction of neurotransmitter availability not leading to an immediate elevation of mood has been variously explained (Julien, 1996). One explanation is that the increased availability of neurotransmitters in the synaptic cleft reduces the hypersensitivity of the post-synaptic neurons (a phenomenon called down regulation) over a period of time, so that post-synaptic neuronal activity normalises. This adaptive change in neuronal behaviour is speculated to take time, hence the delay in observing a clinically significant change in mood following observance of a change at the biochemical level. An alternative explanation is that mood elevation occurs with an adaptive change in the serotonin rather than norepinephrine or dopamine receptors (Brody *et al.*, 1998; Murphy *et al.*, 1998). Adaptive changes in serotonin receptors may take time to be achieved, hence the delay in observing a clinically significant effect after an apparent biochemical effect.

ment. Of interest in this chapter are the mechanisms of action of each of the three major types of anti-depressants. TCAs (e.g., imipramine, doxepin and amitripline) achieve their effect by prolonging neurotransmitter activity through the blocking of pre-synaptic re-uptake of norepinephrine and serotonin. Serotonin-Specific Reuptake Inhibitors (SSRIs) enhance neurotransmitter availability by blocking the pre-synaptic re-uptake of serotonin. Monoamine oxidase inhibitors (e.g., phenelzine and moclobemide) increase the availability of the neurotransmitters norepinephrine, serotonin and dopamine through the inhibition of an enzyme that normally metabolises these neurotransmitters.

With few exceptions (e.g., Prozac and moclobemide), anti-depressants have a side effect profile that includes impaired memory, attention deficits, poor dexterity, and sedation (Brody *et al.*, 1998; Turley, 1999). For that reason, most anti-depressants are best ingested at bedtime so as to minimise major disruption of personal effectiveness during normal day hours. TCAs have historically been preferred over SSRIs and MAOs in treating depression, although SSRIs and the newer class of MAOs may be taking precedence over TCAs as first choice drugs for major depression. TCAs are known for their lower side effect profile compared to SSRIs and MAOs. However, TCAs are as good as SSRIs in treating major depression, and not effective in treating about a third of people with major depression (Julien, 1996). TCAs may interact dangerously with drugs that are used to treat high blood pressure, arthritis, epilepsy and Parkinsonism. Death can result from taking TCAs with some alcohol.

Anti-psychotics

Drugs used to treat major psychosis such as schizophrenia are referred to as major tranquillisers, neuroleptics, anti-psychotics or anti-schizophrenics (Lido, 2000; Turley, 1999). Major tranquilisers are contrasted with minor tranquillisers (e.g., benzodiazepines – see section on anti-depressants), which are effective for treating anxiety and neurotic behaviours, but less effective in treating major psychosis such as schizophrenia. Clonazepam is one benzodiazepam that is effective for treating agitation in people with psychosis (Julien, 1996). The word tranquilliser, as applied to anti-psychotic medications, should not be interpreted to mean that the drugs exert a soothing effect on the person with schizophrenia or a state of calm serenity. The discussion on the side effects (unintended effects) of anti-psychotic medications will show that use of these drugs is associated with a host of debilitating effects, which may incline people with psychosis towards non-compliance with the medication.

People with schizophrenia, for whom these drugs are primarily intended, often present with disturbances in thought, emotional regulation and behaviour with a loss of contact with reality (Byck, 1986; Lane & Reed, 1992; Liddle, 2000). The poor contact with reality has been associated with processes of dissociation of thought, emotion and behaviour. On the one hand, people with schizophrenia may evidence behavioural excesses in the form of auditory, visual, tactile and gustatory hallucinations, delusions and bizarre behaviours. On the other hand, they may also present with blunted affect, uncommunicativeness, apathy and a general disinterest in themselves or the environment. Behavioural excesses (e.g., delusions) in people with schizophrenia are referred to as positive symptoms, whereas the symptoms of behavioural inhibition (e.g., lack of affect) are called negative symptoms (Byck, 1986; Julien, 1996; Liddle, 2000). Anti-psychotic medications are intended to reduce positive and negative symptoms.

The experience of schizophrenia is associated with the proliferation of dopamine receptors in the mesolimbic areas of the brain (i.e. nucleus accumbens, amygdale and hippocampus), the hypothalamic pituitary and the frontal lobe (Julien, 1996). As previously noted, the mesolimbic system is involved with the organisation and retention of memory, the hypothalamic areas, with the regulation of emotions, and the frontal lobe is central to integration. The evidence that a dysregulation of dopamine receptors is related to the experience of schizophrenia comes from post-mortem examinations of people with schizophrenia, which show that they have an elevated presence of dopamine receptors in the brain (Julien, 1996; Taylor & Creese, 2000). Further to that, symptoms of schizophrenia abate with treatment with medications that block a sub-class of dopamine receptors that in proliferation is associated with the experience of schizophrenia. The experience of schizophrenia has also been associated with elevated densities of serotonin receptors in the brain (Julien, 1996; Seeman et al., 1997). An abnormally high prevalence of serotonin receptors is thought to inhibit the release of dopamine. The lack of adequate supplies of dopamine to the brain neurons that require it may cause an adaptive response such as an increase in the number of dopamine receptors to utilise the small quantities of dopamine that may be available.

Drugs used to treat schizophrenia achieve their effect by blocking a sub-class of dopamine receptors. That is particularly true of a class of anti-psychotic medications called phenothiazines (e.g., fluphenazine, trifluoperazine, chlororpromazine and thioridazine) (Byck, 1986; Lane & Reed, 1992; Turley, 1999). Phenothiazines also block other acetylcholine receptors such as those for norepinephrine, histamine and to a lesser extent, serotonin receptors. Evidence for the dual involvement of both serotonin and dopamine receptor proliferation in schizophrenia comes from the fact that risperidone, which blocks both dopamine and serotonin receptors, is more effective in ameliorating both positive and negative symptoms as compared to drugs that block dopamine and norepinephrine receptors (e.g., phenothiazines) or dopamine receptors only (e.g., haloperidol) (Julien, 1996; Marder & Meibach, 1994).

The majority of anti-psychotic medications are more effective with positive symptoms rather than negative symptoms (Lane & Reed, 1992; Lido, 2000;

38.3 RESEARCH INTO SCHIZOPHRENIA

Goal
To compare the efficacy and safety of risperidone and haloperidol in treating schizophrenia.

Method
Thirty-five people (17 males; 18 females) with schizophrenia participated in the study, and over a period of 8 weeks. Participants were randomly assigned to either drug condition. Neither the participants nor the clinicians who administered the medication knew about the goals of the study nor that the participants were receiving different medications.

Results
Treatment effect was similar for risperidone and haloperidol. Risperidone had fewer side effects as compared to haloperidol.

Conclusion
Risperidone is the choice medication over haloperidol in treating people with schizophrenia (Min et al., 1993).

Maxmen & Ward, 1995; Turley, 1999). As previously noted, risperidone is unique in that it is effective in the reduction of both positive and negative symptoms. Phenothiazines have the advantage that they are non-lethal if taken in overdose. They also do not lead to dependency, even with lifetime use. About 30 per cent of people with schizophrenia do not respond to phenothiazines and may have to be treated with risperidone or clozapine (Julien, 1996). Clozapine carries a risk for reduction of white blood cells and resultant susceptibility to infections. People on clozapine need close monitoring of white blood cells count, weekly for the first four to five months, and monthly thereafter (depending on evidence that the white blood cell count is within normal limits). They also should not take another white blood cell depleting drug such as carbamazepine or tegretol.

Anti-psychotic medications carry significant risk for akathisia, dystonia and neuroleptic-induced Parkinsonism (Maxmen & Ward, 1995; See, 2000; Turley, 1999). Akathisia refers to subjective feelings of anxiety, restlessness and repetitive, purposeless actions (e.g., pacing and rocking). Dystonia refers to involuntary muscle spasms and bizarre posturing of the limbs, trunk, face and tongue. Neuroleptic-induced Parkinsonism is evidenced by the experience of tremors of the limbs while at rest, with rigidity, slowness of movement and a lack of spontaneity. Akathisia, dystonia and neuroleptic-induced Parkinsonism are collectively referred to as extra-pyramidal effects. The use of anti-psychotic medications is also associated with the experience of tardive dyskinesia or involuntary twitching movement of the face, tongue, limbs and trunk. Additional symptoms of tardive dsykinesia include sucking or smacking of lips, darting, pushing or twisting of the tongue and lateral movements of the jaws. Low potency phenothiazines (e.g., chlorpromazine and thioridazine) have a lower side effect profile than high potency phenothiazines (e.g., fluphenazine, trifluoperazine and periphenazine) (Julien, 1996; Turley, 1999). Haloperidol, which is a non-phenothiazine medication has a relatively lower side effect profile than the phenothiazines (Julien, 1996; Lido, 2000). Clozapine and risperidone have the least extra-pyramidal and dystonic side effects of the currently available anti-psychotic drugs (Lane & Reed, 1992; Maxmen & Ward, 1995; Taylor & Creese, 2000). However, clozapine is associated with increased salivation, dizziness and weight gain (Taylor & Creese, 2000). The specific role of neurotransmitters in the experience of side effects is incompletely understood, although there is some speculation that the side effects may be from drugs binding at specific receptor sub-types (See, 2000).

Drug dependence and tolerance

Drug dependence (compulsive use of a drug for physical and psychological reinforcement) and tolerance (the need to consume increasing amounts of a drug) are associated with substance abuse or addiction, and are discussed in detail in Chapter 33. For the purposes of this chapter, the neural transmission processes involved in drug dependence and tolerance are briefly discussed. Drug dependence is when a person must maintain a certain level of drug in his or her blood stream in order to function effectively (Chan et al., 1997; Ebadi, 1997; Thompson & Johanson, 1981). Cessation of the drug or lowering of its presence in circulation results in withdrawal symptoms (or abstinence syndrome), and a compulsive need to find and use the drug to restore a drug-induced sense of well-being. Drug dependence seems to be driven by a bio-psychological need to maintain some equilibrium or homeostasis in the drug level present in the person's blood circulation at any one moment since re-taking the drug treats the withdrawal symptoms or restores a sense of well-being. Cross-dependence is a type of drug dependence, which is evidenced by the relief of withdrawal symptoms from use of a different drug from that on which dependence was originally acquired.

Two processes have been linked to the development of drug tolerance: metabolic tolerance and pharmarcodynamic tolerance (Julien, 1996; Valenzuela, 1997). Metabolic tolerance arises from actions of the liver in breaking down psychoactive drugs into usable derivatives or waste matter products for eventual expurgation from the body. It follows that psychoactive drugs typically increase the actions of enzymes of the liver cells that are responsible for metabolising psychoactive drugs. These enzymatic actions are non-specific to drug and are potentiated with repeated use of psychoactive substances. Thus, repeated exposure to psychoactive drugs accelerate the rate at which psychoactive drugs are decomposed by the liver, leading to the need for higher dosages of a drug to achieve the same psychopharmacological effects as before. Pharmacodynamic tolerance, by contrast, derives from cellular adaptation that occurs with repeated or compulsive use of a psychoactive agent. In this case, tolerance develops from the fact that the number of receptors for a particular psychoactive drug increases so that synaptic drug processing is rapid or has a washout effect. Pharmacodynamic tolerance is also possible due to the fact that receptor sensitivity to a drug may be reduced by overexposure. In both cases, greater dosages of the drug will be required to achieve the desired effect. The fact that people who abuse alcohol develop tolerance for it is due to both metabolic and cellular adaptation tolerance. Cross-tolerance is when a person has a lessened response to a drug because of previous exposure to another.

Drug monitoring and side effects

Some psychoactive drugs require frequent medical monitoring of the presence of the drug in the person's blood or plasma (Brody *et al.*, 1998; Evans *et al.*, 1992; Turkey, 1999). Drawing a sample of blood from an individual and carrying out the appropriate laboratory tests that will establish the blood drug presence is essential. There are at least three reasons for the monitoring. One reason may be to determine whether the person is taking the drug and at the prescribed dosage. If the blood drug concentration is lower than expected, and for a drug with known absorption properties, that would suggest that the person was not following prescription. Alternative ways of administering the drug may need to be considered (e.g., through injection rather than orally). Another reason for plasma drug monitoring is to minimise the chances of drug plasma levels reaching toxicity. Toxic levels of psychoactive drugs are associated with dangerous side effects, and should be avoided. A third reason for drug monitoring is to determine the correct dosage for an individual by matching drug blood presence with the impact on the target symptoms. For some psychoactive drugs there is considerable variability in the response of individuals and a need may arise to determine what is the correct dosage level for a particular individual. With drugs that deplete white blood cell count (e.g., carbamazepine and clozapine), drug monitoring is essential to prevent mortality from use of the drugs.

The total amount of a drug in an individual's blood is often directly proportional to the main effect (desired effect) or side effects (unwanted effects) associated with the drug (Brody *et al.*, 1998; Ebadi, 1997; Julien, 1996). A reason for the involvement of many organs in the side-effect profile of psychoactive drugs is due to the fact that the bulk of the drug circulates outside the brain, and does not contribute to the main effect. Instead, the drug interacts with many other organs, and in a manner that may modulate their functioning. It is common practice to consider side effects by examining the functions of the body system that is impacted (e.g., respiratory, gastrointestinal, cardiovascular, and so on). The distinction between main and side effect may depend on the treatment goals. In other words, one person's main effect can be another person's side effect. For example, a well-known side effect of the anti-depressant, paxil, is constipation. However, constipation is a sought after main effect if treating for diarrhoea. People who abuse prescription drugs may be seeking to experience the side effects of the drugs rather than the intended effects.

Conclusion

Psychoactive drugs are substances that alter thoughts, moods and behaviour. The use of psychoactive agents to treat mental health problems is called psychopharmacology. Certain classes of drugs are useful for treating particular mental health conditions. The appropriateness of a psychoactive agent for treating a mental health condition is premised on the way it is thought to interact with neurons. Neurons transit messages across the body and in the form of electrical impulses. To achieve that purpose, they utilise biochemicals called neurotransmitters. These neurotransmitters exist in several types and are sensitive to particular receptor sites in the brain. Mental health problems are associated with abnormalities in the quality of neurotransmitter activity. Psychoactive agents are used to regularise dysfunctional neurotransmission, and thereby restore a level of mental health. They do so by either blocking of enhancing the neurotransmitter activity.

Classification of psychoactive drugs is possible by both their chemical structure as well as by their behavioural effects. Most classifications systems use behavioural effects as the primary criterion because drugs that differ in chemical structure may be similar in their behavioural effects. Often, it is the behavioural effects that are of interest to mental health professionals. Four major classes of psychoactive drugs are discussed in this chapter with regard to uses and effects: central nervous system depressants, mood stabilisers (anti-depressants), psychostimulants and anti-psychotics.

The use of psychoactive agents to manage mental health is not without cost. For instance, psychoactive agents have intended effects (main or treatment effects) and also unintended effects (side effects). Sometimes, the side effects can outweigh the advantages of taking the psychoactive agent. Close monitoring of the blood composition of an individual taking psychoactive agents that put him or her at risk is often necessary. Use of psychopharmacological agents may lead to drug dependency and/or tolerance, which would lower the quality of health care for the individuals concerned.

REFERENCES

Antonovsky, A. (1993). The implications of salutogenesis: An outsiders's view. In A.P. Turnbull & J.M. Patterson (Eds.). *Cognitive Coping, Families and Disability*. Baltimore, MD: Paul H. Brookes, pp. 111-22.

Ariano, M.A. (Eds.). (1998). *Receptor Localization: Laboratory methods and procedures*. New York: Wiley-Liss.

Brody, T.M., Larner, J. & Minneman, K.P. (Eds.). (1998). *Human pharmacology: Molecular to clinical*. St Louis: Mosby.

Byck, R. (1986). *Treating Mental Illness*. New York: Chelsea House.

Chan, F., Reid, C., Kaskel, L.M., Roldan, G., Rahimi, M. & Mpofu, E. (1997). Vocational assessment and evaluation of people with disabilities. *Physical Medicine & Rehabilitation Clinics of North America*, 8:311-26.

Cohen, S. (1988). *The Chemical Brain: The neurochemistry of addictive disorders*. Irvine, CA: CareInstitute.

Ebadi, M.S. (1997). *Core Concepts in Pharmacology*. Philadelphia, PA: Little Brown.

Eckler, J.A.L. & Fair, J.M.S. (1996). *Pharmacology Essentials*. Philadelphia, PA: Saunders.

Evans, W.E., Schentag, J.J., Jusko, W.J. & Relling, M.V. (Eds.). (1992). *Applied Pharmacokinetics: Principles of therapeutic drug monitoring*. Vancouver, WA: Applied Therapeutics.

Hucho, F. (Ed.). (1993). *Neurotransmitter Receptors*. New York: Elsevier.

Janicak, P.G., Davis, J.M., Preskorn, S.H. & Ayd, F.J. (1997). *Principles and Practice of Psychopharmacotherapy*. Baltimore, MD: Williams and Wilkins.

Julien, R.M. (1996). *A Primer of Drug Action: A concise, nontechnical guide to the actions, uses, and side effects of psychoactive drugs*. New York: W.H.: Freeman.

Kalant, H. & Roschlau, W.H.E. (Eds.). (1998). *Principles of Medical Pharmacology*. New York: Oxford University Press.

Katzung, B.G. (Ed.). (2001). *Basic and Clinical Pharmacology*. New York: Mange Medical Books.

Lane, K. & Reed, L. (Eds.). (1992). *Medications: A guide for health professionals*. Philadelphia, PA: F.A. Davis.

Levine, R.R., Walsh, C.T. & Schwarts-Bloom, R.D. (2000). *Pharmacology: Drug actions and reactions*. New York: Parthenon.

Liddle, P.F. (2000). Schizophrenic syndromes. In M.S. Lido (Ed.). *Neurotransmitter Receptors in Actions of Antipsychotic Medications*. Boca Raton, FL: CRC Press, pp. 1-15.

Lido, M.S. (2000). General overview of contemporary antipsychotic medications. In M.S. Lido (Ed.). *Neurotransmitter Receptors in Actions of Antipsychotic Medications*. Boca Raton, FL: CRC Press, pp. 17-29.

MacDermott, B.L. & Deglin, J.H. (1994). *Understanding Basic Pharmacology: Practical approaches for effective application*. Philadelphia, PA: F.A. Davis.

Marder, S.R. & Meibach, R.C. (1994). Risperidone in the treatment of schizophrenia. *American Journal of Psychiatry*, 151:825.

McCormick, D.A. (1998). Membrane properties and neurotransmitter actions. In G.M. Shepherd (Ed.). *The Synaptic Organization of the Brain*. London, Oxford University Press, pp. 37-75.

Maxmen, J.S. & Ward, N.G. (1995). *Psychotropic Drugs: Fast facts*. New York: W.W. Norton & Company.

Min, S.K., Rhee, C.S. & Kang, D.Y. (1993). Risperidone versus haloperidol in the treatment of chronic schizophrenic patients: A pararllel group double-blind comparative trial. *Yonsei Medical Journal*, 34:179-90.

Mpofu, E. (2002). Psychopharmacology in the treatment of conduct disorder in children and adolescents: Rationale, prospects, and ethics. *South African Journal of Psychology*, 32:9-21.

Mpofu, E. & Conyers, L.M. (2003). The neurochemical basis of the comorbidity of conduct disorder and other disorders of childhood and adolescence. *Counselling Psychology Quarterly*, 16:37-41.

Moller, A.R. (2003). Sensory Systems: Anatomy and physiology. Amsterdam, Boston: Academic Press.

Moss, S.J. & Henley, J. (2002). *Receptor and Ion-channel Trafficking: Cell biology of ligand-gated and voltage sensitive ion channels (molecular and cellular neurobiology)*. Oxford, NY: Oxford University Press.

Murphy, D., Andrews, A.M., Wichems, C.H., Li, Q., Tohda, M. & Greenberg, B. (1998). Brain serotonin neurotransmission: An overview and update with an emphasis on serotonin sub-system heterogeneity, multiple receptors, interactions with other neurotransmitter systems and consequent implications for understanding the actions of serotonergic drugs. *Journal of Clinical Psychiatry*, 59:4-12.

Oslon, J.M. (2001). *Clinical Pharmacology Made Ridiculously Simple*. Miami, FL: MedMaster.

Powis, D.A. & Bunn, S.J. (Eds.). (1995). *Neurotransmitter Release and its Modulation: Biochemical mechanisms, physiological function and clinical relevance*. New York, NY: Cambridge University Press.

Racagni, G. & Nicoletta, B. (1999). Physiology to functionality: The brain and neurotransmitter activity. *International Clinical Psychopharmacology*, 14:S3-7.

See, R. (2000). The role of neurotransmitter receptors in the adversive effects of antipsychotic drugs. In M.S. Lido (Ed.). *Neurotransmitter Receptors in Actions of Antipsychotic Medications*. Boca Raton, FL: CRC Press, pp. 221-42.

Seeman, P., Tallerico, T., Corbett, R., van Tol, H.H. & Kamboj, R.K. (1997). Role of dopamine D2 D4 and serotonin (2A) receptors in antipsychotic and anticataleptic action. *Journal of Psychopharmacology*, 11:15.

Taylor, L.A. & Creese, I. (2000). Regulation of neurotransmitter receptors by antipsychotic drugs. In M.S. Lido (Ed.). *Neurotransmitter Receptors in Actions of Antipsychotic Medications*. Boca Raton, FL: CRC Press, pp. 177-98.

Thompson, T. & Johanson, C.E. (Ed.). (1981). *Behavioral Pharmacology of Human Drug Dependence*. Rockville, MD: US Department of Health and Human Services, Public Health Service, Drug Abuse, and Mental Health, Administration, National Institute on Drug Abuse, Division of Research.

Turley, S.M. (1999). *Understanding Pharmacology for Health Professionals*. Upper Saddle River, NJ: Prentice Hall.

Valenzuela, C.F. (1997). Alcohol and neurotransmitter interactions. *Alcohol Health & Research World*, 21:144-8.

Webster, R.A. (Ed.). (2001). *Neurotransmitters, Drugs and Brain Function*. Chichester, NY: Wiley.

Multiple choice questions

1. Psychoactive drugs achieve their intended effect either by _____ or _____ a receptor site, enzyme or DNA molecule
   a) activating; inhibiting
   b) reuptaking; releasing
   c) substituting; providing
   d) imitating; initiating

2. The specific functions of a majority of neurotransmitters that have been identified are
   a) known
   b) unimportant
   c) unknown
   d) emerging

3. Two basic functions that are served by psychoactive drugs are ___ and _____ regulation
   a) dependency; tolerance
   b) prophylactic; dependency
   c) tolerance; side effect
   d) symptom; side effect

4. The potency of a psychoactive drug depends on its _____ compatibility with the specific receptor site
   a) chemical
   b) pre-synaptic
   c) post-synaptic
   d) physical

5. Drugs that tend to be compulsively abused are those that enhance the ___ centres of the brain
   a) reward
   b) visceral
   c) primate
   d) memory

6. Behavioural classification of psychoactive drugs is useful because drugs with a(n) ____ chemical structure may treat the same symptoms
   a) different
   b) similar
   c) equivalent
   d) identical

7. Drugs are selected for treating specific conditions with regard of their ____ and ____ profile
   a) efficacy; side effect
   b) dosage; neurotransmitter
   c) concentration; absorption
   d) reward; side effect

8. Main and side effects are properties of the
   a) chemical structure of the drug
   b) unknown effects of the drug
   c) intended effects of the drug
   d) prophylactic treatment effects

9. In general, psychoactive drugs are able to penetrate cell membranes because they are
   a) fat soluble
   b) made of fat
   c) neurotransmitter soluble
   d) intracellular agents

10. Metabolic drug tolerance increases with the sensitisation of the
    a) caudate nucleus
    b) liver
    c) basal ganglia
    d) mucous membrane

Short answer questions

1. What is a psychoactive drug? How are psychoactive drugs typically used to manage mental health problems?

2. On what criterion/criteria are psychopharmacological drugs classified? How is/are the criterion/criteria you identified better or worse than an alternative classification system? Give reasons for your answer.

3. Why is drug monitoring important to psychopharmacological treatment?

4. Define each of the following:
   a) dependence;
   b) tolerance;
   c) cross-dependence; and
   d) cross-tolerance.

5. Use the information presented in the chapter to complete the following table on psychoactive drug classification, uses and effects. Consult other sources on psychoactive drugs and add to your list. Which drugs would you recommend for specific psychiatric conditions, and why?

Psychoactive drug	Classification	Major uses	Alternative uses	Main effects	Side effects

39

Community Mental Health

Tony Naidoo, Sherine van Wyk & Ronelle Carolissen

CHAPTER OBJECTIVES

After studying this chapter you should be able to:
- conceptualise what is meant by community mental health
- critique the traditional biomedical formulations of mental health
- understand the ecological model of development and the three constituent domains of well-being
- differentiate between protective and risk factors affecting mental health
- describe the historical context for mental health provision and resources in South Africa
- describe and critique mental health provision from a primary health care approach
- provide a schema to describe community mental health interventions.

Nosipho, like many people, had imagined that psychologists worked mainly with individual patients in a consulting room. As she read about community psychology, though, it made perfect sense that psychologists should also take each person's broader environment into account when they thought about the best way to intervene. Her own experience of growing up in a township had taught her a great deal about the importance of a community.

Her neighbourhood had been a particularly supportive one where the women would often get together to talk about general issues for the community and how to improve things for everyone. Her mother had been involved in one particular group where they had helped to set up a crèche for the younger children who had had nowhere to go when their parents went to work. If psychologists could help facilitate this kind of activity within communities, they would be able to reach many more people than they would if they only counselled one person at a time.

Thinking about her community though, Nosipho was also forced to acknowledge that there had also been a great many problems that were common to people living there. While her own family had lived reasonably well on her father's salary, many of those in the surrounding houses had been unemployed and struggled sometimes to even feed their families. Often the families, who had more, like her own, would share with others. While this kind of community support was very important, it did not take away the problems that came along with unemployment. Some of the younger men who couldn't get jobs would hang around on the streets, sometimes drinking and fighting. Although other people in the community got angry with them for doing this, they also understood that the young men were frustrated and angry at not being able to find work. Nosipho could see from this kind of situation that it was just as important for psychologists to think how to change people's environments as it was to focus on changing the people themselves. An intervention that helped to reduce unemployment in her community might have done a great deal to prevent social and psychological problems from developing.

Introduction

Worldwide there is the growing realisation that the health, quality of life, progress and prosperity of individuals are dependent on the health and well-being of the communities of which they form a part. According to the World Health Organisation (2001), epidemiological studies indicate that various social stressors, such as violence, alcohol and substance abuse, poverty, suicide, stress and HIV/AIDS are indicative of problems of modern living. These social conditions seriously erode and undermine the physical and mental well-being of communities as well as individuals. For example, and as we have already seen, people living in unhygienic conditions in squatter camps where there is no sewerage system are more susceptible to contracting tuberculosis (TB).

There is growing concern about the increase in mental health problems and disorders, with estimates that globally 450 million people suffer from some form of mental illness (World Health Organisation, 2001). Adverse social factors such as poverty, unemployment, escalating HIV/AIDS incidence, crime, violence and alcohol and substance abuse affect all sections of South African society. These conditions have grave implications for the mental well-being of South African society. One in five South Africans is estimated to suffer from a diagnosable mental disorder that affects his or her social functioning. Moreover, general practitioners estimate that 25 per cent of all their patients (one in four) are ill due to psychological distress rather than biological causes. Adolescents are especially regarded as a high-risk group. Research indicates that annually at least 20 per cent of adolescents think of injuring themselves (Mental Health Information Centre, 2002). This awareness of the interaction between psychological, social and biological factors in health has brought about a shift from a predominantly biomedical model to a more inclusive and comprehensive bio-psychosocial model of health and disease.

The biomedical approach

In South Africa, health services have been strongly influenced by the traditional biomedical model that primarily focuses on the treatment of physical signs and symptoms of mental illness. This approach regards mental health as being secondary or subordinate to physical health, resulting in mental health being seen as less important, receiving low priority status and hence less attention and resource allocation. The dominance of the biomedical approach, with its partitioning of mental and physical health, has separated and fragmented the provision of health services. Consequently, many mental and behavioural disorders have been neglected, were undetected and left untreated, resulting in much misery and the waste of human potential. Cowen (2000) contends that the traditional biomedical definition of mental health and its main focus on dysfunction, biological causative factors of disease and with the remedial treatment of diagnosed illnesses, has narrowed and restricted the focus of traditional psychology. This has been reflected in psychology's limited focus on individual behaviour and the intra-psychic facets and processes of behaviour, and the assessment, diagnosis and treatment of pathology and dysfunctional behaviour. This has, in turn, led to the neglect of other equally important factors such as the individual's environment, social context, relationships and the interaction among these variables.

The bio-psychosocial approach

In contrast to the dualistic mind/body separation of the biomedical model, the bio-psychosocial approach calls for a more holistic and integrated view of well-being. The bio-psychosocial model of health acknowledges that physical and mental health cannot be fragmented. The model maintains that an individual's physical, behavioural and social contexts are interrelated and integral to mental health. Hence its broader focus is on the holistic treatment of individuals, including rehabilitation, prevention of mental illness and the promotion and enhancement of mental health (Albee, 1982; Cowen, 1994, 1996, 2000; Prilleltensky & Nelson, 2002). Developments in neuroscience, genetics and the behavioural and social sciences have advanced our understanding of mental health and disorders. Recent scientific evidence indicates that the interaction of biological and psychological and social factors (that is *genetic plus environment*) are determining factors in mental and behavioural disorders (World Health Organisation, 2001). As early as 1951, Kurt Lewin advocated that behaviour needed to be construed as a function of the interaction between the person and environment ($B = f(P \times E)$). Instead, many mental health practitioners adhere to a far more limited formula: $B = f(P)$ – that is, behaviour is the function of the person. As a result, many professional programmes continue to perpetuate the individualistic-remedial-intra-psychic approach to psychology even though the communities' needs for mental health services far exceed this limited modality (Lewis *et al.*, 2003).

39.1 PREVENTION IS A NEGLECTED FOCUS

Research indicates that most emotional or behavioural problems have their origins in negative social environments where, for example, poverty, violence, crime, abuse and social injustice abound. Various theorists have shown that early exposure to negative social contexts could drastically limit optimal social development and result in later adult pathology. Despite the knowledge gained from decades of prevention research and the positive benefits of preventive interventions, the commitment to the science and practice of prevention has been limited. The status quo has largely been maintained with traditional diagnostic systems, therapeutic approaches and training methods that perpetuate a victim-blaming stance and adhere to the biomedical model for conceptualising the consequences of social problems. For example, the sequelae of all forms of violence against women and children in South Africa, hold grave implications for the mental health of this society.

Traditional individual curative ways of rendering services to victims of violence, notwithstanding their positive benefits for patients, could be regarded as 'band-aid therapy'. The treatment is merely focused on the symptoms of the problems and does not address the root causes thereof. Such interventions would also not necessarily reduce the incidence of violence against other women and children in the broader population. Prevention science advocates addressing such problems by rendering services as well as harnessing efforts to combat the development of such psychosocial issues. Primary prevention's focus would be to address the core of the problem by confronting the entrenched cultural forces such as, patriarchy and gender inequality that perpetuate male dominance over women and children. Secondary and tertiary prevention would render services to both the victims of violence as well as rehabilitation programmes for perpetrators. Violence prevention interventions should be multi-level and across disciplines, for example, the family, school, traditional leaders, church, media, clinics, hospitals, government and places of work should all be involved. The entire population should be targeted, not merely the victims and perpetrators of violence.

Similarly, the psychological, social and economic implications of the HIV/AIDS pandemic are critical for the development of South Africa. The vulnerability of especially young women to infection and death from AIDS-related illnesses are also indicative of the broader, systemic social inequalities within South African society. Individual interventions to stem the escalating levels of the HIV/AIDS pandemic in South Africa have not met with much success as Western theoretical models of the disease have been applied. These theories emphasise individual personal processes, ignoring the complex interplay of social, economic, cultural and political factors that operate in developing societies. In order to change high-risk sexual behavioural practices and attempt to make some impact on the prevention of the spread of this pandemic, the interaction between the different systems within a society needs to be considered.

In a developing country like South Africa with its historical inequities, backlogs and limited resources, on the one hand, and the vast need for prevention and mental health services, on the other hand, the challenge is to apply resources optimally for the benefit of all. The question can be posed whether it is expedient to continue applying resources to small-scale modes of treatment or whether one should not rather be applying these limited resources more broadly for the prevention of mental health problems. This also raises issues at another level, namely, the nature and relevance of professional training in psychology and the location of mental health professionals within the broader society. Can the training of mental health professionals in a developing country essentially be geared for private practice with a focus on individual-oriented treatment paradigms? Also, can the silence about prevention science and issues of social justice continue to be ignored in the training programmes of psychology?

Few people would argue against the folk wisdom of 'prevention is better than cure' or 'an ounce of prevention is worth a pound of cure', yet psychology as a profession continues to apply its energies at remediation. Thus it makes better economic sense rather to apply resources to prevent mental health problems from developing than the costly expense, both human and material, of treating them. Prevention should not merely address the symptoms, but should confront the deep-seated structural inequalities embedded within a society that give rise to the development of mental health problems.

Defining mental health

Mental health and its more recent reformulations, wellness or well-being, have diverse meanings in different social contexts. There is no single definition that fully encapsulates the essence of these concepts. Cowen (1994) contends that 'wellness' (and, for that matter, sickness) are culturally determined constructs and, given the diversity of cultural values, seeking a uniformly acceptable definition of wellness or mental health is a complex and illusory process. He contends that wellness and pathology (sickness) should be seen as the two anchoring ends of a hypothetical continuum, where wellness is the positive end, a matter of prime concern and an ideal that should be striven for continually, not only when it breaks down (Cowen, 1996, 2000). Further, he argues that 'wellness is not the same as the absence of disease. Rather it is defined by the presence of positive marker characteristics that come about as a result of felicitous combinations of organismic, familial, community and societal elements' (Cowen, 1996:247). These positive markers are *behavioural and psychological*. Behavioural markers refer to actions such as the ability to work productively and form sound interpersonal relationships. Psychological markers include processes such as having a sense of purpose and belongingness, self-efficacy and control over our fate (Cowen, 1994:152). Likewise, Desjarlais *et al.* (1995:7) suggest that mental health is not merely 'the absence of detectable mental disease but a state of well-being in which the individual realises his or her own abilities, can work productively and fruitfully, and is able to contribute to her or his community'.

Dimensions of mental health

In 1981, the World Health Organisation emphasised the social dimensions of mental health and the importance of social environments when it stated that:

Mental health is the capacity of the individual, the group and the environment to interact with one another in ways that promote subjective well-being, the optimal development and use of mental abilities (cognitive, affective and relational), the achievement of individual and collective goals consistent with justice and the attainment and preservation of conditions of fundamental equality (World Health Organisation, 2000a:11).

From this definition it is apparent that mental health:

- goes beyond the biological and the individual;
- is facilitated or undermined by a number of inter-related factors operating on different levels (e.g., a child's well-being is dependent on the family, school, peer groups and whether the parents or caregiver(s) have adequate resources);
- is complex and multidimensional for as one progresses from one life stage to the next, there are a number of systems that can impact on wellness (Cowen, 2000);
- is culturally constructed and rooted in subjective value judgements;
- has a social dimension and is influenced by non-psychological factors (e.g., having a job, housing, access to sanitation and water (Albee, 1982)); and
- is facilitated by conditions of social justice and equality (Prilleltensky & Nelson, 2002).

Thus, if an unemployed pregnant mother is malnourished or prone to substance or physical abuse, such negative stressors will impact on the viability of the growing foetus, affecting its physical and cognitive development and ultimately the mental health of both the child and mother. Thus, there are multiple systems involved in the mental well-being of an individual, some having an impact even before birth.

Interdependence of the dimensions of mental health

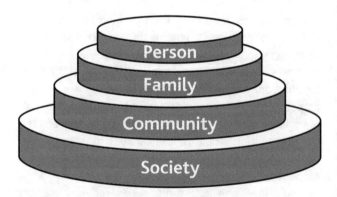

Figure 1 Social interdependence of mental health

Figure 1 illustrates the hierarchical structure and ecological interdependence of mental health or well-being. Any individual is embedded or nested in several interacting social systems such as families, neighbourhoods, communities and broader society. Each of these layers of society exerts a particular influence on the individual, some directly and others indirectly, some negatively, others positively. Hence the mental health and well-being of individuals is shaped by social conditions often beyond the ambit of their control. Any individual's personal well-being is dependent on the well-being of his or her immediate family, which in turn, is contingent on external community and societal conditions. Within this ecological model of development, Prilleltenky and Nelson (2002) describe three domains of well-being (integrating both physical and mental health): individual well-being, relational well-being and collective well-being. These domains are interdependent, with the quality of well-being in one domain likely to impact on the quality of well-being in the other domains; well-being is attained when there is a simultaneous and balanced satisfaction of personal, relational and collective needs.

Personal well-being is fostered when the necessary conditions for the protection of an individual's physical and emotional health are ensured, and where self-determination and personal growth are promoted. Interventions in this domain are aimed at empowerment, giving individuals mastery, control, a voice, and choice over aspects of their emotional and phys-

ical well-being. Counselling and psychotherapy are interventions fostering personal well-being. (An example of this domain where personal well-being is severely undermined is a woman who is being physically and psychologically abused by her partner.)

Relational well-being focuses on the promotion of respect and appreciation for human diversity and for collaboration and democratic participation. Interventions in this domain encourage participation and involvement in decision-making processes and assuming mutual responsibility. (An example here would be relations in the workplace among staff from diverse cultural backgrounds.)

Collective well-being is fostered when vital community structures that facilitate the pursuit of personal and communal goals are established. This provides a sense of community, cohesion and formal support. Equally important for collective well-being is the attainment of social justice, ensuring fair and equitable allocation of bargaining powers, obligations and resources in society. (An apt example of this domain is the activism of the Treatment Action Campaign Group (TAC) for government to provide necessary medication to prevent mother-to-child transmission of HIV.)

39.2 INDIVIDUAL WELLNESS: A CONTEXTUAL UNDERSTANDING

Myers *et al.* (2000) present an interesting integrated holistic model of wellness and prevention over a life span. Their model presents desirable characteristics of an individual necessary for optimal health. The wheel of wellness depicts different facets of an individual's life and wellness in one area, whether positive or negative, affects other areas. Healthy functioning occurs on a developmental continuum. Behaviour at one stage of life impacts on development and functioning at a later stage. Hence wellness stresses prevention and early intervention to enhance social functioning. In the pursuit of wellness an individual engages in five life tasks that are interrelated and interconnected. The first life task and the core of wellness is spirituality as reflected by our moral values and the pursuit of the meaning of life. This is followed by the life tasks of self-direction, work and leisure, friendship and love. These life tasks interact dynamically with life forces within and without the individual. Life forces without refer to the societal institutions such as the family, community, religious, education, government, media and business or industry systems. Further, both natural and human global events such as wars, poverty, unemploy-

ment, economic decline, exploitation, injustice, terrorism, earthquakes, floods and famine have an impact on the life tasks and life forces (Myers *et al.*, 2000).

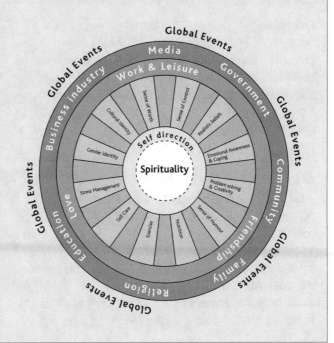

It follows, then, that well-being cannot be conceptualised in a vacuum or be reduced to individual responsibility. 'Personal needs such as health, self-determination, and opportunity for growth are tied to the satisfaction of collective needs such as adequate health care, access to safe water, fair and equitable allocation of resources and economic equality' (Prilleltenky & Nelson, 2002:12).

When health-promoting factors are available on all levels, a positive synergistic effect is likely to ensue. However, when neglect, injustice and exploitation combine with a lack of resources, social fragmentation together with ill-health, suffering and oppression will emerge.

Protective and risk factors

The mental health of communities is affected by social, economic, political and individual factors. The relationship between these factors impacts on psychological well-being, particularly on the nature, intensity and duration of mental health problems and disorders. Mental and behavioural disorders are formal categories as indicated by the DSMIV and the *International Statistical Classification of Diseases and Related Health Problems (ICD-10)*, and refer to conditions that are characterised by alterations in thinking, mood or behaviour in vulnerable individuals (World Health Organisation, 2001). Mental health problems refer to those psychological and social stresses that the majority of people experience, but which lack the intensity and duration to be classified as a mental disorder. Some individuals who are predisposed, may develop mental disorders which are triggered by psychosocial stressors, whereas the majority are able to cope, to a lesser or greater degree, due to protective factors. These protective factors could reside within the individual or in the family or community.

Protective factors refer to those processes that promote resilience within an individual and serve as buffers against the likelihood of developing mental health problems. Cowen (1994:158) highlights five necessary strands that enhance mental health and serve as protective factors against mental illness:

- having and forming healthy, stable early attachments with parents or the primary caregiver(s);
- developing age- and ability-appropriate cognitive and interpersonal competencies;
- exposure to positive settings and social environments that enhance mental health;
- creating empowering conditions that provide people with opportunities to be in control of their lives and enhance decision-making; and
- developing the ability to deal effectively with the major stressors of life.

Risk factors refer to all those characteristics or variables, biological, psychological or social, which are

---

39.3 FATAL INJURIES: THE NEED FOR PREVENTION AND INTERVENTION

Procedure
Data were collected as part of the National Injury Mortality Surveillance System (NIMSS) developed by the Medical Research Council and the Institute for Social and Health Sciences of UNISA from 32 mortuaries in six provinces in South Africa during 2001 to determine the 'who, what, when, where and how' of fatal injuries.

Results
A total of 25 361 fatal injuries were recorded comprising 80 per cent male, 20 per cent female; Africans or Blacks constituted 74 per cent, Coloureds 12 per cent, Whites 11 per cent, and Asians 3 per cent of all cases; the majority of deceased were young adults (72 per cent) between the ages of 15 to 44 years; homicide was the major cause of death, accounting for 44 per cent of all deaths; transport-related deaths accounted for 27 per cent, sui-cide for 10 per cent and other unintentional or accidental injuries for 10 per cent. Firearms accounted for 28 per cent of all cases. For children 1 to 4 years of age, burns were the major cause of death; for children 5 to 14 years, pedestrian injuries. Hanging accounted for 42 per cent and firearms for 29 per cent of suicides with 4.7 male suicides for every female suicide.

Findings
Fatal injuries, especially due to violence and transport accidents, constitute priority threats to South African citizens. The NIMSS data lends itself to the formulation of injury prevention policy and interventions at national and community levels. Interventions within a public health model can be designed to address some of the risk factors identified for potential victim groups (Matzopolous, 2002).

associated with the vulnerability of an individual to develop negative outcomes and the likelihood that these outcomes will occur (Mash & Wolfe, 2002). However, it should be noted that risk factors are not absolutes; an individual's engagement with risk processes could result in adaptive coping strategies to overcome the risks and these processes could further serve as protective mechanisms (Rutter, 1990). Biological factors refer to variables such as age, gender, organic deficits and genetics. Studies of extended multigenerational families indicate that most of the common severe mental and behavioural disorders have a strong genetic component (World Health Organisation, 2001). Individual psychological factors, such as poor or ineffective coping strategies in dealing with stressful life events, could result in certain kinds of mental and behavioural disorders such depression or anxiety. Ainsworth and Bowlby (in Cowen, 1994) have indicated the importance of secure attachment throughout infancy to adolescence for sound development and well-being. The absence of such nurturing relationships poses a threat to wellness and restricts the foundations for future development (Cowen, 1994).

Social factors are integrally linked to well-being and could lead to a wide range of social and psychological consequences. Factors such as the escalation of HIV/AIDS, urbanisation, rapid social and technological change, racism, oppression, escalating levels of crime and violence, gender violence and the lower status of women, poverty and socio-economic status could impact negatively on mental health (World Health Organisation, 2001). The World Health Organisation (2001) contends that women, given their multiple roles they play in society, are at greater risk to develop mental and behavioural disorders. Despite being an integral part of the labour force and being the prime source of income for their families, their status worldwide remains low. Research indicates that there is a strong inverse relationship between social position and well-being and people from low socio-economic status have a higher risk for common mental health disorders (Dohrenwend, 1990; Patel et al., 1999). Further, violence against women has escalated and has become a public health issue because of the devastating consequences for women's mental and physical well-being (Jewkes, 2002). Thus, the mental health and well-being of women is linked to their status in society and has a direct impact on human well-being and the prospects of future generations (World Health Organisation, 2000a).

Oppression and discrimination are further determinants that impact on mental health. In South Africa, apartheid was a form of structural oppression and state-sanctioned violence that directly impacted upon the mental well-being and identities of the majority of South Africans. Its pernicious policies, such as forced removals and the migrant labour system, resulted in the disintegration of families and the social upheaval of established communities. The forced migration of adult men and women to the cities in order to earn their livelihood deprived children of secure attachment to their parents, the loss of role models and a sense of belonging. These adverse social conditions rendered generations of Black South Africans at risk of negative mental health outcomes. In the cities, the loss of the natural social support systems of the extended family often resulted in physical and psychological isolation, poverty, homelessness, alcohol abuse and depression. Despite the political changes in South Africa since 1994, the legacy of apartheid and its impact on the mental health of individuals and communities continues. Indications hereof are the high crime rate, unemployment and alarming rates of abuse of children and women. Psychology, as a discipline and profession, can become a potent force in the reconstruction and development of community mental health in South Africa by developing and providing appropriate accessible mental health services.

Community mental health interventions

Providing mental health services in South Africa

Mental health provision in South Africa has been marked by racial segregation, fragmentation and duplication. It has been described as inadequate, inaccessible (particularly for rural communities), inappropriate, based largely on institutional custodial care and being discriminatory (Lazarus, 1988; Naidoo, 2000), reflecting broader class, race, gender and urban-rural inequalities. These historical legacies were exacerbated by the sparse distribution of mental health personnel such as psychiatrists, psychologists and social workers within the public sector. In South Africa, the ratio of psychiatrist to patient is 1:130 500 whereas the equivalent ratio in developed countries is 1:14 000. The ratio of psychologist to patient is equally limited. The recommended ratio for psychologist to patient is 1:100 000, but provinces such as Mpumalanga have one psychiatrist, two psychologists and 12 social workers to serve the mental health needs of a population of approximately three million people (Freeman & Pillay, 1997). Most mental health professionals work in private practice while those working in the public sector are concentrated in the Western Cape and Gauteng. Mpumalanga and the Northern Province are particularly compromised in terms of mental health workers (Pillay & Petersen, 1996; Pillay et al., 1997). That the majority of psychologists in South Africa are predominantly White, middle-class and in private practice serving predominantly White, middle-class patients (Swartz et al., 1986), underscores that the mental health needs of Black South Africans and disadvantaged communities have largely been neglected (Naidoo et al., 2003). The National Council for Mental Health (South African Institute of Race Relations Survey 1989/90) found that the existing mental health facilities were meeting the needs of 62 per cent of Whites, 2 per cent Indians, 28 per cent Coloureds and 8 per cent of Africans or Blacks (South African Institute of Race Relations, 1990).

Health intervention in South Africa has traditionally been predicated on the biomedical model. Hence even mental health care was predominantly hospital-based with the emphasis on curative relief of symptoms and medication as treatment. Mental health interventions furthermore targeted severe mental illness almost exclusively, resulting in interventions that were largely custodial and focused on chronic care (Freeman, 2002; Freeman & Pillay, 1997). Moreover, mental health service delivery was marginalised within the health system and subservient to the discourse of disease, pathology and treatment. Mental health personnel were trained to deal with problems experienced in developed countries, rather than on those characteristic of a developing country (Kalisky, 1998). This set of factors rendered mental health services in South Africa largely inaccessible and inappropriate to the majority of South Africans, catering mainly for the privileged minority.

Restructuring mental health provision and intervention in South Africa

The restructuring of mental health provision in post-apartheid South Africa has therefore not occurred in a vacuum, nor from a level foundation. To redress the inequities of the past, restructuring the provision of mental health services required a two-pronged approach, at legislative and policy level and in implementation. Firstly, a new health strategy needed to be drafted reconciling the neglect and lessons of the past with current needs and available resources. Secondly, new training strategies to deliver the proposed new health system were needed.

When the new policy for restructuring health services in South Africa was drafted, a broad-based approach rooted in primary health care and driven by a human rights approach was adopted by the National Department of Health in its Health Sector Strategic Framework (1999-2004) (Department of Health, 2002). The intention was to provide access to health care (for both physical and mental health) for all South Africans at community level. In line with this approach more than 495 new primary health clinics have been built since 1994 with 300 undergoing extensive upgrading. This framework has resulted in mental health, and hence the development of mental health services, being defined more broadly to include psychological health and well-being as well as mental illness.

However, Pillay et al. (1997) indicate that this has not yet resulted in any major shifts in resources, or additions to the amounts allocated for mental health services. Further, there is a concern that the added integration of mental health services into the already overburdened and under-funded primary health care system could further contribute to the lack of detection and neglect of mental health problems, and affect the quality of services rendered to communities. Also, primary health care is essentially bio-medically oriented and could perpetuate the medicalisation of social problems and hence the marginalisation of mental health (Nell, 1994).

Significantly, the watchdog of the health professions, the South African Medical and Dental Council, was rationalised and renamed the Health Professions Council of South Africa. This gave increased independence and equity for professions such as psychology, occupational therapy and physiotherapy which were formerly accorded a lower professional status in relation to medical disciplines by being labelled supplementary health professions. Several of the health professions have made adjustments to their training requirements and have instituted compulsory community service before graduates will be allowed to register with their respective professional boards. The Professional Board of Psychology, the body responsible for vetting and monitoring the ethical, training and practice standards of the psychology profession, has also intro-

South African universities have recently instituted a new four-year professional qualification in psychology called the B. Psych degree. Learners completing this degree are eligible to become a registered counsellor with the Professional Board for Psychology. This new professional category was introduced to address the need for mental health services at primary level. The integrated course equips counsellors to provide basic assessment, counselling, psycho-education and lifeskills interventions. Hence B. Psych graduates are trained to work within a community mental health framework that includes both curative and preventative services. As this degree represents an attempt to merge traditional and community psychology, it often sets up interesting dilemmas. Whereas the majority of psychologists tend to work in private practice doing mainly individual therapy, the registered counsellors will be able to be deployed in various community settings (clinics, schools, NGOs, community projects, etc.) utilising group interventions.

Registered counsellors will be challenged with actively having to market the 'new psychology' in community settings as primary health care nurses, for example, have limited conceptions of what psychology can offer. The reason for this is twofold: Psychology has traditionally been a very elitist profession and has dealt with the needs of middle-class South Africans, using predominantly Euro-American individualistic theories and models of practice. Hence the perception is that psychology is of limited value in poor communities because its traditional bias is still prevalent.

There is also an onus on the health care system to provide employment opportunities for registered counsellors to play an active role in the promotion of mental health at community level. This will broaden access to adequate mental health services that should be a right of all South Africans.

duced a new level of training requiring a four-year degree. This Bachelor of Psychology degree will equip registered counsellors with competencies to provide basic interventions at community level in eleven practice fields. These practice fields include community mental health counselling, career counselling, HIV/AIDS, trauma counselling, family counselling, school counselling, sports counselling, human resources, pastoral counselling and employee well-being.

The primary health care approach

The Health Sector Strategic Framework adopted by the Department of Health (2002) adheres to a primary health care approach. The World Health Organisation and United Nations' Children's Fund officially adopted a formal definition of primary health care in 1978 at a conference in Alma Ata, in the Soviet Union. According to the Alma Ata Declaration (World Health Organisation, 2000b), the primary health system of a country should be based on:
• accessibility and acceptability of health services;
• priority to be given to those in need;
• the presence of an integrated, functional and supportive referral system; and
• levels of community participation in the planning and implementation of health care.

The primary health care approach embraces concepts of equity, accessibility and appropriateness of services for communities in which they are rendered, focusing on the prevention and promotion of well-being for individuals and families within the community context. Interdisciplinary and intersectoral collaboration is encouraged requiring health professionals to work collaboratively with other health workers, agencies and departments outside of the health sector when appropriate. The Strategic Framework strongly motivates for the principles of primary health care to be implemented via the public health service.

Mental health structures within the public health service

In the Health Sector Strategic Framework (Department of Health, 2002) the public health service is based on a district health system that operates on a three-tier system. The primary tier consists of community-based clinics that are the primary site of health (including mental health) delivery. These primary health clinics are usually staffed by nurses. On a secondary level, the community is incorporated into a district such as the Boland, which has one district hospital. The third tier consists of a tertiary academic hospital, like Lentegeur

Psychiatric Hospital in the Western Cape. When mental health problems become too severe to be dealt with at primary care level, primary care nurses usually refer patients to subsequent tiers in the health system. A cyclical referral process is envisaged whereby individuals assisted at tertiary level, once stabilised, are discharged into their communities for ongoing maintenance and support (Department of Health, 2002).

Community mental health

Community mental health is practised largely at primary care level in communities within the public health system incorporating both curative and preventive interventions. Community mental health can be conceptualised as a multifaceted approach. In this approach intervention strategies extend beyond traditional methods focusing exclusively on the individual to include interventions such as life-skills training and advocacy which are aimed at preventing mental health problems and enhancing psychological wellness (see Figure 2). Not only are individuals targeted for intervention, but groups, organisations and even the whole community in a given geographical location are seen as necessary targets for intervention. These strategies draw on local resources and strengths to facilitate capacity building and empowerment within communities by working with those communities themselves to address needs and implement programmes identified by them. These initiatives are therefore not only geared to alleviate mental illness but also to promote mental health, to prevent mental health problems and to facilitate broader systemic change.

Caplan (1964) differentiates among primary, secondary and tertiary levels of intervention. Primary prevention ensures that people without psychiatric symptoms remain healthy. Interventions at this level are targeted at improving support for individuals either in terms of resources or coping skills and are intentionally focused on promoting well-being. An example of such an intervention would be the implementation of life-skills programmes for all learners in schools. Secondary prevention assists individuals who are vulnerable or at risk of developing mental health difficulties, to remain symptom-free. Early intervention is essential in this context. Early school programmes that concentrate on assessment and identification of behavioural and cognitive difficulties, with the intention to intervene, typically fall into this category. Tertiary prevention aims to ensure a positive quality of life for individuals who already suffer from a mental disorder or condition. Psychosocial rehabilitation of psychiatric patients is a good example of tertiary prevention. In this regard, psychiatric patients typically receive rehabilitation with regard to employment opportunities, living circumstances and personal care. While curative and preventive work has been viewed as mutually exclusive, theorists and practitioners are increasingly advocating that curative and preventive interventions take place concurrently and complement each other (Naidoo & van Wyk, 2003; Scillepi *et al.*, 2000).

A model of community intervention

Lewis *et al.* (2003:31) propose a useful model of conceptualising mental health service delivery in a community that highlights both the multiple levels of intervention and the expanded roles envisaged for

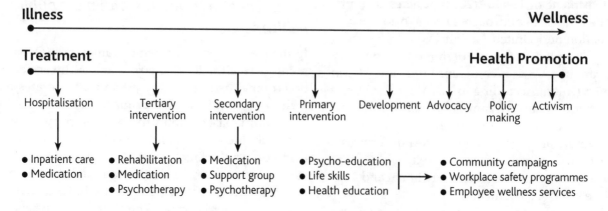

Figure 2 The mental health intervention continuum

psychologists working in communities. This model is summarised in Table 1.

	Community Services	Client services
Direct	Preventive education	Counselling (individual)
Indirect	Influencing public policy	Consultation/ Advocacy

Table 1 A model of intervention in communities

The model outlined in Table 1 differentiates between direct and indirect services and between community and patient services yielding four distinct components that represent different service modalities:

- *Direct community services*: These services provide educational experiences aimed at the community as a whole and are preventive in their intention and objective. The mental health practitioner is typically involved in preventive psycho-education initiatives such as implementing HIV life-skills programmes.
- *Direct patient services*: These services are directed at individuals who have actively sought help and have been identified as experiencing problems or who are at risk of developing future mental health problems. Examples of specific services used in this component include counselling and outreach to vulnerable individuals in the community. This component of intervention is usually implemented within traditional modes of psychological intervention.
- *Indirect community services*: These services and interventions involve efforts intentionally designed to make the social environment more responsive to community needs. In promoting these types of constructive changes, the mental health practitioner collaborates with key community role players in targeted areas to cultivate positive systemic changes, typically by influencing public policy. Initiatives to modify or change the social environment that contributes to poor mental and physical health are central to this role. The expulsion of pregnant teenagers from school is one such example. Psychologists can assist community groups to argue for legislation assisting young girls to return to school after a teenage pregnancy. Their increased levels of education may increase their employability, which in turn will contribute to their psychological wellness.

- *Indirect patient services*: Services and interventions in this component include those environmental interventions that are aimed at meeting the special needs of people presenting with mental health disorders or who may be at risk. Services are primarily aimed at creating new helping networks by providing consultation and patient advocacy assistance to people and agencies within the areas where patients live. By facilitating patients' use of their own personal power as well as resources and networks within their community, the mental health practitioner assists patients in helping themselves. A typical example of an intervention within this component is the provision of staff support groups to overburdened primary health care staff suffering from burnout. By providing this intervention, psychologists indirectly assist the nurses' patients as nursing staff (as a community resource) then are able to provide an improved quality of service to the community (Lewis *et al.*, 2003:49).

In integrating these four components into a unified complementary and interdependent framework, mental health practitioners can begin to conceptualise the types of interventions for the purpose in mind. Such a comprehensive helping framework will necessarily embrace both ameliorative (healing) and transformative (change promoting) agendas. This framework (depicted in Figure 2) should include a range of interventions spanning curative and remedial services to programmes predominant-

39.5 WORLD REPORT ON VIOLENCE AND HEALTH

This report by the World Health Organisation is the first ever global representation of the extent of violence and its impact on health. The report confirms that violence is the leading cause of death in the 15 to 44 age group worldwide. Different types of violence such as sexual violence, youth violence and collective violence, amongst others are examined. The public health approach based on the principles of prevention is forwarded as a meaningful approach to reduce violence. Furthermore, early intervention to prevent children from developing into perpetrators of violence, is encouraged. The report also actively encourages governments to develop plans of action to integrate violence prevention into social and education policy (Krug *et al.*, 2002).

ly focusing on prevention and health-promotion and social change action. It should also provide a continuum of care within which values such as empowerment, participation and social justice can be incorporated within a primary health care approach.

Conclusion

In summary, mental health is a central construct when focusing on intervention and services in psychology. The conceptualisation of mental health needs to be broadened from its traditional encapsulation within the biomedical model of health with its emphasis on illness, the curative role and its focus on the individual. The bio-psychosocial model expands mental health to include an awareness of the role environmental and social contexts play on the health and well-being of individuals, specifical-

ly vulnerable populations and on communities as a whole. Intervention goals of prevention and health promotion and identifying risk and protective factors become important objectives in fostering community mental health. Since 1994, South Africa has adopted a predominantly primary health care system creating new challenges to the health professions for the delivery of health services. A comprehensive model for complementary and interdependent community health interventions proposed by Lewis *et al.* (2003) provides a useful model for conceptualising and planning community mental health initiatives that include direct and indirect services to both patients and communities. Seen within the ambit of the country's 1996 constitution, the provision of optimum mental health needs is considered to be the right of all individuals and communities in South Africa. How to foster and achieve this basic right is the challenge to government, mental health professionals, community role players and the private sector to form collaborative partnerships.

REFERENCES

Albee, G.W. (1982). Preventing psychopathology and promoting human potential. *American Psychologist*, 37(9):1043-50.

Caplan, G. (1964). *Principles of Preventive Psychiatry*. New York: Basic Books.

Cowen, E. (1994). The enhancement of psychological wellness: Challenges and opportunities. *American Journal of Community Psychology*, 22(2):149-79.

Cowen, E. (1996). The ontogenesis of primary prevention: Lengthy strides and stubbed toes. *American Journal of Community Psychology*, 24(2):235-49.

Cowen, E. (2000). Community psychology and routes to psychological wellness. In J. Rappaport & E. Seidman (Eds.). *Handbook of Community Psychology*. New York: Kluwer Academic/Plenum Publishers, pp. 79-99.

Department of Health. (2002). *Health Sector Strategic Framework* 1999-2004, www.196.36.153.56/doh/doc/index.html (accessed 25 February 2002).

Desjarlais, R., Eisenberg, L., Good, B. & Kleinman, A. (1995). *World Mental Health: Problems and priorities in low-income countries*. New York: Oxford University Press.

Dohrenwend, B.P. (1990). Socioeconomic status (SES) and psychiatric disorders. *Social psychiatry & psychiatric epidemiology*, 25:41-7.

Freeman, M. (2002). National mental health structures and priorities in South Africa. Unpublished presentation to 3rd year psychology students. Stellenbosch University.

Freeman, M., & Pillay, Y. (1997).Mental health policy: Plans and funding. In Y. Pillay, D. Foster & M. Freeman (Eds.). *Mental Health Policy Issues for South Africa*. Pinelands, Cape Town: MASA Multimedia, pp32-54.

Jewkes, R. (2002). Intimate partner violence: Causes and prevention. *Lancet*, 359:1423-9.

Kalisky, S. (1998). The Southern African context. In S. Baumann (Ed.). *Psychiatry and Primary Health Care*. Landsdowne: Juta, pp. 29-35.

Krug, E.G., Dahlberg, L.L., Mercy, J.A., Zwi, A.B. & Lozano, R. (Eds.).

(2002). *World Report on Violence and Health*. World Health Organisation: Geneva.

Lazarus, S. (1988). *The Role of the Psychologist in South African Society: In search of an appropriate community psychology*. Unpublished doctoral dissertation, University of Cape Town, Cape Town.

Lewis, J.A., Lewis, M.D., Daniels, J.A. & D'Andrea, M.J. (2003). *Community Counselling: Empowerment strategies for a diverse society* (3rd edition). New York: Brooks/Cole Thompson Learning.

Mash, E. & Wolfe, D. (2002). *Abnormal Child Psychology* (2nd edition). Belmont, CA: Wadsworth.

Matzopolous, R. (Ed.). (2002). *Third Annual Report of the National Injury Mortality Surveillance System. A profile of fatal injuries in South Africa*. Crime, Violence and Injury Lead Programme, Medical Research Council and the Institute for Social and Health Sciences, Unisa, Pretoria.

Mental Health Information Centre. (2002). *The mental health information centre*, www.mentalhealthsa.co.za (accessed 21 February 2002).

Myers, J.E., Sweeney, T.J. & Witmer, J.M. (2000). The wheel of wellness counseling for wellness: A holistic model for treatment planning. *Journal of Counseling & Development*, 78:251-66.

Naidoo, A.V. (2000). *Community Psychology: Constructing community, reconstructing psychology in South Africa*. Published inaugural lecture. University of Stellenbosch.

Naidoo, A.V., Shabalala, N. & Bawa, U. (2003). Community psychology. In L. Nicholas (Ed.). *Introduction to Psychology*. Lansdowne: Juta, pp. 423-62.

Naidoo. A. V. & van Wyk, S. (2003). Intervening in communities at multiple levels: Combining curative and preventive interventions. *Journal of Intervention & Prevention in Community*, 25(1):65-80.

Nell, V. (1994). Critical psychology and the problem of mental health. *Psychology in Society*, 19:31-4.

Patel, V., Araya, R., de Lima, M., Ludermir, A. & Todd, C. (1999). Women, poverty and common mental disorders in four restructuring societies. *Social Science & Medicine*, 49:1461-71.

Pillay, Y. & Petersen, I. (1996). Current practice patterns of clinical and counseling psychologists and their attitudes to transforming mental health policies. *South African Journal of Psychology*, 26(2):76-80.

Pillay, Y., Freeman, M. & Foster, D. (1997). Post script: An update. In D. Foster, M. Freeman & Y. Pillay (Eds.). *Mental Health Policy Issues for South Africa*. Pinelands, Cape Town: MASA Multimedia, pp. 330-42.

Prilleltensky, I. & Nelson, G. (2002). *Doing Psychology Critically: Making a difference in diverse settings*. Palgrave/Macmillan: New York.

Rutter, M. (1990). Psychosocial resilience and protective mechanisms. In J. Rolf, A. Master, D. Cicchetti, K.H. Nuechterlein & S. Weintraub (Eds.). *Risk and Protective Factors in the Development of Psychopathology*. Cambridge: Cambridge University Press, pp. 181-214.

Scileppi, J.A., Teed, E.L. & Torres, R.D. (2000). *Community Psychology: A common sense approach to mental health*. New Jersey: Prentice-Hall.

South African Institute of Race Relations. (1990). *Race relations Survey 1989/90*. Johannesburg: South African Institute of Race Relations.

Swartz, S., Dowdall, T. & Swartz, L. (1986). Clinical psychology and the 1985 crisis in Cape Town. *Psychology in Society*, 5:131-8.

World Health Organisation. (2000a). *Women's Mental Health: An evidence-based review*. Geneva, Switzerland: World Health Organisation.

World Health Organisation. (2000b). *Alma Ata Declaration*, www.who.int/hpr/archive/docs/almaata.html (accessed 1 February 2002).

World Health Organisation. (2001). *The World Health Report 2001. Mental health: New understanding, new hope*, www.who.int/whr/2001 (accessed 2 February 2002).

Multiple choice questions

1. Which of the following statements describe(s) the biomedical model?
   a) focuses on biological causation
   b) stresses remedial treatment
   c) emphasises diagnoses
   d) all of the above
2. The separation of mind and body is characteristic of
   a) the holistic view of well-being
   b) the bio-psychosocial model
   c) community mental health
   d) the biomedical model
3. Which of the following statements is false?
   a) the ability to form sound relationships is a positive behavioural marker
   b) having a sense of self-confidence is an example of a positive psychological marker
   c) risk factors cannot serve as protective mechanisms for the individual.
   d) protective factors serve to buffer the individual against mental illness
4. Which one of the following is an example of tertiary intervention?
   a) a life-skill programme to all grade 7 learners
   b) providing free condoms in public toilets
   c) helping discharged psychiatric patients adjust to living in the community
   d) referring learners with attention problems for assessment
5. Using the Lewis, Lewis, Daniels, and D'Andrea Model, match the correct example
   a) individual counselling is an example of an indirect client service
   b) advocacy is an example of a direct client service
   c) running an AIDS awareness programme is an example of a direct community service
   d) influencing public policy is an example of indirect client service
6. Which of the following is not emphasised in the Alma Ata Declaration?
   a) presence of an integrated, functional and supportive referral system
   b) priority to be given to tertiary intervention
   c) accessibility of health services
   d) community participation in planning and implementation of health care

7. In Lewis et al.'s (2003) intervention model direct community service is most similar in focus to Caplan's
   a) primary prevention
   b) secondary prevention
   c) tertiary intervention
   d) b and c
8. Which of the following statements contradicts Prilleltensky and Nelson's (2002) notions of wellness?
   a) wellness is attained only when there is the satisfaction of personal needs
   b) relational wellness is dependent on how social needs are met
   c) collective wellness is fostered when vital community resources are established
   d) personal wellness is fostered when self-determination and personal growth are promoted
9. _____ refer to those processes and characteristics that serve as buffers against mental illness
   a) risk factors
   b) protective factors
   c) psychosocial stressors
   d) environmental factors
10. Lewin's formula (B=f(PXE)) emphasises
    a) the biomedical model
    b) the internal and external determinants of mental health
    c) the Cartesian split
    d) the need for assessment using the ICD-10

Short answer questions

1. Discuss mental health within an ecological framework with special reference to those factors that promote and impact negatively on mental health. Provide good examples to elaborate your answer.
2. How would you as a psychology student use the wellness wheel of prevention to promote the benefits of mental health in your community?
3. Discuss the nature of protective and risk factors in your community that could impede or promote mental health. Provide good examples in your response.
4. Discuss a model of community mental health intervention in South Africa with illustrative examples.
5. Critically discuss the Primary Health Care approach as a means of providing mental health services to all South Africans.

Glossary

A

ABC model of prevention *Abstinence* or not engaging in sex encourages delaying sexual debut amongst the youth. *Being faithful* involves being mutually faithful to one partner. *Condomise* involves the correct use of condoms at all times.

Academic sport psychologist A sport psychologist who is primarily involved in education and theoretical research.

Accessibility Refers to the fact that service users need to be able to have access to all services, for example, financially.

Activation One general dimension of emotions that describes the level of arousal typically accompanying various emotional states.

Activism The conscious process through which individuals and/or groups engage in protest, advocacy, lobbying and campaigning directed towards the resolution of specific social issues.

Acute stress Short-term stress.

Acute stress disorder A psychological disorder resulting from exposure to a catastrophic stressor. It is similar to post-traumatic stress disorder, but of shorter duration and characterised by dissociation.

Adaptive behaviour Particular skills or abilities needed to survive in a specific environment.

Adolescence In traditional developmental psychology, adolescence refers to that stage of human development that follows middle childhood, and that serves as the transition from childhood to adulthood. It is generally viewed as beginning with the onset of the biological changes of puberty and ending with the cultural identity of adulthood. While adolescence may not necessarily be universally traumatic, as described by much of the literature in most cultures, the beginning of biological puberty and the social and cultural expectations and pressures associated with this tend to signify an important transition for the child.

Adolescent 'egocentricism' Refers to the adolescent's preoccupation with the self and related self-consciousness, which is viewed as a consequence of cognitive changes that take place in adolescent, in particular, the shift to formal operational thinking.

Adrenalin Also known as epinephrine (American term) is a hormone secreted in the adrenal gland that raises blood pressure and increases the heart rate and acts as a neurotransmitter when the body is subjected to stress or danger.

African paths This incorporates a wide range of things, including the ways Africans perceive or see the world, raise children, survive and lead their lives.

Aggression Refers to behaviour, including speech, posture, facial expression and actions, that is intended to create fear, withdrawal or flight in others.

Agrarian economies Organisation of labour, production and human needs based on agricultural activities.

AIDS Refers to, and is the acronym for, Acquired Immune Deficiency Syndrome. Note that AIDS is an acquired disease (not inherited) and is caused by a virus called the HIV or *Human Immuno-deficiency Virus*, which is contracted from outside the body. The term 'immunity' refers to the body's natural ability to defend itself against infections and disease. Deficiency is said to occur when the body's defence system (immune system) has become so weakened that it is unable to defend itself against infections (even those that occur very commonly). 'Syndrome' is a medical term that refers to a collection of specific signs and symptoms that typically co-occur, and that are associated with particular illnesses or diseases.

Akathesia Subjective feelings of anxiety, restlessness, and repetitive, purposeless actions.

Algorithm A step-by-step process that will always ensure that the goal for the task is achieved.

Alienation Refers to a sense of being excluded from and therefore not owing allegiance to social rules and structures.

Alma Ata Declaration An agreement reached at the World Health Organisation conference in 1978 that officially gave birth to the concept of primary health care. The declaration sets out the vision for primary health care.

Alzheimer's disease A degenerative brain disorder that results in a decline in intelligence, awareness and the ability to control bodily functions.

Amnion A group of cells in the trophoblast that becomes the amniotic sack.

Amniotic fluid The fluid that fills the amnion and surrounds the developing embryo and foetus.

Anaemia A condition in which the number of red blood cells is below normal, usually resulting in tiredness.

Androgynous Refers to a personality or social orientation that combines positive characteristics that are typically viewed 'feminine' with positive characteristics that are generally viewed as 'masculine'.

Androgyny The integration of masculinity and femininity within an individual.

Anima aspects of the male psyche.

Animism Attributing human-like qualities to inanimate objects.

Animus Male aspects of the female psyche.

Anti-Islamism An ideology that is premised on a willingness and a commitment to act with hostility and prejudice against Muslims and/or Islam to accomplish other political goals.

Anti-retroviral treatment (ART) Refers to medication that slows that rate at which the HIV multiplies in the body.

Anti-Semitism An ideology that is premised on a willingness and a commitment to act with hostility and prejudice against Jews and/or Judaism to accomplish other political goals.

Anxiety A specific form of arousal characterised by worry, nervousness and physiological activation.

Apgar Scale A commonly used scale to assess the basic physical condition of a neonate.

Applied sport psychologist A sport psychologist who is primarily involved in practice and applied research.

Approaches to learning Ways in which people acquire knowledge, attitudes, perceptions and skills.

Appropriate services Refers to the fact that services must be able to deal with issues presented by service users. Services must not be imposed on groups for whom they were not originally designed.

Archetypes Images of universal experiences contained in the collective unconscious.

Arousal A broad continuum of physiological and psychological activation or energy.

Associative learning phase The second phase of learning characterised by accurate, consistent skill performance and increased environmental and strategic awareness.

Asymmetrical distributions Statistical distributions in which there is either a cluster of extremely high scores (negatively skewed distribution) or a cluster of extremely low scores (positively skewed distribution).

Autobiographical memory Memories of distinctly personal information, such as our name, place and date of birth.

Autonomous learning phase The third phase of learning, characterised by skill mastery and automaticity (performing a skill 'on auto-pilot').

B

Barchart A graph used for discrete variables in which the frequencies of each category are displayed as a vertical bar.

Behaviour modification A form of therapy that applies the principles of reinforcement to bring about desired behavioural changes.

Behavioural neurologists Neurologists who specialise in neuropsychology.

Bimodal distribution Refers to a distribution with two peaks.

Biomedical paradigm A framework that views health from a biological perspective and seeks to understand illness or disease from a pathology orientation. It does not include concepts of wellness in defining health.

Bio-psychosocial model This model of health acknowledges that health is influenced by biological, psychological and social determinants.

Bivariate stem-and-leaf display A stem-and-leaf display of two sets of scores.

Blastocyst A hollow sphere of specialised and organised cells.

Blocked practice Practising different skills in an exhaustive, sequential manner.

Body Mass Index (BMI) One of the anthropometric measures of body mass; it has the highest correlation with skinfold thickness or body density and is calculated by dividing weight by height^2 (kg/m^2).

C

Capitalism A system and ideology, now globally dominant, in terms of which most aspects of social life are governed by the principle of privately owned property.

Career The sequence of jobs, occupations, or positions that a person holds throughout his or her working life.

Castration complex Focuses on a male child's fantasy of his penis being cut off, which induces castration anxiety.

Cathexis The emotional charge associated with an object or the process of investing psychic energy in an instinctual object.

Centration The tendency of children during the preoperational stage to focus on only one aspect or dimension of an object or situation.

Cephalocaudal developmental trend The sequence of growth that proceeds from the head and progresses downwards.

Cerebral anoxia Lack of oxygen to the brain.

Cerebral malaria Refers to malaria that induces changes in mental status and coma.

Child labour Work done by a child that stunts or disrupts a child's normal development and that is not consistent with

his or her culture's normal expectations for that age. A derogatory view of the socialization of children in many African societies through their participation in the work and activities of the family and community.

Child work The activities or duties children perform as an integral component of education in African family traditions.

Chorion A groups of cells that becomes the foetal part of the placenta.

Chronic care Refers to care where persistent and enduring pathology has been diagnosed, for example, the care of patients suffering from schizophrenia.

Chronic stress Long-term stress

Cilia Hair-like projections along the fallopian tubes.

Class consciousness An awareness among poor people that they form an economic group whose interests are fundamentally different from those of rich people.

Clinical sport psychologist A sport psychologist who specialises in the mental health of athletes.

Cognition Mental processes or activities, such as thinking and reasoning.

Cognitive anxiety The mental and emotional components of anxiety (e.g., worry and nervousness).

Cognitive development Refers to the age-related changes that occur in mental activities such as attending, perceiving, learning, thinking and remembering.

Cognitive distortion This occurs when a person commits errors in reasoning and makes faulty assumptions of him- or herself and the world.

Cognitive learning phase The first phase of learning characterised by an intellectual understanding of the skill to be performed.

Cognitive therapy An action-oriented therapy focusing on identifying and changing faulty thinking and beliefs.

Co-joined twins Also known as Siamese twins. Two children that develop from a single fertilised egg cell that has failed to split completely and remains joined in some way.

Cohabitation A term frequently used to refer to two unmarried people living together as intimate partners.

Collective unconscious A part of the unconscious containing memories, instincts and experiences that are shared by all people.

Collective well-being When the well-being of both the individual and the group (community) is promoted through democratic processes.

Collectivist cultures Refers to cultures in which individuals are encouraged to think of themselves as linked to and interdependent on others.

Conception The moment at which the ovum and sperm merge.

Concrete-operational stage This is the third stage identified in Piaget's theory of cognitive development. During this stage children are capable of logical thought in relation to concrete events and phenomena.

Conditioned satiety Animals learn the caloric content of different foods, and anticipate how much of each food they should eat to become satiated.

Conditioned taste aversion (CTA) Animals typically sample new foods, and if any sickness follows in a few hours, they avoid that food on future occasions.

Conditioning The process of learning through which the behaviour of organisms becomes dependent on environmental stimuli.

Conformity A kind of social influence that involves modifying individual behaviour in response to a real or imagined pressure from others. Conformity is the tendency to allow our opinions, attitudes and actions to be influenced by those of the people around us.

Congruence In Holland's theory of vocational types, the correspondence between an individual's work-related personality type and his or her work-related environment. More broadly, this is a core condition for therapeutic change within the person-centred approach. It also refers to the genuineness that the therapist expresses in the therapeutic relationship.

Conscientisation The process that enables us to develop skills to critically analyse our problems and to recognise the roles we may take in changing our social conditions.

Conservation An understanding of the principle that quantities remain the same despite changes in their appearance.

Consistency In Holland's theory of vocational types, when an individual's interests lie adjacent to one another on the hexagonal model of interests.

Constant practice Practising skills under the same conditions.

Construct A psychological phenomenon that can be measured.

Constructivism An approach to psychology which argues that people do not passively take in knowledge, but actively construct their own knowledge through their activities in the world. Piaget is a constructivist.

Consumer culture Refers to the (usually unspoken) assumption that owning more material things will make people happy.

Contextual memory An alternative term for 'source memory'.

Continuous variables In statistics, these are

variables that can take on any value, even a fraction of a value.

Critical thinking This has been seen as another spin-off of formal operational thought and includes both convergent and divergent thinking; the former referring to a strategy of focusing in on one correct answer to a problem, while the latter refers to the opposite process of solving a problem with many possible answers. Critical thinking allows the young person to begin questioning aspects of his or her life that were previously assumed, and is more likely to facilitate creative thinking as well.

Crystallised intelligence The individual's learned abilities to process information, including analysis and problem solving. Vocabulary and general information are also seen as examples of crystallised intelligence.

Cultural imperialism The process of imposing the cultural forms of a stronger country (or countries) onto weaker countries – now usually used in relation to Euro-American cultural imperialism.

Culture Everything that goes into the entire way of life of a particular group of people, including beliefs, attitudes, practices and behaviour patterns, objects, symbols, institutions, etc.

Culture-fair Efforts to specifically design a test to eliminate cultural bias and prejudice.

Culture-free Efforts to develop psychological tests that would measure heredity intellectual potential independently of the influence of cultural background.

Cumulative frequency In statistics, the number of scores that fall into and below a particular class in a frequency distribution.

Cumulative percentage In statistics, the percentage of scores falling into and below a particular class in a frequency distribution.

Curriculum Formal and incidental learning experiences available to learners in a community.

Curriculum development Changes in the goals and processes that comprise the learning opportunities in a specified context.

Custodial care Where patients receive care on a long-term and consistent basis, typically outside their family environment. Long-term hospitalisation of mentally ill patients falls into this category.

Cytokines A class of substances that are produced by cells of the immune system and can affect the immune response in a similar way to hormones.

D

Death instinct The unconscious drive towards death, initially turned inwards on ourselves with a tendency to self-destruct, and later turned outwards in the form of aggression.

Decentration The ability to consider multiple aspects of a stimulus or situation.

Declarative memory Memories that we can consciously recall, such as the score of the 2002 FA Cup final.

Deductive reasoning Reasoning which draws specific conclusions from general statements.

Defence mechanisms A process whereby the ego protects itself against the id by avoiding conscious awareness of conflicts or anxiety-arousing ideas or wishes.

Deferred imitation The ability to imitate an action sometime after it was observed.

Deficit model A pattern or framework for thinking about anything or any situation, which holds that one version of it is superior to all others.

Dementia Refers to the intellectual and personality deterioration sometimes associated with the aging processes of late adulthood.

Dependent variable In statistics, the variable being influenced by the independent variable.

Descriptive statistics Those analytical tools used to organise, summarise and describe data.

Dimensional theories of emotions In this approach, emotions are seen as being constructed of three major attributes: activation, valence and surgency (or power).

Direct violence Refers to acts that result directly in the psychological and/or physical harm of individuals and/or groups, or in the psychological and/or physical well-being of individuals and/or groups being compromised.

Disability A physical, sensory or mental limitation as a result of impairment.

Disability pressure groups Organisations for and of people with disabilities.

Discourse Refers to the symbolic forms that humans use to convey meanings about their social worlds. These symbolic forms may be found in artistic expression, photographs, written language and the spoken word, to mention but a few. Most commonly in psychology, discourse refers to spoken or written language.

Discrete variables These can only be expressed in whole numbers.

Dissociation Refers to an abnormal psychological state in which a person's perception of him- or herself and his or her environment is altered significantly.

Distal factors Socio-cultural and structural factors that occur at a societal level.

Dizygotic twins Also known as fraternal twins. Two children who develop from separately fertilised egg cells.

Domain-general knowledge Knowledge that is fundamental to a wide range of activities, such as formal operational thinking.

Domain-specific knowledge Knowledge that is crucial for particular activities, but not necessarily used in other settings.

Dream analysis A technique of psychoanalysis in which interpretation is applied to the manifest content (a verbal account of the dream experience) of dreams in their effort to reveal their latent content (the underlying or hidden meaning of a dream).

Dyadic model Refer to one-to-one psychotherapeutic models (as opposed to group therapy, family therapy, etc.).

Dystonia Involuntary muscle spasms and bizarre posturing of the limbs, trunk, face and tongue.

E

Ecological interdependence The relationship between the various systems in which the individual lives that exert an influence on his or her behaviour or are influenced by his or her behaviour.

Ecological realities Whatever exists in a given physical place, in terms of what actually exists and what is perceived to exist by whoever perceives it. Two people may perceive 'different ecological realities'.

Education The process and product of teaching and learning.

Effective dose The amount of a drug that produces a desired treatment effect in a person with the minimum side effects.

Efficacy of a psychoactive drug The effectiveness of a psychoactive drug in treating a psychiatric condition.

Ego This is a largely conscious part of the mind, governed mainly by the reality principle, mediating between external reality, the id and the superego.

Ego-ideal An internal notion of personal perfection serving as a model to which strives to conform.

Egocentrism The tendency of children during the preoperational stage to view everything from their own perspective.

Electra complex The unconscious desire of a girl for her father, accompanied by a desire to replace or destroy her mother, which manifests during the phallic stage.

Embryonic stage The six weeks of prenatal development after the germinal stage.

Emotions An umbrella concept for various energetic states of the brain, that have many attributes (autonomic arousal, cognitive, expressive, and feeling aspects). Some emotional responses are intrinsic to the nervous system, others are learned.

Empathy A core element for therapeutic change within the person-centred approach. It refers to the therapist's understanding of the client's thoughts and feelings from the client's perspective.

Environmental factors Factors that occur within the broader social context, such as poverty or cultural influences.

Epidemiological studies Studies that draw on various disciplines such as psychology, medicine, anthropology and sociology, for example, to study disease and illness, their prevalence and distribution in the population and their impact on the environment.

Epidemiology In the context of psychology, the study of the distribution and determinants of mental health problems.

Episodic memory Memory of episodes and events from our own lives, such as our first day at university, the last time we visited the zoo, our first kiss, etc.

Equity Refers to equal rights and access to health services for all service users regardless of race, gender and economic status.

Etiology Reason, cause and basic origin of a disorder.

Ethnicity or Ethnic identity A sociological and anthropological construct that refers to shared social elements and cultural values, such as language, religion, customs, traditions and history, within a particular social group, which in some way contributes to the distinct identity of that group.

Ethnocentrism Refers to the degree to which individuals perceive their own social group as being superior to others, while simultaneously harbouring feelings of negativity towards outgroups.

Eustress refers to 'healthy stress' that is necessary for optimal functioning, health and performance.

Everyday thinking Tacit thought that is part of the mundane practical activities of life.

Evolutionary psychology A school of thought that studies the evolutionary foundations of human behaviour. The claim is that many of our ways of responding and thinking and feeling are a result of the way our brains were designed during the long course of evolution.

Expectancy The anticipation of an outcome (reward or punishment) as a result of an action.

Explicit memory Memories that we con-sciously acquire and recall.

Extinction The process of eliminating a behaviour by withholding reinforcement; the removal of positive consequences (usually following undesirable behaviour).

Extrinsic motivation External factors (like money and praise) that can reinforce behaviour. Many of the causes of motivated behavioral changes are due to environmental conditions.

Extrinsic rewards Those that originate outside the individual, such as money.

Extroversion An attitude of the psyche characterised by an orientation toward the external world and other people.

F

Factor analysis A process of statistical analysis in which patterns of correlation between the various elements of the test are studied.

Fallopian tubes The narrow tubes where the ovum is fertilised and along which the zygote travels.

False memory A mental event that feels like a memory, but recalls an event that never occurred.

Femininity and Masculinity Terms used to refer to characteristics that are traditionally associated with being female or male within specific cultures.

Fimbria The fringed ends of the fallopian tubes.

Focus group interviews A group discussion that explores a particular topic selected by the researcher.

Fine motor skills Skills or capabilities involving small body movements.

Fluid intelligence Fluid intelligence is believed to be based on the speed and efficiency of neurological factors. Fluid intelligence is said to increase until late adolescence and then to decline throughout adulthood.

Foetal Alcohol Syndrome (FAS) A group of symptoms found in babies whose mothers were heavy drin-kers of alcohol during pregnancy.

Foetal stage The stage of prenatal development from the third to the ninth month of pregnancy.

Frequency distribution A table that summarises the frequency with which each value (or category) occurs.

Formal operational thinking This form of cognition which, according to Piaget takes place during adolescence, involves more abstract, less concrete conceptualisation, with the ability to hypothesise and use logical reasoning.

Frequency polygon A graph in which the frequencies of each category are indicated by dots and these dots are then joined by a line.

G

Garden metaphor Use of something that can be grown or cultivated to indicate that the quality of 'growing' or 'increasing gradually' is in whatever the metaphor represents. The idea of tending and cultivating a garden is also important.

Gender This concept usually refers to the social construction of biological, or inherent, sexual differences between men and women. It is assumed that gender is social, while sex is biological, though some theorists question this divide and whether there is anything outside of the social. It is also assumed by most gender theorists that the term encapsulates a notion of power inequality, in which in patriarchal societies, the male gender is imbued with more status and access to power (social, political and economic) than the female gender. Gender refers to cultural and socially meaningful roles and responsibilities ascribed to women and men. Gender identity refers to an individual's sense of self as being either male or female.

General adaptation syndrome Also known as GAS. The general set of reaction to stress that mobilises the organism's resources to deal with an impending threat.

Generativity An Eriksonian term which refers to the individual's urge and commitment to take care of the next generation.

Genital stage The final psychosexual stage characterised by a focus of libido in the genital area which emerges during puberty. During this stage the Oedipus complex reappears and is overcome through mature object choices.

Genocide Refers to violence committed with intent to destroy, in whole or in part, a national, ethnic, racial or religious group, and includes acts such as the killing of members of the group, serious bodily or mental harm to members of the group, the deliberate infliction of conditions intended to result in the physical destruction of the group, measures to prevent births within the group, and the forcible transfer of children from the group to another group.

Germinal stage The first two weeks of prenatal development after conception.

GINI Coefficient A concept named after Corrado Gini (1884-1965), an Italian statistician and demographer, and indicates how far a society deviates from perfect income equality. A Gini Coefficient of 0 indicates perfect income equality, while a 1 indicates perfect inequality (i.e. a single person owns everything). In the real world, Gini Coefficients typically range between 0.26 and 0.60.

Gist recall A recollection that summarises the main points of an event or story.

Globalisation Refers to the process through which the world community has increasingly become integrated into common ideological, economic, social and political systems. This process has been facilitated by easier access to information through advanced information technologies (e.g., the Internet), increased contact with international communities through transportation technologies, and virtually unrestrained and deregulated international trade.

Glucose intolerance A pathological state in which the fasting plasma glucose level is less than 140 mg per deciliter and the 30-, 60-, or 90-minute plasma glucose concentration following a glucose tolerance test exceeds 200 mg per deciliter. This condition is seen frequently in diabetes mellitus but also occurs with other diseases.

Gross motor skills Skills or capabilities involving large body movements.

Group polarisation The tendency for preexisting individual opinions, ideas or positions to become more extreme or polarised following a group discussion.

Grouped frequency distribution In statistics, a frequency distribution in which the values of the variables are grouped into classes.

Groupthink A phenomenon that may lead to faulty decision-making by group members who are more concerned with reaching consensus than with considering alternative courses of action.

H

Handicap An environmental restriction on an individual because of a unique difference (e.g., a disability).

Health Sector Strategic Framework A document detailing the ANC-led government's plan for health in South Africa.

Hegemonic masculinity The most powerful, culturally idealised masculinity at any given time.

Heritage The social transmission of customs, beliefs, values and practices from one generation to another.

Heterosex This term is used to refer to sexual practices between men and women. In most popular culture we simply use the term sex to refer to heterosex. This however assumes that all sexual activity takes place between men and women, and ignores homosexual sexuality.

Heterosexual intercourse Refers to sexual intercourse between a male and female.

Heuristic A rule-of-thumb or a short-cut method that enables us to solve a problem.

Hierarchical There are many levels of control in brain motivational systems, with lower systems providing more simple response tendencies than higher systems.

Hierarchy of needs An arrangement of innate needs, from strongest to weakest, that activates and directs behaviour. The hierarchy of needs includes physiological, safety, belongingness and love, esteem and self-actualising needs.

Histogram A graph used for continous variables in which the frequencies of different classes of scores are displayed as a vertical bar.

HIV This refers to the human immunodeficiency virus.

Homeostasis The bodily motivations such as hunger and thirst have levels of stability (e.g., body energy and water content) which behavioral and physiological changes aspire to sustain.

Hypertension Persistently high arterial blood pressure. Hypertension may have no known cause (essential or idiopathic hypertension) or be associated with other primary diseases (secondary hypertension). Hypertension is a risk factor for the development of heart disease, peripheral vascular disease, stroke and kidney disease.

Hypothesised To make a hypothesis. A hypothesis is a speculative statement about the expected relationship between phenomena, which is then investigated empirically.

Hypothetical-deductive thinking This is the logical component of formal operational thinking, which is manifested in an ability and desire to actively plan and problem solve on the part of the adolescent.

I

Id A reservoir of energy derived from instincts and governed by the pleasure principle. Its contents are unconscious, repressed and it is constant conflict with the ego and superego.

Idealised self-image The self-image for normal people is the idealised picture of them self built on flexible, realistic assessment of their abilities. The self-image of neurotics is based on an inflexible, unrealistic self-appraisal.

Identity Refers to the conceptualisation of the self, and is a key issue highlighted in theories of adolescent personality development. Erikson, who has provided one of the most comprehensive accounts of identity development through the life span, sees adolescence as falling into the fifth of eight stages, namely, that of identity versus identity confusion, where the crisis involves a wrestling and experimenting with conflicting identities as the individual emerges from the security of childhood to the development of an autonomous adult identity. Those who do not adequately resolve the conflict of this stage will suffer from 'identity confusion'.

Identity absorption Prioritising something (e.g., sport) to the point where it becomes the 'be all and end all' of our life and defines who we are.

Ideology Any set of beliefs that is socio-historically specific and that is held by an individual or collectively by a social group, and may either be utilised in a manner which dominates others or in a manner which seeks to challenge such domination.

Immunity Refers to the body's natural ability to defend itself against infections and disease.

Impairment The physical basis of a functional limitation that causes a disability.

Implantation When the blastocyst successfully attaches itself to the uterine wall.

Implicit memory Memories that we acquire and demonstrate without being aware of it.

Incentive A perceived reward or encouragement for exercising a particular behaviour.

Incidental learning Bits of information that we acquire and are able to recall without having intended to.

Independent variable The variable selected, measured or manipulated by the researcher to determine its effect on another variable.

Indigenous That which is authentic or original to, say, a specific culture or environment or community.

Indigenous healing This refers to African healing systems, which incorporate various cultural beliefs and practices in treating psychological distress.

Individualist cultures Cultures in which individuals are encouraged to think of themselves as independent selves.

Inductive reasoning Reasoning which draws a general conclusion from specific occurrences or cases.

Infant mortality rate Refers to the number of infant deaths in a year per 1 000 live births during the year.

Inferential statistics That branch of statistics that are used to draw inferences about populations using data obtained from a sample.

Inheritance That which is acquired, generally without conscious awareness, like the genes a child inherits from parents or the social class a child acquires at birth or the social conditions into which a child is born.

Inner cell mass A membrane of the blastocyst that eventually differentiates into body parts and organs.

Instinct A term used to indicated that there are behavioural and mental functions that are largely due to the way the nervous systems is constructed, and that learning only refines how they operate.

Intelligence The capacity to acquire or learn and use knowledge.

Intelligence Quotient (IQ) an index that summarises the person's performance or level of general intellectual functioning on an individual intelligence scale.

Intercultural Refers to processes taking place between cultures.

Interviewing Involves the researcher asking questions, listening and analysing the responses.

Interdisciplinary service provision Multiple disciplines, for example, psychology, medicine, physiotherapy and occupational therapy must work together in a coherent way to provide an effective service for the users of services, preferably in one location.

Intermittent stress refers to responses to stressors that vary in duration, alternating between periods of stress and calm.

Interpersonal factors Factors that occur within the context of relationships with others, for example, peer influence.

Intersectoral collaboration Different sectors of society, such as justice, education and health, must work together on problems which impact on mental health. Addressing violence is a good example of a problem that necessitates intersectoral collaboration.

Intracultural Refers to processes taking place within cultures.

Intrapersonal factors Factors located within the individual, such as biological causes.

Intrapsychic processes Processes that are internal to an individual.

Introversion An attitude of the psyche characterised by an orientation toward ours own thoughts and feelings.

Internalisation Absorbing a relationship or an instinctual object into our mental apparatus.

Intersection A junction or a point at which more than one thing meets or exists together.

Intrinsic motivation Internal factors (like pride and a sense of achievement) that can reinforce behaviour. Many of the causes of rapid behavioral changes are due to internal brain and bodily conditions.

Intrinsic rewards Rewards from within the individual, such as self-satisfaction.

Irreversibility The inability to mentally reverse perceived actions.

Ischaemic heart disease A low oxygen state, usually due to obstruction of the arterial blood supply or inadequate blood flow leading to hypoxia in the tissue.

L

Latency stage A stage of life characterised by a decrease in sexual activity.

Learning The acquisition knowledge, attitudes, perceptions and skills for effectively interacting with the environment.

Libido The energy of the sexual instinct as a component of the life instinct.

Licensure A legal process that confers the title 'psychologist'.

Life instinct Includes the sexual instinct and the ego instinct (or the self-preservation instinct).

Life expectancy Refers to the expected age at death for a newborn infant.

Lingua franca A common language or language used as a means of communication between people from diverse language backgrounds.

Linguistic determinism The idea that language determines the way in which we think.

Linguistic relativism The idea that language strongly influences the way in which we think.

Long-term memory (LTM) A memory that lasts beyond mere seconds and may be remembered for a lifetime.

M

Mainstream approaches Approaches within psychology which are traditionally adhered to. These approaches typically originated and were developed in Europe and America.

Malnutrition Faulty or inadequate nutrition; under nourishment.

Mean In statistical analysis, the mean is all the scores added together divided by the number of observations.

Measures of central tendency A single value that in some way represents all the values in a distribution.

Measures of variability A single value that describes the spread (variability) of scores in a distribution.

Median Refers to that score in the middle of a distribution when scores are arranged from low to high, that is that score that halves a distribution in two.

Menarche The start of menstrual bleeding and reproductive functioning.

Menopause Occurs during middle adulthood and refers to the end of menstruation and the capacity to bear children.

Mental abilities Qualities of the human mind, which determine the extent to which an individual can learn and use different types or forms of knowledge and experiences or deal with the world.

Mental age This is measured as performance on a test at a level equivalent to that of other persons of the same chronological age.

Mental set An inappropriate heuristic that comes to dominate our thinking and blocks the ability to solve a problem.

Mitosis The process by which the zygote divides into identical cells.

Mode Refers to that score that occurs most frequently in a set of scores.

Model Take something or somebody as an example for our behaviour; to copy someone's behaviour or ways.

Modelling The process of imitating or copying other people's behaviour. Modelling is the learning process which brings about a change in behaviour as a result of observing, reading or hearing about the behaviour of another person (who is the model).

Monogamous When a person has only one sexual partner.

Monozygotic twins Also known as identical twins. Two children who develop after a single fertilised egg cell splits into two.

Motivation That which provokes, initiates, incites and directs or channels behaviour. It is a term that highlights the diverse bodily and brain conditions that promote goal-directed actions, as a result of various internal bodily and brain states, intrinsic organismic responses to various environmental stimuli (incentives), and interact with a host of cognitive and learning processes.

Multigenerational families Extended families in which different generations are still alive.

Myelination Myelin is the sheath which insulates neuronal fibres in the brain and affects the speed of processing of information. Myelination is only complete 10 to 12 years after birth.

N

Narrative A tale, story, composition of facts, especially a story told in first person.

Nationalism Refers to the belief that each nation or group of people should have their own country, with clearly defined borders, and the right to self-determination through self-governance. It encompasses aspects such as loyalty to our country, pride in our country and patriotism.

Nativist An explanation that accounts for phenomena as being innate or internal.

Natural language The everyday languages

that we are familiar with and produce.

Negatively skewed distribution In statistics, a distribution in which there is a cluster of extremely high scores.

Negative reinforcement Removing aversive consequences (usually following desirable behaviour). Negative reinforcement refers to the increased probability of a response occurring as a result of that response preventing or terminating an aversive event.

Neocortex The extensive sheet of neurons (with six distinct neuronal layers) that surrounds lower brain areas and provides the highest level of integration within the brain-mind.

Neonatal period A period of development from birth to approximately the first month of life.

Neonate A newly born infant up to the age of around four weeks.

Neuron A functional unit of the nervous system which comprises a cell, axon and dendrites.

Neuropeptides Short proteins, of several to several hundred amino acids that are manufactured in distinct neurons of the brain and appear to control a variety of distinct emotional and motivational processes.

Neurophysiological functioning The functioning of the nervous system.

Neurotransmitters Biochemical agents available in the central and peripheral nervous system that are involved in nerve impulse conduction.

Non-mainstream approaches These approaches are typically not part of the mainstream and are seldom included in the teaching of psychology.

Non-social groups Collectivities comprised of two or more individuals who are present at the same time and place but are not interacting with each other.

Noradrenalin Also known as norepinephrine (American term) is a hormone, secreted by the adrenal gland and similar to adrenaline, that is also the principal neurotransmitter of sympathetic nerve endings supplying the major organs and skin. It increases blood pressure and rate and depth of breathing, raises the level of blood sugar, and decreases the activity of the intestines. Informally called the 'anger hormone'.

Normal distribution In statistics, a bell shaped curve called a symmetrical distribution since the left and right halves of the distribution are mirror images of each other.

Nosology The classification of diseases.

O

Obedience A social influence process in which individual behaviour is modified in response to a command from an authority figure.

Obesity An increase in body weight beyond skeletal and physical requirements, resulting from an excessive accumulation of fat in the body.

Observed scores The scores obtained for respondents on a psychometric instrument.

Oedipus complex The unconscious desire of a boy for his mother, accompanied by a desire to replace or destroy his father, which manifests during the phallic stage.

Open-ended interviews In open-ended interviews the researcher merely tries to remain focused on an issue of study without any pre-set list of questions.

Operant behaviour Behaviour, emitted spontaneously or voluntarily, that operates on the environment to change it.

Operant conditioning The variety of behaviourist theory developed by B.F. Skinner, which examines how the organism does not only respond to stimuli but also 'operates' on its environment, in order to receive particular stimuli.

Operant learning A learning process whereby the consequences of behaviour influence the likelihood of the behaviour being repeated.

Opioids A family of neuropeptides that have characteristics similar to addictive alkaloids such as morphine. There are several distinct families, and one – the endorphin family that acts on mu receptors – helps reduce various kinds of stress and helps mediate many pleasurable functions in the brain.

Opportunistic infections Refers to infections refer to common illnesses, such as influenza, which we contract when our immune system is weak.

Oral-aggessive phase The second phase of the oral stage, characterised by biting.

Oral-incorporative phase The first of the two phases of the oral stage, characterised by sucking.

Othering Refers to the process of differentiating between ourselves and others, or between our group and others, thereby casting people different from ourselves in a subordinate status, often compromising their human, social and political rights.

Outcome expectations An individual's estimation of the consequences of his or her behaviour.

Outcome-based education (OBE) Educational practices that place an emphasis on the observable or verifiable results of teaching and learning.

Ovum The female reproductive cell.

Oxytocin A nine amino acid peptide that facilitates milk let-down peripherally in nursing mothers, and in the brain controls a variety of social processes, including separation distress, sexuality, maternal nurturance and social memories.

P

Part practice Practising skill in isolated segments.

Participatory learning The process of gaining knowledge or developing by participating or being actively involved as part of whatever is going on, for example, in different activities of the family, community or in a project.

Patriarchy Refers to a system of domination that has systematically treated women as subordinate, inferior beings. Patriarchy refers to a system of domination that has systematically treated women as subordinate, inferior beings.

Peace building Seeks to diminish structural violence through the pursuit of social justice, which is directed at the social transformation of society and the transformation of cultural discourses that maintain oppression and exploitation.

Peacekeeping Implies the presence of neutral forces to prevent or diminish episodes of violence in contexts characterised by conflict and hostility.

Peacemaking Refers to efforts directed at reducing the occurrence and intensity of direct, episodic violence, and promoting non-violence.

Peer culture The atmosphere created by or in which a peer group functions. Some aspects of this 'climate' are peculiar and best understood and appreciated by group members.

Peer group A group of persons of similar age and status who have common interests, goals and activities.

Peer mentoring A learning situation in which a more knowledgeable person, say an older child, adolescent or adult, guides, directs or inspires a less knowledgeable one or novice. Generally, mentoring is regarded in positive terms.

Perceived barrier Our opinion of the tangible and psychological costs of some or other advised action.

Perceived benefit Our opinion of the efficacy of some or other recommended action to reduce risk or seriousness of impact.

Perceived severity Our opinion of the seriousness of a condition and its consequences.

Perceived susceptibility Our opinion of the chances of getting or contracting a particular condition.

Person-centred therapy A therapy that emphasises the centrality of the personal qualities of the therapist and the supportive environment of the therapeutic relationship in helping the client to change.

Person-environment fit The degree of fit between an individual's characteristics and the characteristics of the working environment.

Persona The public face or role person presents to others.

Personal identity Who or what a person is; that which marks someone out as separate from and different to any other person.

Personal well-being A state of optimal physical, cognitive, behavioural and spiritual wellness of an individual.

Personality The sum of characteristics that make us unique, including core variables, typical responses and role-specific responses.

Photographic memory Refers to the exceptional and rare ability to acquire and recall very detailed information. For example, being able to recall the exact words on a particular page of a book.

Physiological arousal A source of self-efficacy information obtained through the level of anxiety or arousal an individual experiences when confronted with a task.

Placenta A complex organ made of tissue from the embryo and the mother.

Population The total number of people or objects that form the subject of the research.

Positive reinforcement Presenting rewarding consequences (usually following desirable behaviour). Positive reinforcement refers to the increased probability of a response occurring as a result of that response being followed by a reinforcer.

Positively skewed distribution A distribution in which there is a cluster of extremely low scores.

Post-traumatic stress disorder A psychological disorder resulting from exposure to a catastrophic or extreme traumatic stressor. It is characterised by re-experiencing of the trauma, avoidance and hyperarousal.

Preconscious Mental contents that are not currently in consciousness, but are accessible to consciousness by directing attention to them.

Primary groups Groups that are characterised by frequent intimate and direct social interactions that play an important role in primary socialisation and personality development.

Primary health care Providing appropriate, acceptable and accessible health care to communities through health promotion and prevention services.

Primary intervention Promotes broad-scale interventions geared towards keeping the general population health and attempting to reduce new incidences of mental health problems.

Primary memory An alternative term for short-term memory.

Principles of learning The underpinnings of successful learning experiences.

Procedural memory The type of memories that we demonstrate through performing particular tasks or skills.

Prolactin A large199 amino acid peptide that regulates milk production peripherally, and in the brain controls separation distress, maternal behaviors and probably various other social tendencies.

Propositional memory Memories that we can consciously recall.

Prospective memory A specific form of memory. It refers to the ability to remember that something needs to be done at some previously specified time.

Protective factors Those influences that limit or reduce the likelihood of high risk behaviour and play a moderating or buffering role. These are processes both within and outside the individual that serve as buffering agents against negative stressors.

Proximal factors Interpersonal relationships and social influences such as peer or social norms as well as factors in a persons immediate environment like the community or workplace.

Proximodistal developmental trend The sequence of growth that proceeds from the centre of the body outward.

Psychiatric illness Any disturbance in mood, behaviour or thought that is abnormal in terms of severity, frequency and duration.

Psychoactive drugs Substances that alter mood, behaviour and thoughts through biochemical action on the central nervous system.

Psychopharmacology The use of psychoactive drugs to treat psychiatric illness.

Psychoanalysis An insight therapy that focuses on uncovering and resolving unconscious conflicts resulting in personality change.

Psychological assessment The process of measuring psychological constructs.

Psychological Skills Training Improving athletic performance through the use of psychological skills.

Psychometric properties These are measures of the extent to which a psychometric instrument adequately measures a psychological construct.

Psychopathology A term used generally to refer to psychological disorders or psychiatric illnesses.

Psychosocial theory of development Refers to Erik Erikson's theory of development. The theory postulates that people must deal with a series of 'crises' as they pass through various stages of development from birth to death.

Psychotherapy A psychological intervention in which the therapist and patient are engaged in a therapeutic relationship so as to bring about change within the patient.

Puberty Puberty has been defined as a period of fairly fast physical maturation involving hormonal and bodily changes that occur mainly during early adolescence. Puberty begins with hormonal increases, which manifest in a range of internal and external bodily changes or what are known as the primary and secondary sex characteristics that signify sexual maturation and gender differentiation. These changes coincide with a growth spurt in height and weight.

Punishment Presenting aversive consequences (usually following undesirable behaviour). Punishment is an aversive stimulus that follows a response for the purpose of eliminating that response.

Q

Qualitative research Qualitative methods produce research and textual research data in the form of words and sentences.

Quantitative research Quantitative methods produce research data that are numeric and can be analysed using statistical techniques.

R

Racialisation Refers to the delineation of group boundaries and the allocation of persons within those boundaries by primary reference to (supposedly) inherent and/or biological (usually phenotypical) characteristics.

Random practice Practising different skills by interspersing them.

Random sampling The process of selecting the sample so that all members of the population have an equal chance of being selected.

Range In statistics, range indicates the difference between the highest and the lowest scores.

Reasoning A form of thinking in which people draw conclusions through a systematic, logical evaluation of statements.

Recent memory Memories that have been stored during the last few hours to months.

Reciprocal determinism A concept applied by Albert Bandura to the interdependence of behaviour, cognitions and the environment.

Reference groups Groups to which a person does not belong but with which she or he identifies.

Reflexes Involuntary, inborn actions over which the neonate and/or young infant has no control.

Reflexivity The research topic, design and process, together with the experience of doing the research are reflected on and critically evaluated throughout.

Reinforcement The act of strengthening a response by adding a reward, thus increasing the likelihood that the response will be repeated.

Rehabilitation The use of medical and psychosocial interventions to support the participation of people with disabilities in the activities of their communities to the same extent as other ordinary citizens of those communities are able to.

Reinforcement schedules Patterns or rates of providing or withholding reinforces.

Relational well-being Having healthy social relationships outside the family where mutual respect and connectedness are valued.

Reliability The extent to which the items on a test measure the same construct. Reliability; the stability or consistency of the measure.

Remote memory Memories that have been stored years or even decades previously.

Resilience The ability to adapt effectively in the face of adverse life circumstances. Successful adaptation to an environment despite exposure to risk.

Respondent behaviour Responses made to or elicited by specific environmental stimuli. Resilience is the capacity that individuals and groups have to thrive in the face of adverse circumstances. Resilience is successful adaptation to the environment despite exposure to risk.

Responsible intelligence The capacity to learn and make positive and useful contribution to life, especially the solution of problems in daily life.

Reversibility Refers to the ability to mentally reverse actions or situations.

Rewards A synonym for positive reinforcers.

Risk Risk occurs when negative or potentially negative conditions threaten normal development.

Risk behaviour Refers to specific forms of behaviour which are proven to be associated with increased susceptibility to a specific disease or ill-health.

Risk factors Refers to biological, psychological, social or economic behaviours or environments which are associated with or cause increased susceptibility to a specific disease, ill health, or injury; processes both within or outside the individual that predispose an individual to succumb to negative stressors.

Risk-taking behaviours These refer to a wide range of behaviours that place an individual at physical and/or emotional risk, including unsafe sexual practices (unprotected sex, multiple sexual partners, etc.), substance abuse (alcohol, drugs) and violent and criminal activities (e.g., gang involvement, violence towards the opposite sex, coercive sexual practices, such as date-rape, or more subtle forms of pressurising partners to have sex, suicidal or other self-destructive thinking and behaviours, etc.). Adolescence is viewed as a period where the particular physical, cognitive and social-emotional changes that place, facilitate vulnerability to risk-taking.

S

Sample A selection of people or objects from the population.

Schema An overarching network of knowledge that is central in our thinking.

School learning The process of gaining knowledge or developing by undergoing well-organised activities or experiences meant to develop specific knowledge or skills in the learner.

Script A set of information that provides the general principles about what to expect in an event, situation or social setting.

Secondary groups Refers to groups that are characterised by few intimate and direct interactions, weak levels of group identification and affection, and functional relationships.

Secondary intervention Attempts to lower the rate of prevalence of a disorder by targeting those at risk or those in the early stages of a disorder to remain symptom-free.

Secondary memory An alternative term for long-term memory.

Self A person's inner qualities, traits or characteristics or feelings of what he or she is.

Selfhood The fact of being a human being with inner qualities.

Self-cleansing tendency A tendency to spontaneously abort severely malformed embryos and/or foetuses within the first three months of pregnancy.

Self-definition The way in which an individual may define him- or herself.

Self-efficacy One of the most powerful self-regulatory processes. It is a belief that concerns ones ability to perform behaviours producing an expected outcome that is desirable. Self-efficacy is our confidence in being able to successfully perform a certain behaviour.

Self-efficacy expectations An individual's belief in his or her ability to complete a task successfully. An individual can have high (positive) or low (negative) self-efficacy expectations.

Self-righting tendency A tendency to develop normally under all but the most adverse conditions.

Semantic memory Our general knowledge of the world, such as knowing the capital of a country, the captain of a sports team, and the meaning of a particular word.

Semi-structured interviews The researcher ensures that certain areas of questioning are covered but there is no fixed sequence or format of questions.

Senescence The increasing decline of all the body's systems (including the cardiovascular, respiratory, endocrine and immune systems) during late adulthood.

Separation anxiety An infant's fear of strangers or of being separated from the caregiver (this include stranger anxiety).

Seriation Refers to the ability to arrange objects in order along quantitative dimensions, such as weight, length, or size.

Sex Biologically determined differences between males and females.

Sexually transmitted infections Or STIs are infections and diseases that are transmitted via sexual contact.

Short-term memory (STM) Associated with store models of memory, a memory that lasts for no longer than a few seconds and requires rehearsal in order to be retained in STM.

Social action Promoting participation of people in community efforts towards a common goal like improved quality of life, social justice and political efficacy.

Social capital Refers to the networks, norms, and sense of trust in a society that facilitate co-operation for mutual benefit. Social Capital means that membership of a social group or network that secures certain benefits for an individual.

Social cohesion Refers to the connections and bonds between people.

Social competence The ability to relate in acceptable ways to other people as well as to notice the needs or problems of others and handle or address them in a positive and acceptable manner.

Social dislocation When we are uprooted from our original community.

Social expectations What other people wish, hope or expect to see as a manifestation of another person's qualities, behaviours or achievements and competencies.

Social facilitation A group process phenomenon that occurs when there is an improvement in individual task performance when working with others or in the presence of an audience.

Social groups Two or more interdependent individuals who influence each other through social interaction.

Social influence The change in judgments, opinions and attitudes that occurs because of exposure to the judgments, opinions and attitudes of others.

Social integration The process of becoming an acceptable and useful member of a social group.

Social loafing A group process phenomenon in which individual performance is relaxed or inhibited because of the assumption that others will compensate.

Socialisation The process of learning how to become a member of given culture. This involves learning that occurs by the mere fact of being part of such a group, learning that is part of the culture's ways of training or bringing up children and learning through more deliberate means like schooling.

Societal groups Two or more individuals who have something in common that they themselves recognise and that affects their behavior.

Sociobiology The study of the biological basis of social behaviour (i.e. examining how humanity's evolutionary history and biological structure determines social behaviour).

Socio-historical approach An approach to psychology, which understands thinking to be a social process linked to activities and relationships with others. Another term for this approach is situated cognition.

Somatic anxiety The physiological components of anxiety (e.g., elevated heart rate and muscular tension).

Source memory Your memory of where and when you learned something.

Sperm The male reproductive cell.

Sport psychology The study of the impact that psychological phenomena have on sport participation and performance (and vice versa) as well as the practical application of that knowledge.

Standard deviation In statistics, the square root of the variance.

State anxiety Anxiety that is situation-specific and ever-changing.

Stem-and-leaf displays A frequency distribution in which values are broken down into a leading digit (called the stem) and a trailing digit (called a leaf).

Stigma the ascription of a negative connotation to a person, event or object because of its difference from the ordinary.

Stress A set of physiological, psychological and behavioural reactions that serves an adaptive function.

Stressors Any situation, activity or experience that causes stress.

Structural violence Includes the more insidious processes of social domination, political oppression and economic exploitation of individuals and social groups, that result in the psychological and physical well-being of these individuals and groups being compromised.

Structured Clinical Interview A structured interview that includes diagnostic criteria contained in the Diagnostic and Statistical Manual of Mental Disorders (Fourth Edition, Test Revised) to diagnose disorders.

Structured interviews The interviewer follows a set list and sequence of questions.

Sub-cortical A term to indicate areas of the brain situated below the neocortex, that are generally much more ancient in evolution, and which mediate many of the intrinsic aspects of emotions and motivations.

Substance abuse A recurrent pattern of drug use with significant adverse effects.

Substance dependence When a person continues to use a substance, despite significant adverse effects related to the substance. There is often tolerance, withdrawal and compulsive drug-seeking behaviour.

Substance misuse A pattern of use where there are some adverse effects, but these are not recurrent.

Successive approximation The acquisition of complex behaviours. This applies to reinforcing behaviour only as it comes to approximate the final desired behaviour.

Superego Originates from a conflict between the id and the ego in the course of development and monitors and controls the ego like a judge.

Surgency One of the general dimension of emotions that describes the 'power' of an emotion, namely how much a certain emotion tends to fill the mind.

Synapse The space between neurons through which electrochemical impulse are conducted.

Syndrome A medical term referring to a collection of specific signs and symptoms that typically co-occur and are associated with particular illnesses or diseases.

T

Tabula rasa A term that was used to highlight the importance of learning in the ability of the brain to have any content; literally, some thought that the brain-mind was a 'blank slate' prior to learning.

Teaching The activities involved in facilitating successful interaction with the environment.

Temperament An individual's characteristic manner of responding to the environment.

Teratogens Harmful environmental agents that interfere with normal prenatal development; an agent that causes physical defects in the developing embryo.

Tertiary intervention Employs strategies to decrease the debilitating effects of an existing disorder and attempts to rehabilitate individuals towards adequate social functioning.

Theory A set of coherent propositions that is helpful for describing, explaining and predicting phenomena.

Traditional education A form of teaching and learning that is an integral component of a given culture, such as education that is consistent with family traditions and routines in many African communities.

Trait anxiety A relatively stable predisposition to experience state anxiety in a wide variety of situations.

Transactional sex When a person exchanges sex for money or goods.

Transductive reasoning Preoperational reasoning in which children reason from one particular event to another particular event.

Transitivity Refers to the ability to recognise relations among elements in a serial order (for example, if A is more than B, and B is more than C, then A is more than C).

Trophoblast A membrane of the blastocyst that eventually divides into the amnion and the chorion.

True scores The hypothetical score obtained by averaging the scores from an infinite number of administrations of a test.

U

Umbilical cord The tube connecting the embryo to the placenta.

Ungrouped frequency distribution In statistics, a frequency distribution in which the actual categories or values of the variable concerned are used.

Unconditional positive regard A core condition for therapeutic change within the person-centred approach. It refers to the therapist's unconditional acceptance of the client as a person.

Unconscious A part of the mind containing repressed instincts and their representative wishes, ideas and images that are not accessible to direct examination.

Unimodal distribution In statistics, a distribution with only one peak.

Universal grammar The basic underlying grammatical structure at the basis of all human languages.

V

Valence The general dimension of emotions that describes the type of positive or negative affective internal experience that accompanies an emotional state.

Validity The extent to which a test measures the construct it intends to measure.

Variable Any property of an object or person that can vary from person to person or object to object.

Variable practice Practising skills under different conditions.

Variance A measure of the average deviation of all the scores in the distribution.

Verbal persuasion A source of self-efficacy information obtained through the spoken word.

Vicarious expectancy People adopt other people's expectancies concerning future events, especially those with whom they share a common experience.

Vicarious learning A source of self-efficacy information obtained through observation of other people's behaviour.

Verbatim memory The ability to recall a passage or conversation word-for-word.

Victomology The study of experiences of victimisation.

Voluntary Counselling and Testing Also know as VCT, which is when you volunteer to have an HIV test which is accompanied by pre- and post-test counseling.

Vulnerability Susceptibility to negative outcomes under conditions of risk. In the case of substance abuse, vulnerability refers to the probability of a person using drugs under conditions of risk.

W

Whole practice Practising skills in their entirety.

Working memory A dynamic conceptualisation of STM that includes the retaining, retrieval and mental manipulation of material.

Z

Zone of viability The time from which a prematurely born foetus may have a chance of survival.

Zygote The single cell formed as a result of the merging of an ovum with a sperm cell.

Index

'inyanga' (doctor), 499
IQ tests, 77
Iraqi war, 281
Irritable Bowel Syndrome, 424
'isangoma' (diviner), 498–9
isiXhosa
    kinship terms, 227
    preschool children's pronunciation, 60
isiXhosa-speaking patients
    schizophrenic condition, 484

J

Jackson, John Hughlings, 111, 115
Japan
    Strange Situation procedure, 102–3
job satisfaction, 377–8 & fig.
Jung, Carl Gustav, 164, 166
    neoanalytic approach, 169–71
Junior South African Individual Scale (JSAIS), 199

K

Kathorus study, 264
Kelly's cognitive theory, 165
Kikuyu culture, 332
kinesiology, 386, 391
Klinger, J., 181
knowledge-driven research, 16
Korsakoff's disease, 118

L

labelling, 478–9
labelling/mislabelling, 494
language, 224
    acquisition, 229–31
    components, 227–9
    development, 59–60, 144
    pragmatic context, 229
    referring to disabled persons, 364
    in South Africa, 231–2
    sport psychologists' proficiency, 401
late adulthood, 93–6
    abuse, 94–5
    nutrition, 443
        see also cognitive development;
            physical development; psychoso-
            cial development
lateral transfer, 355
Laubscher, L., 181
lead exposure
    effects on newborns, 43
learners, disabled
    see disabled learners
learning, 341, 348–9, 356, 395
    Biggs' student approaches to, 353
    practice distribution, 354–5
        principles
            feedback, 352
            motivation, 353
            perception, 355–6
            transfer, 355
    surface/deep level strategies, 351–2
    theories, 350–2
        see also behavioural approach;

humanistic approach; information
    processing approach
learning potential theories (Vygotsky), 204–5
Leipoldt, C. Louis, 199
lesbian feminism, 295
liberal feminism, 295
liberation psychology, 314, 318–19
libido, 166, 170
Lichtheim, Ludwig, 111, 115
Liepmann, Hugo, 111
life cycle squeeze, 92–3
life expectancy, 263–4
life instinct (Freud), 166
life span approach (to personality), 164, 172–4
linguistic determinism, 226
linguistic relativism, 227
Lissauer, Heinrich, 111
localisationist view, 111, 128
long-term memory (LTM), 237
longitudinal design, 4
ludic energies, 130
Luria, Aleksandr Romanovich, 112
lust systems, 126, 129

M

magnetic resonance imaging (MRI), 116
magnification, 494
maladaptiveness, 470–1
malaria, 43, 450, 459
    cerebral, 461
    prevention/treatment adherence
        interventions, 460
males
    see men
malnutrition, 438
    effects on middle childhood, 65–6
    effects on newborns, 48, 439–40
    effects on preschool children, 53, 440–1
mammals
    core emotional systems, 129–34
Marie, Pierre, 111
marijuana
    effects in newborns, 43
Marr, David, 145
marriage, 90
Marx, Karl, 266
masculinity, 293, 296, 397–8
    see also men
Maslow, Abraham
    hierarchy of needs, 124, 175 & fig.
    humanist approach (to personality), 165
massed practice sessions, 354–5
maternal conditions
    illnesses/diseases/infections, 43
    negative attitudes to pregnancy/baby, 44
    nutrition, 42–3
maternal instinct, 129
mean, 23–4
measures of central tendency, 23, 25
measures of variability, 23, 25
median, 23–4
memory, 128, 236
    accuracy, 241

ecological approach, 241
interference, 239–40
and meaning, 240–1
multi-store model, 237
rehearsed information, 237, 238
role of context, 241–3
tactile/olfactory, 240
working memory model, 238 & fig.
men
    care taker education, 129
    sexual identity, 78
        see also masculinity
mental age (MA)/chronological age (CA)
    index, 200
mental competency assessment, 118
mental health, 516
    community level interventions, 521–2
        & fig.
    community service delivery model,
        522–3 & tab.
    impact of HIV/AIDS, 454
    impact of parasites, 460–1
    impact of poverty, 264
    impact of TB, 458
    racism and, 279
    socially interdependent layers, 516–18
        & fig.
    sport specific issues, 391, 394
    violence against women, 294
mental illness
    attitudes towards, 472
    bio-psychosocial approach, 514–15, 524
    biomedical approach, 514, 520
    causes, 514
    classification, 476–9
    cultural context, 481–2
    DSM-IV, 476–7
        disorders listed, 478
    global assessment of functioning, 477
    history, 472–6
        humanitarian reforms, 474–5
        naturalistic view, 472–3
    Kraepelin's classification system, 475
    myths, 471
    protective factors, 518
    psychosocial stressor severity, 477
    risk factors, 518–19
    socio-political factors, 481
Mental Measurements Yearbook, 187
mental retardation, 482
mental sets, 219
metabolic tolerance to drugs, 509
micronutrients, 438
middle adulthood, 91–3
    see also cognitive development; physical
        development; psychosocial
        development
middle childhood, 64–9
middle class
    versus poor people, 265–6
migration
    and TB epidemic, 455–6
Milner, A.D., 147
mind-body problem, 110

mining industry
    alcohol misuse, 432
Minnesota Multiphasic Personality Inventory
    (MMPI), 187
minority influence, 254
Mishkin, M., 146
    two visual systems hypothesis, 147
mode, 23–4
models, 178, 214, 410
modularity (Fodor), 144–6
Moll, J.M., 199
monoamine oxidase inhibitors (MAOs),
    506–7
moral order, 167
morphemes, 228
Moscovici, Serge, 254
motivation, 122, 135
    evolutionary psychology, 125
    hierarchical view, 124
    importance of affective processes, 134–5
    to learn, 353–4
    and memory, 122
    psychobiological view, 123
motor knowledge, 111
multiculturalism, 231–2
Multidimensional Anxiety Theory (MAT),
    389–90 & fig.
multilingualism, 231
multiple disabilities, 362
myelination, 461

N
narrative analysis, 29
National Peace Accord Trust
    Wilderness Therapy, 316
nationalism, 278, 281
nativist theory of language acquisition, 231
nature versus nurture debate, 68
Neighbourhood-Based Safety Promotion
    Programme (UNISA), 319
Neisser, Ulric, 241–2
neonates, 45–8
    see also infants
neopsychoanalysts, 164
networks, 265
neural networks, 112
neuroadaptation, 430
neuroanatomical view, 127
neuroleptic-induced Parkinsonism, 509
neuropsychiatry, 110
neuropsychology, 107–8, 110
    qualitative/quantitative assessment,
        113–14
    research methods, 116, 148
    role of theory, 114–15
    training, 117
        see also clinical neuropsychology;
            neuropsychiatry
neurosis theory (Horney), 171
Neurotic-Extraversion-Openness Personality
    Inventory (NEO-PI), 187
neuroticism dimension, 187
neurotransmitters, 503 & fig., 505

newborns
    see infants
non-organic failure-to-thrive (NOFTT), 441
norepinephrine (NE), 503, 506
normal distribution, 22 & fig., 23
normative social influence, 254
norms
    of groups, 252
    of tests, 206
number of classes, 20
nutrition, 438
    counselling to HIV-infected patients, 444
        see also malnutrition

O
obedience, 254–5
obesity, 438, 442
object recognition, 141, 146
objective personality assessment, 186–8
objectivity, 27
observational learning, 178
occupation, 376
occupito-parietal/occupito-temporal
        syndromes, 147 & fig.
Oedipus complex, 169, 171, 288
open-ended interviews, 28
openness dimension, 187
operant behaviour (Skinner), 176
opioid systems, 133–4
oral-aggressive/sadistic personality types,
        168
oral-passive personality types, 168
Othering, 272
outcome expectations (results of behaviour),
        379
outcomes-based education (OBE), 69, 342–4
oxytocin, 128, 132–3

P
pain tolerance, 179
panic system, 126, 129
'parallel distributed processing' (PDP) models,
        115
parasitic infections, 458–9
    bio-psychosocial factors, 460
    impact on cognitive development, 461
    psychology's role in control, 462 tab.
parasitic worms/hookworms, 43
parent-adolescent relationship, 80, 431
parenthood, 90–1
    styles, 57–8
patriarchy, 155
Pavlov, I.P., 176, 475
peace education, 320
peace psychology, 314, 320
peacebuilding, 317–18 & tab.
peacemaking, 314–15, 318 & tab.
    cultural context, 315–16
peer groups, 80, 331, 333
    and safe sex practices, 453
    and substance abuse, 431, 432
'penis envy', 169, 288
peptic ulcers, 424
perception, 140, 355–6

performance enhancement, 387 & fig.
person-centred therapy, 491 tab., 495–7
person X environment theory, 376
persona (Jung), 170
personal distress, 471
personal myth, 76
personalisation, 494
personality assessment
    Big Five dimensions, 187
    criterion-based approach, 187
    cross-cultural applications, 188
    objective personality assessment, 186–8
    projective personality assessment, 188–9
    questionnaire/test result reliability, 190
    test controversies, 189
        see also assessment
personality factors
    substance abuse, 430–1
personality psychology, 155
    and culture, 156–8
    Euro-American views, 160, 180–1
    integration of construction of meaning,
        159 & fig.
    loci of control, 158
    non-Western views, 180–1
    in South Africa, 154
personality theories, 164
    Bandura, A., 178–9
    Erikson, E., 172–4
    Freud, S, 166–9
    Horney, K., 171–2
    Jung, C.G., 169–71
    Skinner, B.F., 176–7
personologists, 164
pharmacodynamic tolerance, 509–10
phenomenological approach to learning,
        350–1
phenothiazines, 508–9
phonetics, 227
phonological loop (memory), 238
physical development, 36
    adolescence, 74–5
    late adulthood, 93–4
    middle adulthood, 91–2
    middle childhood, 64–6
    preschoolers, 52–3
physical disabilities, 362
Piaget, Jean, 36
    cognitive development theory, 58, 68,
        290
    constructivist approach to cognition,
        215–17
    formal operational thinking, 75
    thought/language debate, 225
Plaatje, Sol, 262
play, role of, 65, 130, 135
play system, 126
    gender differences (Erikson), 174
pleasure principle (Freud), 167
polarised thinking, 494
politicisation of ethnicity, 280
positional-level theory, 256
positron emission tomography (PET), 116

post-traumatic stress disorder (PTSD), 306, 419–20, 482–3
potency dimension, 127
poverty, 262–3
    AOD micro-enterprises, 432
    and elderly, 93, 94
    impact on children, 56, 264–5, 441
    role in HIV/AIDS pandemic, 452–3
    spiral of hopelessness, 265
    and TB, 455–6
    uncertainty about future, 265–6
poverty trap, 265
practice sessions, 354–5
preconscious (Freud), 166
predictive validity (test scores), 192
pregnancy, unplanned, 79–80
prejudice, 277, 305, 365, 367
prenatal development stages
    embryonic stage, 41
    foetal stage, 41–2
    germinal stage, 40
    influences, 42
    nutrition, 439–40
        see also infants; maternal conditions
preoperational stage, 58–9
preschool development
    cognitive development, 58–9
    physical, 52–3
    risk and resilience protection, 60
    social and emotional, 53–4
preventative interventions, 515
primacy effect (memory), 238
primary groups, 251
primary health care, 521
primary-process thought (Freud), 167
Primary School Nutrition Programme (PSNP), 441
principle of reality (Freud), 167
proactive interference, 239
problem-driven research, 16
problem solving, 218
procedural memory, 240
Progressive Muscular Relaxation (PMR), 390
projective personality assessment, 188–9
prosopagnosia, 142–4
protective factors, 409
    community social networks, 411, 433
    'social capital', 267, 411, 452
    substance abuse vulnerability, 429
proximity principle, 355–6
psychiatry, 110
    attitudes towards, 472
psychoactive drugs
    classification by behavioural effects, 504–9
    main effect/side effect, 510
    mechanisms of action, 502–4 & fig.
    medical drug monitoring, 510
    potency/efficacy/dose, 504
psychoanalytic approach (to personality), 155
psychoanalytic psychotherapy, 490–3 & tab.
psychobiology, 136
psycholinguistics, 229–30

psychological distress
    cognitive therapeutic view, 493 fig.
    person-centred view, 495 fig.
    psychoanalytic view, 491 fig.
psychological factors
defence mechanisms, 480
substance abuse, 430–1
Psychological Skills Training (PST), 387 & fig., 388
psychology
    in Africa, 13–14
    assessment, 184
    attitudes towards, 472
    career opportunities, 7–8
    contribution to control of infectious/ parasitic diseases, 462 tab.
    cross-cultural trauma assistance, 309
    evaluating information, 4–6
    research terminology, 8
    role in treatment adherence interventions (TB), 457–8
    training programmes, 515, 520–1
psychometrics, 187
    culture-fair tests, 206
    culture-free tests, 206
    questionnaire reliability, 190, 206
    reliability coefficients, 190–1
    test scores, 190
    theories, 202
    validity of test scores, 191–3, 206
psychopathology, 104, 470
    biomedical approach, 477, 479
    cognitive behaviour perspective, 480–1
    community psychology perspective, 481–2
    context-dependency, 476
    psychodynamic approach, 479–80
        see also mental illness
psychopharmacology, 475, 502
psychosexual development theory (Freud), 168
psychosis, 484
psychosocial development
    adolescence, 77–81
    early adulthood, 90–1
    late adulthood, 94–6
    middle adulthood, 92–3
    theory (Erikson), 36, 172–4
psychosocial stressors, 477
psychostimulants, 506
psychotherapy
    cognitive-behaviour therapy, 491 & tab., 493–5
    cross-cultural issues, 498–9
    efficacy studies, 497
    person-centred, 495–7
    psychoanalytic, 490–3 & tab.
psychotropic drugs, 475
puberty, 75, 78–9
punishment, 396

Q

qualitative research, 16, 27
    data verification, 31

quantitative research, 16–17

R

R-I-A-S-E-C types of people/occupations, 376–7
racism, 278–9
    and ethnicity, 279–80
    in sport, 399
radar graph, 23 fig.
radiation effects on newborns, 43
radical feminism, 295
rage system, 126, 129
random sampling, 17
range, 20, 25
rape, 294
realistic conflict theory, 256
realistic environment/personalities, 376–7
reasoning, 216
recency effect (memory), 238
receptor sites, 502
recognition disorder, 142–3
Recommended Dietary Intakes (RDI), 438
reconciliation, 316–17
reference groups, 251
reflexes, 45–6
reflexivity, 27
rehabilitation programmes, 118
reinforcement concept (Skinner, Bandura), 176–7, 178, 410, 430
relative deprivation theory, 256
relaxation techniques, 425
reliability coefficients
    equivalent-forms reliability, 191
    internal consistency reliability, 191
    split-half reliability, 191
    test-retest reliability, 190–1
religious healing, 499
religious organisations
    and substance abuse, 432
research
    abuse of women, 29
    cycle, 31 fig.
        see also knowledge-driven research; problem-driven research
resilience, 104, 265, 409
resistance to psychoanalysis, 492
resource mobilisation theory, 256
resource rooms, 365
respondent behaviour, 176–7
retirement, 94
retroactive interference, 239
reversibility, 69
Rey Auditory Verbal Learning Test, 238
Rh incompatibility, 43
rich people
    consumer culture, 266
rickets, 65
risk behaviour, 408
    community influences, 411
    individual influences, 409, 430
    interpersonal influences, 410–11
    societal influences, 411–12
    structuralist influences, 412
risk/resilience matrix, 413 tab.